Drawings by Guercino

from British Collections

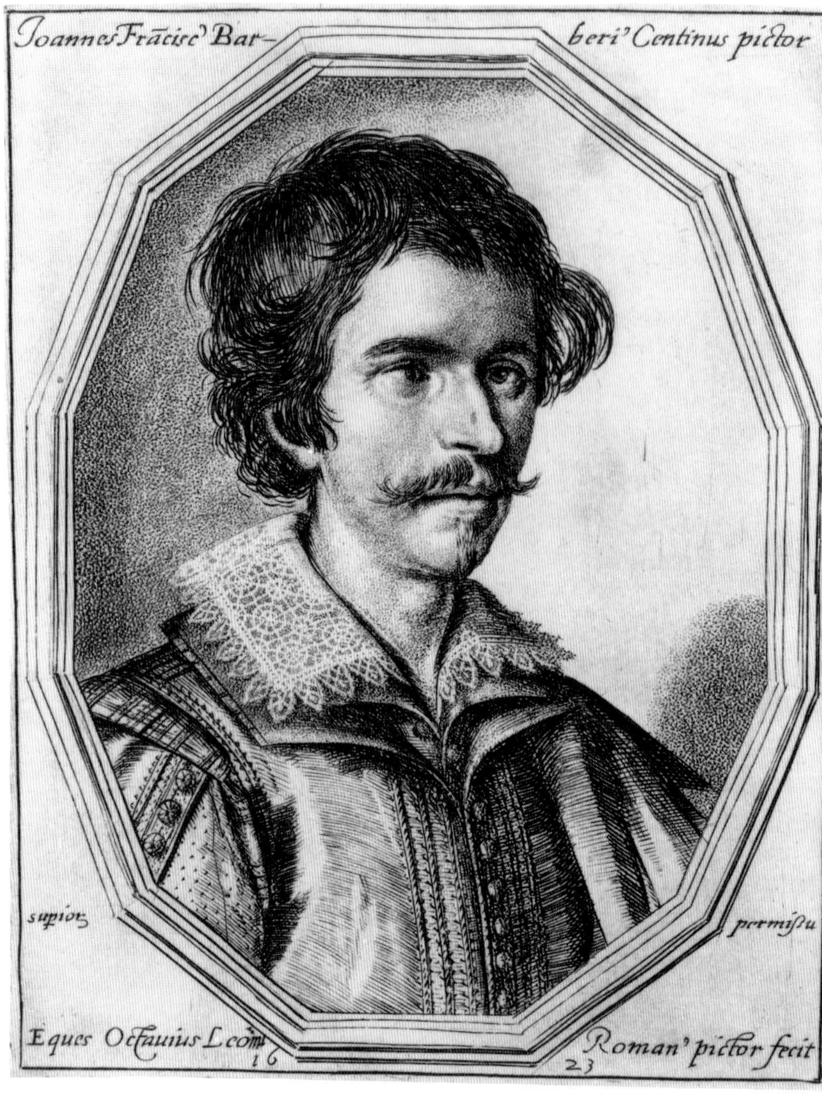

Ottavio Leoni, *Portrait of Guercino*. Engraving (Bartsch, XVII, 253, 18)

Drawings by Guercino

from British Collections

with an Appendix describing the
drawings by Guercino, his School and his Followers
in the British Museum

Nicholas Turner and Carol Plazzotta

Published for The Trustees of the British Museum
by British Museum Press
in association with Leonardo-De Luca Editori

To Sir Denis Mahon
Guercino enthusiast *par excellence*

The Trustees of the British Museum
acknowledge with gratitude generous assistance
towards the production of this book
from Leonardo Mondadori

Published by British Museum Press
A division of British Museum Publications Ltd
46 Bloomsbury Street, London WC1B 3QQ
in association with
Leonardo-De Luca Editori
Via di S. Anna 16, 00186 Roma

British Library Cataloguing in Publication Data

Guercino, *1591–1666*
Drawings by Guercino from British collections: with an appendix describing the drawings by Guercino, his school and his followers in the British Museum.
1. Italy
I. Title II. Turner, Nicholas, *1947–* III. Plazzotta, Carol IV. British Museum, *Department of prints and drawings* V. Giovanni Francesco Barbieri
741.945

ISBN 0-7141-1643-2 (British Museum Press)
ISBN 88-7813-344-2 (Leonardo-De Luca Editori)

Designed by James Shurmer

Printed in Great Britain by BAS Printers Limited,
Over Wallop, Hampshire

Contents

continued overleaf

Contents *continued*

Preface

This exhibition commemorating the 400th anniversary of the birth of Guercino consists of a selection of the artist's drawings from British collections, in which he is superbly represented. It takes its place as one of a series of exhibitions being organised in 1991 in a number of museums and galleries in Europe and North America, the most important of which will be that held in Bologna, beginning in September. The present publication is made up of two main parts: the Catalogue and the Appendix. The Catalogue, consisting of 217 entries, accompanies the loan exhibition of drawings by Guercino from British collections which takes place at the British Museum from 17 May to 18 August. The Appendix, consisting of 126 entries, describes those drawings by Guercino, his School and his followers in the British Museum's permanent collection; with the exception of seventeen of the more important sheets, these drawings are not shown in the exhibition. Given the special interest in the artist's work in the quatercentenary year of his birth, it seemed appropriate to publish the British Museum's drawings in conjunction with the Catalogue to the exhibition, ahead of the permanent catalogue of the Bolognese drawings in the British Museum.

Guercino has long been admired in this country. While still a young man, he was invited to England in 1625 as court painter to King Charles I, an invitation he chose to decline; his place was taken by the Tuscan artist Orazio Gentileschi (1562–1647). From shortly after the middle of the seventeenth century Guercino's paintings and drawings began to attract the attention of British collectors, and as the eighteenth century progressed what began as a modest flow of works into this country soon became a steady stream. The demand for his work from abroad diminished soon after the middle of the nineteenth century as it fell out of favour, along with that of most other Italian Baroque artists. Guercino was still out of fashion until just before the middle of the twentieth century, when a long overdue reappraisal of his work was championed by the distinguished British collector and scholar Sir Denis Mahon, a generous friend and benefactor of this Department.

Guercino's drawings exerted their strongest appeal to English collectors in the eighteenth century. As a contemporary, the distinguished French connoisseur and collector P.-J. Mariette observed, 'Les Anglois sont passionnés pour les desseins de Guerchin'. So strong indeed was this admiration that for a period of more than 100 years, from shortly after the middle of the eighteenth century until just after the middle of the nineteenth, most of Guercino's vast output of drawings, amounting to many hundreds, had passed from the artist's heirs into two collections in this country: the Library of King George III, now in the Royal Collection at Windsor Castle, and the Bouverie collection. Only with the beginning of the dispersal of the Bouverie collection in 1859 did this virtual monopoly of the artist's drawings begin to weaken, a process much accelerated with the advent of the twentieth century, as further sales from this same collection took place. Yet, in spite of the dispersal of the Bouverie collection, Guercino's drawings are nowhere more magnificently represented than in Britain.

After the individual entries of the Catalogue and Appendix had gone to press, the compilers discovered that the Bouverie collection of Old Master drawings of all Schools, including the magnificent group of many hundreds of drawings by Guercino, had been purchased by John Bouverie (*c.*1722–50) and not by his younger second cousin, the Hon. Edward Bouverie (1738–1810), as had hitherto been thought. How John Bouverie's name came to be detached from the collection he had formed with such good taste and discernment is one of the minor mysteries in the history of collecting. His reinstatement as a collector and connoisseur has wider implications beyond its importance for the provenance of many of Guercino's drawings and is a topic to which the compilers will return at a future date.

The sequence of ownership for just under a quarter of all the drawings in the exhibition which share this provenance (see n. 92 to the Introduction) may therefore be corrected to the following: John Bouverie (d. 1750); his brother-in-law John Hervey (d. 1764; inherited through his wife, Anne Bouverie, d. 1757); his son Christopher Hervey (d. 1786); his aunt Elizabeth Bouverie (d. 1798; surviving sister of John Bouverie); by bequest to Sir Charles Middleton, later 1st Baron Barham (1726–1813); his grandson Charles Noel, later 1st Earl of Gainsborough (1781–1866), and thence by descent. This revised provenance similarly applies to many drawings in the Appendix.

For help in the publication of this volume the Trustees are grateful for the generous support of Mr Leonardo Mondadori, who has made a significant contribution towards the production costs. The Trustees are also greatly indebted to Mr John Morton Morris, who provided funds for the employment of a Special Assistant, Miss Carol Plazzotta, who, with Mr Nicholas Turner, Assistant Keeper in the Department of Prints and Drawings, is joint author of the Catalogue. A further contribution to these funds was generously made by Sir Denis Mahon.

This exhibition would not have been possible without the gracious loan from Her Majesty The Queen of 100 drawings from the nearly 350 autograph sheets that make up the 836 by Guercino, his entourage and his followers in the Royal Library, Windsor Castle. This magnificent collection was recently catalogued by Sir Denis Mahon and Nicholas Turner, with the support of the Director and Trustees of the British Museum, the volume being published in the summer of 1989. Around this nucleus the other loans from British collections have been disposed. In addition to representing Guercino's career as a draughtsman as effectively as possible, the organisers have also sought to represent British collections both large and small, public and private. Their requests for loans have met with a generous response, though they are conscious that there are many further drawings by Guercino in private collections of which they remain unaware. The greatest disappointment among those drawings that could not be lent was from a public collection: *Youth wearing a Hat, half length*, in the Public Library, Museum and Art Gallery, Folkestone (Fig. 1), a study in reverse for a print by Francesco Curti (Bertelà, 1973, no. 550). The drawing will be included in a touring exhibition of the Folkestone collection later this year.

The Trustees and Director of the British Museum wish to thank those whose generous willingness to lend has made this exhibition possible: Her Majesty The Queen, the

Duke of Devonshire and the Trustees of the Chatsworth Settlement, Viscount Coke, Sir Denis Mahon and nine private collectors who wish to remain anonymous. The Trustees also thank the Visitors and Director of the Ashmolean Museum, the Committee of Management and Director of the Courtauld Institute Galleries, the Trustees and Director of the Victoria and Albert Museum, the Syndics and both the former and present Director of the Fitzwilliam Museum, the Trustees and Director of the National Gallery of Scotland, the Trustees of the National Museums and Galleries on Merseyside, the Director of the Walker Art Gallery, and the Arts Department and Director of the Nottingham Castle Museum.

Thanks are also due to the Librarian, Mr Oliver Everett, the Curator of the Print Room, the Hon. Mrs Roberts, Miss Theresa-Mary Morton and Miss Gwyneth Campling of the Royal Library, Windsor Castle; Mr Peter Day, the Keeper of the Collections at Chatsworth; Mr F. C. Jolly of the Holkham Estate Office; Mr Timothy Wilson, Keeper of Western Art at the Ashmolean Museum, and Dr Jon Whiteley and Dr Catherine Whistler; Mr William Bradford of the Courtauld Institute Galleries; Miss Susan Lambert, Curator of the Department of Designs, Prints and Drawings at the Victoria and Albert Museum; Mr David Scrase, Keeper of Paintings and Drawings, the Fitzwilliam Museum; Mr Hugh Macandrew, Keeper of Prints and Drawings, the National Gallery of Scotland; Mr Julian Treuherz, Keeper of the Art Galleries, the Walker Art Gallery, Liverpool; and Mr Neil Walker, Keeper of Fine Art at the Nottingham Castle Museum. The Museum is also grateful to Mr Richard Day of Richard Day Ltd, Miss Gabriel Naughton of Thos. Agnew & Sons Ltd. and Mr Thomas Williams of Thos. Williams Fine Art Ltd.

In writing the Catalogue and Appendix, the compilers have greatly benefited from the help of many friends and colleagues, among whom they should like to mention Miss H. M. Argar, Mr Prisco Bagni, Dr Piero Boccardo, Dr Gianvittorio Dillon, Mr Alan Donnithorne, Dr Mirjam Foot, Sir Brinsley Ford, Miss Kate Ganz, Mr Antony Griffiths, Dr Thomas Keymer, Mr William Keymer, M. Stéphane Loire, Mr Francis Rus-Russell, Dr Kim Sloan, Mrs N. Steele, Dr David Stone, Dr Carel van Tuyll and Miss Rachel Watson. The compilers also wish to thank Mrs Jane Shoaf Turner, who carefully edited the text of the Introduction, Catalogue and Appendix and Sir Denis Mahon, who read the whole typescript, correcting numerous errors as well as making many valuable suggestions. We are especially indebted to him for his enthusiasm and encouragement.

Miss Teresa Francis of British Museum Press and Mr James Shurmer undertook the onerous task of preparing the text for the printers, while much of the work in the later stages of the organisation of the loans for the exhibition was provided by Miss Janice Reading of the Department of Prints and Drawings. The compilers wish to express their gratitude to them.

J. K. Rowlands
Keeper, Department of Prints and Drawings,
British Museum

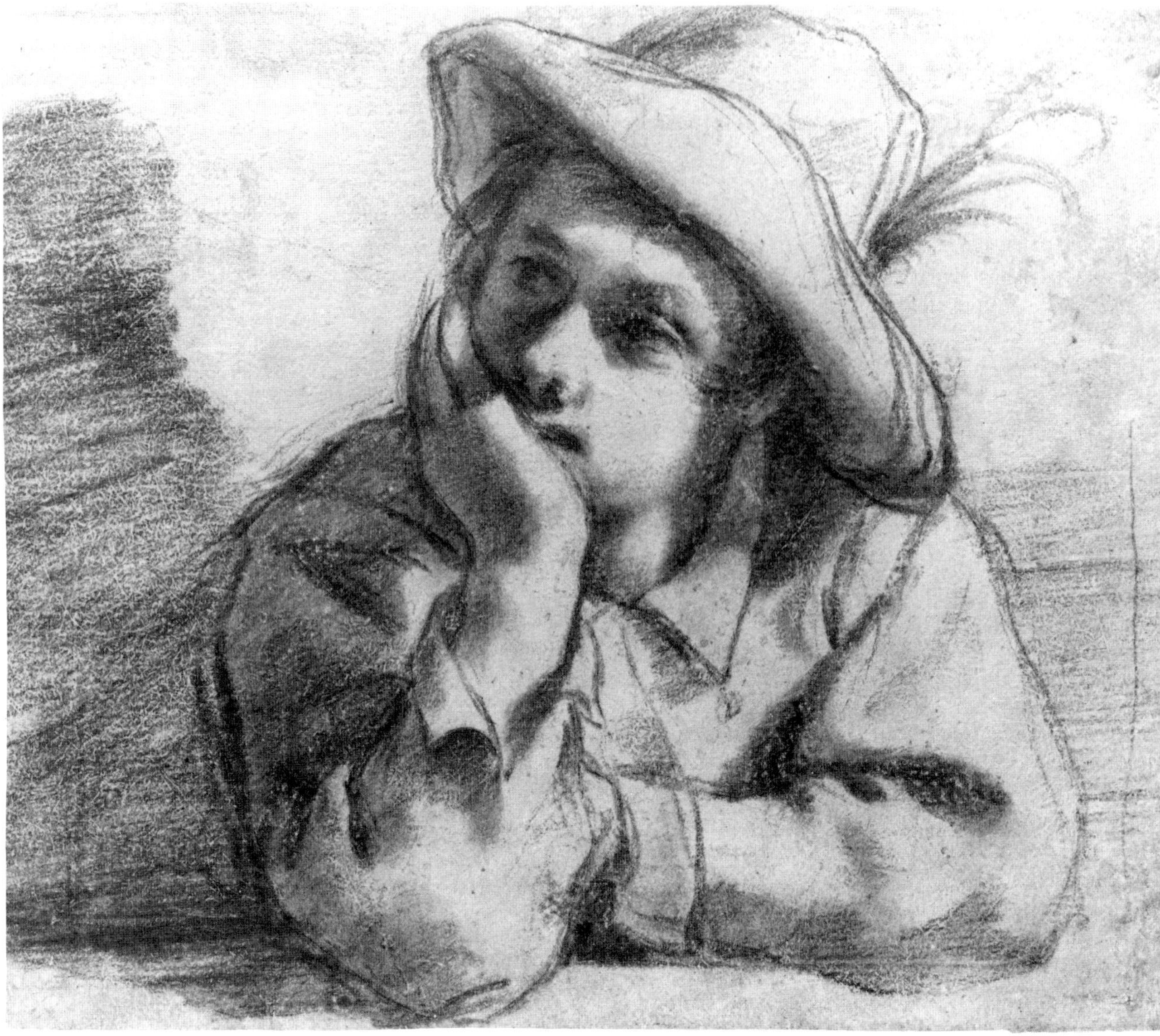

Fig. 1 *Youth wearing a Hat, half length.* Red chalk, 127 × 171 mm (Folkestone, Public Library, Museum and Art Gallery, inv. no. 102; 637/35/3). See Preface

Introduction

Guercino: A biographical Note

Giovanni Francesco Barbieri, the son of Andrea Barbieri and Elena Ghisellini, was born on the outskirts of Cento in Emilia and baptised in that town on 8 February 1591.[1] He was nicknamed Guercino (Italian: 'squinter') at an early age, on account of the squint that he is said to have suddenly developed from a shock he received while in the care of his nurse. Count Carlo Cesare Malvasia (1616–93), who knew Guercino personally in later life and published the artist's official biography in 1678, noted that by the age of six Guercino was already beginning to demonstrate 'la vehemente inclinatione c'havea al dissegno'.[2] Other early biographers, such as Francesco Scannelli (1613–63), stressed his natural aptitude for painting ('dipinse portato dal solo istinto di natura'),[3] which was all the more remarkable given the fact that Guercino was largely self-taught, having at no time in his early career been affiliated to a painter of renown. He nonetheless did receive some rudimentary training in the studios of local artists while a youth at Cento. The early sources report that when aged only nine he studied with a 'pittore di guazzo'; there followed an apprenticeship with the *quadraturista* Paolo Zagnoni (though this was perhaps at Bologna). From these brief spells of apprenticeship Guercino presumably gleaned only technical knowledge such as the mixing of pigments. In 1607, Guercino's father placed him in the studio at Cento of the painter Benedetto Gennari the elder, with whose family the artist was to be closely associated for the rest of his life. Quick to appreciate the skill of his young apprentice, Gennari formed a fruitful partnership with him within a year; this lasted until the older artist's death in 1610. It is harder to determine what training Guercino would have received in his native town. Such instruction as there was would have been strongly affected by what was happening in more important centres nearby, such as Ferrara, Modena and Bologna.

Guercino himself professed that the bulk of his artistic education was formed on his own;[4] it was based upon his dedicated application to drawing and his appreciation of the work of important Emilian forerunners and contemporaries, including Ferrarese artists such as Ippolito Scarsella, called Scarsellino (1551–1620), and Carlo Bononi (1569–1632). But of far more critical importance for his development as an artist was the influence of the Bolognese artist Ludovico Carracci. Several sources register Guercino's great admiration for Ludovico's *Holy Family with St Francis* of 1591, which was then in the church of the Cappuccini in Cento. According to Malvasia, Guercino referred to this work as his 'Cara cinna' (a pun on the name Carracci), signifying, in local dialect, the breast from which the newly-born derives nourishment.[5] Guercino was especially inspired by the older painter's strong chiaroscuro and, in some cases, his way of orchestrating figures within the composition. Malvasia also claimed that the young artist made visits to Bologna to study the work of the Carracci (Annibale, Agostino and Ludovico), presumably in the second half of the first decade of the century.[6] By shortly after the middle of the second decade Ludovico's influence was certainly joining that of Scarsellino in Guercino's paintings.

No trace of Guercino's work has survived from before 1612, the year in which he was 'discovered' by Padre Antonio Mirandola, Canon of S. Salvatore in Bologna and later President of the Monastery of S. Spirito in Cento, who befriended him, becoming a regular patron and a staunch advocate of his work. It was through Mirandola that Guercino received the important commission from Don Biagio Bagni of the *All Saints in Glory*, an altarpiece, now lost, painted in 1613 for the church of S. Spirito in Cento; it is the earliest altarpiece from Guercino's hand of which we have a visual record, a copy of it having been formerly in Bridgewater House, London (S, 1988, no. 3). In the following few years Guercino received several commissions to provide mural decorations in tempera for private residences in Cento, such as the Casa Provenzale (now Benazzi) in 1614 and the Casa Pannini (with other local artists) in the following year. Malvasia particularly praised Guercino's technique in the latter enterprise, commenting that his work looked as though it had been carried out in oil, a still more subtle medium. In 1616, Guercino made the enlightened gesture of setting up his own *Accademia del nudo* in rooms in the house of one of his Centese patrons, Bartolomeo Fabri, thereby placing himself, perhaps somewhat self-consciously, in the tradition of the famous Carracci, pioneers of the academic discipline for artists. According to Malvasia, Guercino quickly accumulated a significant following of students, who numbered twenty-three by 1617. Already by this date Guercino was beginning to suffer the effects of the sudden increased demand for his paintings from influential patrons. He was forced in that year, for instance, to reach a compromise with the marquis Enzo Bentivoglio over the proposed decoration of the latter's palace: in a letter to Bentivoglio, written on his behalf by Padre Mirandola, he undertook to work on the project for just one month in every year, while his apparently less successful colleague

Pierfrancesco Battistelli proceeded at once with the frieze, leaving blanks for Guercino to fill in when he found time.[7] Mirandola's letter emphasises the 'tanti oblighi di lavori, che ha e con il Gran Duca [Cosimo II of Tuscany], e l'Ill.mo Cardinale Lodovisi, et altri Sig.ri che ha dodici ancone, e undeci quadri'. Guercino's career had clearly taken off.

In 1617 Guercino is also documented as working on a number of pictures for Cardinal Archbishop Alessandro Ludovisi, one of his most influential Bolognese patrons. This information is provided in two letters to Don Ferrante Carlo from Ludovico Carracci, who enthusiastically endorsed the manifest talents of the younger artist, reciprocating Guercino's admiration for him. The second letter, dated 25 October 1617, is particularly unrestrained in its eulogy: 'Quà vi è un giovane di patria di Cento, che dipinge con somma felicità d'invenzione. È gran disegnatore, e felicissimo coloritore: è mostro di natura, e miracolo da far stupire chi vede le sue opere. Non dico nulla: ei fa rimaner stupidi li primi pittori: basta il vedrà al suo ritorno.'[8]

It was at the request of Padre Mirandola that in 1618 Guercino made a series of anatomical drawings for the instruction of novice artists. These passed into the possession of a colleague of Mirandola, Padre Pietro Martire Pederzani, who took them to Venice, accompanied by Guercino, to show to Jacopo Palma il Giovane, one of the major exponents of Venetian painting of the period. Palma was apparently duly impressed and concluded that there was nothing he could teach Guercino; instead he showed him the works of Titian, 'del quale il Sig. Gio. Francesco fù sempre mai innamorato, portandolo scolpito nel cuore per l'idea de' pittori'.[9] The influence of Titian's rich, sombre palette and vibrant textures can indeed be felt in Guercino's paintings from the end of the second decade of the seventeenth century: lush blues, purples, burgundies and oranges emerge imperceptibly from the twilight of his compositions (many of them set under a glowering overcast or night sky), subtly modulating the intensity of the chiaroscuro.

Guercino continued to be beset by the difficulty of clashing demands from different, equally illustrious patrons. In 1619, again at Mirandola's request, his series of exemplary drawings was engraved by Oliviero Gatti and bound in a volume with a dedication to Ferdinando Gonzaga, Duke of Mantua, to whom it was sent. The Duke subsequently approached Guercino to paint pictures for him, but Guercino replied from Ferrara that, while desiring to serve the Gonzaga household, he would not be able without the Duke's intervention to release himself from his current commitments with Cardinal Serra, Legate of Ferrara. By 1620 Guercino had managed to produce only one painting for the Duke, *Erminia and the Shepherd*, which he delivered in person; he was received as an honoured guest and collected not only his fee but also a knighthood. Not to be outdone, Cardinal Serra also knighted Guercino on 8 December 1620. The same year, again through Padre Mirandola, Guercino was awarded his most prestigious ecclesiastical commission to date, the *St William receiving the monastic Habit* for the church of St Gregory in Bologna (see Nos. 26–8). The picture acquired a tremendous reputation as soon as it was in place, and Malvasia referred to it with understandable admiration: 'Questo è quel quadro che atterrisce tutti, che spaventa ogn'altro; e infelice Lodovico ivi prossimo col suo bellissimo S. Giorgio, se si trovava più vivo'.[10]

When in 1621 Cardinal Ludovisi was elected Pope Gregory XV, he summoned Guercino to Rome to decorate the Loggia delle Benedizioni in St Peter's. This Roman sojourn proved to be a turning-point in Guercino's career, both in terms of the prestige it brought and the significant effect it had on his style. His work in Rome comprised a mixture of private, public and ecclesiastical commissions, mainly for the Ludovisi and their entourage. For the papal treasurer, Monsignore Costanzo Patrizi, he painted a ceiling fresco representing *The sleeping Rinaldo abducted by Armida* (see No. 30); and for the Ludovisi themselves, he provided a more ambitious scheme to decorate their villa in Rome, known as the Casino Ludovisi. One ceiling was dedicated to *Aurora* (see Nos. 32–5), in direct competition with the ceiling of the same subject painted by Guido Reni (1575–1642) in 1614 for Cardinal Scipione Borghese; and in another room, Guercino painted the allegorical figure of *Fame*. It was perhaps no coincidence that Borghese sought out the newcomer the following year to paint a ceiling canvas depicting *St Chrysogonus in Glory* for the church of S. Crisogono in Trastevere. However, the crowning achievement of Guercino's Roman period was the great *St Petronilla* altarpiece for St Peter's, commissioned in 1621 by Pope Gregory XV but finished two years later (see Nos. 38–43).

During this period, Guercino lived in the Strada Paolina, in the company of two assistants, Guido Cagnacci (1601–81) and Lorenzo Gennari (1595–after 1665, a presumed cousin of Benedetto the elder who is first documented as a member of Guercino's entourage when working on the Casa Pannini frescoes in 1615). A fourth name on the census register, Giovan Battista Croce, was probably that of a servant.[11] Guercino's physical appearance at this time is recorded in a drawing by Ottavio Leoni (1578–1630), who used it as the basis of his engraving of 1623 (see Frontispiece; the drawing is in the Biblioteca Marucelliana, Florence, vol. H 7, reproduced in S, 1988, p. xix). The portrait shows Guercino to have had somewhat delicate features, with a long nose, a generous mouth concealed by a wispy moustache and the characteristic squint by which he became known.

With the death of Pope Gregory in 1623, the project that had brought Guercino to Rome in the first instance, the decoration of the Loggia delle Benedizioni, fell through, and the artist returned to Cento, where he worked in close association with several assistants, including Bartolomeo (1594–1661) and later his brother Ercole Gennari (1597–1658), who married Guercino's sister Lucia in 1628, cementing the considerable bond that already linked the two families. Guercino's two nephews, Benedetto (1633–1715) and Cesare Gennari (1637–88), who were the product of this union, also grew up to become his assistants. Although Guercino himself never married, he nevertheless assumed the role of paterfamilias, as the main breadwinner. Despite his considerable success and the continuing demand for his work, Guercino apparently preferred to remain very much in the bosom of his family and somewhat off the beaten track, in the small country town where he was born. His love for his rural surroundings and the rustics who made up such a significant part of the local population is best revealed in the drawings he made without specific commissions in mind, namely his landscapes and caricatures; these also seem to substantiate Malvasia's report that he was 'amatore dei Poveri, che sempre mai aveva intorno quando usciva di Casa, onde pareva il padre di essi; e si prendeva gusto discorrer con loro'.[12]

In spite of living in a backwater, Guercino remained very much on the artistic map. Soon after King Charles I's accession to the English throne in 1625, Guercino was invited to court, with the offer of an annual stipend in return for his services as a painter.[13] He characteristically declined and the post was accepted in 1626 by the Tuscan painter Orazio Gentileschi (1562–1647). The English monarch apparently had to make do with two pictures by Guercino which his agent despatched from Rome in 1626. Guercino's growing fame abroad is attested in 1629 by a letter from Cardinal Bernardino Spada, Papal Legate of Bologna, to Maria de' Medici, Queen Mother of France, reporting his failure to persuade Guido Reni to work for the Queen in Paris but putting forward instead the name of Guercino, who 'per havere un dissegno vigoroso et un colorito di grandissima forza, e vivezza, vien judicato da ogn'uno, e da Guido istesso, attissimo à rappresentamenti di battaglie e d'attioni grandi e maestose'.[14] The painting that Guercino made as a sample of his talents for Maria de' Medici, the *Death of Dido* of 1631 (see Nos. 81–2), was in fact never delivered due to the contemporary political upheavals in France and the Queen's subsequent flight. It was nevertheless displayed to the public in Bologna for three days and was universally praised, even in verse, bringing Guercino further acclaim. In 1632 he went to Modena to paint the portraits of the Duke and Duchess and was again invited to stay at court; although he did not establish himself there, he worked regularly for the Duke over a number of years. Malvasia recorded yet another invitation to go and work at the French court in 1639, this time for King Louis XIII.

Notwithstanding the many illustrious patrons on his books, Guercino retained a surprisingly down-to-earth attitude to his art, which he treated as a plain job of work. This much is clear from his detailed Account Book which survives for the period from 1629 to his death in 1666. The document reveals that, like many eminent Italian painters of the time, he charged set rates for his paintings according to the number and length of the figures they contained.[15]

After his Roman visit, Guercino was based in Cento for nearly twenty years. One factor influencing his decision to remain faithful to his home town is likely to have been the presence in Bologna of Guido Reni, an older artist with a towering reputation to whom Guercino had to play second fiddle, all too often receiving commissions that Reni had previously turned down. This much is borne out by the fact that within weeks of Reni's death in 1642, Guercino had installed himself in Bologna (thereby also avoiding the dangers of violence in Cento, caused by the war of Castro). Two years later he purchased the family house, later known as the Casa Gennari, at what is now no. 3, Via S. Alò. Ironically, Guercino's paintings of this later period at Bologna, with their idealised figures, classicising forms and pale colours, are analogous in some respects to the example left behind by Reni, particularly in his later years. Guercino's output continued to be prodigious, thanks to his capacity to work extremely quickly and efficiently: Malvasia pointed out 'la sua formidabile velocità nell'oprare, e alla prima bozzando, e finendo nello stesso tempo; e talvolta dando compire due teste il dopo pranzo di una giornata estiva'.[16] Guercino's undisputed position as the city's leading painter assured him of public commissions in its principal churches as well as those of many other Italian cities, together with a host of private contracts for both secular and religious paintings. He also maintained his high profile abroad, working for foreign patrons such as Louis Phélypeaux de La Vrillière, Secretary of State to King Louis XIII of France, the Maréchal de Plessis-Praslin, Duc de Choiseul, and the Emperor Ferdinand III.

Guercino appears to have maintained his links with Cento despite the move to Bologna with most of his close family. The Account Book records payments in 1642 and 1645 for the construction of a family chapel in the church of the Rosario in Cento, for which Guercino painted an altarpiece (see No. 138) and ceiling panels depicting his own patron saints, John the Baptist and Francis; the project was very much a reflection of the artist's rising status.

In 1649, Guercino's brother, Paolo Antonio Barbieri (b. 1603), a painter of still lifes in his own right, died suddenly after a brief illness at the age of 46. Until his death, Paolo Antonio, in Malvasia's words, the 'esatto Economo', was responsible for the general administration of the household and all Guercino's accounts (prior to 1649 the Account Book is in his hand), taking on these tasks to allow his brother to concentrate on his painting without distraction. His death was a considerable blow to the artist, and Malvasia relates the various strategies of one of his most devoted patrons, the Duke of Modena, to divert him from his 'maninconia inconsolabile', inviting him to Modena in the company of other artists to view the Este collections and visit the Duke's country seat at Sassuolo. Guercino and members of the Gennari family kept up the Account Book after his brother's death and it shows that the artist was as much in demand as ever in the 1650s and 1660s. In 1655 Queen Christina of Sweden visited Guercino in his studio in order to pay homage to his talent.

Towards the end of his life Guercino was beset by ailing health. In 1661 he became seriously ill but recovered enough to continue painting, though he had to rely increasingly on the support of his nephews, Benedetto and Cesare. In 1665 Don Antonio Ruffo asked Guercino for a painting of the Magdalen 'in piccolo', a request that provoked an extremely reluctant response: 'non sò sè la vista è l'ettà mal [*sic*] permetterà per il nocumento che provo quando voglio troppo minutamente aplicare perchè a queste cose vi si ricerca la gioventù sì per l'acutezza della vista, come per la fermezza del polso'.[17] It appears from the same correspondence that Guercino did nevertheless carry out his patron's request. That Ruffo himself recognised a change in Guercino's style is reflected in his stipulation that the half-length figure that he commissioned from him as a pendant to one by Rembrandt in 1660 was to be in his 'prima maniera gagliarda'.[18] Elsewhere, it emerges that Ruffo also wanted from Guercino 'qualche quadro fatto in [sua] Gioventù'.[19] The latest drawing for a history subject in the Catalogue (No. 163) shows something of the tremulous quality of his late manner.

Guercino died on 22 December 1666 and was buried in Bologna in the church of S. Salvatore.

Guercino as a Draughtsman

From the very outset of Guercino's long career – which lasted for more than fifty years – every picture or large-scale decoration of any importance was preceded by a series of preparatory studies, many of which he kept. These ranged from rapid sketches made to clarify his first ideas, to studies of figures and groups of figures, to carefully drawn studies of heads, limbs and draperies for the more important figures within a given composition. Since he produced scores of paintings over his career, his parallel output of preparatory drawings was immense. If one adds to this the drawings he made for pleasure, such as landscapes, genre studies, *capricci* and caricatures, it becomes clear that the total would have been truly prodigious, amounting to a vast corpus for which numerically there are only few rivals among other artists of the Italian School. Thus the drawings known today, numerous though they may seem, must constitute only a fragment of the original total. Although for many of Guercino's pictures several related studies exist, for others there are none at all. However, enough drawings have survived to allow one to gauge his practice as a draughtsman and to understand some of the complex processes that lay behind the creation of his paintings.

Guercino's working drawings, although not made with an audience in mind, are characterised by a certain natural charm. This attractiveness is apparent irrespective of medium and is one of their most persistent qualities. That astute eighteenth-century French connoisseur P.-J. Mariette described it as 'une *Vaghesse* qu'on ne trouve dans les Desseins d'aucun autre Maitre'.[20] Why do Guercino's drawings so please the eye? Perhaps it is the clever alliance of two opposing forces, chance and intention, through which the artist allowed felicitous accidental effects as much scope as passages of controlled drawing. The resulting variation in tempo conveys a lively sense of movement, somehow preserving the life and energy that gave rise to the drawing in the first place.

Mariette pointed to another essential quality of Guercino's draughtsmanship, his ability to represent light: 'il y a dans la distribution de son clair-obscur, une intelligence & des effets merveilleux.'[21] Guercino's remarkable ability to evoke the appearance of light was a consistent feature of his drawings throughout his career. This brightness animates the figures in his working drawings and caricatures, and defines the open spaces of his landscapes. The emphatic darkness of the cast shadows in many of the pen-and-wash studies conveys immediately the strong Mediterranean sunlight. The sensation of being out of doors is vividly suggested in drawings such as No. 197. To take another random example of this effect, in No. 45 an outdoor setting is implied by the pronounced 'chiaroscuro', particularly extreme in the head of the woman wearing a voluminous dress seated on the right. The brightness of the ambient light is indicated by the intense contrast between the dark shadow of her neck, as she turns her head, and the lights on the side of her face, on the tip of her nose and on her lips. The bold suspension of drawing on the front of her dress, where the white paper has been left blank, functions as a highlight because of its contrast with the broad passages of mid-tone washed in at her side. This same 'chiaroscuro' method recurs in constantly varying degrees both in the pen-and-wash drawings and in those in pen and ink alone. In the latter, the mid-tones are indicated by passages of open cross hatching, and the few dark accents with heavy touches of the pen (e.g. No. 80).

Unlike the finished pictures, which were of course intended as public statements, Guercino's working drawings were private exercises made very much for his own ends in order to prepare his paintings. To show them as works of art in themselves in an exhibition such a this is to a certain extent to misunderstand their purpose. They were evidently not sold to his patrons, and only in excep-

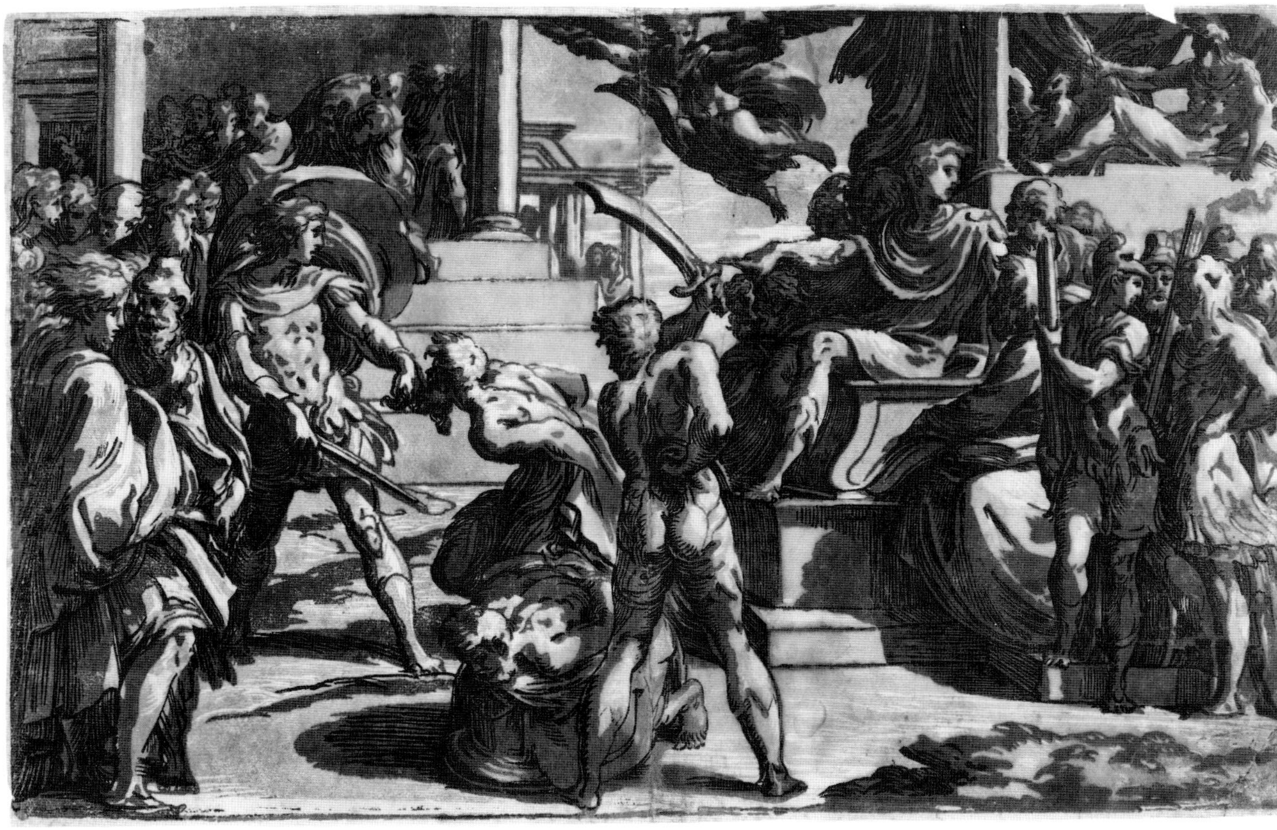

Fig. 2 Antonio da Trento after Parmigianino, *The Martyrdom of Sts Peter and Paul*. Chiaroscuro woodcut (Bartsch, XII, 79, 28)

tional circumstances were they given away to admirers.[22] Those that the artist felt worth preserving he kept almost jealously, not just because he liked them but also because they served as a repertory of figural poses and compositional ideas that would inspire other motifs. They were thus an essential resource for the studio and, among other things, helped Guercino to remember the pictures that he had already painted and long since despatched. Many of his drawings may be grouped according to category: whole-length figures, half-length figures, head and shoulders, and heads. Such a division must reflect their intended function as well as the system of set rates according to which he priced his pictures. Thus, when he needed to, he could pick out, for example, a suitable head or group of heads and, like a joiner, would fit them together as a unit to fill a particular space.

The recycling of motifs, which we have frequently remarked upon in the Catalogue and which was almost certainly in part the result of preserving such a rich fund of drawings, must have occurred for every class of drawing, from the compositional studies to the separate studies for figures. A good instance of the migration of a figural idea, almost certainly through the re-use of old preparatory drawings, is the repetition of the powerful group of a standing executioner and his crouching victim in two pictures of 1632, the *Damon and Pythias* (see Nos. 83–4) and the *Martyrdom of Sts John and Paul, with the Madonna and Child above* (see especially Nos. 86–8). Although the source for this group was the chiaroscuro woodcut of the *Martyrdom of Sts Peter and Paul* by Antonio da Trento after a design by Parmigianino (see Fig. 2),[23] Guercino studied it so exhaustively himself, endlessly varying the figures, that the idea became absorbed into the composition as if it were his own. The group was repeated in both pictures with only a few changes, thereby saving much effort.

One can easily imagine how such a borrowing of motifs might have happened among the category of studies for draperies and limbs, and of putti. Although drawn with a particular figure in mind, a finished drapery study, such as No. 93 (otherwise App. no. 17), could well have been re-used, with some modifications, for another similar standing female figure. A glance at Guercino's pictures, especially those from the mid-1630s onwards, will show how often the hands and feet of the figures conform to a number of stereotypes, for which he would almost certainly have depended upon existing drawings. It is equally likely that Guercino re-used his drawings of putti from time to time, for they too fall into certain stock types that change surprisingly little over his long career. Studies of drapery, feet and hands have always had only a limited appeal to the collector, and it is not surprising that they have not survived in large numbers (the only known group of such studies is in the Staatsgalerie, Stuttgart, on deposit from the Koenig–Fachsenfeld Collection: see the discussion under App. no. 17).

There seems not to have been a stage in the preparation of a composition when Guercino brought together his numerous working studies to make a single finished composition study or *modello*, either drawn or painted, that would represent the definitive design. This was the sort of study that many others of his contemporaries would have drawn on paper and then squared in order to transfer the design either onto a cartoon or directly onto the surface to be painted; but Guercino apparently side-stepped the practice (see No. 62). The one drawing in the exhibition made specifically as a *modello* is not squared (No. 41). It is very much an exception, and the design it embodies was not put into effect. Perhaps because of his desire to keep his options open, even to the very last moment, Guercino was reluctant to commit the composition to paper in this way, preferring instead to work exclusively from his series of miscellaneous studies of single figures and groups of figures, enlarging them in his head and combining them together into a painted whole, the final composition effectively coming together first on the full-size canvas rather than beforehand on a piece of paper. Malvasia suggested as much when he commented that Guercino was so proficient in 'disegno' that he could paint his composition directly onto a given surface rather than making an intermediate cartoon (see No. 77). The evidence of this working method is borne out in the paintings themselves: the compositions are at times fragmented, appearing to be the sum of a number of disparate parts.

Guercino's search after a satisfactory arrangement for a given subject required both a literary and a figurative understanding of the 'story'. The formal and psychological disposition of each participant within the painted composition revealed the quality of the artist's 'invention' – the novel, yet pleasing way that he told his 'story'. The sheer quantity of studies from Guercino's hand, embodying widely different thoughts as he went about solving a composition, is very much the result of his quest as a dramatist. The drawings show the fertility of his imagination as well as an almost touching lack of certainty as to how to proceed. What was Guercino looking for when he rejected one pose in favour of another? He seems to have been searching for a series of abstract correspondences between his figures and their gestures, a harmony akin to that which a choreographer might wish to establish. The four drawings exhibited here for the *Assassination of Amnon* show how the various options for the composition were considered in precisely these terms (Nos. 69–72). Following his visit to Rome, this process of attempting to arrange his figures within a given design took on certain marked characteristics. Increasingly his drawings reveal a desire to modify the adventurous 'Baroque' solutions of his first ideas in favour of a more 'classical' solution, which seems to have found favour with much of his clientele.

Even in his most severely classical pictures, the fruits of Guercino's close observation of everyday life are clearly visible. His old male saints, young Madonnas and benign God the Fathers are intimately related to their real-life counterparts from the market-places and streets of Cento or Bologna. His audiences must have recognised the connection and applauded the accessibility of his stories. In his drawings he was playing the same game. To take just one instance, the *Madonna and Child with St Anne* (No. 36), the protagonists might have come from any Emilian household. Popular subjects were, of course, the basis of his genre drawing, but the presence of ordinary people is also implicit in his working drawings for history subjects. Guercino would certainly have employed models to draw them, since he could not have achieved the variety and energy in his figures simply from his own imagination, as anyone who has ever drawn a figure will realise. Thus the curly-locked youth who modelled the figure of Marsyas in No. 6 was used to model Apollo in No. 7; he seems to crop up again as Adonis in Nos. 17 and 18. The same bearded model appears to have been engaged to pose for St Prosper in No. 51 as well as for St Jerome in No. 56 and in a drawing at Genoa (see Fig. 10). And one cannot imagine how the complicated poses of Nos. 69–72 could have been captured without the services of at least two models, one bearded and the other clean-shaven.

There is evidence to suggest that the distinctive way in which Guercino's compositions evolved in his drawings through an almost tortuous process of trial and error may have owed something to Ludovico Carracci's own similar preparatory method, in which, among other things, a given design was often reversed in order to refresh the artist's ideas for the grouping of the figures.[24] There is no doubt that the influence of Ludovico's work on Guercino's early development as a draughtsman – probably even more so than as a painter – was fundamental. Considerable knowledge of Ludovico's drawing style is already apparent in what is generally agreed to be Guercino's earliest surviving study, the composition sketch in the Louvre for his lost picture of *All Saints in Glory*, painted in 1613 for the church of S. Spirito at Cento.[25] In this study there are also important echoes of Scarsellino and, more particularly, Carlo Bononi, whose influence on Guercino's early style of drawing deserves further examination.[26] Yet it was the impact of Ludovico that proved the more enduring. In the pen-and-wash studies of Guercino's pre-Roman period, resonances of Ludovico's fluid, calligraphic line and pale washes occur time and again (see Nos. 5, 7, 8, 9, 11 and 20). These same traits remained consistent features of Guercino's drawings in the medium almost to the very end of his career, though they were quickly tempered by his maturing personality.

It was perhaps through Ludovico's drawings that Guercino first came to understand fully an even earlier Emilian tradition of drawing, as practised by the Parmese artists Correggio (*c.*1489/94–1534) and Parmigianino (1503–40). Hints of Guercino's knowledge and appreciation of this tradition, especially as exemplified by Parmigianino, are betrayed by the elegance of line in some of his earliest studies. As we have just seen, Guercino was well acquainted with one of Parmigianino's printed compositions, from which he derived a certain figural motif later in his career. At a more prosperous moment in his life Guercino very probably owned original studies by both Correggio and Parmigianino.[27] It is worth calling attention to another instance of Guercino borrowing from a print, since he undoubtedly made use of them to inspire his own ideas. Lucas van Leyden's woodcut of *Jael and Sisera* (see Fig. 3) seems to have prompted Guercino's own unusual treatment of the pose of Sisera, with his feet locked together in agony, in No. 25. Certain analogies between the figure of Jael in the print and No. 25 would appear to confirm the connection.[28]

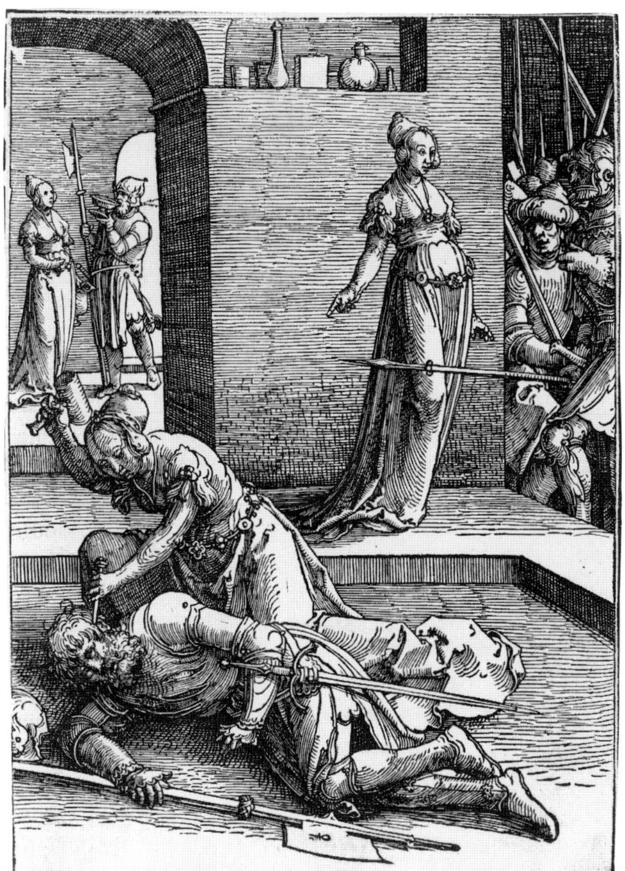

Fig. 3 Lucas van Leyden, *Jael and Sisera*. Woodcut (Bartsch, VII, 440, 7)

Guercino was also receptive to other Bolognese influences. On his periodic visits to the city in the second decade of the century he would also have seen the drawings of Ludovico's cousin Annibale Carracci (1560–1609) and of Pietro Faccini (*c.*1562–1602). Guercino has been described as Annibale's 'spiritual successor as a draughtsman, vividly continuing his distinctive Bolognese style'.[29] Both artists expressed a strong sense of humour in their drawings as well as a capacity to reflect the popular culture of their time. Like Annibale, Guercino drew ceaselessly and was capable of a very great range of different types of drawing, from landscape and caricatures to studies of genre. Guercino's acknowledged admiration for the drawings of Faccini is recorded in a manuscript note by Malvasia, based on a conversation with Guercino: apparently Padre Mirandola had access to drawings by Faccini and showed them to Guercino, who 'si incapriciava, et incontrando il suo genio quel modo di fare gl'imitava'.[30]

Guercino's red chalk drawings owe much to those by Annibale, though he may also have been influenced during his visit to Rome by those of Florentine artists active there at about the same time, for whom the technique was also a favourite one. In choosing the unusual technique of oiled charcoal for some of his nude figure drawings (e.g. Nos. 1, 4, 16 and App. no. 3), Guercino no doubt had in mind prototypes by Faccini for whom this was the preferred medium for drawings of the type. But it is not always clear why one moment Guercino decided to pick up his red chalk to draw a given group of figures, then in the next opted for pen, and then finally switched to drawing them with his pen in combination with brush and wash (see Nos. 90–92). Technique, function and the sources for Guercino's different types of drawing are so closely interrelated that it is not easy to separate them satisfactorily. No hard-and-fast rules seem to have existed for his choice of medium, though his preference for one rather than another for certain purposes is open to some interpretation.

Guercino's favourite technique – and the one in which he perhaps excelled above all – was pen and brown ink and wash (usually brown, but sometimes grey); early in his career he occasionally heightened his pen-and-wash drawings with white (e.g. No. 8). Just under half of all the drawings in the Exhibition are in pen and wash. Besides enabling him to create remarkable suggestions of light and shade, the technique allowed him to work quickly and gave him ample scope for highly pictorial (as opposed to graphic) effects. As drawings, these are therefore closest in feel to his paintings.

Guercino used pen-and-wash for most of the composition and figure studies, as well as most of the caricatures and *capricci*. He even used it for categories of drawings for which he usually preferred other media. Thus some of the studies from the nude model, which he normally carried out in oiled charcoal, are drawn in this way (see No. 6 and probably No. 14), as are occasionally some landscapes, which are usually executed in pen and ink alone (those in the Catalogue in which some passages of wash appear include Nos. 166, 169–70 and 182). Although apparently none of the detailed drapery studies are in pen and wash, some of the detailed studies of heads are (e.g. No. 140).

Just under a quarter of the drawings in the Exhibition are in pen and ink. As a medium it is, of course, related to pen and wash and similarly permits great speed of execution. When using this material, the artist lacked the option of a mid-tone which could be quickly and easily applied; instead he had to create it rather laboriously by cross hatching. By way of compensation, however, he had at his command the varied qualities of pure line, with all its expressive potential. As well as speed, the technique also permitted greater precision, and Guercino cleverly exploited both properties.

In the late twentieth century, when pens with all types of reservoirs and sophisticated 'points' are taken thoroughly for granted, it is worth pausing to consider that Guercino had only two basic kinds available to him – the quill and the reed pen. A fine line could be achieved with the quill pen and this was probably the type that he would have used more frequently. Both sorts would have needed frequent refilling from an inkpot as the artist drew. Yet Guercino was so proficient in this technique that the lines of his pen-and-ink drawings are remarkably consistent: only rarely do passages betray those moments when the pen was going dry, thus producing only a faint line, or when the freshly loaded nib was drawing too darkly and making blobs (but see No. 202). Invariably in Guercino's drawings the lines from the recently filled pen coincide admirably with the areas of dark where the artist wished to place his accents.

Guercino most often used iron-gall ink, which appealed to him because of its darkness. Unfortunately the medium fades with time to a lighter brown; it also has a destructive power peculiar to itself and degrades the paper regardless of the conditions under which the sheet is kept.[31] This is the reason why so many of Guercino's drawings are damaged in the areas of greatest shadow. He also sometimes used a lighter, bistre ink, especially in combination with extensive passages of light wash (e.g. Nos. 103–4 and 110).

Among the pen drawings displaying Guercino's pleasing sense of rhythm are those rapid scribbles embodying his first ideas for compositions and figures, mostly the latter. Guercino made several drawings of this type during the first part of his career, up to and including his Roman period of 1621–3 (e.g. Nos. 9, 25–7 and 30). Similar rapid pen studies can also be found later on (e.g. No. 143). Pen alone was occasionally also employed for more careful studies of figures and groups of figures (e.g. Nos. 89, 107).

The precision possible with pen and ink no doubt inspired Guercino's choice of that technique for the great majority of his landscape drawings. In them he adopted a careful, engraver-like style to which the pen was admirably suited. Pen was also used for other categories of finished drawing, being employed with great proficiency in his finished designs for prints (e.g. Nos. 31, 94 and 105), in which he occasionally also introduced a touch of wash, smudging it with his finger to interrupt the monotony of passages of regular cross hatching. In another category of finished drawing (No. 36), possibly made for presentation, one witnesses a similar, almost fastidious use of the pen. Finally, Guercino sometimes used pen and ink instead of chalk at the very end of the preparatory process to make finished studies of heads, to which he could then refer when painting that particular detail. No. 80 is probably the only study of this type in the Catalogue, but the picture for which it was drawn is lost (App. no. 32 is probably another example, and others are discussed under Nos. 50 and 126).

Guercino was also skilled in the use of red chalk, obtaining with it many outstanding effects. Red chalk limits the draughtsman to a narrower tonal range than black chalk or pen and wash, but it facilitates more subtle gradations within the range; it also provides an attractively warm hue, which Guercino exploited to the full to bring his figures to life in all their sensuousness. He began using the medium regularly only after his visit to Rome, though Nos. 3 and 22 show that he was aware of its potential well before then. Once he had decided that a certain figure was to be included in a composition, he often studied its pose in red chalk (e.g. Nos. 32–3, 35, 44, 58, 63, 77–8, 116, 118–19 and 135). As his career progressed he came to depend upon it more and more, also using it frequently for his composition studies (e.g. Nos. 75, 113, 125, 137, 151, 155, 157, 159, 160 and 163). At the very end of his life red chalk took over from pen and wash as the most frequently used technique, for almost all categories of drawing.

Stumping is a particular device associable with Guercino's drawings in red chalk, though it was also sometimes used for those in black. The artist delicately smudged the chalk, either with his finger or with the stump, a stick of soft paper tightly rolled together and pointed at the end. The extra-subtle gradation of the mid-tones thereby achieved was especially suitable for modelling the flesh of women and putti (e.g. Nos. 53, 67–8 and 76). Besides the figure studies, invariably drawn on white paper, Guercino also used red chalk for many of his highly finished detail studies of heads, limbs and drapery (see Nos. 50 and 93), which he made at the end of the preparatory process. For these drawings he often chose a coarse, buff-coloured paper and touched in the highlights sparingly with white chalk.

In general, black chalk did not hold much appeal. He sometimes used it for the odd figure or composition study at the very beginning of his career, but more often towards the end, in the 1640s and 1650s (e.g. Nos. 142, 144 and 156). He turned to it more regularly as an occasional alternative to red chalk for his detailed studies of drapery, when he likewise worked on a coarse, buff-coloured paper, smudging or stumping the chalk to obtain the mid-tones and sometimes picking out the highlights with white chalk. Pure charcoal, which is cheap and similar in appearance to black chalk but less permanent, is a material he seems to have by-passed altogether. Most seventeenth-century Italian painters would have used it for drawing cartoons (full-size drawings, usually on pieces of cheap brown- or blue-tinted paper stuck together, made at the end of the preparatory process to transfer the outlines of the composition onto the surface to be painted, either by pricking through the outlines or indenting them with the stylus); but Guercino seems not to have used this method of transfer at all (see above and No. 77). On the other hand, he did employ oiled charcoal (charcoal soaked in oil, thereby making it more permanent) for some of his working drawings. In his early career he especially reserved the medium for large-scale drawings from the nude model (e.g. Nos. 4 and 16) and for certain other categories of study (e.g. No. 12). For these drawings he invariably chose a tinted paper, very often touching in the highlights with white chalk.

In the sixteenth and seventeenth centuries paper was expensive and not always easy to obtain, with the result that many artists were understandably careful not to waste it. The frequent habit of some to draw on every available square inch of both sides of the sheet is surely evidence that this scarce resource was carefully husbanded. There are, however, few signs that Guercino stinted himself over paper. His successful business as a painter must have enabled him to keep a plentiful supply. Although he occasionally drew on both sides of the sheet (e.g. Nos. 42, 62, 71, 79, 89, 92, 145, etc.), he undoubtedly preferred not to do so. A strong reason for his unwillingness was that the paper he most liked to draw on, a light, white, rag paper, was too thin to allow a study to be drawn on the back without the marks showing through the sheet. This was especially so with drawings in pen or in pen and wash, but even red chalk showed through the paper slightly. Another reason for not drawing on the back was that it was easier to see the image on the front reversed, by turning the paper round and holding it up to the light (see No. 147). In the Catalogue we have often commented upon Guercino's habit of reversing figures in his compositions as the design for a picture progressed.

Guercino only occasionally used tinted papers, except, as we have seen, when he was making his detailed studies of limbs and draperies or when he was working in oiled charcoal (e.g. Nos. 4, 12, 16 and 37). A tinted paper was only exceptionally chosen for drawings in pen and ink (e.g. No. 214). Just as rare was his use of a coloured surface that he himself had prepared by brushing a lightly tinted wash onto the paper (e.g. No. 8). Although choosy about good paper, from time to time he used scrap, the commonest sort being discarded drafts of letters (e.g. No. 107), though sometimes it was account-book paper – good quality paper torn from an old ledger. Paper of this latter type is easily recognised from the parallel lines ruled towards one side of the sheet (e.g. No. 101). Guercino seems to have had a good source of such paper around the middle of the 1630s.

Drawings by Guercino and British Collections

Drawings by Guercino are well represented in most of the great Print Rooms of Europe and North America, but nowhere are they more numerous than in British collections. That they survive in such abundance today is due primarily to the artist's habit of keeping them in his own lifetime; on his death his effects included not only several of his own paintings, but also an 'infinità di dissegni'.[32] Malvasia, who was granted access to the Casa Gennari when researching the artist's life, observed that the drawings were preserved in albums, which he described as follows: 'Dieci Libri di dissegni, parte à penna, parte di lapis rosso, e nero, con diversi paesini dissegnati con esquisitezza'.[33] The custodians of this formidable collection were Guercino's nephews and heirs, Benedetto and Cesare Gennari, who seem to have regarded their uncle's work with due veneration, keeping the corpus as intact as possible. However, at the time Malvasia was writing his biography (first published in 1678), he noted that some of Guercino's drawings had already found their way into prestigious collections: 'Sono anche mostruose, e formidabili le falangi de' disegni, che schierandosi più de gli altri ne' più adorni gabinetti, sfidano coraggiosamente qual siasi mai stat'altra leggiadra penna'.[34] Malvasia himself certainly owned a substantial number of the artist's drawings, which he must have acquired, if not from Guercino himself, directly from his heirs.[35] Several drawings also found their way into British and French collections before the main dispersal of the Casa Gennari collection in the mid-eighteenth century. A likely explanation is that Benedetto Gennari, who visited the courts of King Louis XIV of France in Paris (1672–4) and Kings Charles II and James II of England in London (1674–89) and in exile in Saint-Germain-en-Laye (1689–92), took with him drawings by his famous uncle, as a way of eliciting the interest of prospective clients. Examples, for instance, were owned by the artist and collector Sir Peter Lely (1618–80), with whom

Benedetto would have come into contact at the English court. It was certainly through the mediation of Benedetto that fourteen landscape drawings by Guercino, which were engraved by Jean Pesne in Paris, found their way into the collection of the 4th Earl, later the 1st Duke, of Devonshire, presumably before Benedetto's hurried departure from England in the wake of the exiled court in 1689.[36]

In spite of this gradual erosion of the collection, an inventory of the property of the Gennari family dated 31 October 1719 attests to the fact that much of Guercino's prodigious output of drawings still survived in the family's possession and, furthermore, amounted to a sizeable proportion of the total value of their entire estate, which included both the family's house in Bologna and its country retreat, the so-called 'Casino' at Bel Poggio outside the city. The inventory was drawn up after the death in 1715 of Benedetto Gennari, who never married, to help settle the distribution of his property between his two nephews (Cesare's sons), Gianfrancesco (1671–1727) and Filippo Antonio Gennari (1677–1751). It is not known how the collection was divided between these second-generation heirs, nor exactly how it was passed on subsequently, though speculation is aided by the further researches on the Casa Gennari by Prisco Bagni, published recently.[37] The drawings inherited by Gianfrancesco would have passed at his death in 1727 to his son Carlo (1716–90), then aged eleven. Bagni has surmised that those that had belonged to Filippo Antonio, who died in 1751, also went to Carlo, since Filippo Antonio's three children were female.[38] It was Carlo, Guercino's great-great-nephew, who began to sell off sizeable portions of his inheritance, in the face of the relentless interest and enthusiasm of eighteenth-century collectors for authenticated drawings of this type, though Filippo Antonio almost certainly sold some of his own share before his death. And with so great a quantity of drawings, the obvious way to sell them most effectively was piecemeal.

The inventory reveals that the drawings in the possession of the Gennari family in 1719 were kept in three different ways: framed and hanging on the wall; preserved in eleven large albums (probably corresponding in part to the 'Dieci Libri' seen by Malvasia); and loose, presumably in folders.[39] The framed drawings were distributed between the houses in Bologna and at Bel Poggio, but the albums and the loose sheets appear to have remained together in the Casa Gennari. Of the framed drawings, almost half were by Italian artists other than Guercino and his two nephews. Since almost all these drawings were by Guercino's contemporaries and their precursors, the later Bolognese painters of the generation of Benedetto and Cesare having been scarcely represented, it seems plausible to deduce that the collection was assembled either by Guercino himself or on his behalf. This hypothesis accords with Malvasia's assertion that Guercino had a discerning eye: 'avea [. . .] perfettissima intelligenza nel discern[er]e le diverse maniere de' pittori'.[40] Just under a quarter of the framed drawings were by Guercino himself, numbering some 136 in all. Three drawings in the Exhibition can be matched with items described in this part of the inventory (Nos. 36, 54 and 188). The remainder of the framed drawings were by Benedetto and Cesare Gennari.

Of the eleven albums, eight (five imperial and three royal) contained drawings by Guercino, numbering 1,689 in all, one (royal) contained offsets of drawings by Guercino (177 drawings) and two (royal) contained drawings by the Gennari (287 drawings). The drawings were laid down on one side of each folio, with some three to four drawings per folio in the imperial albums and usually only one sheet per folio in the royals. The sheets were attached to the folios by spots of glue in the corners and consequently many drawings with a Casa Gennari provenance have losses at these points, where the paper tore as the drawing was removed from the album. Apart from such damage, sustained only later when the albums were dismantled and their contents sold, the drawings remained in excellent condition, the paper flattened and protected from sunlight, damp, dust and damage.

The loose sheets listed after the albums in the inventory comprised a miscellaneous selection of material by Guercino, the Gennari and others, divided into categories such as 'Schizami' or slight sketches, drapery studies, studies of hands, arms, legs and feet, caricatures and academic studies from the nude.

By all accounts, this remarkable corpus was still relatively intact until shortly before the middle of the eighteenth century, when it suddenly became the focus of interest, above all for English connoisseurs. In a passage in his note on Guercino in the *Abecedario*, Mariette commented on the vogue for collecting his drawings: 'Les Anglois sont passionnés pour les desseins de Guerchin'; and he went on to mention specifically the dealer William Kent, who was probably among the first to gain access to the Casa Gennari collection: 'Un des leurs, je crois M. Kent, fit graver, étant à Florence, quelques desseins de ce maître, et y employa le Zocchi'.[41] Since Kent is documented as being 'at Florence buying up Pictures' in 1758,[42] it seems likely that he had somehow got hold of a selection of drawings by Guercino by this date, probably directly from the Casa Gennari, and employed Giuseppe Zocchi (1711–67) to engrave them during his stay in Florence. Mariette also stated that Kent acquired 'à Bologne' a group of plates by Domenico Bonaveri (1653–1731) after drawings by Guercino, and since these very plates are documented as being in the possession of Guercino's heirs in the 1719 inventory, one can assume that Kent's source was indeed the Casa Gennari.[43] During this period Kent also managed to secure two important collections in their entirety, that of Francesco Maria Niccolò Gaburri in Florence in 1758 and that of the artist Benedetto Luti in Rome in 1759, both of which were subsequently offered for sale in England. Kent seems to have incorporated his purchases from the Casa Gennari into the Luti collection, which he presented for sale anonymously in London between 8 and 11 December 1762. Scattered among the drawings that Luti had amassed are both the 'anonymous' copper-plates by Bonaveri after Guercino and the seventeen drawings by Guercino with corresponding plates by Zocchi mentioned by Mariette, confirming Kent's identity as the anonymous vendor; also included in the sale were three drawings by Guercino with corresponding plates by the young Florentine engraver Francesco Bartolozzi (1727–1815); three drawings by Guercino with corresponding plates, collectively described as by Zocchi and Bartolozzi; five unengraved drawings also by Guercino; and two by 'Gennari, nephew of Guercino'. All of the twenty-eight drawings by Guercino, as well as the two by Gennari, are more likely to have been among Kent's own prize purchases from the Casa Gennari than to have come from Luti's collection.

Kent was only one of several English dealers combing Italy for Old Master drawings at this time. Particularly stiff competition presented itself in the form of the unscrupulous Richard Dalton who, from 1755, was employed as Librarian to George, Prince of Wales, afterwards King George III, to purchase works of art for the Royal Collection. Dalton had toured Italy extensively as a young man, making many influential contacts there; he was ideally qualified to act as agent, and his activity in this capacity is well documented in his correspondence with the Prince's favourite, Lord Bute, himself an enthusiastic collector of drawings. Yet despite the wealth of information that can be extracted from this exchange, there is only one documented instance of a purchase by Dalton of Guercino drawings on behalf of his royal patron. In a letter from Florence dated 17 November 1758 Dalton revealed that he had secured, among other *trouvailles*, a group of some forty drawings by Guercino: 'Now I have the pleasure to say that a fine collection of Drawings are sent to Leghorn carefully packt for HRH to the Number of near 700, one Rafaele amongst them, about 40 fine ones of Guercino and several of the Carracci & other eminent Masters'.[44] Although he does not mention his source, Dalton probably acquired the Guercino drawings directly from the Casa Gennari. Surprisingly, there is no firm evidence to explain how the remaining 800-odd drawings by Guercino and his School acquired during the reign of King George III were actually obtained. It seems more than likely that Dalton played a significant role in their procurement.

Dalton followed the despatch of drawings back to England in the summer of 1759, returning to Italy after the Prince of Wales' coronation in 1760 as King George III. He went to Venice in 1762 to assist in negotiations over the purchase of the collection of Consul Smith and possibly also of that of Cardinal Alessandro Albani in Rome. A further visit to Italy in 1763–4 took him to Bologna, and it is generally assumed that Dalton made further, much more wide-ranging purchases from the Casa Gennari during this period.[45] He was certainly in contact with Bartolozzi at this time, since the latter is documented as making drawings after pictures that the Royal Librarian was considering as possible purchases for the King, who would thus be able to judge their desirability. Dalton himself recorded that he employed Bartolozzi on the basis of his 'matchless Imitations of the Drawings of *Guercino*',[46] and it is possible that during the same period Bartolozzi made copies after drawings in the Casa Gennari to be sent back to England for the approval of the King and Lord Bute. One such copy, after a drawing by Guercino that never reached the Royal Library, was later engraved by Bartolozzi and is now itself at Windsor; it was said by the compiler of MS. Inv. A (a late eighteenth-century manuscript inventory of drawings at Windsor Castle, called 'King George III, Inventory A'), to be 'from one at Bologna that the family cou'd not then dispose of'.[47] Dalton subsequently commissioned Bartolozzi to make a series of prints after the drawings by Guercino that did enter the Royal Collection, to which purpose the engraver moved to England in 1764.

King George III's role in amassing the unique collection of Guercino drawings that remains in the Royal Library today was clearly (indeed understandably) a largely passive one; the credit for the discovery of the cache of original drawings in the custody of Guercino's heirs in Bologna and the excellence of the selection made from it clearly lies with Dalton. Something of the King's own appreciation is revealed in a recently discovered document, in which he registered his pleasure in receiving one of perhaps several batches of Guercino drawings that make up the present collection. The letter (unfortunately undated) is addressed to Lord Bute, who apparently made a gift of the drawings to the King: 'My D. Friend: I have this instant receiv'd from Dalton the collection of Guercinos you gave him for me. They are very beautiful, but their value is much encreased from the pleasure as whenever I examine them that must occur, of knowing from whom I have got them.'[48] Dalton's efforts were therefore by no means wasted on this illustrious, yet discerning patron.

The other important group of Guercino's drawings brought to England in the eighteenth century was the Bouverie collection. In Henry Reveley's short account of the artist's drawings in his collector's guide to Old Master drawings (1820), this group was described as 'perhaps the finest collection of Guercino's drawings in England'.[49] For so worthy a connoisseur as Reveley, who knew the collection of the master's drawings acquired by King George III, this was praise indeed.[50] In spite of the great importance of the

Bouverie collection, it has not been known until now precisely when or by whom in the eighteenth century it was acquired, nor, indeed, how it passed from one successive owner to another.

A 'Mr. Bouverie' is said by Reveley to have bought the drawings from a certain 'Francesco Formi at Bologna, into whose possession they had come, from a great grandson of Guercino; being the same which are noticed by Carlo Malvasio, in his Lives of the Bolognese Painters'.[51] At some point before 1820, when Reveley's account was published posthumously by his son, the Bouverie collection of Guercino's drawings had passed into the possession of a 'Mr. Hervey of Welbeck Street', London, who is said to have been Mr Bouverie's nephew; while in Hervey's possession the collection was described as having been contained 'in about twelve volumes' (one of which is here catalogued as No. 217).[52] The Bouverie/Hervey collection is next documented with the Earls of Gainsborough, who began slowly to break it up at auction, beginning with a sale in 1859 (we shall return to the matter of its dispersal, which is also touched upon in the Introduction to the Appendix below).

Hitherto the entire 'Bouverie' collection was thought to have been bought *en bloc* sometime towards the end of the 1760s by the Hon. Edward Bouverie (1738–1810) of Delapré Abbey, Northamptonshire.[53] It now seems almost certain, however, that the drawings by Guercino were acquired, probably in two or more phases, in the 1740s by John Bouverie (*c.*1722–50), the cousin of Sir Jacob Bouverie, later 1st Viscount Folkestone (1694–1761), who was Edward's father and an important collector of pictures as well as the first President of the Society of Arts.[54] If true, this would mean that the drawings (after the group brought in 1674 by Benedetto Gennari) were the first very large collection by the artist to enter England, arriving at least ten years before those of Kent and almost twenty years before those of Dalton and King George III.

The evidence for an acquisition date of the Bouverie Guercino drawings in the 1740s rather than 1760s – and thus in John's lifetime – is provided by several different sources. In a letter dated 23 October 1742 from Horace Walpole to Sir Horace Mann in Florence, Walpole asked his friend to buy for him the 'book' of drawings by Guercino that he had seen there on his last visit:

> P.S. I must add a postscript, to mention a thing I have often designed to ask you to do for me. Since I came to England I have been buying drawings (the time is well chosen, when I had neglected it in Italy!) I saw at Florence two books that I should now be very glad to have, if you could get them tolerably reasonable: one was at an English painter's, I think his name was Huckford, over against your house in the Via Bardi; they were of Holbein: the other was of Guercino, and brought to me to see by the Abbé Bonducci [*sic*]; my dear child, you will oblige me much if you can get them.[55]

In Mann's reply of 11 December of that same year he reported as follows:

> I have made search for the drawings you mention, but they are gone. Mr Bouverie bought those of Holbein of Hugford and those of Guerchin of Bondocci [*sic*], at a very high rate near two years ago. Mr Chute saw them and did not think them all originals, and if they had been not near worth the price he gave.[56]

This exchange of information tells us much. It demonstrates not only that some of Guercino's drawings were available for sale as early as about 1740, but also that a number of Englishmen were after them, including Horace Walpole, Mr Chute and a certain Mr Bouverie, who was their successful purchaser and who can be identified as John Bouverie.[57] He cannot have been Sir Jacob Bouverie, who would not have been referred to by Mann, well-versed in British etiquette, as plain 'Mr'; he was clearly John Bouverie, who, with a number of companions travelling at his expense, had in fact stayed in Mann's house in Florence in 1741.[58]

As an antiquarian, collector and connoisseur, John Bouverie attained remarkable eminence in his short life, though sadly today his contribution in these spheres has been almost completely forgotten. He was educated at Oxford, matriculating from New College on 13 October 1737 and receiving the degree of MA on 17 November 1742.[59] He had earlier inherited a large fortune, following the death of his father, Sir Christopher Des Bouveries, in 1732/3 and of his older brother, Freeman Bouverie, in 1734.[60] Before being awarded his MA, John Bouverie went abroad on the Grand Tour, principally in Italy, under the care of his 'bearleader' or tutor, the Scottish physician John Clephane (d.1758): it was presumably on this trip that he bought in Florence the album formerly with the 'Abbé Bonducci' that was referred to in the Walpole–Mann correspondence.[61]

What was the source of the drawings that Bonducci was selling? As previously stated, the main dispersal of the drawings from the Casa Gennari seems to have taken place with the sales from the late 1750s to about 1780 instigated by Carlo Gennari, Guercino's great-great-nephew. It must have been Carlo who sold the drawings to both Kent and Dalton.[62] Nonetheless the dismantling of the collection must have begun earlier, as the letters of Walpole and Mann imply. A likely explanation is that the drawings by Guercino in the 'book' that was with the 'Abbé Bonducci' in Florence about 1740 probably came originally from Carlo's uncle, Filippo Antonio Gennari, who did not die until 1751, though it is not impossible that it might have come from the young Carlo's part of the estate.

Another piece of evidence for an early acquisition date comes from a number of independent claims that in the first half of the 1740s the young Joshua Reynolds (1723–92) made copies after drawings by Guercino then available in England. The originals that Reynolds copied would almost certainly have been those from the album brought back to England by John Bouverie from his Grand Tour.[63] James Northcote (1746–1831), Reynolds's pupil and biographer, reported how Reynolds himself remembered that when apprenticed to Thomas Hudson (1701–79), around 1742–3, his master had encouraged him to copy the drawings of Guercino.[64] According to Northcote, '. . . thc youthful and tractable pupil executed his task with such skill, that many of those early productions are now preserved in the cabinets of the curious in this kingdom; most of which are actually considered as originals by that master [i.e. Guercino]'. This account is confirmed by the inscription on the *verso* of Reynolds's copy of No. 126, which begins 'This drawing is by Sir Joshua Reynolds while Pupil to M. Hudson' (the inscription is quoted in full under No. 126). Besides the drawings referred to under Nos. 126–7 and App. nos. 46 and 48, other copies by Reynolds after Guercino are known.[65]

Reynolds's master Hudson is known to have had contacts with the Bouveries. In 1749 he was commissioned by Jacob Bouverie, then newly created 1st Viscount Folkestone, to paint a series of ten portraits of members of his family for his seat at Longford Castle, the last of which was completed by Reynolds in 1757.[66] That the two artists may have had contacts with other branches of the family in the first half of the 1740s is thus entirely possible. Hudson may also have acted as the family's adviser in art collecting. He himself had been the pupil of that distinguished collector and dealer in Old Master drawings, Jonathan Richardson senior (1665–1745), whose daughter he had married, and was in his turn an important collector of Old Master drawings. And it was Hudson who first owned several of Reynolds's copies after Guercino, including that after No. 126.

One 'book' of drawings by Guercino cannot, however, account for the extensive numbers that survive today with a Bouverie/Hervey/Earls of Gainsborough provenance. Other drawings, if not acquired later as has always been supposed, could also have been acquired in the 1740s, though almost certainly not through the 'Abbé Bonducci'. Bouverie was again in Italy in 1745 and 1746, where he seems to have moved in the Jacobite circles that centred on the Court of the Old Pretender, Prince James Edward Stuart (1688–1766), who was in Rome under papal protection.[67] In May of 1745 he spent a week in Bologna in the company of the painter James Russell (recorded in Rome in 1740; died 1763), the archaeologist James Dawkins (1722–57) and Richard Phelps (*c.*1720–71), their self-styled travelling tutor.[68] There Bouverie may well have met the 'Francesco Formi' mentioned by Reveley. His surname, according to the recent research of Bagni, was Forni, not 'Formi', and he was apparently the son of Antonio Forni, the leading dealer in Old Master drawings in Bologna in the second quarter of the eighteenth century.[69] Forni senior is described by Zanotti as 'onesto cittadino bolognese, e mercatante, vago al sommo di ra[d]unar disegni d'ottimi maestri, e n'ha cumulati insieme tanti, e sì belli, e pregiati, che non v'ha raccolta in Bologna in tali cose, che possa la sua pareggiare.'[70] In addition, Bagni has pointed out that Forni senior was apprenticed to Giuseppe Magnavacca, who had compiled the inventory of the property of Casa Gennari in 1719, and it is likely that he was on good terms with the Gennari family and advised them in their affairs.[71] Clearly, this association was maintained by his son Francesco, who is named by Reveley and who seems to have acted as agent, perhaps on behalf of his father, in another, this time far larger, sale of Guercino's drawings to John Bouverie.

Bouverie was back in England in 1747, since he is reported as being at his country seat of East Betchworth (Beachworth), Surrey, in December of that year.[72] Indeed, he was already in England as early as 22 January 1747, when the sale took place in London of the magnificent collection of Old Master drawings formed by Richardson, from which he bought in person a sizeable group of drawings (for which see below). He was again in Rome and Naples in 1749, preparing for the journey for which he is best remembered: this was the voyage from Naples in the spring of 1750 to '. . . the most remarkable places of antiquity on the coast of the Mediterranean', undertaken in the company of two distinguished fellow archaeologists, Robert Wood (?1717–71) and James Dawkins (1722–57), both also formerly of Oxford, and the Italian topographical artist Giovanni Battista Borra (1712–86).[73] While on their journey, Bouverie died at Magnesia in Turkey on 8 September, his body being taken to Smyrna for burial.[74] His beautiful Latin epitaph, perhaps composed by Wood, a considerable classical scholar, praises Bouverie's cultivation in the arts (he is described as possessed of 'Artium elegantissimarum Peritia'), the extensiveness of his travels in Europe and his learnedness as a collector of the Antique.[75] Wood, Dawkins and Borra proceeded on their journey in Asia Minor and reached Palmyra and Baalbeck in March of 1751, Wood on his return to England publishing an account of the two sites in his famous *Ruins of Palmyra* (1753) and *Ruins of Balbec* (1757), in the former of which an obituary of Bouverie appears.[76]

A tantalising reference to Bouverie's various collections is provided in a letter of 1 February 1755 from the Italian artist and antiquarian Domenico Augusto Bracci (1717–95) to the 10th Earl of Huntington, in which Bracci offers his assistance to the Earl in the formation of a collection of medals, adding a little boastfully by way of encouragement that he was 'instrumental in the formation of the greater part of the collection of prints, designs [i.e. drawings], engravings, cameos and medals belonging to the late Mr J. Bouverie'.[77]

Although we have so far uncovered not a trace of John Bouverie's collection of prints, cameos and medals, some idea of his collection of Old Master drawings – besides the several hundred sheets by Guercino – may be gleaned from the 1859 Christie's sale catalogue of 'The Bouverie Collection', held on 20 July.[78] Regrettably, the larger section of the collection sold at Christie's on 27 July 1922, consisting of fourteen lots comprising at least 468 drawings (probably well over 200 by Guercino), gives a less reliable impression of the collection's scope, for the simple reason that only a few drawings were singled out for description. In both the 1859 and 1922 sale catalogues the provenances, where given for the drawings by other artists, are all of late seventeenth- and early eighteenth-century sources, above all the collection of Richardson sold in 1747, which John Bouverie attended and at which he was understandably an important buyer (the lots he bought being given in a note below); according to the much more detailed 1859 sale catalogue, not a single drawing bears the mark of a collector active only in the second half of the eighteenth century, thus confirming that the collection had already been formed by 1750.[79]

The 1859 sale catalogue shows that among the Italian schools there were represented, besides the 116 sheets by Guercino, drawings by Florentine, Roman, Venetian and other Emilian artists, with groups by or attributed to Correggio, Michelangelo, Parmigianino, Raphael, Guido Reni, Giulio Romano, Salvator Rosa, Titian, Leonardo da Vinci and others. The Dutch and Flemish schools were represented by groups of drawings by Jordaens, Ostade, Rembrandt (13), Rubens (6) and Snyders; the French by good groups by Claude (15) and Poussin (3); the German by two drawings given to Dürer; and the Swiss by a drawing attributed to Holbein the younger. Many of the drawings from this sale can still be identified today, and many are of surprisingly high quality. The collection seems to reveal Bouverie's intention to form around the nucleus of drawings by Guercino a more representative collection of drawings of all schools.

The 1859 sale catalogue, ironically, provides the only argument against John Bouverie's having acquired the drawings by Guercino in the 1740s. On the title-page it is stated that the 'series of drawings, by Guercino, [was] purchased by Mr. Bouverie about 80 years since, from the Descendants of the Artist'. This would point to a date of *c.*1779, nearly thirty years after John's death.[80] Despite this, the accumulated evidence seems to us to be very much weighted in favour of the earlier date. As we have just seen, this theory is further supported by the circumstantial evidence of the early provenances of the drawings by other artists included in the same sale. If another 'Mr Bouverie' had been responsible for forming the collection and buying the Guercino drawings, it is difficult to account for the apparent gap of about thirty years in his collecting activity.

However, conclusive proof of the fact that it was John Bouverie who formed the Bouverie collection is provided by its subsequent ownership in the second half of the eighteenth century and the early nineteenth. From Reveley it is known that the drawings by Guercino passed from Mr Bouverie into the hands of his nephew, a 'Mr Hervey' of Welbeck Street, London. When John Bouverie, a bachelor, died in 1750, he left his estate to his two sisters, Anne Bouverie (d.1757), who was married to John Hervey, Esq. (1696–1764), a Welsh circuit judge then resident in Leicester Fields, London, and Elizabeth Bouverie (d.1798), who never married.[81] Reveley's 'Mr Hervey' can thus now be identified as Christopher (d.1786), the elder of two sons of Anne and John Hervey.[82] John Bouverie's former seat at East Betchworth passed by agreement between the two sisters to the Herveys in 1752.[83] Christopher Hervey succeeded to the ownership of the estate on the death of his father John, who had only a lifetime interest in it. Christopher's younger brother, also called John, died unmarried before him, and so when Christopher died in 1786 without issue, the entire estate went to his aunt, Elizabeth Bouverie.

Already in 1772 Elizabeth Bouverie had inherited, from her cousin Sir Philip Boteler,[84] the manor of Barham Court at Teston, near Maidstone, Kent, which she set about improving – to the extent that by 1782 it was considered 'one of the greatest ornaments' of that part of the county.[85] At her death in 1798 she devised the manor-house at East Betchworth to her third cousin, the Hon. William Henry Bouverie (1752–1806), second son of the 1st Earl of Radnor. But the collection of drawings that had come to her with the property at Betchworth she bequeathed, along with the manor at Teston, to the distinguished naval officer Sir Charles Middleton (1726–1813),[86] who from 1805 was Admiral of the Red and Lord Barham of Barham Court and Teston, Kent. The precise connection between Elizabeth Bouverie and Sir Charles and his family is not yet known, but three of his grandchildren were born at Betchworth in the early 1790s when it was still in the possession of Elizabeth.[87] In 1780 Sir Charles's only child, Diana (d.1823), who inherited the Barham peerage, had married Sir Gerald Noel Noel (1759–1838). Altogether they had eighteen children, sixteen of whom survived infancy. The Bouverie collection of drawings passed to their eldest son, Charles Noel (1781–1866), either via his mother, Lady Barham, who passed her peerage on to him, or direct from his grandfather.[88] In 1841 Charles Noel was created 1st Earl of Gainsborough, and it was from his property that the first group of Bouverie drawings was sold in 1859.

The collection seems to have remained more or less intact until this sale. One alienation that took place before then was that of a small group of drawings by Guercino (and apparently some by Salvator Rosa also) which seems to have been acquired, probably by purchase, by the avid collector of pictures John Rushout, 2nd Lord Northwick (1770–1859), from whose collection the drawings were eventually sold at auction in 1919 and 1920.[89] At some other point another group passed from the Earls of Gainsborough to the Fowell Buxtons, almost certainly via the marriage in 1862 between the 1st Earl's daughter Victoria (d.1916) and Sir Thomas Fowell Buxton, 3rd Bt (d.1915).[90] The next major dispersal of the Bouverie collection took place in 1922, with a sale from the collection of the 3rd Earl of Gainsborough, followed by a number of lesser sales, including one in 1953, from the 5th Earl.[91] Since then a great number of the Bouverie Guercino drawings have passed into continental European and North American collections; nonetheless there are nearly fifty drawings with this remarkable provenance in the present Exhibition of the artist's drawings from British collections (amounting to just under a quarter of the whole).[92]

Whatever their complex and fascinating history, drawings by Guercino with a Bouverie collection provenance share many features in common. They are in general in remarkably fine, even pristine condition, which implies, as

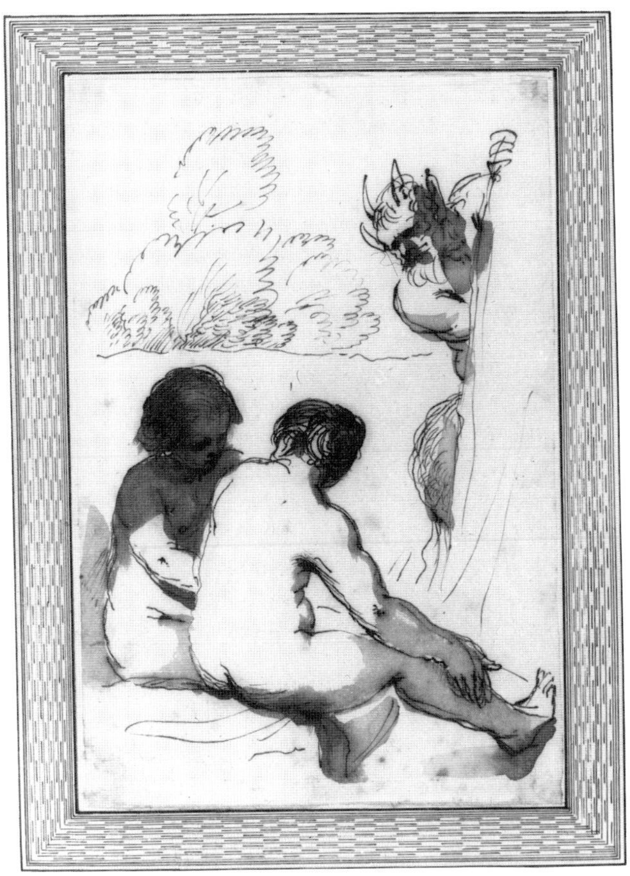

Fig. 4 *Two Nymphs and a Satyr* (No. 203, complete with 'Casa Gennari' mount). Pen and brown ink and brown wash, 203 × 137 mm (London, Courtauld Institute Galleries, Witt Collection)

Reveley was the first to observe, that they were very largely the drawings once preserved in the albums described by Malvasia as being in the master's house. (The exceptions are some of those drawn in iron-gall ink, where the paper has been eaten away in the darks in the manner previously described.) Although the drawings now at Windsor remain the single most impressive group of Guercino's drawings in existence, they were probably *in toto* rather less fine a corpus. Included among the Windsor drawings are some that had become faded and damaged from having been kept on the walls in the Gennari family's two households,[93] while others that were clearly from the albums tend to be studies of groups of figures, single figures and heads rather than the more desirable pictorial composition studies in which the Bouverie collection was so rich.

Many of the Bouverie drawings carry the collection mark, a small *B* stamped in black ink in a corner of the sheet.[94] Cryptic Italian inscriptions in pen and ink of the late seventeenth century or early eighteenth, the significance of which, with one or two exceptions, remains unknown, occur on several of the drawings or their mounts.[95] Often a number written in pencil, likewise obscure in origin but inscribed at some point in the nineteenth century almost certainly by an English hand, is also to be found on either the drawing or its mount.[96] Many of the more spectacular drawings were mounted on a backing with a highly individual, somewhat modernistic ruled border (see Fig. 4).[97] The ruled lines vary widely in pattern, but are usually drawn in a blackish-grey ink. Sometimes red or brown ink is used, most frequently if the drawing, for instance one in red chalk, itself implies such a colour.[98] For other drawings plainer mounts were adopted, while still others were simply tipped in loose into the 'twelve volumes'. In spite of the recent fashionable trend, now fortunately over, to remove drawings from what were thought to be extraneous, later accretions, many of the special ruled mounts have survived, much enhancing the drawings they surround. The combination of mount and drawing appeals again today, perhaps as a result of our understanding of the intended contrast between the austere, abstract decoration of the border and the energetic drawing of the sheet it encompasses.

Although these backings have acquired the denomination 'Casa Gennari mounts', it remains unclear when and by whom they were applied to the drawings. The vast majority of drawings with a 'Casa Gennari mount' are by Guercino or occasionally by members of his School, but they are in some rare instances found supporting drawings by other masters similarly once in the 'Bouverie collection'.[99] It is generally thought that the mounts were made in Italy, since their design seems not to be English and the paper is almost certainly Italian. Perhaps it was Forni who first bought the drawings and then arranged for them to be mounted in this

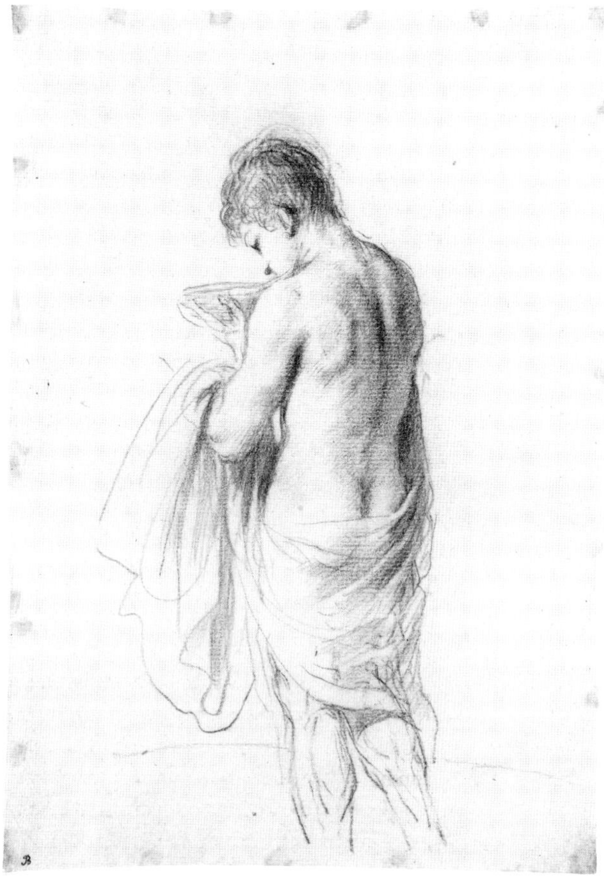

Fig. 5 *Study for the Figure of Ganymede*. Red chalk, 265 × 189 mm (New York, Metropolitan Museum of Art, inv. no. 63.75.2)

way before their acquisition by Bouverie.[100] Drawings were attached to these 'Casa Gennari mounts' by small paper tabs pasted along the edges of the sheet; most of the drawings had previously been torn from the artist's albums, hence the tears and glue stains often found at the corners where they had been stuck down first. Fig. 5 reproduces a red chalk drawing on such a mount (with the border now trimmed away but leaving a trace of a red ruled line) showing the discolouration of the paste at these points along the edge.[101] A campaign of repairs clearly preceded the mounting of the drawings onto 'Casa Gennari' backings. Already in the Casa Gennari the iron-gall ink had eaten through the paper of many of the drawings, probably as early as about 1700, and the tinted patches of paper stuck to the back of some of the drawings from the 'Bouverie collection' (see the reproduction of the *versos* of Nos. 124 and 132) are identical with those found on many sheets with similar damage now in the Royal Collection at Windsor.[102]

With the second half of the nineteenth century, following the sale of an important part of the Bouverie collection in 1859, the story of British collecting of Guercino's drawings becomes more complex. As it is partly told in the Introduction to the Appendix, the details need not detain us here.[103] During the twentieth century dispersal rather than accumulation has become the dominant trend. Nevertheless, a number of significant collections of drawings by the master have been formed within this period, three of which will be discussed here. From this point onwards the history of British collecting merged with another strand in the story, the growth and maturity of the scientific study of Guercino's work as an artist. (Indeed, it is interesting how these two phenomena have progressed hand in hand.) The initial stimulus for this revival of interest was the second divestment, on 27 July 1922, at Christie's, London, of another section of the Bouverie collection by the 3rd Earl of Gainsborough, the number of drawings in this sale being much greater than the first, as is evident from a cursory glance at the five lots, each with scores of drawings (lots 81–5).

Among those to take greatest advantage of this event was the art collector Sir Robert Witt (1872–1952),[104] who is today best remembered for his collection of photographs and reproductions of works of art, which he started to assemble while an undergraduate at Oxford and which in 1944 he made over to the newly established Courtauld Institute.[105] In parallel with his collection of reproductions and photographs, Witt formed a collection of Old Master drawings that was intended to complement it. Given the difficulty of being able to afford choice examples by the great masters, he instead:

> . . . concentrated on obtaining representative works by artists who, while interesting or charming, were slightly below the highest rank, or who were temporarily out of fashion. In this way his collection, while it contained many more works of great intrinsic beauty, became to some extent an accumulation of documents of use to the art historian.[106]

Rarely studied as a whole, the importance of his collection remains to be fully appreciated, but the passing of time has undoubtedly made it more than an 'accumulation of documents'. The fine series of Guercinos is unquestionably one of its glories. For decades they provoked no special interest, and the patronising recognition of the group by the art critic Clive Bell in a review of the collection when it was on exhibition at the Victoria and Albert Museum in 1943 must have been typical of the period: 'As for the grand Italian style, Guercino was no giant, but that amateur must be hard to please who cannot enjoy the choice examples of his calligraphy from Sir Robert Witt's collection.'[107]

There is no reason to believe that Witt had any particular passion for Guercino before the 1922 sale. The artist is not mentioned at all in his early popular book on the appreciation of art, *How to Look at Pictures*, published in 1902. Like all good collectors, however, he responded to the opportunity of securing an unparalleled group of the master's drawings. Witt appears to have commissioned the firm of Meatyard to bid on his behalf for lot 81,[108] in quality probably the best single surviving group of drawings by Guercino from that sale and thus from the distinguished Bouverie/Hervey/Earls of Gainsborough provenance. Of the twenty drawings in the Exhibition on loan from the Courtauld Institute Galleries, only two were not apparently from this source.[109] Many of the drawings from lot 81 were not, however, bequeathed to the Gallery at Witt's death, as he was in the habit of turning over his collection, selling some drawings to buy others. An example of a fine Guercino drawing disposed of in this way is cited under App. no. 102.

Another amateur and collector on the scene at the time of the 1922 sale was Archibald Russell (1879–1955), Lancaster Herald of Arms and the author of the first book on the drawings of the master, *Drawings by Guercino*, which was published in 1923.[110] With one exception, the five drawings from his own collection reproduced in the book have an Earls of Gainsborough, and therefore Bouverie, provenance, as did all five from that of Sir Robert Witt.[111] Even though he wrote at a time when appreciation of Italian Baroque art was still much affected by the strong dislike for it of the preceding Victorian era, he described the artist's drawings with sympathy and understanding:

> In the lightness of touch, in the transparency of effect, as well as in the luminous use of the untouched spaces of white paper, which are characteristic of the best of these [pen-and-wash] sketches, he is the forerunner of Tiepolo, who, it may be observed, is known to have held the drawings of Guercino in the highest esteem and to have formed a collection of them. . . .[112]

Russell also realised that the great corpus of surviving drawings of different type and quality presented alarming problems of connoisseurship. To ensure a proper understanding of the artist he recommended a 'rigid process of selection' in order to '. . . safeguard his name from a multitude of copies, imitations and school pieces, not to speak of wholly unrelated drawings, that have been assigned to him.'[113]

He then went on to advocate what today seems an unorthodox line of enquiry:

> For any profitable purpose of study we may, however, eliminate not these alone [the copies, imitations, etc.] but the great majority of the sketches which are indisputedly from his hand, since were he to be judged by the general level of his performance he would have little claim to higher distinction than that of capable mediocrity.[114]

Equally surprising is Russell's generalisation that most of the drawings were made 'for their own sake' rather than as working studies for pictures.[115] According to him, the number of such preparatory drawings was extremely small, and this apparent lack of rapport between the artist's drawings and his painted work denied the critic the possibility of dating the drawings properly.

The first to realise the importance of connecting the drawings with the pictures in order to establish a proper chronology for the former was the collector and leading art historian Sir Denis Mahon (b.1910), whose fine collection of drawings is now on loan to the Ashmolean Museum, Oxford; it is generously represented in this Exhibition by no less than twenty-nine drawings. Sir Denis has devoted a lifetime to the study of Guercino, transforming our understanding of the master's work in the process and forming at the same time an unrivalled collection of Guercino's pictures and drawings.[116] His research on the entire *œuvre* was published for the first time in the catalogue accompanying two exhibitions (one of paintings, the other of drawings) held at Bologna in 1968 in honour of the 300th anniversary of the artist's death.[117] Mahon is now organising another exhibition to take place in Bologna in September 1991 to mark the occasion of the 400th anniversary of the artist's birth – likewise the purpose of this Catalogue.

No work on Guercino can go forward without acknowledgement of Mahon's formidable contribution, and the reader will be aware of our great debt to him on every page. His achievement in this and other spheres was succinctly and admirably outlined in an essay by James Byam Shaw, entitled 'Denis Mahon: a sketch', which prefaced the catalogue to an exhibition held at the Ashmolean in 1986 to draw attention to Mahon's deposit there of his collection of drawings by Guercino.[118] As was fully evident then and now, Mahon belongs to a distinguished tradition of British collectors of drawings by Guercino, whose perspicacity – as well as Guercino's own brilliance – is, we hope, well reflected in this Exhibition. His enthusiasm has continued unabated since at least 1934, when he bought his first painting by the artist: he is, as Mariette would say, 'passionné pour le Guerchin'.

Notes

1. APSB, baptisms, 1585–96, fol. 82*v*; M, *Dipinti*, 1968, p. 4.

2. Malvasia, 1678, II, p. 361; 1841, II, p. 257.

3. Scannelli, 1657, p. 360.

4. Malvasia, 1678, II, p. 360; 1841, II, p. 256.

5. Malvasia, 1678, II, p. 360; 1841, II, p. 256; M, *Dipinti*, 1968, pp. 9–10, n. 26.

6. Mahon (1937, p. 117, n. 18) published a passage which he found in Malvasia's manuscript notes (Biblioteca Comunale dell'Archiginnasio, Bologna, MS. B. 16): '[Guercino] soggiongeva che egli . . . veniva spesso à Bologna à vedere le cose de Carracci, et ad osservarle, e à fare memoria, e poi tornava à Cento ad operare.'

7. B, 1984, p. 269, document 3.

8. Bottari, 1754–8, vol. I, pp. 208–9; see also M, *Dipinti*, 1968, p. 45.

9. Malvasia, 1678, II, p. 363; 1841, II, p. 259.

10. Malvasia, 1678, II, p. 364; 1841, II, p. 259.

11. B, 1984, p. 225 and n. 14.

12. Malvasia, 1678, II, p. 383; 1841, II, p. 272.

13. Malvasia, 1678, II, p. 366; 1841, II, p. 261 (under the year 1624); M, 1949, p. 221.

14. Guiffrey, 1876, pp. 252–4; M, *Dipinti*, 1968, pp. 132–3, and n. 24.

15. But see Loire, 1990, p. 24 and n. 34.

16. Malvasia, 1678, II, p. 374; 1841, II, p. 266.

17. Ruffo, 1916, p. 112.

18. Ibid., p. 101.

19. Ibid., p. 106.

20. Mariette, 1741, p. 57. 'Vaghesse' is a rendering in French of the Italian *vaghezza* (charm).

21. Ibid.

22. See M, 1968, pp. 346f. and M & T, 1989, p. xviii.

23. Particulars of the prints are given under No. 86.

24. This was the central theme of a paper on the drawings of Ludovico Carracci presented by Turner at a meeting of the College Art Association of America, held in New York in February 1990, to be published shortly.

25. M, *Disegni*, 1969, no. 1.

26. Bononi's drawings have been the subject of a number of articles in *Master Drawings*: VII, 1969, pp. 413–24 (E. Schleier); VIII, 1970, pp. 387–90 (L. Frerichs); X, 1972, pp. 363–78 (E. Schleier); and XIX, 1981, p. 444 (N. Turner). The monumental simplicity of Bononi's drapery studies – illuminated in much the same subtle way as those by Guercino – makes it plausible that there is some stylistic connection between the work of the two artists at this time. Furthermore, the way Guercino simplifies the structure of hands in his early drawings also has something in common with Bononi.

27. For what was almost certainly Guercino's collection of drawings by other Italian masters, which included drawings by Correggio and Parmigianino, see M & T, 1989, p. xix.

28. Particulars of the print are given under No. 25.

29. M & T, 1989, p. xv.

30. M, *Disegni*, 1969, under no. 7; M & T, 1989, p. xv, n. 4.

31. M & T, 1989, p. xx.

32. Malvasia, 1678, II, p. 384, 1841, II, p. 273.

33. Malvasia, 1678, II, p. 385, 1841, II, p. 273.

34. Ibid.

35. Mariette, 1741, p. 58; M & T, 1989, p. xviii and n. 13.

36. See Nos. 166–70.

37. B, 1990, pp. 11–13.

38. Ibid., p. 11.

39. For a detailed analysis of the 1719 inventory, see M & T, 1989, pp. xviii–xxii.

40. Malvasia, 1678, II, p. 383, 1841, II, p. 272.

41. Mariette, 1851–60, I, p. 64.

42. Stainton, 1983, p. 12; M & T, 1989, p. xxviii.

43. See further M & T, 1989, p. xxviii and under nos. 588–9.

44. Mount Stuart Archive, Mount Stuart, Rothesay, Isle of Bute, 17 November 1758, from Florence; see M & T, 1989, p. xxvi and n. 29.

45. M & T, 1989, pp. xxix–xxxi.

46. Richard Dalton, *Remarks on Prints intended to be published, relative to the Manners, Customs, &c. of the present Inhabitants of Egypt*, London, 1781, p. 10 n.; M & T, 1989, p. xxx and n. 44.

47. See M & T, 1989, p. xxx.

48. Extract from the letters of King George III to the 3rd Earl of Bute (no. 401), Cardiff Public Library, Manuscripts Department, Bute Collection. We are grateful to the Hon. Mrs. Roberts of the Royal Library, Windsor Castle, for kindly bringing this document to our attention.

49. Reveley, 1820, p. 77. The author of the text, Henry Reveley, died in 1798, but his book was published posthumously by his son Hugh. Russell (1923, p. 16) first drew attention to the importance of this short description of the Bouverie collection. See also n. 82 below.

50. Reveley, 1820, p. 76: 'In the Royal one [collection] at the Queen's palace, there are fourteen large volumes full, besides many loose in portfolios. They are executed in different manners: some are in chalks; others are penned; and many are washed and shaded with bistre, in a masterly style.'

51. Ibid., p. 77. Guercino of course had no great-grandsons, only nephews and great-nephews etc. through his sister. The reference to the original albums is in Malvasia, 1678, II, p. 385; 1841, II, p. 273.

52. Ibid., p. 77.

53. The first to comment upon the Bouverie collection of drawings,

erroneously associating the *B* mark with the ownership of the Hon. Edward Bouverie's son, also called Edward (1767–1858), was Louis Fagan in his *Collector's Marks*, London, 1883, p. 8. This identification was continued by Lugt in his *Marques de collections*, no. 325. Lugt revised his earlier account in his *Supplément*, under no. 2858c, giving the collection instead to the Hon. Edward Bouverie, as Russell had already done (1923, p. 16); he was followed in this view by later writers, including Mahon (M, 1968, pp. 348f. and *Disegni*, 1969, p. 11).

The Hon. Edward Bouverie was educated at Christ Church College, Oxford, matriculating on 17 January 1757, aged 18. He succeeded to the Clarke estates in Northamptonshire in 1759 and was MP for New Sarum in 1761 and 1768 and MP for Northampton in 1790. He is said to have bought Delapré Abbey in 1764 for £22,000, in the same year that he married Harriet, daughter of Sir Everard Fawkener and a well-known beauty of the time. He died on 3 September 1810 in Old Burlington Street, St James's, London. In his will dated 14 December 1808 (PROB11/1515/455), Edward nominated his wife Harriet as his Residuary Legatee. In 1811 she married Lord Robert Spencer, son of the 3rd Duke of Marlborough, who died without offspring in 1831. We are grateful to Mr William Keymer for kindly providing us with the above information.

54. Jacob Bouverie succeeded to the baronetcy of his brother in 1736 and was elevated to the peerage on 29 June 1747, with the titles of Lord Longford, Baron of Longford and Viscount Folkestone. His wife, whom he married in 1723, was Mary Clarke, daughter and sole heiress of Bartholomew Clarke of Hardingstone in the County of Northamptonshire. From this union there are references to the following births/baptisms: William (1725), Mary (1726; ?deceased in infancy), Jacob (1727), Bartholomew (1728), Ann (1729), Mary (1730), Harriet (1731; ?deceased in infancy), Charlotte (1732), Edward (1734; ? deceased in infancy), Harriot (1736), and Edward (1738; the future Hon. Edward, with whom the Guercino drawings have been traditionally associated). Lady Bouverie died in 1739, the year after Edward's birth. In 1741 Sir Jacob married a second time, Elizabeth, daughter of Lord Romney.

For details about John Bouverie as well as pedigrees of the Bouverie and Clarke families, we are most grateful to Miss Rachel Watson, County Archivist, Northamptonshire Record Office, Delapré Abbey, Northampton.

For Jacob Bouverie's interest in art collecting, see Lippincott, 1983, pp. 48, 58–9, and 113.

55. Lewis, *Walpole*, 1937–83, XVIII, pp. 91–2. We are grateful to Dr Tom Keymer for bringing this and the following reference to our attention. 'Huckford' was Ignatius Hugford (1703–78), an English painter and engraver settled in Italy. The identity of a 'Bonducci' is discussed by Lewis, *Walpole*, 1937–83, XVII, p. 64, n. 40.

The so-called Holbein drawings are the thirty-two portrait drawings, which, together with their title-page, are now in the British Museum, placed under Clouet, inv. nos. 1910–2–12–52 to 84 (see L *Suppl*, under no. 1468a and J. Fleming, *Connoisseur*, 1955, pp. 106–10 and 197–206). Interestingly, the drawings are mounted on backings decorated with ruled lines not unlike the 'Casa Gennari mounts' referred to below (see also Fig. 4), thereby providing an independent indication that mounts of this kind were not unusual in about 1740. The drawings, which do not seem to be by either Holbein or Clouet (and appear not to have been included in the 1859 Bouverie sale catalogue, for which see below) were bequeathed to the Museum by George Salting (1835–1909).

56. Lewis, *Walpole*, 1937–83, XVIII, p. 116.

57. According to the Index in Lewis, *Walpole*, the 'Mr Bouverie' referred to was John Bouverie (*c.*1722–50).

Chute's disparaging comment about the authenticity of the drawings in the albums Bouverie had secured might have been legitimate in some cases, especially that of the so-called Holbeins, which would indeed have been rarities if genuine – but they were not! On the other hand, he might have been piqued at not having himself bought the albums, which had evidently also caught the eye of Walpole. For the Mr Chute concerned, whose Christian name, as we have been kindly informed by Mr Francis Russell, was Challoner, see L. Lewis, *Connoisseurs and Secret Agents in Eighteenth-Century Rome*, London, 1961, pp. 128–32 and 137. As it turned out, the Chute family did at some point acquire an album of drawings by Guercino. The folio volume, bound in half roan, contained twenty-eight drawings by the master and was sold at Sotheby's on 22 June 1949, as the property of C. L. Chute, The Vyne, Basingstoke. The following drawings in the Catalogue once belonged to this album: Nos. 55, 66, 73, 125, 135 and 138.

58. In 1741 Sir Jacob had released a considerable sum of money to an intermediary in Rome, who was apparently negotiating the purchase of a 'Guercino' (presumably a painting) on his behalf. This much can be deduced from an entry in Sir Jacob's Account Book held in the Muniment Room at Longford Castle, which is dated 20 November 1741: 'Claude Aubert's bill being money remitted to Rome for a Guercino. £146. 12. 0.' Unfortunately no such picture is recorded in the inventories of Longford Castle. We wish to thank Miss Argar of the Estate Office of Longford Castle for bringing this transaction to our notice and for kindly informing us that the account books in the Muniment Room at Longford Castle (which cover the years of the 1st Viscount Folkestone and the 1st and 2nd Earls of Radnor, from 1720 to 1823, and which provide details of the prices for nearly all the more important pictures purchased within that period) do not mention the purchase of any drawings by Guercino.

For John Bouverie's visit, see Lewis, *Walpole*, 1937–83, XVII, pp. 63–4, 67, 70, 83, 116–17, 146 and 153–4.

59. Papers of Sir Brinsley Ford (under J. Bouverie), Mellon Centre for British Art, London, quoting from *Alumni Oxonienses*.

60. W. Page (ed.), *The Victoria History of the Counties of England: History of Surrey*, III, London, 1967, pp. 167f.

61. For Clephane, see *DNB*, XI, London, 1887, p. 37. Mr Francis Russell refers to the journey of Clephane and Bouverie in his typescript *Dr Clephane in Italy . . .*, which he has kindly allowed us to consult, most of which was published in the *Burlington Magazine*, CXXVII, 1985, pp. 890ff. According to Russell, Clephane and Bouverie set out on their journey on 1 October 1740. In April 1741 the two men travelled from Genoa to Milan, when Bouverie fell seriously ill; at the end of May they were in Venice, and in early June in Bologna. They arrived in Florence on 10 June, making expeditions to Pisa and Leghorn soon after, staying at Mann's 'little house over the Arno' until October. From Florence they journeyed to Rome, arriving there in November; they seem to have returned to England in the spring or early summer of 1742.

Further notice of Bouverie's presence in Florence in the summer of 1741 (on 24 June and 10 September) is provided in the Papers of Sir Brinsley Ford (under J. Bouverie), MCBA (see n. 59 above), quoting from letters from Horace Mann to Walpole and from F. Whithed to T. Puckeridge (the latter in the Hampshire Records Office).

It is worth noting that while in Italy, Clephane was also acting for Sir Jacob Bouverie in the purchase of pictures (see Russell).

62. M & T, 1989, pp. xvii and xxvff.

63. Mahon had previously suggested that Reynolds's copies could have been made when he was painting the twin portrait of the Hon. Mrs Edward Bouverie together with Mrs John Crewe contemplating a tomb marked 'Et in Arcadia Ego' (M, 1967, p. 73, under no. 45; *Disegni*, 1969, p. 210, under no. 225); this portrait was exhibited at the Royal Academy in 1769 (Waterhouse, 1941, p. 60) and was followed by one of the Hon. Mrs Edward Bouverie with her child exhibited at the Academy in the following year (Waterhouse, 1941, p. 60).

64. Northcote, 1813, I, p. 13.

65. Mahon tentatively attributed two drawings after Guercino in his own collection to Reynolds (1967, nos. 49–50) and also pointed out that a third copy attributable to Reynolds (after a drawing by Guercino with a Bouverie/Hervey/Earls of Gainsborough provenance that also belongs to him) was in the collection of John Nicholas Brown, Providence, Rhode Island (M, 1967, no. 45; M, *Disegni*, 1969, no. 225; M & E, 1986, no. 44). Byam Shaw catalogued as Reynolds three copies after Guercino in the Fondation Custodia, Institut Néerlandais, Paris (1983, I, nos. 355–7). What is probably yet another example is in the Weld collection, Lulworth Manor (inv. no. 107; Courtauld Institute of Art, neg. no. 504/15/22), and bears the collector's mark of Thomas Hudson; it is an important piece in the puzzle since it was copied from a drawing by Guercino of *Sts Roch and Sebastian*, formerly in the Bouverie/Hervey/Earls of Gainsborough and Sir Robert Witt collections and now in the Snite Museum of Art, Notre Dame (we were informed of the present whereabouts of this latter drawing by Dr David Stone). There are many others. So far every traceable Guercino drawing copied by Reynolds appears to have a Bouverie provenance.

66. Miles, 1979, unpaginated, but tenth page counting from the beginning of the introduction. For some of Sir Jacob's children who could have sat for Hudson, see n. 54 above.

67. For Bouverie's 1745 visit, see the Papers of Sir Brinsley Ford (under J. Bouverie), MCBA (see n. 59 above), quoting both from a letter of James Russell of 13 July 1745 and from a note among the Clephane Papers, Scottish Records Office, of 24 October 1745. For Bouverie's presence in Italy in 1746, see Lewis, *Connoisseurs and Secret Agents*, London, 1961, p. 134, where he is described as having left Rome '. . . in suspicious circumstances in March 1746 and was thought to have gone on some mission from the Pretender to the Court of Vienna'.

68. Papers of Sir Brinsley Ford (under J. Bouverie), MCBA (see n. 59 above), quoting from a letter of James Russell, dated Florence, 13 July 1745: 'On May 5th I [Russell] left Rome, in company with Mr Dawkins, Mr Bouverie, and Mr Phelps, taking the road to Loretto from whence we went to Ancona, and so to Bologna, where we arrived the 12th [May]. After a week's stay at which place, we set out for Venice, in order to be there at the feast of the Ascension.' On 4 June Russell took leave of Dawkins, and with Bouverie and Phelps, came to Florence.

69. Bagni, 1990, p. 12.

70. Zanotti, 1739, II, p. 333.

71. Bagni, 1990, p. 12.

72. Papers of Sir Brinsley Ford (under J. Bouverie), MCBA (see n. 59 above), quoting from a letter of James Russell of 9 December 1747 to T. W. Drake, British Library, Dept. of MSS., Add MS. 41169. John Bouverie inherited the manor at East Betchworth on the premature death of his brother in 1734. The estate had descended from their mother Elizabeth Freeman, daughter and sole heiress of Ralph Freeman of Betchworth.

73. For Wood, see *DNB*, LXII, London, 1900, pp. 373–5; for Dawkins, see *DNB*, *Supplement*, ii, London, 1901, pp. 119–20; and for Borra, see *Dizionario biografico degli italiani*, XII, Rome, 1970, pp. 807–9.

74. His death is recorded in *Gentleman's Magazine*, 1750, p. 525.

75. His epitaph is published in Sir E. Brydges, ed., *Collins's Peerage of England*, V, London, 1812, pp. 32–4.

76. R. Wood, *Ruins of Palmyra*, 1753, p. 6: 'Besides those virtues, the loss of which we regret in common with all his friends . . . the great objects of his private entertainment were almost every thing which comes within the circle of Virtù, in which he had acquired such knowledge, by several journies to Rome, that his opinion in those matters had authority among the connoisseurs of that country; and indeed his collection of drawings, medals, intaglio's and cameo's, (which would have grown very considerably had he lived) are proofs of the correctness of his taste.'

77. Papers of Sir Brinsley Ford (under J. Bouverie), MCBA (see n. 59 above), quoting from HMC, Hastings MS., III, 1934, p. 91. Bracci's credentials as a scholar of the Antique were subsequently questioned by the famous J. J. Winkelmann, who came to Rome in 1755.

78. The manor-house at East Betchworth was said (W. Page, ed., *The Victoria History of the Counties of England: History of Surrey*, III, London, 1967, p. 168) to contain '. . . some antiquities brought from Italy . . . in the eighteenth century'; these may have been purchased by John Bouverie rather than by John Hervey as stated there. It is also possible that Mr Hervey, who was John's executor after his death, travelled to Italy to bring back objects previously acquired by Bouverie. See also n. 81 below.

As Mahon (1968, p. 350) pointed out, the owner of the property of the 1859 sale was the 1st Earl of Gainsborough (1781–1866).

79. According to the copy of the Richardson sale catalogue in the Department of Prints and Drawings at the British Museum (shelfmark A. 1. 8(8)), which is annotated with prices and (only sporadically) with buyers' names, 'Bouverie' was buying on the 11th to 12th and 16th to 18th nights of the sale (3–4 and 9–11 Feb. 1747, respectively). He was the purchaser of the following lots: 18, 40, 61–2 on the 11th night; 61, 63, 66 and 68 on the 12th night; 37, 49, 57 and 63 on the 16th night; 50, 52, 56 and 69 on the 17th night; and 55, 60, and 69 on the 18th night. Of these purchases, many reappear in the 1859 sale catalogue. 'Bouverie' cannot, of course, have been the Hon. Edward, who was then aged only nine; nor could he have been Sir Jacob Bouverie, created Viscount Folkestone later that same year, since the annotator, attentive to the correct form of title of the noble and gentlemen buyers, would have referred to him as 'Sir J. Bouverie'.

In the 1859 sale catalogue, forty-four drawings are cited as coming from the collection of Richardson, five from that of Sir Peter Lely (sold in 1688 or 1694), two from that of Prosper Henry Lankrink (sold in 1693 or 1694), two from that of J. P. Zoomer (sold after 1724) and one from Jean-Denis Lempereur. (Although Lempereur's principal sale was in 1773, six years before his death, he is known to have sold parts of his collection in Paris as early as 26 March 1749.)

80. A sale of Guercino material did take place from the Casa Gennari at this time, as has been noted by Bagni (1990, p. 12). The transaction is described by Oretti, a Bolognese writer of the late eighteenth century, who compiled an extensive series of manuscript notes relating to the arts. Oretti reports that towards the end of October 1779, Carlo Gennari's son Francesco 'andò a Firenze e portò seco delle Pitture del Guercino da Cento e quantità di disegni del detto Guercino e delli Gennari per esitarli'; in a following note he then states, 'verso la fine di questo Mese [October 1779] il Sig. Francesco Gennari ritornò da Florenza doppo la vendita de Libri de disegni del Guercino e delli Gennari, lasciò le Pitture da vendersi' (Biblioteca Comunale dell'Archiginnasio, Bologna, Oretti, MS. B 106, c. 98).

81. Sir E. Brydges (ed.), *Collins's Peerage of England*, V, London, 1812, pp. 34. It is there stated that John Hervey was also of Beachworth (i.e. Betchworth), but this estate he acquired only as a result of John Bouverie's demise, at which time Hervey was a resident of London. When Anne Hervey's cousin Sir Edward Des Bouverie of Longford Castle died in 1736 he left a bequest of £100 each to the Herveys, described as of Leicester Fields, London. A further family connection between the Bouveries and the Herveys is documented: in his will dated 1761, Sir Edward's brother Jacob Bouverie, Viscount Folkestone, bequeathed 20 guineas to a John Hervey, presumably also his cousin Anne's husband. (Information from notes compiled by Mr William Keymer; the wills of Jacob and Edward are PROB11/863/92 and PROB11/680/264 respectively.) John Hervey was still at the Leicester Fields address on 24 October 1751 when the Rev. Mr Russell wrote to James Russell suggesting that he contact him as John Bouverie's executor concerning a statue of Apollo that Mr Bouverie had left with James before his death (Papers of Sir Brinsley Ford (under J. Bouverie), MCBA (see n. 59 above), quoting from a letter of the Rev. Russell).

82. Rev. O. Manning and W. Bray, *The History and Antiquities of the County of Surrey . . .*, II, London, 1809, p. 208. The death date of 1786 for Christopher Hervey confirms that Reveley's account of the collection of drawings by Guercino was written by Henry well before his death in 1798 and not updated in this respect by Hugh Reveley for the 1820 publication, as has sometimes been thought (M, 1968, p. 348f.).

For Christopher Hervey, see the Papers of Sir Brinsley Ford (under C. Hervey), MCBA (see n. 59 above). In his youth Hervey was at one time considered as a possible match for Lady Mary Wortley Montagu (see *Letters*, 2nd ed., 1837, III, pp. 100–101), but he is better known for his own extended visits abroad, one of which is recorded in his *Letters from Portugal, Spain, Italy and Germany, in the Years 1759, 1760, and 1761* (3 vols, London, 1785: these are described by Ford as 'digressive and anecdotal – the author not particularly interested in antiquities and works of art').

83. Rev. O. Manning and W. Bray, *The History and Antiquities of the County of Surrey . . .*, II, London, 1809, p. 207f., gives the complete history of the ownership of East Betchworth until 1809. For the subsequent history, see also W. Page (ed.), *The Victoria History of the Counties of England: History of Surrey*, III, London, 1967, p. 167f.

84. He was the only son of her aunt Anne Bouverie (d. 1717), who in 1690 married Sir Philip Boteler, Bt (d. 1719), of Teston, Kent.

85. E. Hasted, *The History and Topographical Survey of the County of Kent . . .*, II, Canterbury, 1782, *ad vocem* 'Teston'. According to Pevsner, *Buildings of England: West Kent and the Weald*, Harmondsworth, 1976, p. 568, the house was remodelled *c.*1791–2 by Benjamin H. Latrobe (1764–1820). It was apparently the first commission of this British-born architect, who subsequently emigrated to the United States, where he was an enormous success.

86. Sir E. Brydges (ed.), *Collins's Peerage of England*, V, London, 1812, p. 34.

87. Ibid., IX, p. 248.

88. In his will Lord Barham, who died in 1813, left each of his then fourteen grandchildren the considerable sum of £10,000 (V. Gibbs (ed.), *The Complete Peerage*, I, London, 1910, p. 422, *ad vocem* 'Barham').

89. Sales were held on 18 November 1919 and 1 November 1920, at Sotheby's, London. The group has been discussed by Mahon (M, 1968, p. 350; and M, *Disegni*, 1969, p. 12). Long before, there had been an anonymous sale of drawings from the Bouverie collection at Sotheby's on 6 March 1888, of which twenty-eight were sold as by Guercino (see M, *Disegni*, 1969, p. 13, n. 25 and no. 221).

90. This group until recently belonged to Sir Thomas Fowell Buxton, 6th Bt, at Woodredon, Waltham Abbey, Essex, and comprised about ten drawings, perhaps the most important of which was the *St Michael* (M, *Studies*, 1947, fig. 16), the present whereabouts of which are unknown. Some of the group was sold at Sotheby's, London, on 23 March 1978.

91. The sale on 27 July 1922 has been discussed above; another took place on 22 July 1953 at Sotheby's, London.

92. They are as follows: Nos. 6, 10, 12, 14, 23–4, 27, 33, 38, 44, 46, 54, 56, 71, 81, 87–8, 96, 103–4, 107, 109–11, 113–14, 120–21, 124, 126–7, 132, 134, 140–41, 152–4, 158, 189–91, 194, 196, 203, 209, 211–12.

93. The sort of damage sustained by drawings kept in this way was considered by Mahon and Turner (M & T, 1989, pp. xviiiff.).

94. L 325: see also the discussion under n. 53 above. The following drawings in the Catalogue are stamped with this mark: Nos. 12, 54, 113, 120, 134, 141 and 154. Mahon (M, 1968, pp. 349f.) argued convincingly that the stamp was only applied, with some few exceptions, to the drawings in the 1859 sale; this explains its absence from so many drawings with the same provenance sold later. The mark was very probably applied by Christie's, the auction house responsible for the sale.

95. See M, 1968, p. 350. The following drawings in the Catalogue carry such inscriptions: Nos. 10, 14, 24, 27, 38, 44, 46, 103, 124, 126–7 and 196.

96. The examples where this numbering occurs are listed under No. 10.

97. For a discussion of these mounts, see L *Suppl*, 2858c; M, 1967, p. 20, where a number of examples of both borders and inscriptions are reproduced; and M, 1968, p. 350f. The following drawings in the Catalogue are mounted in this way: Nos. 10, 23–4, 27, 38, 87, 96, 110, 114, 127, 132, 141, 154, 194 and 203.

98. No. 154 is such an example.

99. A drawing attributed to the Florentine painter Agostino Ciampelli (1565–1630) of the *Adoration of the Magi* in the British Museum is mounted in such a way (inv. no. 1946–7–13–1480); on the verso (?) John Bouverie's attribution to *Paolo Farinati*, inscribed top centre in pen and brown ink. So too is one of a *Group of Peasants*, perhaps by Ercole Bazicaluva (*c.*1610–after 1641), in an English private collection. It remains possible that such drawings could also have come from the Casa Gennari, since we know from the inventory of 1719 that Guercino had possessed drawings by other artists.

100. See M, 1968, p. 351; and M, *Disegni*, 1969, p. 11. An inscription in Italian on the back of one of these mounts (that of No. 27) reads: *Ricercata del terribile Quadro del S. Guglielmo nella Chiesa di S. Gregorio in Bologna*. This, as Mahon has pointed out (1967, p. 30), clearly shows familiarity with two of Malvasia's comments on the altarpiece; further, Mahon (1968, p. 351) draws attention to the fact that this could indicate the mounts were 'supplied in Bologna'.

A proper analysis of the watermarks on the backing sheets on which the borders have been drawn remains to be undertaken.

101. The drawing, in the Metropolitan Museum of Art, New York, is Bean, 1979, no. 245, where the reproduction does not completely show the edges of the drawing.

102. Such repairs are visible through the paper of No. 127, a drawing with a Bouverie provenance laid down on a 'Casa Gennari mount'. There are numerous examples in the Royal Library, Windsor Castle, of damaged pen-and-ink drawings repaired in this way, the patches similarly showing through the paper; many of these drawings are still laid down onto the late eighteenth-century (?probably English) paper backings to which they were stuck when they entered the collection. A further discussion of these tinted repair patches is to be found under App. no. 49.

103. See pp. 231ff. below.

104. Witt was partner in, and eventually head of, the firm of Stephenson, Harwood and Tatham, solicitors. He helped found the National Art-Collections Fund in 1903. He was a Trustee of the National Gallery, the Tate Gallery and the Watts Gallery, Compton. For an account of his career, see the notice by Alec Martin in *DNB*, 1951–60, ed. E. T. Williams and Helen M. Palmer, Oxford, 1971.

105. Blunt, 1956, p. i, states that 600,000 reproductions of paintings were contained in his bequest. For many years this fine collection was available to specialists at his house in Portman Square. The visitors' books covering the 1920s to the mid-1940s read like a roll-call of the most distinguished art historians, collectors and museum officials of the day.

106. Blunt, 1956, p. 1.

107. *New Statesman and Nation*, 6 March 1943.

108. The drawings in the Catalogue originally from lot 81 are Nos. 6, 33, 38, 44, 46, 56, 71, 88, 96, 107, 111, 121, 132, 141, 189–91 and 203.

109. The two not from that lot are No. 154, said to have come from either lot 82 or 83, and No. 47, purchased by the Galleries after the death of Witt.

110. Referred to in the Bibliography as Russell, 1923. A pleasing vignette of this amateur and collector is to be found in the autobiography of the modern British Surrealist painter and printmaker Eileen Agar (b. 1899), who describes the ménage at his house, 'Scarbank', on the cliffs above Swanage as follows:

It was full of fascinating objects and paintings . . . He kept a Doge's hat under a glass case. It was of yellow silk and fashioned in that delightful shape which recalls Bellini . . . He even had a small moth room built on the flat roof of his house, completely empty save for an electric light bulb, which used to burn all night long to entice the moths in. He went about on summer nights with a miner's lamp on his head, wearing very little else during the hot weather, collecting midnight moths and startling the loving couples in the grass. (Eileen Agar, in collaboration with Andrew Lambirth, *A Look at my Life*, London, 1988, pp. 110f.)

We are grateful to Antony Griffiths for kindly bringing this passage to our attention.

111. On pp. 15f. he explains that many of the drawings reproduced were 'acquired by their present owners from the lately dispersed and remarkably fine collection of Guercino's drawings in the possession of the Earl of Gainsborough'. The drawings from Russell's own collection are Russell, 1923, pls. V, XVII, XVIII, XIX and XXIII (only for this last drawing is an Earls of Gainsborough provenance not stated); those from the collection of Sir Robert Witt are pls. III, VI, VII, VIII and X.

112. Russell, 1923, p. 20.

113. Ibid., p. 18.

114. ibid., p. 18.

115. Ibid., p. 22.

116. For Mahon's collection of drawings by Guercino, see M, 1967, and M & E, 1986.

117. These catalogues are abbreviated throughout in our text as M, *Dipinti*, 1968, and M, *Disegni*, 1969.

118. M & E, 1986, pp. viiif.

I Studies for History Subjects, including Drawings for Prints and Studies from the Live Model (Nos. 1–163)

The majority of Guercino's drawings were made as working studies to prepare the compositions of his paintings. By far the largest number of drawings in the exhibition fall within this category. Also included under this heading are Guercino's preparatory studies for prints as well as his rare studies from the nude model, since both types of drawing are more compatible with his work for history subjects than with any other aspect of his activity as a draughtsman.

More so than most of his contemporaries, Guercino diligently explored his ideas on paper before picking up the brush. His attitude towards his working drawings was therefore primarily utilitarian: he clearly regarded them as a means to an end and as an entirely subordinate excercise to the business of painting. The great number of his surviving drawings should not obscure this fact. As his career developed, he did come to use drawing as a pastime, but in such moments he drew landscapes, scenes from everyday life and caricatures (see Parts II and III of the Catalogue).

Guercino's drawings for pictures give a remarkable insight into the often complex stages of development through which his ideas passed before a compositional solution was reached. His procedure is marked by a lengthy process of trial and error, according to which a given design was often reversed in order to refresh his ideas for the grouping of the figures. This practice was already well developed before Guercino visited Rome in 1621 and is first fully apparent in his studies for the altarpiece of *St William receiving the monastic Habit* of 1620 (see Nos. 26–8). However, it can best be seen in the Catalogue in the groups of studies for the *Assassination of Amnon* of 1628 (Nos. 69–72), the *Visitation* of 1632 (Nos. 89–93), the *Christ appearing to St Teresa* of 1634 (Nos. 97–102) and the *Atlas* of 1646 (Nos. 144–8).

Guercino's professional activity as a painter lasted for more than fifty years. In this period his approach to drawing remained surprisingly consistent, especially in the way his compositions evolved on paper. Also much the same throughout was his rapid touch and the special skill he always possessed in evoking a sense of light. On the other hand, the change in his style within that same span was dramatic. This can be judged when two typical studies in red chalk (e.g. Nos. 3 and 163), made at the beginning and end of his career respectively, are compared. The unsteadiness of his hand in his late chalk drawing, which gives the marks a looser texture, is also apparent when the exercise is repeated for his pen-and-wash studies (e.g. Nos. 5 and 158). To illustrate the gradual evolution in his style over such a long period, the drawings in this first part of the Catalogue have been arranged as far as possible chronologically, within six subsections that correspond approximately to its major phases of development (which by no means correspond with those of his development as a painter).

With a draughtsman as prolific as Guercino, it is especially fortunate that two fundamental early sources have survived to provide a secure means of dating his paintings and thus, by extension, the many drawings related to them. One source is the long list of Guercino's commissions recorded in the life of the painter by his biographer Malvasia (1678, II, pp. 361–83; 1841, II, pp. 257–72). The other is the artist's own Account Book (the *Libro dei Conti*), kept from 1629 until his death in 1666 to note the payments for his pictures. This detailed, month-by-month register of his activities is as revealing of the business footing of the studio as of the date when a given work was finished; it is especially precious since nothing as complete survives for any other important painter of the time.

These two sources provide the basic framework for the sequence of drawings in the exhibition. However, several of the drawings cannot be connected with any known or documented works and these have been interspersed on the grounds of style among those that are securely dated, so that they might be viewed and reassessed in the context of other examples thought to be from approximately the same period. Needless to say, their precise position, before or after specific drawings in the chronology, will always be open to speculation.

1 The pre-Roman Period (Nos. 1–29)

The brilliance of Guercino's early, pre-Roman pictures was appreciated at once by his contemporaries. Their bold 'naturalism', compositional inventiveness, powerful chiaroscuro and robust brushwork must have seemed dazzling in the context of the small Emilian town of Cento. Largely due to Padre Antonio Mirandola, who first discovered the artist's talent and became his promoter and life-long friend, Guercino not only began to attract the attention of local dignitaries, but increasingly became known to more cosmopolitan figures such as Cardinal Alessandro Ludovisi, then Archbishop of Bologna and later Pope Gregory XV; Ferdinando Gonzaga, Duke of Mantua; Cardinal Serra, Papal Legate of Ferrara, and others.

In this early period of Guercino's career, the full force of his prodigious creative powers manifested itself more in his paintings than in his drawings. Nonetheless that 'Scarsellinesque' elegance that pervades his first pictures and gives his early figure types their characteristic 'Ferrarese' appearance is also apparent in his drawings. But compared with the technical virtuosity and freshness of his early pictures, his drawings of this same period seem more restrained: at this earliest moment, they are delicate in touch and highly attractive in their overall effect but their tempo is sedate. There quickly followed the more potent impact of the Emilian tradition of drawing, whose exponents were such artists as Correggio (1494–1534), Parmigianino (1503–40) and, above all, Ludovico Carracci (1555–1619). This more forceful lesson, however, was not fully absorbed until about 1618–19, and it was at this point that Guercino's personality as a draughtsman began to be properly formed.

The earliest drawings in the exhibition date from *c.*1615–18, when the artist would have been in his mid- to late twenties. During this period the largely self-taught Guercino was establishing himself in his home town of Cento. Many of the following drawings are studies for altarpieces destined for churches in provincial Emilian towns, such as Cento itself (No. 8), possibly Renazzo di Cento (No. 1), Brisighella (No. 9) and Carpi (No. 13). In 1620 Guercino was awarded his most prestigious ecclesiastical commission to date, *St William receiving the monastic Habit* (see Nos. 26–8), for S. Gregorio in Bologna, which Malvasia singled out for special praise, commenting that it outshone the fine *St George* by Ludovico Carracci which hung nearby (1678, II, p. 364; 1841, II, p. 259). Guercino also made studies for smaller devotional and mythological paintings (Nos. 3, 17–18, 19, 23–5, 29). Two drawings (Nos. 2 and 5) can be connected with the various mural paintings and frescoes Guercino painted in this early period. In 1616 Guercino set up his own *Accademia del nudo*, and Nos. 4 and 16 are probably examples of the sort of drawings from the life that he would have made there.

1 St Francis kneeling

Charcoal crayon, heightened with white, on buff paper. 301 × 226mm.

Mahon Collection, on loan to the Ashmolean Museum, Oxford, M & E, 1.

Provenance: (?)P. Crozat (his number *3* inscribed in brown ink bottom right); T. Hudson (L 2432; possibly the drawing in his sale, Langford's, London, 27 March 1779, lot 43, bt *C. Rogers, £3–6–0*); Sir J. Reynolds (L 2364); W. Mayor (L 2799); G. Branch; Lady P. Branch; R. Buhler, R.A. (anonymous sale, Christie's, London, 24 July 1953, lot 91, as 'Venetian School'), purchased pseudonymously by Sir Denis Mahon.

Literature: Mayor, 1871, no. 179 (as Annibale Carracci); M, 1967, no. 34; M, 1969, no. 7; M & E, 1986, no. 1.

Guercino's early paintings are notable for their bold chiaroscuro effects and this preoccupation is evident here, especially in the manipulation of the coarse grain of the paper to achieve a dappled, granular effect, the courageous understatement of some of the lightest areas of the drawing, such as the back of the figure's skirt, and the subtlety of the white highlights.

Mahon has always connected this drawing, together with a similar one of a kneeling friar in the British Museum (App. no. 4), with the figure of St Francis in the altarpiece, the *Madonna and Child with Sts Francis, Antony Abbot and Bovo*, painted for the church of S. Sebastiano in Renazzo di Cento (S, 1988, no. 9); although Mahon and Salerno were inclined to date the picture *c.*1615, Mahon now believes it may date in the period 1616–17. Although the present drawing is certainly early in date, showing the influences of both Pietro Faccini (1562–1602), as Mahon pointed out, and Ludovico Carracci, its connection with any of Guercino's surviving paintings from his pre-Roman period is more problematic than one might think. Neither the British Museum drawing nor No. 1 fits unequivocally with any of the surviving representations of St Francis from this period. We feel that the two drawings may have been made at different times and possibly for different commissions. No. 1 is perhaps the earlier of the two, since it fits with the Renazzo di Cento picture in a number of respects, most notably in the bend of the saint's body and in the flattish profile of his uptilted head, though obviously the gestures of the two figures differ substantially.

However, a drawing in the Accademia di Belle Arti, Perugia (Cresti, *et al.*, 1977, no. 2, repr. as Pietro Faccini, though accepted by us and others as by or after Guercino or even from his circle), which was pointed out to us by Dr David Stone, must inject a note of caution into the whole

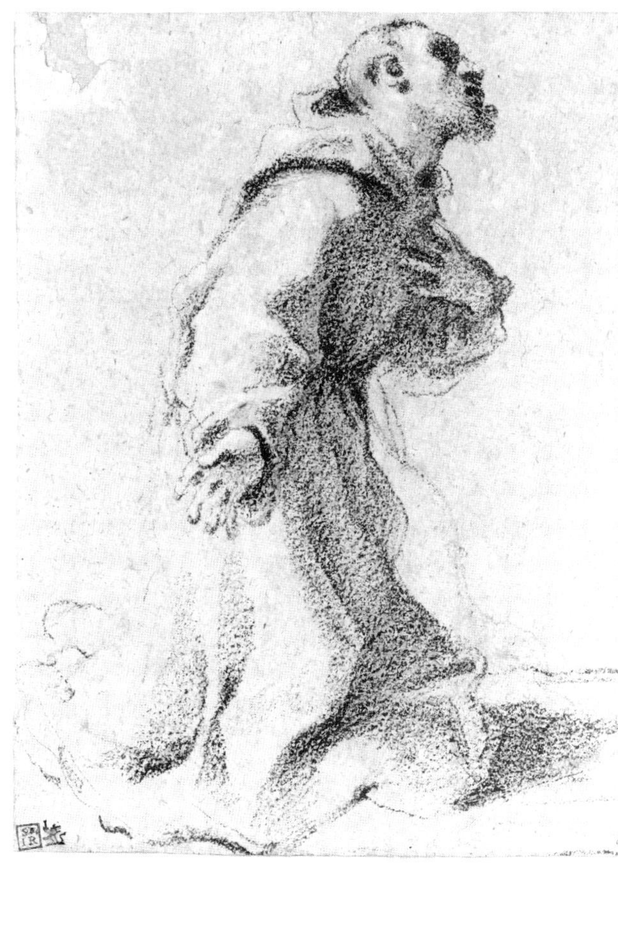

1

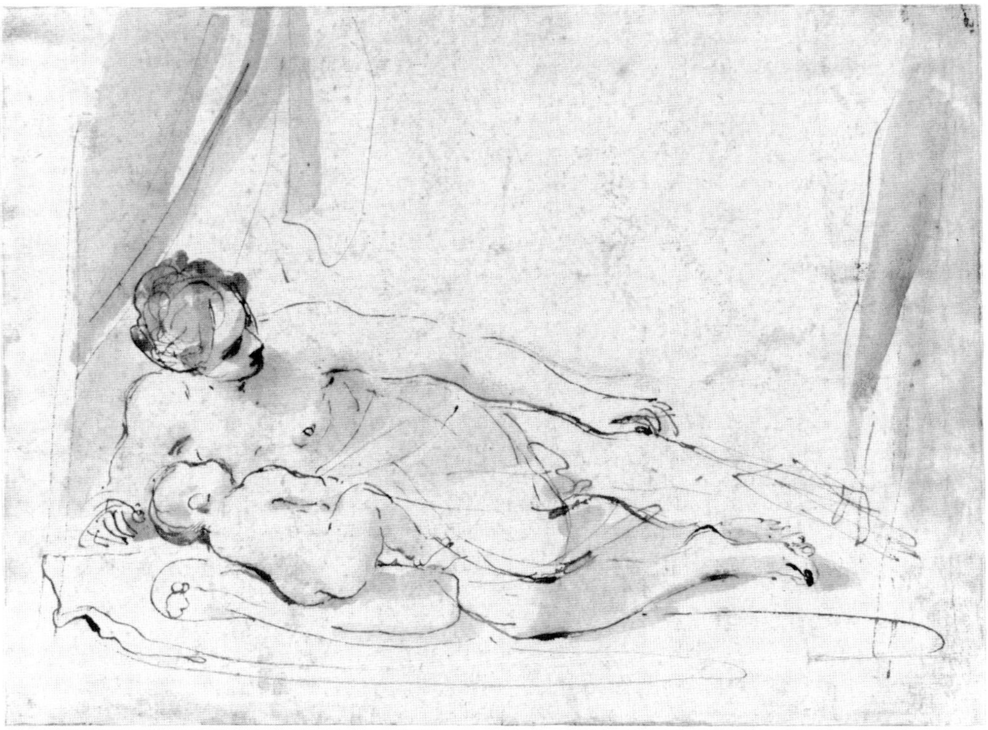

2

debate. It shows two friars kneeling in a landscape, facing each other but looking upwards, as if in supplication or prayer. The figure on the left of the drawing is undoubtedly connected with that represented in No. 1, and the comparison is far more compelling than that afforded by the Renazzo St Francis. The Perugia drawing itself, however, begs many questions. If it was executed with a picture in mind, no such work exists today. Furthermore, the subject is extremely unusual, particularly for an altarpiece, and even the identity of the saints is not obvious.

To complicate matters still further, the figure on the right of the Perugia sketch is extremely close in pose to that of St Bernardino of Siena in the painting of *Sts Bernardino of Siena and Francis of Assisi with the Madonna of Loreto* of 1618, now in the Pinacoteca Civica, Cento (S, 1988, no. 44), with which we have tentatively connected the British Museum study. It is worth noting that the figure on the left in the Perugia drawing (and by extension No. 1) actually has certain points in common with the figure of St Francis in the same altarpiece, especially in the facial type and the gesture of the hands. All of this must call into question whether the Mahon drawing can really be preparatory for the Renazzo picture after all, though of course it is conceivable that it simply served as a reference for the later Perugia drawing. For the time being at least, one is forced to concede that the question of the interrelationship of the various drawings and early pictures of St Francis must remain unresolved.

2 Venus suckling Cupid

Pen and brown ink and light brown wash. 166 × 231mm.

Windsor Castle, Royal Library, inv. no. 2532.

Provenance: Casa Gennari; King George III.

Literature: M, *Disegni*, 1969, no. 14; B, 1984, pp. 142, 148, pl. 118; S, 1988, under no. 24 I; M & T, 1989, no. 1.

A preparatory study for the much-damaged fresco painted on the chimney-breast of an upper-floor room of the Casa Pannini at Cento. The fresco, detached and laid onto canvas, is now in the Pinacoteca Civica at Cento (S, 1988, no. 24 I). In 1615 the Centese dignitary Bartolommeo Pannini commissioned the young Guercino to decorate several rooms in his town house, which still stands in the main street of Cento. Guercino completed the work in 1617.

The figures of Venus and Cupid correspond closely with their painted counterparts, except in the angle of Venus's head and in the position of the quiver. In both works Cupid is represented lying on a cushion on the ground, being breast-fed by his mother. Venus takes one of Cupid's arrows from its quiver, which lies on the ground, in front of Cupid in the painting but at Venus's feet in the drawing.

Another drawing for the composition is in the Fondazione Cini, Venice (inv. no. 36.122; M, *Disegni*, 1969, no. 13). Drawn in red chalk, it appears to have been studied from the life, though the figures are in reverse to those in No. 2 and the final painting. A drawing of *Venus and Cupid in a Chariot drawn through the Clouds by a Dove* in the Cleveland Museum of Art (inv. no. 25. 1188) may represent an early phase of the same commission, though it was clearly intended as a design for a ceiling decoration. The idea was presumably abandoned, for the two ceilings that Guercino painted on the staircase of the Casa Pannini represent *Apollo* and *Diana*; in both cases, however, the figures are shown riding in chariots. (For further discussion of this possibility and previous bibliography for the Cleveland drawing, see M, *Disegni*, 1969, under nos. 13 and 14; B, 1984, p. 151, pl. 119; and M & T, 1989, under no. 1.)

Guercino returned to a variation of the theme of Venus suckling Cupid in a drawing of *Venus and Mars with Cupid and Time* from the Morelli Collection in the Civiche Raccolte d'Arte, Milan (Bora, 1988, no. 57), which has been related to a lost picture dated 1656. In the Milan drawing Venus reclines on a bed, with the sleeping Cupid beside her breasts, as she leans forward to take an arrow from Cupid's quiver which lies in the middle foreground in front of the two figures. She is watched by Time and Mars who stand behind her, to the left and right respectively.

3 Dead Christ with an Angel

(*see colour pl. 1*)

Red chalk. 120 × 262mm.

Windsor Castle, Royal Library, inv. no. 2755.

Provenance: Casa Gennari; King George III.

Literature: M, *Dipinti*, 1968, under no. 23; S, 1988, under no. 37; M & T, 1989, no. 3.

A preparatory study with many differences for the small painting on copper of the *Dead Christ mourned by two Angels* in the National Gallery, London, which is usually dated 1617–18 (S, 1988, no. 37). Guercino went to some trouble to arrive at a suitable pose for the figure of Christ, probably working directly from the model as he did so. Other drawings for the picture are in the Statens Museum for Kunst, Copenhagen (inv. no. 11133; M & T, 1989, p. 3, repr. fig. 1), and in the Hermitage Museum at Leningrad (inv. no. 18308).

4 Nude Youth seated on the Ground

(*see colour pl. 2*)

Oiled charcoal, on greyish-buff paper. 300 × 263mm.

Windsor Castle, Royal Library, inv. no. 2415.

Provenance: Casa Gennari; King George III.

Literature: Russell, 1923, pp. 19 and 42, pl. ix (where the provenance is given incorrectly as from the collection of Consul Joseph Smith); M, *Disegni*, 1969, no. 250; M & T, 1989, no. 149.

As this example well demonstrates, Guercino's studies from the living nude model are masterly in their suggestion of light, their confident handling, and their economic simplification of form. To understand their function, however, they have to be seen in the context of contemporary drawings of the same type. These, usually known as 'academies', are invariably finished studies and are normally drawn in red chalk, rather than black chalk or oiled charcoal. In them the artist strives to render as accurately as possible the musculature of the figure by the careful modulation of light and shade. They originated in the life-drawing class, usually held at an academy (hence their name). Here the master offered instruction to his pupils in front of the model, his own often large-scale drawings from the nude frequently being used as exemplars (their size was presumably related to their need to be visible in this context). 'Academies' were therefore undertaken as exercises in their own right – as ends in themselves. They were not conceived as preparatory works for a picture or sculpture, although they are sometimes reflected in the pose of a figure in the master's painted work (see No. 16). It is important to emphasise the formal nature of such life studies and to make the distinction between them and the master's working drawings, which, by their very nature, are more spontaneous and experimental.

Most of Guercino's drawings from the nude apparently date from his pre-Roman period. They were probably made at the time when the young painter, still little known outside his native town of Cento, directed a small academy for life drawing there. According to Malvasia, this *Accademia del nudo* was founded in 1616 when Bartolomeo Fabri placed at the artist's disposal two rooms in his house, the Casa Fabri (Malvasia, 1678, II, pp. 362; 1841, II, p. 258). On the chimney-breast of one of the two rooms of this academy was Guercino's painting of *Prometheus bringing the Statue of Clay to Life with a burning Torch*, now in the collection of the Cassa di Risparmio at Cento (B, 1984, pl. 5; S, 1988, no. 26), also referred to under No. 19. Guercino's drawings of parts of the anatomy, published in 1619 in a series of engravings by Oliviero Gatti intended to instruct beginners in the art of drawing, may also date from this same moment (see Nos. 20–21). The reasons why Guercino apparently discontinued the practice of making life drawings later in his career remain obscure, but a likely explanation is that once he had become established as a painter he ceased teaching drawing outside his own studio. Indeed, drawings by Guercino of the same type as Nos. 4 and 16 are virtually unknown after the middle of the 1620s at the latest.

When making his drawings from the nude, Guercino invariably chose the medium of oiled charcoal which he used on coarse, tinted paper, occasionally touching in the highlights sparingly with white chalk. The same technique, but with greater recourse to white heightening, had been the favourite of the Bolognese painter Pietro Faccini for his studies from the life and some of his working drawings; Guercino apparently told Malvasia that he much admired the drawings of Faccini (see M, *Disegni*, 1969, p. 44, and M & T, 1989, p. xv, n. 4). Pure charcoal, which for a long time was the cheapest and simplest to manufacture of all the drawing materials, can be easily rubbed out. On the other hand, oiled charcoal, made from pure charcoal soaked in oil, has the advantage of being more adhesive to paper and more permanent (fixatives not yet being available), though a trace of yellow staining from the oil can sometimes appear on either side of the line. Thus its handling requires a greater assurance on the part of the artist. Guercino used oiled charcoal only rarely for his working drawings (for

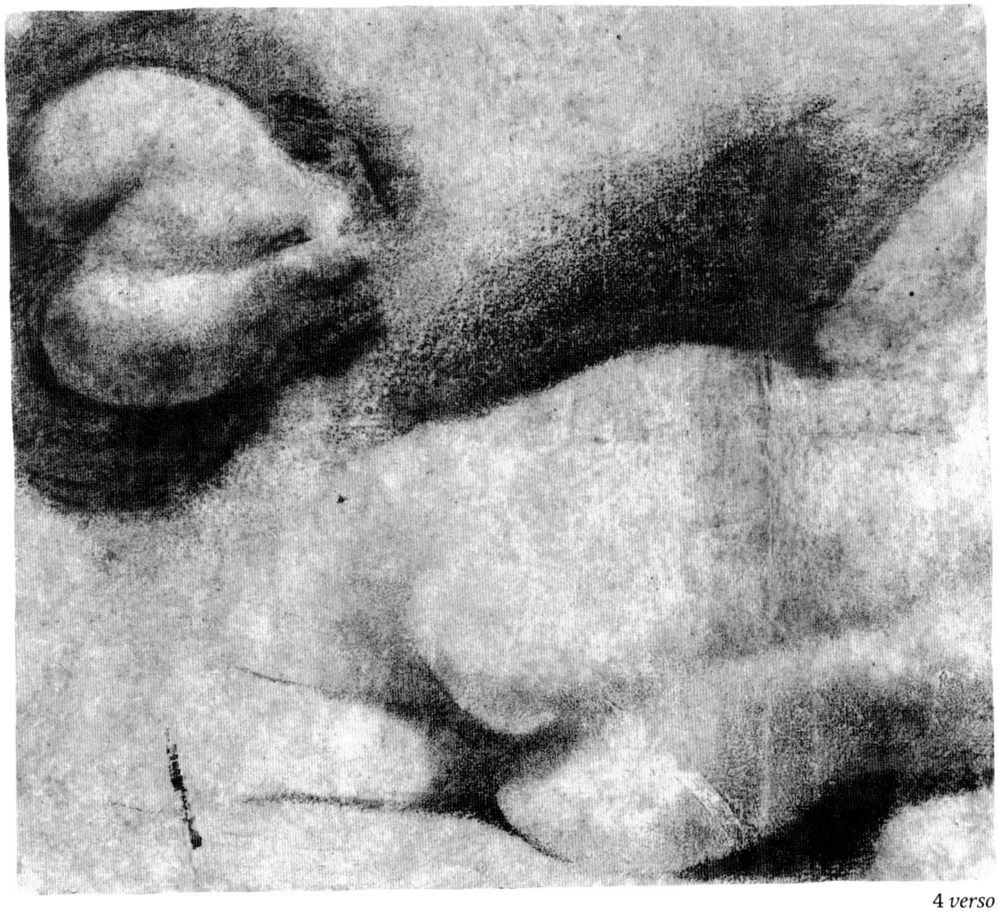

4 *verso*

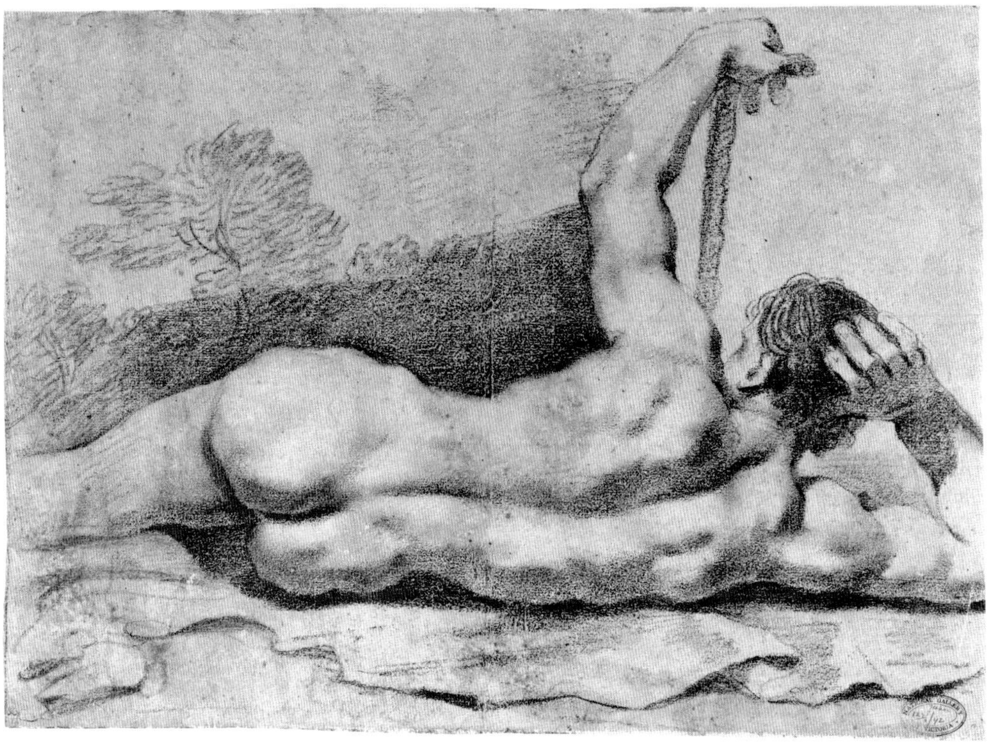

Fig. 6 (right) *Reclining male Nude seen from the rear.*
Oiled charcoal,
542 × 890 mm
(Melbourne, National Gallery of Victoria,
inv. no. 1278/3). See No. 4

which he vastly preferred the media of pen, pen and wash, and red chalk), but he evidently found that it had many advantages for drawing the nude in particular. Among these must have been the consistency of tone that could be achieved when oiled charcoal was lightly shaded, which made it ideal for rendering shadow on flesh. Also, when used on a coarsely textured paper the poor penetration of the oiled charcoal gave a subtle and lifelike effect of reflected light in the passages of shadow, for example in the back and thigh of the figure in No. 4. Finally, a wide range of tone could be suggested, including a heavy dark that could effectively contrast not only with the lightness of the paper but with the passages of mid-tone of the lighter shading: thus most of Guercino's drawings in the medium either have heavily accented areas of dark within the figure itself, such as the hair of the youth in the present example, or patches of dark behind the figure to throw into relief the areas of highlight on the model.

No. 4 has been recently lifted to reveal two further studies in oiled charcoal on the *verso*. The main study is of the lower back, posterior and thighs of a figure reclining on the ground, seen from the rear; the subsidiary study seems to be an abstract form of the artist's own invention, inspired, as it were, by the buttocks drawn in the other study, though it must not be ruled out that this form may have been intended to represent a pair of testicles. Guercino does appear to have indulged in erotic fantasies elsewhere in his drawings: see App. no. 78 *verso*, in which an erect male member complete with testicles is seen approaching a female pudendum. The principal study on the *verso* of No. 4 may be compared with a drawing in oiled charcoal of a reclining male nude seen from the rear, formerly in the collection of Sir Thomas Lawrence and now in the National Gallery of Victoria, Melbourne (inv. no. 1278/3; 542 × 890mm; see Fig. 6).

5 David with the Head of Goliath

Pen and brown ink and brown wash over red chalk. 165 × 127mm.

Windsor Castle, Royal Library, inv. no. 2487.

Provenance: Casa Gennari; King George III.

Literature: M, *Disegni*, 1969, no. 26; M & T, 1989, no. 4.

A study for the detached fresco of *c*.1618, now in the Nelson–Atkins Museum of Art, Kansas City (S, 1988, no. 41). It is not known for whom or what purpose the fresco was made; Mahon has suggested that it may have been undertaken as an exercise in *buon fresco*. Two other drawings for the composition are in the Uffizi, Florence, and the Louvre, Paris (inv. nos. 1638-F and 6862; see M, *Disegni*, 1969, no. 27, and Roli, 1972, no. 13 respectively).

No. 5 is an attractive example of Guercino's early draughtsmanship. The red chalk underdrawing combined with pen and brown wash lend a vibrancy to the sheet. As a figure type, the *David* strongly suggests those of the Ferrarese painter Ippolito Scarsellino (1551–1620).

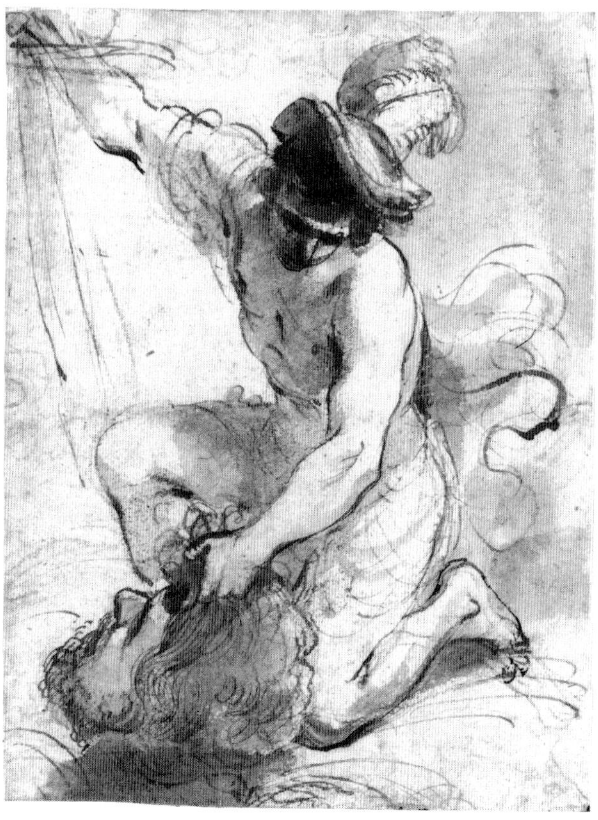

5

6–7 Studies for *Apollo flaying Marsyas* (1618)

Florence, Palazzo Pitti

6 Nude Figure of a Youth lying on his Back, with his left Arm and Leg raised

Pen, point of the brush and brown wash on pale blue-grey paper. 228 × 239mm.

London, Courtauld Institute Galleries, Witt Collection, inv. no. 1376.

Provenance: Casa Gennari; Mr Bouverie; Mr Hervey; the Earls of Gainsborough (sale, Christie's, London, 27 July 1922, lot 81, with others, bt *Meatyard*); Sir Robert Witt.

Literature: M, *Disegni*, 1969, no. 32; Hammer, *et al.*, 1977, no. 34; M & T, 1989, under no. 5.

Probably an early study for the figure of Marsyas in the *Apollo flaying Marsyas* in the Palazzo Pitti, Florence, which Guercino painted in 1618 for Cosimo II, Grand Duke of Tuscany (S, 1988, no. 47). In colour, mood and compositional treatment, the painting is strongly redolent of Titian and other sixteenth-century Venetians. The drawing was evidently executed early in the genesis of the composition since the pose is quite distinct from that selected for the finished painting. The figure extends his left arm as if to

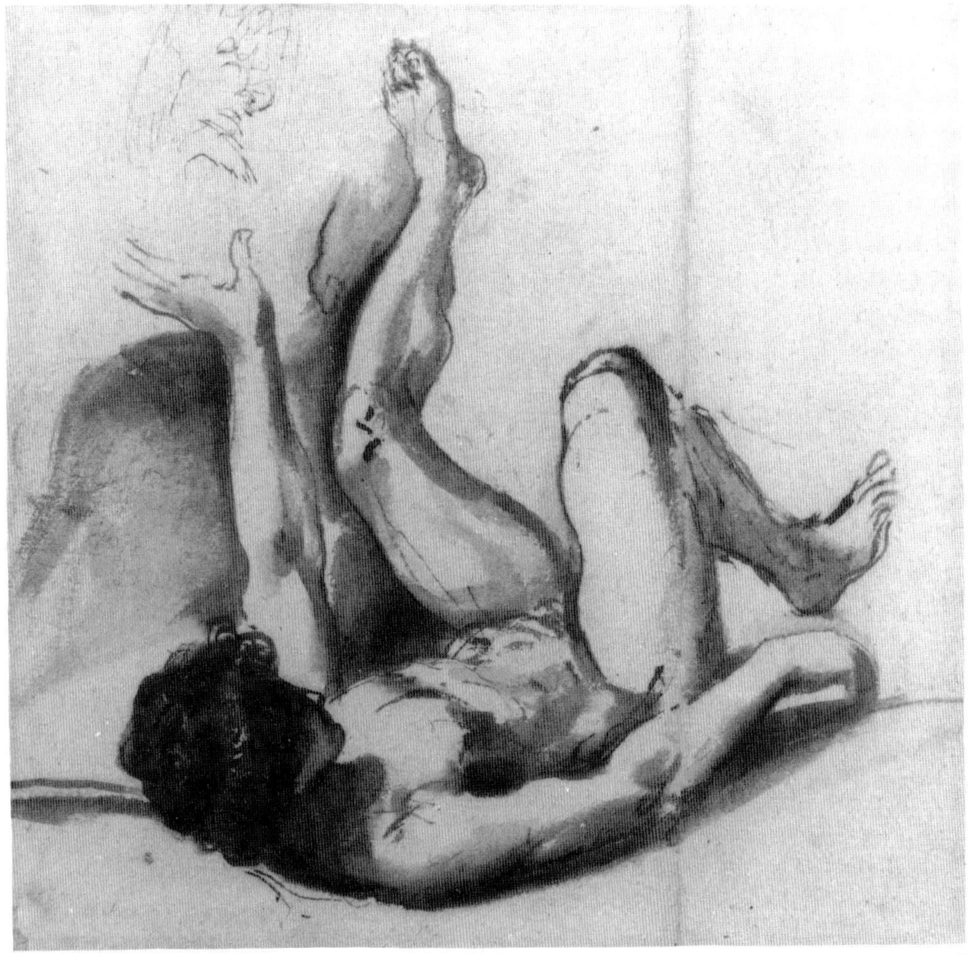

6

fend off an assailant. His left leg is also raised (as is the right leg of Marsyas in the painting), presumably as though submitting to the knife of Apollo. Guercino experimented with several different poses for the figure of Marsyas, as can also be seen in two composition studies, No. 7 and a drawing in the Albertina, Vienna (inv. no. 2362; Stix & Spitzmüller, 1941, no. 218; M, *Disegni*, 1969, no. 34). A fine charcoal study for the same figure, shown in the pose eventually chosen for the picture, is in the Ecole des Beaux-Arts, Paris (inv. no. 156; M, *Disegni*, 1969, no. 35).

The curly-locked, youthful head of Marsyas in the drawing was replaced in the painting (and indeed already in the other preparatory studies) by a much older, often bearded type. As Hammer *et al.* rightly pointed out, the youthful head was used instead, with little variation, for the figure of Apollo in the painting, the face remaining in dark shadow but for the light catching the tip of the nose. It would seem therefore that Guercino used the same model for studying both figures.

In the top left corner is a grotesque head drawn in ink. Another head, drawn in black chalk, can be seen beneath the brown wash at the centre left edge.

7 Apollo flaying Marsyas

Pen and brown and black ink and brown wash. 194 × 265mm.

Windsor Castle, Royal Library, inv. no. 2469.

Provenance: Casa Gennari; King George III.

Literature: M, *Disegni*, 1969, no. 33; S, 1988, under no. 47; M & T, 1989, no. 5.

A particularly good example of Guercino's early style of draughtsmanship. In the painted version of *Apollo flaying Marsyas*, for which see No. 6, the nude Apollo is more actively engaged in his gruesome task: he stands almost in the centre of the composition, with his left foot on the stomach of Marsyas (who lies in agony on the ground with both hands tied above his head to a tree stump on the right), and begins to flay him by the legs rather than by the arms. The drawing reverberates with echoes of the style of the Bolognese Ludovico Carracci.

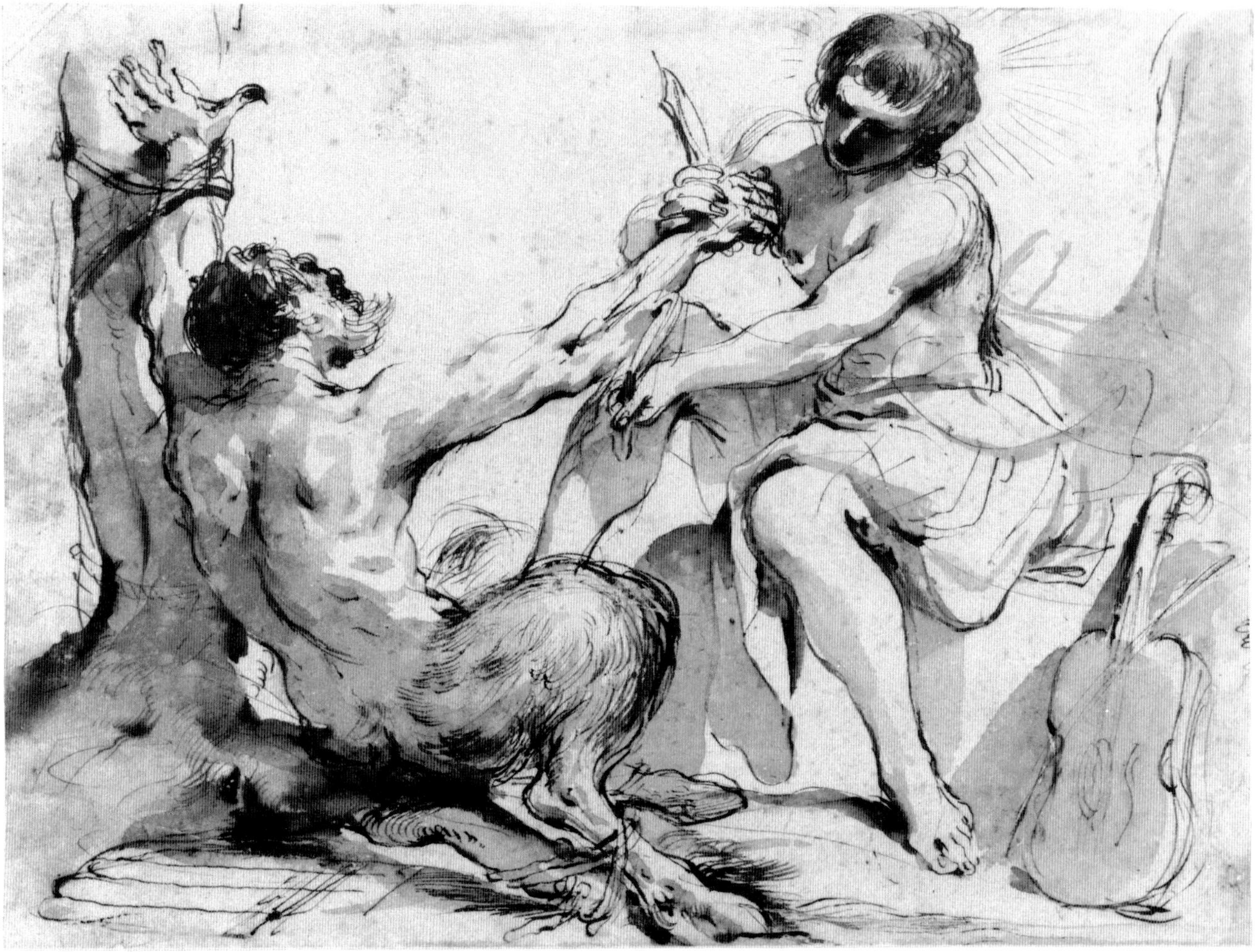

7

8 Christ handing the Keys to St Peter and pointing to the papal Chair

Pen and brown ink and greyish-brown wash, heightened with white (partly oxidised), on paper washed light yellowish-brown. 344 × 240mm.

Windsor Castle, Royal Library, inv. no. 2727.

Provenance: Casa Gennari; King George III.

Literature: M, *Dipinti*, 1968, under no. 28; M & T, 1989, no. 6.

A study, with the composition reversed, for the altarpiece of 1618, formerly in S. Biagio and now in the Pinacoteca Civica at Cento (S, 1988, no. 46). In a later compositional drawing, now in the collection of HRH Queen Beatrix of the Netherlands (M & T, 1989, p. 5, repr. fig. 2), Guercino altered the direction of the design to that adopted in the painting. Throughout his career Guercino was in the habit of switching around the composition as he worked in order to refresh his ideas (see Introduction).

In both drawings the question of how to close the subject at the top has not yet been resolved, though in the second a heavy awning or drapery covers the architecture and some of the sky. In the painting there is a youthful angel raising this drapery; this figure is studied on the *verso* of a double-sided drawing formerly in the collection of Rudolf Joseph and now in a Swiss private collection.

No. 8 is unusual in Guercino's graphic *oeuvre* in being drawn on a prepared ground with the addition of white heightening. This technique allowed the artist greater scope to explore the effects of light than was normally open to him using just pen and wash on white paper. Guercino was so accomplished a draughtsman and so expert in suggesting the effects of light by the simplest of means that his recourse to this method was only occasional and seems to have taken place exclusively at the beginning of his career. Ludovico Carracci, on the other hand, frequently adopted it, as did some of his followers, for example Giacomo Cavedone (1577–1620). It is not surprising therefore that reminiscences of Ludovico Carracci should seem so strong in this drawing.

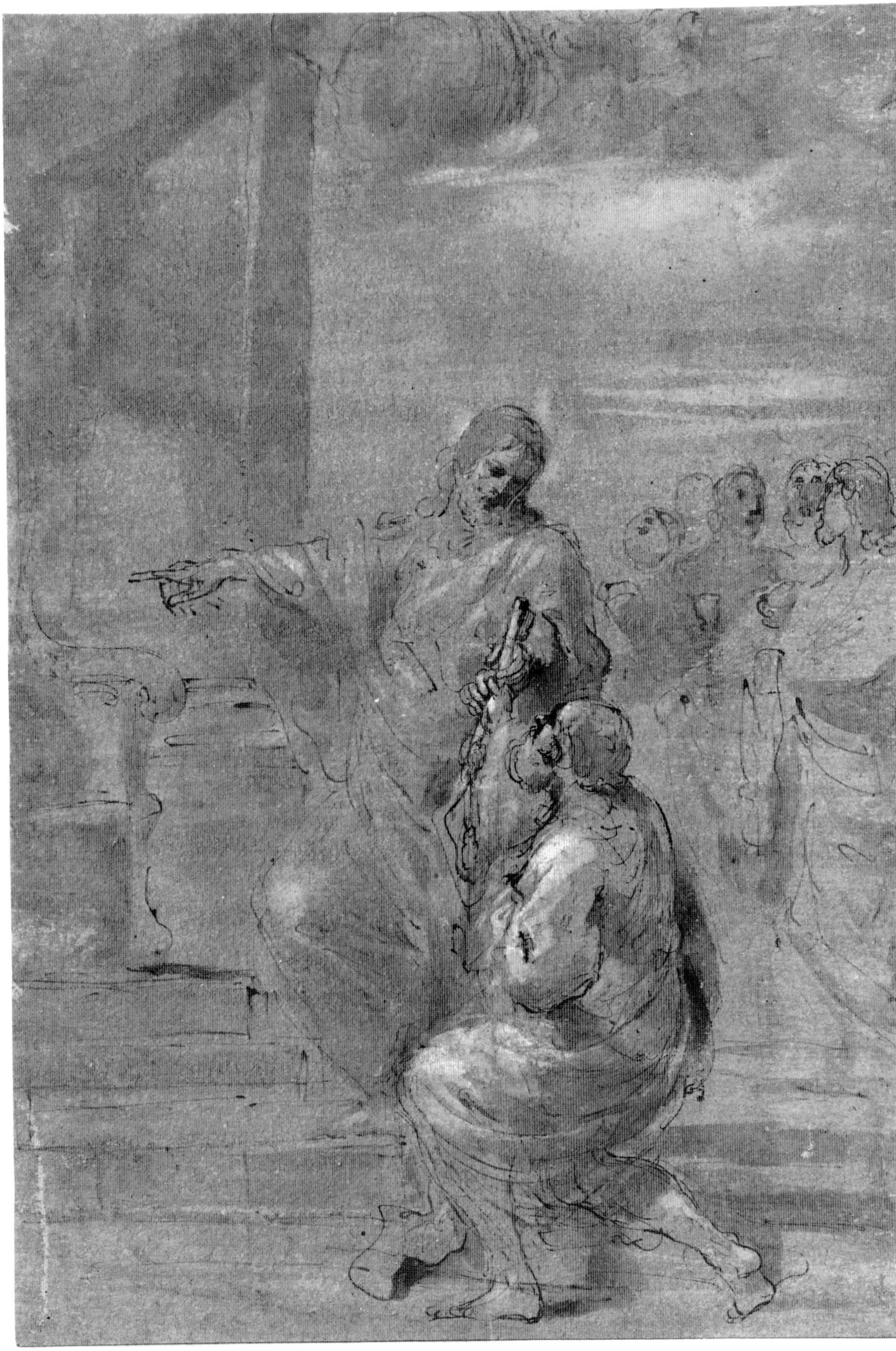

8

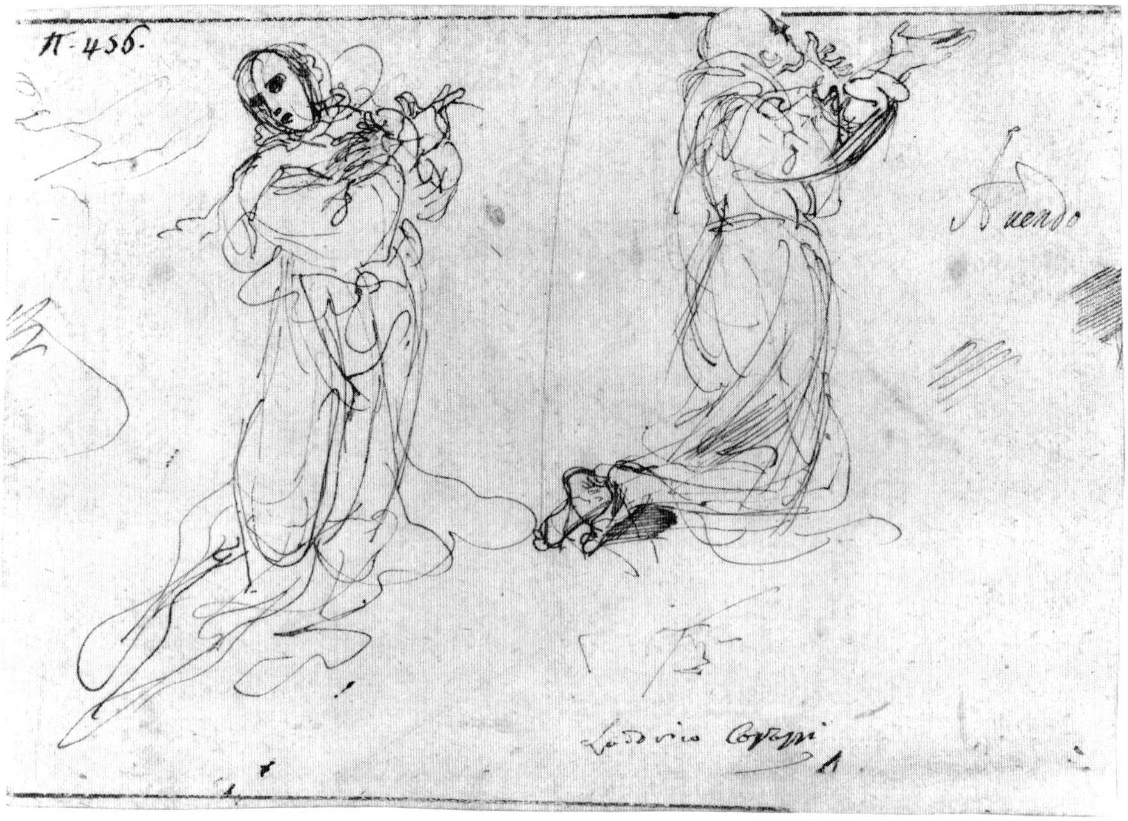

9

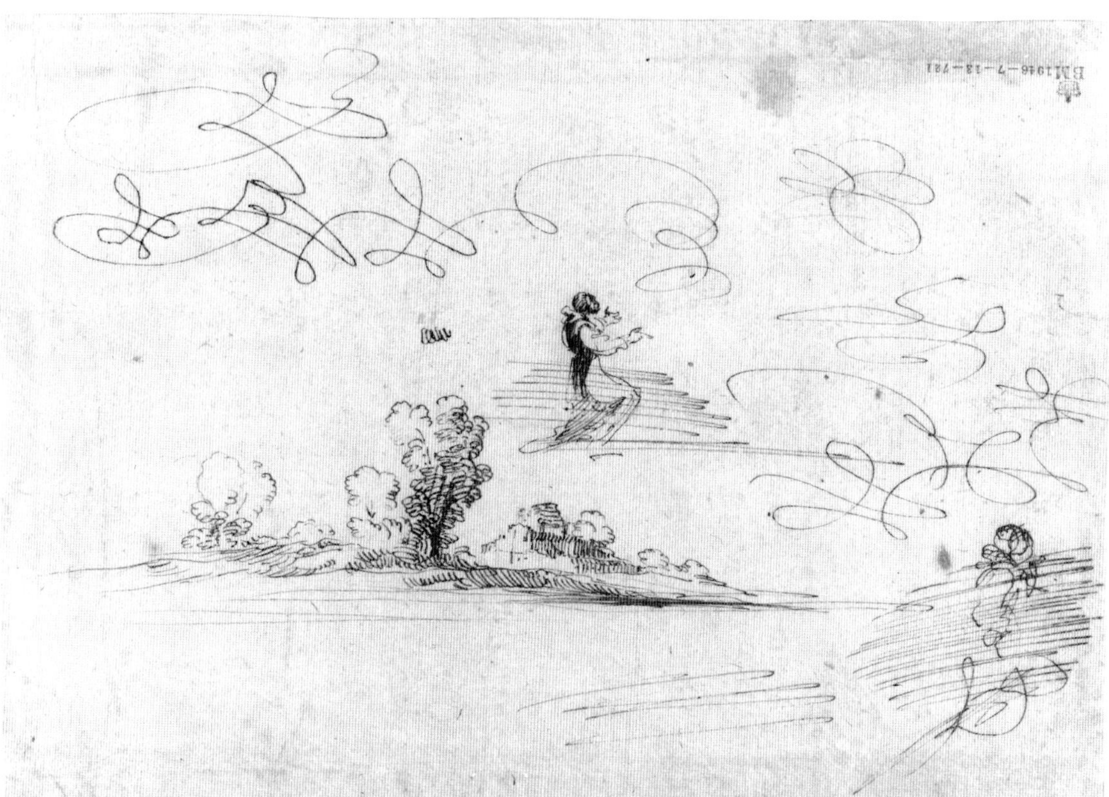

9 verso

9 Studies for a kneeling St Francis

London, British Museum, inv. no. 1946–7–13–721.

(For other details, see App. no. 2.)

A study for the altarpiece of *Sts Francis and Louis of France kneeling in Adoration* in the church of S. Francesco at Brisighella, dated 1618 (S, 1988, no. 40). The handling recalls Ludovico Carracci's style of pen drawing and this would explain the old attribution to the master in the bottom right. Two of the studies are taken to a fairly high degree of finish, while a third, on the extreme left, partly cut by the edge of the sheet, is only sketchily drawn. It more or less repeats the pose of the figure in the study on the right. This latter is, interestingly, closed off on the left by a faint vertical line indicating the edge of the altarpiece. The two minute studies of the saint on the *verso* are surely no more than doodles and must have been done after the drawings on the other side.

Two other drawings connected with this same altarpiece, both studies for the whole composition, are in the Metropolitan Museum of Art, New York (inv. no. 1987.21; repr. Turner, 1981, pl. 35), formerly in a private collection in Zurich; and in the Staatsgalerie, Stuttgart (Koenig–Fachsenfeld Collection, inv. no. III/119; repr. Turner, 1981, pl. 38).

10 A Monk receiving the Child from the Madonna; a seated Nun with an Angel below, and two music-making Angels above

Pen and brown ink and brown wash. 278 × 164mm.

Mahon Collection, on loan to the Ashmolean Museum, Oxford, M & E, 2.

Provenance: Casa Gennari (the drawing retains its fine Casa Gennari mount, for which see L *Suppl*, 2858c, and M, 1967, p. 20); Mr Bouverie; Mr Hervey; the Earls of Gainsborough (sale, Sotheby's, London, 22 July 1953, lot 5), purchased by Sir Denis Mahon.

Literature: M, 1967, no. 35; M, *Disegni*, 1969, no. 20; Roli, 1972, no. 9; M & E, 1986, no. 3.

Inscribed in ink in the bottom left corner, *58 Pr. Fo.* (For similar inscriptions, see No. 46 and M & T, 1989, nos. 200 and 297.) It is likely that this annotation is a reference to the drawing's original location in the series of albums of drawings by Guercino preserved by the artist's heirs until the dispersal of the collection in the eighteenth century, the letters perhaps standing for 'Primo Foglio'.

Numbered in graphite on the old mount, below the bottom left corner of the drawing: *14*. This is an example of a numbering system which is associated with drawings with a Bouverie – Hervey – 1st Earl of Gainsborough provenance (for other instances in this catalogue see Nos. 14, 24, 27, 44, 56, 88, 96, 107, 109, 132, 152, 153, 189, 194 and 196).

This study is one of several of the same subject, all datable *c.*1616–19, presumably preparatory to a painting which, if it was ever completed, remains untraced. Besides No. 10, Mahon discussed three others: one in the Uffizi, Florence (inv. no. 12427-F; M, *Disegni*, 1969, no. 19), another, now untraced but formerly in the collections of the Earls of Gainsborough and later Sir Robert Witt, and one in a Swiss private collection, which had formerly belonged to P.-J. Mariette and J. P. Heseltine. To these four can be added one more for the same composition in pen and wash; this is in the Wadsworth Atheneum and is shortly to be published by Andrew Blume in a forthcoming article in *Master Drawings*. The Wadsworth drawing and two of the four others, those in the Uffizi and formerly in the Witt Collection, represent only a section of the finished painting, focusing intimately on the group of the Madonna, the saint and the Child. No. 10, on the other hand, is far more elaborate, with a greater number of figures including a kneeling nun and several angels. Of all the drawings, it gives the best idea of the image's function as an altarpiece with the diagonal composition carefully worked out in typically Ludovico-like fashion and the corners satisfyingly filled with subsidiary figures. Guercino has also indicated the confines of his composition with drawn lines at the lateral top

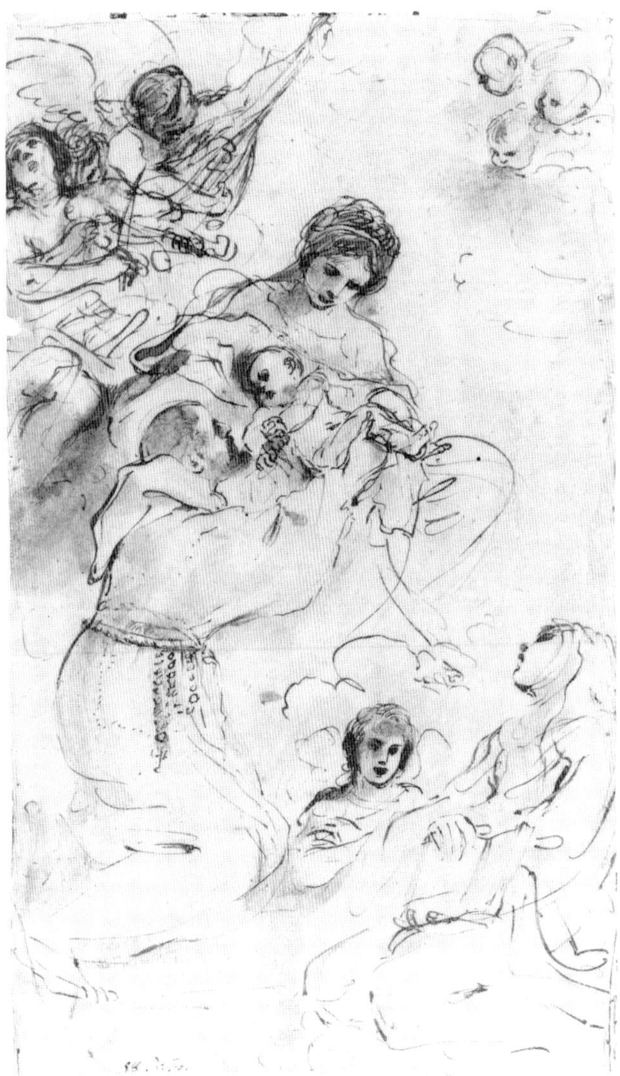

10

edges of No. 10, implying that he had already decided on the shape of the eventual composition and the rough scale of the figures. Blume is thus surely wrong in suggesting in his forthcoming article that this complicated study is the earliest of the surviving drawings for the project.

Mahon identified the saint as St Antony of Padua or possibly St Felice Cappuccino, whereas Blume believes him to be St Francis. On the evidence available, it is impossible to ascertain which saint is represented in the series.

11 Madonna and Child with Sts (?)Catherine, Francis and Louis of France

Pen and brown ink and brown wash. 273 × 221mm.

Private collection.

Provenance: (?)Earl of Shrewsbury (on his mount); Rev. William Turner of Trent (inscribed on the mount in pen and brown ink: *from the Rev. W. Turner of Trent*).

Literature: Russell, 1973, p. 271.

When Russell first published this drawing, he drew attention to the analogies in composition and subject with the *Madonna and Child with Sts Joseph, Augustine, Louis, Francis, and a Child Donor*, an altarpiece datable 1616, formerly in the church of S. Agostino at Cento and now in the Musées Royaux des Beaux-Arts, Brussels (S, 1988, no. 27). He saw an even stronger connection, however, with Guercino's study of the *Madonna and Child with Sts Louis and Francis*, formerly in the collection of the distinguished French connoisseur P.-J. Mariette and now in the Musée des Beaux-Arts at Marseille (inv. no. 76; Bacou, 1967, no. 58). The Marseille study is drawn in much the same attractive pen-and-wash style, but there are many differences, including the omission of the figure of the female saint seen in the present drawing and the idea of closing the composition with an arched top. Moreover, the amount of space taken up by the composition of the Marseille sheet is reduced. St Louis appears on the left, three-quarter length, while St Francis is seated in the centre, with the lower part of his legs disappearing behind the ledge on which he is seated. The Madonna and Child appear immediately behind him, with the Christ Child reaching towards the small wooden cross which the Madonna picks up with her left hand from a lectern on the right. A copy of the Marseille drawing by Charles Natoire (1700–77), also formerly in Mariette's collection, was recently on the Paris art market (sale, Drouot Richelieu, directed by M. Paul Renaud, 5 April 1989, lot 88, repr.).

Although the Marseille drawing is often associated with the Brussels picture, Russell hinted that both it and No. 11 could have been conceived for another work, one a little later in date. Russell's contention is supported by the stylistic difference between these two drawings and the more intricate handling of the studies undoubtedly related to the Brussels picture, such as that in the Brera, Milan (inv. no. 25; M, *Disegni*, 1969, no. 18), which so strongly reflects the Ferrarese influences that affected Guercino's style at this still juvenile moment in his career. By contrast, both No. 11 and the Marseille drawing show a greater exuberance, as well as some knowledge of the drawings of Ludovico Carracci, with whose work Guercino showed greater familiarity in the second half of the second decade of the century. A date of around 1618 for both drawings is suggested by stylistic parallels with other drawings of about this date. For example, the figure of St Louis in No. 11 may be compared with that of Christ in the *Christ handing the Keys to St Peter* (No. 8), and its general fluency of handling with that of the *Apollo flaying Marsyas* (No. 7).

In No. 11 Guercino had not fully decided how to show the figure of St Louis, whose right hand was first drawn extended further to the left, apparently holding the sleeve of the Madonna; it was then indicated further back, as if pointing towards her. The saint's sceptre, drawn with the point of the brush, appears to have no visible means of support and may at first have been intended to appear where the short vertical pen lines are to be found, near the right edge of the sheet. In type St Francis somewhat resembles in reverse the figure in No. 1.

12 Bearded Man wearing a Turban

(*see colour pl. 1*)

Black chalk (or ?oiled charcoal), with occasional touches of white chalk, on blue-grey paper. 349 × 272mm.

Private collection.

Provenance: Casa Gennari; Mr Bouverie (L 325); Mr Hervey; the Earls of Gainsborough (?sale, Christie's, London, 20 July 1859, lot 79: 'Head of an old man' (by Guercino, in black chalk), bt in on the vendor's behalf by *Hogarth* and re-offered ?sale, Christie's, London, 27 July 1922, lot 82, which included 'Head of an Old Man, by Guercino', with others, bt *Davis and Orioli*, presumably the London dealers).

When acquired by the present owner, the traditional attribution of this beautiful drawing had been lost sight of. It was instead given to the English artist Thomas Worlidge (1700–66) – 'who copied and imitated Rembrandt prints and also made a reputation with his portrait heads'. The drawing was restored to Guercino by J. A. Gere in 1968, when it was brought into the British Museum for an opinion; Gere also pointed out its early provenance.

The style suggests the period immediately before Guercino's departure for Rome in 1621. A similar, slightly exotic bearded type appears in his painting of *St Sebastian succoured*, of 1619, in the Pinacoteca Nazionale, Bologna (S, 1988, no. 54; see also No. 15). This figure, presumably a physician, is seen in the centre of the composition pulling out a broken arrow from the saint's left forearm. He has a full beard, wears a large hat and looks down intently at his task. An analogous head, looking downwards and this time wearing a turban, occurs in the figure on the left of the *Erminia discovering the wounded Tancred*, of 1618–19, in the Galleria Doria-Pamphili, Rome (S, 1988, no. 53), though this second figure is not as close to that in the present drawing.

It is also possible that No. 12 may have been made as

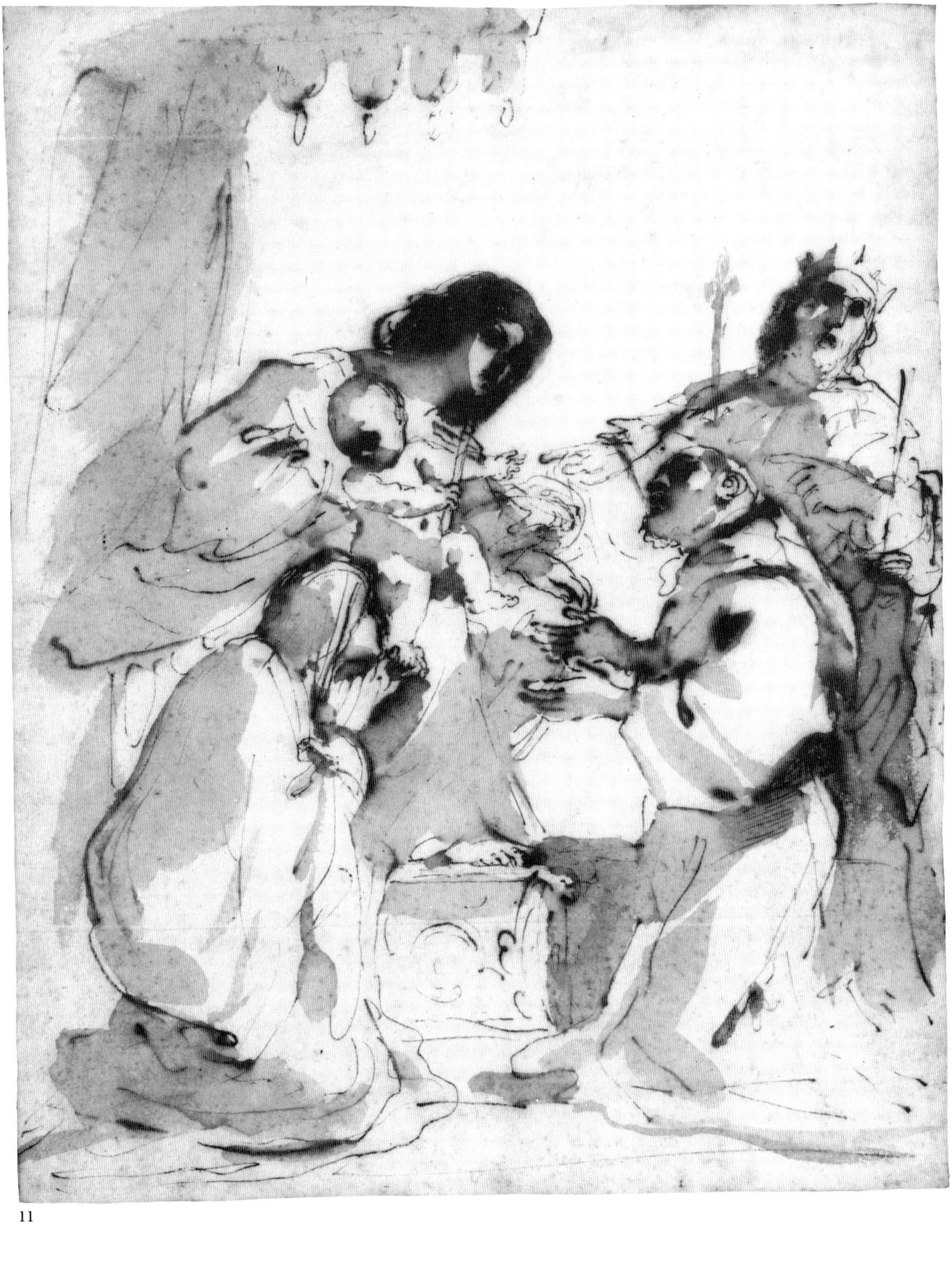

11

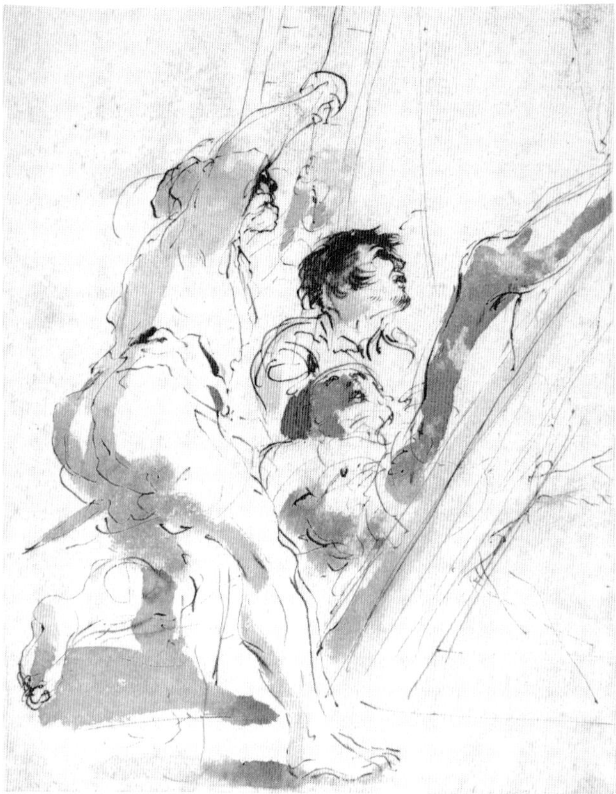

13

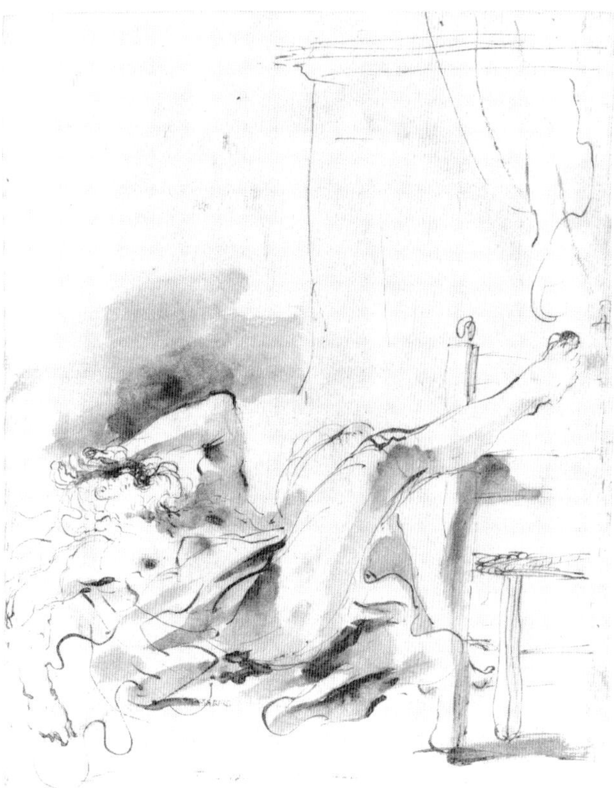

14

an exercise in drawing in its own right. A not dissimilar head of a bearded man, though seen in profile, appears in one of the series of prints engraved in 1619 by Oliviero Gatti as models for training young artists how to draw (Bertelà, 1973, no. 666): see also under No. 20. In technique, conception and handling, No. 12 resembles a drawing of the head of a bearded man in the Royal Library at Windsor Castle (M & T, 1989, no. 148), until recently placed with the drawings of Cavedone (1577–1660). The Windsor drawing, with its medium of oiled charcoal, its broad simplifications of form and its largeness of scale, has so much in common with Guercino's 'academies' of much the same date (for which see Nos. 4 and 16) that it may well have originated in a similar context.

13 The Crucifixion of St Peter

Pen and brown ink and brown wash. 202 × 161mm.

Windsor Castle, Royal Library, inv. no. 2907.

Provenance: Casa Gennari; King George III.

Literature: M, *Disegni*, 1969, no. 38; S, 1988, under no. 52; M & T, 1989, no. 8.

No. 13 is now generally accepted as a study, with substantial variations, for the altarpiece painted by Guercino in 1618–19 for the church of S. Bernardino at Carpi and now in the Galleria Estense at Modena (S, 1988, no. 52). The drawing shows the dramatic moment in which St Peter, only partly attached to the cross, is being raised upon it by one of the executioners, who strains at a rope above his head, presumably attached to a pulley. The body of this executioner and the angle made by the main beam of the cross articulate the composition of the drawing in two parallel diagonal lines. In the picture, however, the compositional solution is strikingly different, with St Peter seated on his cross which lies flat on the ground. Nevertheless some echoes of the ideas formulated in No. 13 remain: the position of the legs of the executioner on the left in the picture is much the same as that of his counterpart in the drawing; and the diagonal line made by St Peter's drapery, coarsely pulled from his body by another executioner, recalls the line made by the cross in the drawing.

Two other drawings for the picture survive, one for the drapery of St Peter in the Koenig–Fachsenfeld Collection on deposit in the Staatsgalerie, Stuttgart (inv. no. Barbieri 86; M, *Disegni*, 1969, no. 39), and a study for an executioner in the Musée des Beaux-Arts, Montreal (inv. no. Dr. 946.82; M & T, 1989, under no. 8).

14 An old bearded Man lying on the Ground, shielding his Eyes with his Hands

Pen and brush and grey-black ink and grey-brown wash with traces of bodycolour. 265 × 210mm.

Mahon Collection, on loan to the Ashmolean Museum, Oxford, M & E, 6.

Provenance: Casa Gennari (see the inscription *5 T. Fo.* on a fragment attached to the *verso*); Mr Bouverie; Mr Hervey; (?)1st Earl of Gainsborough; R. H. Randall Davies (though it does not bear his mark, L *Suppl*, 2903a); from whom acquired by Sir Denis Mahon in 1938.

Literature: M, 1967, no. 4; M, *Disegni*, 1969, no. 48; M & E, 1986, no. 6; Loire, 1990, under no. 2.

Numbered in graphite on the old mount, below the bottom left corner of the drawing: *67* (for a discussion and further instances of sheets numbered in this way, see No. 10).

The presence of the chair, along with the dresser or bed in the background, and the hint of a curtain at the right, suggest that this is a narrative or genre anecdote set in a domestic interior. The drawing seems to represent an old man who has fallen to the ground, perhaps off the chair. On closer inspection, however, it becomes clear that he is using the seat as a prop for his legs, to help him sustain a difficult pose. The drawing must therefore be a study from the life, constructed with the aid of studio props. As such, it conveys an unusual immediacy, with the artist boldly applying the wash to create a sense of movement and depth.

Mahon (1967) suggested that this might be a preparatory study from the life for the saint in *The Angel appearing to St Jerome* of *c.*1619–20, painted probably for the Ludovisi family and now in the Louvre (S, 1988, no. 60). The manner in which the figure shields his eyes in both works is very similar, although the figure is reversed. The subject that this pose most obviously suggests is the Conversion of St Paul. There is no documentary evidence to suggest that Guercino ever tackled this theme at such an early date, but a drawing of the subject exists in the Biblioteca Reale, Turin (inv. no. 16114 D. C.; M, *Disegni*, 1969, no. 177; Sciolla, 1989, no. 100). It shows the saint in a somewhat similar pose, but in reverse, and surprisingly, not shielding his eyes, but raising one hand in the direction of the apparition of Christ above. It must be said that, if anything, the Turin drawing appears to date a little earlier than No. 14, *c.*1614–17.

15 St Sebastian succoured

Pen and black ink and grey wash. 186 × 266mm.

Windsor Castle, Royal Library, inv. no. 2468.

Provenance: Casa Gennari; King George III.

Literature: M, *Disegni*, 1969, no. 43; M & T, 1989, no. 9.

A study for the painting of 1619, commissioned by Guercino's important early patron, Cardinal Jacopo Serra, Papal Legate of Ferrara, and now in the Pinacoteca Nazio-

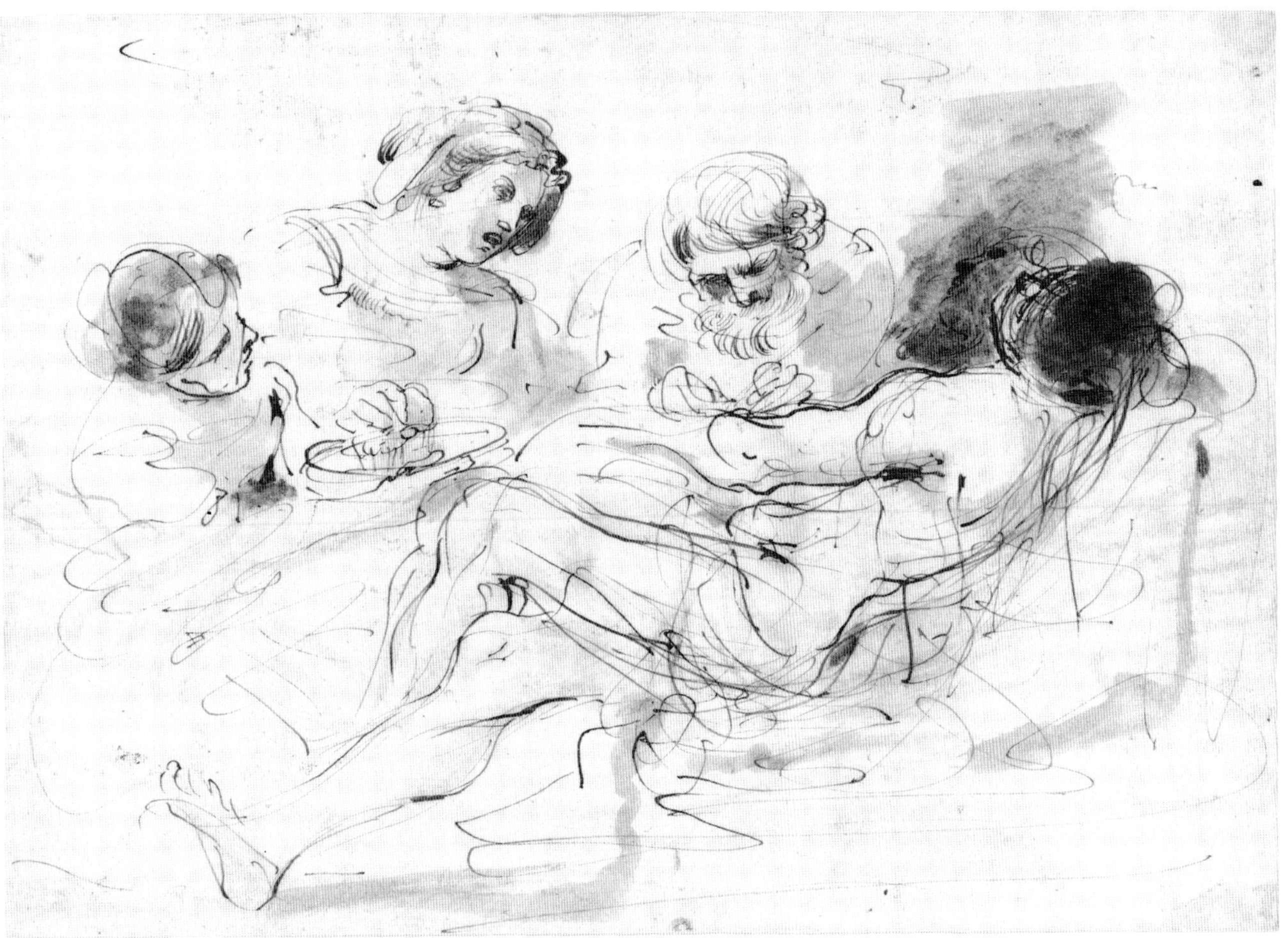

15

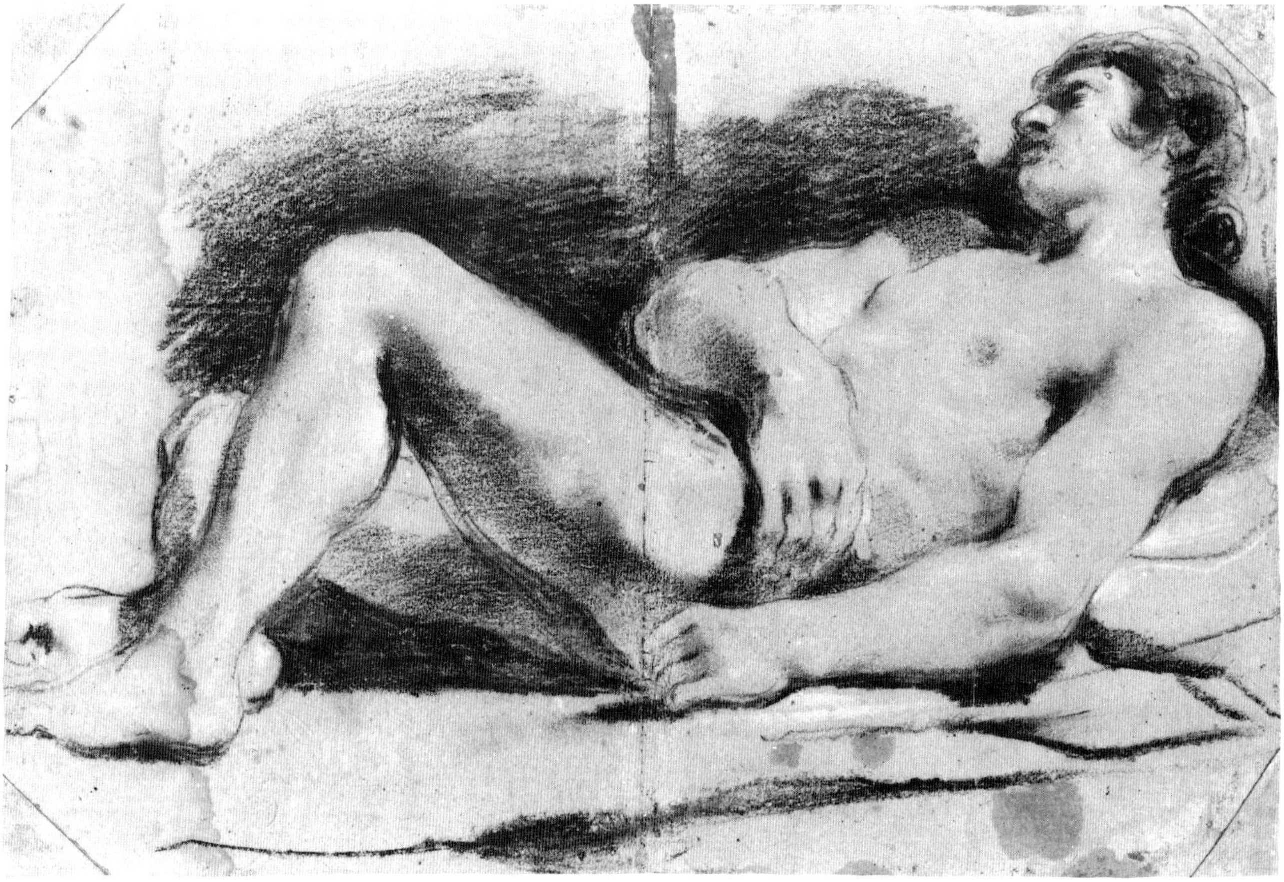

16

nale, Bologna (S, 1988, no. 54). So far as it goes, the drawing corresponds reasonably closely to the finished work, but it lacks the figure of the youth on the right who supports the head of the saint with a cushion. Indeed, it is in this right-hand section of the drawing that the artist has been most indecisive, correcting the position of the saint's head, altering that of his left arm and leaving vacant the area where his body would seem to require support. The dark wash cancellation of the pentiment for the saint's head has been cleverly exploited to enhance the light on the face of the head in its new position, thrown slightly back.

Two drawings in the Uffizi, Florence (inv. nos. 12475-F and 1615-F; M, *Disegni*, 1969, nos. 41 and 42), show the composition at an earlier stage. In both the youth on the right is also absent and, similarly, only three attendant figures are shown.

16 Nude Youth lying on the Ground

Oiled charcoal, with some white heightening, on buff paper. 385 × 576mm.

Windsor Castle, Royal Library, inv. no. 01227.

Provenance: Casa Gennari; King George III.

Literature: M, *Disegni*, 1969, no. 247; M & T, 1989, no. 150.

This magnificent study probably came into being as an exercise in life drawing rather than as a working drawing for a picture. For a discussion of Guercino's life studies of the nude, known as 'academies', see No. 4. As in the present example, Guercino invariably used the uncommon medium of oiled charcoal for such studies.

The pose of the figure may be compared either with that of Tancred in the *Erminia discovering the wounded Tancred*, datable 1618–19, in the Galleria Doria-Pamphili, Rome (S, 1988, no. 53), where the figure is, however, in reverse compared with that in No. 16, or with that of St Sebastian in the *St Sebastian succoured*, datable 1619, in the Pinacoteca Nazionale, Bologna (S, 1988, no. 54; see also No. 15). These two painted figures share several features with the figure in No. 16. They are so close that it seems likely that the drawing was made at roughly the same date as the two pictures, perhaps as a by-product of his work on them, though no direct preparatory relationship with either can be demonstrated.

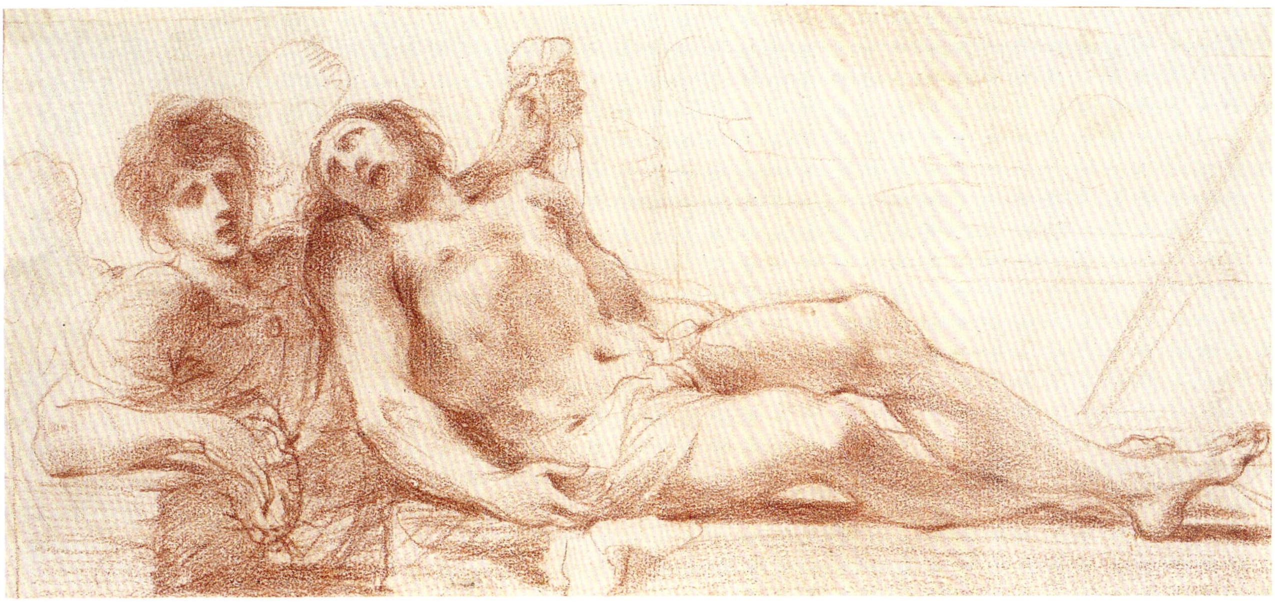

3 (above) *Dead Christ with an Angel.*
Windsor Castle, Royal Library

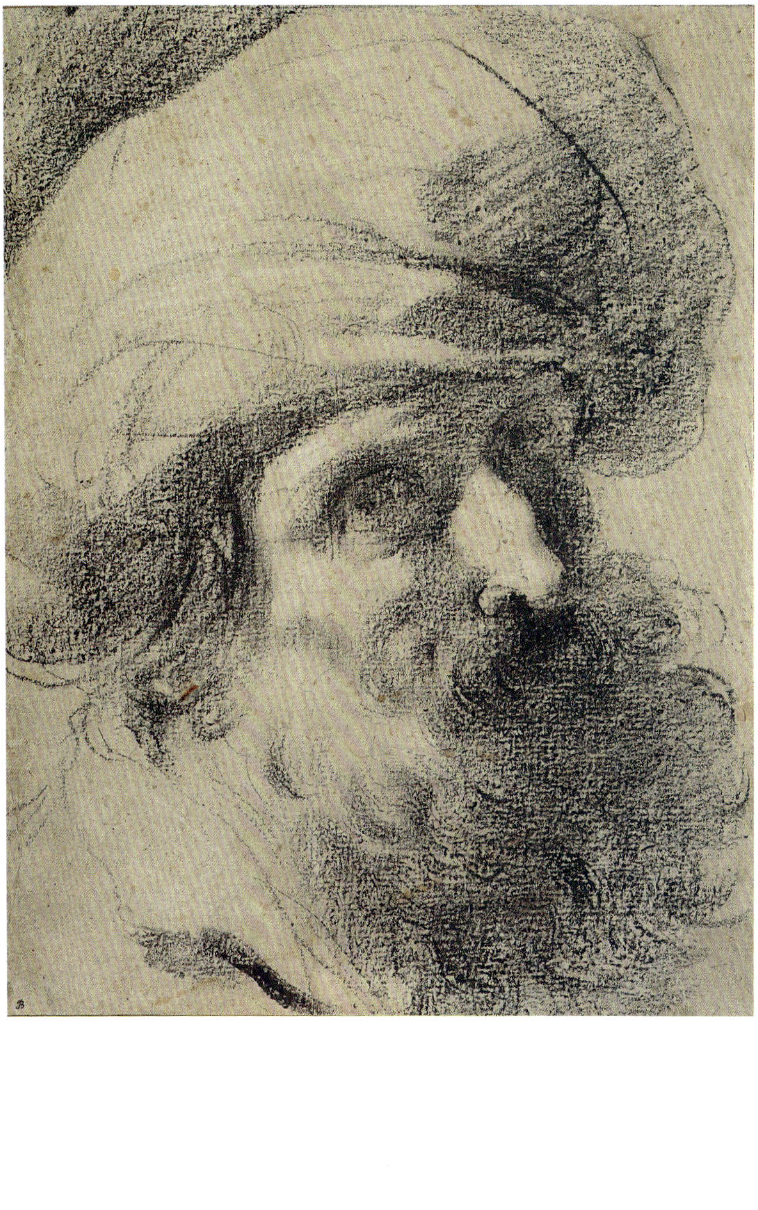

12 (right) *Bearded Man wearing a Turban.*
Private Collection

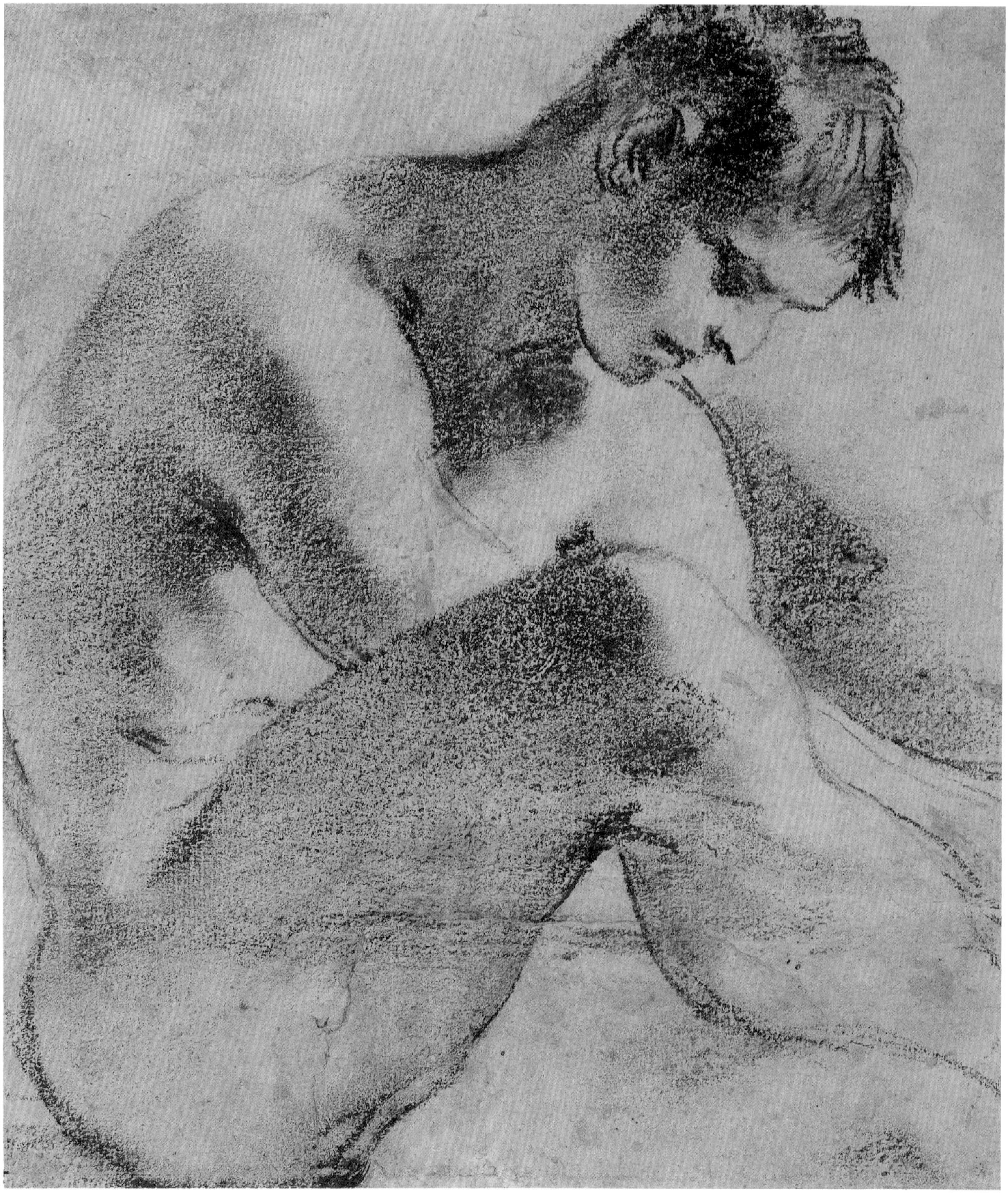

4 *Nude Youth seated on the Ground*. Windsor Castle, Royal Library

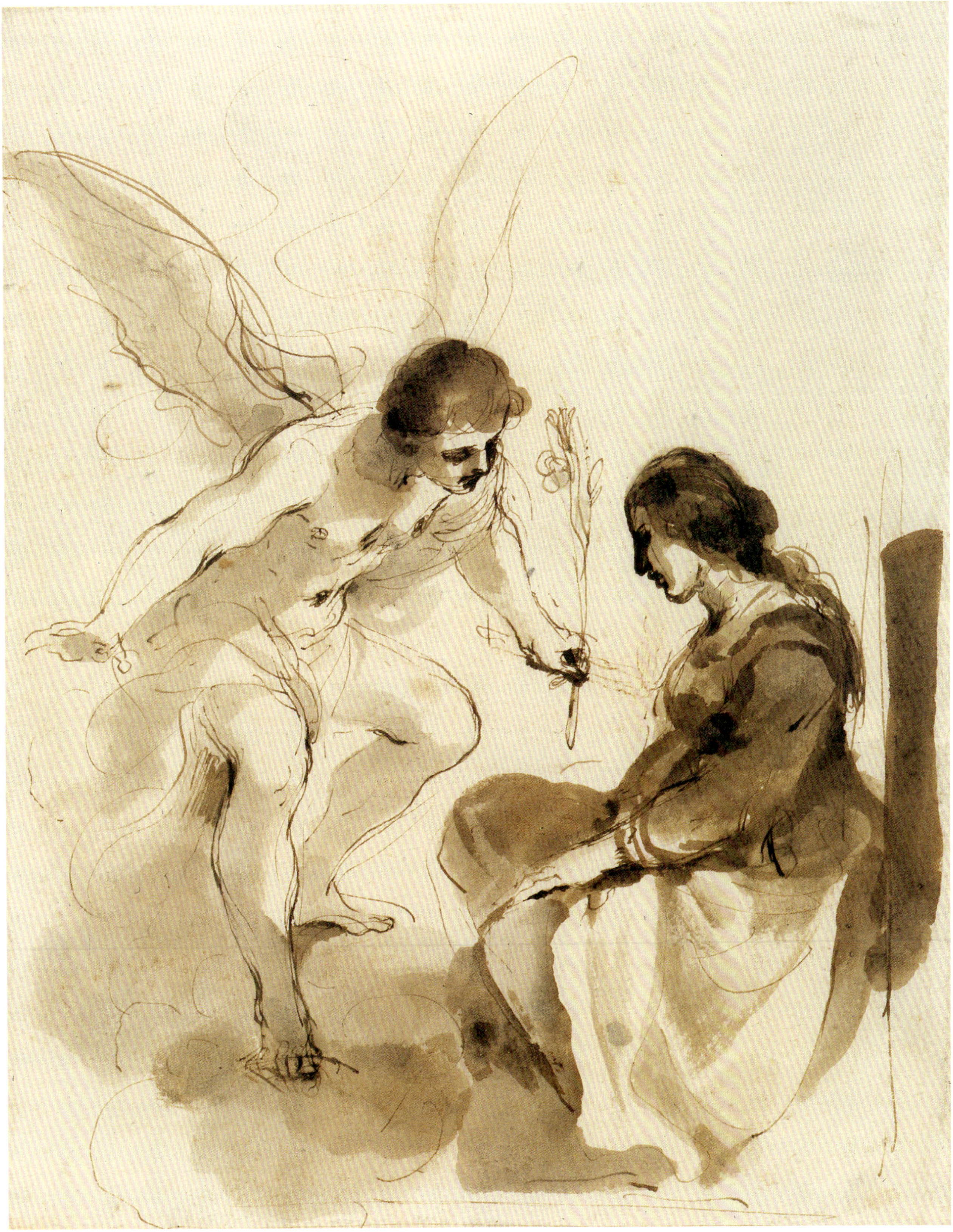

19 *The Annunciation*. Windsor Castle, Royal Library

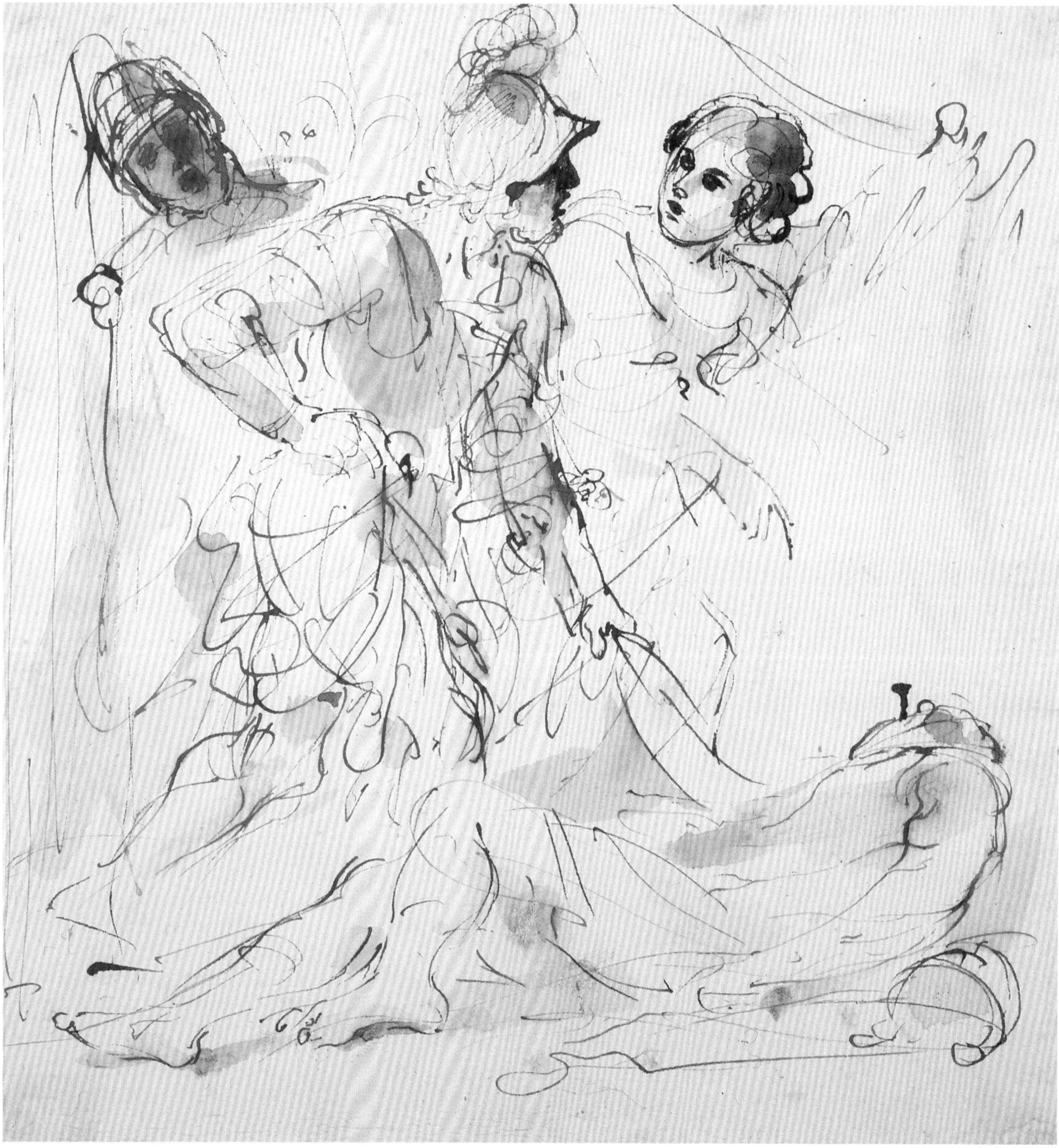

23 *Jael showing Barak the Corpse of Sisera*. Mahon Collection, on loan to the Ashmolean Museum, Oxford

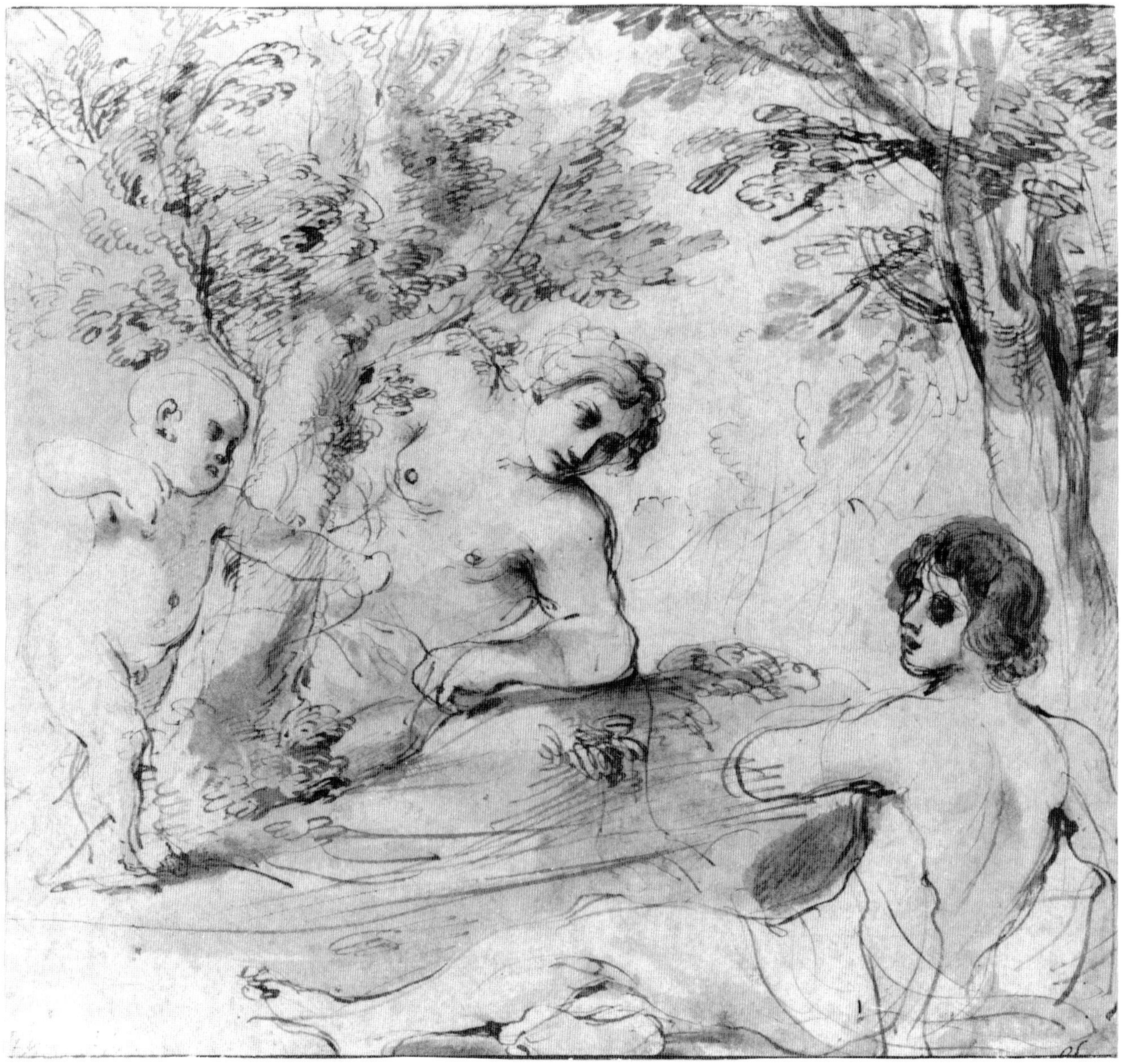

17

17–18 Studies for *Venus, Adonis and Cupid* (*c.*1618–19)

Engraving by G. B. Pasqualini, dated 1620

17 Venus, Adonis and Cupid in a Landscape

Pen and brown ink and brown wash with traces of greyish wash. 180 × 196mm.

Mahon Collection, on loan to the Ashmolean Museum, Oxford, M & E, 4.

Provenance: (?)Pierre Crozat; (?)Count Gustav Tessin; Sir Thomas Lawrence (L 2445); H. M. Calmann; from whom purchased by Sir Denis Mahon on 28 March 1963.

Literature: Mariette, 1741 (?lot 545: see M, 1967, p. 25); M, 1967, no. 2; M, *Disegni*, 1969, no. 36; M & E, 1986, no. 4.

From its style and technique, the drawing seems to date from around 1618–19, being executed in a grey-black ink typical of this period. The curly-headed figure of Adonis is reminiscent of the model used for the *Apollo flaying Marsyas* of 1618 (see No. 6). A more fully developed drawing of the same subject is at Chatsworth (see No. 18) and was engraved by Pasqualini with the date 1620. As Mahon has pointed out, the existence of two connected preparatory drawings suggests that Guercino was planning a painting of this subject, though no such work has yet to come to light.

In the Mahon drawing Venus was originally positioned above Adonis rather than beyond him; in order to establish

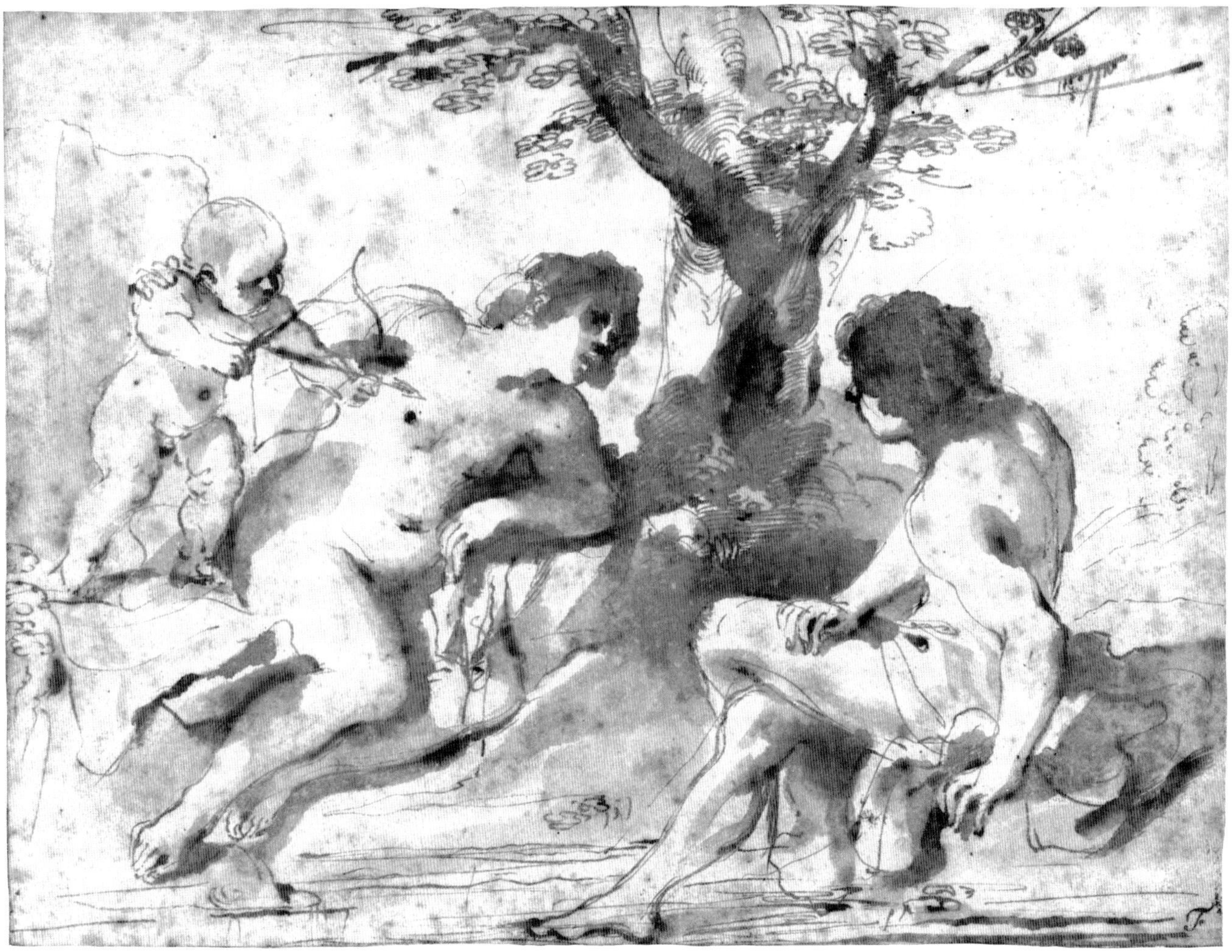

18

some depth Guercino masked part of her figure with a tree, which explains why she appears unnaturally large (she is, in fact, drawn to the same scale as Adonis in the foreground). There are also interesting pentiments for the figures' arms which suggest a rather more intimate encounter than that ultimately depicted in the Chatsworth drawing. Adonis was originally shown leaning back, propping himself up on both arms as though yielding to Venus, whose outstretched left arm formerly strayed in his direction.

18 Venus, Adonis and Cupid

Pen and brown ink and brown wash. 188 × 251mm; drawn on paper apparently from an account book.

Chatsworth, inv. no. 522.

Provenance: N. A. Flinck (L 959); probably William Cavendish, 2nd Duke of Devonshire; thence by descent.

Literature: M, *Disegni*, 1969, no. 37; B, 1988, no. 22.

The drawing was engraved in reverse by Giovanni Battista Pasqualini (1595–1631) with the date 1620 (Bertelà, 1973, no. 818; B, 1988, no. 21). Guercino may have made the drawing specifically for the engraving, a conclusion partly justified by its careful execution. On the other hand, the composition may also be connected with a painting, though none is known.

The execution of the passages of wash, especially in the areas of flesh, is particularly effective. Employing the brush with a darker tone of the same wash, Guercino also achieved varied effects in the hair of the two principal figures and in the background shadows.

19 The Annunciation

(*see colour pl. 3*)

Pen and brown ink and brown wash. 220 × 174mm.

Windsor Castle, Royal Library, inv. no. 2792.

Provenance: Casa Gennari; King George III.

Literature: Russell, 1923, pp. 20 and 55, pl. XVI (where the provenance is given incorrectly as from the collection of Consul Joseph Smith); M, *Disegni*, 1969, no. 178; M & T, 1989, no. 139.

No painted version of this composition is known but the drawing surely dates from about 1616–18 and may have been for a small devotional picture.

Mahon and Turner noted that the pose of the angel closely resembles, in reverse, that of the figure of Prometheus seen on the clouds on the right of *Prometheus bringing the Statue of Clay to Life with a burning Torch*, now in the Cassa di Risparmio, Cento, which Guercino painted in 1616 (while he was working on the decoration of the Casa Pannini) on the chimney-breast in one of the two rooms of his Accademia in the Casa Fabri at Cento (see B, 1984, pl. 5; S, 1988, no. 26). Indeed, one wonders whether the idea of an Annunciation did not occur to Guercino as he was in the middle of a study for the Prometheus composition, for the resemblance is extremely close, with a pentiment for the burning torch near the Madonna's breast and calligraphic swirls of drapery indicated between the angel's wings. Certainly the torch would be most unusual in the iconography of the Annunciation, and it was in fact replaced with Gabriel's more conventional lily.

The drawing is executed in a painterly style, the Madonna being modelled almost entirely in wash.

20–21 Studies for the *Allegory of Painting* (1619)

Engraved frontispiece by Oliviero Gatti

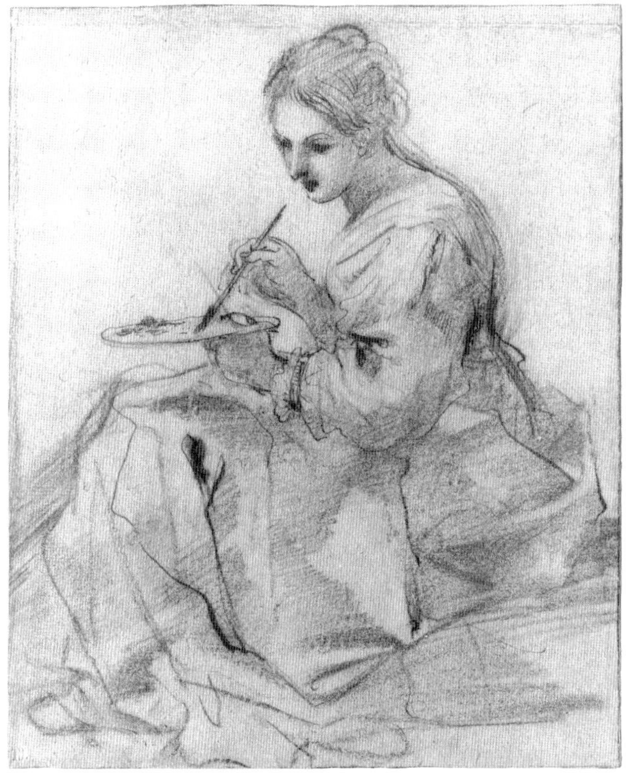

20

20 A Woman painting

Red chalk with some pen and brown ink. 194 × 161mm.

Oxford, Ashmolean Museum, KTP 859.

Provenance: Sir T. Lawrence (L 2445); S. Woodburn; purchased 1948.

Literature: Parker, 1956, no. 859; M, *Disegni*, 1969, no. 30; M & E, 1986, no. I.

A study for the allegorical figure of Painting in the engraved frontispiece, dated 1619, of the *Allegory of Painting* by Oliviero Gatti (*fl.* 1596–1626), which introduces a series of twenty-one prints by the same engraver, also after Guercino, of anatomical and figure subjects intended for the instruction of beginners in drawing (Bartsch, 1803–21, XIX, p. 30, no. 118, I; Bertelà, 1973, no. 653; and B, 1988, no. 4 for the engraved frontispiece only).

The figure of the woman is similar to that in Gatti's print, except that the head is not in profile to the left but turned very slightly in the direction of the spectator. The female type that Guercino selected for this allegorical figure is one that recurs frequently in his early works, robust in form, with sloping shoulders and rounded features (compare, for example, Nos. 19, 22, 24, 32, 37 and 45).

21 Woman painting a Coat of Arms on a Canvas

Pen and brown ink and brown wash, over black chalk. 160 × 216mm.

Windsor Castle, Royal Library, inv. no. 2730.

Provenance: Casa Gennari; King George III.

Literature: M, *Disegni*, 1969, under no. 30; M & E, 1986, under no. I; M & T, 1989, no. 11.

A study, in the same direction, for the *Allegory of Painting*, an engraved frontispiece by Oliviero Gatti, for which see No. 20. In the print, the plinth on the right bears a dedication to Duke Ferdinando Gonzaga of Mantua; and the coat of arms, rendered only in outline in the drawing, is completed as that of the Gonzaga family. (Malvasia mentioned this work in his table of Guercino's commissions under the previous year (1678, II, p. 363; 1841, II, p. 259), though it is clear that he was aware that the date of Gatti's print was 1619 (1678, I, p. 109; 1841, I, p. 90).)

In the drawing Guercino was at first undecided as to where to place the putto on the right. Originally he peeped out from behind the canvas, but the awkward proximity of his head to the woman's profile caused the artist to erase the figure (though his left hand, clasping the edge of the stretcher, is still clearly visible just above the end of her brush). He was then moved to the space in the air above to hold the upper right corner of the canvas, but even here, with more room in which to draw the figure, Guercino still

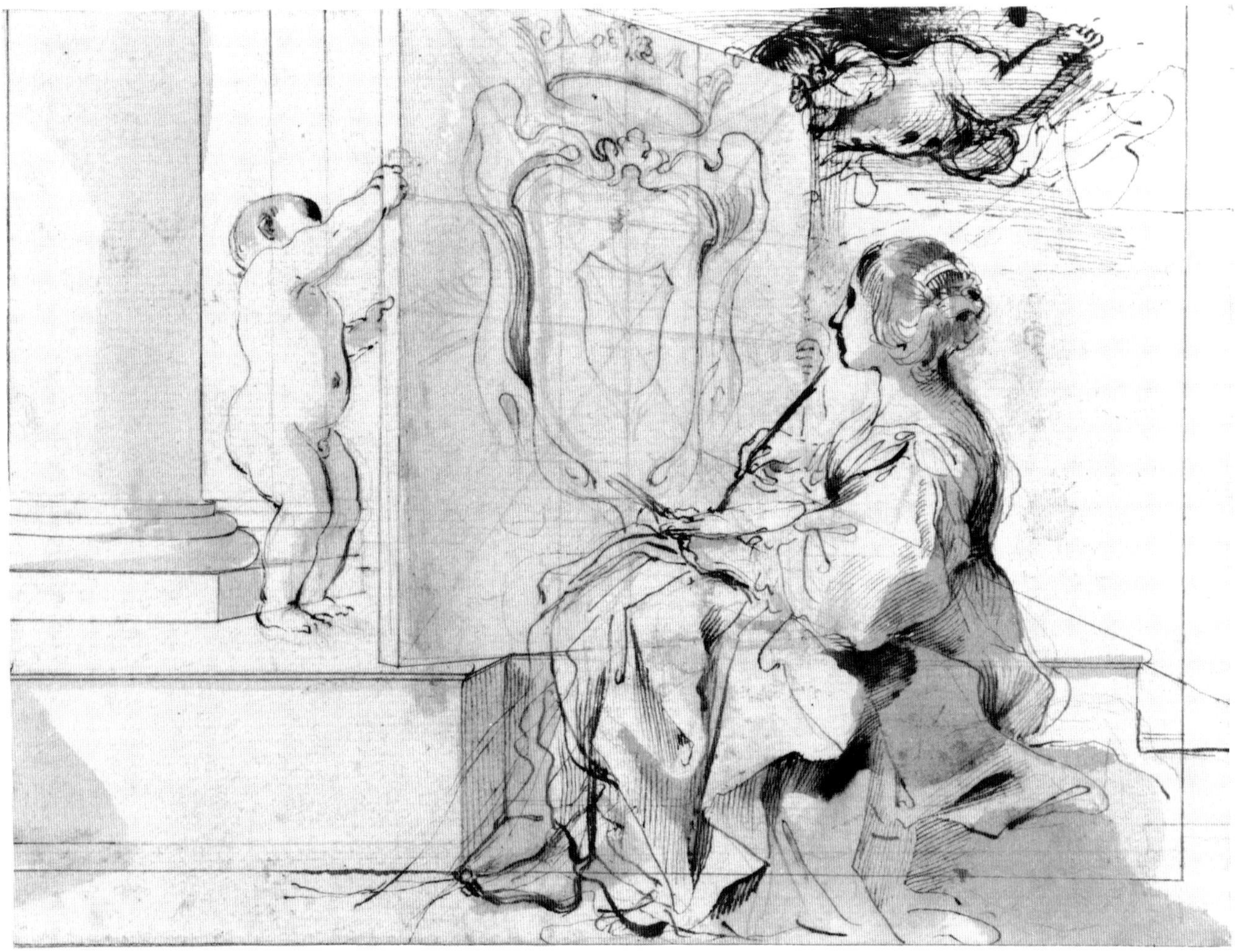

21

had some difficulty in fixing its pose. Among the several differences between the drawing and the print is the position of the figure of Painting, who, in the print, is moved further away from both the plinth and the canvas and looks down intently at her palette.

22 Erminia

Red chalk, with some stumping, on light buff paper. 348 × 256mm.

Windsor Castle, Royal Library, inv. no. 2898.

Provenance: Casa Gennari; King George III.

Literature: S, 1988, under no. 61; M & T, 1989, no. 12.

A finished study, with differences, for the figure of Erminia in the painting *Erminia and the Shepherd*, commissioned by Ferdinando Gonzaga, Duke of Mantua, in 1619–20 and now in the Birmingham City Museum and Art Gallery (S, 1988, no. 61). In the picture Erminia appears bareheaded, while her helmet and collar lie on the ground by her right foot. Erminia's disconcertingly broad nose is noteworthy in both the painting and the drawing.

Finished studies of this sort for a whole figure are rare in Guercino's graphic *œuvre*. The handling, however, is characteristic, especially in the richly textured shadow behind Erminia's right shoulder and in the suggestion of light falling on her skirts. In type, the drawing anticipates the studies in red chalk that the artist perfected in his Roman period, 1621–3. Indeed, Guercino went back to this figure in 1621 in an early drawing at Windsor (M & T, 1989, no. 17) for the pose of Aurora in his decoration of the ceiling in the Casino Ludovisi in Rome (for drawings for this fresco and further particulars of the commission, see Nos. 32–5). He returned to this same figure in 1622 in another drawing at Windsor (M & T, 1989, no. 20), this time for the pose of St Chrysogonus in the painting on canvas for the ceiling of the church of S. Crisogono in Rome (S, 1988, no. 86), now at Lancaster House, London.

App. no. 95 is a feeble copy of No. 22.

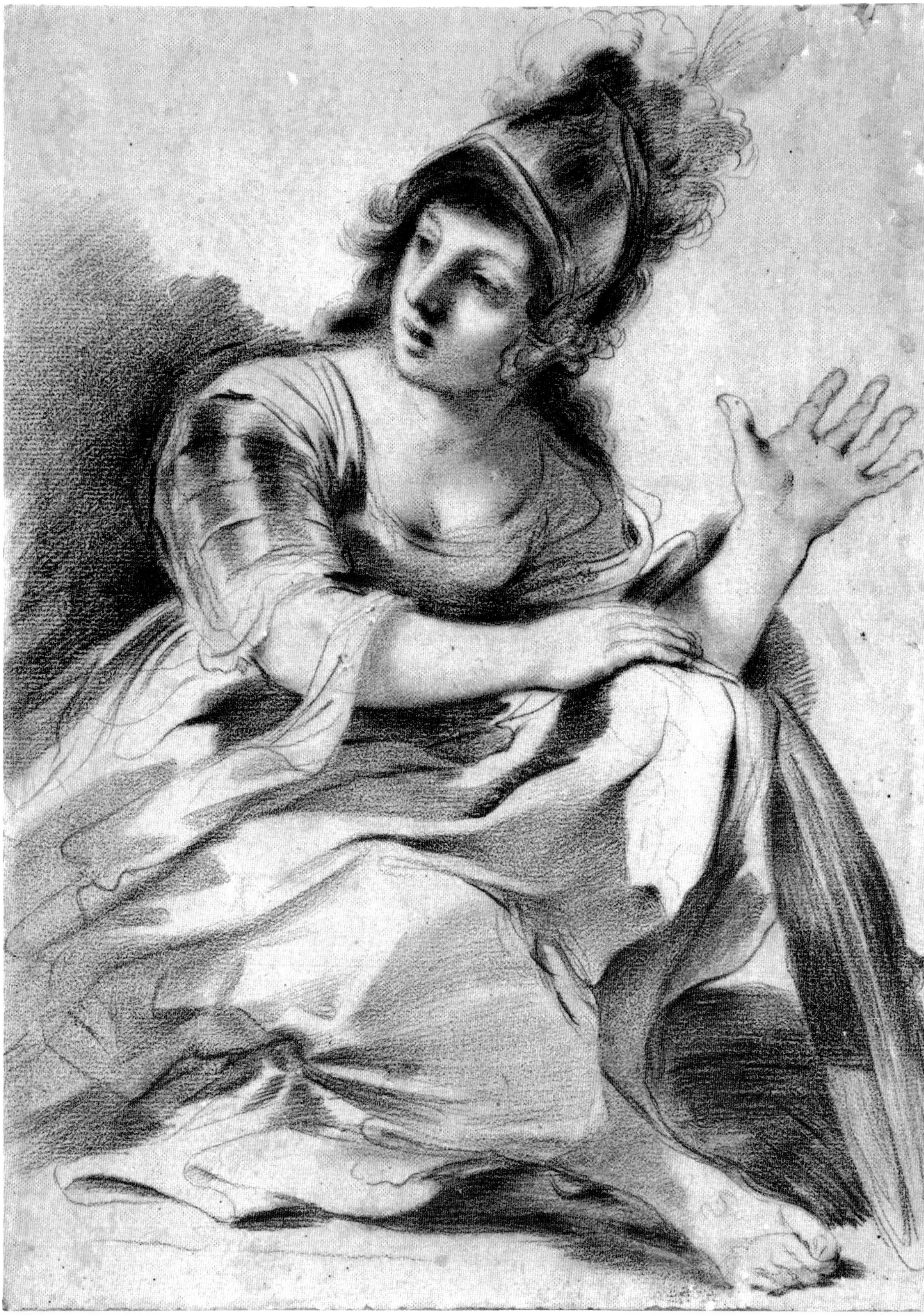

22

23–25 Studies for *Jael and Sisera* (*c*.1619–20)

Lost

23 Jael showing Barak the Corpse of Sisera

(*see colour pl. 4*)

Pen and brown ink and brown wash with traces of greyish wash. 204 × 194mm.

Mahon Collection, on loan to the Ashmolean Museum, Oxford, M & E, 7.

Provenance: Casa Gennari (the drawing is laid down on a fine Casa Gennari mount, for which see L *Suppl*, 2858c, and M, 1967, p. 20); Mr Bouverie; Mr Hervey; John Rushout, 2nd Lord Northwick; P. & D. Colnaghi, London; from whom purchased by Sir Denis Mahon on 28 December 1937.

Literature: M, 1967, no. 5; M, *Disegni*, 1969, no. 49; M & E, 1986, no. 7.

Nos. 23–5 are studies for a lost painting of *Jael and Sisera*, probably painted *c*.1619–20 before Guercino went to Rome; the picture's appearance is recorded in a small photograph from the Fiocco Collection in the library of the Cini Foundation, Venice (M, 1981, p. 175, fig. 6; S, 1988, no. 63; for a discussion of the painting in the photograph and an analysis of the sequence of the preparatory drawings for this commission, see M, *Disegni*, 1969, under nos. 49–52). The lost painting shows a very early moment in the biblical narrative, with Jael poised to strike the first blow on the hammer which will drive the nail into the sleeping Sisera's head. According to Mahon, Guercino must have started with the idea of representing a later point in the story, with Jael showing Barak the corpse of the dead Sisera (Nos. 23–4); he then went on to explore the more dramatic scene of the murder itself (No. 25). A drawing in the Lugt Collection, Paris (inv. no. 1050; M, *Disegni*, 1969, no. 52; Byam Shaw, 1983, no. 338), the latest in the sequence, shows both Jael and Sisera in the same poses as in the finished work.

The violence of the subject, considerably understated in the rendering of No. 23, is revealed only in the deliberation with which the nail piercing Sisera's skull has been drawn. A copy of this drawing by Francesco Bartolozzi is in the Albertina, Vienna (inv. no. 1368; Stix & Frölich-Bum, 1926, no. 441).

24 Barak finds Jael with the Corpse of Sisera

Pen and brown ink and greyish wash. 206 × 293mm.

Mahon Collection, on loan to the Ashmolean Museum, Oxford, M & E, 8.

Provenance: Casa Gennari (the drawing is laid down on a fine Casa Gennari mount, for which see L *Suppl*, 2858c, and M, 1967, p. 20); Mr Bouverie; Mr Hervey; 1st Earl of Gainsborough (sale, London, Sotheby's, 22 July 1953, lot 6), purchased by Sir Denis Mahon.

Literature: M, 1967, no. 6; M, *Disegni*, 1969, no. 50; M & E, 1986, no. 8.

Inscribed in dark brown ink in the bottom left corner of the old mount: *51 non com.* (for a similar annotation, see No. 27). Numbered on the mount in graphite below the bottom left corner of the draw-

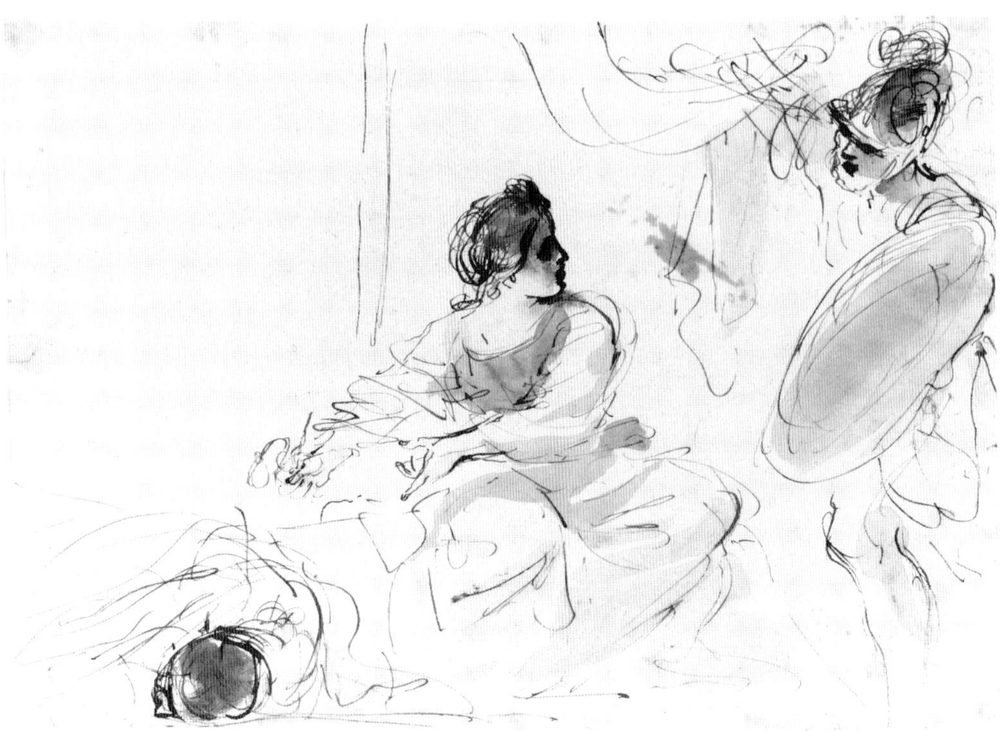

24

ing: *6* (for a discussion and further instances of sheets numbered in this way, see No. 10); numbered in graphite above the drawing: *26*, and below it to the right: *46*.

A study for a lost painting of *Jael and Sisera*, for which see No. 23.

25 Jael killing Sisera

Pen and brown ink. 123 × 139mm.

Mahon Collection, on loan to the Ashmolean Museum, Oxford, M & E, 9.

Provenance: Dr Ludwig Pollak (L *Suppl*, 788b); Prof. Antonio Muñoz; Sir Denis Mahon, who acquired the drawing in 1960.

Literature: M, 1967, no. 7; M, *Disegni*, 1969, no. 51; M & E, 1986, no. 9.

This is the most violent of all the studies for the lost painting of *Jael and Sisera*, for which see No. 23. It represents Jael in the act of murdering Sisera, who is still very much alive, writhing under her blows. The finished painting shows an earlier moment with Sisera still asleep and Jael poised to strike the first blow. Pentiments for the arms of both figures in No. 25 create an impression of frenzied movement. One, for Sisera's left arm, reveals that Guercino at first intended to show him pushing Jael away. Jael's face, like the detail of the nail in No. 23, was so heavily – almost brutally – drawn, that the iron-gall ink has subsequently corroded the paper, exaggerating her harsh mask-like features.

In the bottom right corner at the edge of the sheet are various small sketches, one of which represents a woman's head, turned to the right. These subsidiary sketches suggest that the main study once formed part of a larger sheet on which Guercino made other attempts at the composition, reversing it according to his customary procedure.

Guercino seems to have been inspired by a version of this subject painted much earlier by Ludovico Carracci (the composition of which is known from two preparatory drawings, one, perhaps autograph, in pen and brown ink over red chalk in the Louvre, Paris, inv. no. 7898; and another, in black and white chalk on grey paper and in reverse, in the Biblioteca Ambrosiana, Milan, Codice Resta F. 215, no. 238 *recto*: see Bohn, 1984, no. 5 in her checklist, repr. pl. 4). Although Guercino's early studies for the painting (Nos. 23 and 24) explore independent solutions, he seems to have been affected by the older master's composition, both in the moment he chose to depict and in the arrangement of the figures. Another study by Guercino for this composition in the Lugt Collection, Paris (inv. no. 1050; M, *Disegni*, 1969, no. 52; Byam Shaw, 1983, no. 338), which is closer than

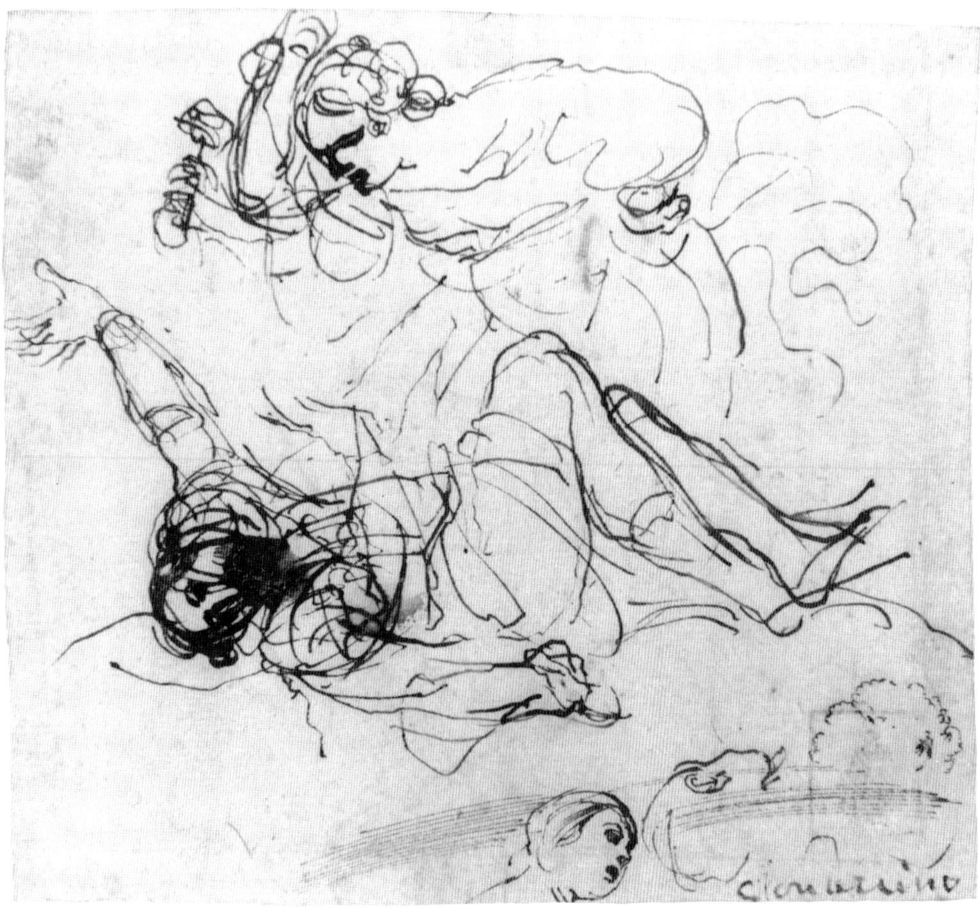

25

any of the drawings exhibited here to its painted counterpart, does seem to imply some knowledge of Ludovico's design as revealed in both the Ambrosiana and Louvre drawings, though in reverse.

Another likely influence on Guercino's composition is a woodcut of *Jael killing Sisera* (Bartsch, 1803–21, VII, p. 440, no. 7; see Fig. 3), by the Netherlandish artist Lucas van Leyden (1494–1533). In the print, Sisera is lying on his right side asleep, and although in general his pose does not appear to correspond with Guercino's solution, the position of his legs, with one foot hooked behind the other, seems directly relevant to No. 25. There are also analogies between the figure of Jael in the print and in No. 25, the Lugt drawing and the lost painting. In the 1719 inventory of the effects of the Casa Gennari there are references to works by named Northern artists, and although Lucas van Leyden is not specifically mentioned, it is not impossible that Guercino knew or even owned prints by him.

26–28 Studies for *St William receiving the monastic Habit* (1620)

Bologna, Pinacoteca Nazionale

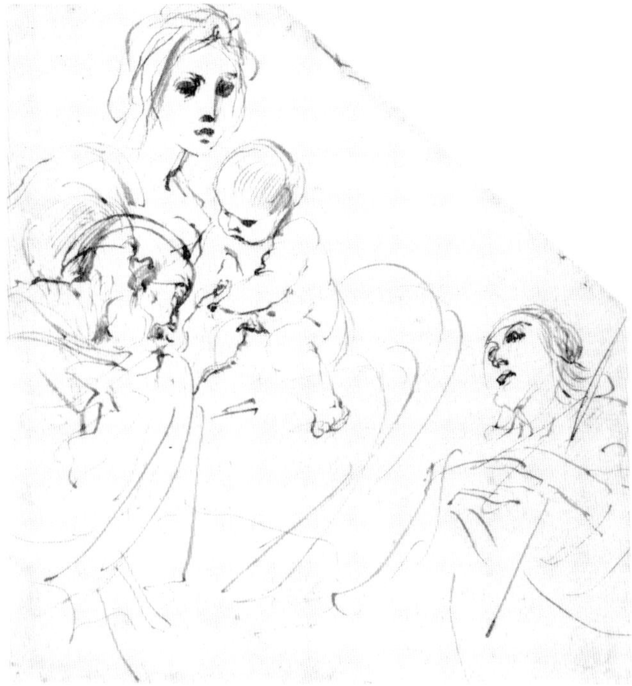

26

26 Madonna and Child with two Saints

Pen and blackish-brown ink. 175 × 164mm; the top right corner cut.

Windsor Castle, Royal Library, inv. no. 2482.

Provenance: Casa Gennari; King George III.

Literature: M, *Disegni*, 1969, no. 60; S, 1988, under no. 69; M & T, 1989, no. 13.

A study for the Madonna and Child with two saints (probably Sts Joseph and James the Greater) in the upper part of the altarpiece of *St William receiving the monastic Habit*, painted in 1620 for the church of S. Gregorio in Bologna and now in the Pinacoteca Nazionale of that same city (S, 1988, no. 69). This celebrated picture, Guercino's early masterpiece, represents the culmination of the painter's early, pre-Roman style and was the most important commission he had received before his departure for Rome in 1621. The genesis of the composition may be followed in an unrivalled series of more than twenty preparatory studies which bear witness to the extraordinary process that lay behind the invention of the composition. During this lengthy evolution every conceivable alternative for each figure seems to have received due consideration (see M, *Disegni*, 1969, nos. 57–76, where the sequence of the drawings is admirably expounded; studies that have come to light since the 1969 catalogue are discussed in S, 1988, under no. 69 and in M & T, 1989, under nos. 13 and 14; see also under No. 27 below).

The figures in No. 26 are different in nearly every respect from their painted counterparts. Three further studies for the same group are in the Albertina, Vienna, the Brera,

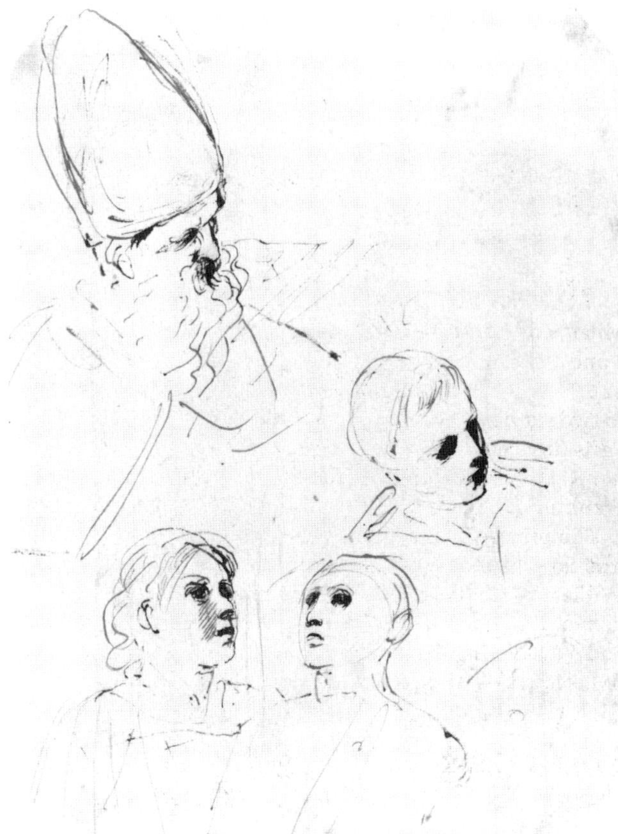

Fig. 7 *Sheet of Studies for St William receiving the monastic Habit.* Pen and brown ink, 190 × 140 mm (Kate Ganz Ltd, London). See No. 27

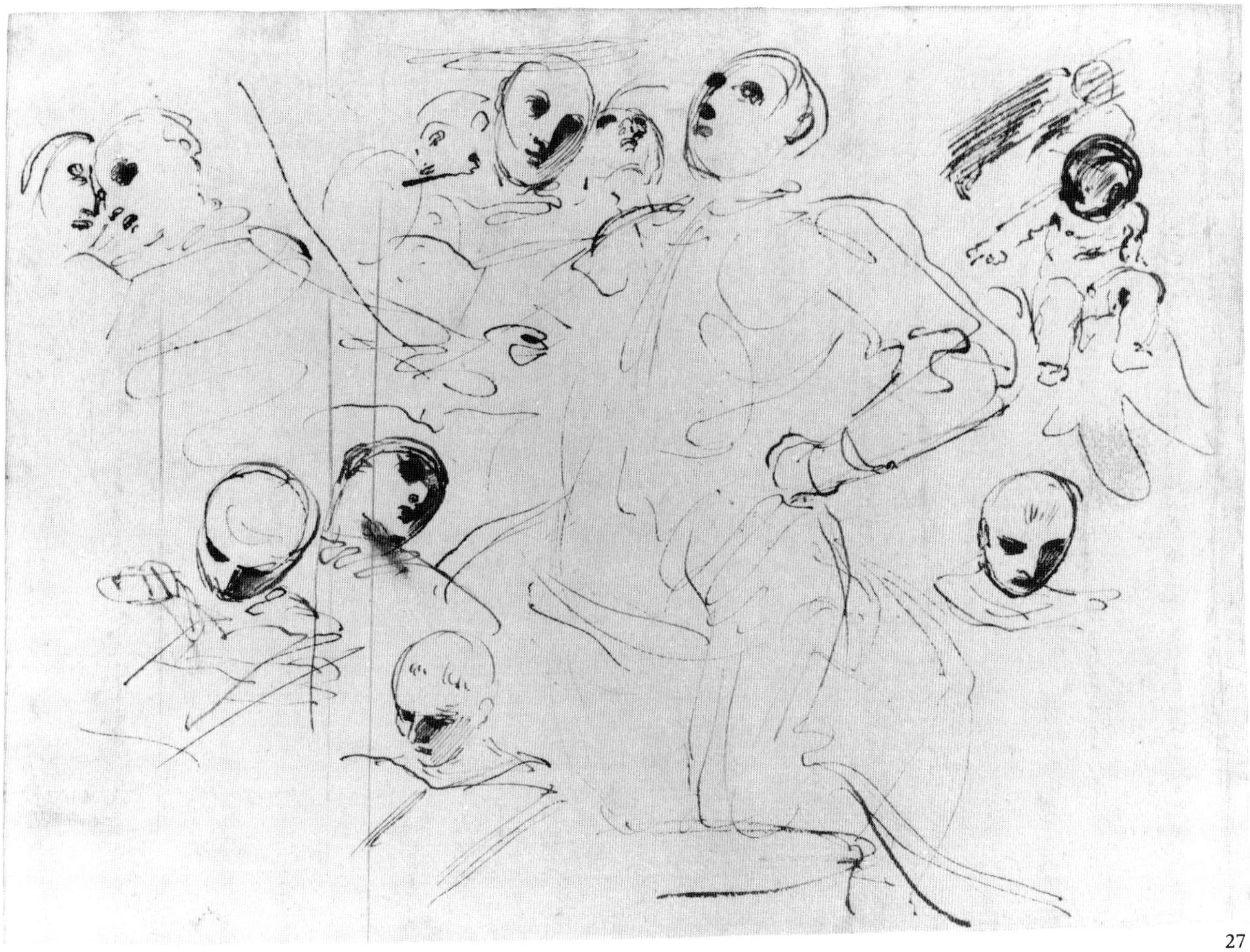

27

Milan, and in the Teylers Museum, Haarlem (inv. nos. 2343, 1 and H. 16 respectively; M, *Disegni*, 1969, nos. 59, 61 and 62). The group appears once more, only summarily drawn, in two studies for the whole composition, one in the Louvre, Paris (inv. no. 6884; M, *Disegni*, 1969, no. 58; Loire, 1990, no. 31), and the other in the Städelsches Kunstinstitut at Frankfurt (inv. no. 3922; Bean, 1969, p. 430, fig. 2).

The picture's iconography is not altogether explicit, but it is now usually supposed that the saint represented is St William of Aquitaine, who is sometimes confused with William of Gascony or Gellone, William of Gascony and Poitou and William of Malavalle (for a discussion of the problem of his identification, see M, *Dipinti*, 1968, p. 99).

27 Sheet of Studies for St William receiving the monastic Habit

Pen and brown ink, with slight touches of brown wash. 196 × 270mm.

Mahon Collection, on loan to the Ashmolean Museum, Oxford, M & E, 10.

Provenance: Casa Gennari (the drawing retains its fine Casa Gennari mount, for which see L *Suppl*, 2858c, and M, 1967, p. 20); Mr Bouverie; Mr Hervey; the Earls of Gainsborough (sale, Sotheby's, London, 22 July 1953, lot 8), purchased by Sir Denis Mahon.

Literature: M, 1967, no. 8; M, *Disegni*, 1969, no. 69; M & E, 1986, no. 10.

Inscribed in brown ink in the bottom left corner of the old mount: *9 non com.* (for a similar annotation, see No. 24). Numbered in graphite below and to the left of the bottom left corner of the drawing: *4* (for a discussion and further instances of sheets numbered in this way, see No. 10); numbered in graphite above the drawing: *13*, and below it to the right: *59*.

Guercino must have begun No. 27 by drawing the kneeling figure of St William, who is studied both in relation to the arms of the bishop on the left and to the heads of the novices seen just behind, one of whom holds an open book. His concentration then shifted to a more careful study of the heads of these assistants, which he proceeded to draw again, as a pair (top left) and as a series of separate studies (bottom left and bottom right); on the right of the sheet he also drew the infant Christ, who appears in much the same pose in the finished picture.

He seems to have failed in his several attempts to draw the heads of the two novices in their correct position immediately behind the saint's right shoulder, first drawing them too low and then in unconvincing relation to each other; the result is that five heads eventually appeared in the principal study competing with the main focus of attention, the saint himself. The idea of uniting the two novices behind an open book was elaborated in three of the subsequent studies, in one of which a leaf is shown being turned, but this motif was abandoned in the painting, as it would have introduced an unnecessary complication into a composition already dense with varied actions.

The detail of the two novices was an important element in the final picture. This passage together with the detail of the cavalry seen in the distance on the right are the only ones that allow the spectator to gauge recession in the lower half of the painting. The variation in scale between the horsemen, the acolytes and the dominant foreground figures, which are placed in roughly the same plane as each other but on different levels, is no more than a dramatic device to delude the eye into judging depth.

A sheet of studies by Guercino, with Kate Ganz Ltd, London, in the summer of 1990 (pen and brown ink, 190 × 140mm; see Fig. 7), is carried out in an identical style to No. 27 and must belong to the same creative moment. It consists of four separate studies of heads, one of which is of the bishop; of the remaining three, one is certainly a trial for one of the same two acolytes.

28 St William receiving the monastic Habit

Pen and brown ink, with some brown wash. 155 × 142mm; all four corners are cut irregularly.

Windsor Castle, Royal Library, inv. no. 2475.

Provenance: Casa Gennari; King George III.

Literature: M, *Dipinti*, 1968, p. 98; M, *Disegni*, 1969, no. 76 and pp. 85f.; M & T, 1989, no. 14.

A study for the figure of St William in the altarpiece *St William receiving the monastic Habit*, for which see No. 26.

That the drawing was made after the artist had begun painting the figure onto the canvas, rather than before, can be established from a scientific examination of the picture, which reveals a pentiment for the saint's left arm with the hand resting on the hip. Guercino must first have painted the figure in this position, following the solution for its pose adumbrated in several preparatory drawings (e.g., No. 27; one in the collection of Pierre Rosenberg, Paris (M, *Disegni*, 1969, no. 71); and another in the Museum der Bildenden Künste, Leipzig, inv. no. N.I. 239; M, *Disegni*, 1969, no. 72). At some point when the picture was already in progress, Guercino decided to make clearer the central action of the saint's assumption of the monastic life and his renunciation of the military: to do this he focused for the first time on William's gesture of donning the monastic habit over his armour. No. 28 thus helped Guercino prepare his alternative idea before effecting this important change on the canvas. However, even in this drawing he had not quite arrived

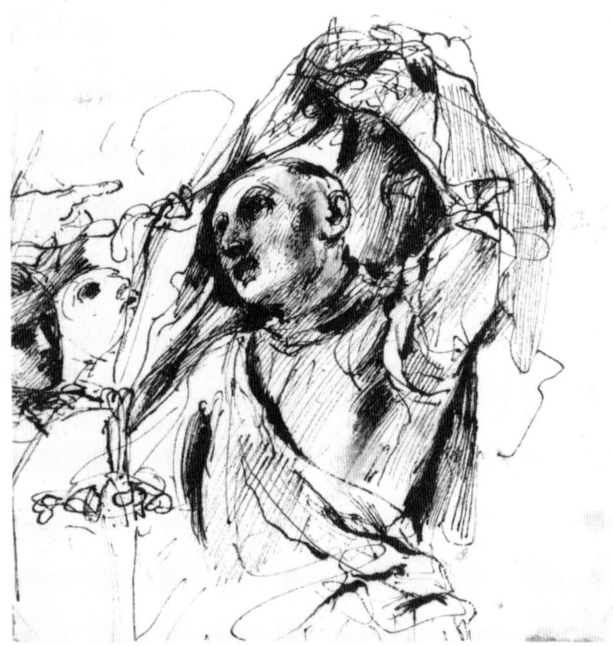

28

at the solution seen in the picture, for the saint's head still leans down a little awkwardly, while in the picture it is thrown further back. Another drawing exploring this same detail was formerly on the London art market (sale, Sotheby's, 4 July 1988, lot 60), likewise drawn after Guercino had begun the picture. There the saint's head is shown bent further back, though the position of the accompanying acolyte is different from that of his painted counterpart. Drawings from such a late phase in the creative process are unusual in Guercino's graphic *œuvre*, as Mahon was the first to point out.

In No. 28 Guercino's use of stippling can be seen in the face of the saint. Another of the artist's favourite graphic devices is also apparent: he has touched in part of the shadow with brown wash, which he has then partly smudged in the area near the neck and ear. A similar passage of wash occurs in the saint's breast-plate. He has thus varied the texture of the drawing by creating a different type of half-tone from the hatching with the pen, which accounts for most of the shading.

29 The Mystic Marriage of St Catherine

Pen and brown ink and brown wash over black chalk. 256 × 203mm.

Oxford, Ashmolean Museum, KTP 856.

Provenance: Anonymous sale, Sotheby's, London, 15 February 1939, lot 21.

Literature: Parker, 1956, no. 856; Waterhouse, 1960, under no. 369; Bottari, 1966, pl. XXII; M, *Disegni*, 1969, no. 53; Macandrew, 1980, p. 298; M & E, 1986, no. IV; S, 1988, under no. 67.

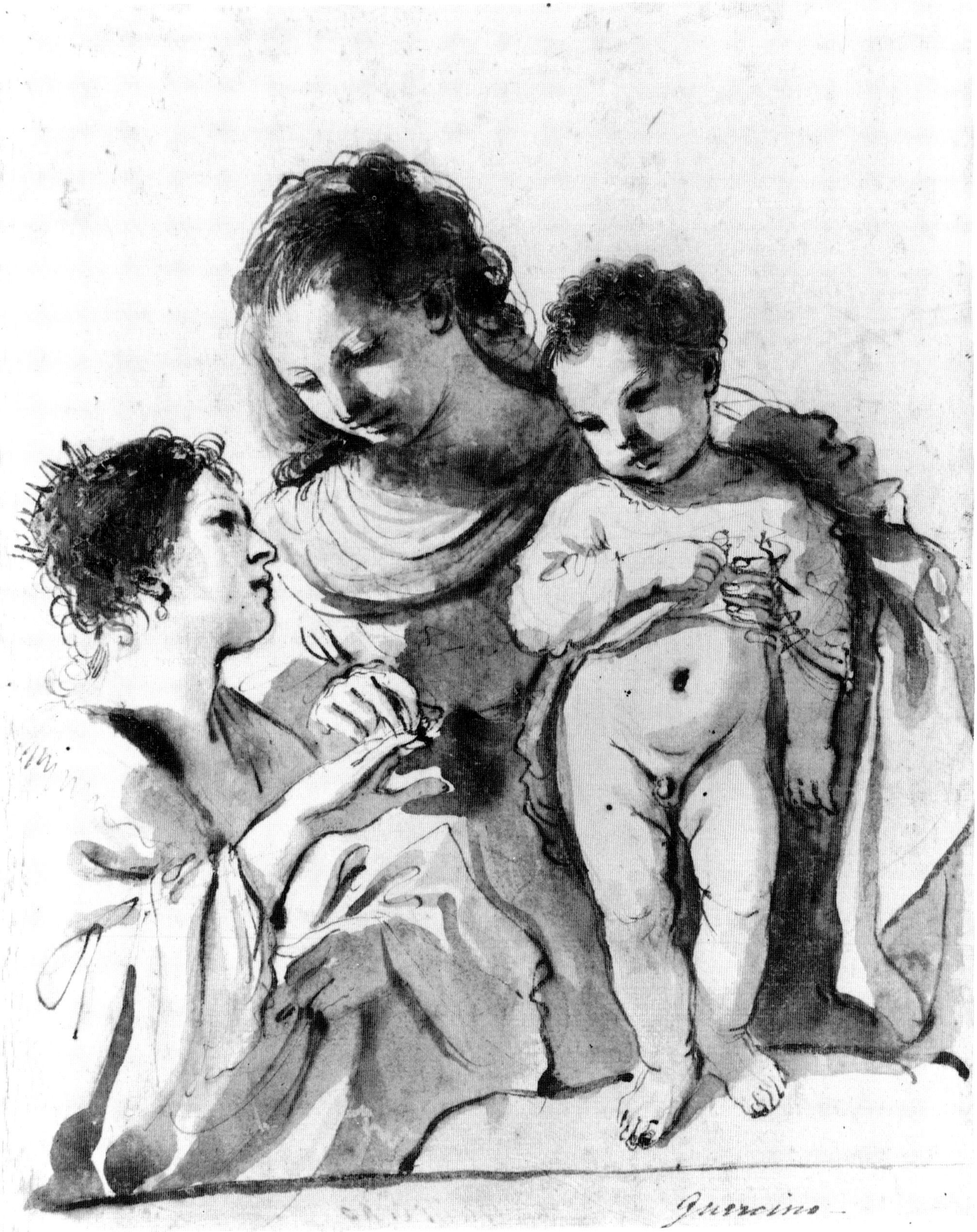

29

A preliminary study for a painting of the same subject formerly in the Mahon Collection, London, and now in the Gemäldegalerie, Berlin–Dahlem (S, 1988, no. 67). According to Malvasia (1678, II, p. 364; 1841, II, p. 259), this was painted for the Cavaliere Piombino of Cento in 1620; it well represents the type of relatively small commission Guercino was receiving from local dignitaries before his departure for Rome the following year. The drawing is unusual in so fully anticipating the finished work. On the whole, Guercino's compositions underwent a complex process of development and only rarely does a surviving drawing match the finished painting more or less exactly; although connections between his studies and painted solutions are usually readily apparent, so too are several alterations and changes.

In this instance, the most significant of the few slight differences between the two works is their scale. In the drawing, the figures are noticeably more spread out, more of each is shown and the figures themselves are more slender. In the painting, the solution is more daring, with the figures brought even closer to the view of the spectator by the three protagonists being slightly enlarged to fill the whole picture plane, a process that somehow forces the spectator to become aware of the picture's abstract qualities seen in the wonderful bravura of its painted surface. It is also interesting to note how at this period in Guercino's career the painted solution was in fact more adventurous in composition than the preparatory drawing that led up to it. In the later part of his career, it was the other way round. Time and again the more dynamic and inventive compositional ideas studied in the drawings were abandoned in favour of a more static solution expressed in paint.

2 The Roman Period, 1621–3 (Nos. 30–43)

In 1621 Guercino was summoned to Rome by his patron Alessandro Ludovisi, the former Archbishop of Bologna who had recently been elected Pope Gregory XV. To an ambitious young painter, the invitation to work in the Holy City must have seemed the opportunity of a lifetime, giving him the chance to prove himself not only alongside the work of the great painters of the High Renaissance but also that of his immediate predecessors of the Bolognese School, such as Annibale Carracci (1560–1609), Guido Reni (1575–1642), Domenichino (1581–1641) and others, who had also felt the lure of this great political and artistic centre. The challenge must have been awesome.

According to Malvasia, Guercino was called to Rome in order to paint the Loggia delle Benedizioni in St Peter's, an enormously costly project which was never executed owing to the untimely death of the Pope in 1623 (1678, II, p. 365; 1841, II, p. 260). Nevertheless Guercino received many other prestigious commissions from the papal entourage. Two of these were ceiling decorations for private palaces, the *Rinaldo and Armida* for Monsignor Costanzo Patrizi, treasurer to the Pope (No. 30), and the *Aurora* for Ludovico Ludovisi, the Pope's nephew (Nos. 32–5). Most important of all was the huge altarpiece *The Burial and Reception into Heaven of St Petronilla*, commissioned by the Pope himself and destined for St Peter's (Nos. 38–43).

The 'naturalistic' style of painting that Guercino brought with him from Cento, with its inventive brushwork and narrow range of saturated colours, may not have had as wide an appeal as he might have liked. There is good evidence to show that fashion in this sophisticated milieu no longer favoured the type of painting represented by Guercino's work, and it was probably criticised as being too dark and not sufficiently classical (this point of view is further considered under No. 41). The effect of this realisation on the whole of the painter's subsequent work was fundamental and marked the beginning of a gradual shift towards a more classical style of painting, with an attendant lightening of his palette and a transformation in his method of composing figures within a given composition. This process seems to have begun with the *St Petronilla* altarpiece and fully matured only in his work of the 1640s.

In spite of the considerable impact of Guercino's short visit to Rome on his work as a painter, its influence on his style as a draughtsman was less profound and did not cause nearly such a sudden switch in direction. His working drawings continued to develop according to the pattern established in the series of studies for the *St William*, as can be seen in his preparatory work for his major Roman commissions. At the same time his drawings for the *Aurora* and the *St Petronilla*, in particular, attained new heights in their vigorous handling, their suggestion of form and their sensuous feeling for light. And at no other time in his career was his use of red chalk as brilliant (see Nos. 33 and 35). This was a medium he had previously used only spasmodically, but whose full potential he more or less discovered in the short period of his visit. He was to come to rely on it greatly thereafter.

30 The sleeping Rinaldo abducted by Armida

Pen and brown ink. 178 × 258mm.

Cambridge, Fitzwilliam Museum, inv. no. 2737.

Provenance: Dr Barry Delany (L 350); Hugh Gatty, by whom presented to the Fitzwilliam in 1945.

Literature: Van Hasselt, 1959, no. 48; M, *Disegni*, 1969, no. 77; Bean, 1979, under no. 243; S, 1988, under no. 77.

A study for the ceiling fresco in the Palazzo Costaguti, Rome (S, 1988, no. 77), painted for Monsignor Costanzo Patrizi, treasurer to Pope Gregory XV (previously Cardinal Alessandro Ludovisi). The subject is taken from Tasso's *Gerusalemme liberata* (XIV, 68).

Malvasia mentions the fresco as follows (1678, II, p. 365; 1841, II, p. 260): 'Fece uno sfondato à Monsig. Patritio Tesoriero del Papa à fresco.' This reference follows those to the various commissions from the Ludovisi family (the *Aurora*, the *St Petronilla* altarpiece, and the portrait of *Gregory XV*, painted at different moments during the Pope's short reign, 1621–3); it also comes after the mention of the decoration of the ceiling for the church of S. Crisogono (now in Lancaster House, London), against which in the margin Malvasia placed the year 1622 (the accuracy of which is confirmed by the fact that the final payment for the ceiling was received on 2 October 1622). The order in which the works are given by Malvasia could imply that the Costaguti ceiling was painted after that for S. Crisogono (see M, *Dipinti*, 1968, p. 6, n. 12), but Mahon has given detailed reasons for believing that Malvasia's sequence of Guercino's Roman work ought not to be read chronologically (M, *Dipinti*, 1968, pp. 108–10). In his opinion, the survival of certain Ferrarese elements in the Costaguti painting suggest that it could have been painted soon after Guercino's arrival in Rome in May 1621, during the period before the villa on the Pincio, acquired by the Ludovisi in June, could be made ready for decoration. We have preferred to follow Mahon in placing it before the *Aurora*.

In No. 30, the composition is studied in reverse, in the same direction as the *Aurora* which it closely resembles, particularly in the foreshortened chariot and the backward glance of Armida. In the fresco, the poses of the two protag-

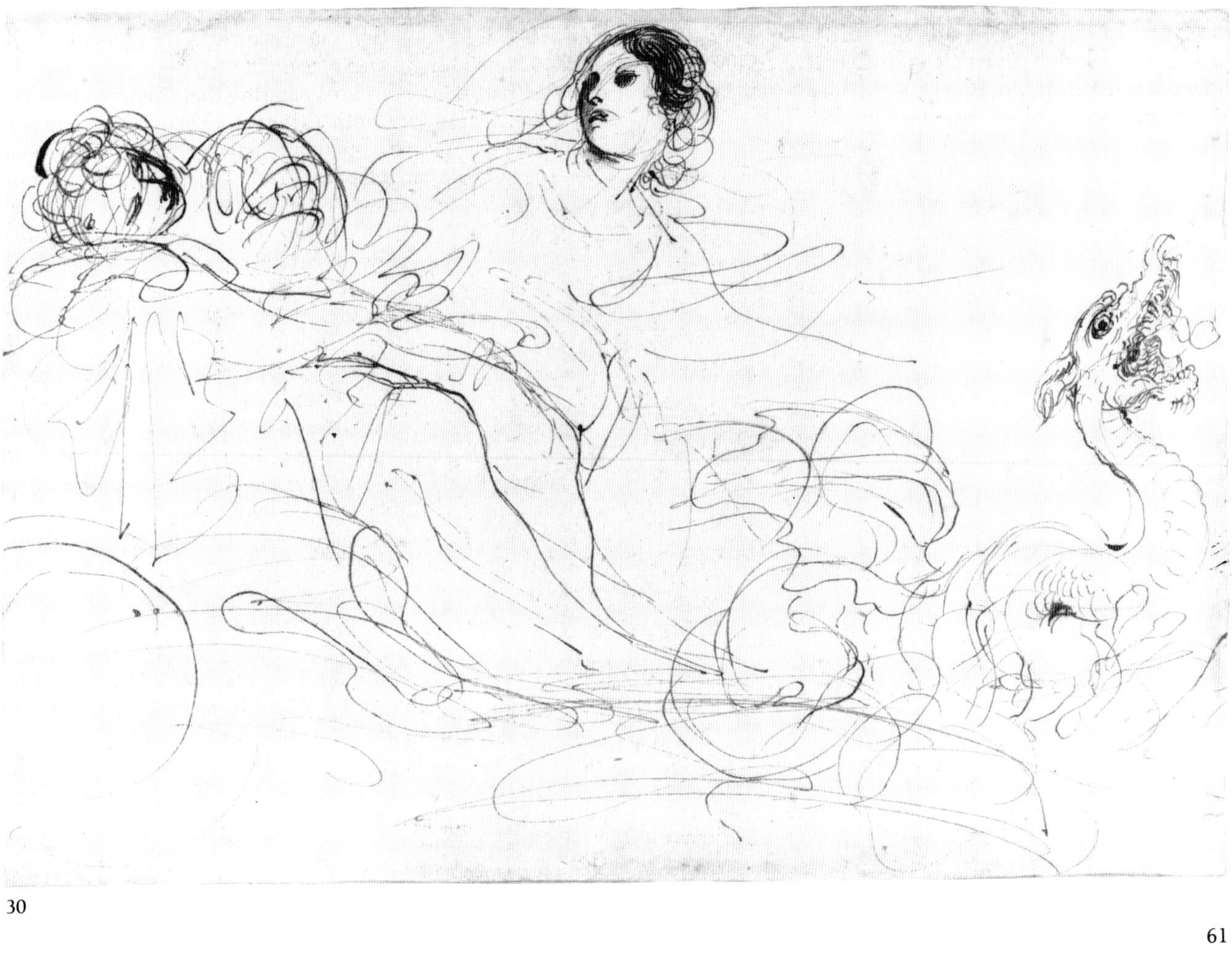

30

onists are somewhat altered, with Rinaldo reclining, his head resting on his left arm, and Armida flying above waving a dart instead of driving the chariot as in this study. Mahon (1969) pointed out that the unusual iconographic motif of a chariot drawn by dragons instead of horses was used by Guercino in an earlier commission, namely in his fresco decorations depicting scenes from the *Gerusalemme liberata* in the Casa Pannini in Cento of *c.* 1615 (detached frescoes now in the Pinacoteca Civica, Cento; B, 1984, pp. 154f., figs. 123–30).

A pen-and-wash drawing in the Metropolitan Museum of Art, New York (inv. no. 80.3.294; Bean, 1979, no. 243), has plausibly been connected with the *Rinaldo and Armida* fresco. However, as Bean pointed out, the male figure certainly does not appear to be asleep, as Rinaldo should be.

31 Holy Family with Sts John the Baptist and Anne

Pen and brown ink. 183 × 242mm.

Windsor Castle, Royal Library, inv. no. 2754.

Provenance: Casa Gennari; King George III.

Literature: B, 1988, no. 39; M & T, 1989, no. 15.

A study in reverse for the engraving by G. B. Pasqualini, inscribed and dated *in Roma 1621* (Bertelà, 1973, no. 794; B, 1988, no. 38). Until recently, Guercino's preparatory studies for prints were little known or understood (for other examples in this exhibition, see Nos. 20–21, 57, 94–5 and 105) and were often dismissed as copies or School works. It is important to grasp the function of such drawings, for at the end of the preparatory process the artist carried them to an unusually high degree of finish in order to provide the engraver with as exact a guide for his print as possible. It is probably true to say that he did not find it as sympathetic to work on so small a scale. These drawings certainly lack Guercino's characteristic fluency, which may well have led to their neglect in the past. Nonetheless, in spite of their usually careful finish, they contain passages of extraordinary refinement: for example, in the present drawing the transparent veil that the Madonna delicately draws over the naked body of the sleeping Christ Child casts a scarcely perceptible shadow over his right leg, a subtle detail that was completely lost on the pedestrian Pasqualini.

The several pin holes that appear regularly at intervals in the wide margins of the drawing were made in order to keep the drawing in place while the design was being transferred to the copper-plate. The sheet has recently been lifted: the blackening on the back of the sheet is not powdered black chalk, as Mahon and Turner supposed, but an oxidised preparation of white whose purpose likewise would have been to facilitate the transfer of the design. Curiously, there is no evidence on the *recto* of stylus work, which was the usual means by which outlines were indented from a drawing onto another surface, usually the copper-plate.

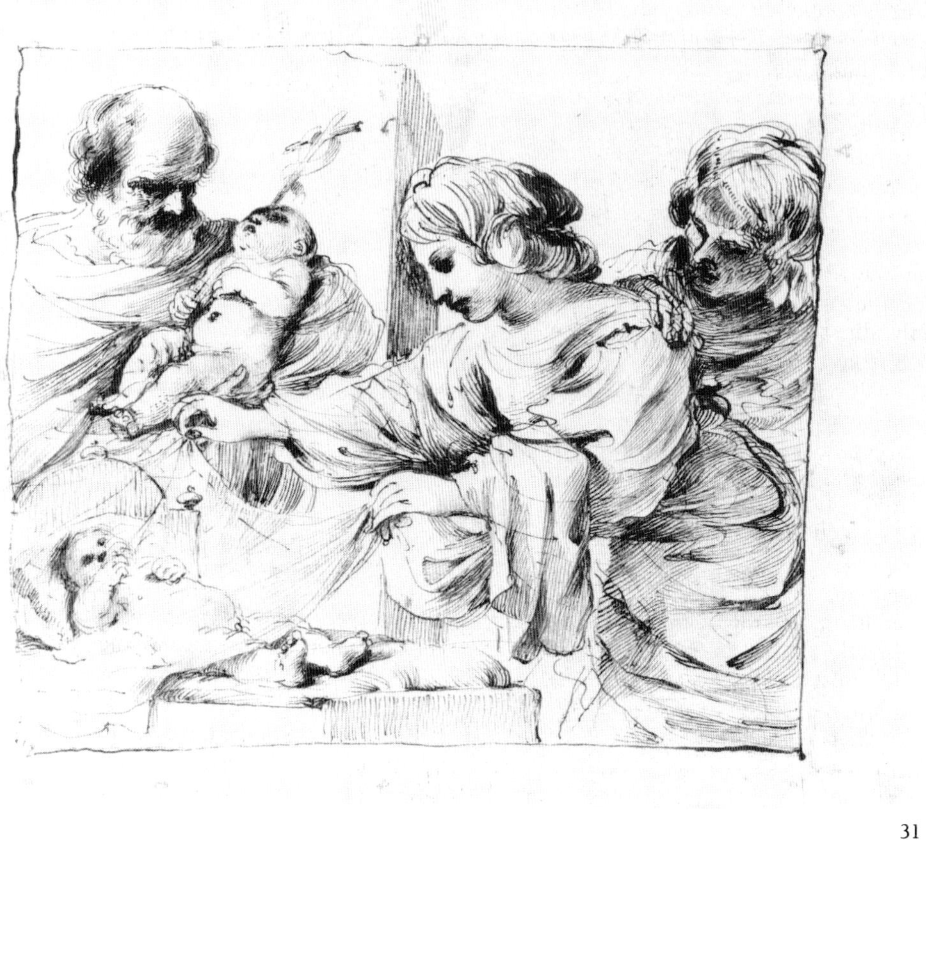

31

32–35 Studies for *Aurora* (1621)

Rome, Casino Ludovisi (fresco in room on ground floor)

32 Seated Figure of Aurora

Red chalk. 255 × 205mm.

Windsor Castle, Royal Library, inv. no. 2814.

Provenance: Casa Gennari; King George III.

Literature: M, *Disegni*, 1969, no. 80; M & T, 1989, no. 16.

A study from the life for the figure of Aurora in the ceiling fresco of that subject painted by Guercino for Pope Gregory XV and his nephew Cardinal Ludovico Ludovisi in the main *sala* of the villa known as the Casino Ludovisi (S, 1988, no. 83). The villa was acquired by the Cardinal in June of 1621 and Guercino's fresco was executed in the second half of that same year. Nos. 33–5 are for this same fresco (for a further discussion of drawings connected with the project, see M, *Disegni*, 1969, under nos. 78–85, and M & T, 1989, under nos. 16–19).

Although the figure is facing the same direction as that of Aurora in the fresco, the pose is not nearly as fully developed as it is in No. 33, where Aurora, despite being turned to the left, is already shown seated in her chariot, wearing a garland of flowers on her head, and raising her right arm to scatter flowers. No. 32 shows Guercino at the very early stage of working out a pose for Aurora. Although he drew the figure seated on the ground, as his model would have been posed in the studio, with no indication of the chariot, the notion of speed is already implied in the way the figure is thrown back upon herself, not merely holding, but tugging with her left hand at the summarily sketched reins. In the finished work Aurora is a far more static, even statuesque figure, and the idea of movement is conveyed less through her actions than by the presence of billowing drapery and the prancing horses, an effect surely influenced by Guido Reni's *Aurora* of 1614 (for which see Pepper, 1984, no. 40 and pls. 67–8). Reni had painted a fresco of this subject for Cardinal Scipione Borghese, for the *casino* in the grounds of his palace on the Quirinal Hill. The Ludovisi commission was certainly directly competitive with the earlier decorative project, from the point of view of both the patron and the artist, and it was plainly a strong reaction against the earlier fresco. Guercino's scheme departs from Reni's, for example, in showing Aurora as the principal figure, being drawn in a chariot; in Reni's more formal, classical rendering, it is Apollo himself who is at the helm of the chariot, surrounded by an *entourage* of handmaidens, while Aurora merely flies ahead of them.

In all Guercino's subsequent preparatory drawings for the figure of Aurora, she is shown looking outwards, either up, as in the fresco, or directly at the spectator. Perhaps prompted by his desire to enlist the participation of the spectator, Guercino apparently decided to abandon this early, more dynamic formulation showing Aurora absorbed in checking the pace of her horses.

All the known chalk studies for this commission are executed in red chalk. Another example for the figure of Aurora, also from the life and therefore without the chariot, is in the Royal Library, Windsor Castle (M & T, 1989, no. 17); here the figure's pose is strongly reminiscent of that of Erminia in another drawing at Windsor (No. 22). Finally, yet another red chalk drawing, this time for the head of Aurora, much as it is depicted in the fresco, is in the Mahon Collection, on loan to the Ashmolean Museum, Oxford (M & E, 1986, no. 12).

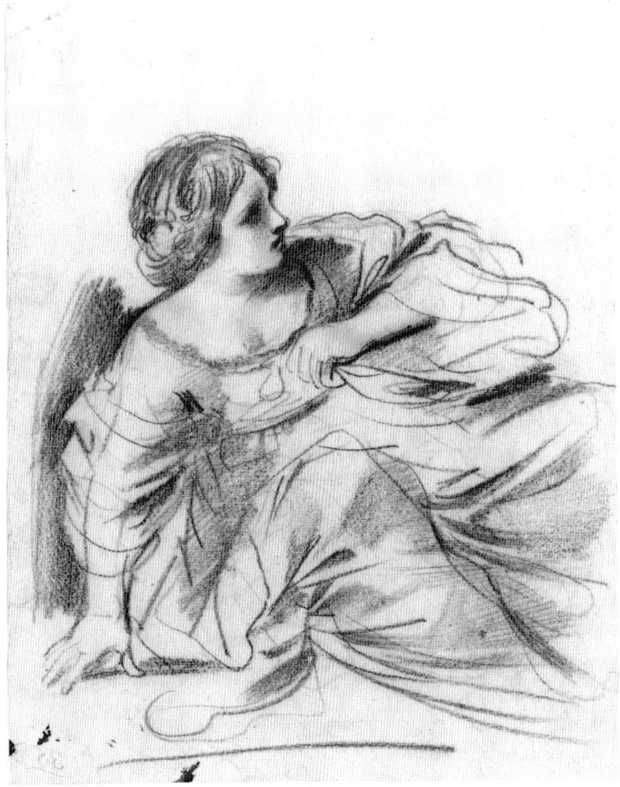

32

33 Aurora

(see colour pl. 5)

Red chalk with some stumping. 248 × 271mm.

London, Courtauld Institute Galleries, Witt Collection, inv. no. 1328.

Provenance: Casa Gennari; Mr Bouverie; Mr Hervey; the Earls of Gainsborough (sale, Christie's, London, 27 July 1922, lot 81, with others, bt *Meatyard*); Sir Robert Witt.

Literature: M, *Disegni*, no. 78; Hammer, *et al.*, 1977, no. 28.

A study in reverse for the figure of Aurora in the ceiling fresco of that subject in the Casino Ludovisi, for which see No. 32. The drawing differs from the finished work in showing the figure with wings and wearing a garland of flowers on her head (whereas in the fresco a putto is about to crown her with one). These discarded attributes are among those recommended by Cesare Ripa in his *Iconologia*, the popular iconographic manual of the day, though Guercino followed Ripa in other respects, most notably in his colour scheme and in showing Aurora scattering flowers. The drawing differs further from the painting in that the figure gazes out at the spectator instead of up in the direction of the putto who, in the fresco, is in the act of covering Tithonus (the aged and abandoned lover of Aurora) with a drapery. A copy in the Uffizi, Florence (inv. no. 3671-S; Bottari, 1966, pl. XXVIII), after a lost drawing by Guercino shows Aurora in a very similar pose to that of the figure in No. 33, but with her legs bare and her chariot drawn by Pegasus, the winged steed; both these ideas conform to Ripa's recommendations for the figure of Aurora but were later abandoned. It seems that at the time of making these two drawings, Guercino was working with the text firmly in mind, possibly at the suggestion of his patron, whereas in the finished version his approach was far less literal.

No. 33 and the drawing recorded in the Uffizi copy must indeed have been made fairly early on in the evolution of the composition, since in both Aurora's chariot is being drawn to the left instead of to the right as in the fresco, such reversals in the design being entirely typical of Guercino's creative procedure. The bold *di sotto in su* foreshortening evident in the chariot and the legs of the figure in No. 33 shows that Guercino was taking into account, even at this early stage, the spectator's position when viewing the finished work.

Drawings showing Aurora's chariot moving towards the right are in the Mahon Collection, on loan to the Ashmolean Museum, Oxford (M & E, 1986, no. 11), and in the Ashby Collection, Vatican Library, Rome (Bodart, 1975, no. 147, repr., the *verso* of which also shows Pegasus, this time bearing a mysterious rider; repr. in M & T, 1989, pp. 9–10, figs. 3 and 4). A red chalk study for the figure of Tithonus is in the Metropolitan Museum of Art, New York (inv. no. 1970.168; Bean, 1979, no. 237).

34 Two Amorini among Tree-tops

Pen and brown ink, with traces of brown wash. 144 × 200mm.

Windsor Castle, Royal Library, inv. no. 2608.

Provenance: Casa Gennari; King George III.

Literature: M, *Disegni*, 1969, no. 82; M & T, 1989, no. 18.

A study for two of the *amorini* among the cypress trees in the ceiling fresco of *Aurora* in the Casino Ludovisi, for which see No. 32. Neither of these *amorini* was included in the finished work, though the one holding a bow and drawing an arrow from his quiver appears at the top of a red chalk study of five *amorini* for this same group in the Mahon Collection, on loan to the Ashmolean Museum, Oxford (M & E, 1986, no. 13). The other four figures in this drawing are roughly as they appear in the finished work, so Guercino must, for some reason, have decided at a late stage to exclude the *amorino* with the quiver. The motif was not forgotten,

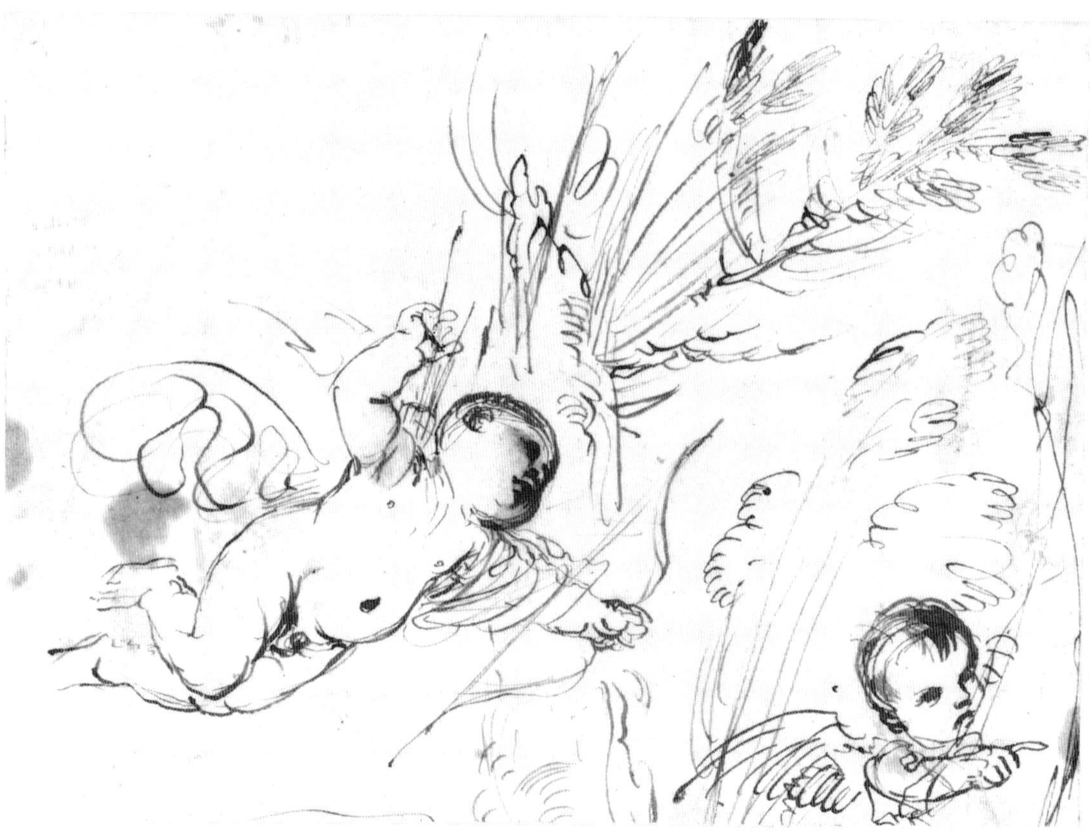

34

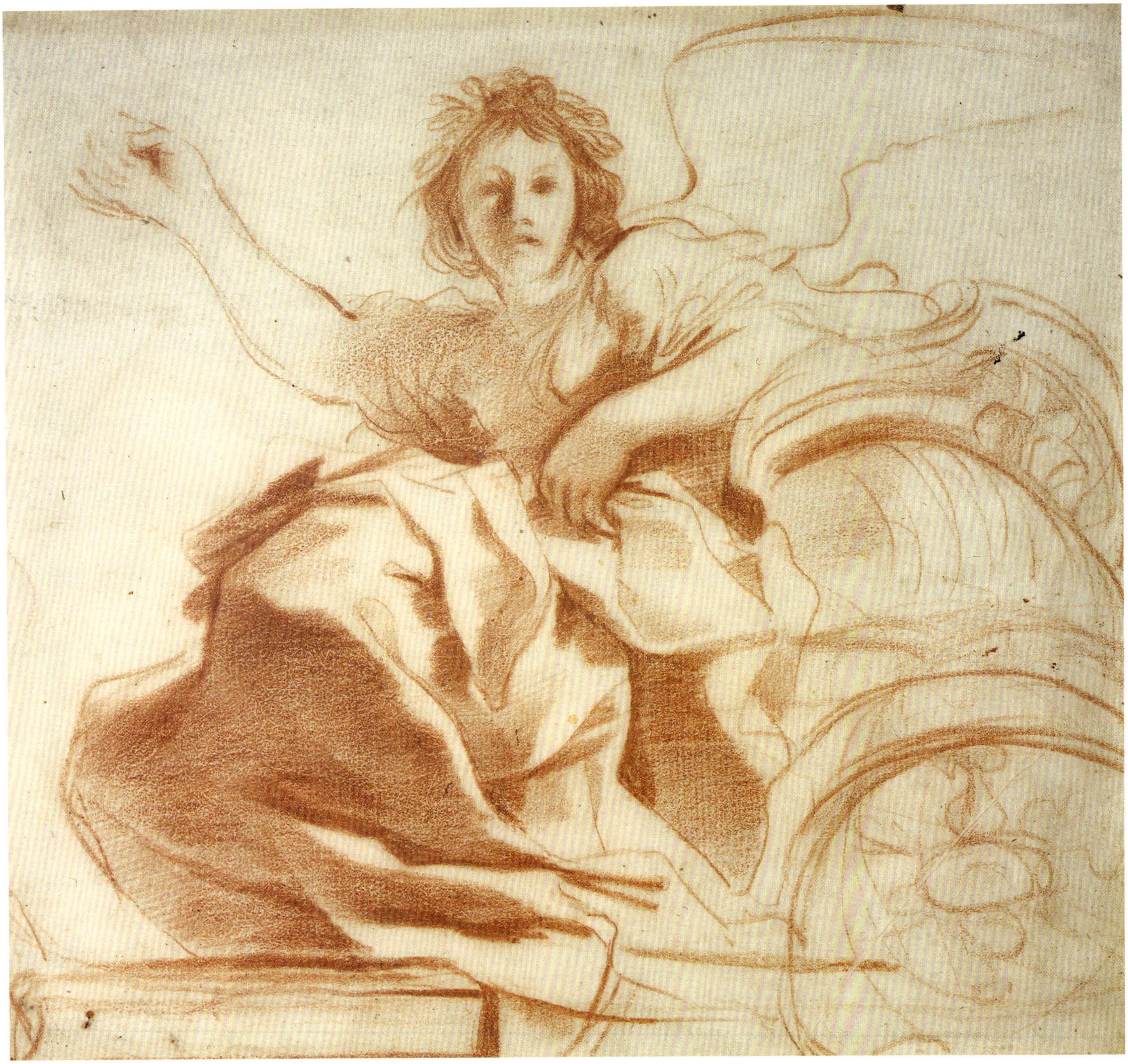

33 *Aurora*. London, Courtauld Institute Galleries

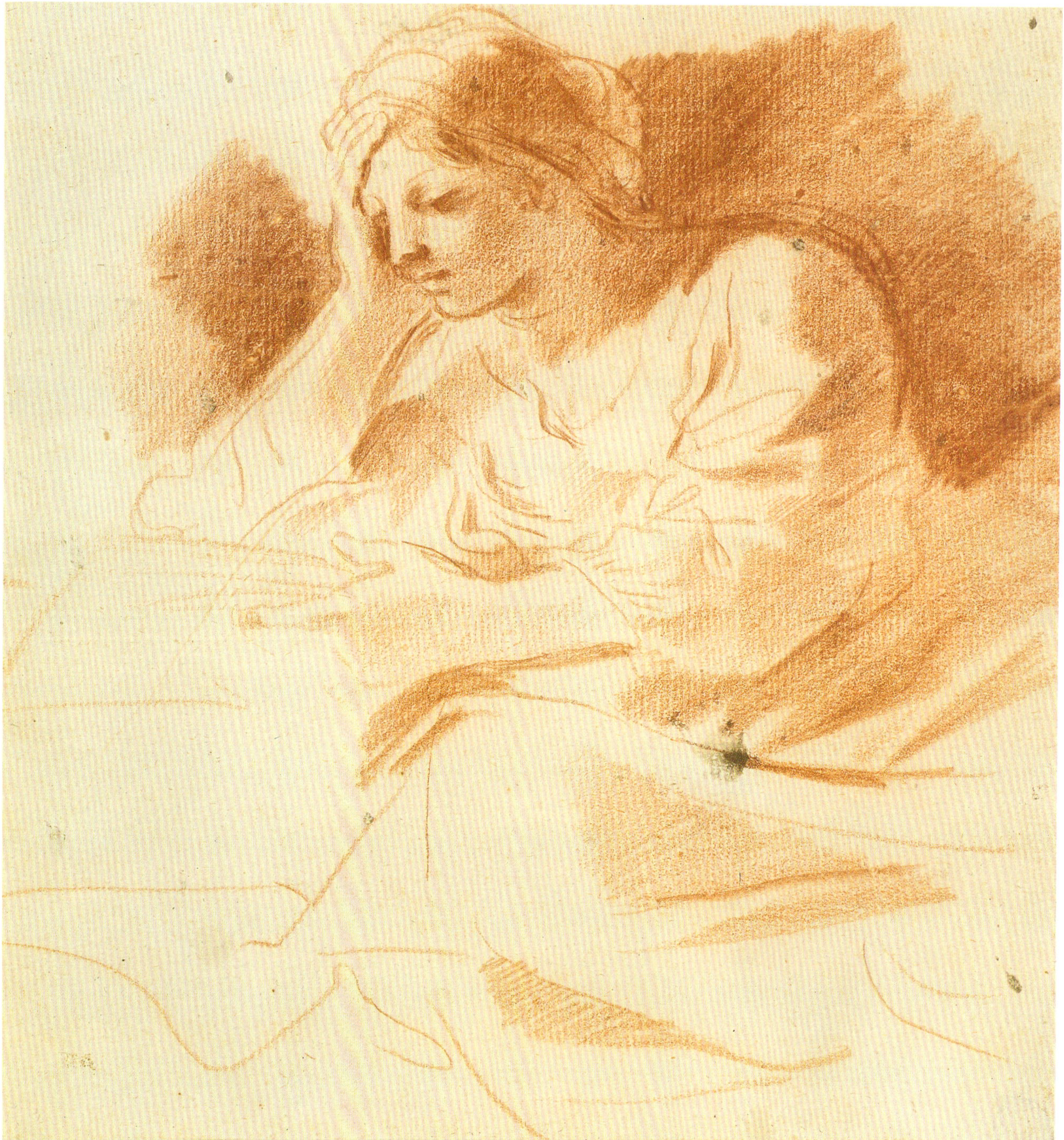

35 *Seated Woman reading a Book*. Windsor Castle, Royal Library

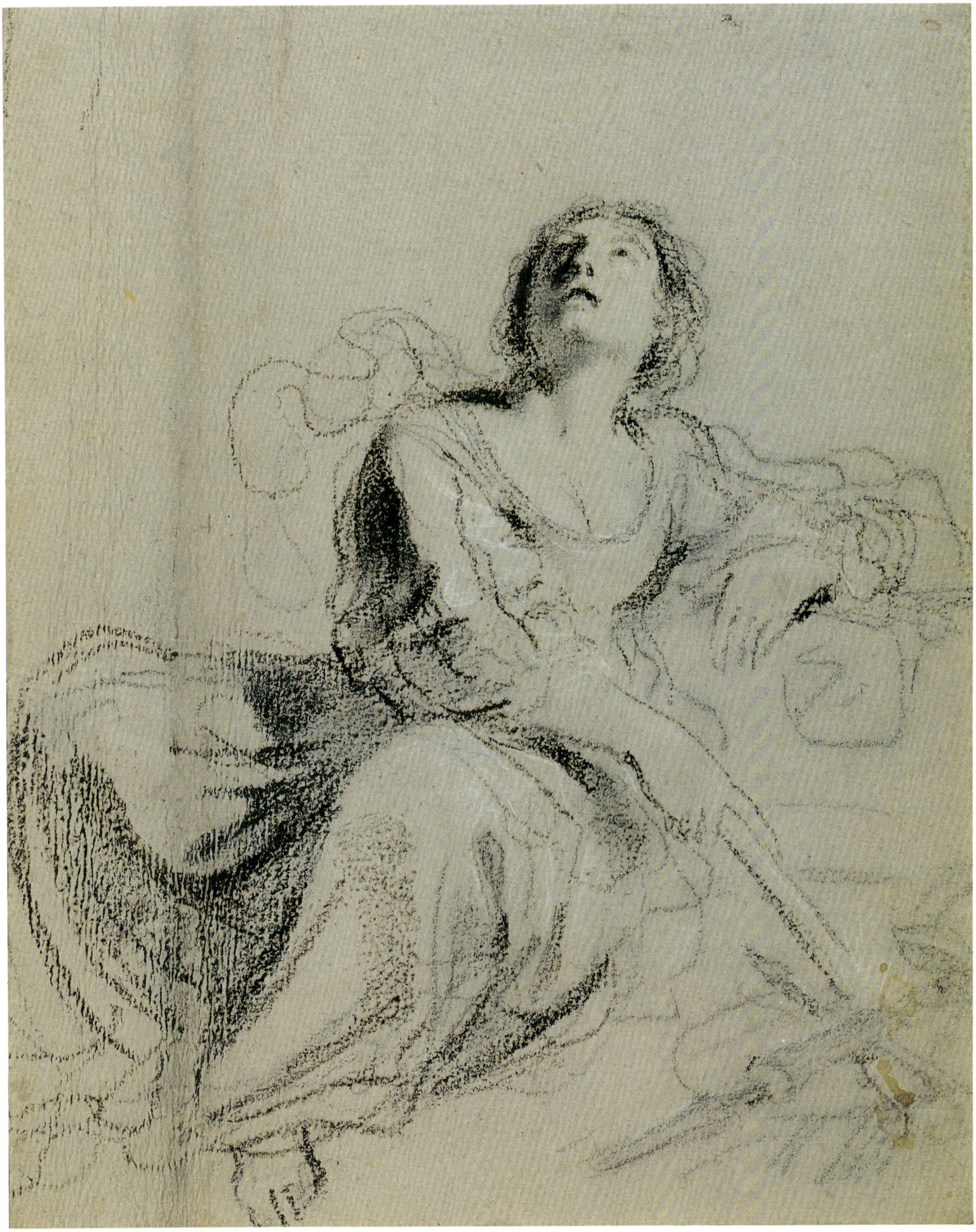

37 *Peace*. Windsor Castle, Royal Library

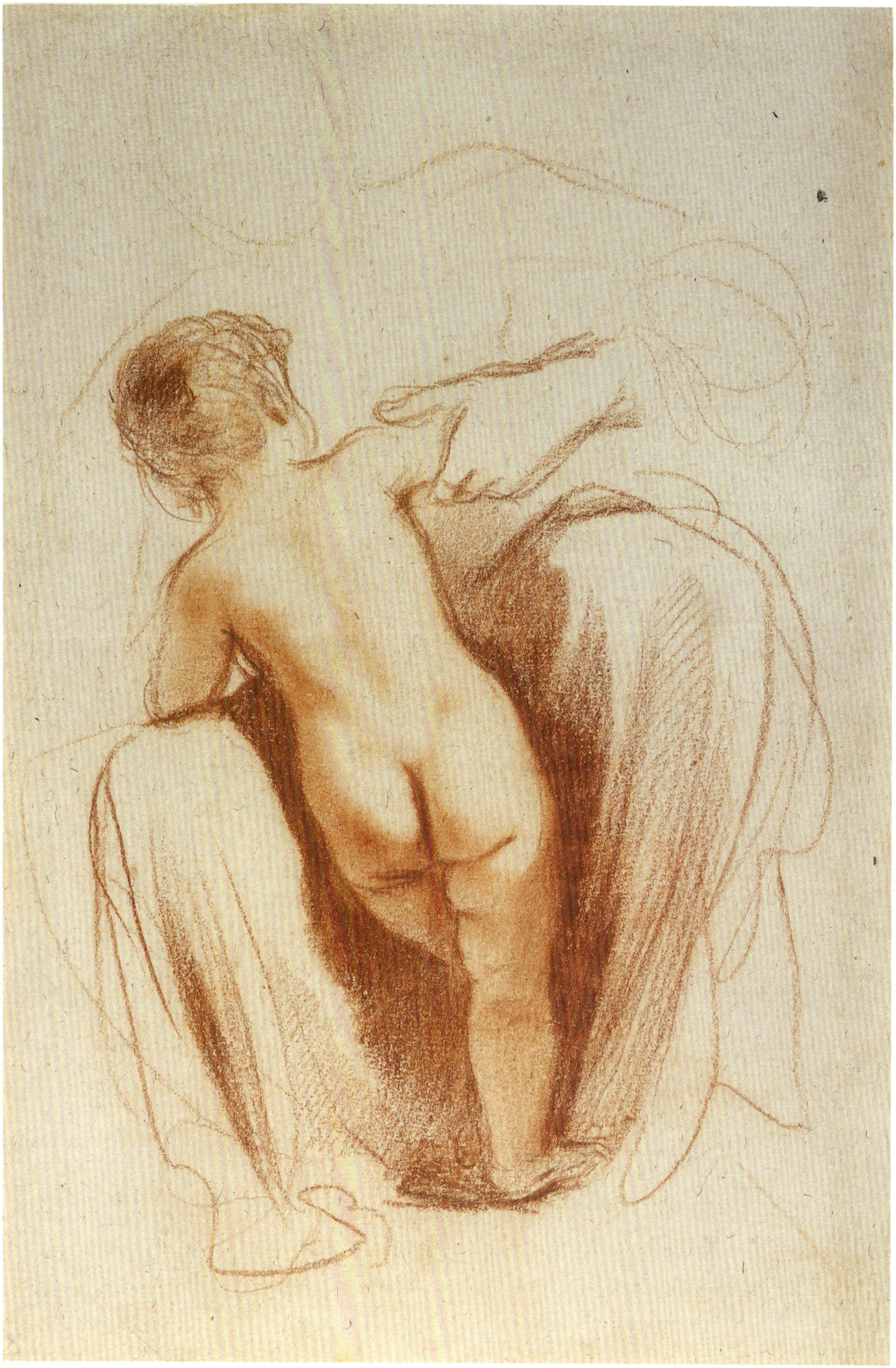

44 *Child standing between its Mother's Knees.* London, Courtauld Institute Galleries

however; as Mahon and Turner have noted (M & T, 1989, under nos. 16–19), Guercino used it again, with slight variations, in a chimney-breast painting of *Venus and Cupid*, painted in 1632 for Count Filippo Aldrovandi, in the Villa Giovannina, Cento (S, 1989, no. 144).

35 Seated Woman reading a Book

(*see colour pl. 6*)

Red chalk. 244 × 232mm.

Windsor Castle, Royal Library, inv. no. 2744.

Provenance: Casa Gennari; King George III.

Literature: M, 1951, p. 57, no. v, repr.; M, *Disegni*, 1969, no. 84; M & T, 1989, no. 19.

A study, probably from the life, for the figure of *Night* in one of the painted lunettes at either end of the main *sala* of the Casino Ludovisi, beneath the frescoed ceiling depicting *Aurora*, for which see No. 32. In the drawing the figure is reading a book, shrouded in darkness, whereas in another drawing in the Albertina, Vienna (inv. no. 2298; M, *Disegni*, 1969, no. 85), and in the finished fresco she is shown asleep over her book, her head still propped up on her hand. As Mahon has pointed out (1969, p. 92), Guercino, in order to establish his own particularly apt personification of Night, seems to have departed from Cesare Ripa's conventional iconography (as he had done in his depiction of Aurora). By contrast, the figure of *Day* at the other end of the *sala* does conform to Ripa's recommendations.

In the fresco the figure of Night is illuminated by the approaching dawn (in the person of Aurora), whose light shines through the hole in the crumbling architecture above her to the left. The emphatic chiaroscuro, occasioned by this strong daylight penetrating the darker recesses of Night's archway or cave, is anticipated in the present drawing in the heavy diagonal shading with the chalk. Instead of merely acting as a foil in the background, this shading boldly cuts across contours, penetrating the form of the figure to create a sense of enveloping atmosphere.

The figure of Night, like that of Aurora, embodies the physical type characteristic of Guercino's female subjects of this period: they are robust, with broad faces, heavy chins, and sturdy limbs, quite different from the more refined but, by the same token, less expressive types of his later years.

36 Madonna and Child with St Anne

London, British Museum, inv. no. Pp. 4–62.

(For other details see App. no. 5.)

The purpose of the drawing is not known, but the artist evidently took great pains not only over its meticulous execution but also, presumably, in arriving at the sympathetic juxtaposition of the figures as a single coherent group. It could well have been made as a drawing in its own right, but it is equally possible that it was made for a print, though none is known. The long parallel hatchings in different directions and (to a lesser extent) the areas of shade made up of dots are reminiscent of the drawings made by Guercino in the early and mid-1620s and subsequently engraved by G. B. Pasqualini; two such examples are in the Royal Library, Windsor Castle: the *Holy Family with Sts John the Baptist and Anne* (No. 31), engraved in 1621, and *Three Soldiers casting Lots over Christ's Garments* (M & T, 1989, no. 34), engraved in 1625. No. 36 can also be compared stylistically with No. 184, which, however, is of a genre subject.

The drawing was first described in the Casa Gennari inventory of 1719 (see App. no. 5).

37 Peace

(*see colour pl. 7*)

Charcoal, partly oiled, and some black chalk, with touches of white chalk, on greenish-grey paper. 395 × 321mm.

Windsor Castle, Royal Library, inv. no. 2876.

Provenance: Casa Gennari; King George III.

Literature: M, 1951, p. 57, no. iv; Bottari, 1966, pl. IV; M, *Disegni*, 1969, no. 180; Roberts, 1986, no. 92; M & T, 1989, no. 147.

The figure, who holds a lighted torch to a pile of arms, corresponds with Cesare Ripa's description of the allegorical figure of Peace in his iconographic manual, *Iconologia*. The drawing would appear to be related in some way to another, in pen and wash, in the Biblioteca Reale, Turin, representing *Peace and Time* (inv. no. 16115; M, *Disegni*, 1969, no. 179; Sciolla, 1990, no. 101); there Peace's upturned head is explained by the presence of Father Time approaching her from the rear, his arms outstretched. Guercino seems to have been planning a painting along these lines, but no corresponding work is known.

There are many parallels between No. 37 and Guercino's preparatory studies for the Ludovisi *Aurora* (see Nos. 32–5). Besides the stylistic conformity, the female type is extremely similar, and one is tempted to suggest that Guercino was using the same model, with her scooped neckline and plump features, as he had for No. 32. The figure's head mirrors closely that in a study for the raised head of Aurora in the Mahon Collection (on loan to the Ashmolean Museum, Oxford; M & E, 1986, no. 12). Furthermore, No. 37 is reminiscent of the figure of Virtue in another fresco in the Casino Ludovisi, *Fame with Honour and Virtue* (S, 1988, no. 83, fig. 4), but in reverse. In the light of these analogies, it seems appropriate to date the drawing *c.* 1621, though it must be said that the related Turin drawing appears to be somewhat earlier, *c.* 1618–20, before Guercino's visit to Rome.

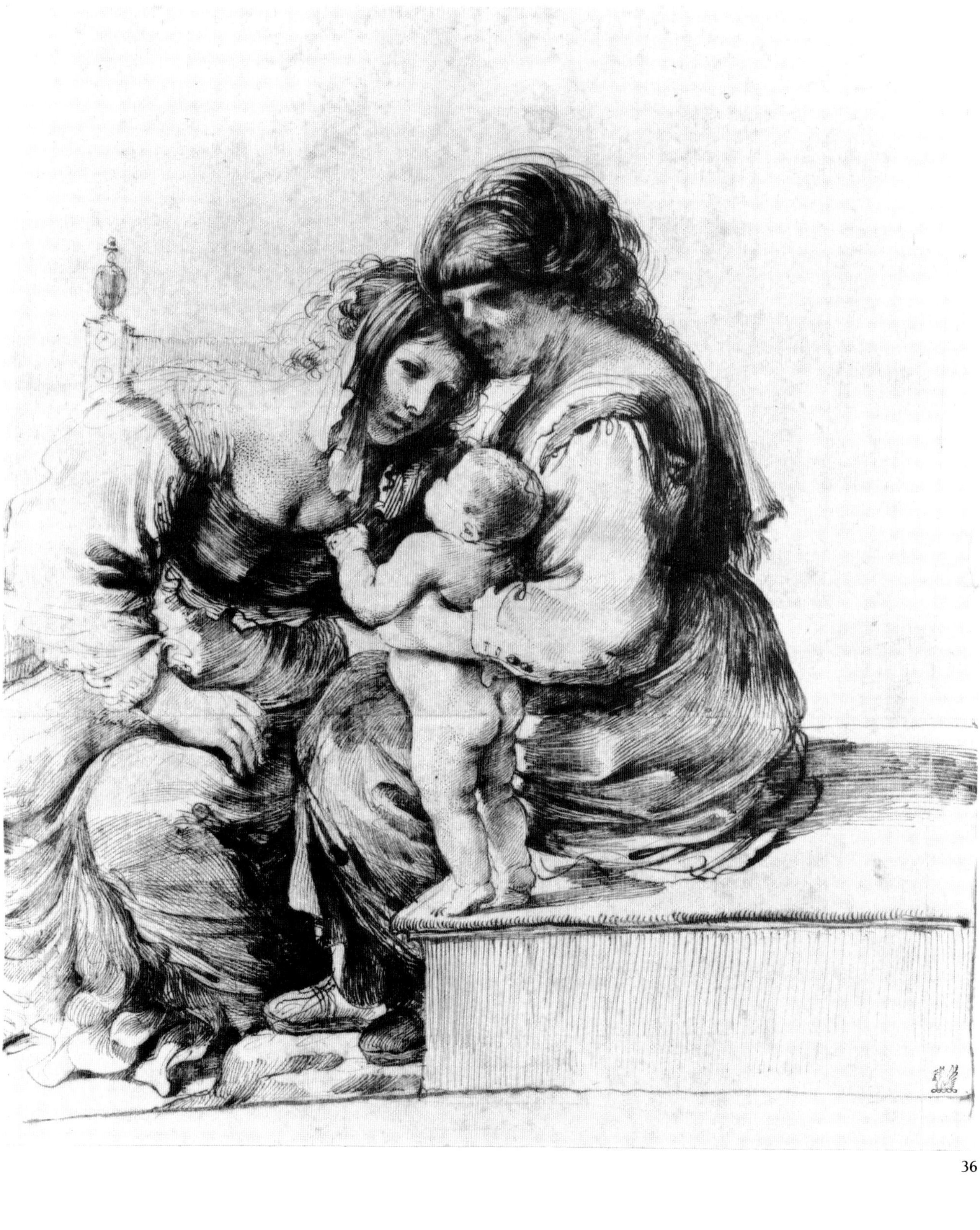

36

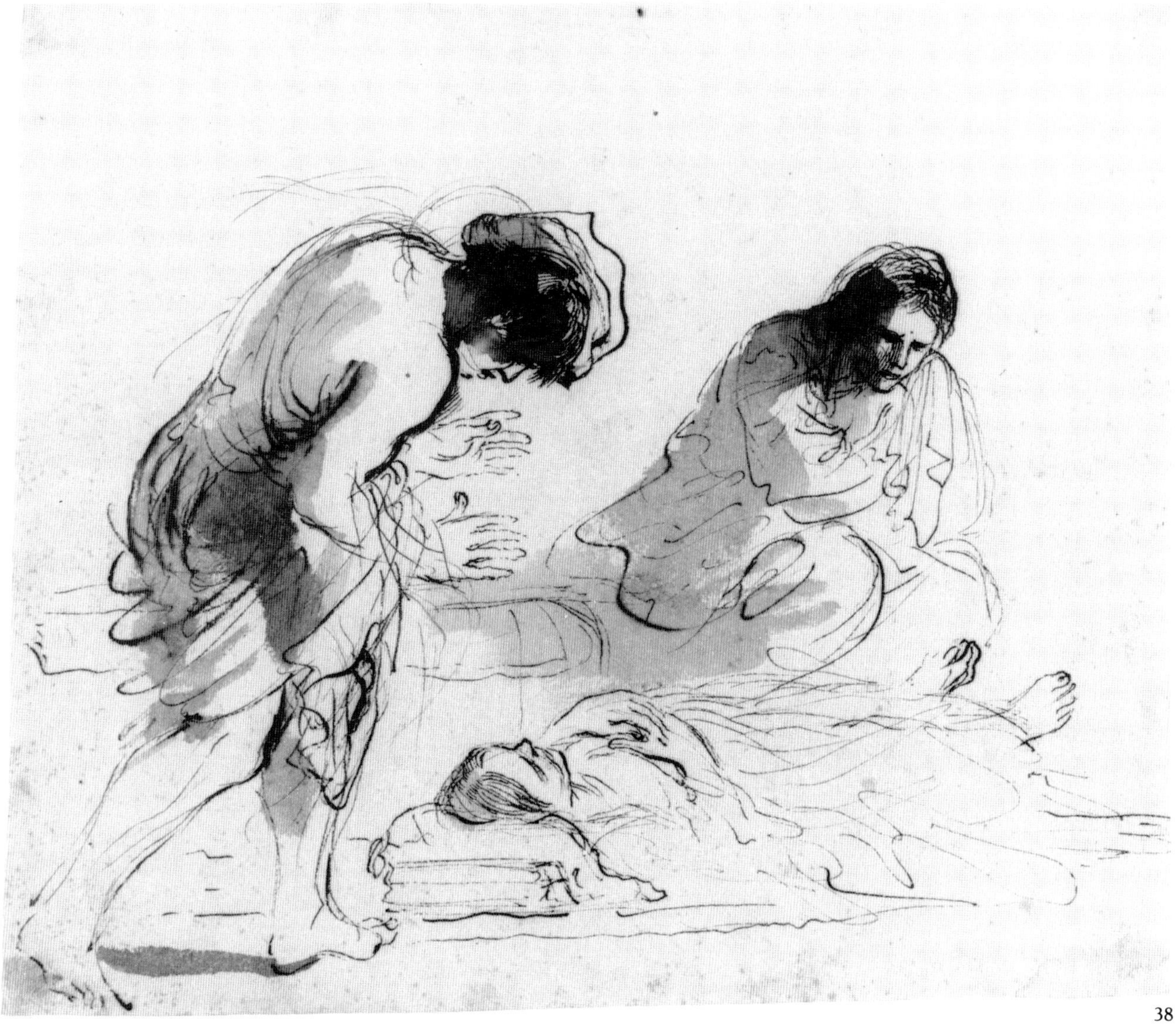

38

38–43 Studies for the *Burial and Reception into Heaven of St Petronilla* (1621–3)

Rome, Pinacoteca Capitolina

38 The Mourning of St Petronilla

Pen and brown ink and brown wash with a touch of bodycolour. 215 × 257mm.

London, Courtauld Institute Galleries, Witt Collection, inv. no. 1345.

Provenance: Casa Gennari (the drawing retains its fine Casa Gennari mount, for which see L *Suppl*, 2858c, and M, 1967, p. 20); Mr Bouverie; Mr Hervey; the Earls of Gainsborough (sale, Christie's, London, 27 July 1922, lot 81, with others, bt *Meatyard*); Sir Robert Witt.

Literature: M, *Disegni*, 1969, no. 87; Hammer, *et al.*, 1977, no. 20; M & T, 1989, under nos. 21–5.

Inscribed in brown ink on the *verso*: *L. 1. F. 200. di sopra.* Similar annotations (see M & T, 1989, under no. 200; see also no. 297) refer to the placing of the sheets in the series of large volumes of drawings formerly preserved in the Casa Gennari. These volumes were recorded in the inventory of works of art in the family's possession after the death in 1715 of Guercino's nephew and heir, Benedetto Gennari (see M & T, 1989, pp. xviii–xx). The inscription on the present sheet probably indicates that it was the upper item on folio 200 of book 1. (For similar inscriptions see Nos. 10, 46, App. no. 89, and others.)

The drawing is an early preparatory study for the large altarpiece, *The Burial and Reception into Heaven of St Petronilla* of 1621–3, commissioned by Pope Gregory XV for St Peter's and now in the Pinacoteca Capitolina, Rome (S, 1988, no. 92). This prestigious commission followed on directly from Guercino's ceiling decoration depicting

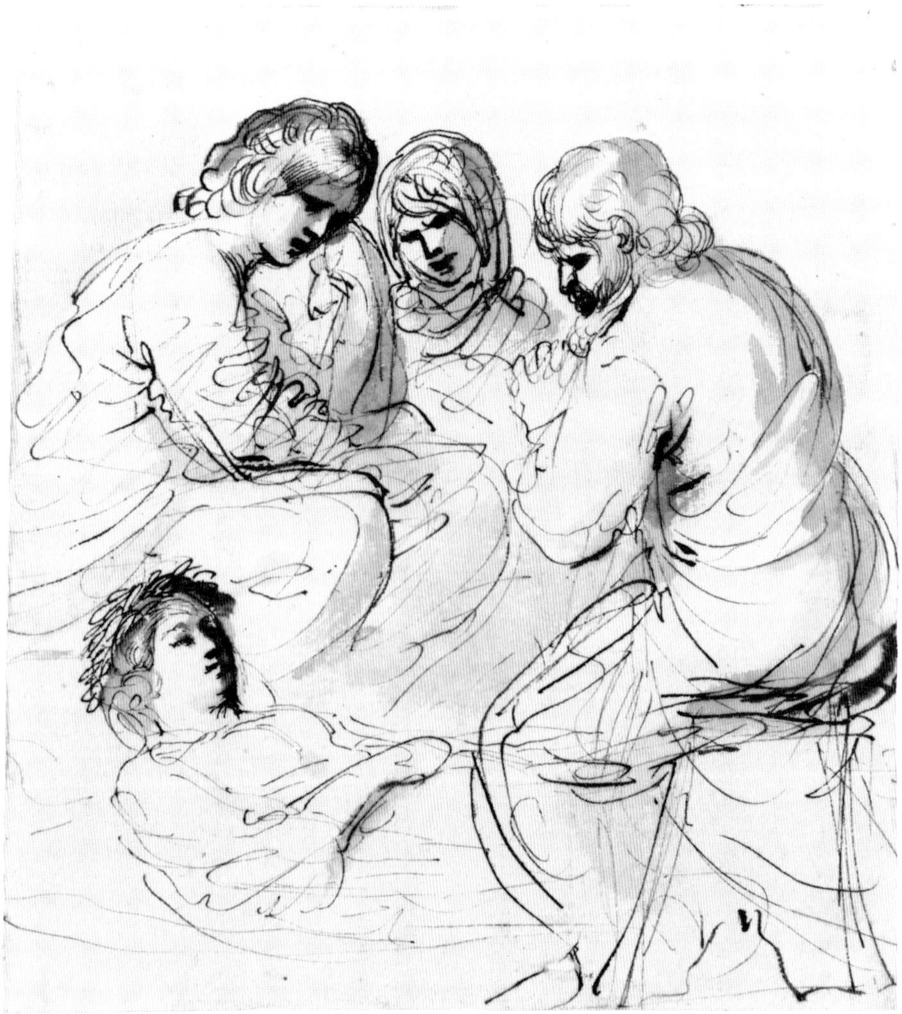

39

Aurora in the Casino Ludovisi, the villa purchased on behalf of the Pope by his nephew, Cardinal Ludovico Ludovisi (for drawings related to this project, see Nos. 32–5). That Guercino was engaged to work in such a key location and on such a grand scale at this early point in his career is an indication of the esteem in which he was already held by his cultivated patrons.

No. 38 occupies an important place in the genesis of Guercino's composition (see M & T, 1989, under nos. 21–5). In it the artist relied on designs for a previous commission, the *Raising of Tabitha* of 1618, now in the Palazzo Pitti, Florence (S, 1988, no. 45), which was made for the same patron, Alessandro Ludovisi, while he was still Cardinal Archbishop of Bologna (he was elected Pope Gregory XV in 1621). In representing the body of St Petronilla lying on the ground being mourned rather than at the subsequent moment of burial, No. 38 differs radically from later preparatory drawings and indeed from the painted composition. The swiftly executed study contains a number of pentiments, most notably those for the left leg and head of the man on the left and the right arm of the mourning woman, who previously held the handkerchief to her face with her right hand instead of her left.

39 The Mourning of St Petronilla

Pen and brown ink and brown wash. 208 × 192mm.

Windsor Castle, Royal Library, inv. no. 2550.

Provenance: Casa Gennari; King George III.

Literature: M & T, 1989, no. 21.

Like No. 38, this belongs to the early phase of the composition, in which the dead saint is still shown lying on the ground being lamented. To avoid taking up too much of the composition, the corpse has been slightly foreshortened and the legs concealed by the mourner seated in the right foreground. The mourner on the left repeats with variations that on the right of No. 38.

In the present drawing St Petronilla wears a wreath, anticipating the wreath of flowers worn by her counterpart in the painting.

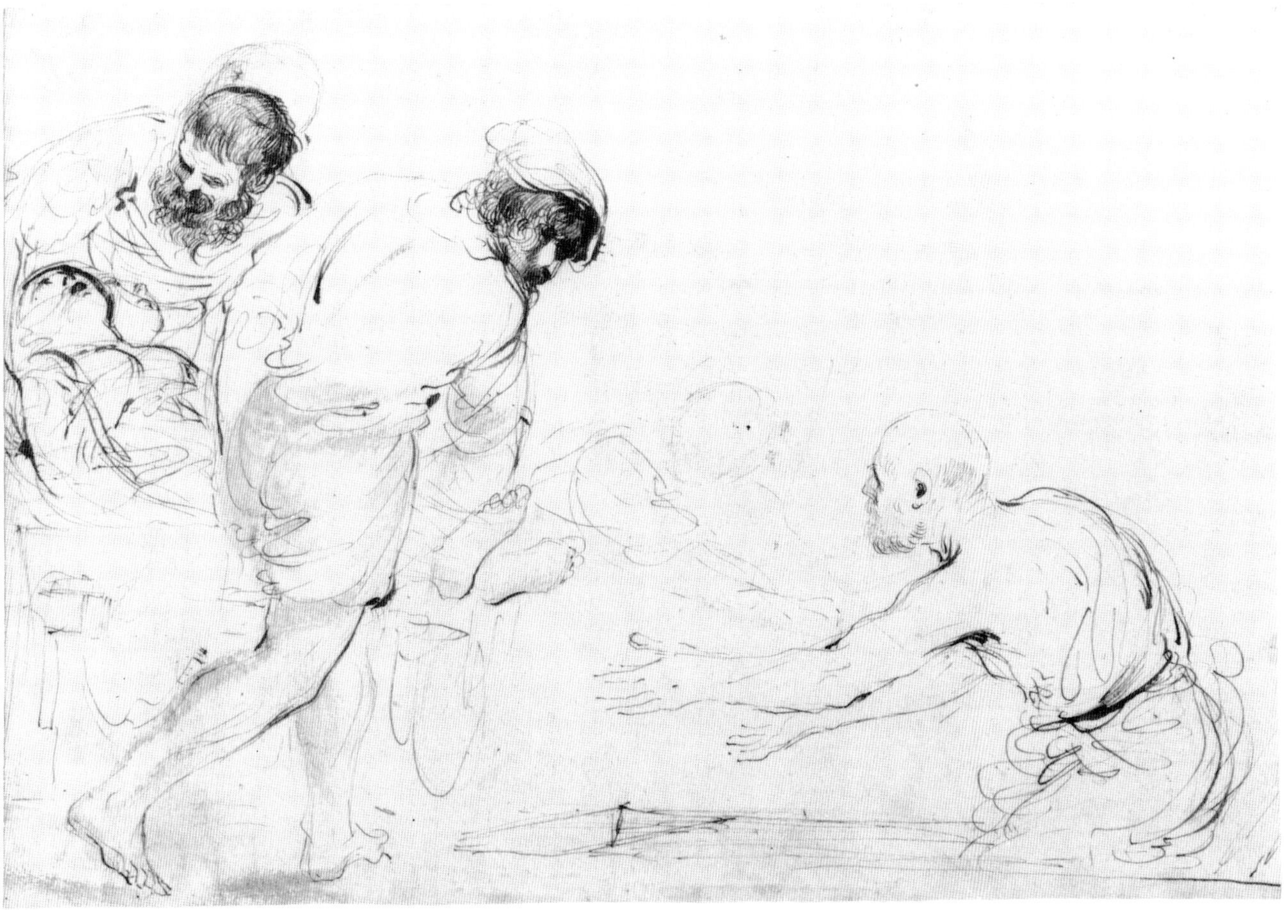

40

40 The Body of St Petronilla raised from the Bier

Pen and brown ink and some grey wash. 211 × 309mm.

Windsor Castle, Royal Library, inv. no. 2574.

Provenance: Casa Gennari; King George III.

Literature: M, *Disegni*, 1969, under nos. 87–91; M & T, 1989, no. 22.

By this stage Guercino had rejected the idea of representing the body of the saint lying on the ground being mourned, deciding to show the actual moment of burial, an interpretation of the subject that gives a greater dynamism to the composition. The present drawing belongs to this subsequent phase and shows the saint being raised from the bier and carried towards an opening in the ground, where a man, presumably standing on some steps, stretches out his arms to receive the body. The corpse has again been slightly foreshortened to prevent it from taking up too much space. There are pentiments for the head of the saint and for the head and left arm of the bearer at the left of the drawing.

41 Composition Study for The Burial and Reception into Heaven of St Petronilla

Black chalk, with some stumping; touches of red chalk in the area of St Petronilla's sleeve. 516 × 378mm; creases at the centre of the sheet indicate that the drawing was probably once folded horizontally across the middle.

Windsor Castle, Royal Library, inv. no. 2756.

Provenance: Casa Gennari; King George III.

Literature: M, *Studies*, 1947, pp. 86 and 91; M, *Dipinti*, 1968, p. 116; M, *Disegni*, 1969, no. 91; Steinberg, 1980, pp. 212, 222f., and 227; M & T, 1989, no. 23.

No. 41 is exceptional among Guercino's surviving drawings in being the only example of a large-scale, finished *modello* for a painting. Almost certainly prepared for presentation, it must itself have been preceded by numerous preparatory studies. Yet in spite of its completeness, the composition was not put into effect and differs markedly – especially in the lower part – from that of the altarpiece. This inevitably raises the question of why such a finished design should have been further modified. It is possible that the authorities who commissioned the picture disliked certain aspects of the composition. On the other hand, the decision to make further changes might well have been taken by

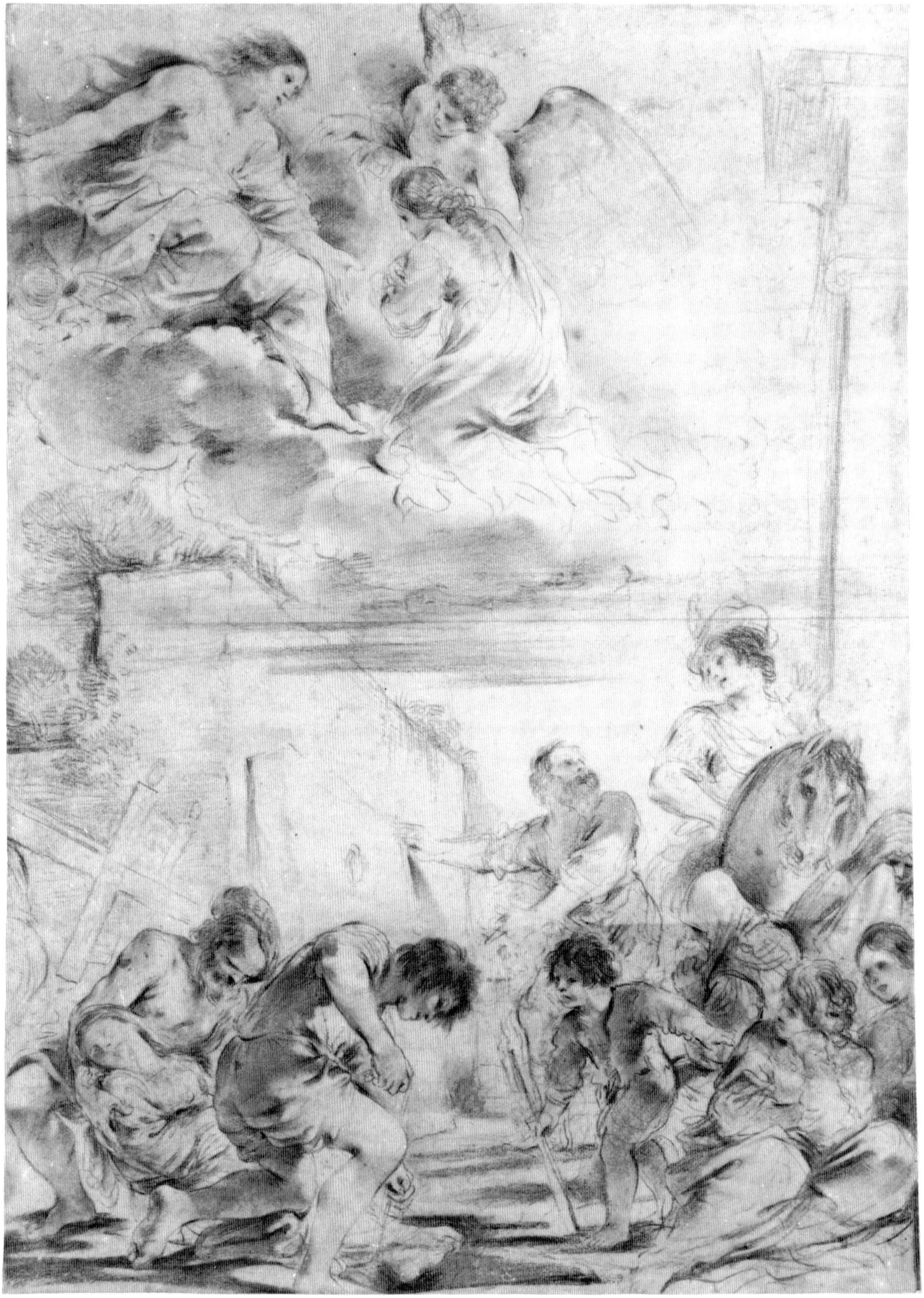

41

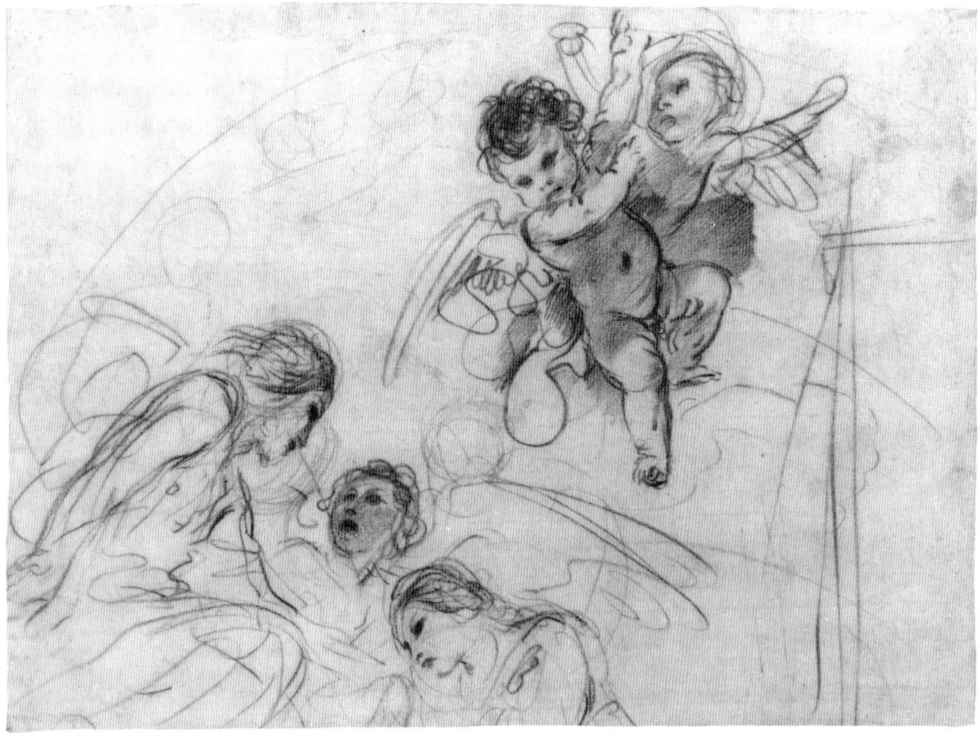

42

Guercino, whose rigorous self-criticism is so frequently encountered in his numerous drawings for important public commissions. His uncertainty could perhaps have been compounded on this occasion by his awareness of the difficulties in finding an interpretation of the subject that would be acceptable to the cultivated milieu surrounding the papal court.

Mahon has argued that the *St Petronilla* altarpiece represents an important turning-point in Guercino's stylistic evolution as a painter (M, *Studies*, 1947, pp. 83–92; M, *Dipinti*, 1968, pp. 113–16, and 118, n. 32; and, more recently, in M & T, 1989, pp. 14–15). According to his thesis, Guercino's gradual abandonment of the 'naturalism' of his early work and his progressive adoption of a more 'classical' vocabulary of form – a tendency that increasingly dominated his later painted work – can be traced to this picture. The differences between No. 41 and the altarpiece therefore lie at the very heart of this change of style. These differences have been interpreted as indicating a preference for a 'classical' rather than a 'baroque' solution for the composition. The biggest change between No. 41 and the altarpiece, as Mahon has emphasised, is in the more fluid spatial organisation of the lower part of the composition. In the picture spatial depth is described by a series of clearly defined receding planes and the figures are more clearly isolated from each other. It is worth noting that the change in style so marked in Guercino's paintings is hardly perceptible in his drawings, a fact not surprising given their functional role; this is not to say, however, that the drawings do not reveal gradual stylistic changes as the artist grows older, simply that these changes are of a different nature.

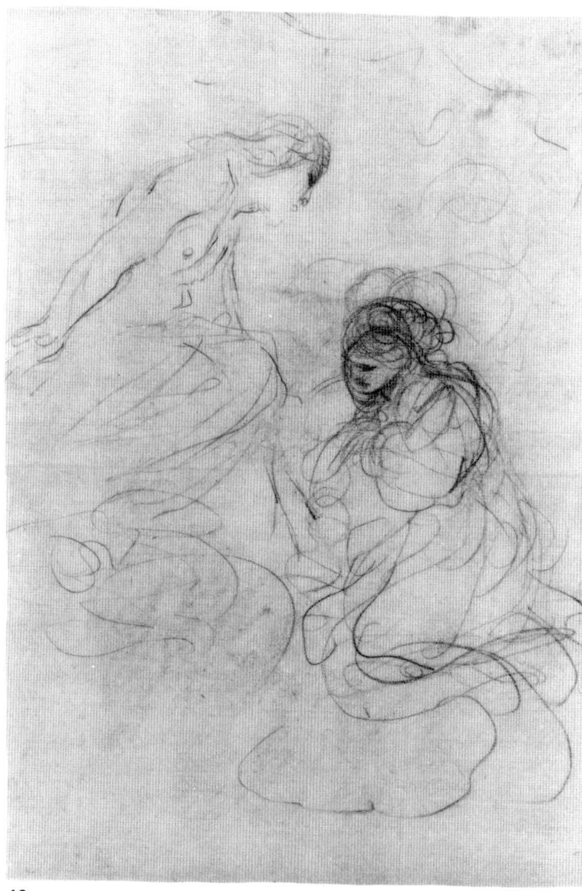

42 *verso*

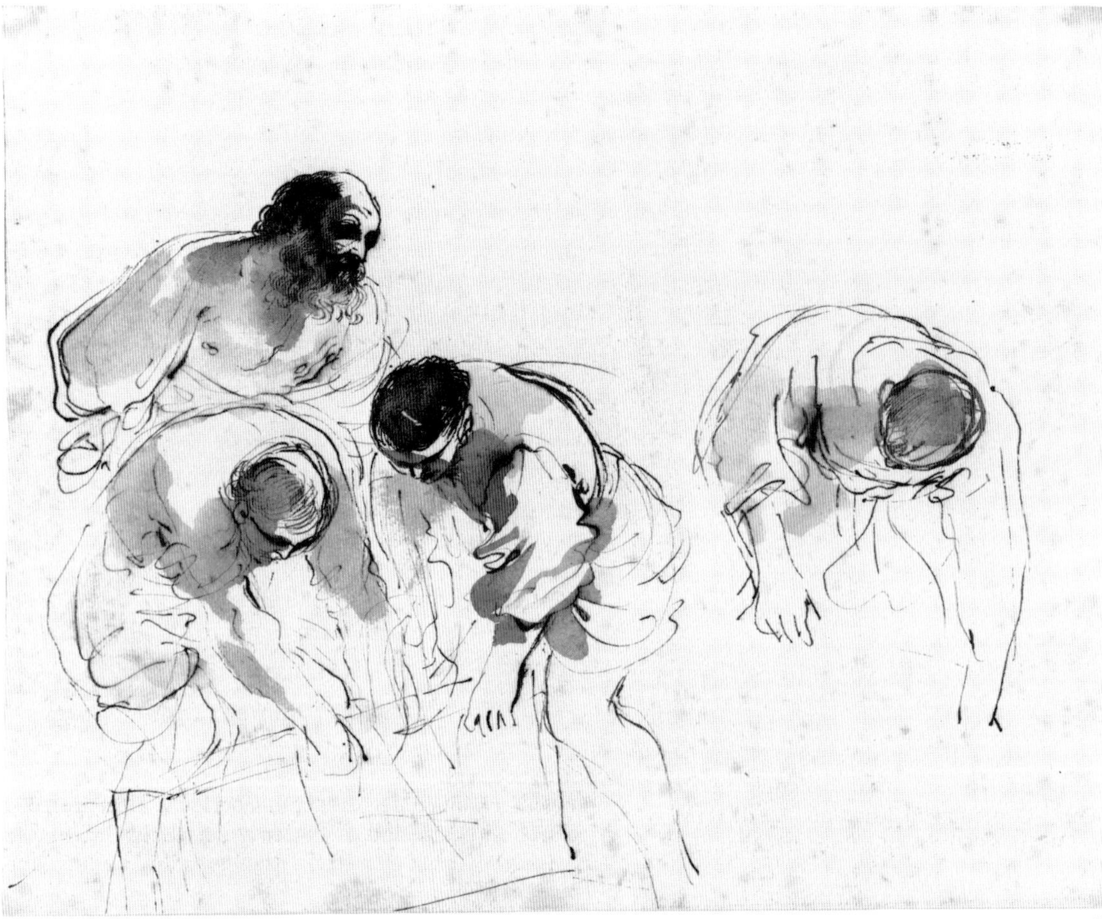

43

42 The Reception of St Petronilla into Heaven

Red chalk. 215 × 297mm.

Windsor Castle, Royal Library, inv. no. 2392.

Provenance: Casa Gennari; King George III.

Literature: M, *Studies*, 1947, p. 86, n. 139; Bottari, 1966, p. 5, and pl. XXIX; M, *Disegni*, 1969, no. 89; Roli, 1972, pl. 27 (in reverse); M & T, 1989, no. 24.

Both the *recto* and *verso* studies are for the upper part of the altarpiece of *The Burial and Reception into Heaven of St Petronilla*, showing Christ receiving the saint into Heaven. The over-prominent putti at the top right of the *recto* study were omitted from the picture, as was the winged angel who appears between Christ and the saint. The relationship between the two principal figures, however, seems to have been more or less established, except that the figure of Christ is shown more in profile in the drawing. The *verso* study explores further the rapport between the two protagonists. The artist obviously had particular difficulty in finding a

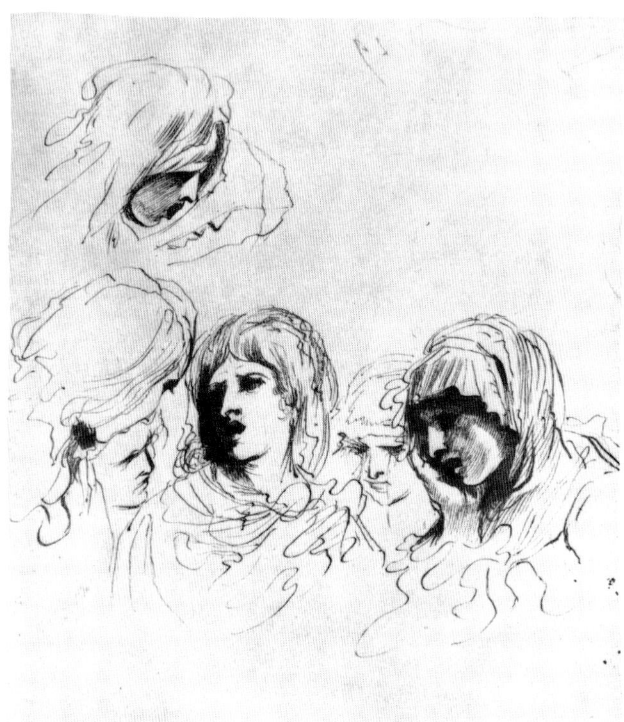

Fig. 8 (right) *Sheet of Studies of female Mourners*. Pen and brown ink, 233 × 202 mm (Madrid, Prado, inv. no. FD 11). See No. 43

satisfactory position for the saint's head, for he made several attempts at drawing and redrawing this detail.

The two studies should be compared with the upper part of the earlier study for the whole composition, No. 41, in which Christ assumes a pose roughly equivalent to his painted counterpart, while St Petronilla, accompanied by a winged angel, kneels with her back half turned towards the spectator and with her face in lost profile.

43 Group of three Men and a separate Study of a Fourth

Pen and brown ink and brown wash. 254 × 320mm.

Windsor Castle, Royal Library, inv. no. 2781.

Provenance: Casa Gennari; King George III.

Literature: M, *Disegni*, 1969, no. 88; Steinberg, 1980, pp. 209 and 236; M & T, 1989, no. 25.

No. 43 belongs to a later phase in the development of the composition than No. 41. At this moment Guercino was in the process of revising his ideas for the lower part of the composition, abandoning his earlier 'baroque' solution and choosing instead one in which 'the figures are related more within planes and less in terms of recession' (M & T, 1989, p. 13). The evidence for placing No. 43 at this stage is based on its close similarity in style to the magnificent drawing for the whole of the bottom half of the picture in the Thorvaldsen Museum, Copenhagen (inv. no. D. 473; M, *Disegni*, 1969, p. 97; Bean, 1969, pl. 35; Roli, 1972, pl. 28), which, it is now generally agreed, belongs to this later step in the evolution of this difficult design. Not only does the use of the dark pools of wash in combination with the confident, rather sparse pen lines in the two drawings suggest that they arose from much the same creative moment, but also an exact counterpart of the man in the centre of the group of three in No. 43 appears in the Copenhagen drawing as one of the gravediggers – that on the left, who lowers the corpse of the saint into the ground.

A pen drawing in the Prado, Madrid (inv. no. FD 11, 233 × 202mm; Mena Marqués, 1983, p. 107, fig. 189, as follower of Guercino; see Fig. 8), appears to be by the master and is perhaps related to the female mourners who are seen in the background of the Copenhagen drawing and on the left in the finished painting. The head of the woman at the top left in the Prado study also compares well with the mourner seated on the left in No. 39.

A pen-and-wash drawing in the Kupferstichkabinett, Berlin–Dahlem (inv. no. KdZ 5184, 230 × 135mm; Gernsheim, photo no. 33801), appears to us to be a study for the group of spectators at the burial. In technique and style it resembles that in Copenhagen.

3 The middle and late 1620s (Nos. 44–74)

On his return to Emilia, Guercino began to receive more significant ecclesiastical commissions in key churches in the province of Emilia. The first of these was the great *Crucifixion, with the Madonna, the Magdalen, St John the Evangelist and St Prosper, Bishop of Reggio,* commissioned in 1624 to hang in one of the principal chapels of the Madonna della Ghiara at Reggio (Nos. 51–2). Although the job was originally offered to Guido Reni (as was so often the case until Reni's death in 1642), Guercino was ultimately chosen as a swifter, more reliable alternative. His working drawings for this project are somewhat different in approach from those for the *St Petronilla* altarpiece of only a year or two before. Guercino seems to have worked much faster on the Ghiara altarpiece (admittedly a far simpler composition) and with greater economy of means. Although he made a large number of studies for this picture, the artist was more selective in his approach, determining a number of suitable poses and groupings from the start, and subsequently trying these out in every permutation, transferring them between protagonists, reversing and modifying his ideas as he proceeded. This deft juggling of his raw material was increasingly typical of Guercino's working method.

The other major enterprise of this period was the frescoed cupola of the Cathedral at Piacenza, the only instance in Guercino's *oeuvre* of church decoration in this medium and on such a grand scale (see Nos. 58–64). It was a project that he took over from the Lombard painter il Morazzone (1573–1626), who had completed only two compartments of the cupola before his untimely death. The commission certainly presented Guercino with a great challenge, since he was required to decorate the remaining six compartments in the last seven months of 1626, and the large historiated lunettes and friezes in the following year. Guercino's drawings for this commission are unusually free and even more experimental than those for the Ghiara *Crucifixion*; the breadth of these drawings and their numerous pentiments surely reflect the pressure of time against which he was battling.

Guercino's drawings in pen and wash are particularly spectacular during this period, and it may be no coincidence that this medium particularly lends itself to speed of execution. The drawings in this technique are, by their very nature, more painterly than others in pen or chalk, and indeed at this moment in his career Guercino's drawing and painting styles seem particularly attuned. The drawings of the middle and late 1620s are still characterised by the monumentality and robustness of the Roman period, but the chiaroscuro is less pronounced, the tones appearing more evenly distributed about the forms, and the touch is freer and more flexible.

44 A Child seen from behind, standing between its Mother's Knees

(*see colour pl. 8*)

Red chalk with stumping. 301 × 211mm.

London, Courtauld Institute Galleries, Witt Collection, inv. no. 1327.

Provenance: Casa Gennari; Mr Bouverie; Mr Hervey; the Earls of Gainsborough (sale, Christie's, London, 27 July 1922, lot 81, with others, bt *Meatyard*); Sir Robert Witt.

Literature: Russell, 1923, p. 38, pl. VII; M, *Disegni*, 1969, no. 187; Hammer, *et al.*, 1977, no. 43.

Numbered in graphite in the bottom left corner: *4* (for a discussion and further instances of sheets numbered in this way, see No. 10).

The study is a masterpiece of Guercino's technique of drawing in red chalk. The beautifully drawn body of the infant, whose soft, palpable skin is delicately suggested by the smudging (stumping) of the chalk, is contrasted with, on the one hand, the far more heavily drawn, cavernous folds of drapery covering the mother's lap and, on the other, the sketchy outlines of the upper half of her body. The subtlety of the drawing's tonal contrasts was apparently lost on Francesco Bartolozzi (1727–1815), whose copy of it, with the bust of the woman completed, is in the Albertina, Vienna (inv. no. 1370; Stix & Frölich-Bum, 1926, no. 453).

Although the child appears to be about to climb into its mother's lap, it is more likely that she is preparing to suckle the infant. This idea is supported by comparison with another red chalk drawing, in our opinion also by Guercino, in the Städelsches Kunstinstitut, Frankfurt (inv. no. 448; 293 × 191mm; see Fig. 9), which represents a child standing between his mother's legs in the same way, but with its mouth very clearly to her breast. We believe that the Frankfurt study is directly connected with No. 44 and that both were preparatory to a project undertaken in the mid-1620s. It is even tempting to suggest that both drawings might be early studies for the *Rest on the Flight into Egypt*, one of the frescoed lunettes in the cupola of Piacenza Cathedral which Guercino decorated in 1627. In several studies for this lunette (B, 1983, nos. 53–5, 57 and 59; see Nos. 61–2 and App. no. 97) and in the finished work (S, 1988, no. 114 L), the Madonna holds one hand to her bodice, as she prepares to suckle the Christ Child, who pushes his way towards her from Joseph's lap. It is possible that Guercino originally thought of showing a slightly later narrative moment, with the Infant actually at his mother's breast.

Alternatively, both No. 4 and the Frankfurt drawing may well be preparatory for a drawing in coloured chalks of the *Madonna suckling the standing Christ Child with St Joseph looking on*, in the Pierpont Morgan Library, New York (inv. no. I, 99; Roli, 1972, p. 26 and pl. 35), datable in the 1620s.

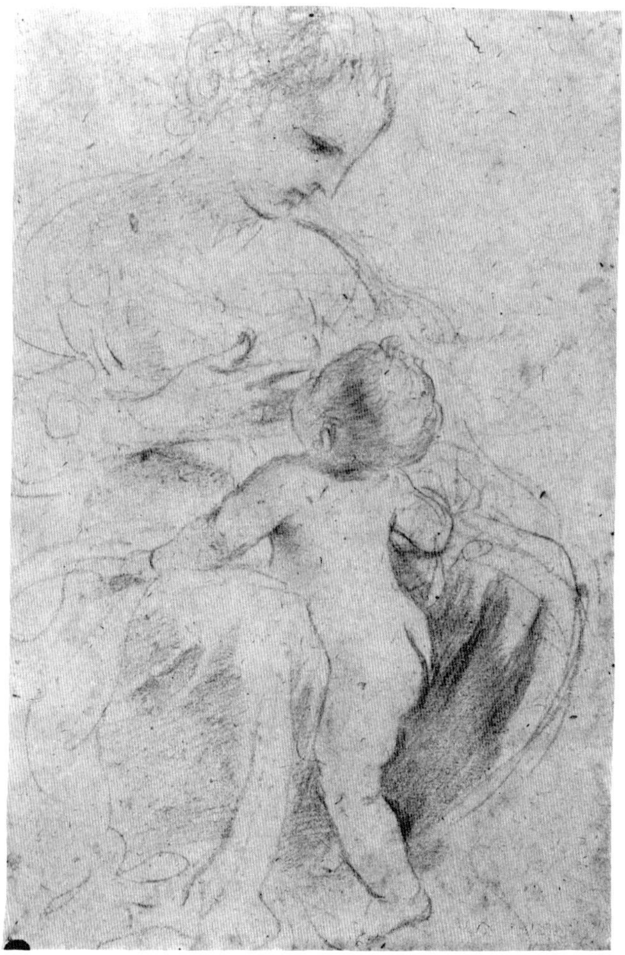

Fig. 9 *Standing Child suckled by his Mother*. Red chalk, 293 × 191 mm (Frankfurt, Städelsches Kunstinstitut, inv. no. 448). See No. 44

45 Woman with a Putto

Pen and brown ink and brown wash. 228 × 181mm.

Windsor Castle, Royal Library, inv. no. 2476.

Provenance: Casa Gennari; King George III.

Literature: M & T, 1989, no. 26.

The drawing appears to date from the first half of the 1620s. Mahon and Turner related this and two further drawings in the Royal Library, Windsor Castle (M & T, 1989, nos. 27–8), to the painting of *The Toilet of Venus*, formerly in the Minneapolis Institute of Arts and now in the Goethe Academy, Renaissance, California (S, 1988, no. 93). It was made for the Ludovisi family and is mentioned in a manuscript inventory dated 1623 of paintings in both the family's Casino and Palazzo (providing a *terminus ante* for the painting). Although none of the figures in the painting is posed in the same way as those in the drawing, it is probable that the female figure was transformed into the attendant with the low neckline taking jewels from a coffer in the painting and the putto is one of those carrying Venus' towel (he is most like the one on the left). An untraced composition drawing in red chalk, formerly in the collection of Charles Rogers, is recorded in an etching by W. W. Ryland, published in 1767 for Rogers's *Imitations* (1778). The pose of the attendant in that drawing is much closer to that of the female figure in No. 45, but in reverse, substantiating the connection. Although the woman and the putto are here studied as a coherent group, in the painting they are separated by other figures.

A drawing for this composition was formerly in the Kunsthalle, Bremen, but was lost in the Second World War (inv. no. 09/697; Marangoni, 1959, pl. 10). Another drawing, whose relationship to the composition rests on the figure of Venus in the ex-Bremen study, is in the British Museum (see App. no. 8).

46 Nude Woman seated, embracing a Child

Pen and brown ink and brown wash with some smudging. 234 × 181mm; damages in the darks repaired.

London, Courtauld Institute Galleries, Witt Collection, inv. no. 1358.

Provenance: Casa Gennari; Mr Bouverie; Mr Hervey; the Earls of Gainsborough (sale, Christie's, London, 27 July 1922, lot 81, with others, bt *Meatyard*); Sir Robert Witt.

Literature: Russell, 1923, p. 43, pl. X; Popham, 1938c, p. 19; Marangoni, 1959, pl. 16; M, *Disegni*, 1969, no. 220; Hammer, *et al.*, 1977, no. 44.

Inscribed in brown ink in the bottom left corner: *34 Pr. Fo.* (For similar inscriptions, see No. 10.) It is likely that this annotation is a reference to the drawing's original location in the series of albums of drawings by Guercino preserved by the artist's heirs until the dispersal of the collection in the eighteenth century, the letters perhaps standing for 'Primo Foglio'.

Popham (1938b, no. 465, and 1938c, p. 19) suggested convincingly that the composition was adapted from Nicolò Boldrini's woodcut of *Venus and Cupid* after Titian (Bartsch, 1983b, p. 203, no. 29 [126]). Although at first sight the image is apparently that of a mother and child embracing, the sensuous interpretation of the subject – with the bold juxtaposition of the figures' faces and lips, the voluptuous treatment of the flesh, together with the additional detail of the stocking which has slipped down the woman's outstretched leg, emphasising her nudity – forces one to consider the possibility that it might indeed have been intended to represent Venus and Cupid.

We endorse Mahon's dating of the drawing in the mid-1620s.

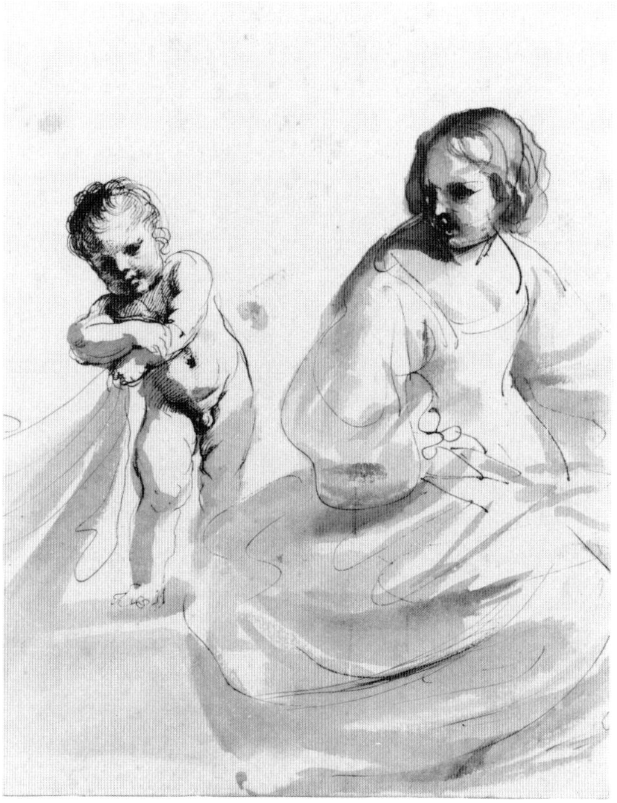

45

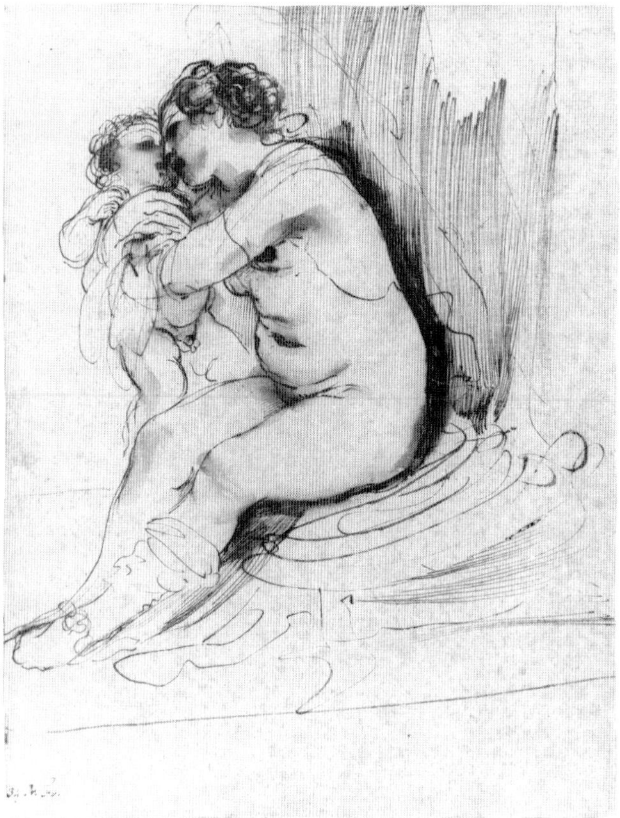

46

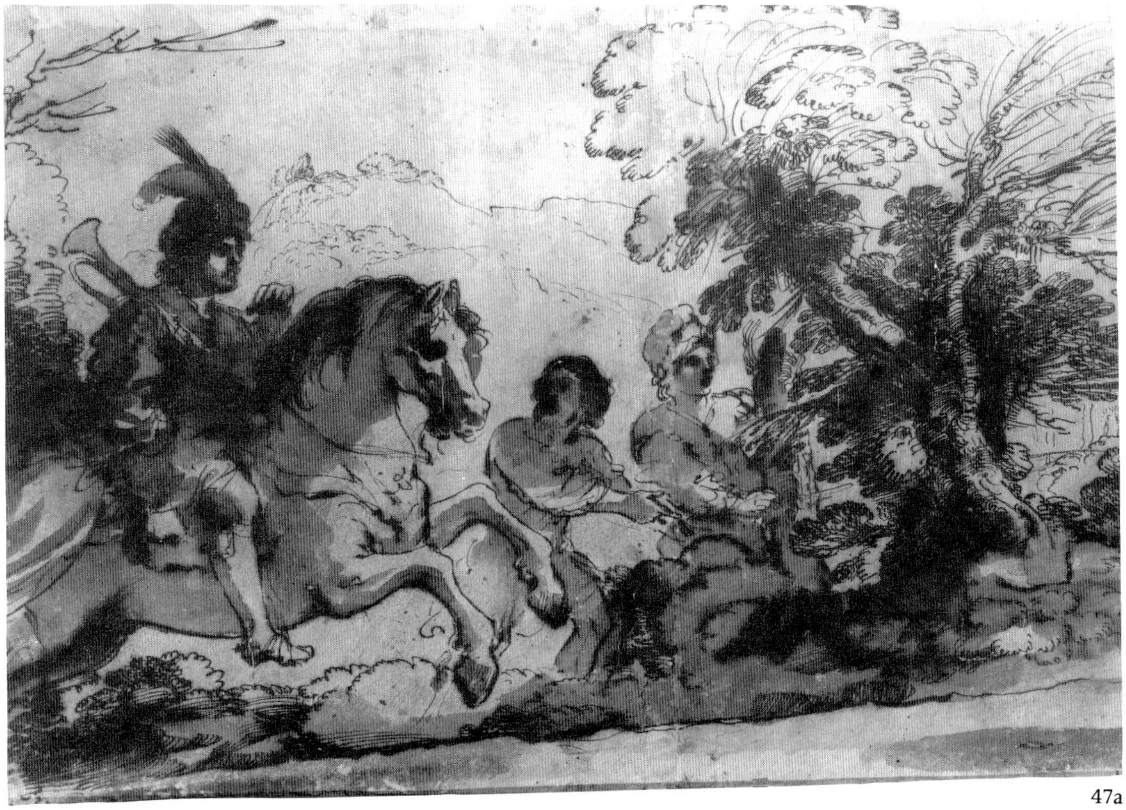

47a

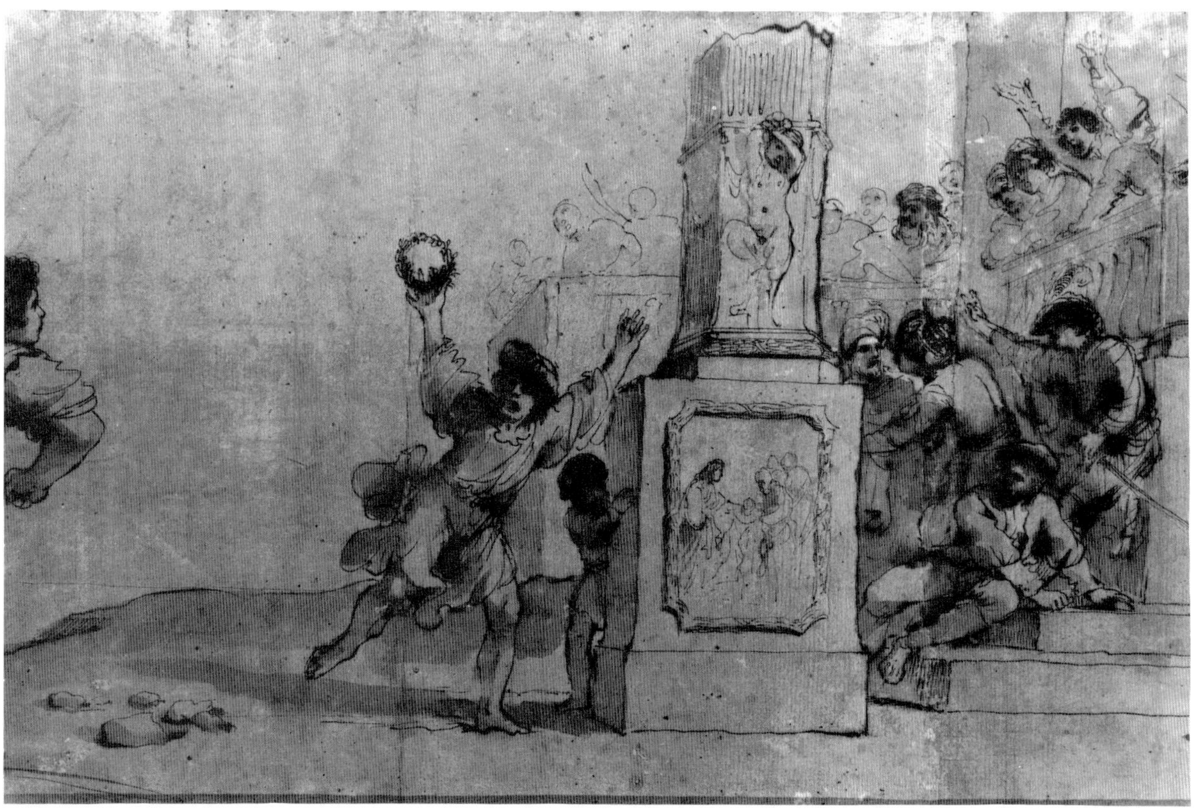

47c

Because of its length, No. 47 is reproduced in four sections, a–d

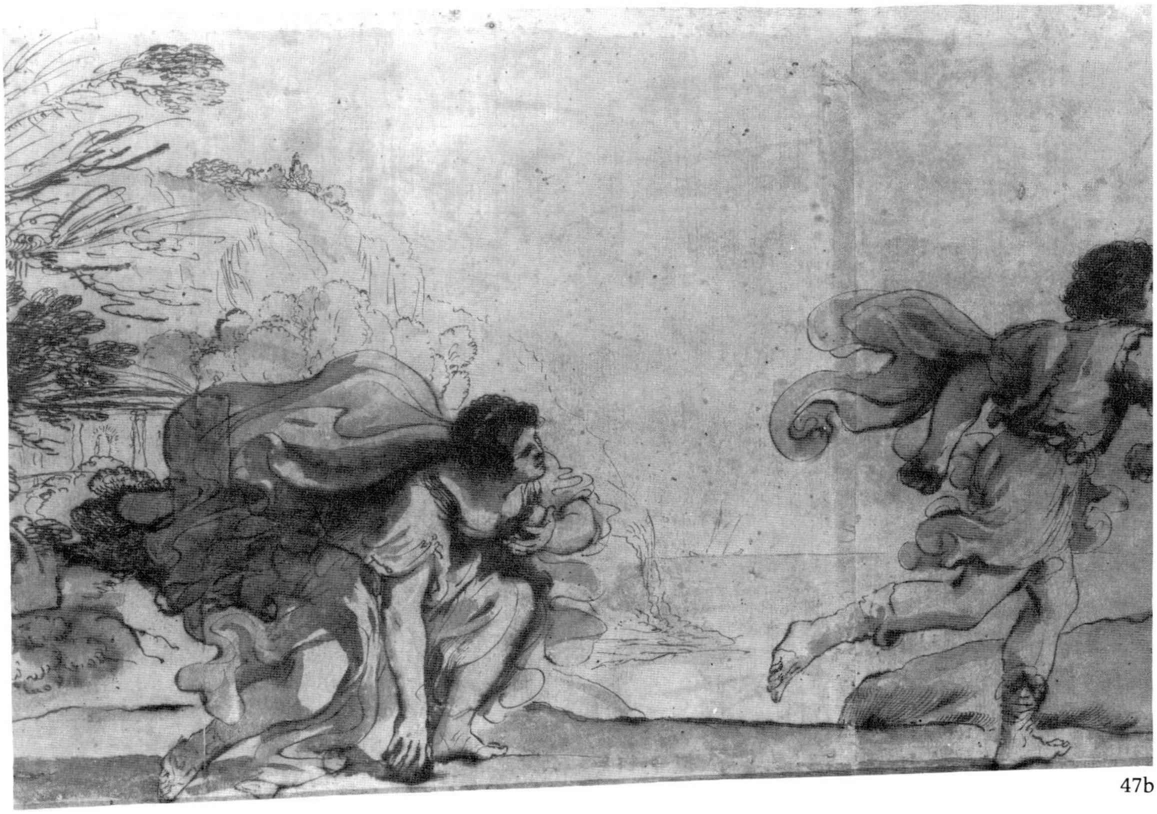

47b

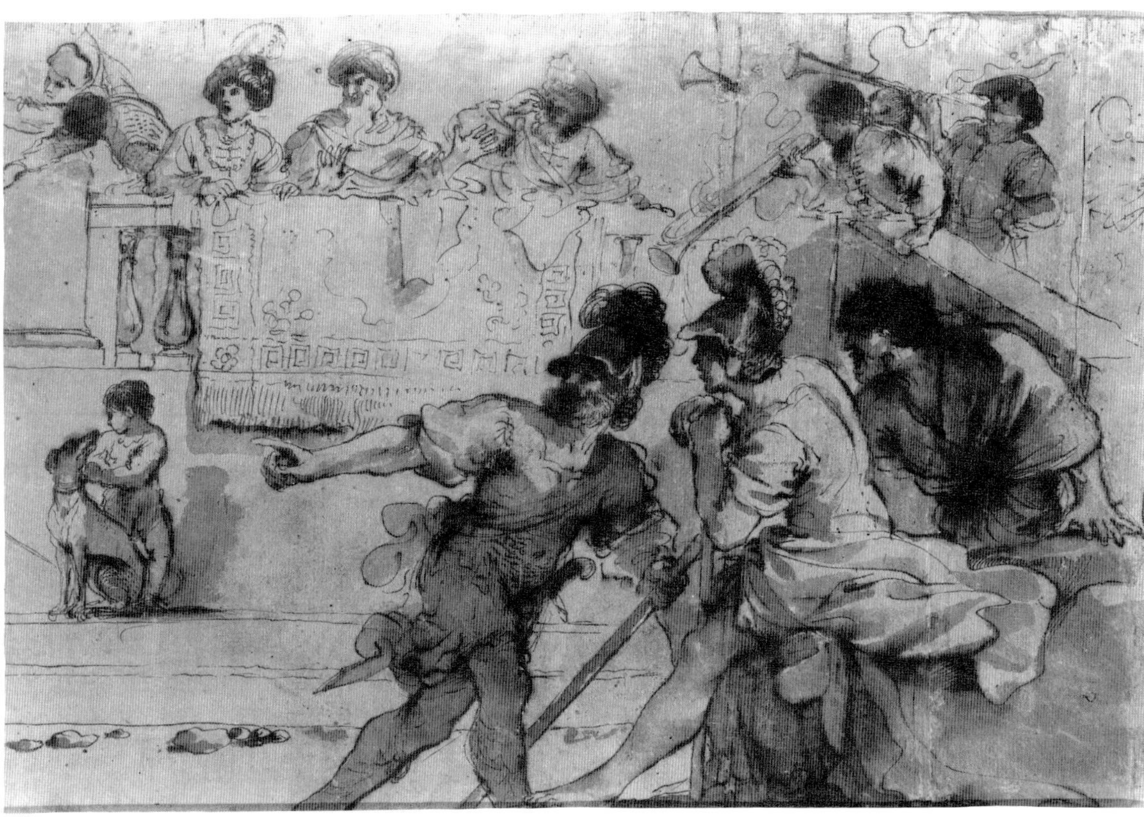

47d

47 The Race of Atalanta

Pen and brown ink and brown wash over some traces of black chalk. 285 × 1595mm; the sheet is made up of five pieces of paper joined together and laid down on canvas. It has suffered considerable damage as a result of having been exposed to light. Losses, especially to the left of the figure of Atalanta, have been made up with brown slips of paper and the drawing completed, probably in the nineteenth century.

London, Courtauld Institute Galleries, Witt Collection, inv. no. 4593.

Provenance: G. Vallardi (L 1223); Sir Matthew Digby Wyatt; purchased 1953, Witt Fund.

Literature: Hammer, *et al.*, 1977, no. 42.

The drawing's remarkable size and elongated shape immediately raises the question of its original function. Certainly, with its canvas support and discoloration, it bears all the hallmarks of having once been hung, framed, on the wall, in all probability along with the many others in the collection of the artist's heirs in the Casa Gennari (see M & T, 1989, pp. xviiif.). Whether or not it was originally intended as a decorative object in its own right is more difficult to determine. It seems more likely that it may have been an elaborate composition study for an overdoor or frieze, or for part of a piece of furniture. On the other hand, the sheet, particularly in the right half, is reminiscent of genre drawings such as the Ashmolean's *Tavern Scene* and the British Museum's *Outdoor Theatre* (see Nos. 185–6), which must surely have been compositions in their own right and not preparatory works for paintings. On stylistic grounds, No. 47 may date from the same period as these examples, but it seems to us more likely that it was drawn in the period 1621–3 when the artist was working in Rome, or possibly a little later. What appears to be a copy of the central section of the drawing was formerly on the London art market (*Old Master Drawings*, presented by Jean-Luc Baroni, exhibited at Douwes Fine Art, 30 June–12 July 1980, no. 7).

The subject is taken from Ovid's *Metamorphoses*, X, 560–707. Atalanta was an athletic huntress who challenged any suitor who presented himself to her to a race in which the loser forfeited his life. She remained unbeaten and a virgin until Hippomenes took her on. As they ran, he dropped three golden apples given to him by Venus and, since Atalanta could not resist stopping to pick them up, she lost the race. The couple later consummated their love in a temple dedicated to Cybele, so enraging that goddess that she turned them both into lions.

Guercino's famous Bolognese contemporary and rival, Guido Reni, also painted this subject, two versions of which survive, one in the Prado, Madrid (usually accepted as the original), and the other in the Pinacoteca di Capodimonte, Naples. Pepper (1984, under no. 59) dates the Madrid painting 1618–19. It is possible that Reni's painting prompted Guercino's choice of subject, although the two compositions clearly bear no resemblance to each other.

A late nineteenth-century oil sketch of *The Race of Atalanta* by Sir Edward John Poynter, P.R.A. (1836–1919), recently on the London art market (sale, Christie's, 9 February 1990, lot 253), is interesting in that it shows clear knowledge of Guercino's composition, as recorded in No. 47, rather than of Reni's more famous work. Poynter's sketch, signed and dated 1875 (though probably completed in 1876), is a design for a picture commissioned by the Earl of Wharncliffe as part of a series to decorate the Billiard Room of his seat, Wortley Hall, near Sheffield. Begun in 1871, the cycle was one of Poynter's most important decorative schemes; it was sadly destroyed in the Second World War. The composition of Poynter's picture, as recorded in the sketch sold at Christie's, is similar to Guercino's drawing in its elongated frieze-like shape; more significantly, the pose of the figure of Hippomenes is derived directly from the Italian master's composition, and even that of Atalanta, pausing to pick up one of the golden balls right at the front of the pictorial field, has several points in common with its counterpart in Guercino's drawing. Moreover, the architectural setting, with spectators watching the race from behind a balustrade, although transferred from the right to the left of the image, clearly owes much to Guercino's composition. As far as one can tell, Poynter never acknowledged his debt to his Bolognese precursor. When the finished canvas was exhibited at the Royal Academy in 1876, it was applauded by the critics for the extraordinary energy of the two running lovers and the sense of frozen movement, as though these were the products of Poynter's own invention. How Poynter came to study Guercino's drawing is not known, but it is possible that he gained access to it when it was in the collection of the architect Sir Matthew Digby Wyatt (1820–77).

48 Old bearded Man seated on the Ground (?St Jerome)

Pen and brown ink and brown wash. 224 × 251mm.

Mahon Collection, on loan to the Ashmolean Museum, Oxford, M & E, 38.

Provenance: Queen Christina of Sweden; Marchese Pompeo Azzolino; Prince Livio Odescalchi; Pierre Crozat; Marquis de Calvière; P. & D. Colnaghi; from whom purchased by Sir Denis Mahon in 1938.

Literature: M, 1967, no. 36; M, *Disegni*, 1969, no. 184; M & E, 1986, no. 38.

Inscribed at the bottom centre of the sheet in pen and brown ink in three different hands: (1) *di Gio: fran. co da Cento*; (2) *Guarcini*; (3) *vient du Prince Dom Livio*. As Mahon was the first to note (1967, no. 36, and *Disegni*, 1969, no. 184), these three inscriptions were written by (?)Giovanni Pietro Bellori, Pierre Crozat and P.-J. Mariette respectively.

Mahon is inclined to date the drawing in the period 1622–4, either during the latter part of the artist's Roman period, or immediately following. We agree with this dating, which in our view is supported by the stylistic analogies between No. 48 and other drawings of around this same period, for example Nos. 39–40 and No. 51.

The figure is presumably intended for a St Jerome rather than an Evangelist. No corresponding painting is known,

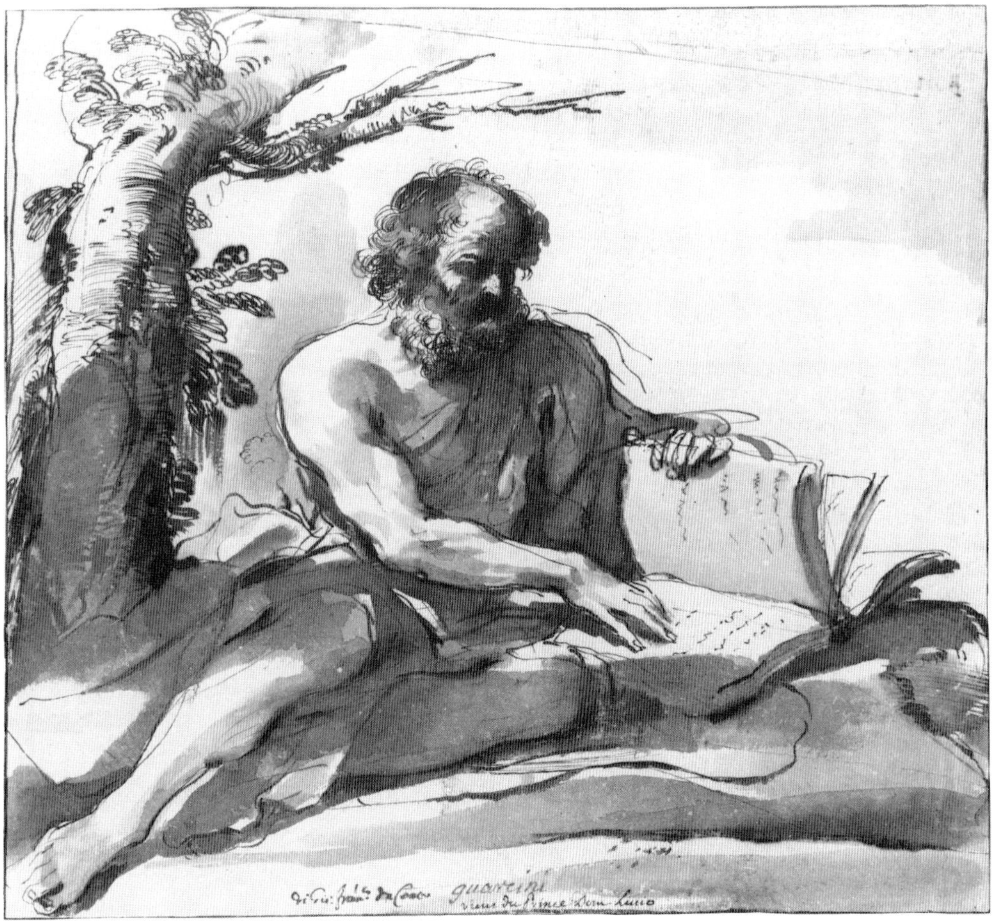

48

though, as Mahon noted (1967, no. 36, and *Disegni*, 1969, under no. 184), there is an unfinished picture by Guercino of *St Jerome seated on the Ground reading from a Book* in the Graf Harrach'sche Collection, Rohrau (Heinz, 1960, no. 123; not in Salerno), which displays some analogies in composition with No. 48, though it is probably pre-Roman in date (i.e. before 1621).

49 St Jerome

(*see colour pl. 9*)

Pen and brown ink and brown wash. 202 × 222mm.

Oxford, Ashmolean Museum, KTP 857.

Provenance: J. C. Robinson (L 1433).

Literature: Parker, 1956, no. 857; Bottari, 1966, pl. XXIII; M, 1967, under no. 36; M, *Disegni*, 1969, no. 183; Macandrew, 1980, p. 298; M & E, 1986, no. VII.

As with the previous drawing, no directly corresponding painting seems to exist. Both drawings are much the same in date and, in the opinion of Mahon (1967, under no. 36, and *Disegni*, 1969, no. 183), may have been conceived with the same painted work in mind. The two drawings are nonetheless very different from each other in composition.

The lines drawn free-hand at the bottom and right edges indicate the composition's extremity at these points. For Guercino's use of this device elsewhere in his drawings, see Nos. 9, 10, 31, 56, 79, 132, 136, 145, 147 and 148.

50 Study for the Head of St Laurence

Red chalk, with slight stumping, on greenish-grey paper. 347 × 245mm; the sheet is slightly foxed throughout.

Windsor Castle, Royal Library, inv. no. 0235.

Provenance: Casa Gennari; King George III.

Literature: Kurz, 1955, no. 718 (as anonymous Bolognese); M & T, 1989, no. 128.

As Plazzotta has pointed out, this is a study for the head of St Laurence in the *Madonna and Child with St Laurence*, the altarpiece painted for the Chiesa del Seminario in Finale nell'Emilia in *c.*1624 (S, 1988, no. 101). Mahon and Turner connected the drawing with a later commission, *The Calling of the Blessed Luigi Gonzaga* of 1650–55, in the Metropolitan Museum of Art, New York (S, 1988, no. 276); however, both in its style and in the type and pose of the figure, the drawing corresponds so closely with the earlier painting that there can be no doubt of the identification.

The drawing is almost life-size and was meticulously executed in red chalk, a rare example of its kind in Guercino's *oeuvre*. The foxing of the paper, now much diminished with restoration, makes it difficult to appreciate (particularly in reproduction) the subtlety of the draughtsmanship in such areas as the shading in the corner of the youth's mouth. This type of detail study would have been made at the very last stage in the preparatory process, which explains why Guercino incorporated the head into the painting with scarcely any modifications. Another example, also in red chalk, is the *Head of God the Father* in the Museum of Fine Arts, Budapest (inv. no. 2323; Czére, 1989, no. 37), for the *God the Father with a Putto* of 1620, now in the Gallerie d'Arte del Comune in Palazzo Bianco, Genoa (S, 1988, no. 70). Other detail studies of heads certainly do survive, particularly from the 1630s, but these are invariably on a somewhat smaller scale and are carried out in pen and brown ink. In addition to the three examples recently discussed by Turner (1990, pp. 653–4, figs. 31–2), a fourth may be No. 80, while a fifth, the *Head and Shoulders of a helmeted Warrior*, is in the British Museum (see App. no. 32).

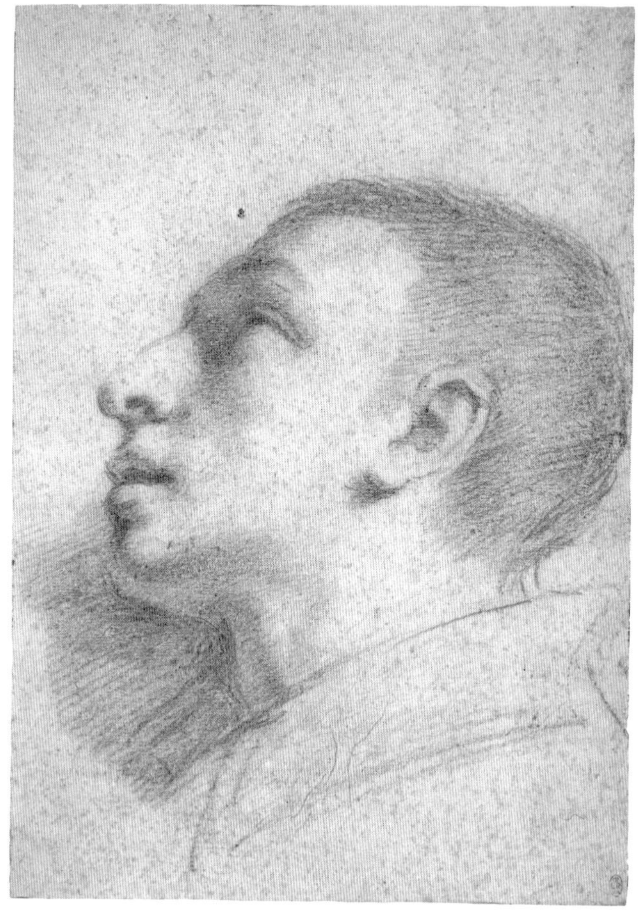

50

51–52 Studies for the *Crucifixion, with the Madonna, the Magdalen, St John the Evangelist and St Prosper, Bishop of Reggio* (1624–5)

Reggio Emilia, Madonna della Ghiara

51 St Prosper, a Woman, and a Putto carrying a Model of Reggio Emilia

Pen and brown ink and brown wash. 257 × 165mm.

Windsor Castle, Royal Library, inv. no. 2553.

Provenance: Casa Gennari; King George III.

Literature: M, 1951, pp. 56f., no. ix; M, *Disegni*, 1969, under nos. 92–100; Roli, 1972, pl. 32; M & T, 1989, no. 31.

A preparatory study for the most important commission of the period immediately following Guercino's return to Emilia from Rome, namely the *Crucifixion, with the Madonna, the Magdalen, St John the Evangelist and St Prosper, Bishop of Reggio*, which was painted in 1624–5 for one of the principal churches in the region, the Madonna della Ghiara at Reggio (S, 1988, no. 105). There are numerous preparatory studies, exploring a wide variety of different poses and positions for each of the figures in this work (these are discussed at length in M, *Disegni*, 1969, under nos. 92–100, and M & T, 1989, under nos. 30–33; a further drawing probably for this same commission is in the British Museum, see App. no. 11). The documents relating to the commission are published in Artioli & Monducci, 1982, pp. 93–6.

No. 51 was made fairly early on in the painstaking genesis of this altarpiece, before Guercino had definitively opted for placing both women on the left of the cross. Interesting pentiments for the female figure's arms, scarcely visible in reproduction, would at first suggest that it is the Magdalen who is represented here, though Mahon and Turner believe that it is more likely to be the Madonna. The two arcs either side of the woman's head must be rudimentary marks denoting the figure's raised arms (this cursory shorthand appears elsewhere in Guercino's work, e.g. No. 135). The same wonderfully expressive gesture features in four other drawings in the series, always being reserved for the Magdalen. These are in the Gabinetto Nazionale delle Stampe, Rome (inv. no. FN 120; M, *Disegni*, 1969, no. 95); the Teylers Museum, Haarlem (inv. no. H. 44; Mahon, *Disegni*, 1969, no. 96); the Kupferstichkabinett, Berlin–Dahlem (inv. no. KdZ 16367; M & T, 1989, under nos. 30–33, fig. 5); the fourth, now untraced, was formerly in the Donnadieu and Usslaub collections (M, *Disegni*, pp. 101f.) and a copy was published by Bean (1969, p. 430 and pl. 36). In all of these studies, however, the Magdalen is on the left of the cross, as in the finished work.

On the other hand, in the Rome and Haarlem drawings and in a third also in the Teylers Museum, Haarlem (inv. no. H. 3; M, *Disegni*, 1969, no. 94), the lamenting gesture actually elaborated for the woman in No. 51, with one hand raised to her cheek, is given to the Madonna. Guercino had explored this gesture, in reverse, in a preparatory drawing, in the Royal Library, Windsor Castle (No. 39), for one of

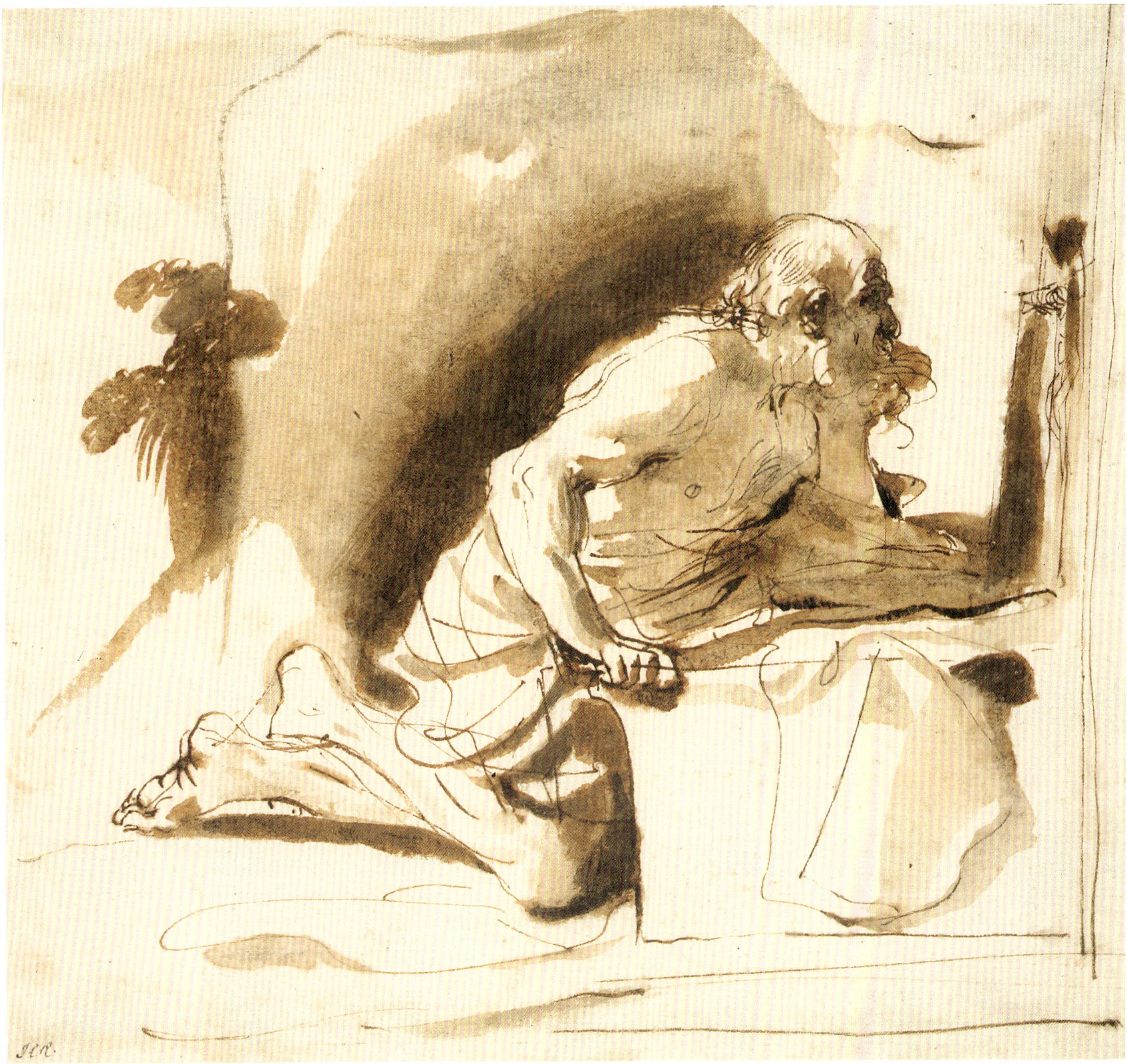

49 *St Jerome*. Oxford, Ashmolean Museum

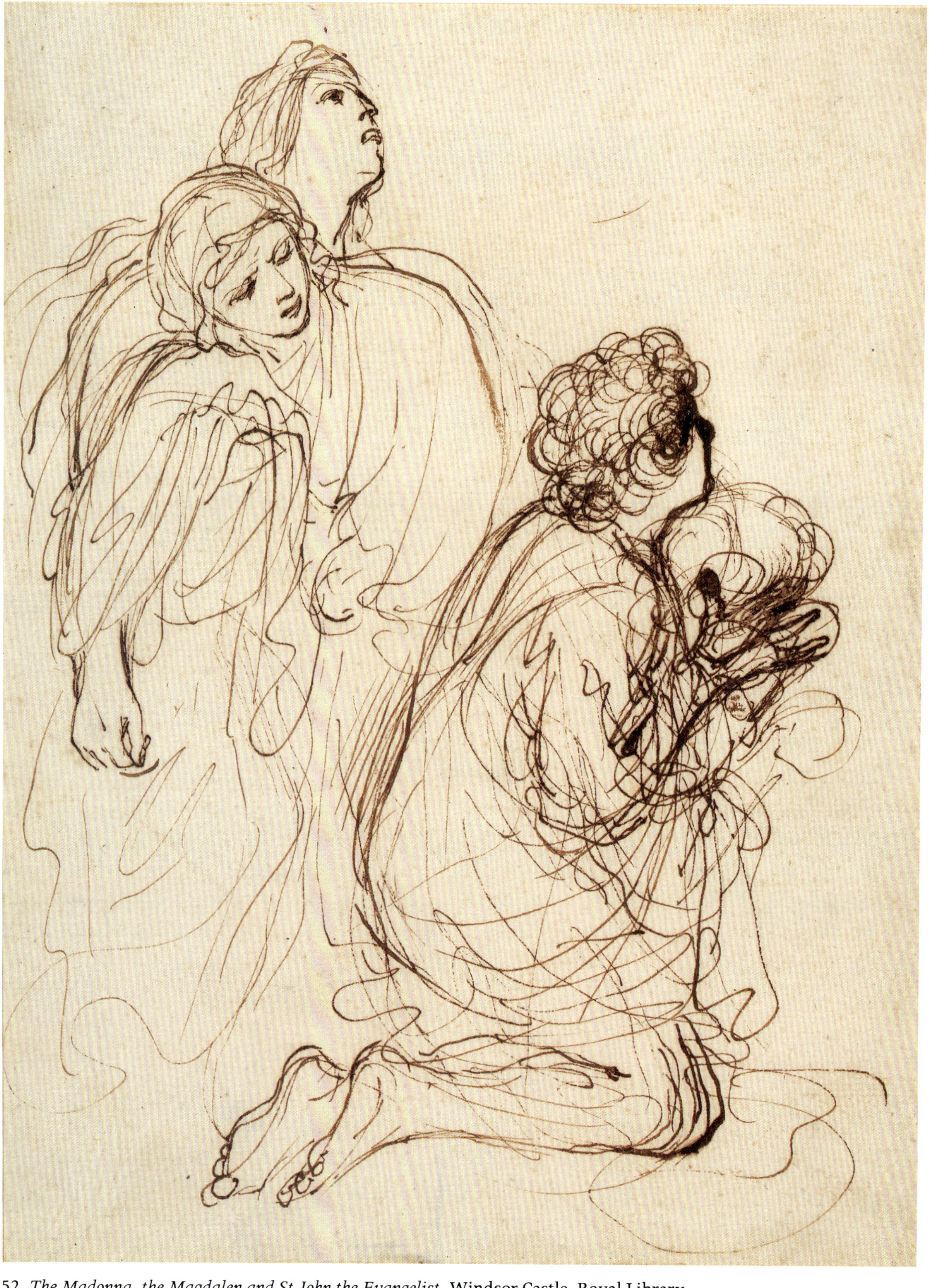

52 *The Madonna, the Magdalen and St John the Evangelist*. Windsor Castle, Royal Library

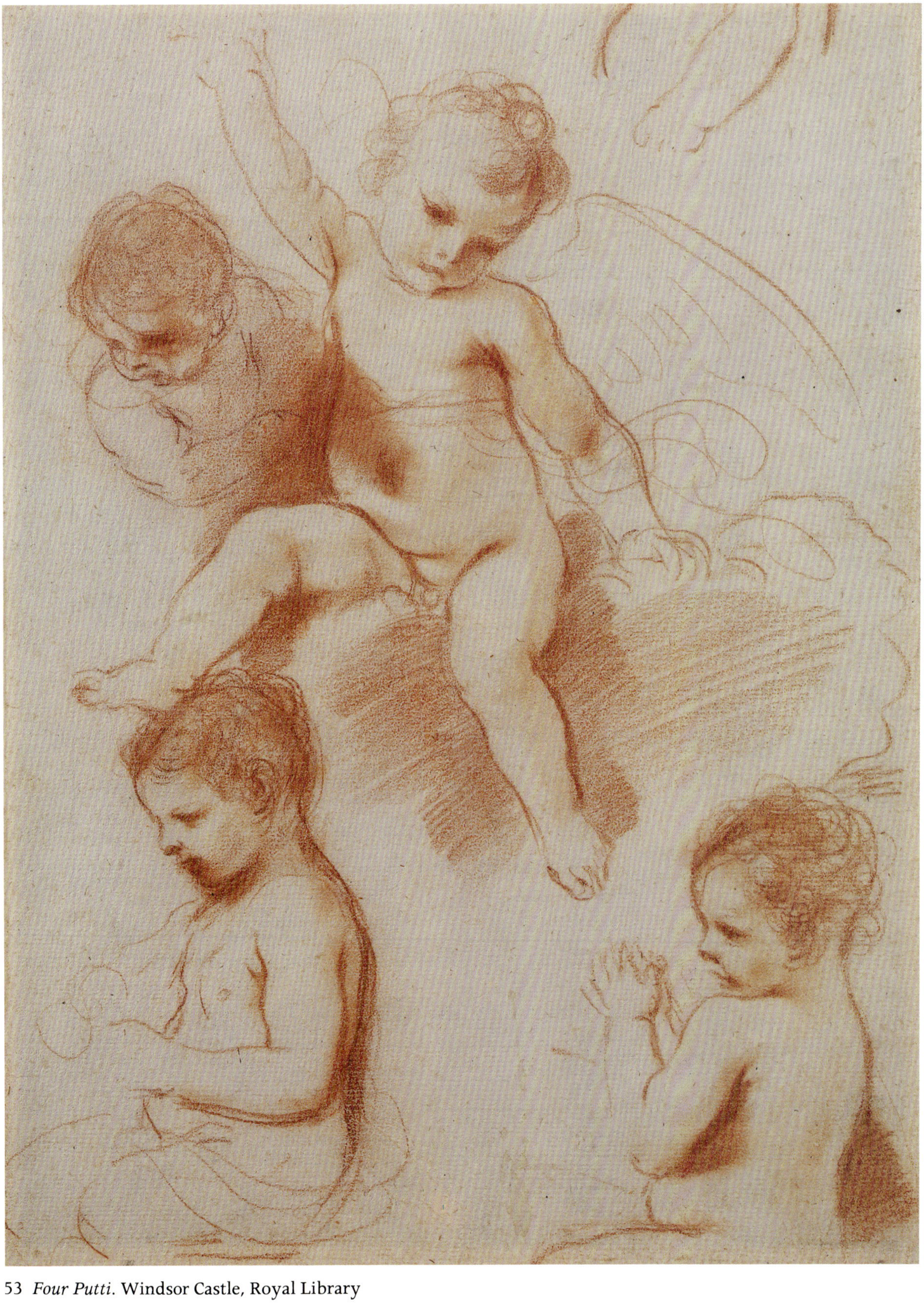

53 *Four Putti*. Windsor Castle, Royal Library

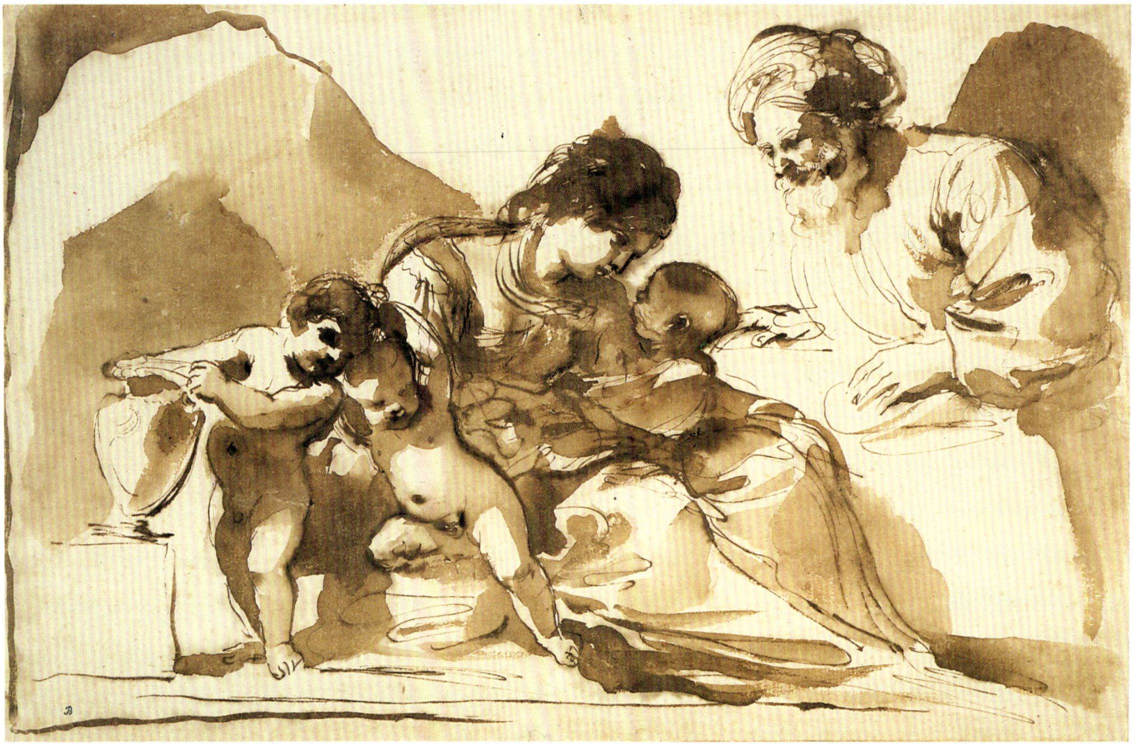

54 *Charity, with an old Man*. London, British Museum (see also App. no. 9)

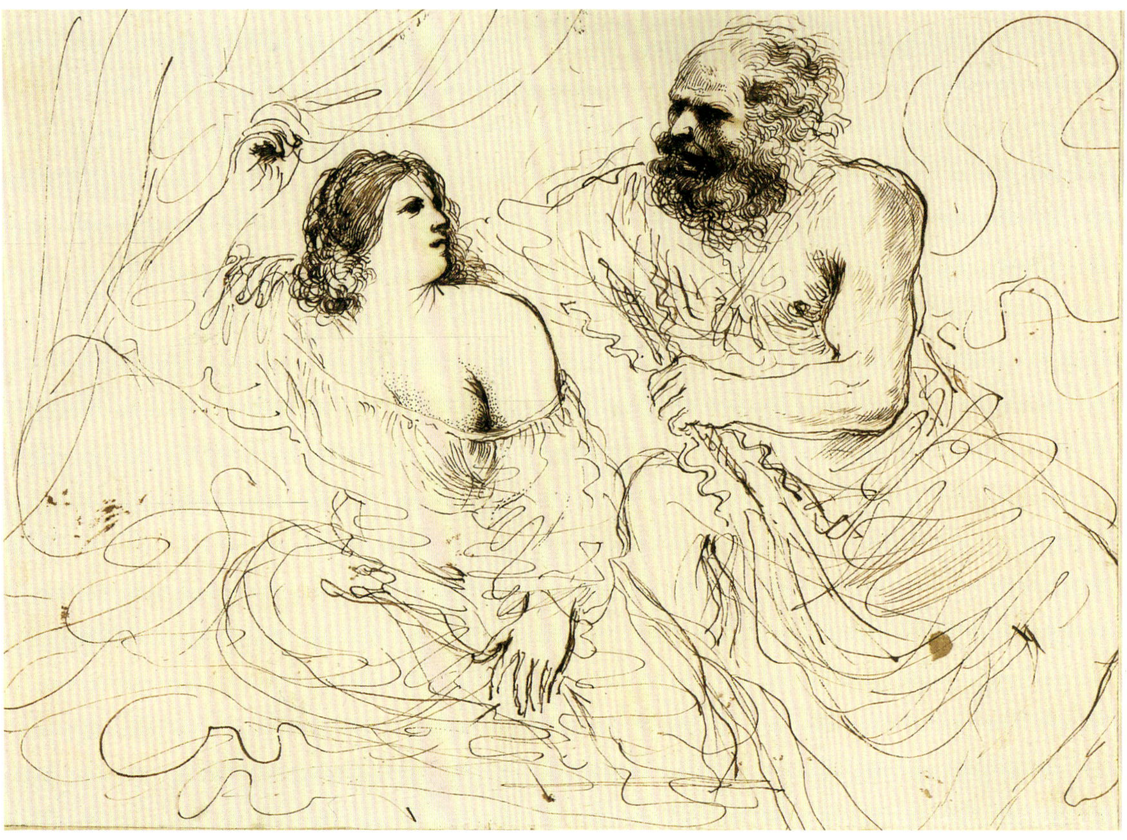

57 *Jupiter and Semele*. Windsor Castle, Royal Library

the mourners in the great *St Petronilla* altarpiece of 1621–3 (S, 1988, no. 92). It may be that when he first roughed out No. 51, Guercino thought of showing the Magdalen but then quickly changed the figure into the Madonna. As was his wont, Guercino opted for neither gesture in the finished work.

The figure of St Prosper is shown in the painting facing forward and kneeling on one knee, gesturing to the model of Reggio Emilia below and looking up at the crucified Christ, an idea anticipated (with variations) in an earlier drawing in the Teylers Museum, Haarlem (inv. no. H. 20; M, *Disegni*, 1969, no. 92) and defined on the *recto* of another sheet at Haarlem (inv. no. H. 80; M, *Disegni*, no. 98). As can be proved time and again, the logic of Guercino's ideas is rarely sequential, since he frequently returned to motifs sketched out in the earlier stages of a composition's design.

The brushwork is particularly bold in this drawing, as, for example, in the rectangular daubs down the side of the saint's face, which, despite their crudity, magically evoke the curves and hollows of the skull beneath the old man's skin.

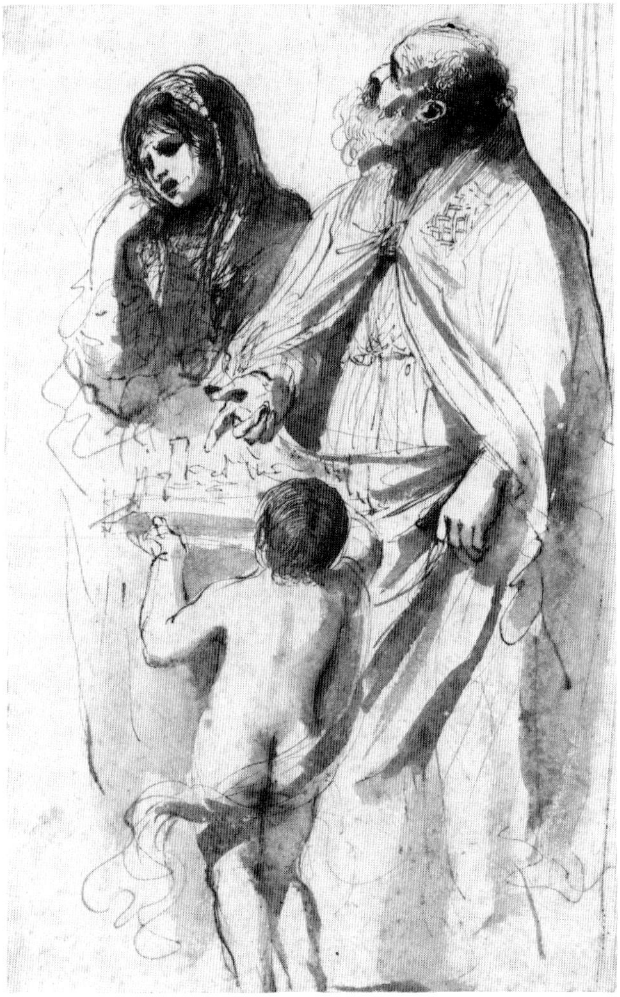

51

52 The Madonna, the Magdalen and St John the Evangelist

(*see colour pl. 10*)

Pen and brown ink. 236 × 178mm.

Windsor Castle, Royal Library, inv. no. 2585.

Provenance: Casa Gennari; King George III.

Literature: M, 1951, pp. 57f., no. viii; Bottari, 1966, no. XXXIX; M, *Disegni*, 1969, no. 97; M & T, 1989, no. 32.

A study for the *Crucifixion, with the Madonna, the Magdalen, St John the Evangelist and St Prosper, Bishop of Reggio*, for which see No. 51. The drawing comes late in the extensive series of preparatory studies for this commission, the positions, if not the precise poses, of the three protagonists to the left of the cross having been established. Guercino appears to have drawn the Magdalen supporting the Madonna effortlessly, with few pentiments, as though the problem of their interaction, so extensively explored in earlier studies, was no longer an issue. His attention was focused principally on the figure of St John, as is evident from the extensive changes in the head and hands, and the robust outlines darkened by repetition. The two alternatives for his pose are drawn in such a way that the figure seems simultaneously to look up to the right and to clasp his bowed head in his hands.

The painted figure of St John kneels to the right with his head turned to the left to regard the Madonna and the Magdalen. His hands are extended in the direction of the base of the cross and hold a drapery to catch the blood dripping from Christ's feet. The contrived pose in the painting does not do justice to the vast gamut of expressive ideas explored on paper. As his career progressed, Guercino regrettably fell more and more into the habit of suppressing the *slancio* of his first ideas as his thoughts for a given composition developed.

53 Four Putti

(*see colour pl. 11*)

Red chalk, with stumping. 323 × 245mm.

Windsor Castle, Royal Library, inv. no. 2891.

Provenance: Casa Gennari; King George III.

Literature: M, *Studies*, 1947, p. 105, n. 177; M, 1951, p. 58, no. x; M, *Disegni*, 1969, no. 102; Turner, 1985, p. 796; M & T, 1989, no. 35.

This is an exceptionally fine example of Guercino's drawing in red chalk. The studies must have been drawn from the life, and to enhance the appearance of the softness of flesh, Guercino has smudged, or stumped, the chalk, obtaining thereby a more delicate range of mid-tones than the chalk itself could provide even when shaded at its lightest.

No. 53 is a preparatory study for the altarpiece of *St Gregory the Great with Sts Ignatius Loyola and Francis Xavier* of *c.*1625–6, probably first painted for Cardinal Ludovico Ludovisi and now in the Mahon Collection, London (S, 1988, no. 112). Sts Ignatius Loyola and Francis Xavier were canonised in 1622, and its seems likely that the picture was intended to decorate one of the altars of the new church of S. Ignazio in Rome. A rapid study in pen for the whole composition is in the Mahon Collection, on loan to the Ashmolean Museum, Oxford (M & E, 1986, no. 14).

The study of a pair of putti in the middle of No. 53 is probably an early idea for the group seen in the top right of the picture; Guercino may have borrowed the pose of the winged putto in this study from a picture by Ludovico Carracci (see Turner, 1985, p. 796). A drawing for the putto on the left of this painted group is in the Collection Wicar at Lille (inv. no. 23; Châtelet, 1967–8, no. 41). The putto in the bottom right of No. 53 corresponds closely with that on the right of this same pair; the putto in the bottom left seems to be a study for the one seated on the ground holding St Gregory's tiara in the bottom right of the picture.

54 Charity, with an old Man

(*see colour pl. 12*)

London, British Museum, inv. no. 1895–9–15–706.

(For other details, see App. no. 9.)

No related painted composition exists for this exceptional example of Guercino's technique of drawing in pen and wash. In it the artist has achieved an effect remarkable even for him in its liquidity and almost sensual feeling for light. As Mahon has suggested, the drawing may be dated on stylistic grounds in the period 1622–6; a later rather than an earlier moment in this span seems to us more likely.

The drawing was first described in the Casa Gennari inventory of 1719 (see App. no. 9).

55 A Woman with two Putti carrying a Model of Bologna

Pen and brown ink and brown wash. 268 × 405mm.

Oxford, Ashmolean Museum, KTP 862.

Provenance: C. L. Chute, The Vyne, Basingstoke (sale, Sotheby's, London, 22 June 1949, lot 1, one of a folio volume of 28 drawings by Guercino, bt *Wilson*); R. E. A. Wilson, from whom purchased in February 1951.

Literature: Parker, 1956, no. 862; Macandrew, 1980, p. 299; M & E, 1986, no. X.

The subject of this drawing is enigmatic and no corresponding painting is known. The model supported by the two putti is clearly identifiable by its two leaning towers as the city of Bologna. In altarpieces it is usually the attribute of St Petronius, the patron saint of Bologna, though the dubious propriety of showing him in the company of a semi-nude woman makes it unlikely that his presence was intended here. The woman may be a personification of the city or some other allegorical figure.

There are many analogies, both stylistic and compositional, with a genre drawing in the Courtauld Institute Galleries (No. 189), which we have dated in the early to mid-1620s. The putto on the left supporting the model of Bologna is reminiscent of the backturned infant in No. 189 who reaches up to grasp a platter of food, and the female figure in profile to the left and holding out her right arm again finds an echo in the youth on the right of the Courtauld drawing who points in the direction of the offending child. These analogies are surely accidental, the artist unconsciously drawing on stock configurations and motifs

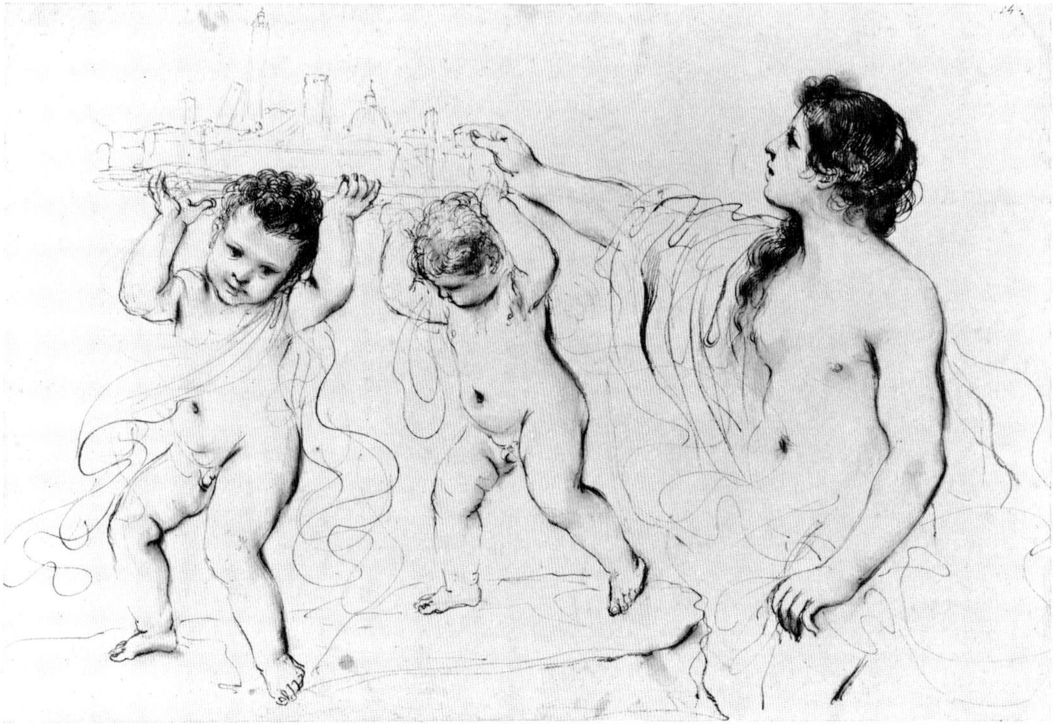

55

from his personal artistic vocabulary. It seems likely, however, that the two drawings were executed at approximately the same time.

A half-length pen-and-wash study of a putto, similar to the one on the left in No. 55, is in the Louvre, Paris (inv. no. 6906; Loire, 1990, no. 38).

56 Seated Figure of St Jerome

Pen and brown ink and grey-brown wash. 251 × 197mm.

London, Courtauld Institute Galleries, Witt Collection, inv. no. 1365.

Provenance: Casa Gennari; Mr Bouverie; Mr Hervey; the Earls of Gainsborough (sale, Christie's, London, 27 July 1922, lot 81, with others, bt *Meatyard*); Sir Robert Witt.

Numbered in graphite in the bottom left corner: *60* (for a discussion and further instances of sheets numbered in this way, see No. 10).

A study for the figure of St Jerome in the altarpiece of the *Assumption of the Virgin with St Peter as Pope and St Jerome* of 1626 for the Cathedral at Reggio Emilia (S, 1988, no. 113). In the altarpiece the saint is shown kneeling on his right knee instead of seated, as in No. 56, and his head is at a slightly different angle. By the time Guercino made this drawing he must have known almost exactly where the saint was to be positioned in the altarpiece, since the lines to the right of the figure in the drawing surely indicate the edge of the eventual composition.

Numerous studies for this picture survive, the majority of them devoted to the figure of St Jerome alone, with whose pose Guercino seems to have been particularly preoccupied. Although the artist apparently planned to place the saint on the right of the picture from the start, his first instinct was to show his body facing inwards, to the left. Several drawings record this early phase. The first is a pen-and-wash study almost certainly for this project in the Palazzo Rosso, Genoa (inv. no. 1683, 262 × 144mm, formerly in the collection of Clemente Nicoli; see Fig. 10), which shows the saint kneeling and looking up, in profile to the left; a good copy of the Genoa drawing, formerly in the Morelli collection, is in the Gabinetto dei Disegni, Civiche Raccolte d'Arte, Milan (inv. no. B 105 (225); Bora, 1988, no. 55, as Guercino). Another study, in pen and brown ink, showing the figure in a very similar pose, is on the *verso* of a sheet recently on the London art market (sale, Christie's, 6 July 1982, lot 40, 242 × 163mm; the sheet is laid down, but the *verso* study is clearly visible through it; see Fig. 12). The *recto* of this same sheet, also in pen, marks another stage in the evolution of the figure's pose, showing him still facing left, but kneeling on one knee only, and with his left hand on his breast. In a third drawing, in pen and brown ink and three tones of brown wash, also double-sided and recently on the London art market (sale, Christie's, 1 April 1987, lot 64, 251 × 199mm), the saint, still facing left and in an almost identical pose to that on the *recto* of the other ex-Christie's drawing, is represented together with St Peter. On the *verso* is a further study (see Fig. 11), in pen and brown ink, for St Jerome alone, in which he is shown in the same position, kneeling on one knee, but with his body turned to the right. This is an important transitional sheet in the composition's design, apparently recording the moment at which Guercino had the idea of reversing the whole figure, but for his head, which obviously had to remain turned in the direction of the Madonna.

The Courtauld drawing seems to belong to a later phase, showing the saint with his torso definitively facing right and his head turned to the left, but also seated and writing in a book. Among the further studies belonging to this same phase are a lost drawing engraved by Bartsch (*Recueil*, XXIII, 962b) showing the figure in a similar pose as in No. 56 but looking downwards; a School sketch in the Royal Library, Windsor Castle (M & T, 1989, no. 458), showing a bearded, semi-draped old man in a very similar attitude to the Bartsch figure, except that his hands are pressed together as in prayer (this Studio work fits very well with other later drawings for the altarpiece and may record another lost sketch); and finally a splendid pen-and-wash drawing in the Moatti collection, Paris (Di Giampaolo, 1987, no. 54), showing the saint half-length but otherwise exactly as he is in the painting. The Moatti drawing is probably the latest of the extant preparatory studies for the figure of St Jerome.

The late group of studies shows how Guercino was inspired by Guido Reni's altarpiece of the *Madonna and Child with Sts Crispus, Crispianus and Jerome*, now in Dresden, painted just a few years earlier in 1620–21 for the church of S. Prospero in Reggio Emilia, less than a quarter of a mile away from the Cathedral (Pepper, 1984, fig. 106). Although the pose of Reni's St Jerome is never directly quoted by Guercino, an echo can be felt in the later studies, in such details as the figure's exposed, flexed arm, his bare shoulders and the motif of the open book. Guercino appears to have looked initially to the kneeling figure of St Crispianus in the same altarpiece as the model for his St Jerome, as can be seen in the Genoa drawing and that on the *verso* of the 1982 Christie's sheet, though in both studies he reversed the pose.

Only one preparatory study for the rest of the composition is known, the drawing for the upper part of the picture, showing the Madonna, an angel and putti, which was formerly in the collection of Claude Lucas (sale, Christie's, London, 9 December 1949, lot 78, with one other, bt *Calmann, 60 gns*); a copy by Robert Shipster is in the British Museum (see App. no. 114).

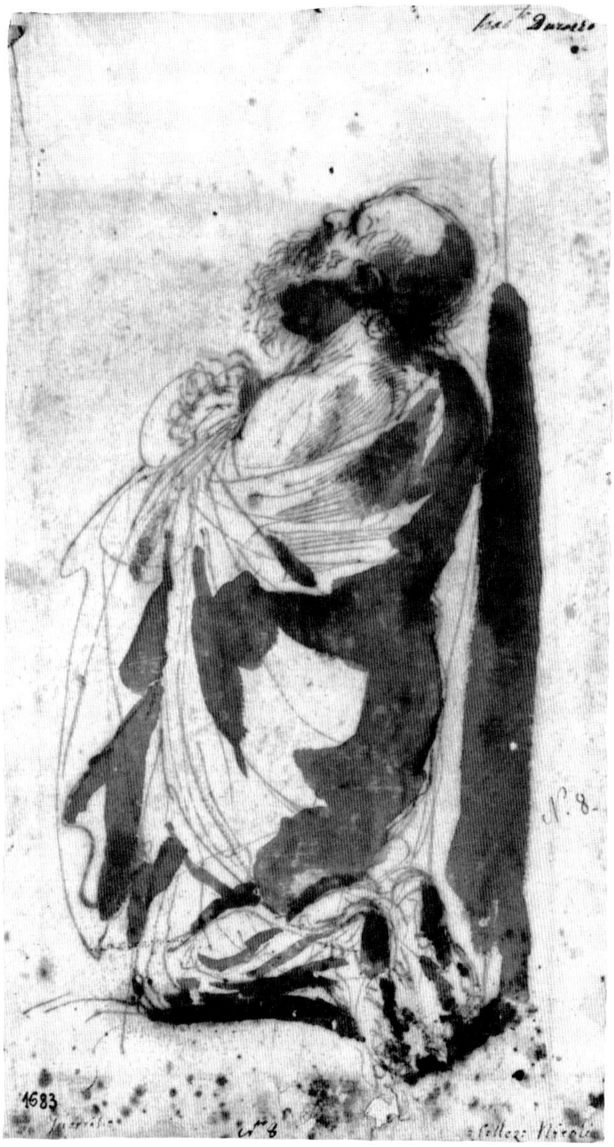

Fig. 10 (above) *Study for a kneeling Figure of St Jerome.* Pen and brown ink and brown wash, 262 × 144 mm (Genoa, Palazzo Rosso, inv. no. 1683). See No. 56

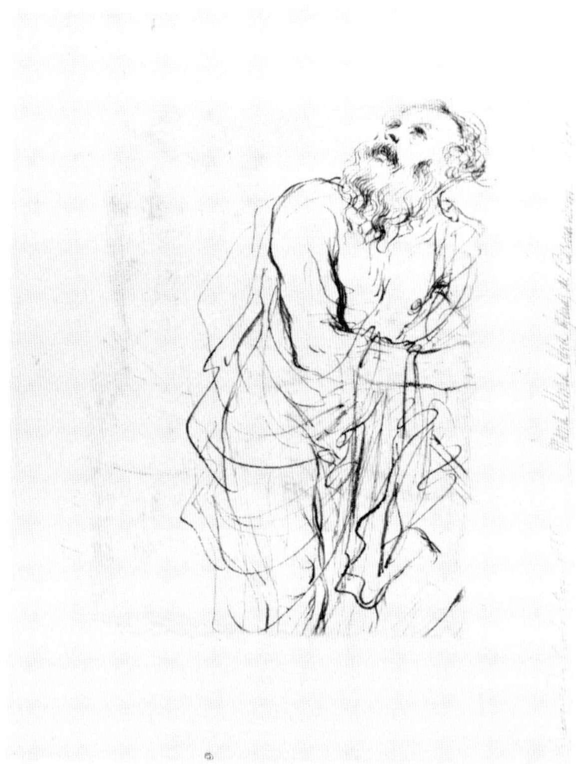

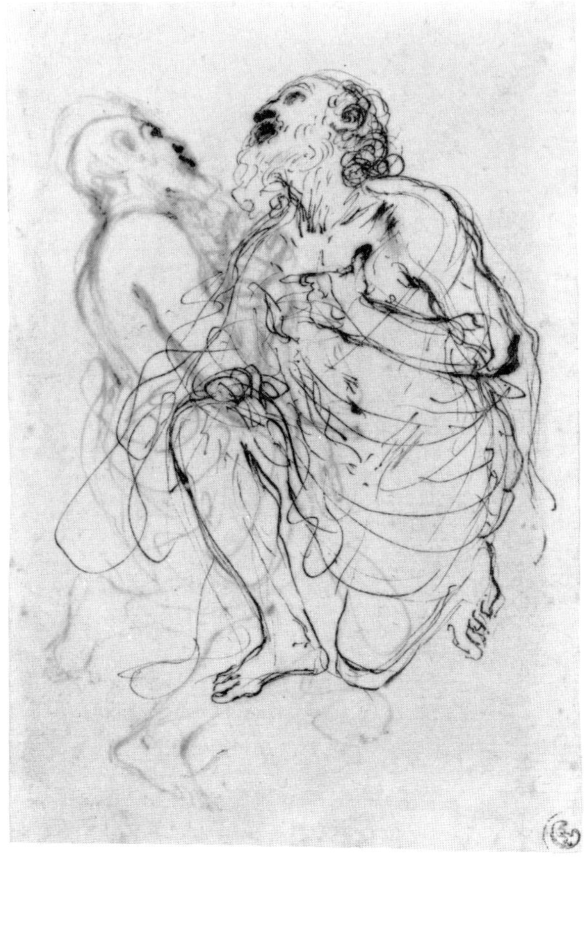

Fig. 11 (top right) *Study for a Figure of St Jerome.* Pen and brown ink, 251 × 199 mm (*verso* of a drawing formerly Christie's, London). See No. 56

Fig. 12 (bottom right) *Study for a Figure of St Jerome.* Pen and brown ink, 242 × 163 mm (*recto* of a drawing formerly Christie's, London). See No. 56

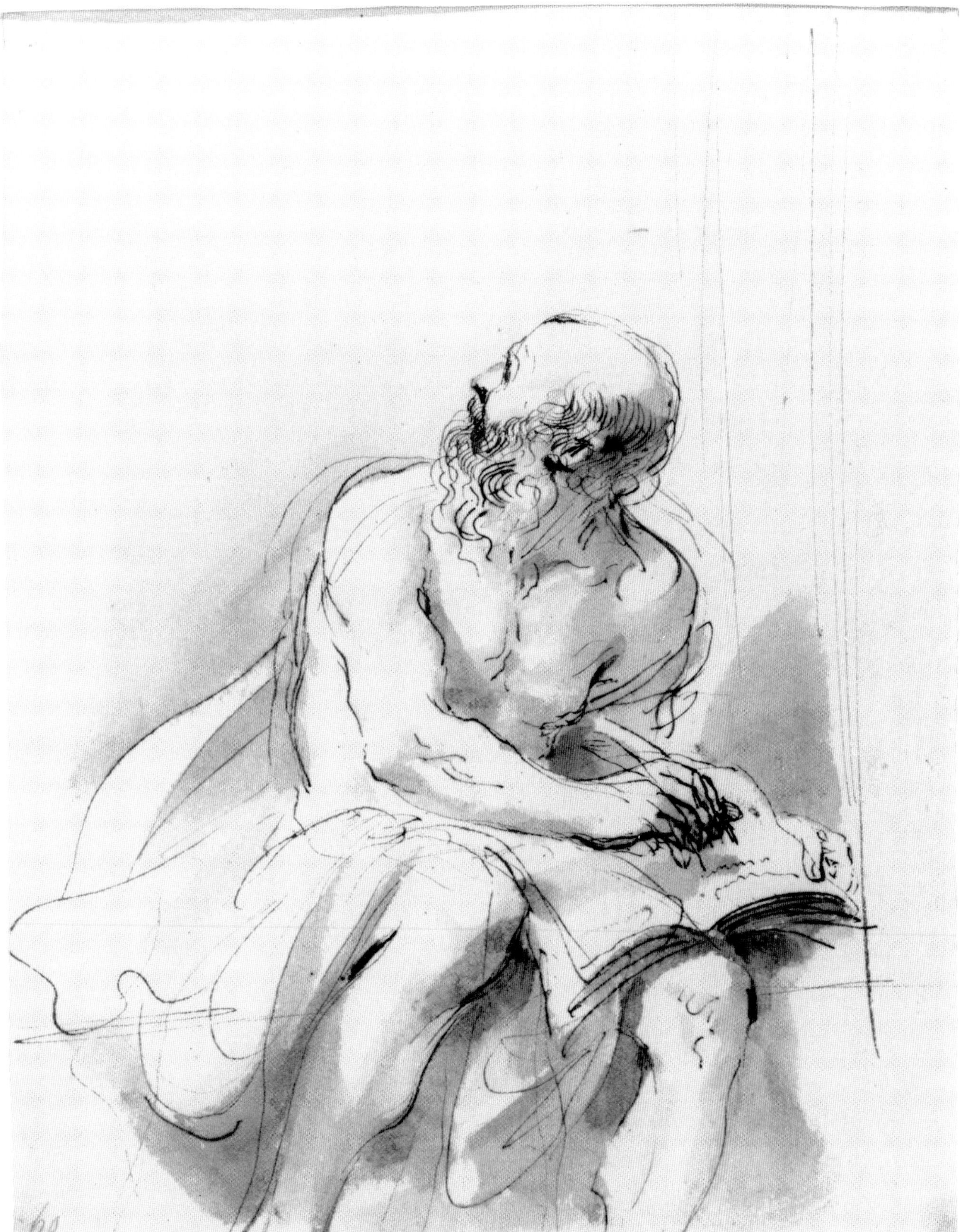

56

57 Jupiter and Semele

(*see colour pl. 12*)

Pen and brown ink. 171 × 240mm

Windsor Castle, Royal Library, inv. no. 2758.

Provenance: Casa Gennari; King George III.

Literature: M & T, 1989, no. 36.

Semele was the daughter of Harmonia and Cadmus, who founded the city of Thebes. She was beloved by Jupiter, by whom she was with child. Juno, prompted by jealousy, appeared to Semele in the form of her aged nurse Beroë and persuaded her to ask Jupiter to visit her in the same splendour and majesty with which he appeared to Juno. Jupiter warned Semele of the danger of her request; but as he had promised to grant her whatever she desired, he had to comply with her prayer. He thus appeared before her as the god of thunder and Semele was consumed by the lightning. Mercury, however, saved her unborn child (who became the wine-god Bacchus) by sewing him into Jupiter's thigh.

An engraving by Giovanni Battista Pasqualini, dated 1626 and dedicated to the Marchese Nicolò Estense Tassoni (Bertelà, 1973, no. 817; B, 1988, p. 64, no. 91; and M & T, 1989, p. 21, fig. 7), records, in reverse, the appearance of the composition to which No. 57 is related. Pasqualini's acknowledgement to Guercino in the print offers no help as to whether it was based upon a painting or a finished drawing, stating simply, '*Jo.s Fran.cus Centensis inv.*'.

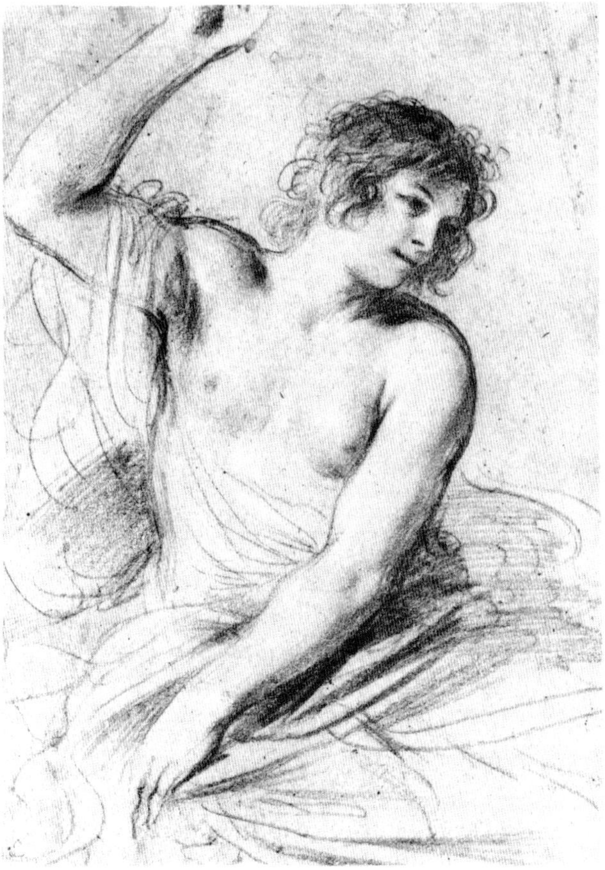

Fig. 13 *Study for a Figure of Semele*. Red and white chalk on blue-grey paper, 299 × 212 mm (Vienna, Albertina, inv. no. 2395). See No. 57

The early sources on Guercino's *oeuvre* are silent about a painting of *Jupiter and Semele* from the middle of the 1620s, or, for that matter, from any other period in his career. No such work appears in Malvasia's list of the artist's commissions. Nor is one mentioned in the Account Book (the *Libro dei Conti*), though this fact is not surprising since it was started only in 1629. However, D.ssa Arabella Cifani and Dott. Franco Monetti have kindly brought our attention to two references to a picture by Guercino of *Jupiter and Semele* once in the collection of the royal House of Savoy, which might well have corresponded to the composition of Pasqualini's print. In an inventory drawn up in 1635 by the Roman painter Antonio della Cornia of the pictures belonging to His Royal Highness Duke Vittorio Amedeo I in the Palazzo di Torino at Mirafiori, outside Turin, item no. 318, in the Camera delle Muse, was a 'Giove col fulmine in mano, che viene alla volta di una donna mezzo ignuda. *Del Guercino*. Buono. A. p. $2\frac{1}{2}$; L. p. 3.' (Vesme, 1897, p. 47). What is clearly the same picture is described in another seventeenth-century inventory as decorating the Palazzo di S. Giovanni (now the Palazzo Vecchio) also in Turin: 'Altro alto piedi doi et largo doi e mezzo, rappresentante *Giove col folgore in mano che si avicina ad una donna meza nuda*, di mano del pittore Guercino da Cento' (Rovere, 1858, p. 59).

Moreover, Cifani and Monetti have noted that the Roman painter Agostino Tassi (1580–1644), when acting as artistic agent to the Cardinal Prince Maurice of Savoy, is documented as having received 37 scudi on 30 April 1625 to buy ultramarine for the picture which 'il signor Giovanni Guercino' was painting 'per servizio di S. A.' (Vesme, 1963–8, III, p. 1038). The fact that this payment was made on behalf of a Prince of the House of Savoy during the year before that given on Pasqualini's print of *Jupiter and Semele*, together with the appearance of a picture of this very subject-matter in the 1635 inventory, leads one to suppose that Pasqualini's print of 1626 is likely to have been made after the painting which Guercino had in hand for the Cardinal Prince in 1625. Unfortunately the present whereabouts of the picture are not known.

No. 57, which is drawn to a smaller scale than Pasqualini's print, shows a line as brilliant and fluid as that seen in the best of Guercino's pen studies for his decoration in Piacenza Cathedral (see Nos. 59–60). There are numerous variations in detail between the composition adumbrated in the drawing and in the finished result, as recorded by Pasqualini. That Guercino was working towards a picture is further supported by the existence of a previously unidentified chalk study from the life for the figure of Semele, apparently drawn from the male model, in the Albertina, Vienna (inv. no. 2395, Sc. B. 457, red and white chalk on blue-grey paper, 299 × 212mm; Stix & Spitzmüller, 1941, no. 238; see Fig. 13). It is unlikely that Guercino would have gone to such lengths to prepare a figure if the end result was simply to have been a small-scale finished drawing. Another drawing for a similar figure, now apparently lost but presumably by Guercino, is recorded in an engraving by Clemente Nicoli (*fl.* 1786) in a volume of prints entitled *Dissegni d'eccellenti pittori italiani incisi di maniere diverse da Clemente Nicoli* (Bologna, 1786); an impression of the print is in the Bibliothèque Nationale, Paris.

58–64 Studies for the Fresco Decoration in the Cupola of Piacenza Cathedral (1626–7)

58 Zechariah

Red chalk. 311 × 200mm.

Windsor Castle, Royal Library, inv. no. 2693.

Provenance: Casa Gennari; King George III.

Literature: M, *Disegni*, 1969, p. 110; Thiem, 1979, pp. 403–4, fig. 3, and 414, n. 10; B, 1983, pp. 70–71, no. 22; M & T, 1989, no. 38.

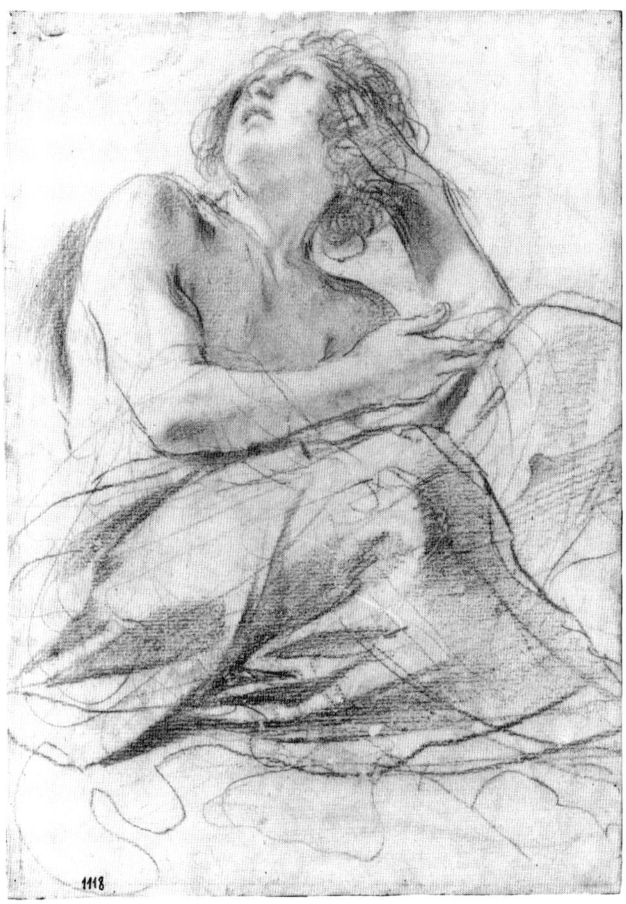

Fig. 14 *Study for a Figure of Zechariah.* Red chalk with stumping, 240 × 172 mm (Genoa, Palazzo Rosso, inv. no. 1118). See No. 58

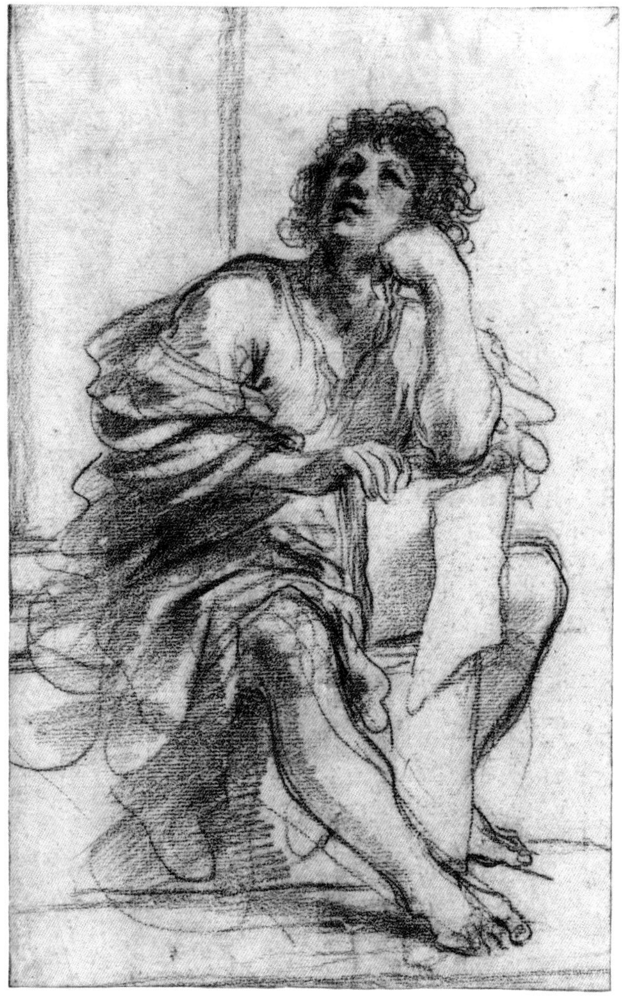

58

No. 58 is now generally accepted as an early preparatory study, presumably from the life, for the figure of the prophet *Zechariah* in one of the eight compartments of the cupola of the Cathedral at Piacenza (B, 1983, no. 21; S, 1988, no. 114 C). In 1625 the Lombard painter Pier Francesco Mazzucchelli, called il Morazzone (1573–1626), had been commissioned by the Cathedral authorities to decorate the cupola with frescoes of the *Prophets*. By the time of his death early in the following year, he had completed only the *Isaiah* and *David*. Guercino was then called upon to finish the decoration, painting the remaining six compartments in the relatively short period between May of 1626 and the end of the year (almost certainly using the same scaffolding that had been erected for Morazzone). In the following year Guercino then went on to decorate the eight arched lunettes on the walls supporting the cupola and the narrow frieze of putti immediately beneath (see Nos. 61 to 64).

The completion of the decoration of the cupola was certainly an ambitious project for Guercino to undertake. It was also an unusual one, since his work was inevitably somewhat constrained by what Morazzone had already painted before him: the scale of the prophets had to be the same, their accompanying putti and angels had to be engaged in similar actions, such as flourishing scrolls with inscriptions and the like, and the overall colouring and lighting within the compartments had to be compatible. A less flexible artist would have refused the commission. Guercino's six prophets are therefore no more than variations on a single theme previously established by Morazzone, that of a seated man accompanied by putti and angels; but Guercino's figures are inevitably more monumental and life-like, and less histrionic in their gestures.

In addition, not only were the six remaining compartments in themselves a substantial area to cover, but also the very height of the cupola from the ground was considerable, bringing with it attendant difficulties of transporting paints and other materials. Also, Guercino was inexperienced in the testing technique of *buon fresco*; his previous commissions for wall paintings had almost invariably been for private patrons and painted *a secco*. It should be remembered that the *Aurora* (see Nos. 32–5), a private commission for a fresco *a secco* and the one closest in date to the decoration at Piacenza, was painted in a room with a relatively low ceiling. Furthermore, from about 1618 until 1621, when he transferred to Rome, Guercino had specialised almost entirely in painting in oil on canvas; and it was only when he was in Rome that he once more began to paint walls or ceilings. After Piacenza Guercino only rarely returned to the *a secco* medium (see Nos. 77–8).

The figure of Zechariah in No. 58 differs so profoundly from its painted equivalent that even the experienced connoisseur would be forgiven for challenging the connection. But enough is known of Guercino's working method to understand that his starting-point was frequently a far cry from the finished result. The claim that the two are related rests principally upon the similarity in the position of the head leaning on the figure's left hand, and in the upward-looking gaze. It is further supported by the drawing's style, which agrees well with others in the same technique with a stronger formal connection with this decoration.

An unpublished double-sided drawing with a study for the *Zechariah* on the *recto* and another probably for the *Jeremiah* on the *verso* is in the Palazzo Rosso, Genoa (inv. no. 1118, red chalk with stumping, 240 × 172mm); in the *recto* study (see Fig. 14) the youthful model, conceivably the same as that drawn in No. 58, is represented in more or less the same pose as his painted counterpart, though the position of the legs is different; in both works the figure is illuminated from the left. The most significant of the many differences in pose between No. 58 and the Genoa drawing is the positioning of the whole figure: in No. 58 the model is seated bolt upright as if he had been drawn directly in the studio; in the Genoa drawing, on the other hand, the figure is shown in strong foreshortening, as would be natural for a figure seen from below.

The other surviving studies for the *Prophets* have been extensively discussed in the recent literature (see B, 1983, pp. 62ff.; S, 1988, pp. 195ff., in the notes to nos. 114 A to F; and M & T, 1989, under nos. 38–45). To these a number of others can now be added. Also in the Palazzo Rosso, Genoa, is a study for the figure of *Hosea* (inv. no. 1157, red chalk on buff paper, 290 × 213mm), of which there exists another, slightly weaker version in a private collection in New York. A third drawing in the Palazzo Rosso (inv. no. 1681, pen and brown wash, 282 × 195mm) is harder to interpret because of its poor condition (and, indeed, Guercino's authorship is not altogether clear); it appears to be related to either the *Hosea* or the *Jeremiah*.

In addition to these drawings in public collections, mention should also be made of the beautiful, but damaged, large-sized study in black and white chalk on buff paper for the *Ezekiel*, formerly on the London art market (sale, Christie's, 3 July 1990, lot 50). A more tenuous connection with the Piacenza *Prophets* exists for a study of a seated nude youth, also formerly on the London art market (sale, Christie's, 4 July 1989, lot 14): the possibility that it too may be an early study from the life for the *Zechariah* should not be lightly dismissed; with its technique of red chalk with stumping it compares well with the study for *Zechariah* in the Palazzo Rosso.

59 Haggai

Pen and blackish-brown ink. 278 × 191mm.

Mahon Collection, on loan to the Ashmolean Museum, Oxford, M & E, 15.

Provenance: R. Udny (L 2248); Lt Col. J. C. Dundas (sale, Sotheby's, London, 6 March 1946, lot 132), purchased by Sir Denis Mahon.

Literature: M, 1967, no. 13; M, *Disegni*, 1969, no. 103; Roli, 1972, pl. 36; B, 1983, no. 18; M & E, 1986, no. 15; S, 1988, under no. 114 A; M & T, 1989, under nos. 38–45.

For the compartment containing the prophet Haggai in the cupola of the Cathedral at Piacenza (B, 1983, no. 17; S, 1988, 114 A). In the fresco, as in the drawing, the figure is shown beardless and apparently engaged in intense discussion with a child angel. (For further discussion of the decoration of the cupola with *Prophets*, see No. 58.)

Throughout his career Guercino's style of drawing with the pen was unusually free, but at times during his work on the Piacenza Cathedral commission it seemed to attain an extra breadth, unusual even for him in its degree of spontaneity (this 'Piacenza' style of drawing was briefly considered by Turner, 1986, p. 843). The simple explanation may be that the painter had to work at very great speed. No. 59 is a fine example of Guercino's pen drawing at this time: the drawing of the lower part of the figure, in particular, constructed by an apparently chaotic mesh of intertwining lines, seems to show the abandon with which this sheet has been executed. There are also several pentiments in the principal study. Guercino habitually made such changes to his figure studies as the drawing evolved, testing different alternatives as he went along. The alteration of the prophet's right arm from a recumbent position on his lap to a more active one pointing outwards was significant, since both the prophet and his child companion adopt variations of this pose for the right arm in the finished

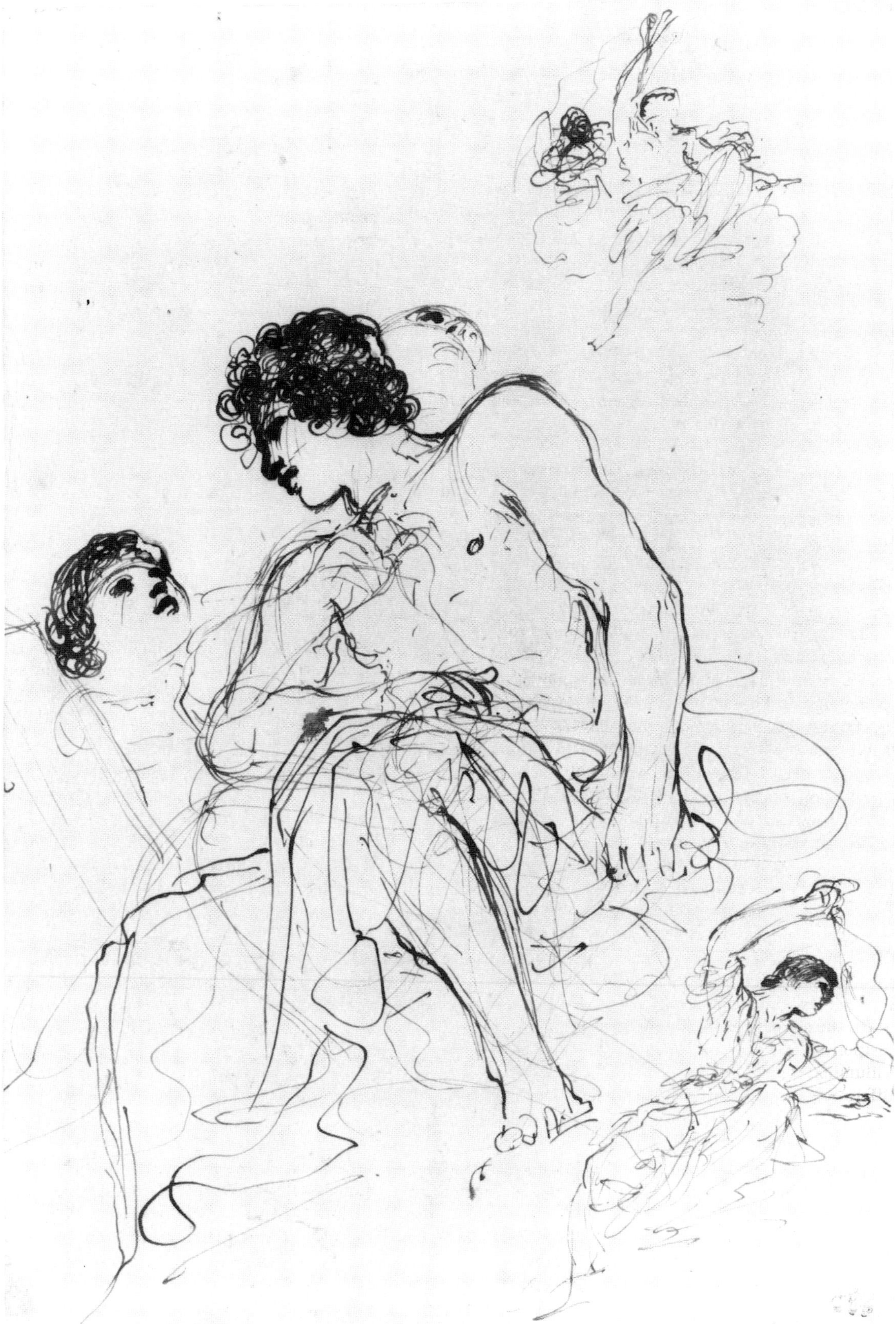

59

fresco. The change to the pose of the prophet's head, showing it looking upwards to the right instead of downwards to the left, was probably made at the same time as the alteration to the right arm, although it was not in the end adopted.

No. 59 is remarkable for its inclusion of two related subsidiary studies drawn to a smaller scale in the margins of the sheet. Although the habit of making such separate studies – invariably alternatives for details of the main study – was common practice in Italian drawing of the seventeenth century, it is encountered only rarely in the work of Guercino. Indeed, the present drawing is the only incidence of the type among the drawings in the present Catalogue. The separate study at the top right appears to show a variation for the main group, with the prophet looking to the left at his companion behind his raised right arm. The other, at the bottom right corner, is of a youthful angel apparently holding a scroll and possibly intended as a substitute for the boy angel. In the finished fresco a similar youthful angel reclines at the bottom of the triangular space of the compartment, holding out an open book in his raised left hand; it seems more likely that the study was intended for this figure.

A red chalk study for the arms of Haggai is in the Koenig–Fachsenfeld Collection, now on deposit in the Staatsgalerie, Stuttgart (inv. no. Barbieri 87; Thiem, 1979, no. 2, pl. 11; B, 1983, pp. 64–5).

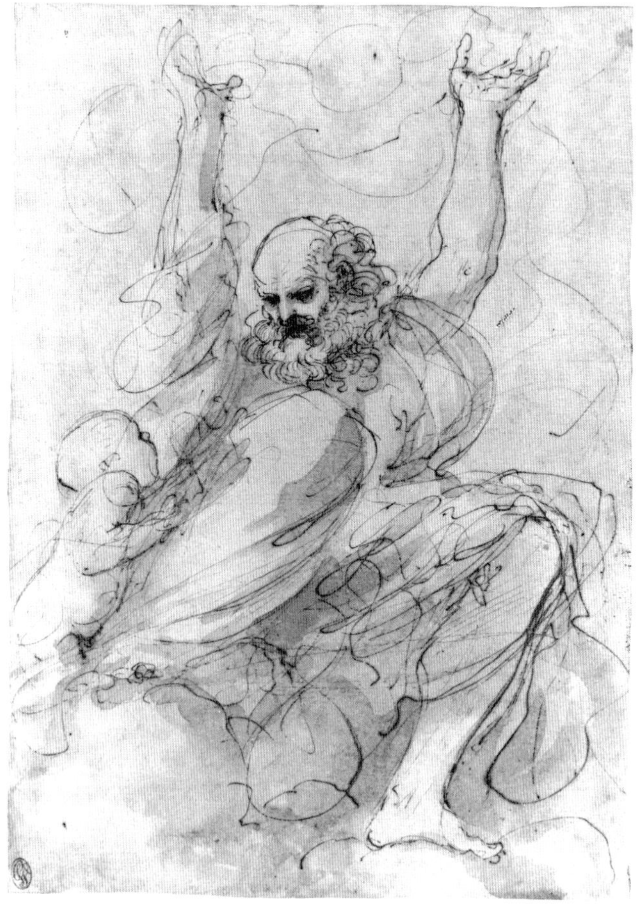

60

60 Jeremiah

Pen and brown ink and reddish-brown wash. 274 × 196mm.

Mahon Collection, on loan to the Ashmolean Museum, Oxford, M & E, 16.

Provenance: G. Vallardi (L 1223); Dr W. Gernsheim; from whom purchased by Sir Denis Mahon on 14 July 1936.

Literature: M, 1967, no. 14; M, *Disegni*, 1969, no. 104; B, 1983, no. 30; M & E, 1986, no. 16.

A study for *Jeremiah*, one of the prophets in the cupola of Piacenza Cathedral (B, 1983, no. 29; S, 1988, 114 F). In the drawing the prophet appears to hold a scroll in his raised hands as he looks downwards at a nude infant at his side. His painted counterpart is substantially different: he wears a turban, looks upwards and holds the scroll in his outstretched left hand, while the accompanying putto assists him by holding it in the middle with both hands above his head (somewhat recalling in attitude the figure of Jeremiah in the present drawing). (For further discussion of the decoration of the cupola with *Prophets*, see No. 58.)

In technique, No. 60 is less experimental than No. 59, there are fewer changes or pentiments in the drawing, and the artist has taken the whole to a greater degree of finish by applying wash, thereby establishing the lights and darks with greater clarity than could be achieved with pen and ink alone. There are four other published drawings for the figure of Jeremiah, in the Gabinetto Nazionale delle Stampe in Rome (inv. no. FN 20023), in the Prado, Madrid (inv. no. FD 327), and two in private collections (see B, 1983, nos. 31–4). In addition to these is a study possibly connected with the *Jeremiah* on the *verso* of a double-sided drawing in the Palazzo Rosso in Genoa (see under No. 58). The seated bearded man on the *verso* of the Genoa drawing is not accompanied by a putto but he holds what is apparently a scroll in both hands above his head, as in No. 60.

61 Rest on the Flight into Egypt

Pen and brown ink and grey wash. 200 × 267mm.

Mahon Collection, on loan to the Ashmolean Museum, Oxford, M & E, 17.

Provenance: R. Udny (L 2248); Sir R. Mond (L *Suppl*, 2813a); Mrs F. H. Brackley (sale, Christie's, London, 1 May 1962, lot 21, repr.), purchased by Sir Denis Mahon through P. & D. Colnaghi.

Literature: M, 1967, no. 15; M, *Disegni*, 1969, no. 106; B, 1983, no. 55; M & E, 1986, no. 17.

A study for the fresco of the *Rest on the Flight into Egypt*, painted on one of the arched lunettes beneath the cupola of Piacenza Cathedral (B, 1983, no. 50; S, 1988, no. 114 L). For another drawing for this same composition, see No. 62.

Early in 1627 Guercino was continuing work for the Piacenza Cathedral authorities, having completed in the previous year the decoration of the cupola with *Prophets* (see

Nos. 58–60). During this second phase of decoration he painted the walls beneath the cupola, alternating four *Scenes from the Nativity of Christ* (of which the *Rest on the Flight* is one) with four pairs of *Sibyls*, each pair separated by a central window. Each of the arched lunettes in which the *Scenes from the Nativity of Christ* appear had originally contained a window, which was blocked to allow the entire area to be painted. Underneath the lunettes Guercino painted a frieze of putti, which also alternated between two types. The four sections of frieze below the *Scenes from the Nativity of Christ* were painted in grisaille in the form of *stucchi finti*, the design of which remains virtually unchanged; by contrast, the four sections below the *Sibyls* were painted in colour and show life-like putti – the poses of which are different in every case – supporting swags of fruit. As with the painting of the *Prophets*, Guercino seems to have worked rapidly but carefully in this second phase. The large number of surviving preparatory drawings for the decoration show how much thought he gave to the design of each scene as well as to the pose of each sibyl.

The central action of the *Rest on the Flight* is that of Joseph surrendering a hungry Infant Christ to the Madonna to be fed; and this same idea was explored by the artist in No. 61. It is typical of Guercino that he should have fixed upon this intimate, human moment in his representation of the theme. Joseph supports the Infant on the ground and guides him towards his mother, while in the fresco, the Infant eagerly propels himself forward, but from Joseph's lap. In both fresco and drawing the Madonna, seated on the ground, undoes her bodice to prepare to give suck to her baby.

No. 44, a study of a mother and her baby, may possibly be for the *Rest on the Flight*, since the baby in that drawing is apparently being suckled. If such a connection exists, then a slightly later narrative moment than that shown on the *recto* of No. 61 was also at one time contemplated.

Besides No. 62, Guercino made several other composition studies for the *Rest on the Flight*: one is in the National Gallery of Art, Washington D.C. (inv. no. B. 30–696), another in the Uffizi, Florence (inv. no. 1677-E), and two in private collections (B, 1983, nos. 51, 52, 56 and 57 respectively). Two detailed studies for the drapery of the Madonna are in the Koenig–Fachsenfeld Collection, now on deposit in the Staatsgalerie, Stuttgart (inv. nos. II/73 and II/91; B, 1983, nos. 58 and 59). Two further composition drawings, recently on the London art market, came to light after the appearance in 1983 of Bagni's study of Guercino's Piacenza decoration (see M & T, 1989, p. 24).

62 Rest on the Flight into Egypt

Pen and brown ink and brown wash. 208 × 300mm.

Mahon Collection, on loan to the Ashmolean Museum, Oxford, M & E, 18.

Provenance: Sir P. Lely (L 2092); (?)W. Gibson (an inscription in ink on the *verso*, *Guercino. 5.2.*, is a method of pricing known to have been used by Gibson); Comte de Pourtalés-Gorgier; J. P. Heseltine; P. & D. Colnaghi; from whom purchased by Sir Denis Mahon on 29 June 1935.

Literature: M, 1967, no. 16; M, *Disegni*, no. 107; B, 1983, no. 54; M & E, 1986, no. 17; M & T, 1989, p. 24.

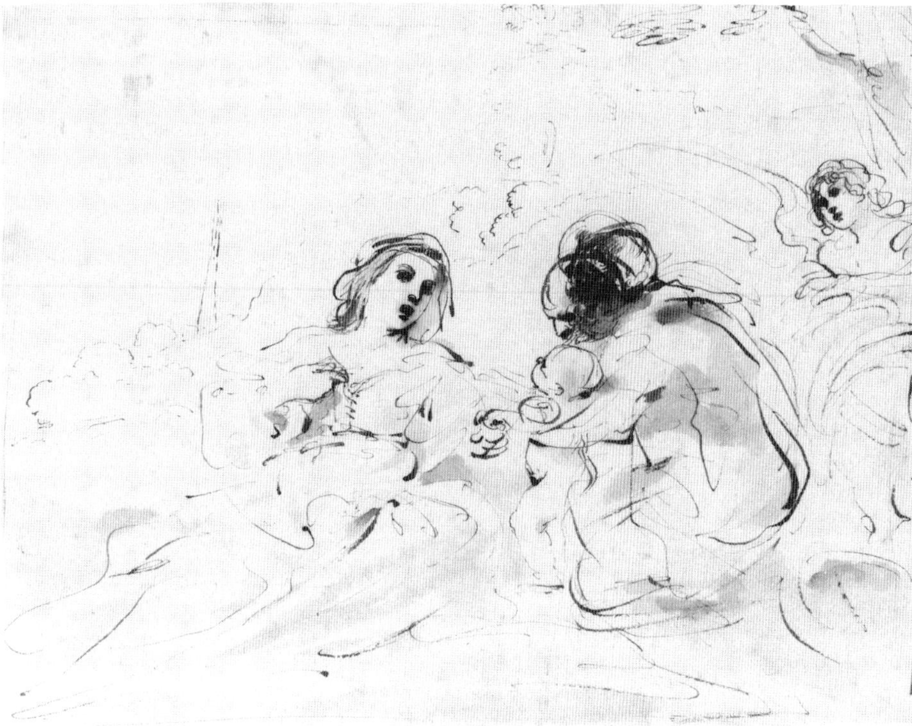

61

Like No. 61, both the *recto* and *verso* studies of the present sheet are for the *Rest on the Flight into Egypt* in Piacenza Cathedral. The *recto* study is unusual among Guercino's composition studies for the four *Scenes from the Nativity of Christ* in its relatively high degree of finish; yet in spite of the artist's pains to complete the study, placing the figures in a landscape setting, the connection with the finished fresco is indirect. The drawing on the *verso* is by comparison no more than a rapidly drawn sketch in which another solution for the placing of the main group is considered: the group is reversed so that the Madonna appears on the right and Joseph in the middle; a winged angel with a donkey is introduced on the extreme left. The highly finished *recto* study compares well with another, probably earlier study for the same composition now in the National Gallery of Art, Washington D.C. (inv. no. B. 30–696; B, 1983, no. 51). This drawing is also carefully finished, but is still further removed than No. 62 from the solution decided upon in the final work. App. no. 97 is a copy of the Washington drawing.

The Washington sheet is noteworthy among Guercino's drawings for the presence of faint squaring in black chalk, one of the few examples of this method of transfer in the artist's surviving drawings. Among Italian seventeenth-century painters squaring was a commonly used method for the transfer and enlargement of a composition from a small-scale though substantially resolved sketch, usually drawn on paper, to another surface, most frequently a canvas or a cartoon for a fresco. An enlarged grid of squares, drawn to the same proportion as those in the sketch, was made onto the other surface and the artist then copied in turn the configuration of lines within each square, thereby obtaining a remarkably accurate, enlarged replica of his design. The appearance of squaring in the Washington drawing is all the more surprising given the lack of an exact correspondence between its composition and that of the fresco; the only explanation for its presence (providing that it was applied by Guercino) may be that the artist simply transferred the composition of the drawing onto another sheet. Since he was not in the habit of using squaring, the question remains unresolved as to how he transferred his compositions from his drawings to his paintings and why so many solutions for a given idea were tested, carefully elaborated and then put aside (for further consideration of this issue, see Introduction, p. 16).

A previous owner of No. 62, the English miniaturist William Gibson (d.1703), was one of the principal purchasers at the sale in 1688 of Sir Peter Lely's collection.

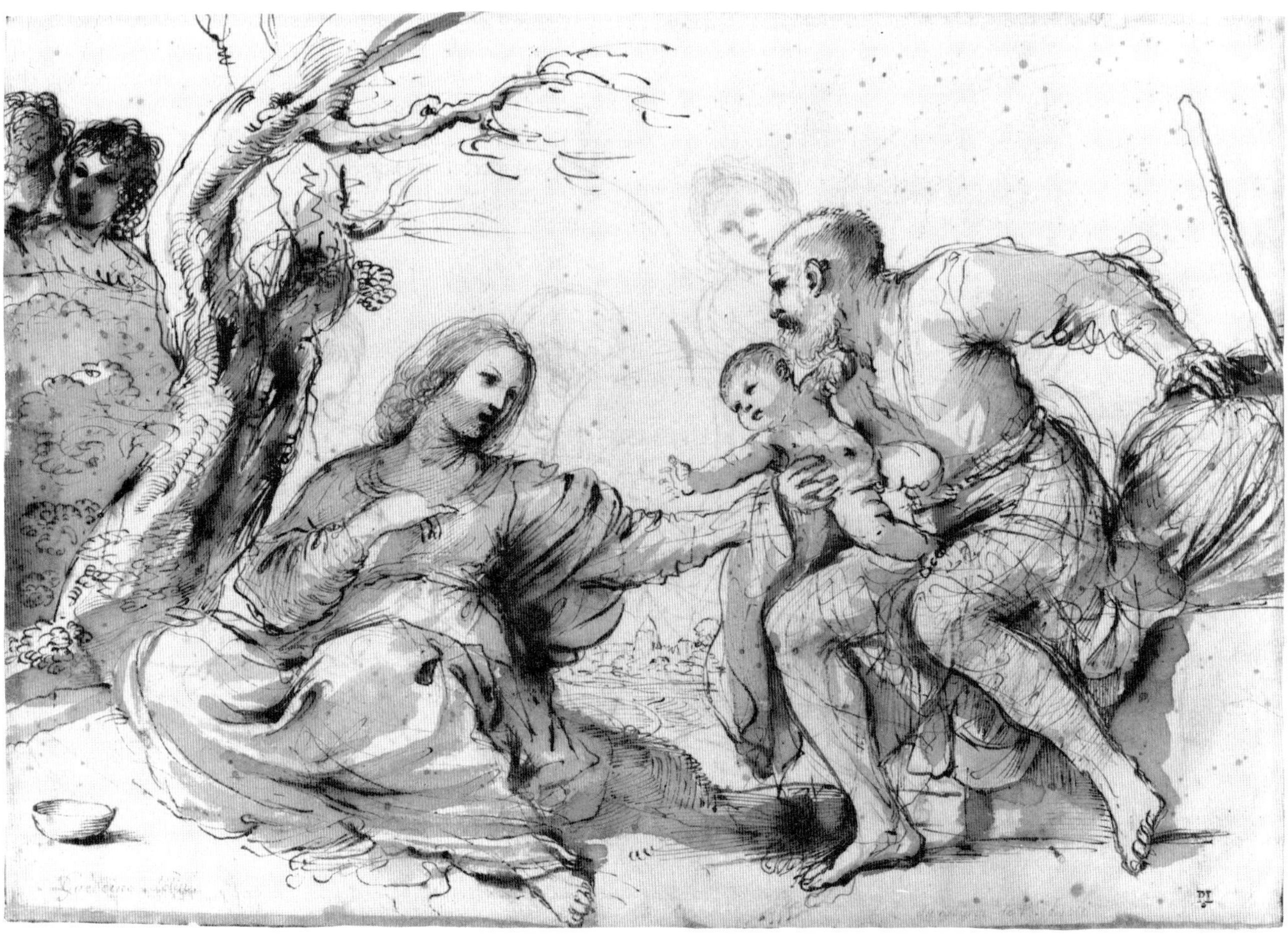

62

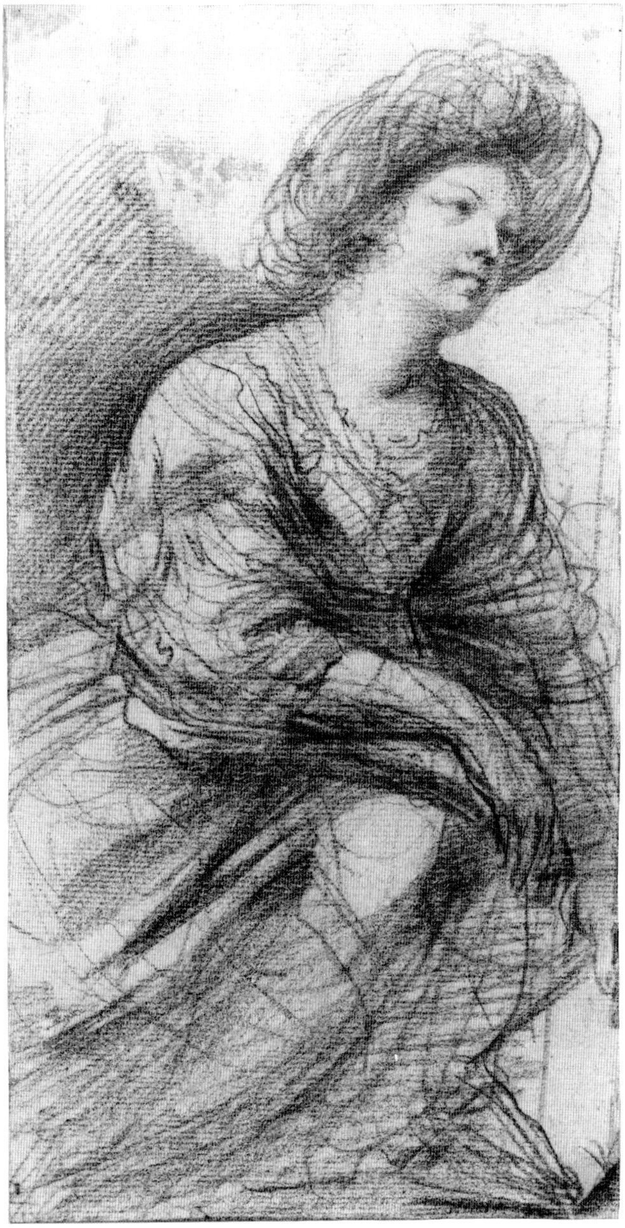

63

Gibson used a coded price system which he inscribed on the back of his drawings, following the name of the artist to whom they were attributed (see L *Suppl*, no. 2885). The inscription on the *verso* of No. 62 corresponds with those on other drawings owned by Gibson.

63 Seated Sibyl

Red chalk. 255 × 132mm.

Windsor Castle, Royal Library, inv. no. 2688.

Provenance: Casa Gennari; King George III.

Literature: M, *Disegni*, 1969, p. 111; Thiem, 1979, pp. 405 and 414, n. 12; B, 1983, no. 68; Turner, 1986, p. 843; M & T, 1989, no. 43.

A study for the *Sibyl* seated to the left of the window in the arched lunette beneath *Ezekiel* in the cupola of Piacenza Cathedral (B, 1983, no. 66; S, 1988, no. 114 O); for Guercino's decoration in 1627 of the alternate walls beneath the cupola with pairs of sibyls, see No. 61. The pose of the figure is much the same in both painting and drawing, except that in the painting the sibyl rests her left forearm on an upright tablet and points outwards and to the left with her left hand. The figure in the drawing has been slightly foreshortened to enable the viewer to understand more easily its pose when seen from below. In his haste to put down his thoughts, the artist has paid little heed to the final appearance of the sheet, the forceful execution of which, with its meandering criss-cross of lines, recalls the handling in pen of No. 59.

A beautiful pen-and-wash drawing of a sibyl in the Nasjonalgalleriet in Oslo (inv. no. B 15246; B, 1983, no. 67) is probably an early study for this same figure, though it differs in pose from both No. 63 and the painted figure in almost every respect. A drawing in the Museum of Fine Arts, Budapest (inv. no. 2318), and another in the Royal Library, Windsor Castle (M & T, 1989, no. 355), have also been tentatively related to the same sibyl (see Turner, 1986, p. 843, and Czére, 1989, no. 38).

64 Three nude Putti with a Swag of Fruit

Red chalk, with some slight stumping. 155 × 288mm.

Windsor Castle, Royal Library, inv. no. 2887.

Provenance: Casa Gennari; King George III.

Literature: M, *Disegni*, 1969, p. 111; B, 1983, no. 74; M & T, 1989, no. 44.

An early idea for one of the four sections of the frieze of fruit-bearing putti painted in colour, just above the arcade in the drum of Piacenza Cathedral. The decoration of this frieze of putti belongs to the second phase of the Piacenza Cathedral commission, which was carried out in 1627 (see No. 61). No. 64, though very different, was probably drawn in relation to that section of the frieze beneath the two *Sibyls*, below the *Isaiah* painted by Morazzone (B, 1983, no. 60; S, 1988, no. 114 M).

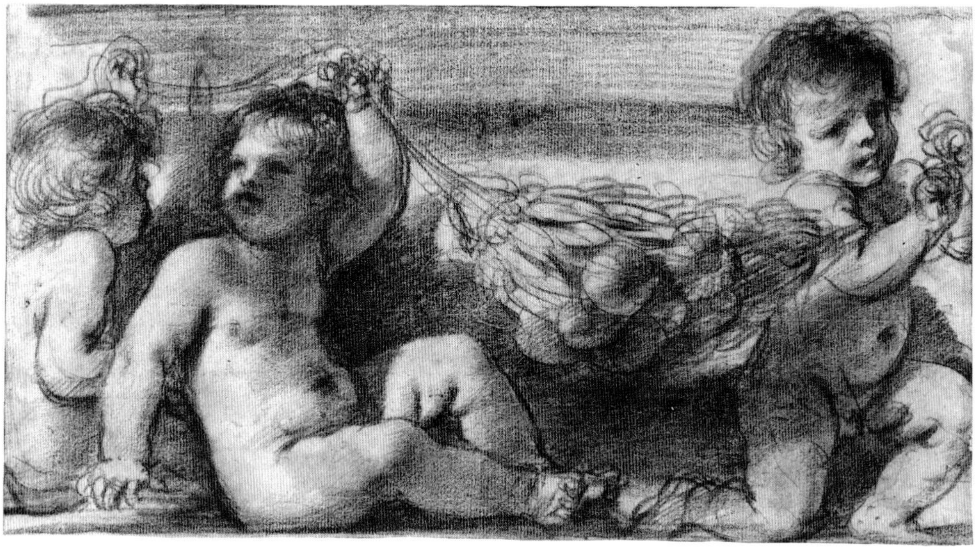

64

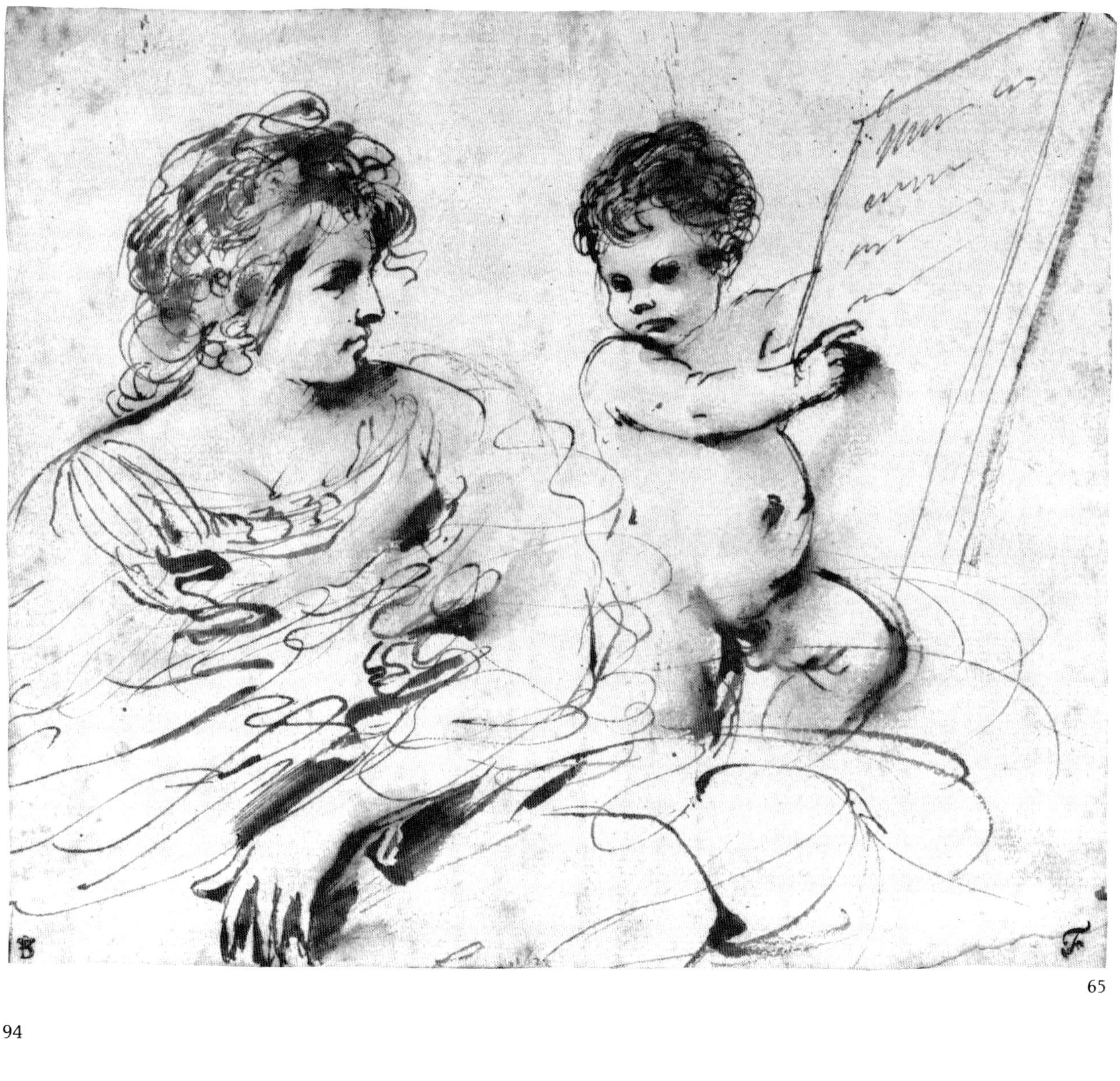

65

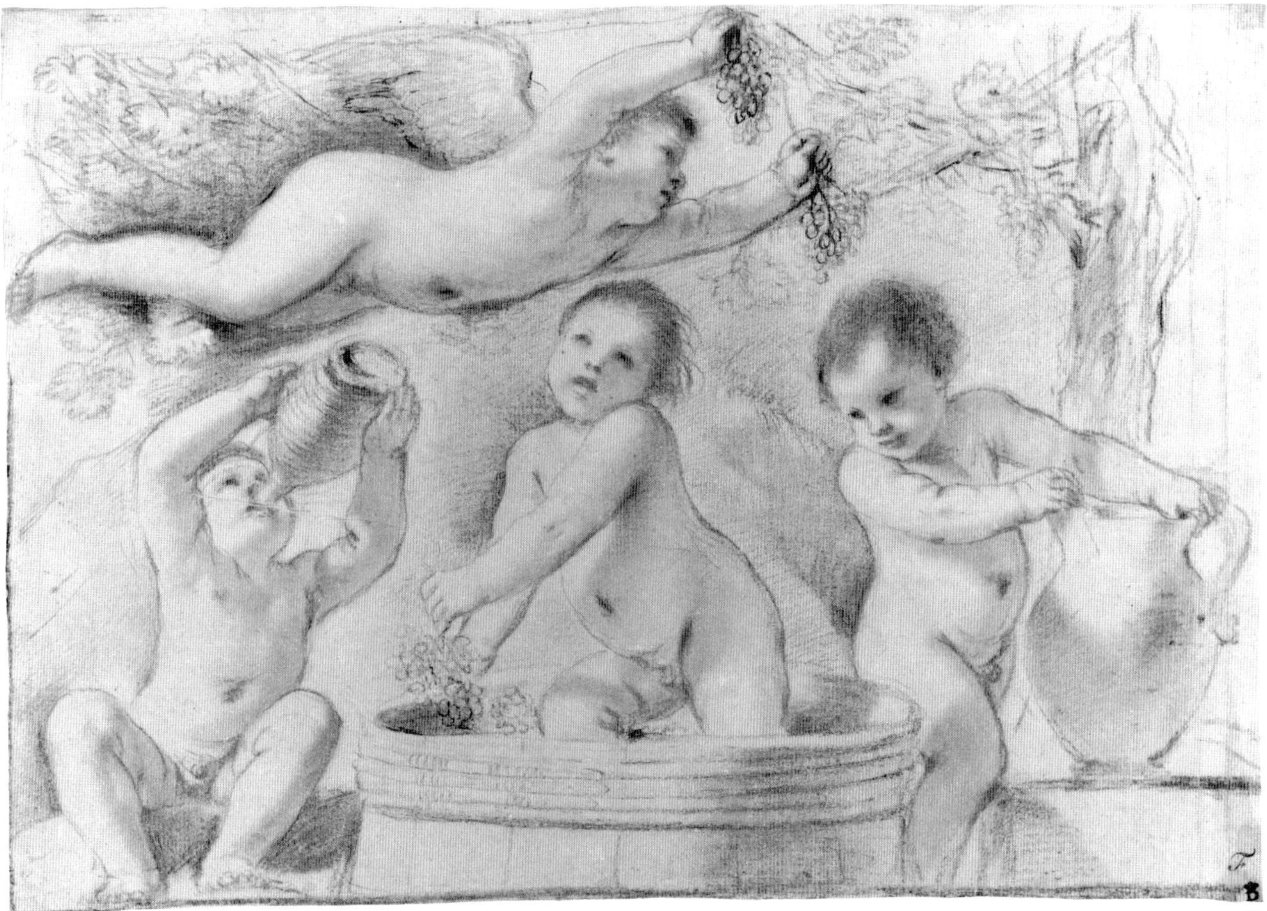

67

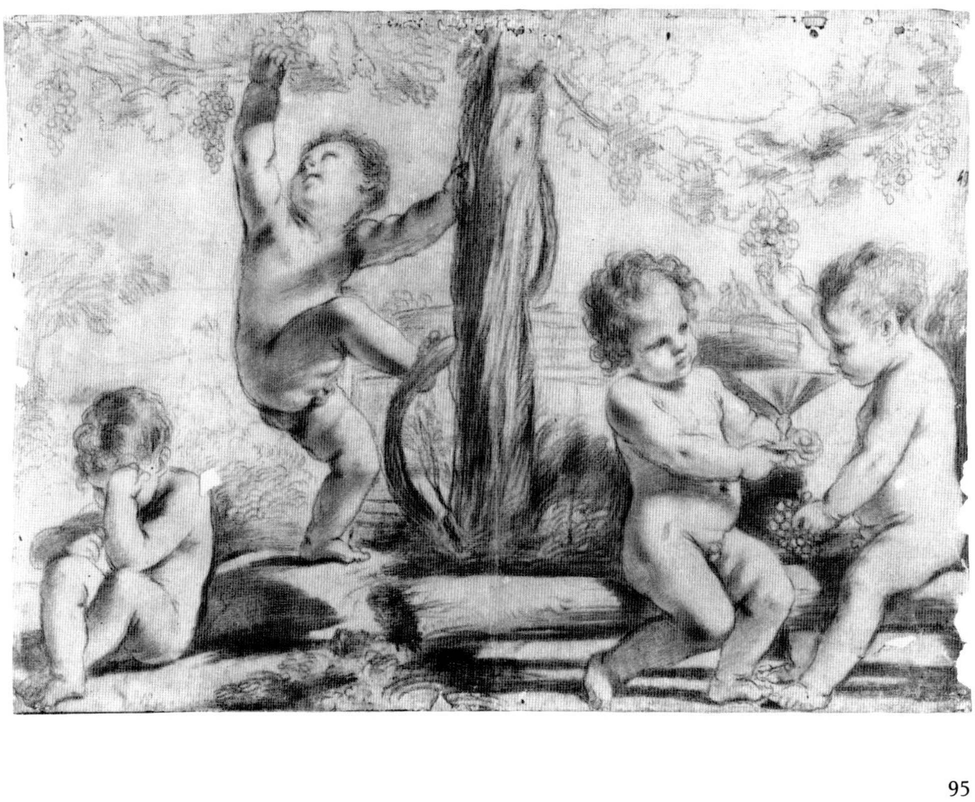

Fig. 15 (right) *Putti wine-making*.
Red chalk, 274 × 396 mm (Modena, Galleria Estense, inv. no. 1147). See No. 67

65 Seated Sibyl accompanied by a Putto

Pen and brown ink and some brown wash. 180 × 214mm.

Chatsworth, inv. no. 514.

Provenance: N. A. Flinck (L 959); William Cavendish, 2nd Duke of Devonshire (L 718); thence by descent.

Inscribed faintly in graphite in the bottom centre, the date: *1623*.

The figure of the sibyl recalls those painted in 1627 in the arched lunettes beneath the cupola of Piacenza Cathedral (S, 1988, nos. 114 M to P, and No. 63 in this Catalogue), none of which is shown accompanied by a putto. The sympathetic psychological rapport between the two figures does, however, resemble Guercino's treatment of the *Prophets* and their attendant figures painted in the preceding year in the cupola above (S, 1988, nos. 114 A to F, and Nos. 58–60 in this Catalogue); some of these are similarly shown in dialogue with putti or youthful angels. In the frescoes of *Prophets*, as in the present drawing, Guercino exploited the contrast between a heavily draped adult figure and the often nude child assistant. The draughtsmanship is compatible with Guercino's style at the time of his work on the Piacenza commission and shortly before. The drawing of the putto can be compared, for example, with that in front in the pair of putti in one of the studies for the *St Petronilla* altarpiece (see No. 42).

66 Three Putti with a Cartouche and a Vase

(*see colour pl. 13*)

Red chalk, partly stumped. 270 × 243mm; drawn on paper apparently from an account book.

Oxford, Ashmolean Museum, KTP 862.

Provenance: C. L. Chute, The Vyne, Basingstoke (sale, Sotheby's, London, 22 June 1949, lot 1, one of a folio volume of 28 drawings by Guercino, bt *Wilson*); R. E. A. Wilson, from whom purchased in July 1949 (Campbell Dodgson Bequest Fund).

Literature: Parker, 1956, no. 872; M & E, 1986, no. XI; M & T, 1989, under no. 212.

As Parker (1956) was the first to point out, No. 66 is a faint offset extensively reworked by Guercino himself. Despite the slight blurring of the image, which offsetting inevitably entails, the artist has succeeded in achieving some remarkable tonal effects, particularly in areas of shading such as the winged putto's forehead. There are also parallels between his prominent belly and the curiously liquid, bulging cartouche.

The purpose of the drawing is not known, although Mahon and Ekserdjian suggest that it may have been a design for the frontispiece of a book. They drew analogies with a drawing in the Royal Library, Windsor Castle (M & T, 1989, no. 212), in which two putti are shown with a similar baroque cartouche. In No. 66 it is not clear whether the three putti were designed as a single, coherent group or whether the seated putto represents an alternative idea. The winged putto bears a striking resemblance to that holding a pitcher on the right of No. 67, but in reverse. It is highly likely that the latter drawing and the study from which No. 66 was offset were made at the same time, probably in the mid-1620s given the emphatic chiaroscuro which is typical of Guercino's work of that period. The original drawing was probably offset and worked up shortly after it was made, although, as Mahon and Ekserdjian point out, retouching was not always carried out at the same time that offsets were made.

67 Allegory of Wine-making, with four nude Putti

Red and black chalk, both with stumping; some touches of pen and brown ink. 207 × 297mm.

Chatsworth, inv. no. 550.

Provenance: N. A. Flinck (L 969); William Cavendish, 2nd Duke of Devonshire (L 718); thence by descent.

Literature: Jaffé, 1987, no. 39.

This and No. 68, possibly drawn at the same time, demonstrate Guercino's remarkable ability to represent the softness of flesh by means of stumping. The technique is achieved by simply smudging the chalk, either with the finger or with a stick of soft paper tightly rolled together and pointed at the end (the stump) or by touching in with the brush a mixture of water and powdered chalk. In Nos. 67 and 68 the former method was probably adopted. Both drawings are unusual in being carried out with two different coloured chalks. Normally when Guercino used stumping, it was only with red chalk (see, for example, No. 53). In the present drawing the two chalks are delicately smudged together in some areas of shadow, for instance in the children's bodies. To the nineteenth-century purist of academic draughtsmanship, smudging was much looked down upon as an effect too easily obtained, and therefore to be avoided. By applying pen and brown ink to emphasise some of the more detailed parts of No. 67 – thus mixing his media – Guercino would have committed a further offence against this over-censorious canon.

Two other drawings by Guercino of much the same date as No. 67 showing putti wine-making should be mentioned here. One, in red chalk, is in the Galleria Estense, Modena (inv. no. 1147, 274 × 396mm; see Fig. 15); the other, in pen and brown ink, is in the Victoria and Albert Museum, London (inv. no. Dyce 321; Ward-Jackson, 1980, no. 725, as School of Guercino). Their precise relationship to No. 67 remains unclear, though it is possible that they may be alternatives, or else related to what may have been a series of representations of this subject. Two further drawings of the same subject, now untraced, are recorded respectively in a School drawing, in red chalk, at Windsor (M & T, 1989, no. 531) and a pen-and-brown ink copy by Bartolozzi in the Albertina, Vienna (inv. no. 1399; Stix & Fröhlich-Bum, 1926, no. 446).

No. 67 is the only drawing by Guercino to have been singled out for mention by the celebrated German connoisseur Gustav Waagen (d.1868) in his notes to his study tour

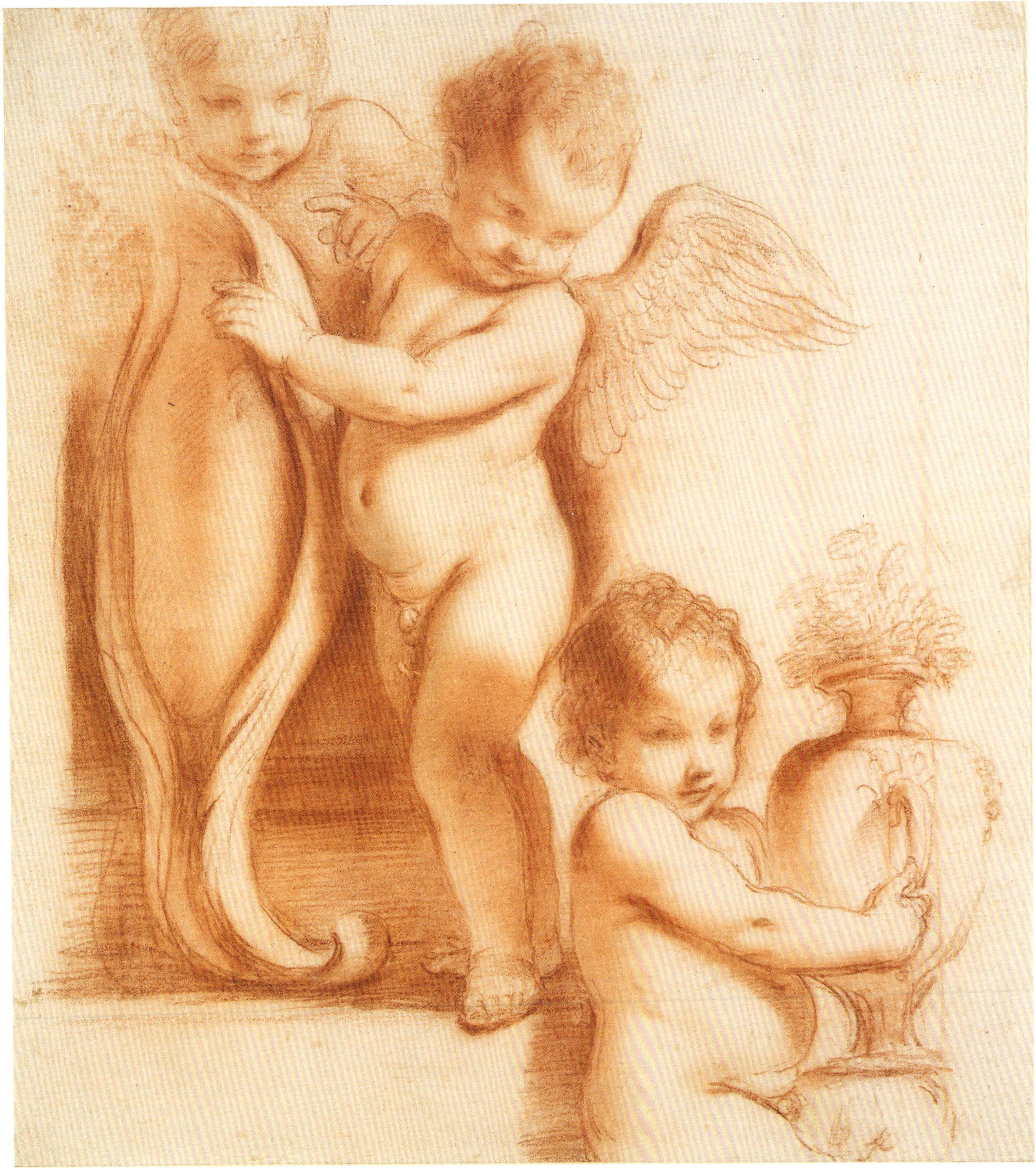

66 *Three Putti with a Cartouche and a Vase*. Oxford, Ashmolean Museum

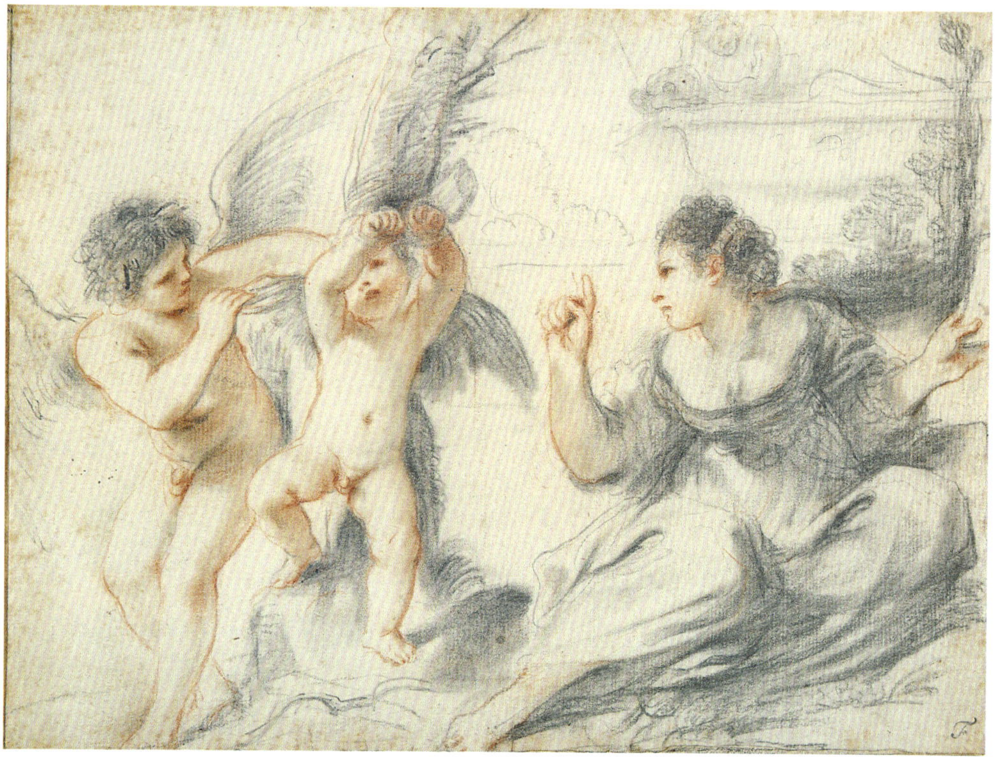

68 *Venus scolding Cupid.*
Devonshire Collection, Chatsworth

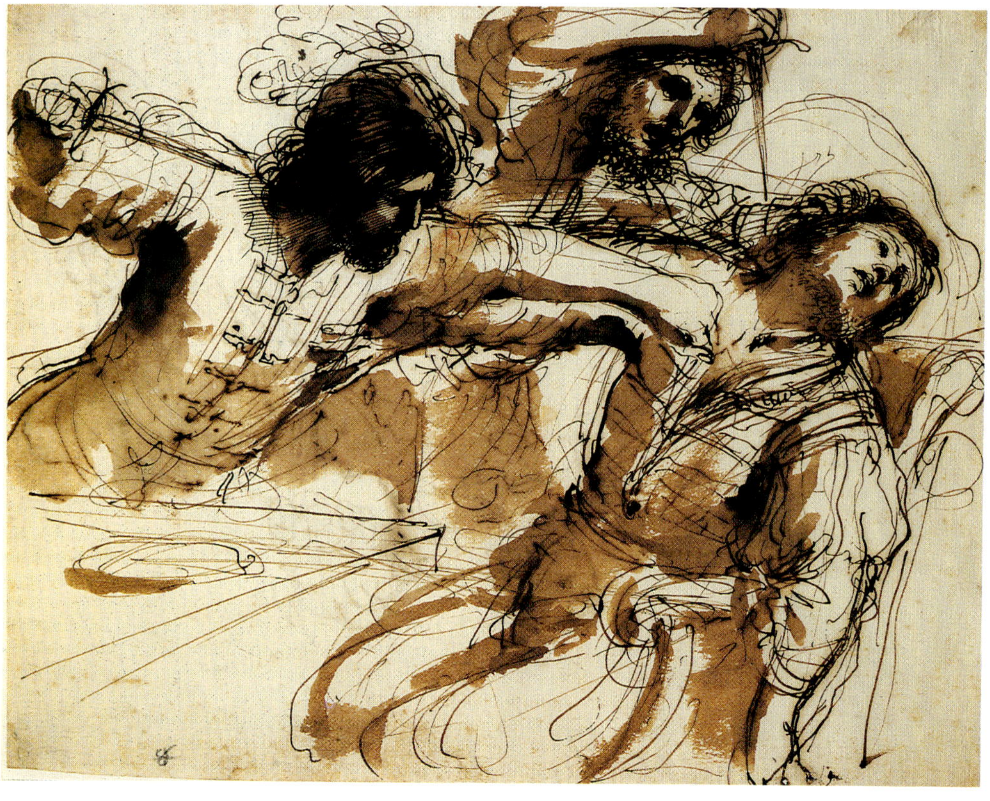

71 *The Assasination of Amnon at the Feast of Absalom.*
London, Courtauld Institute Galleries

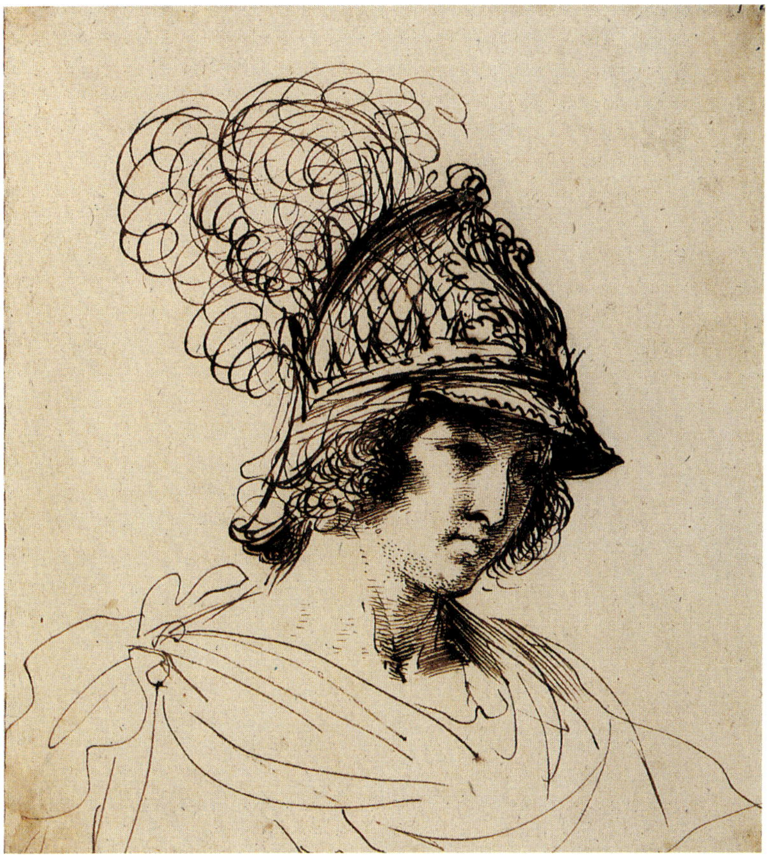

80 *Alexander the Great wearing a plumed Helmet.* Windsor Castle, Royal Library

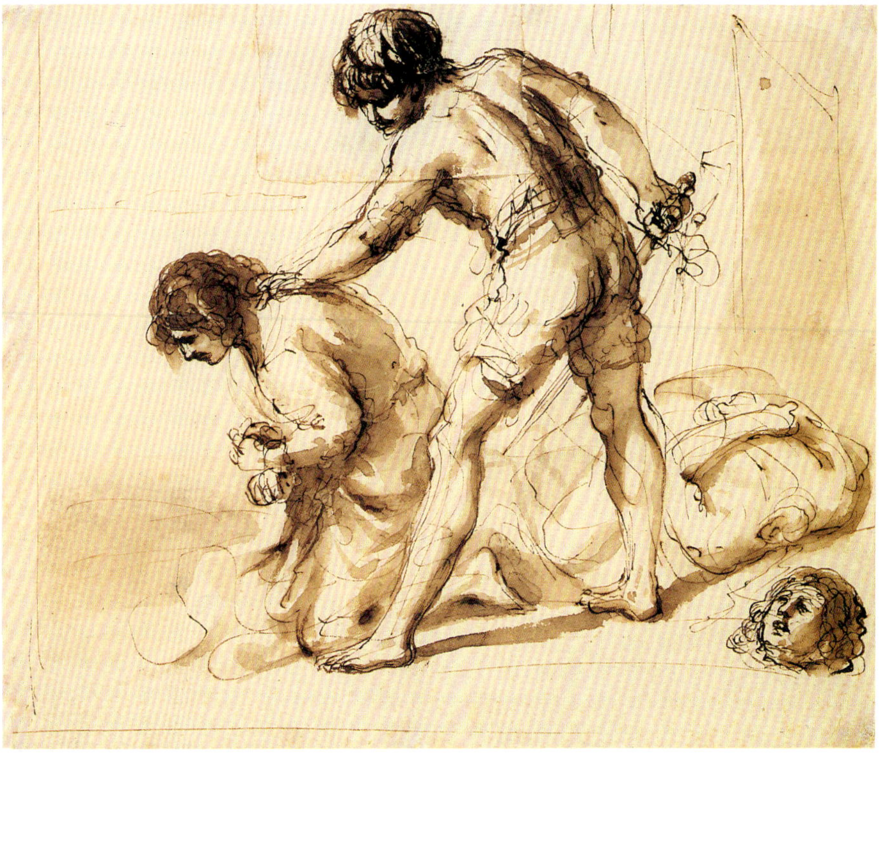

87 *The Martyrdom of Sts John and Paul.* Mahon Collection, on loan to the Ashmolean Museum, Oxford

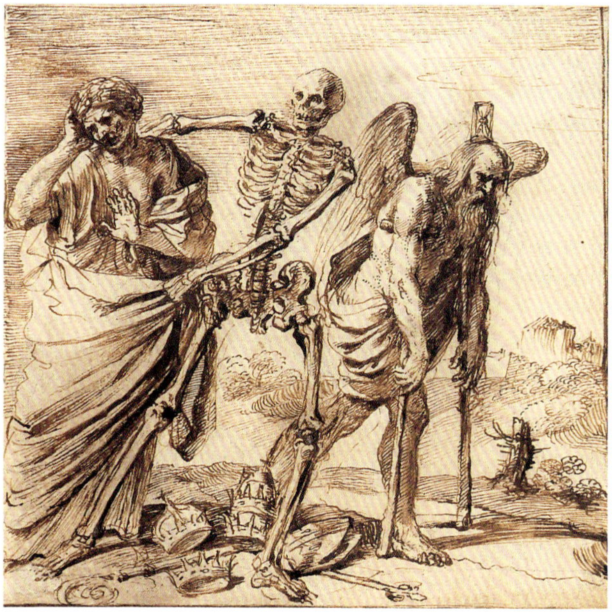

105 *Allegory of the Toll of Death*. Windsor Castle, Royal Library

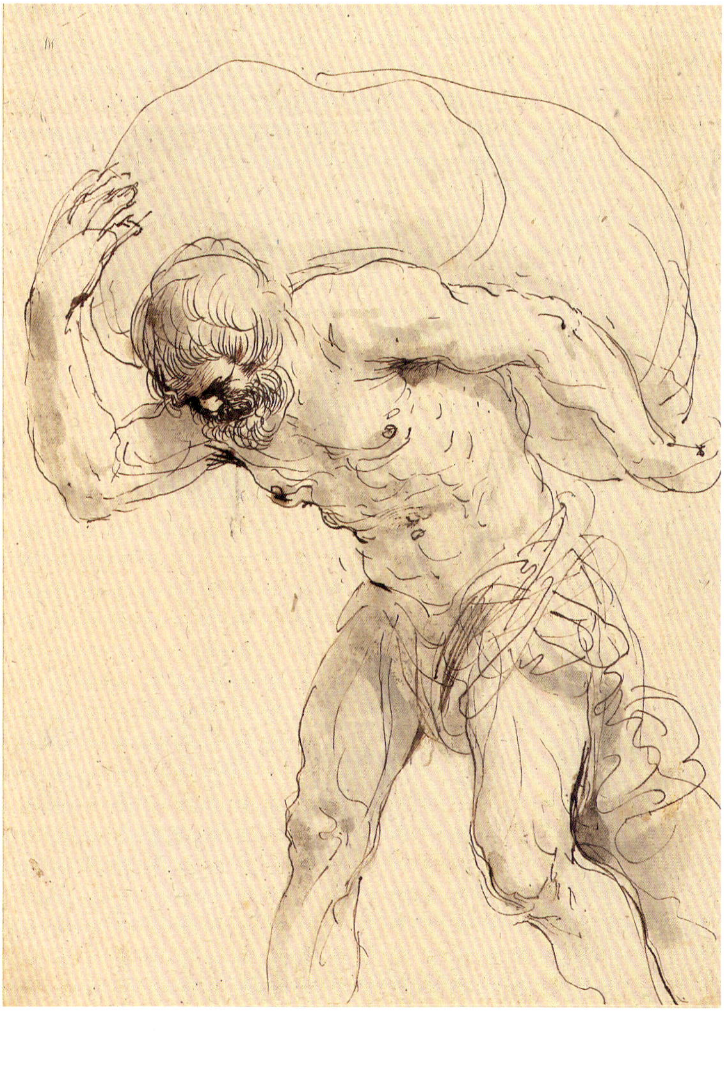

108 *Sisyphus*. Windsor Castle, Royal Library

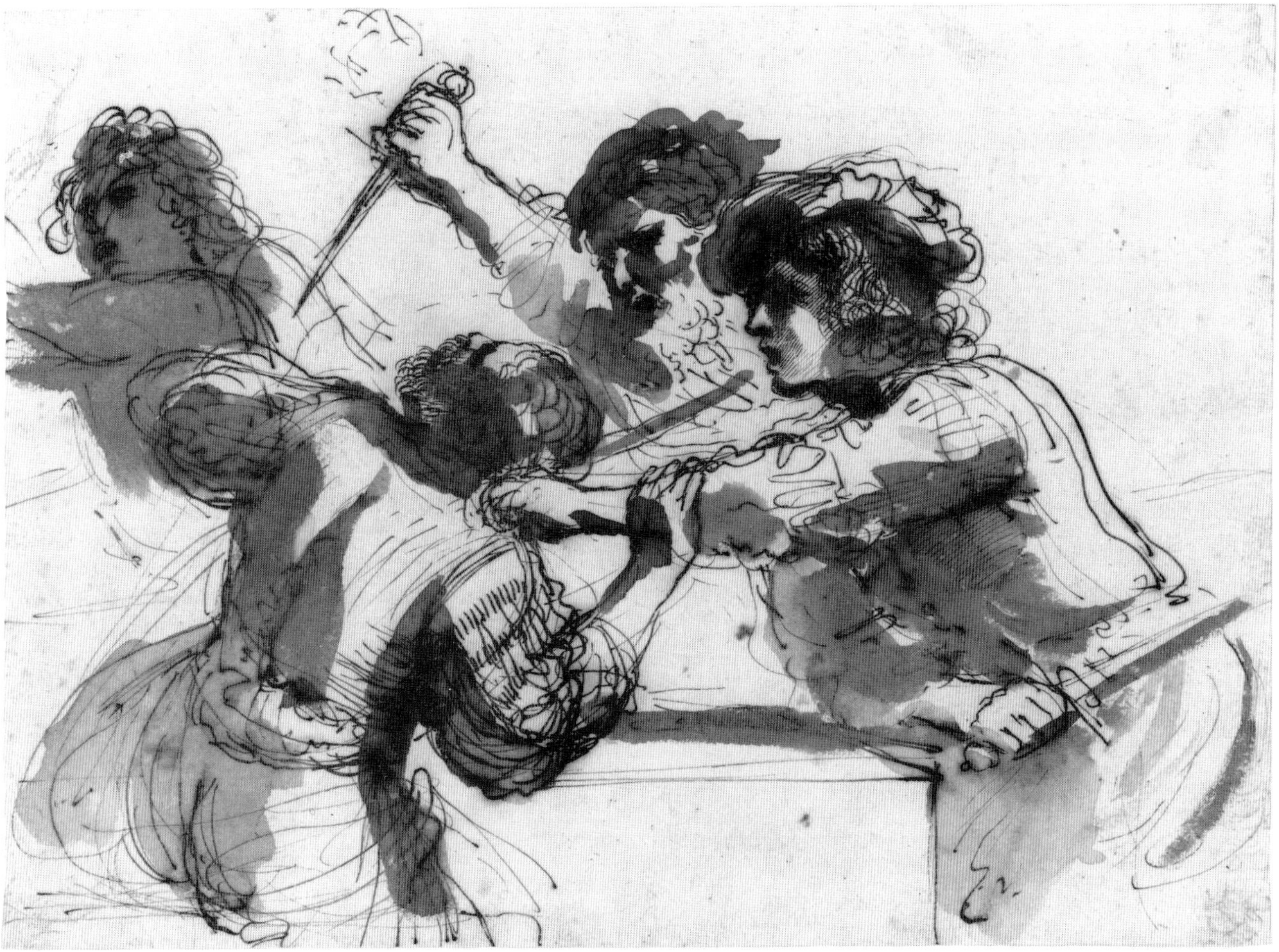

69

of the picture collections of Great Britain published in 1854 (Waagen, 1854, III, p. 359), though he must have seen many other drawings by the master during his visit.

68 Venus scolding Cupid

(*see colour pl. 14*)

Black and red chalk, both with stumping. 192 × 262mm.

Chatsworth, inv. no. 551.

Provenance: N. A. Flinck (L 969); probably William Cavendish, 2nd Duke of Devonshire; thence by descent.

Literature: Popham, 1962–3, no. 31.

From its style, this would seem to date from Guercino's Roman period (1621–3) or shortly after. The artist has well exploited the erotic potential of his subject. The beautiful rendering of the nude figures of Sacred and Profane Love seen in the full sunlight has no parallel in the drawings of any of Guercino's Italian contemporaries.

See also No. 67, possibly drawn at the same time as No. 68.

69–72 Studies for the *Assassination of Amnon at the Feast of his Half-brother Absalom* (1628)

Whereabouts uncertain

69 The Assassination of Amnon at the Feast of Absalom

Pen and brown ink and brown wash. 196 × 273mm.

Windsor Castle, Royal Library, inv. no. 2399.

Provenance: Casa Gennari; King George III.

Literature: M, *Disegni*, 1969, no. 117; M & E, 1986, under no. 19; M & T, 1989, no. 53.

Nos. 69–72 are studies for a picture of the *Assassination of Amnon* painted for Lorenzo Fioravanti and recorded by Malvasia under the year 1628 (Malvasia, 1678, II, p. 367; 1841, II, p. 261). Several renderings of this painting are known (e.g. S, 1988, no. 122), but it is not clear which, if any, might be the original; however, a faithful copy exists in the Pinacoteca Nazionale at Bologna (inv. no. 932).

Absalom and Amnon were half-brothers, both sons of

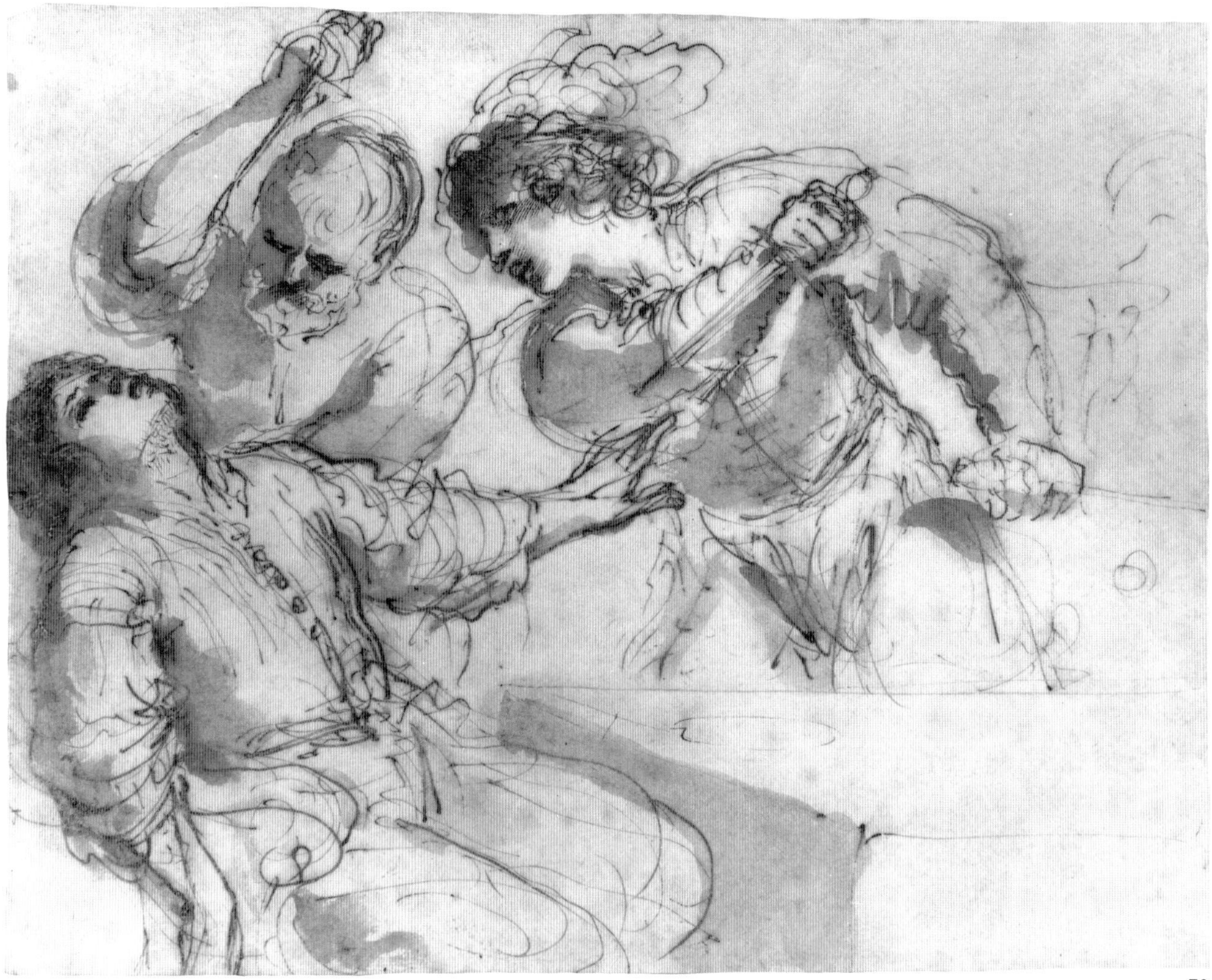

70

King David. Amnon had feigned illness in order to induce Absalom's sister Tamar to feed him in bed, and then raped her, only to reject her afterwards. Absalom later took his revenge: 'Now Absalom had commanded his servants, saying, Mark ye now when Amnon's heart is merry with wine, and when I say unto you, Smite Amnon; then kill him, fear not: have not I commanded you? be courageous, and be valiant' (II Samuel 13:28). Both in the finished painted composition and in the preparatory drawings that led up to it, Guercino's interpretation of the subject is not so much as a Biblical episode but as a contemporary event, with the figures in everyday costume.

In the painted work Absalom is on the left, pointing to his brother Amnon on the right, who is being attacked by two assailants armed with daggers. It is difficult to determine an order for the group of preparatory drawings, since many of the same motifs recur, either pivoted, reversed or transferred from one figure to another. Nos. 69 and 70 both show Amnon on the left with his attackers approaching from the right, in contrast to the finished painting. No. 69 is unusual in showing Amnon seen from the rear, unlike the much more stage-like arrangement of the remaining drawings and the finished work, in which each protagonist's head is in some measure facing the spectator. The figure fleeing in the left background is a motif peculiar to this drawing.

70 The Assassination of Amnon at the Feast of Absalom

Pen and brown ink and brown wash. 204 × 259mm.

Mahon Collection, on loan to the Ashmolean Museum, Oxford, M & E, 19.

Provenance: Charles Rogers (engraved by W. W. Ryland, 1764, when in his collection); George Hibbert; Nathaniel Hibbert; Viscounts Knutsford; sale, Sotheby's, London, 11 April 1935, lot 115; from which purchased by Sir Denis Mahon.

Literature: M, 1967, no 17; M, *Disegni*, 1969, no. 116; Hammer, *et al.*, 1977, no. 22; M & E, 1986, no. 19.

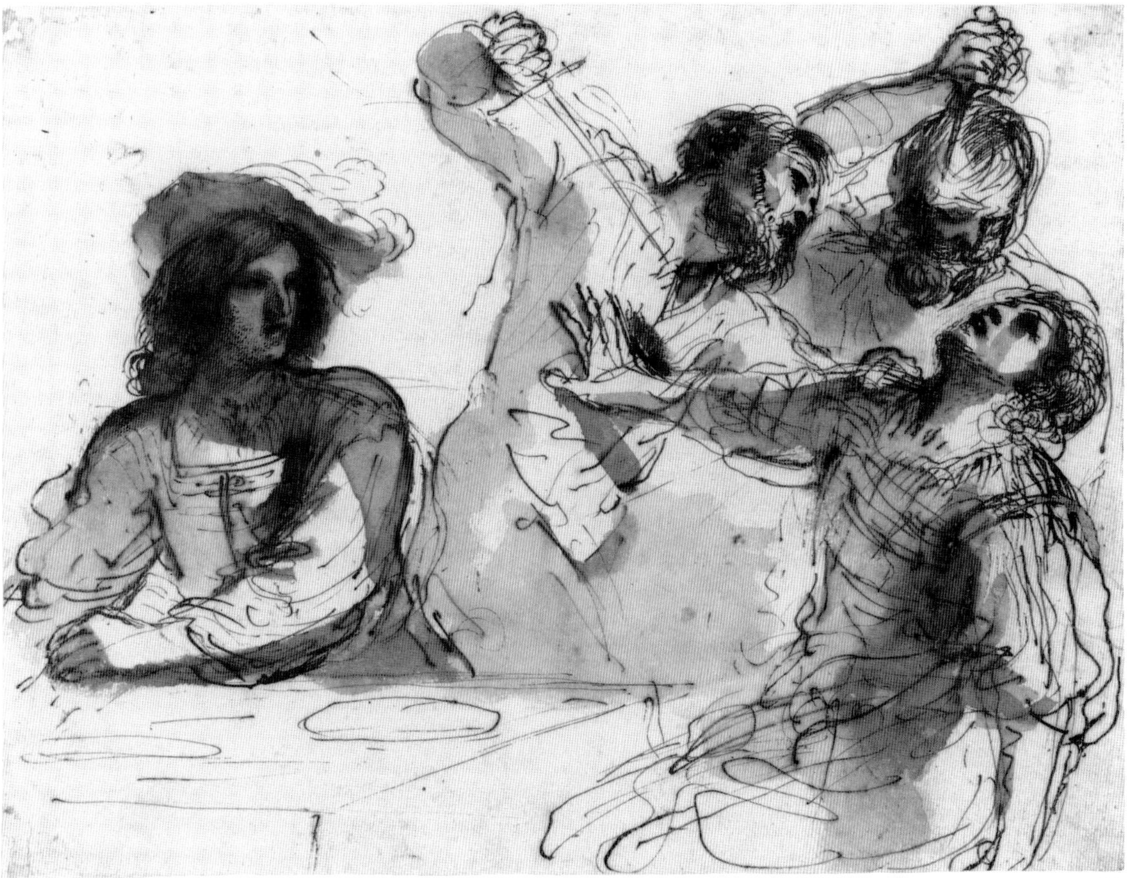

72

A study for a picture of the *Assassination of Amnon*, for which see No. 69. The drawing is similar to Nos. 71 and 72, but in reverse. Like these two drawings, it shows Amnon slumped in his chair with his head flung back and one arm outstretched to fend off one of his assailants, the other hanging limply at his side.

The pose of the older assassin, holding a dagger aloft in his right hand and pinning Amnon down with his left, was repeated not only in other drawings (most notably No. 72), but also in the finished work. Although the pose remains the same, Guercino has shown the figure at a slightly different angle at each attempt.

71 The Assassination of Amnon at the Feast of Absalom

(*see colour pl. 14*)

Pen and brown ink and brown wash. 200 × 263mm.

London, Courtauld Institute Galleries, Witt Collection, inv. no. 1344.

Provenance: Casa Gennari; Mr Bouverie; Mr Hervey; the Earls of Gainsborough (sale, Christie's, London, 27 July 1922, lot 81, with others, bt *Meatyard*); Sir Robert Witt.

Literature: M, *Disegni*, 1969, no. 118; Roli, 1972, pl. 38; Hammer, *et al.*, 1977, no. 21; M & E, 1986, under no. 19.

A study for a painting of this subject, for which see No. 69. Like No. 70, this drawing, in which Amnon is shown on the right as in the finished composition, explores the relationship between the victim and his assailants alone. It is surely the most aggressive of all of Guercino's solutions for this composition, the vehemence of the drawing style echoing the violence of the subject. It appears to have been swiftly executed and contains many pentiments, most notably one for Amnon's right arm flung back behind his head. In the face of such frenetic and dynamic studies, Guercino's painted version is disappointingly static, as is so often the case following the transfer of his ideas to canvas. For example, the powerful horizontal motif of the outstretched arm, which Guercino had toyed with both for the younger assailant and for Amnon, is converted into the static and highly artificial gesture of Absalom pointing at his half-brother in the painting.

A much more cursory sketch on the *verso* of No. 71 also shows Amnon on the right with only one attacker. According to Mahon (*Disegni*, 1969, p. 118), a similar drawing showing only these two figures is in the collection of Signora Valentina Latini at Jesi. Finally, a drawing similar in composition to No. 71, reproduced in a Savile Gallery catalogue of 1929, is in the Albertina, Vienna (inv. no. 34–529).

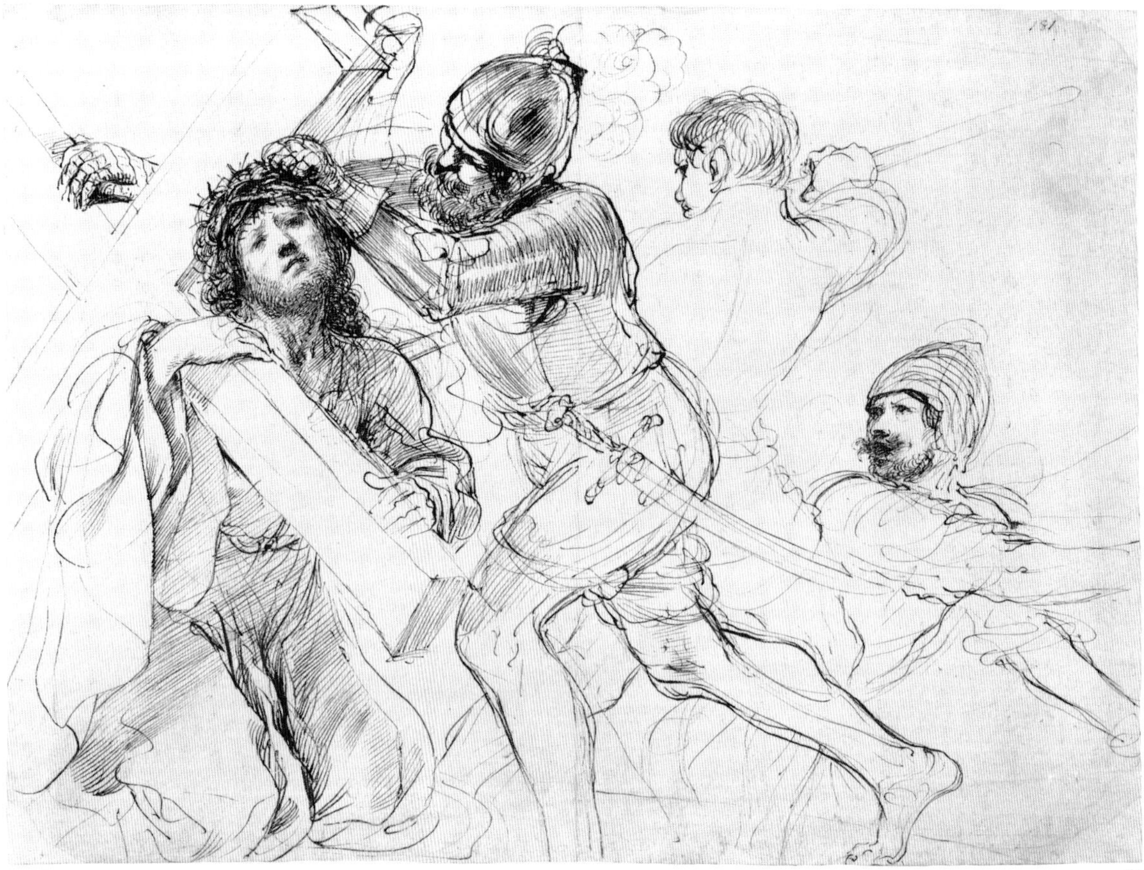

73

72 The Assassination of Amnon at the Feast of Absalom

Pen and brown ink and brown wash. 204 × 271mm.

Windsor Castle, Royal Library, inv. no. 2398.

Provenance: Casa Gennari; King George III.

Literature: Popham, 1938b, no. 461; M, *Disegni*, 1969, no. 119; M & T, 1989, no. 52.

A study for the picture of the same subject, for which see No. 69. The drawing must have been made at a fairly late stage in the development of the composition. It shows, for the first time, all four protagonists together, in approximately the same relationship to each other as in the painting. There is little discrepancy between the two assassins in the drawn and painted works, except that both are shown bearded in the drawing. Guercino decided to mitigate the forward thrust of the assassin who appears in the middle of the composition by concealing his outstretched left arm behind Amnon. Only the poses of Absalom and Amnon are changed. A red chalk drawing showing Absalom standing and pointing to the right as in the finished work was identified by Mahon in the Brera, Milan (inv. no. 614; Emiliani, 1959, no. 72, repr.).

73 Christ carrying the Cross

Pen and brown ink. 279 × 380mm.

Oxford, Ashmolean Museum, KTP 858.

Provenance: C. L. Chute, The Vyne, Basingstoke (sale, Sotheby's, London, 22 June 1949, lot 1, one of a folio volume of 28 drawings by Guercino, bt *Wilson*); R. E. A. Wilson; P. & D. Colnaghi, from whom purchased on 31 May 1950.

Literature: Scharf, 1953, pl. 2, facing p. 352; Parker, 1956, no. 858; M, 1967, under no. 37; Macandrew, 1980, p. 298; M & E, 1986, no. VIII.

One of several studies dated by Mahon (1967) to around 1625–8 and connected by him to a painting of this subject of which no trace remains today. No. 73 is closely related, above all in terms of style, to the *recto* study on a double-sided sheet first cited by Mahon (ibid.) as in the collection of Mrs Jacob Kaplan, which was afterwards on the London art market (exh. cat., P. & D. Colnaghi, *Exhibition of Old Master Drawings*, 25 June–12 July 1974, no. 38, *recto*, repr.). This half-length study shows Christ with only one soldier standing behind him. The position of the soldier, with his head twisted round to the left but both arms extended to the right and the right hand raised to strike Christ with a stick, is extremely similar to that of the half-length soldier seen in the right background of No. 73. The study on the *verso* of the ex-Kaplan sheet shows the figure of Christ alone.

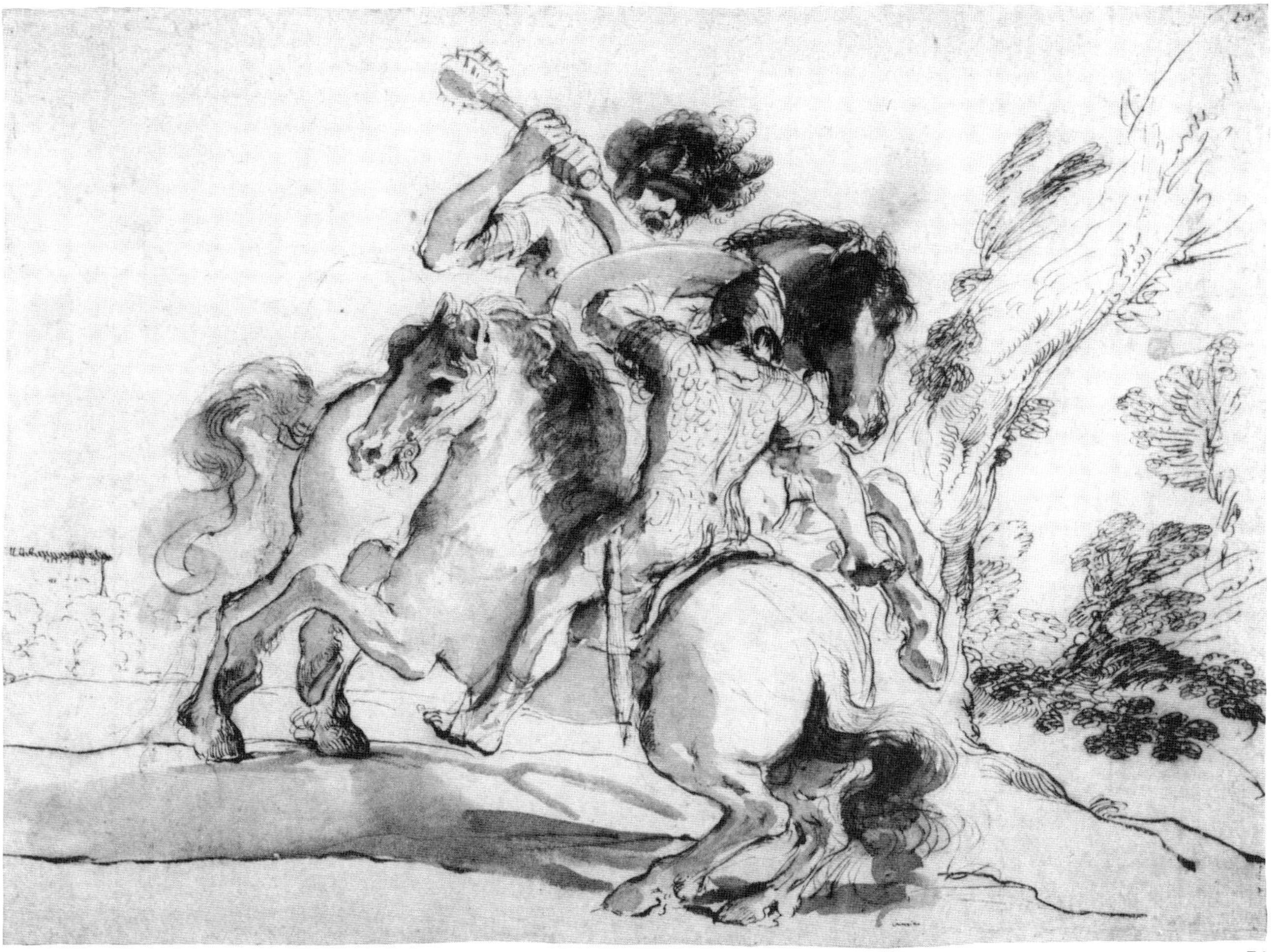

74

There are two other drawings of this subject, which compare interestingly with each other and with the further two studies discussed above. The first is in the Mahon Collection, on loan to the Ashmolean Museum, Oxford (M, 1967, no. 37; M & E, 1986, no. 39). This shows Christ kneeling, as in No. 73, but with his body turned to the left, where a soldier and one onlooker are present. The head of the soldier in the Mahon drawing is reminiscent of that of Christ's principal assailant in No. 73. However, the pose of this figure in the Mahon drawing bears an even closer resemblance to that of its counterpart in a School drawing, presumably recording an untraced original by Guercino himself in the Palazzo Rosso, Genoa (inv. no. 1733, black and red chalk, 222 × 314mm), which shows Christ looking over his shoulder towards a fourth figure, of Veronica, on the right. There are certain analogies between the figure of Christ in this drawing and the ex-Kaplan *recto* study, though in reverse. In view of these many formal echoes, Mahon is probably correct in connecting all the studies (with the exception of that at Genoa which he does not discuss) with the same lost composition, presumably dating from the mid-1620s.

74 Two Horsemen fighting

Pen and brown ink and brown wash. 275 × 379mm.

Holkham Hall, Popham & Lloyd, 142.

Provenance: 1st Earl of Leicester; thence by descent.

Literature: Popham, 1948, no. 17; Whitfield, 1977, no. 49, repr.; Popham & Lloyd, 1986, no. 142.

The purpose of this impressive study remains unknown. From its style, it may date from the second half of the 1620s or possibly slightly earlier. It is an outstanding example of Guercino's work in pen and wash, the wash miraculously fleshing out the forms within the contours, particularly in areas such as the horses' heads. An eighteenth-century copy is in the British Museum (see App. no. 112).

4 The 1630s (Nos. 75–127)

Henceforth, Guercino's work was in great demand. A glance at the list of his commissions in Malvasia's life of the painter shows the varied nature of his work in this decade (1678, II, pp. 367–72; 1841, II, pp. 261–5). This was also the period when Guercino became better known outside Italy. In 1631 Maria de' Medici of France, the Queen Mother, was on the point of asking Guercino to come and work at the French court, when the invitation had to be withdrawn because of the political troubles that occasioned her hasty departure from Paris in July of that year (see Nos. 81–2). (Guido Reni had been Maria de' Medici's first choice, but he had already declined the invitation.) Cardinal Bernardino Spada, Papal Legate of Bologna, who was instrumental in negotiating Guercino's employment by the French Queen Mother, may have gained for him at least one other important French commission (see Nos. 97–102), though he was probably not responsible for the commission from another influential French patron, Louis Phélypeaux de La Vrillière, Secretary of State to Louis XIII (see Nos. 114–15 and 141–2).

Most of Guercino's patrons, however, were local noblemen and gentry from nearby Modena and Bologna, though increasingly he received commissions from other Italian cities further afield. He was now treated with greater respect: in 1632 Francesco I d'Este, Duke of Modena, sent his carriage to Cento to collect Guercino and his assistants, Bartolomeo Gennari and Matteo Loves, to take them to Modena, where the master was to paint the portraits of the Duke and the Duchess. In response to his growing renown, and in the awareness of being constantly compared with Guido Reni, Guercino appears to have developed a still more refined 'classical' style of painting. This stately manner, in which there still survives something of the strong forms associable with his work of the mid-1620s, is seen at its best in two pendant pictures painted in 1632, the *Martyrdom of Sts John and Paul, with the Madonna and Child above* and the *Visitation* (see Nos. 85–8 and 89–93 respectively).

The change towards a greater degree of classicism is reflected in his drawing style in a much more elegant use of the pen, with frequent calligraphic turns (e.g. Nos. 82, 97, 118 *verso*, 124). The tendency to reduce contrasts and create instead broader areas of more neutral mid-tone is also apparent in his drawings in red chalk (see No. 120). In the very middle of the decade Guercino conceived a great liking for indicating these broad areas of mid-tone with extensive passages of fine, diaphanous wash (Nos. 86, 98, 100–102, 104, 112, 115), the graphic equivalent of the clearer, lighter colours of the paintings. These washes are particularly pleasing and powerfully evoke the effect of bright sunlight – their lightness and delicacy anticipating the drawings in this same medium of an artist working a century later, Giovanni Battista Tiepolo (1696–1770). In these pen-and-wash drawings of the mid-1630s the penwork is deliberately limited so as not to impair the effect of the washes, and the ink is often sympathetically lighter in tone than the iron-gall ink usually employed. Several of the genre and caricature drawings seem also to have been made at this same time (e.g. Nos. 191, 195–6, 198 and 208).

75 Ste Geneviève de Paris

Red chalk. 318 × 212mm.

Windsor Castle, Royal Library, inv. no. 2675.

Provenance: Casa Gennari; King George III.

Literature: M & T, 1989, no. 168.

A preparatory study for a composition featuring Ste Geneviève, the patron saint of Paris, which, if it was ever completed, is no longer known. The style and technique of the drawing suggests a date in the early 1630s, even though no such work is recorded in the Account Book kept by Guercino from 1629.

The iconography is complex (see the discussion in M & T, 1989, no. 168): the saint is shown interceding against the plague, and the presence of the angel sheathing a flaming sword above indicates that her mission will be successful. One of Ste Geneviève's distinguishing attributes is a candle or taper blown out by a demon and then relit by an angel,

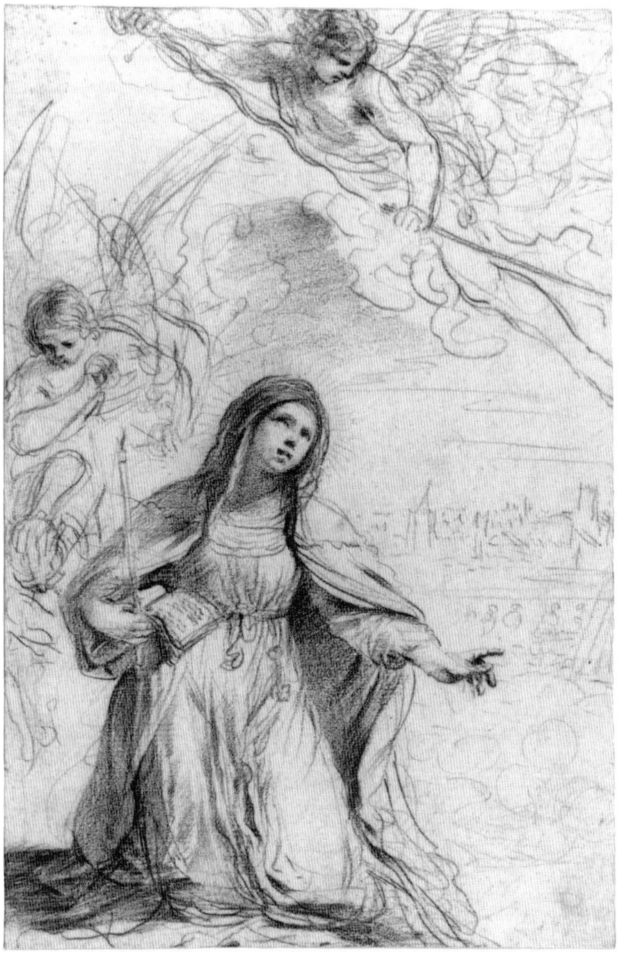

75

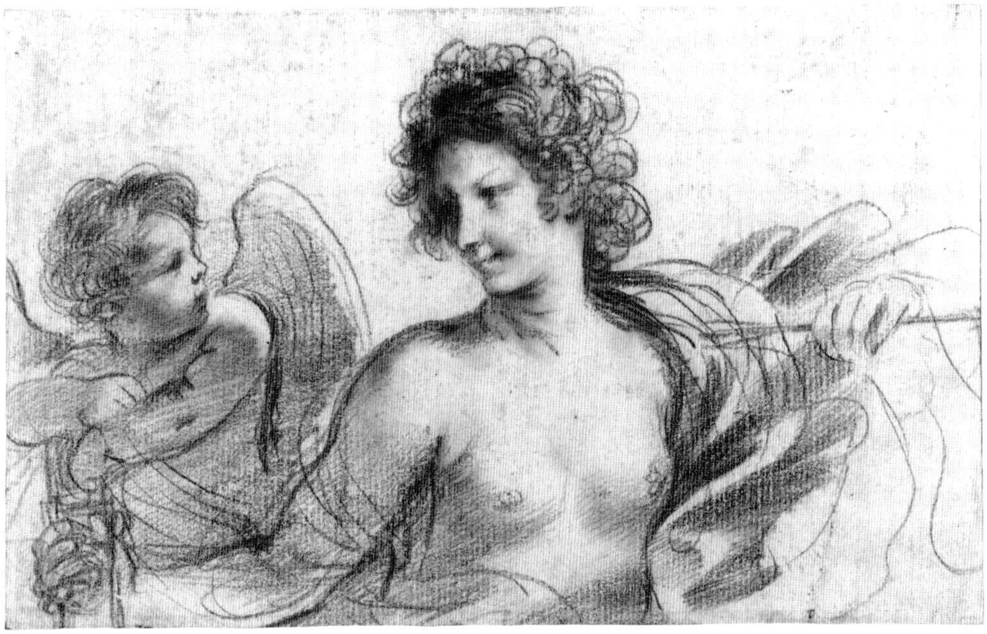

76

an allusion to the conflicting sentiments that her prophetic utterances aroused in others. In No. 75 she holds a candle in her right hand, as the angel relights it with his left while fending off the demon below.

It is not known how Guercino came to be involved in a project with such manifestly French overtones or who the patron could have been. The artist's reputation in France seems to have been promoted by the efforts of his patron and admirer, Cardinal Bernardino Spada, who was Papal Nuncio there between 1624 and 1627, and it is possible that the project came about as a result of his intervention. Mahon and Turner noted that around 1630 northern Italy was afflicted with the plague, which had also ravaged France in the period immediately before this. The commission may therefore have been an extremely topical one at a time of scourge in several parts of Europe.

A pen-and-wash drawing connected with this project, for the lower half of the composition only, was presented to the Pinacoteca Civica at Cento in 1965 (see M & T, 1989, under no. 168, repr. fig. 28). The drawing shows more clearly than No. 75 that it is towards a group of corpses that the saint gesticulates with her left hand.

76 Venus and Cupid

Red chalk, with some stumping. 148 × 241mm.

Windsor Castle, Royal Library, inv. no. 2886.

Provenance: Casa Gennari; King George III.

Literature: S, 1988, under nos. 130–31; M & T, 1989, no. 55.

Mahon and Turner connected this drawing with a painting of *Venus and Cupid* in the Wellington Museum, Apsley House, London, which is paired with a half-length figure of *Mars* (Kauffmann, 1982, nos. 60–61; S, 1988, nos. 130–31). They regarded the style of the pair of paintings and of the drawing as consistent with a date of 1630; and the paintings are almost certainly those mentioned by Malvasia as having been made for Lorenzo Fioravanti, for which three payments were received in 1630 (Malvasia, 1678, II, p. 367; 1841, II, p. 261; *Libro dei Conti*, 1808, pp. 60–61; 1841, p. 308). The figure of Venus is remarkably similar in the drawing and the painting, both in her expression and in the way she is lit; her pose, too, is mirrored closely in the two works, but for the position of her arms. Only in the figure of Cupid does the painting diverge significantly from the preparatory study. In the latter, he is winged and stands facing the spectator on Venus's right as he draws an arrow from the quiver she holds out to him; in the painting, on the other hand, he is on her left, with his wingless back to the spectator, pointing his bow to the left, in the direction of the pendant *Mars*.

77–78 Studies for *Hercules wrestling with Antaeus* (1631)

Bologna, Palazzo Talon

77 Hercules wrestling with Antaeus

Red chalk. 379 × 285mm.

Mahon Collection, on loan to the Ashmolean Museum, Oxford, M & E, no. 22.

Provenance: Dr B. Geiger (sale, Sotheby's, London, 8 December 1920, lot 150); P. & D. Colnaghi; from whom purchased by Sir Denis Mahon in 1958.

Literature: M, 1967, no. 20; M, *Disegni*, 1969, no. 125; M & E, 1986, no. 22; S, 1988, under no. 134; M & T, 1989, under no. 57.

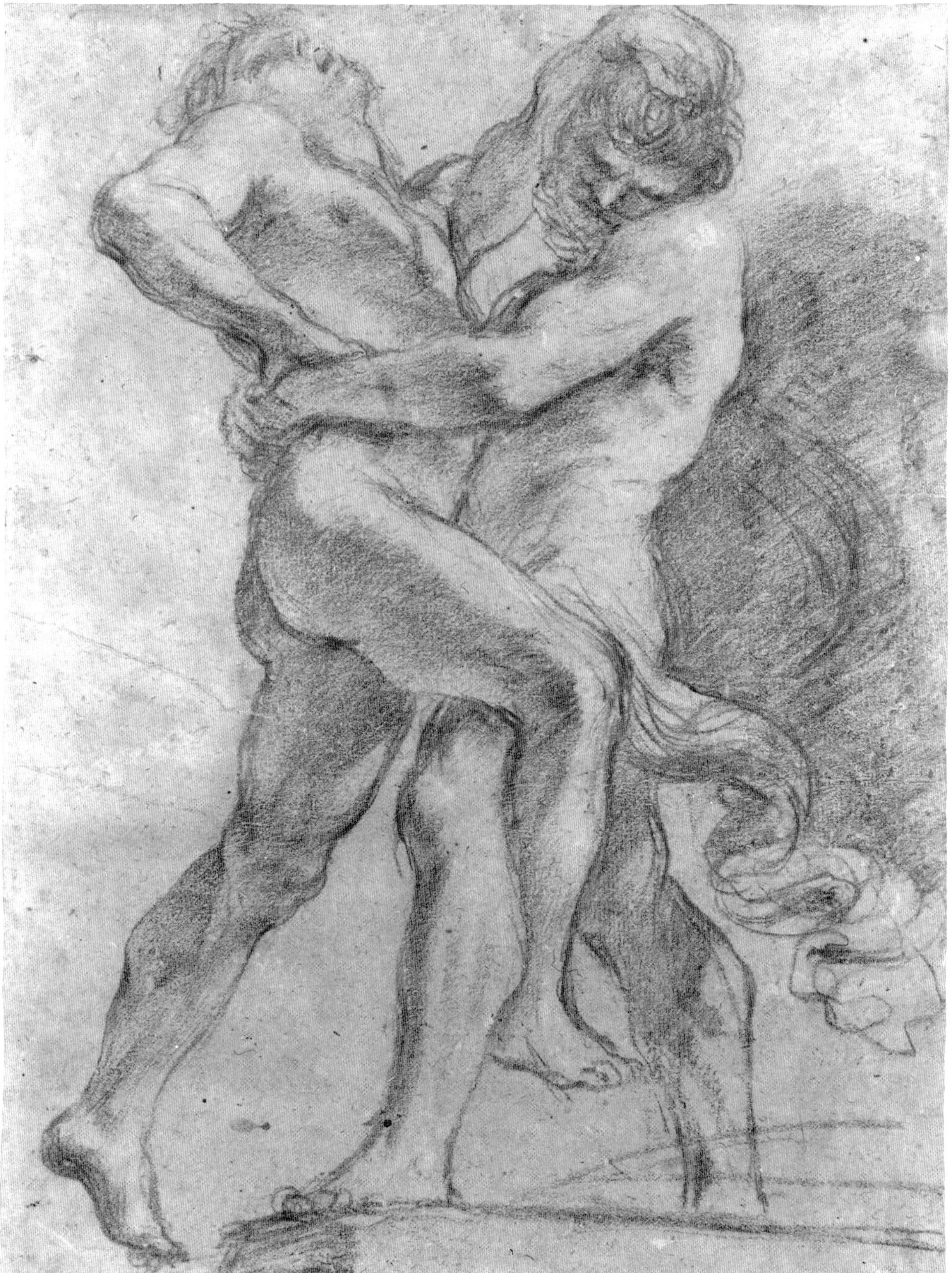

77

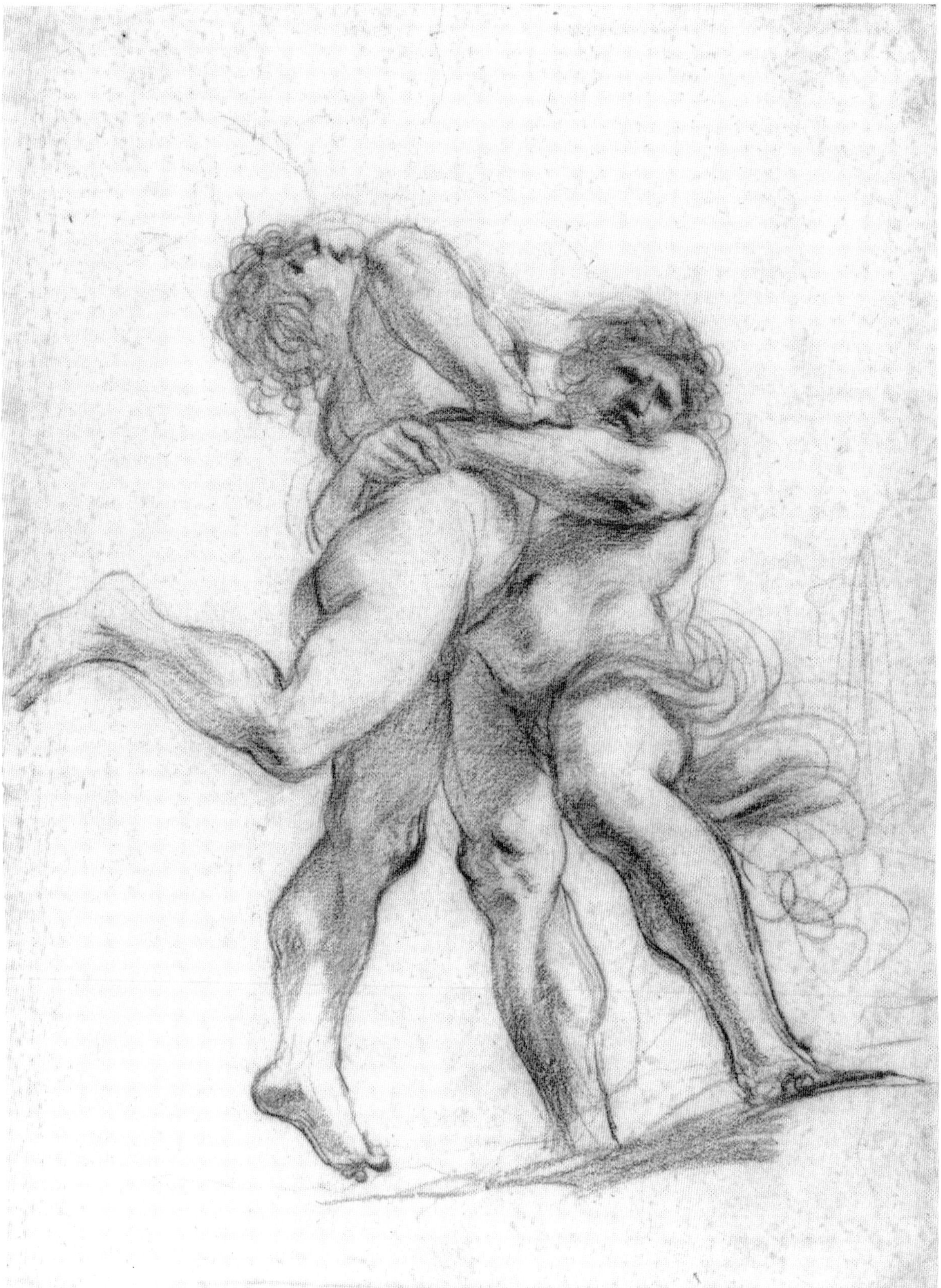

78

In October 1631 Guercino was paid by the Abate Sampieri for the ceiling fresco of *Hercules wrestling with Antaeus*, painted in one of a suite of rooms in the Palazzo Sampieri, now Talon, Bologna (S, 1988, no. 134); three of the rooms of this same suite had previously been painted by the Carracci. Guercino had been in Bologna in the spring of that same year to paint the portrait of *Cardinal Spada*, now in the Galleria Spada, Rome (S, 1988, no. 132), and it seems likely that he worked on the Sampieri commission at the same time. Of the fresco, which is painted *a secco*, Malvasia made the revealing comment, 'è mirabile averlo fatto senza cartone, tanto era pratico nella eccellenza del disegno' (Malvasia, 1678, II, p. 368; 1841, II, p. 262). Most painters of the period made finished cartoons, worked out from preparatory drawings, in order to transfer accurately the design for a given composition onto the surface to be painted. Guercino seems to have ignored this procedure in this and other frescoes (see No. 62).

The wrestling match between Hercules and Antaeus occurred on Hercules' return from the Hesperides. The Libyan giant Antaeus was invincible so long as some part of him touched the earth, from which he derived his strength. Hercules thus held him around the waist and lifted him clean off his feet, keeping him in this position until the power had sapped from his body and he died. In his fresco Guercino responded fully to the dramatic potential of the subject. He focused the spectator's attention on the legs of Antaeus thrashing in the air above his head, with his body writhing in the stolid grip of his opponent.

No. 77 shows an early phase in the working out of the composition in which the figures are not yet foreshortened to the same degree as in either No. 78 or the finished fresco. Although the upper part of the figure of Antaeus agrees in many respects with that of the painted figure, there are numerous other differences. Guercino developed further the idea of representing Hercules standing at the very extremity of a ledge: in the finished fresco the ledge runs across the entire length of the bottom of the composition and its edge is inscribed with the Latin motto *SIC PEREAT QUISQUIS TERRA GENITRICE SVPERBIT* (May whoever takes pride in his earthly ancestry perish thus).

78 Hercules wrestling with Antaeus

Red chalk. 361 × 265mm.

Windsor Castle, Royal Library, inv. no. 2382.

Provenance: Casa Gennari; King George III.

Literature: M, 1951, p. 58, no. xi; Bottari, 1966, pl. LIV; M, *Disegni*, 1969, no. 126; Roli, 1972, p. 28 and pl. 43; M & E, 1986, under no. 22; S, 1988, under no. 134; M & T, 1989, no. 57.

In No. 78 Hercules and Antaeus are shown *di sotto in su*, as in the fresco, but rather differently posed. While the legs of the two figures correspond approximately to their painted counterparts, especially those of Antaeus, the upper parts of their bodies are still significantly different. The legs of Antaeus are studied separately in a double-sided sheet in red chalk in the Koenig–Fachsenfeld Collection, now on deposit in the Staatsgalerie, Stuttgart (inv. no. Barbieri 450; Thiem, 1979, nos. 8a and b, pls. 17 and 18).

79–80 Studies for *Alexander the Great enjoining Secrecy on his Friend Hephaestion* (1631)

Lost

79 *Recto*: Alexander the Great enjoining Secrecy on his Friend Hephaestion *Verso*: The Horse 'Belladonna'

Pen and brown ink and brown wash. 176 × 188mm.

Windsor Castle, Royal Library, inv. no. 2840.

Provenance: Casa Gennari; King George III.

Literature: M & T, 1989, no. 58.

The painting with which the *recto* study is connected is untraced. It is presumably identical with that referred to by Malvasia under the year 1631 as an 'Alessandro Magno' (Malvasia, 1678, II, p. 368; 1841, II, p. 262) and cited in the Account Book in an entry dated 11 May 1631 as a composition of 'due mezze figure, cioè Alessandro magno, ed Efestione', paid for by a 'Sig. Gio. Battista Vaccari da Bologna' (*Libro dei Conti*, 1808, p. 63; 1841, p. 309). The horizontal lines drawn freehand at the bottom of the sheet demarcate the lower extremity of the composition, which shows the two figures half length. Another, probably later rendering of this same composition, with several variations, is recorded in a black chalk drawing at Christ Church College, Oxford, classified as from the Studio of Guercino (Byam Shaw, 1976, no. 1004; M & T, 1989, under nos. 58–60).

The incident represented is from Plutarch's life of Alexander the Great (chap. XXXIX). Alexander's mother Olympias apparently often wrote him private letters, which he kept hidden. On one occasion, however, his great friend Hephaestion, who was usually privy to the King's papers of state, saw one of Olympias' letters. Alexander allowed him to read it, but by pressing the seal of his signet ring to Hephaestion's lips he indicated that he trusted his friend to keep its contents secret.

The pen drawing of a horse on the *verso* is evidently related to another untraced picture painted by Guercino in the same year. This commission was referred to by Malvasia immediately preceding his notice for the *Alexander and Hephaestion*: 'il ritratto à olio d'un cavallo detto Belladonna al sig. Co. Filippo Aldrovandi. Questo cavallo era stato donato dall'Imperatore à Papa Gregorio XV. per la sua bellezza, havendo le crine del collo, che si estendevano sino à piedi: e perche s'infermò, il sudetto sig. Aldrovandi lo comprò, e lo tenne sempre per bellezza'. Count Filippo Aldrovandi's payment for the picture was entered in the Account Book on 24 April 1631 (*Libro dei Conti*, 1808, p. 62; 1841, p. 308). There can be no doubt that the horse

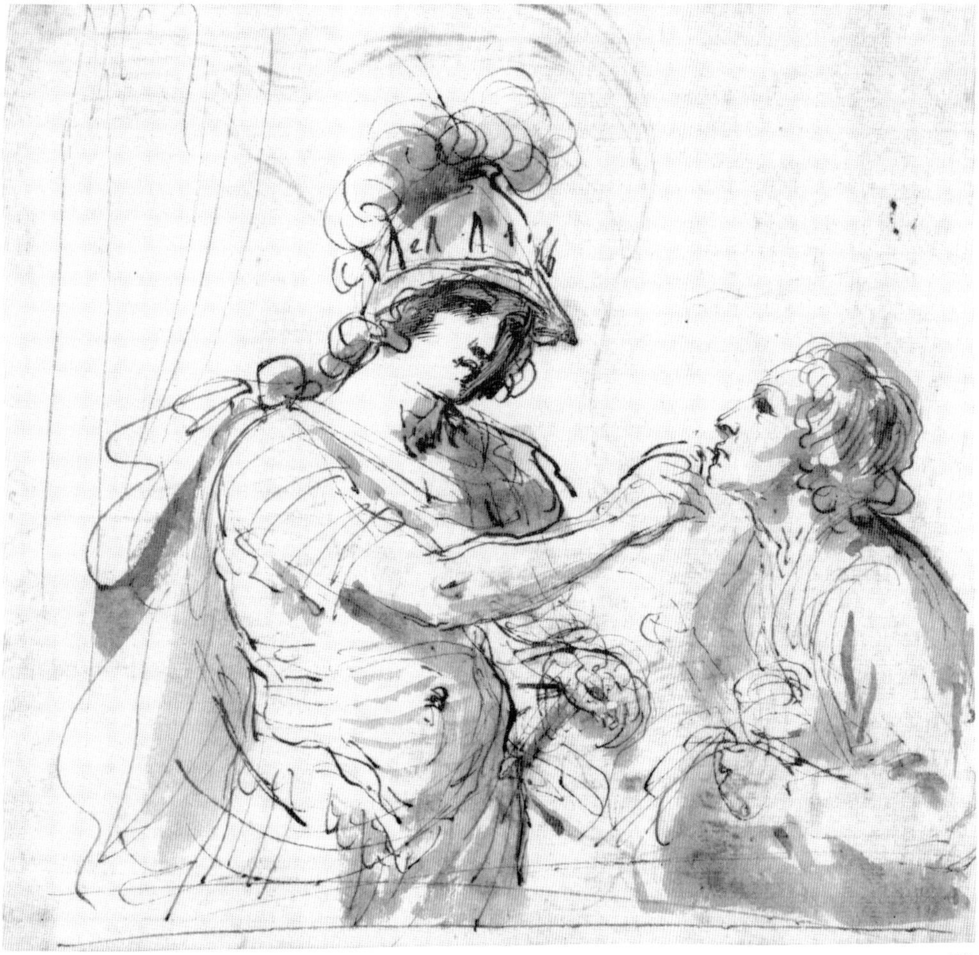

79

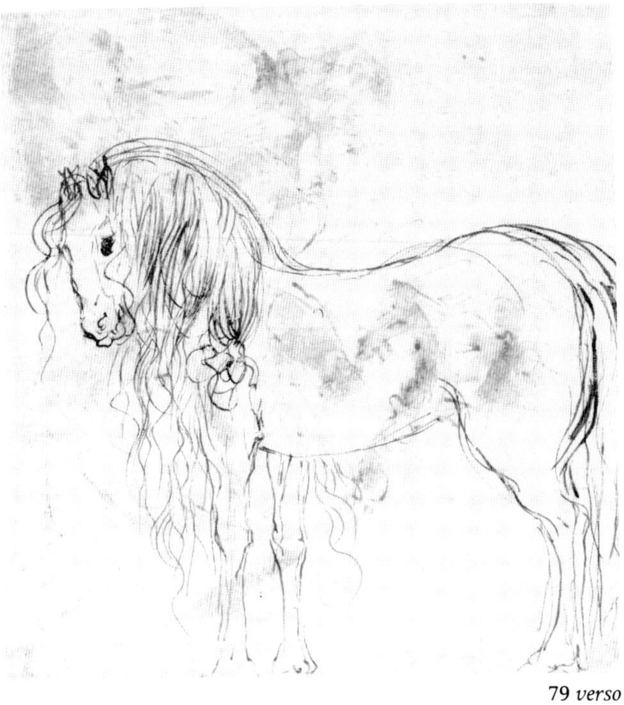

79 *verso*

on the *verso* of No. 79 with its long mane is none other than *Belladonna*.

Guercino painted a portrait of a dog, apparently for this same patron, which survives in the Norton Simon Museum at Pasadena, California (S, 1988, no. 104).

80 Alexander the Great wearing a plumed Helmet

(*see colour pl. 15*)

Pen and brown ink. 179 × 164mm.

Windsor Castle, Royal Library, inv. no. 2625.

Provenance: Casa Gennari; King George III.

Literature: M & T, 1989, no. 60.

For the head of Alexander in the composition studied in No. 79. Guercino has dwelt with obvious satisfaction upon the drawing of the plume, the ornate helmet with the coronet and the figure's hair, demonstrating as he does so his fluent use of the pen. Two studies for the same head, but turned a little more in the direction of the spectator, appear in another pen drawing at Windsor (M & T, 1989, no. 59),

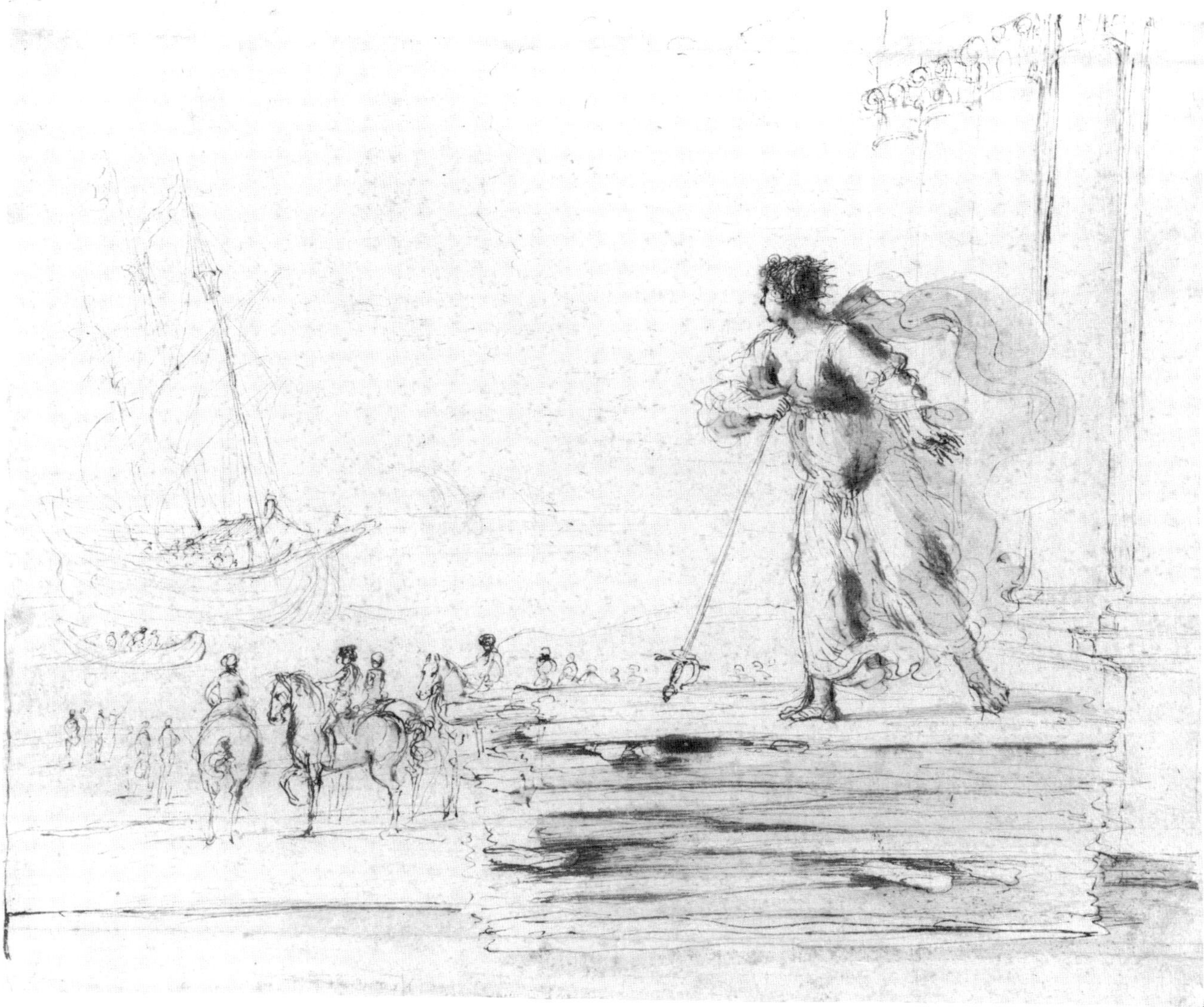

81

which is close in style to the present drawing. In one the King appears a little more than head and shoulders and his summarily drawn right arm is raised much as it is in No. 79.

81–82 Studies for the *Death of Dido* (1630–31)

Rome, Galleria Spada

81 The Death of Dido

Pen and brown ink and brown wash. 279 × 345mm.

Mahon Collection, on loan to the Ashmolean Museum, Oxford, M & E, 21.

Provenance: Casa Gennari; Mr Bouverie; Mr Hervey; John Rushout, 2nd Lord Northwick; thence by descent (sale, Sotheby's, London, 1 November 1920, lot 13); H. S. Reitlinger (L *Suppl*, 2274a; sale, Sotheby's, London, 9 December 1953, lot 54), purchased pseudonymously by Sir Denis Mahon.

Literature: M, 1967, no. 19; M, *Disegni*, 1969, no. 123; B, 1984, p. 153, fig. 121; S, 1988, under no. 135; M & T, 1989, under no. 61.

An early preparatory study for the *Death of Dido* of 1630–31, in the Galleria Spada, Rome (S, 1988, no. 135), a picture first commissioned by Cardinal Spada on behalf of the Queen Mother of France, Maria de' Medici. New documentary evidence has shed much light on the complex circumstances of the commission, casting doubt on the previously accepted account provided by the German painter and writer on art, Joachim von Sandrart (1608–88), who claimed that the *Dido* and the *Rape of Helen*, a masterpiece by the Bolognese painter Guido Reni, had been exhibited together in Rome in June 1631 (see Dirani, 1982–3, pp. 83–94; and the summaries of her findings in S, 1988, no. 135, and M & T, 1989, under no. 61).

The idea that Guercino should paint a *Dido* was probably

first mooted in a letter to the painter from Cardinal Spada, a former Nuncio in France and friend of the Queen Mother. The letter is dated 27 October 1629, shortly after Spada had begun his attempts to buy for the same patron Reni's *Rape of Helen*, which he obviously intended to pair with the *Dido*. The *Rape of Helen* was itself first commissioned in January of 1628 by a Spanish patron for presentation to King Philip IV, but when this plan failed, the picture became the subject of detailed negotiations on the part of Spada for its sale to the Queen Mother in the summer of 1629. The commission of the *Dido* to Guercino was apparently connected with a proposal, with which the Cardinal was also much involved, that the Queen Mother might eventually invite Guercino to France in place of Guido Reni, who had recently declined her invitation; the *Dido* would thus have provided the Queen with an example of Guercino's work by which to judge his suitability. However, the political upheavals in France that began in the autumn of 1630 and eventually led to the Queen fleeing the country on 18 July 1631 caused both schemes to be abandoned. Cardinal Spada took over the commission of the *Dido*, but the finished picture was stuck in Bologna because of the ban on the movement of persons and objects out of Emilia during the plague of 1631; it was only in April of 1632 that it eventually made its way to Spada's palace in Rome. Meanwhile the *Rape of Helen* remained in Rome until as late as 1638, passing eventually into the hands of a French buyer, Louis Phélypeaux de La Vrillière, for whom see No. 114.

It seems likely that No. 81 belongs to a very early phase in the gestation of the work, before Guercino became aware that it was to have been paired with a picture by his rival, Guido Reni. The composition is therefore radically different from the finished picture, with the scale of the figures much smaller in relation to the whole: Dido, standing on the funeral pyre with her sword at her breast, watches the embarcation of the fleeing Aeneas accompanied by his horsemen. The ideas it embodies must soon have been rejected: a pen-and-wash drawing by Guercino in the Staatliche Graphische Sammlung, Munich (inv. no. 2890; M & T, 1989, p. 35 and fig. 11), is a rapid copy by Guercino of Reni's *Rape of Helen*, probably made as a record in order to gauge the scale and number of figures to include in the revised composition of his own 'rival' picture.

82 Three Women Spectators at the Death of Dido

Pen and brown ink and brown wash. 242 × 184mm.

Windsor Castle, Royal Library, inv. no. 2834.

Provenance: Casa Gennari; King George III.

Literature: M & T, 1989, no. 61.

No. 82, which is remarkable for its very great freedom of touch, is a study for three of the women spectators in the *Death of Dido*, for which see No. 81. It was drawn at the time when the painter was thinking of placing the group on the right of the composition instead of on the left, as

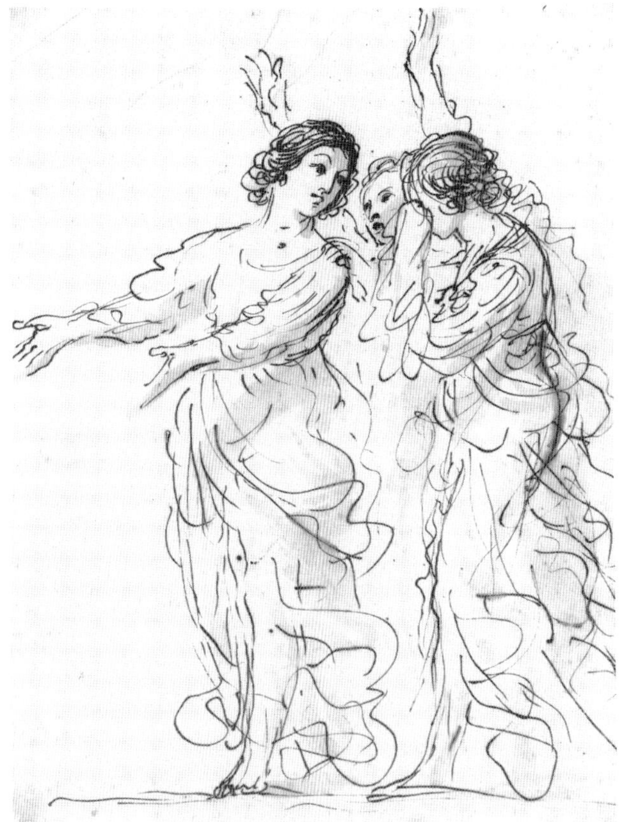

82

in the finished picture. The three figures are nonetheless recognisable, in reverse and with many other variations, in their painted equivalents.

Other drawings for this picture also document the painter's unusual, but frequent habit of exploring his compositions in different directions. A retouched offset in the Royal Library at Windsor Castle (M & T, 1989, no. 622) records another study, in red chalk, now lost, in which the three women were also originally drawn in the same direction as No. 81.

83–84 Studies for *Damon and Pythias* (1632)

Lost

83 Damon and Pythias

London, British Museum, inv. no. 1969–9–20–17.

(For other details see App. no. 16.)

A study for the picture painted for Cardinal Palotta, the Papal Legate of Ferrara, for which Guercino received payment in May 1632. The appearance of this picture, now lost, is known from a copy on loan from the Galleria Rospigliosi to the Federazione dei Consorzi Agrari, Palazzo Rospigliosi–Pallavicini, Rome (S, 1988, no. 138).

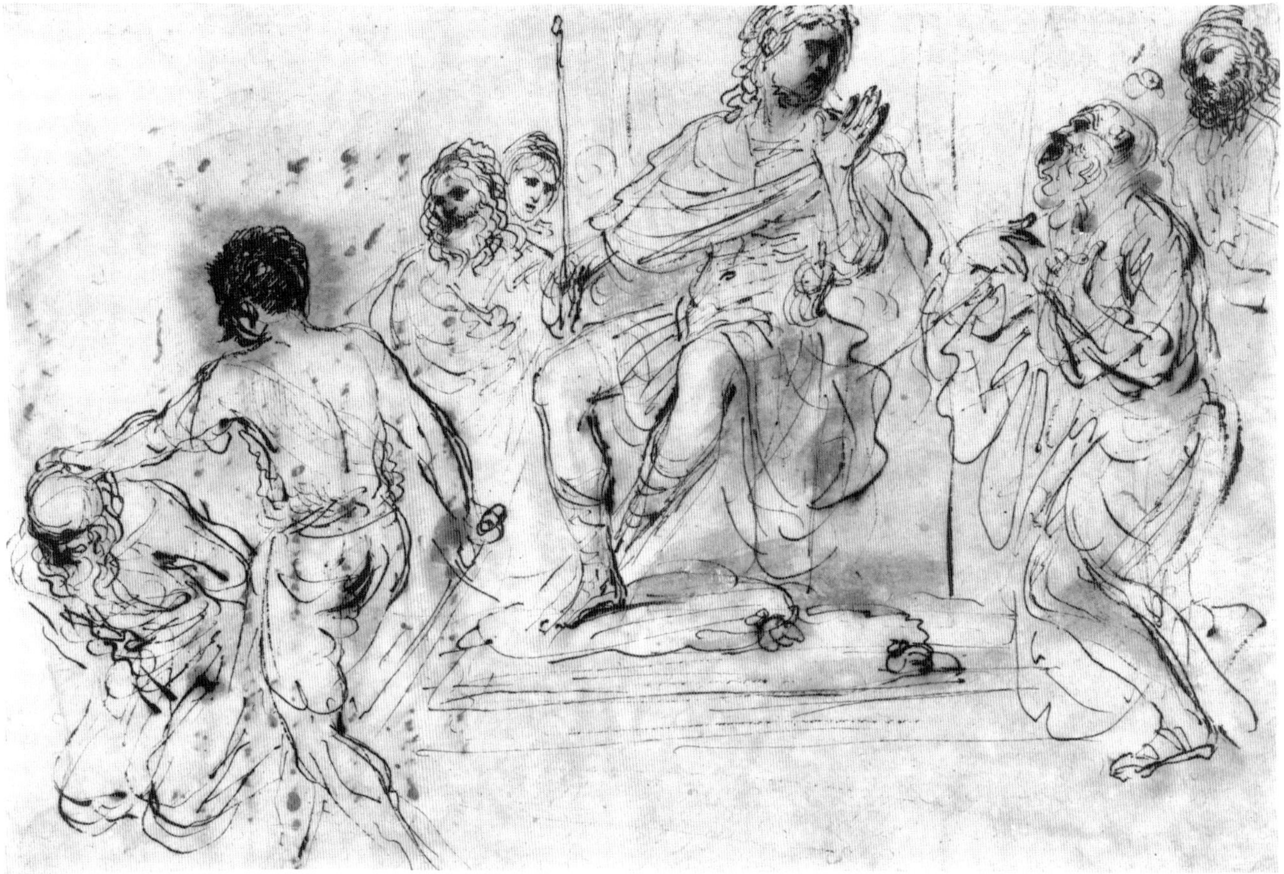

83

The subject is an unusual one and illustrates the important episode in the friendship of two Pythagoreans, Damon and Pythias. Pythias, wrongly accused of an attempt on the life of the tyrant Dionysius the Younger, was condemned to death. Protesting his innocence, he was given a few days' liberty in which to arrange for the future care of his family, but on the condition that Damon would act as surety for his return. When Pythias reappeared at the appointed time of his execution, the tyrant was so impressed by his faithfulness that he asked to be admitted to their friendship.

Four other drawings related to this picture are known. One is a compositional study in the Kunsthalle, Bremen (inv. no. 1953/50; referred to by Turner, 1980, under no. 45); it clearly post-dates the British Museum drawing since the positions of Damon and the executioner have already been resolved, although the right half of the drawing showing Pythias kneeling before the tyrant is still reminiscent of No. 83. A second compositional study was formerly on the London art market (sale, Sotheby's, 16 November 1960, lot 3; see M & T, 1989, under no. 70, where the sale date is incorrect). The other two drawings are detailed studies for individual figures: one is No. 84 and the other is the retouched red chalk offset for the head of the tyrant Dionysius, in the Royal Library, Windsor Castle (M & T, 1989, no. 70).

84 Study of an old Man kneeling on the Ground

Red chalk, slightly heightened with white. 242 × 174mm.

London, Victoria and Albert Museum, inv. no. Dyce 303.

Provenance: Sir J. Reynolds (L 2364); Dyce Bequest, 1869.

Literature: Reid, 1874, no. 303; Ward-Jackson, 1980, no. 722, repr. (as School of Guercino); S, 1988, under no. 138; M & T, 1989, under no. 70.

A study for the kneeling figure of Damon about to be executed in Guercino's composition of *Damon and Pythias* of 1632, for which see No. 83. The figure closely resembles its counterpart in the painting, except for a few minor discrepancies in the angle of the head and the folds of the drapery. Damon also appears in this pose in a composition drawing in the Kunsthalle, Bremen (inv. no. 1953/50; see Turner, 1980, under no. 45).

The drawing is essentially a drapery study, on coarse-grain paper, very much in the manner of those in the Koenig–Fachsenfeld Collection in the Staatsgalerie, Stuttgart, a selection of which was published by Mahon (*Disegni*, 1969), the whole group later being the subject of an article by Thiem (1979). For an example of such a drapery study in the British Museum, see No. 93 for Guercino's *Visitation*, also of 1632. As in that drawing, No. 84 already anticipates

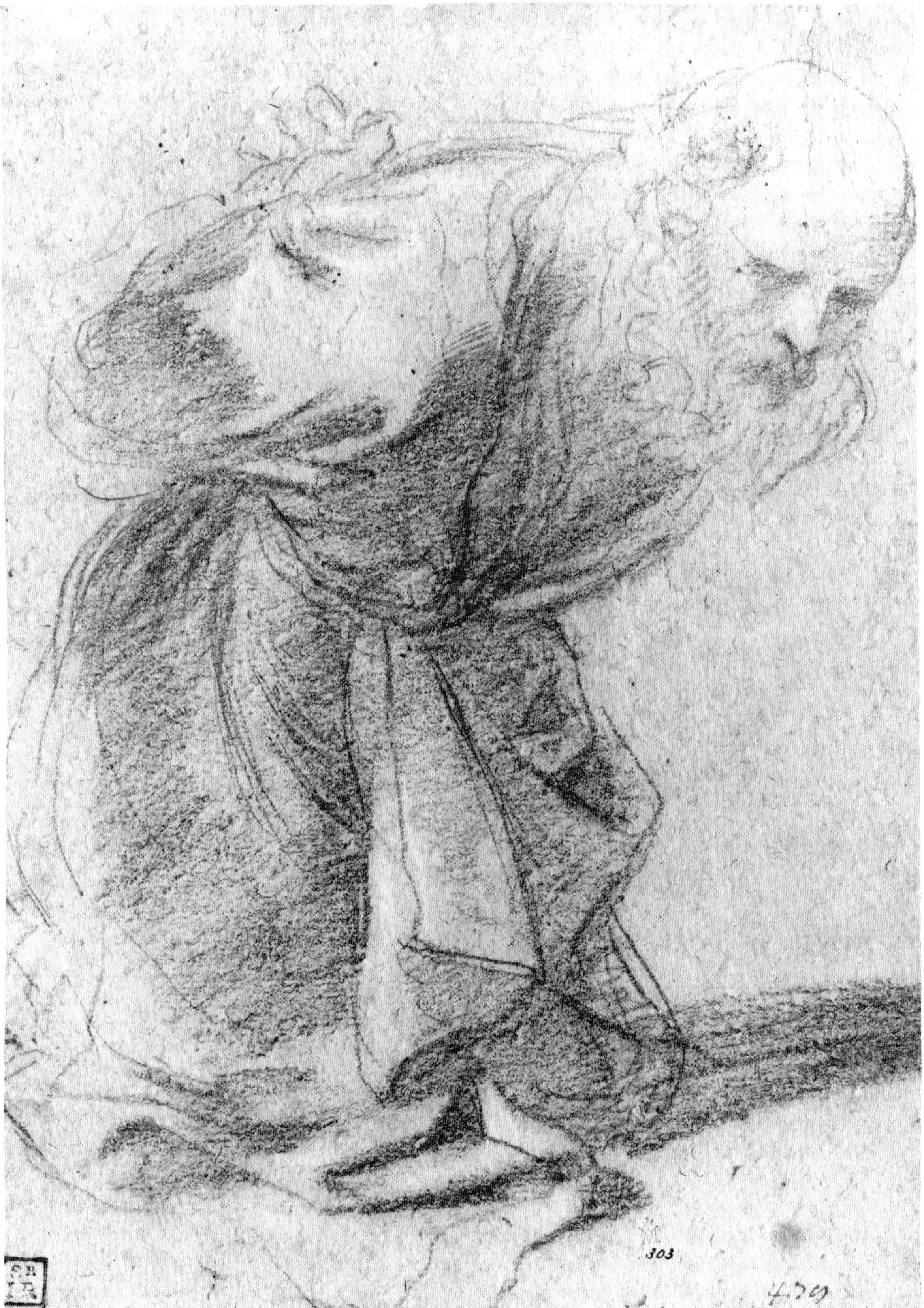

84

the lighting of the painting fairly accurately, the most prominent highlights falling on the saint's right shoulder, the back of his neck, and his bald pate. Needless to say, such studies were carried out when the composition was at an advanced stage of preparation.

The theme of execution was one that Guercino repeated on more than one occasion in the first half of the 1630s, in his *Martyrdom of Sts John and Paul* of 1632 and the *Martyrdom of St Maurelius* of 1634–5. Studies for the former certainly interrelate with the composition eventually arrived at in the *Damon and Pythias* (see the *verso* of No. 88); and they, in turn, appear to have been in the artist's mind when he was preparing the *St Maurelius*.

85–88 Studies for the *Martyrdom of Sts John and Paul, with the Madonna and Child above* (1632)

Toulouse, Musée des Augustins

85 The Madonna and Child seated

Pen and brown ink. 272 × 250mm.

Windsor Castle, Royal Library, inv. no. 2738.

Provenance: Casa Gennari; King George III.

Literature: M & T, 1989, no. 62.

Nos. 85–8 are studies for the *Martyrdom of Sts John and Paul, with the Madonna and Child above*, one of a pair of pictures painted for the side walls of the Giroldi Chapel in the Cathedral at Reggio Emilia, for which Guercino received payment in 1632; the painting is now in the Musée des Augustins, Toulouse (S, 1988, no. 139). For a drawing in the British Museum related to this picture, see App. no. 18. For drawings related to its pendant, the *Visitation* (now in the Musée des Beaux-Arts, Rouen), see Nos. 89–93.

Guercino made a large number of studies for both lateral paintings (see M, *Disegni*, 1969, under nos. 127–31, and M & T, 1989, under nos. 62–8). The altarpiece of the chapel, representing the *Assumption of the Virgin with St Peter as Pope and St Jerome* (still *in situ*), had also been painted by Guercino some six years earlier, in 1626 (S, 1988, no. 113); for a drawing related to this picture, see No. 56.

No. 85 is a study in reverse for the Madonna and Child, who, in the picture, are seated on a cloud looking down on the martyrdom below. However, in the drawing the Madonna's gaze is boldly directed outwards at the spectator. The painting also differs from this preparatory sketch in that the Child no longer props himself up with one arm, but instead holds onto the Madonna's veil. Another pen drawing for the Madonna and Child, which is considerably closer to the finished painting, was formerly in the Meissner collection, Zurich (*Hundert Zeichnungen aus fünf Jahrhunderten*, exh. cat., Galerie Meissner, Zurich, 1984, no. 45, repr.), and is now on the London art market.

No. 85, executed in pen only, is notable for its prominent hatching to denote shadows. Such hatching applied as an alternative to wash, particularly in the face, is characteristic of Guercino's work, especially of the mid-1630s (see, for example, Nos. 80, 91–2 and App. no. 32).

A fine study for the drapery about the knees of the Madonna is in the Koenig–Fachsenfeld Collection, now on deposit in the Staatsgalerie, Stuttgart (inv. no. Barbieri 63; M, *Disegni*, 1969, no. 131). It makes an interesting complement to No. 85, which is curtailed at the level of the Madonna's knees. At this stage, Guercino was interested in resolving the poses of the Madonna and Child and was working rapidly in pen, scarcely bothering with the drapery. In the Fachsenfeld study, on the other hand, all but the right hand of the Madonna's upper body has been omitted, with a blank space left for the Child. This meticulous study, in red chalk with white heightening, is extremely close to the finished work and must have been completed right at the end of the design process, after the attitudes of the two figures had been established.

Mahon and Turner have suggested that another drawing in the Royal Library, Windsor Castle (M & T, 1989, no. 175), may be an alternative study for the Madonna and Child in this composition, and that two offsets (M & T, 1989, nos. 626–7) might also have been taken from related drawings.

It is interesting that all the drawings for this picture are either for the Madonna and Child or for the figures below but never the two groups together, a fact that might explain the curious two-tier effect of the painting.

86 Body of a Man with a severed Head

Pen and brown ink and brown wash. 191 × 259mm.

Windsor Castle, Royal Library, inv. no. 2849.

Provenance: Casa Gennari; King George III.

Literature: M, *Disegni*, 1969, under no. 131; M & T, 1989, no. 63.

This is a study for the decapitated saint in the background of the *Martyrdom of Sts John and Paul, with the Madonna and Child above*, now in Toulouse, for which see No. 85. Of the several drawings for the lower half of the composition (discussed under No. 87), this one is exceptional in representing the corpse of the beheaded saint in isolation. For a drawing of the kneeling saint about to be beheaded, see App. no. 18.

Despite being a detail study, the artist has not neglected to give some indication of setting in No. 86. Particularly subtle is the delicate film of wash (now partially removed through cleaning) used to denote a faint shadow effectively marking the extent of the courtyard at the back of the composition.

Guercino appears originally to have drawn the saint's body on top of a block, though its outlines are interrupted by other marks which make its presence ambiguous. The block is evident in only one other drawing for this work, in the Rijksmuseum, Amsterdam (inv. no. 64:38; M, *Disegni*,

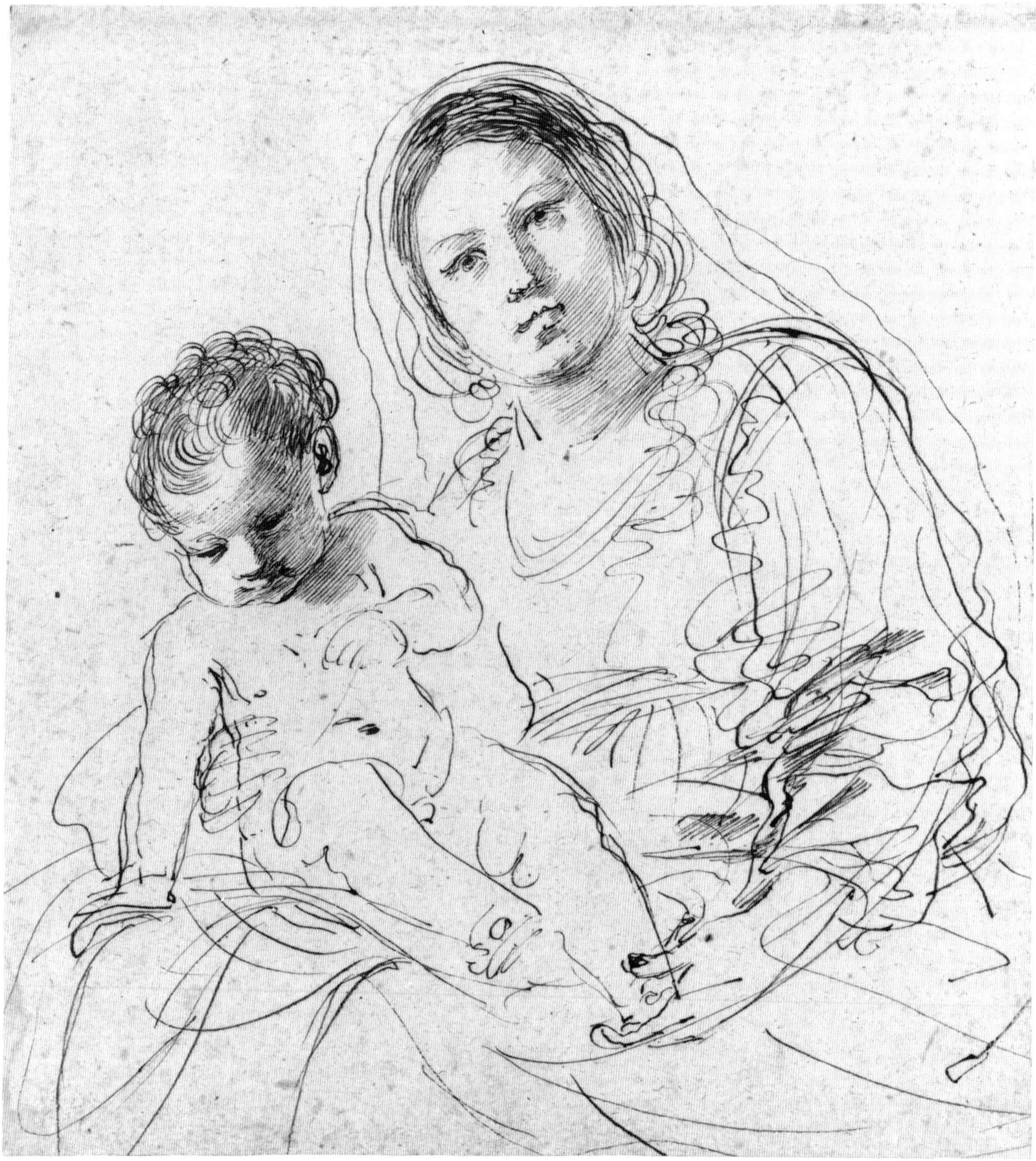

85

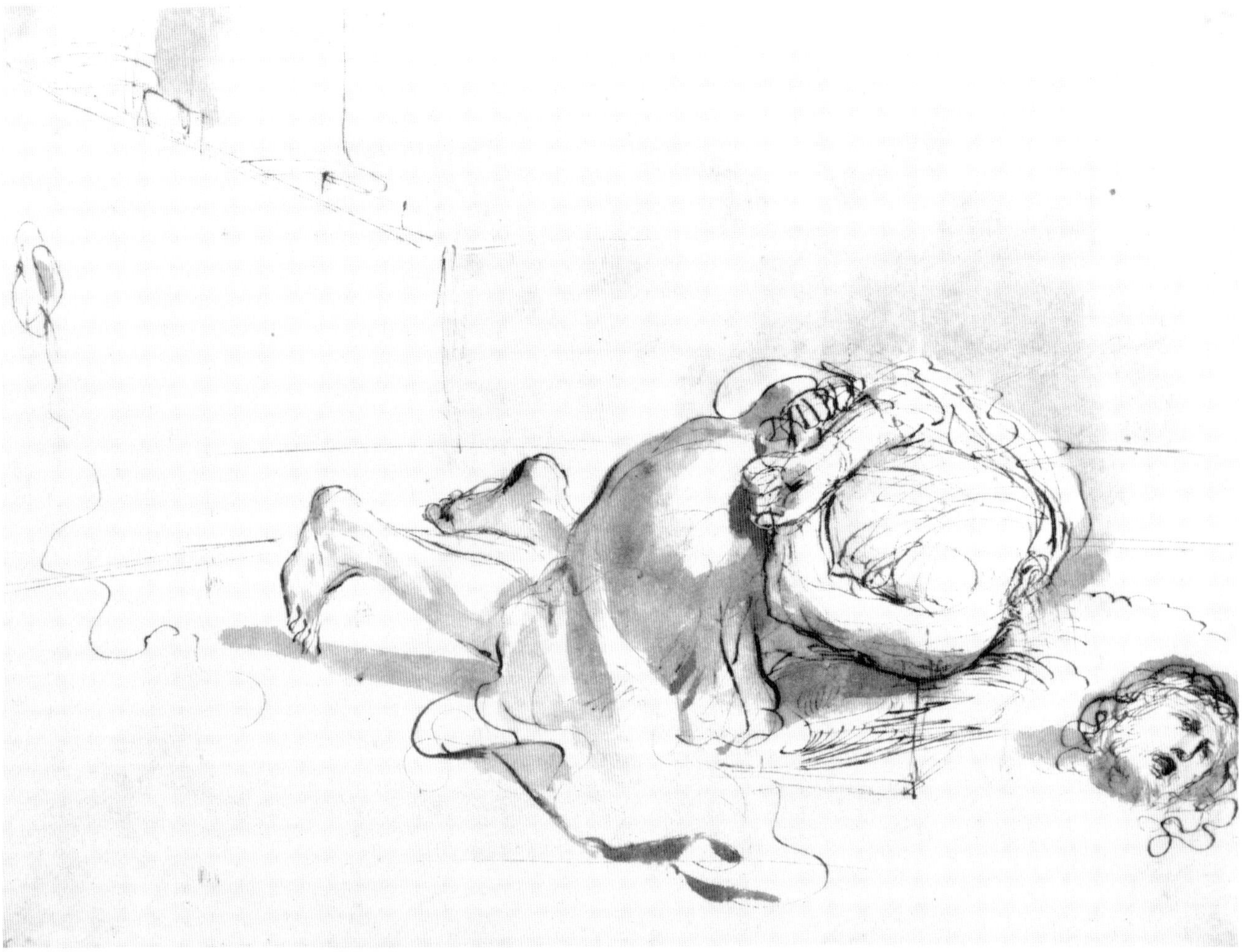

86

1969, no. 127); there, however, it is the second saint who is sprawled over it, in the process of having his throat slit, while the first decapitated corpse lies in the background. In the finished painting the dead saint's severed head appears at the lower right, above which his body is shown lying with its shoulders at the edge of a stone step, in a manner not unlike that in No. 86, except that his hands are folded under his body rather than tied behind his back.

There are interesting analogies between the Toulouse painting and a chiaroscuro woodcut by Antonio da Trento after a design by Parmigianino (and made under his supervision) of *The Martyrdom of Sts Peter and Paul* (Bartsch, 1803–21, XII, p. 79, no. 28; see Introduction and Fig. 2). This is particularly true of the executioner in Guercino's painting (and No. 88, the latest of the group exhibited here) and his juxtaposition with the saint about to be beheaded. However, the latter figure in Antonio da Trento's work also resembles extremely closely the corpse in No. 86, although in reverse and with his head not yet severed. The saint in the woodcut is kneeling with his head over the edge of a circular plinth and with his arms tied behind his back in a strikingly similar pose to the saint slumped over the block in No. 86. Other drawings related to the Toulouse picture also reflect different aspects of the print. Judging from this evidence, there can be no doubt that Guercino knew the Parmigianino composition intimately (and possibly possessed an impression in his own collection).

87 The Martyrdom of Sts John and Paul

(*see colour pl. 15*)

Pen and brown ink and brown wash, with faint traces of greyish wash in the brown. 188 × 229mm; a piece of paper, 45 × 70mm, with an alternative for the head and shoulders of the executioner, is attached to the sheet with a hinge, over the first attempt at this part of the drawing, enabling the viewer to see both versions.

Mahon Collection, on loan to the Ashmolean Museum, Oxford, M & E, 23.

Provenance: Casa Gennari (the drawing retains its fine Casa Gennari mount (concealed), for which see L *Suppl*, 2858c, and M, 1967, p. 20); Mr Bouverie; Mr Hervey; John Rushout, 2nd Lord Northwick; Henry Oppenheimer (sale, Christie's, London, 10 July 1936, lot 102A), purchased by Sir Denis Mahon.

Literature: M, 1967, no. 21; M, *Disegni*, 1969, no. 129; M & E,

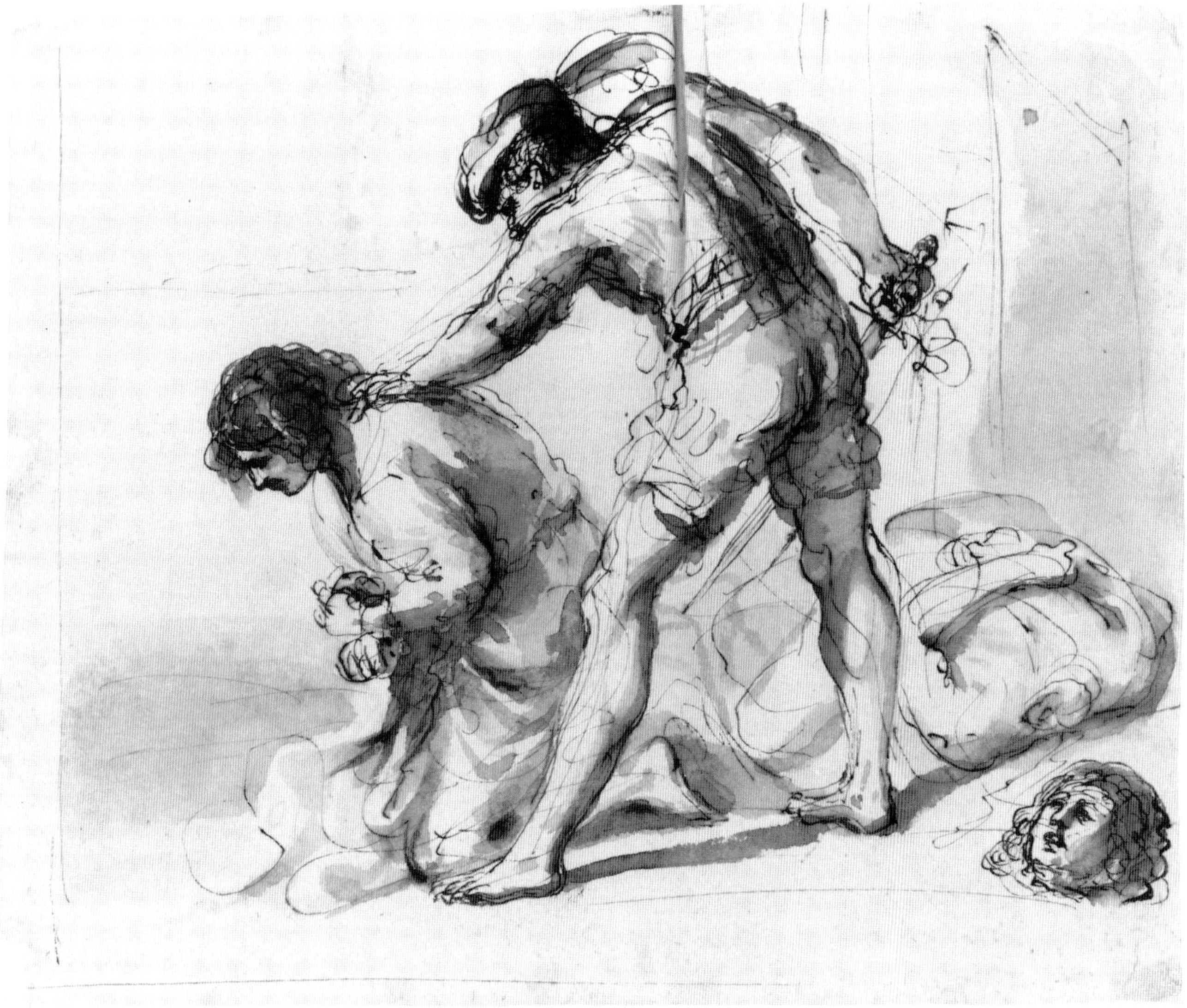

87 (with paper correction open)

1986, no. 23; S, 1988, under no. 139; M & T, 1989, under nos. 62–8.

A study for the lower half of the *Martyrdom of Sts John and Paul, with the Madonna and Child above*, for which see No. 85. In his search for a satisfactory composition, Guercino experimented with several different ideas for the group of the two martyrs with their executioner midway through his task. Apart from Nos. 87–8, there is a composition study in the Rijksmuseum, Amsterdam (inv. no. 64:38; M, *Disegni*, 1969, no. 127), and another, double-sided, in the Pierpont Morgan Library, New York (inv. no. I, 101h; M, *Disegni*, 1969, no. 128). An engraving by William Hebert, made in 1762 after an untraced drawing, then in the collection of George, Earl Cholmondeley, records a further rendering of the group (Rogers, 1778, numbered 46 in the Department's copy, shelfmark 163 c. 26). The disposition of the figures in the engraving is similar to that adopted in No. 87, with the executioner seen almost in profile to the left as he approaches the kneeling saint, rather than from the rear as in No. 88 (*recto*) and the finished work. It is impossible to tell whether the engraving reverses the lost drawing. Finally, a second engraving, by Bartolozzi, dated 1792, records yet another, lost, preparatory drawing for the executioner and the kneeling saint alone, in similar attitudes to the figures in the painting (Calabi, no. 2191; two impressions are in the British Museum, inv. nos. S. 5–39 and 1873–7–12–414).

The presence of the paper correction, or *Klebe-korrektur*, is very unusual in Guercino's *œuvre*. The artist must have been satisfied with the appearance of the drawing – which indeed begins to resemble the painted composition fairly closely – except in the area of the head of the executioner. Yet in spite of the careful correction, Guercino did not go on to paint the substitute head, which is somewhat awkwardly twisted to the left. He instead reverted to his original

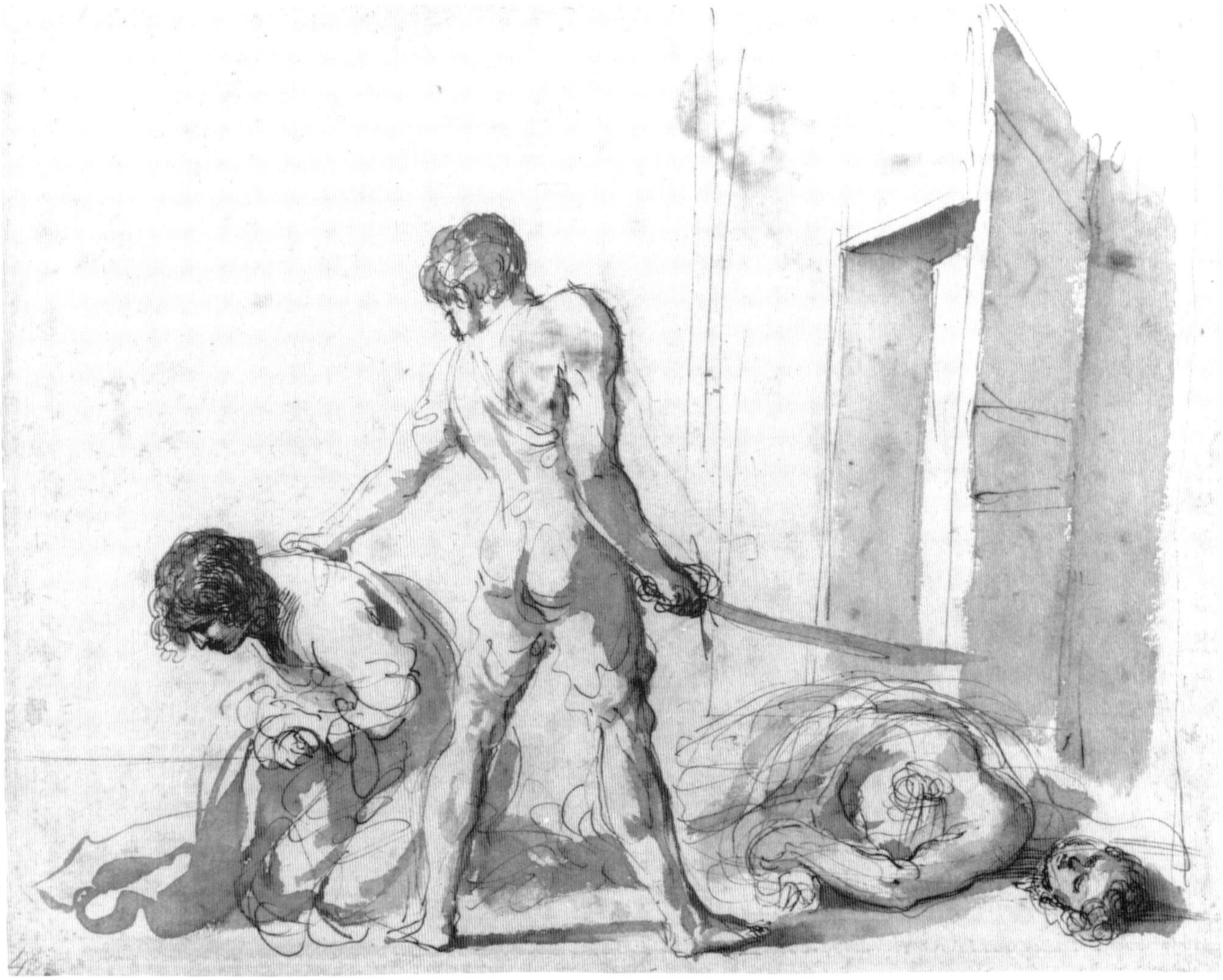

88

idea, with the head half-hidden by the figure's left shoulder, but with the right shoulder twisted considerably further to the right (as in the *recto* of No. 88), thus achieving the *contrapposto* he was presumably seeking.

The lines demarcating the edges of the composition at the left and along the bottom indicate that Guercino already had the format of the finished work in mind.

88 The Martyrdom of Sts John and Paul

Pen and brown ink and brown wash. 239 × 310mm.

London, Courtauld Institute Galleries, Witt Collection, inv. no. 1341.

Provenance: Casa Gennari; Mr Bouverie; Mr Hervey; the Earls of Gainsborough (sale, Christie's, London, 27 July 1922, lot 81, with others, bt *Meatyard*); Sir Robert Witt.

Literature: M, *Disegni*, 1969, no. 130; Hammer, *et al.*, 1977, no. 23.

Numbered in graphite in the bottom left corner: *4* (for a discussion and further instances of sheets numbered in this way, see No. 10).

On both the *recto* and the *verso* are studies for the lower part of the composition of the *Martyrdom of Sts John and Paul, with the Madonna and Child above*, for which see No. 85.

The *recto* of No. 88 comes closer to the finished painting than any other composition study for this section of the picture, both in the pose and the disposition of the figures. The two works differ most significantly in terms of the setting, with the open door in the right background of the drawing being replaced in the painting by a ruined wall and the base of a column in the left background (an idea already anticipated in No. 86). It was unusual for Guercino to indicate his protagonists' surroundings so fully in his figure studies. Although the figures of the two saints had been more or less established in previous studies, the executioner's pose is here resolved for the first time.

Curiously, the study on the *verso*, unlike the *recto*, is very remote from the final solution. One even wonders whether the drawing on the *verso* may have been made at an earlier moment in the design process and the sheet re-used

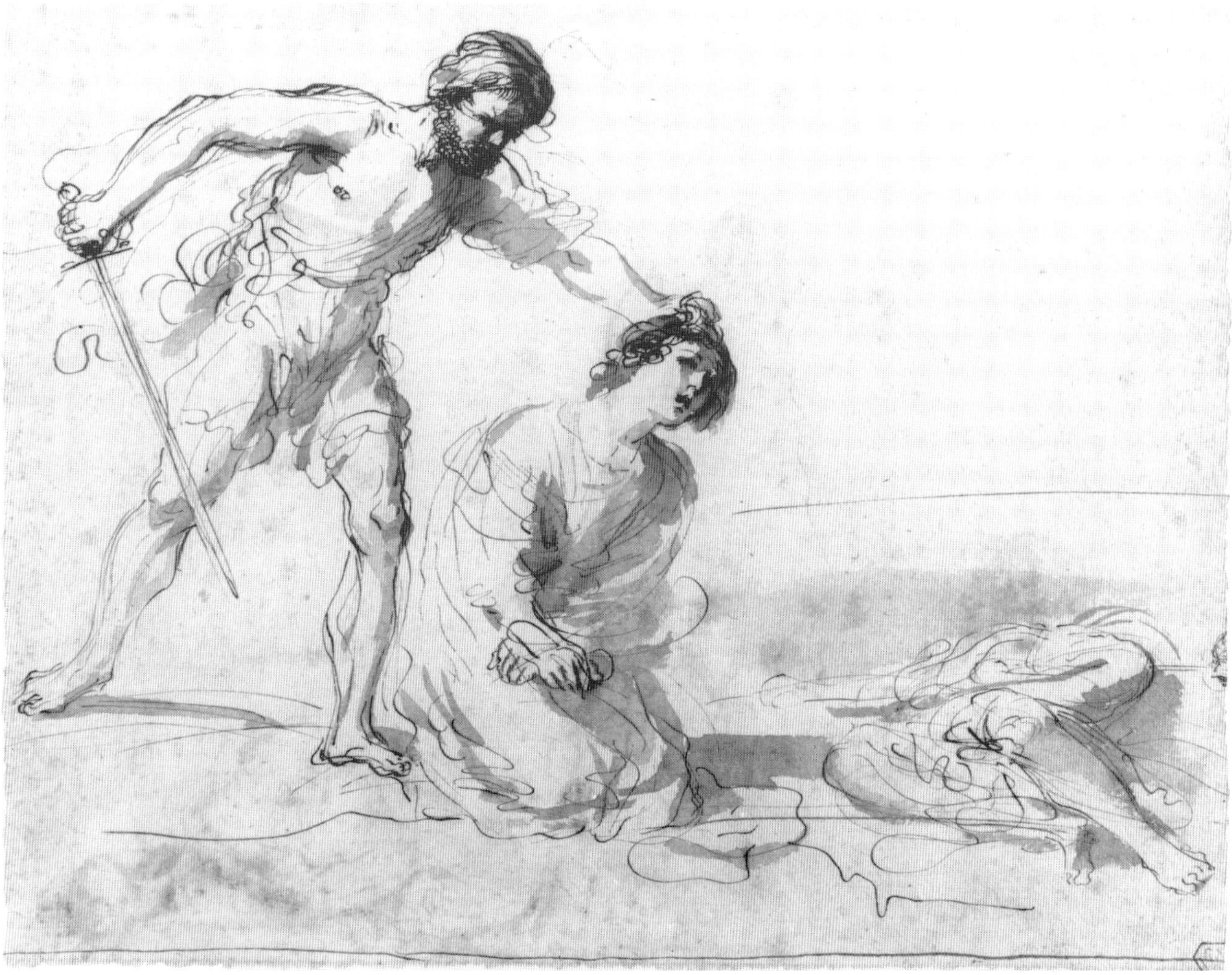

88 *verso*

later, when the design of the composition was nearing completion.

These two preparatory sketches, like the others in this series, are remarkable for the chiaroscuro effects achieved with the wash. This is especially true of the drapery of the kneeling figure on the *recto*, which is executed almost entirely in that medium. The dancing line and fluid finish of the wash synthesise forms only sketchily realised in the more frenetic penwork.

89–93 Studies for the *Visitation* (1632)

Rouen, Musée des Beaux-Arts

89 The Visitation

Pen and brown ink. 203 × 178mm.

Windsor Castle, Royal Library, inv. no. 2747.

Provenance: Casa Gennari; King George III.

Literature: M & T, 1989, no. 67.

Nos. 89–93 are for the *Visitation* now in the Musée des Beaux-Arts at Rouen (S, 1988, no. 140), one of a pair of pictures painted in 1632 for the side walls of the Giroldi Chapel in the Cathedral at Reggio Emilia. The pendant picture of the *Martyrdom of Sts John and Paul, with the Madonna and Child above*, painted in the same year, was studied in Nos. 85–8 and App. no. 18. Some of the complex details of the commission for the two pictures are briefly summarised under No. 85. In 1626 for this same chapel Guercino had

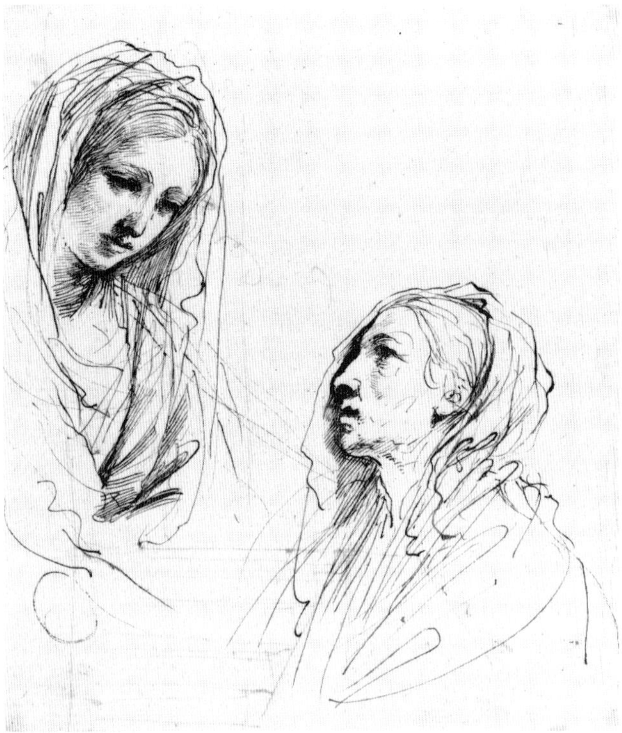

89

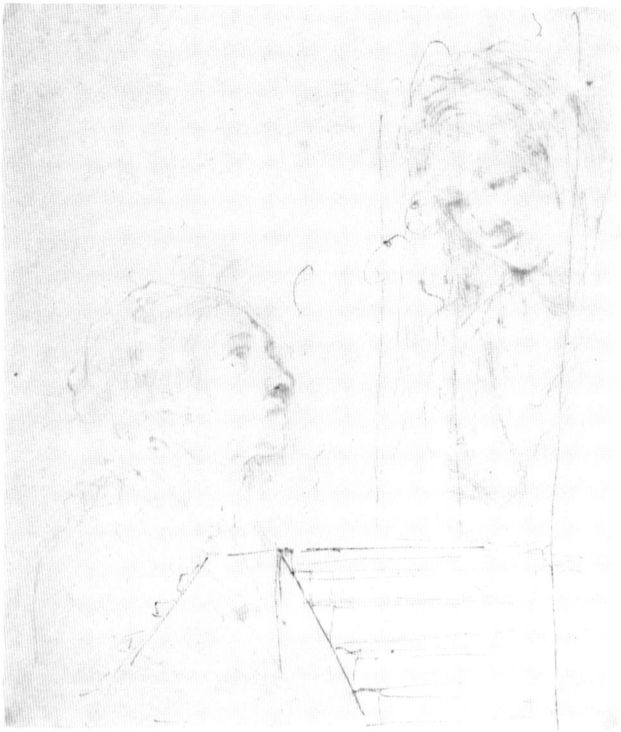

89 *verso*

painted the altarpiece with the *Assumption of the Virgin with St Peter as Pope and St Jerome*, for which see No. 56.

In exploring a solution for the composition of the *Visitation*, Guercino made numerous preliminary studies. One first idea was to show the Madonna dismounting from a donkey as she arrived with Joseph at the house of Zacharias, husband of her cousin Elizabeth, who was then in her sixth month of pregnancy. This unconventional interpretation of the two women meeting, with one of them on horseback, appears in a pen-and-wash drawing on the *recto* of a sheet in the Fodor Collection in the Historisch Museum at Amsterdam (inv. no. A 11010; Koevoets, 1976, no. 24) and in a pen-and-wash drawing on the *recto* of another sheet in the Art Museum, Princeton University (inv. no. 48–745; M, *Disegni*, 1969, no. 132; Gibbons, 1977, no. 274). Since in No. 89 the Madonna is represented a good head above her companion, it seems reasonable to associate the drawing with the *recto* of the Princeton sheet, where the Madonna, on the left, is shown being helped to the ground by Elizabeth. This seems to be the most likely explanation for the Madonna's more elevated position, since it was not her part in the story to receive Elizabeth, which is what she would otherwise appear to be doing. The only other possibility might be that Elizabeth is shown curtseying, but this is not the case in any of the other drawings. In both No. 89 and the *recto* of the Princeton drawing the Madonna seems to reach out as if to embrace Elizabeth, though the two protagonists are shown in closer proximity in No. 89. In No. 89 Guercino has also emphasised the difference in age between Mary and the previously barren Elizabeth who, with Zacharias, is described in the Bible as 'well stricken in years'.

No. 89 has been lifted since the publication of Mahon and Turner, who pointed out the existence of the study on the *verso* of the drawing. It shows two flights of steps, back to back, leading up to either side of a door on the right; there are also indications of the figures of Elizabeth in the doorway and of the Madonna below ascending the steps at the rear. This solution for the architectural setting, highly schematic though it is, conforms essentially to that of the final picture, although there the steps are much less obtrusive.

A drawing formerly on the London art market (pen and brown ink, 159 × 249mm; Yvonne Tan Bunzl, *Old Master Drawings*, London, 1987, no. 34, repr.), apparently of Elizabeth and Joseph, head and shoulders, is stylistically extremely close to No. 89 and may perhaps be associated with the same phase of the composition as that on the *recto*.

90 The Visitation

Red chalk. 248 × 183mm.

Windsor Castle, Royal Library, inv. no. 2676.

Provenance: Casa Gennari; King George III.

Literature: M & T, 1989, no. 64.

Most representations of the *Visitation* feature the moment when the Madonna is being greeted by Elizabeth on the steps of her house, which the two women are about to enter.

Such an interpretation was studied, in opposite directions, in two composition drawings in the Pierpont Morgan Library, New York. In the first (inv. no. I, 101f; M, *Disegni*, 1969, no. 133) the composition is in reverse to that of the picture: Elizabeth, standing on the left at roughly the same level as her visitor, appears to take the Madonna by the hand to show her up a small flight of steps towards the door of the house, which is on the left instead of the right. In the second, more rapidly executed study (inv. no. 1956.21, pen and brown ink and brown wash, 223 × 166mm; Stix & Leporini, 1927, no. 55; see Fig. 16) the composition is in the same sense as the picture: the Madonna, in the centre, ascends a low flight of steps towards the right and is about to be shown through a doorway on the right by Elizabeth, who stands on the right at the top of the steps, again roughly on the same level as her visitor; Joseph and Zacharias, with the assistance of a winged angel, attend to the donkey in the left background.

No. 90, with Elizabeth shown standing on the left greeting Mary who advances towards her from the right, seems to belong to an intermediate phase in the evolution of the design, being closer to the first Pierpont Morgan Library drawing. Although both figures are shown half length, Elizabeth is at a slightly higher level, as if at the top of a flight of steps. Unlike in the painting, she wears a large turban, and the Madonna is shown bareheaded; there is less of a contrast in age between the two women than in the previous drawing (No. 89).

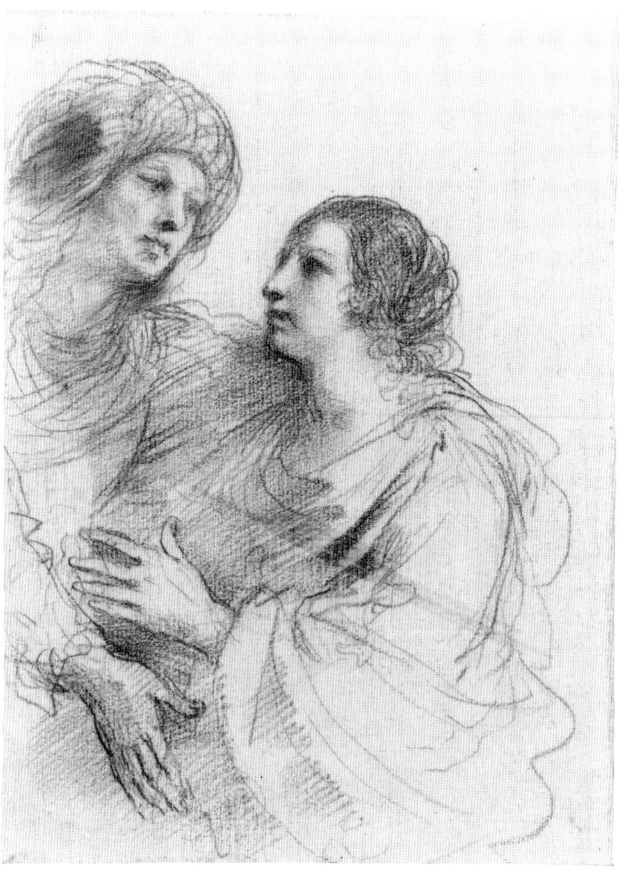

90

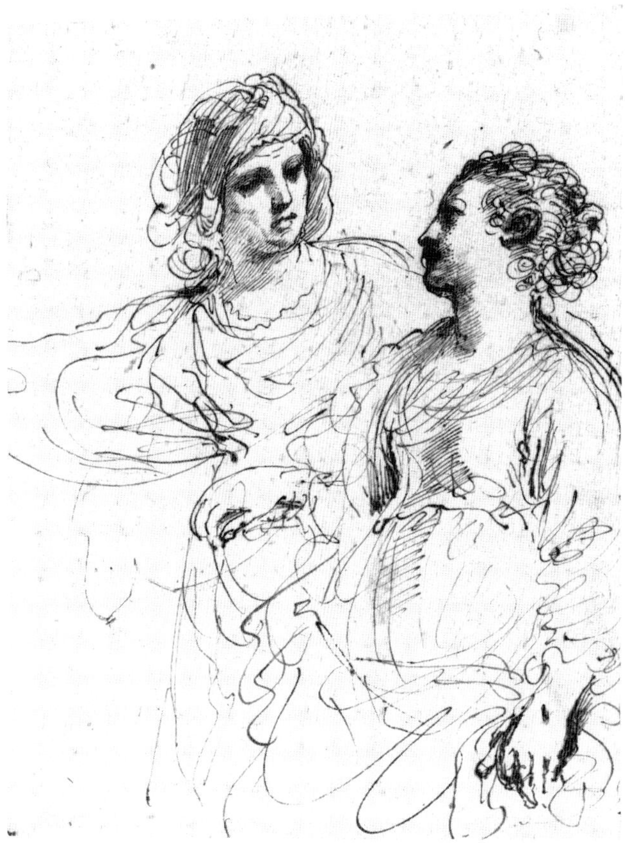

91

91 The Visitation

Pen and brown ink on light buff paper. 253 × 193mm.

Windsor Castle, Royal Library, inv. no. 2793.

Provenance: Casa Gennari; King George III.

Literature: M & T, 1989, no. 65.

Like No. 90, the present drawing belongs to an intermediate phase in the evolution of the composition of the *Visitation* when the principal figures were studied in reverse to their final appearance in the picture. The fluent, confident execution of No. 91 compares well in style with No. 85, a study for the pendant picture of the *Martyrdom of Sts John and Paul, with the Madonna and Child above*.

Guercino invariably used thin paper for drawing; the strong pen lines of the present drawing would have been easily legible had the artist turned the sheet over and held it up to the light, allowing him thereby to see his sketch in reverse.

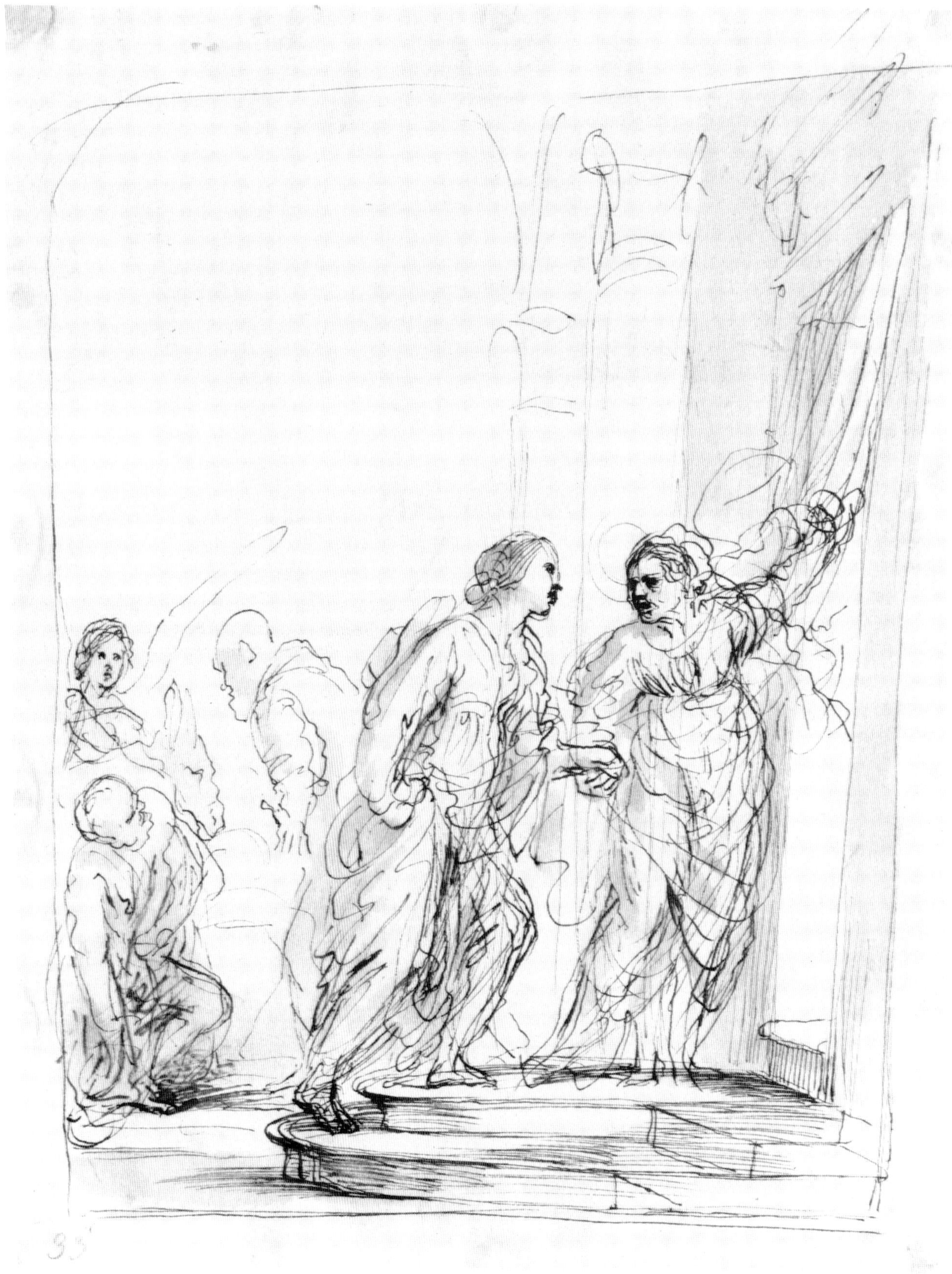

92 The Visitation

Pen and brown ink and brown wash. 212 × 185mm.

Windsor Castle, Royal Library, inv. no. 2870.

Provenance: Casa Gennari; King George III.

Literature: M, *Disegni*, 1969, no. 134; S, 1988, under no. 140; M & T, 1989, no. 68.

Inscribed on the *verso*, possibly in Guercino's hand, now almost completely indecipherable, but possibly reading: . . . *p. altra spesa da pagare p. d. to C*[. .]*pello dico è* △ *500*.

In No. 92 the two protagonists are disposed in much the same relationship to each other as in the painted result. One minor difference is that in the drawing the veil covering the Madonna's head falls forward, slightly in front of her face, creating an area of dark shadow that emphasises her attractive, almost classical profile. In the picture this detail was abandoned in favour of neater headgear or a scarf worn on the back of her head, allowing her profile to be contrasted directly against the dark background. In a separate study for the head of the Madonna in the Fitzwilliam Museum, Cambridge (inv. no. 3011, pen and brown ink, 174 × 152mm), in which the form of the profile is even closer to that in the painting, part of the veil is still shown falling forward in much the same way as in No. 92. However, the shadow is not as deep, as if the artist had begun to realise that the device might not be necessary.

No. 92 was recently lifted to reveal a study and inscription on the *verso*, unfortunately cut by the top of the sheet (their presence had been previously noted in M & T, 1989, no. 68). So far as they go, the schematically drawn outlines of the four figures and their setting correspond very closely to the painting, even to the extent of showing the rounded steps of the porch; the artist seems to have paid particular attention to the rhythms of the Madonna's drapery (for which see No. 93). The late phase in the evolution of the composition marked by the *verso* study is also exactly that of the drawing in the Pierpont Morgan Library, New York (inv. no. 1956.21; referred to under No. 90), which is similar in its rapid tempo and even in some of the abbreviations of the figures (see Fig. 16).

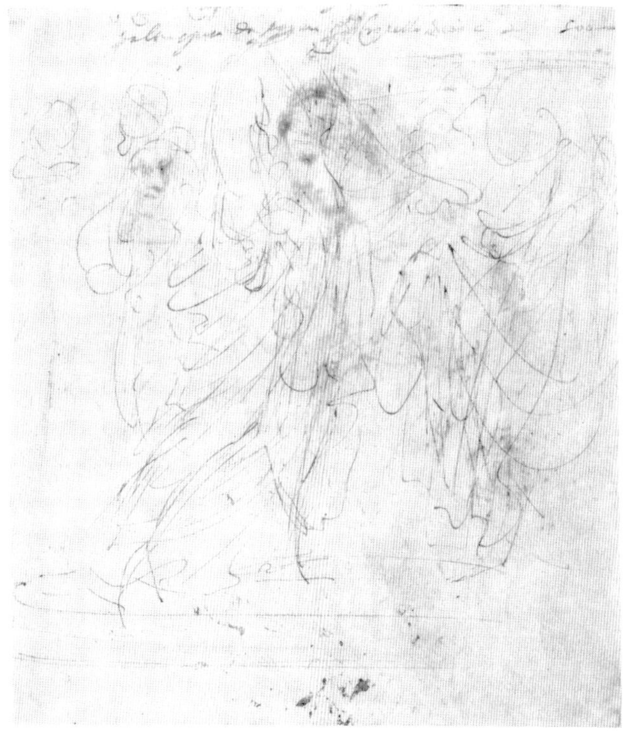

92 *verso*

93 Study for the Drapery of the Madonna in the Visitation

London, British Museum, inv. no. 1986–6–21–14.

(For further details, see App. no. 17.)

A study for the drapery of the Madonna in the *Visitation*, for which see No. 89.

When Guercino had decided upon the positions that his figures would assume within a given composition, after having completed what was sometimes an exhaustive series of preparatory studies, he then considered how the draperies of each figure should be represented. To arrive at their form he made studies either from the clothed model posed in the same attitude as the principal figures, or from a mannequin covered with linen and similarly positioned; these drawings, such as No. 93, are almost invariably in red chalk, heightened with slight touches of white, on light buff paper and are remarkable for their delicate rendering of light and shade. A sizeable group of such drawings has survived in the Koenig–Fachsenfeld Collection, now on deposit in the Staatsgalerie, Stuttgart, a selection from which was exhibited at Bologna in 1968 (e.g., M, *Disegni*, 1969, nos. 75, 99, 100, 105, 108, 109, etc.). No. 93 appears to be the only drawing of this type to have survived outside this group in Stuttgart.

Although the correspondence between the drawing and the painted detail is close, there are subtle differences which serve to remind one that Guercino was in the practice of qualifying his thoughts, even at this late juncture in the preparatory process. For example, the few light areas at the back of the lower part of the skirts, which are mostly in shadow, are eradicated in the painting, and there is even less light on the small bunch of drapery behind the Madonna's right hand; there are also several other adjustments of this sort.

Fig. 16 (opposite) *The Visitation*. Pen and brown ink and brown wash, 233 × 166 mm (New York, Pierpont Morgan Library, inv. no. 1956.21). See Nos. 90 and 92

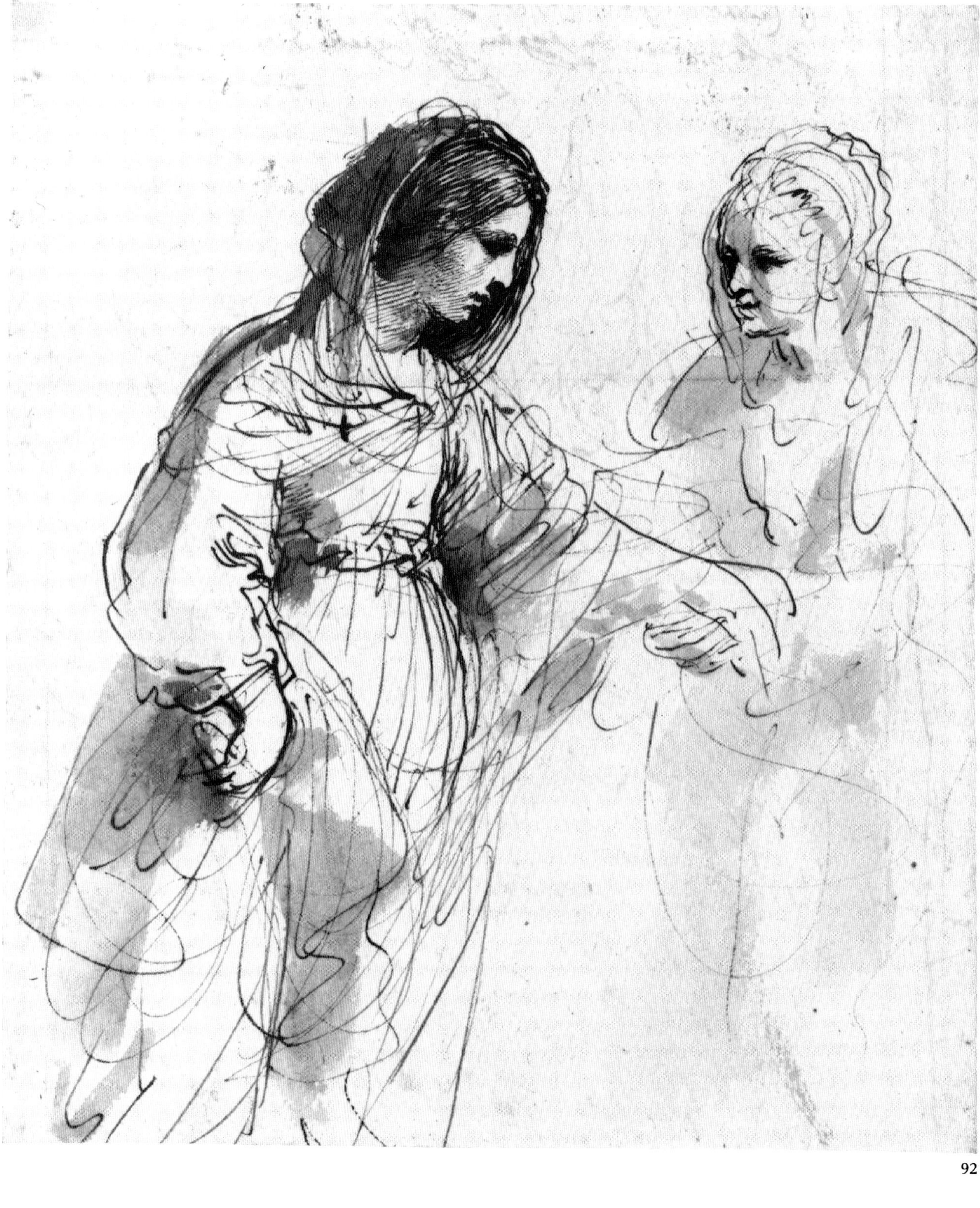

92

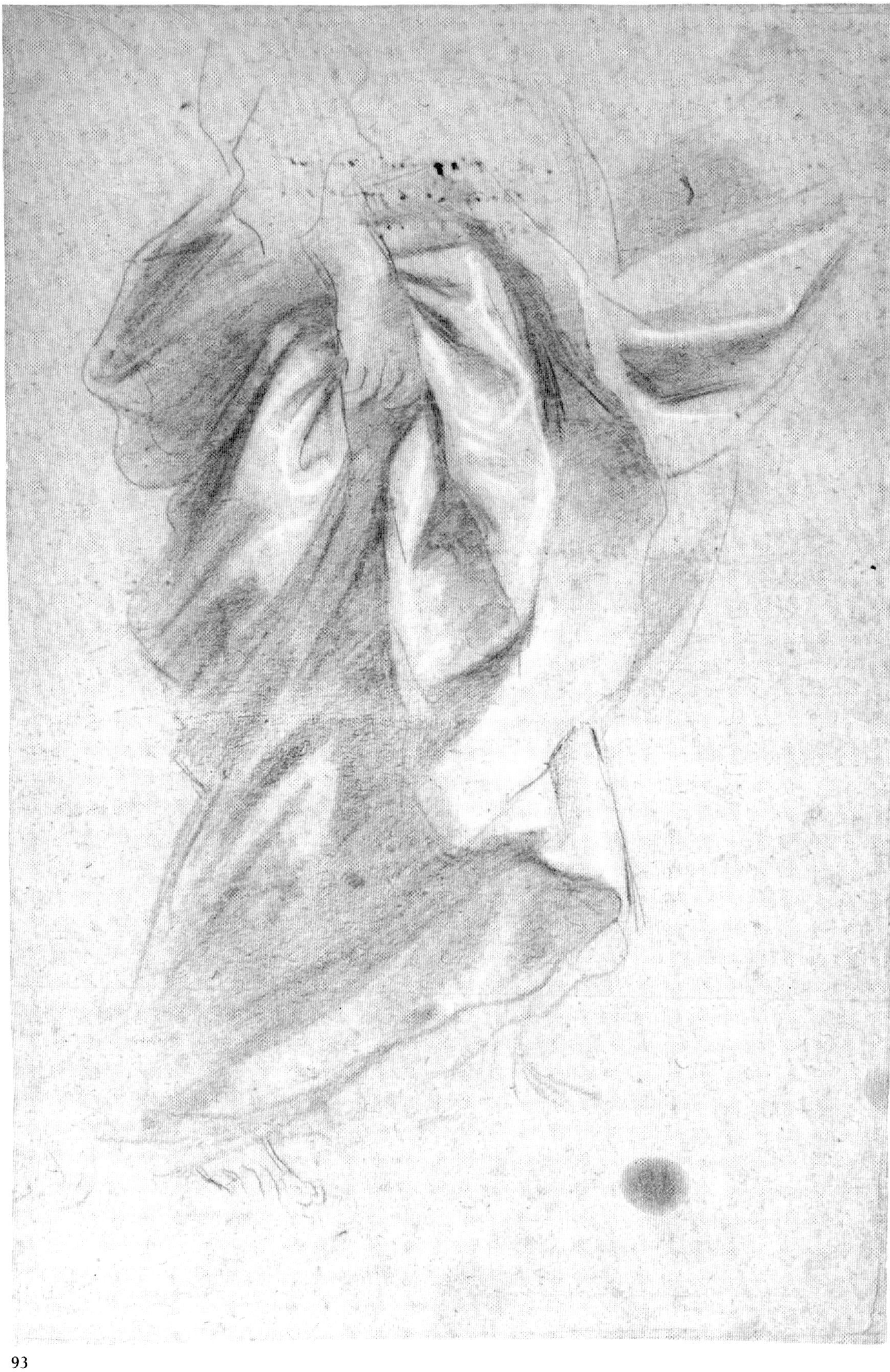

93

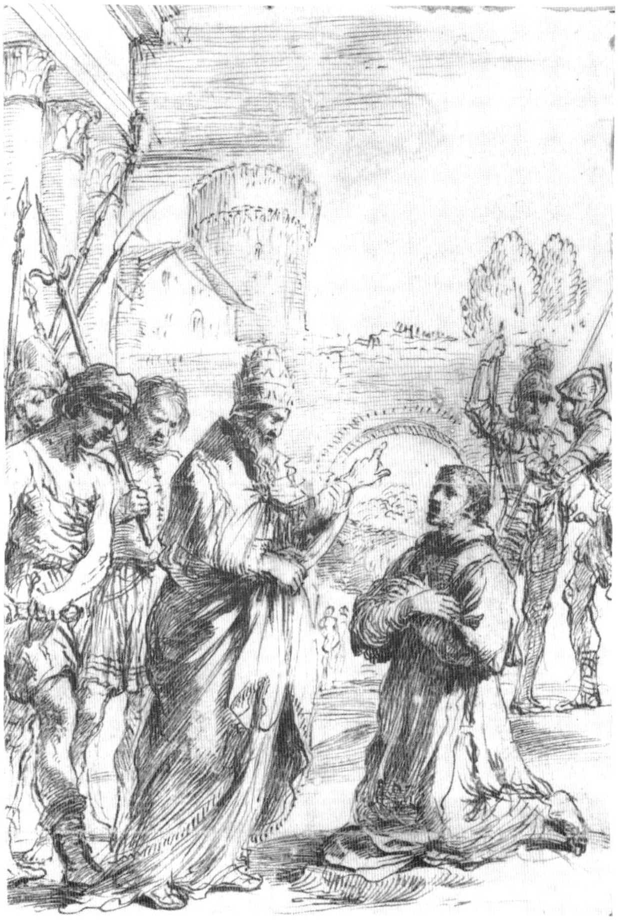

94

94 St Laurence kneeling before Pope St Sixtus II

Pen and brown ink, with very slight traces of black chalk. 190 × 133mm.

Windsor Castle, Royal Library, inv. no. 2914.

Provenance: Casa Gennari; King George III.

Literature: M & T, 1989, no. 73.

No. 94 is unusual among Guercino's drawings for its high degree of finish – a quality largely explained by its purpose as a design for an engraving. It is a preliminary study, in reverse and with slight variations, for a print by Giovanni Battista Coriolano (*fl.* in the first half of the seventeenth century) (Bartsch, 1803–21, XIX, p. 40, no. 7; Bertelà, 1973, no. 378), one of a set of five made after drawings by Guercino illustrating the life of St Laurence for the poem in five cantos by Francesco Toschi, entitled *Il trionfante Levita, poemetto sacro di S. Lorenzo*. The poem was dedicated to Cardinal Lorenzo Magalotti on 30 March 1633, but the volume's colophon states that it was published in Bologna in 1632. The engraving precedes the second canto on p. 56 of the volume. No. 94 is drawn to a slightly larger scale than the corresponding print, whose platemark measures 176 × 114mm. There are also a number of passages that show that the artist was still uncertain over the resolution of certain details, for example the pitch of the roof in the building just to the right of the colonnade, the placing of the legs of the soldiers both on the left and right of the composition, and the outline of the cornice on the colonnade at the top left. The careful hatching and stippling throughout the drawing anticipate the marks that the engraver had to reproduce with the burin.

A second study in reverse for this same print, evidently drawn immediately after No. 94, is in the Ecole des Beaux-Arts, Paris (inv. no. 2699, pen and brown ink, 174 × 111mm; see Fig. 17). It is even more laborious in its handling and is drawn to precisely the same scale as the engraving. Moreover, the uncertainties noted above have been corrected, though there is a slight pentiment for the helmet of the soldier on the extreme right.

Unlike No. 94, the principal contours of the Paris drawing have been gone over with a stylus, the means by which

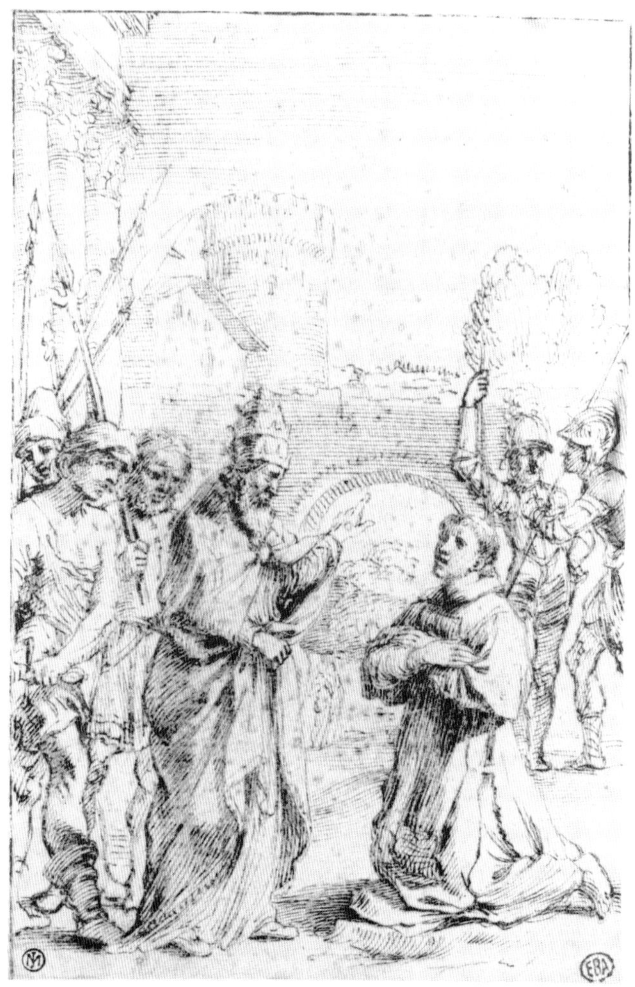

Fig. 17 *St Laurence kneeling before Pope St Sixtus II*. Pen and brown ink, the outlines indented with the stylus, 174 × 111 mm (Paris, Ecole des Beaux-Arts, inv. no. 2699). See No. 94

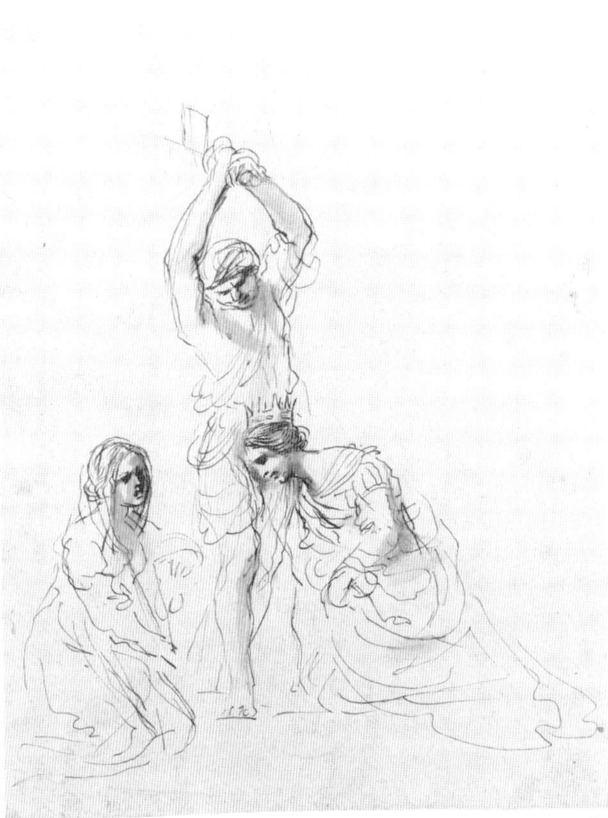

95

the engraver transferred the composition onto the copperplate. In this method of transfer either the back of the paper or the surface of the copper itself was prepared in such a way as to allow a line corresponding to the stylus indentations to appear on the metal surface. This line then served as a guide for the engraver to begin cutting the plate with his burin. When an image was transferred in this way (it was not the only method used), the image of the drawing was repeated in the same direction onto the plate, with the result that when the plate was printed the image was reversed.

95 The Execution of Mary Queen of Scots

Pen and brown ink and brown wash. 237 × 187mm.

Windsor Castle, Royal Library, inv. no. 2790.

Provenance: Casa Gennari; King George III.

Literature: M & T, 1989, no. 74.

The subject of No. 95 can be identified with certainty owing to its connection, in reverse, with a drawing in the Hessisches Landesmuseum at Darmstadt (inv. no. AE 1676; pen and brown ink and brown wash, 217 × 152mm; see Fig. 18). The Darmstadt drawing, formerly in the collections of Pierre Crozat (his number *65* in the bottom right corner) and Sir Thomas Lawrence (for this latter provenance, see M & T, 1989, no. 74), is inscribed in the lower margin, probably in Guercino's hand: *MARIA REG* [the word is interrupted at the centre of the line by the arms of Pope Urban VIII (1623–44)] *INA DI SCOTIA/ poema* . . .. It is a more complete rendering of the composition than that of No. 95. The execution of the Queen is seen taking place on some steps; there are figures of soldiers and spectators in the background; and the executioner wields a sword in his right hand instead of an axe in both hands. Otherwise the general relationship of the three principal figures to each other is much the same in both drawings. The kneeling woman attendant holding a crucifix in one hand and pointing to it with the other, seen on the right of the Darmstadt drawing, explains the action of her counterpart on the left in No. 95.

The composition of both No. 95 and the Darmstadt drawing bears some relationship to that of an engraved frontispiece by the Bolognese printmaker Agostino Parisini (*fl.*1625–36). This introduces a poem by Bastiano Gatti entitled *Maria Regina di Scotia Poema heroico*, published in Bologna in 1633. So crude is the design of this print that its invention is almost certainly not directly based on one

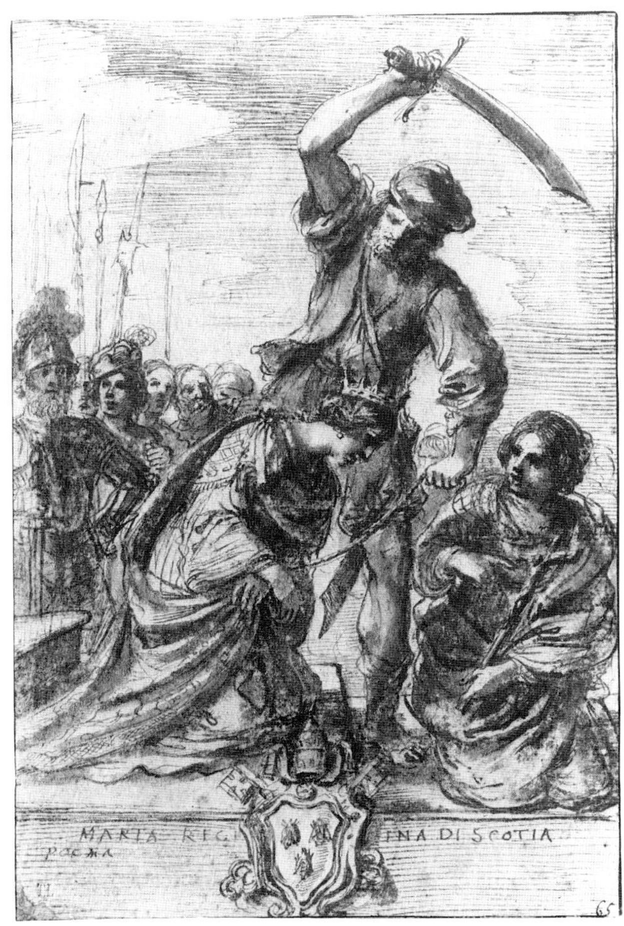

Fig. 18 *The Execution of Mary Queen of Scots*. Pen and brown ink and brown wash, 217 × 152 mm (Darmstadt, Hessisches Landesmuseum, inv. no. AE 1676). See No. 95

by Guercino, though the similarity of individual elements seems to point to knowledge of the present composition. The image in Parisini's engraving also corresponds in size with that of the Darmstadt drawing and includes the arms of Urban VIII in the bottom centre.

96 St Francis receiving the Stigmata

Pen and brown ink and brown wash. 256 × 184mm.

London, Courtauld Institute Galleries, Witt Collection, inv. no. 1369.

Provenance: Casa Gennari (the drawing retains its fine Casa Gennari mount, for which see L *Suppl*, 2858c, and M, 1967, p. 20); Mr Bouverie; Mr Hervey; the Earls of Gainsborough (sale, Christie's, London, 27 July 1922, lot 81, with others, bt *Meatyard*); Sir Robert Witt.

Literature: Hammer, *et al.*, 1977, no. 38.

Numbered in graphite in the bottom left corner: *31* (for a discussion and further instances of sheets numbered in this way, see No. 10).

Guercino painted several versions of this subject, five of which are known. These are in the Chiesa delle Sacre Stimmate, Ferrara (1632); the Chiesa dei Cappuccini, Piacenza (1633); the Mittelrheinisches Landesmuseum, Mainz (1642); the Galleria Nazionale d'Arte Antica, Rome (1646); and the Chiesa di S. Maria di Carignano, Genoa (1649). All five (S, 1988, nos. 142, 147, 201, 229 and 265 respectively) are similar in format and composition: the saint kneels in the foreground of a rocky landscape, with his arms outstretched to receive the stigmata. In our opinion the drawing dates from the 1640s, discounting the possibility of its connection with the two earliest of the extant versions.

Mahon (his opinion is quoted by Hammer, *et al.*) connected the drawing with what is probably the latest of the paintings of this subject, that now in the Chiesa di S. Maria di Carignano, Genoa, which is thought to be the picture painted for Cardinal Francesco Maria Macchiavelli and recorded in the Account Book under the year 1649. Although the Witt drawing compares well with the Genoa picture in terms of the pose of the figure and the direction of the lighting, it seems to us that it has more in common with the painting now in Mainz, though in reverse. As well as his general pose, the bent arms of the saint in the drawing relate extremely well to those of the figure in the painting; also the block of stone on the left of the drawing corresponds to the makeshift altar on which St Francis rests his book, skull and crucifix in the Mainz painting, whereas in the Genoa picture such items rest on a slab of stone at the figure's feet.

Guercino initially drew the figure of St Francis higher up the sheet and on a slightly larger scale. He then concealed this draft with sketches of foliage, particularly over the figure's raised right arm.

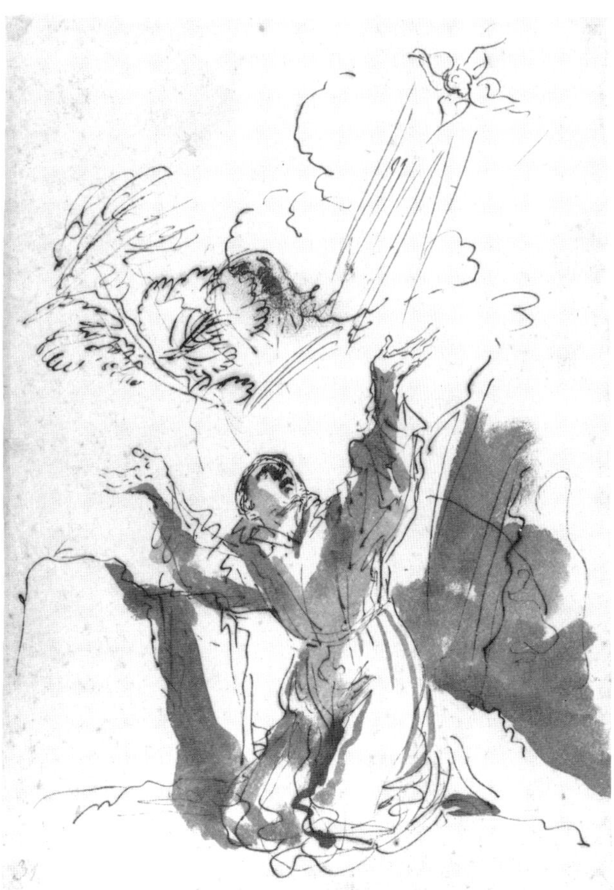

96

97–102 Studies for *Christ appearing to St Teresa* (1634)

Aix-en-Provence, Musée Granet

97 Christ appearing to St Teresa

Pen and brown ink and brown wash. 290 × 198mm.

Windsor Castle, Royal Library, inv. no. 2806.

Provenance: Casa Gennari; King George III.

Literature: M, *Disegni*, 1969, under nos. 137–8; S, 1988, under no. 152; M & T, 1989, no. 79.

Nos. 97–102 are studies for the altarpiece painted in 1634 for Barthélémy Lumague, destined for his family chapel in the church of the Convent of the Barefooted Carmelites, Lyon, and now in the Musée Granet, Aix-en-Provence (S, 1988, no. 152). Lumague was a banker and merchant of Italian extraction who had settled in Lyon. As was first suggested by Mahon, it is likely that he acted as banker to the French Queen Mother Maria de' Medici in her attempt to purchase Guido Reni's *Abduction of Helen* (Pepper, 1984, no. 132); and it is also possible that it was Cardinal Spada, the Legate of Bologna, with whom Lumague surely negotiated, who put Guercino forward as a candidate to take on the banker's own private commission (see Loire, 1990, p. 14).

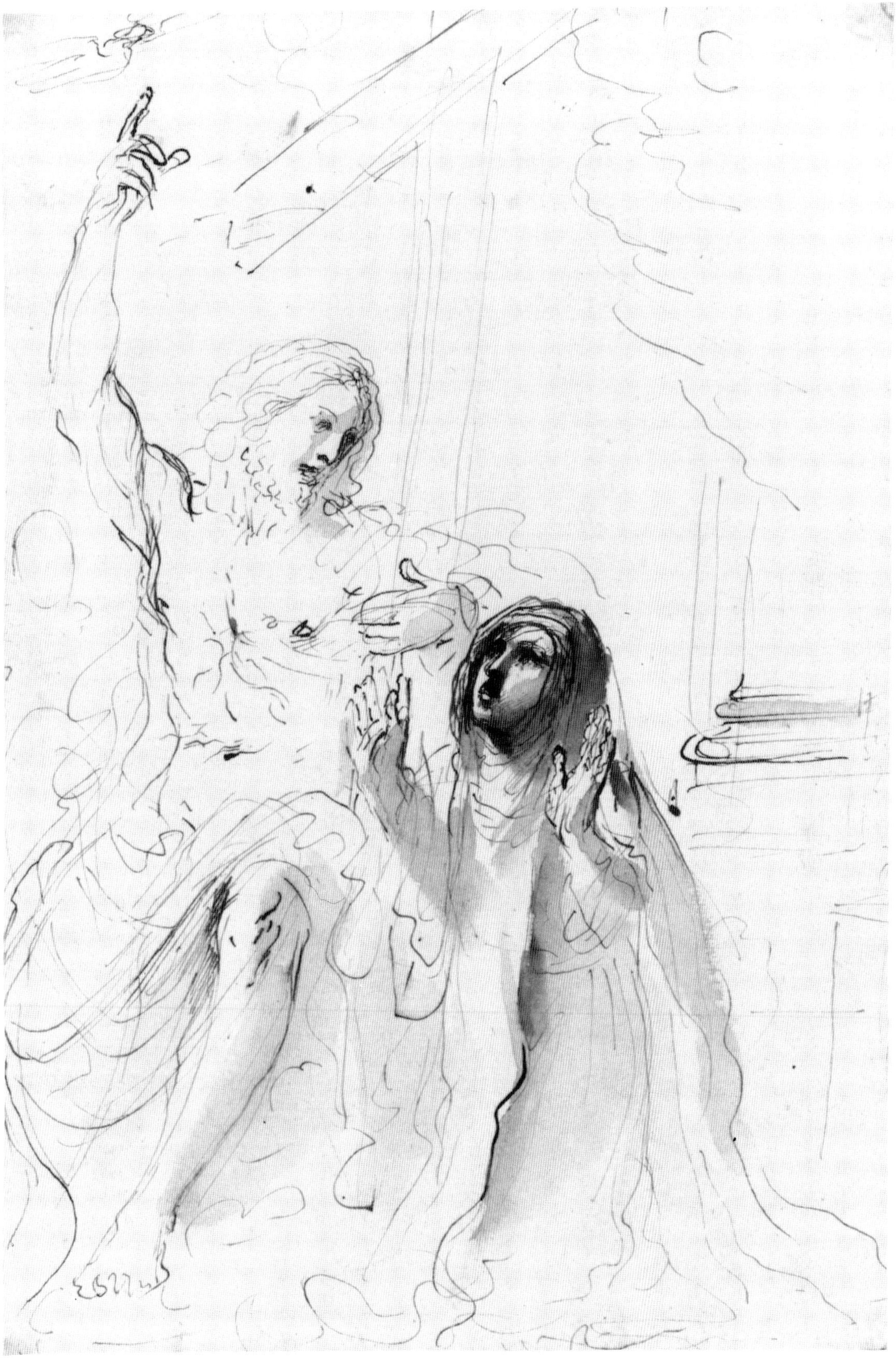

97

The present study differs most notably from the finished work in showing Christ seated and supporting a large cross with his left hand. His right hand is raised, pointing upwards as in the finished work. A drawing in the Teyler's Museum, Haarlem (inv. no. H. 13), shows Christ in a very similar position, with St Teresa again kneeling at his left side, though with her hands clasped. No. 97 instead shows the saint's hands raised in wonder at the apparition of Christ, rather than crossed as in the finished work. Another drawing in which she is shown in this pose, this time in response to Christ drawing a nail out of his left hand, is in the Musée Turpin de Crissé, Angers (inv. no. MTC 5028; Huchard & Laing, 1977–8, no. 52, repr.). The large cross that features in No. 97 and in the Haarlem drawing is also in the background of the Angers study.

Dr David Stone has kindly brought to our attention a pen-and-wash drawing in the Seattle Art Museum, Seattle, Washington (inv. no. 51.155; 244 × 235mm), which shows St Teresa kneeling with both arms raised above her head, flanked by two angels, one of whom draws back the saint's habit to reveal her heart, into which the other is poised to plunge an arrow. This unusually daring treatment of the subject was clearly inspired by St Teresa's own account of a recurring vision in which an angel appeared to her and repeatedly plunged a fiery spear through her heart into the depths of her body. We have followed David Stone in his suggestion that this is an early work for the Aix picture on the grounds of style. The saint's uplifted arms in the Seattle drawing seem to echo or even foreshadow her gesture of surprise in No. 97 and the Angers study. It seems that Guercino was experimenting with several ways of depicting Teresa's visions while the composition was at an early stage. The three ideas explored – namely, St Teresa and the angels, Christ revealing his wounds and Christ holding the cross – were all eventually abandoned in favour of a far more restrained result, which scarcely acknowledges the visionary nature of the scene.

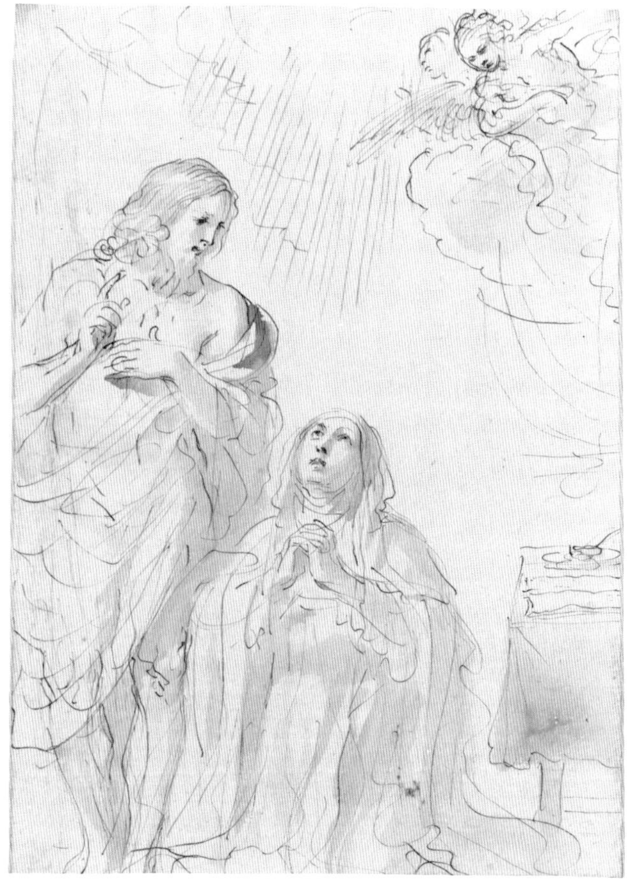

98

98 Christ appearing to St Teresa

Pen and brown ink and grey wash, with slight traces of brown wash. 295 × 210mm.

Windsor Castle, Royal Library, inv. no. 2696.

Provenance: Casa Gennari; King George III.

Literature: M, *Disegni*, 1969, no. 137; S, 1988, under no. 152; M & T, 1989, no. 78.

A study for Guercino's altarpiece of this subject of 1634, for which see No. 97. In the present study Christ's gesture at first sight appears to be one of instruction or admonishment, whereas in fact he is indicating God the Father and the Holy Ghost above to St Teresa. This ambiguity might explain Guercino's choice of the more emphatic gesture for Christ in the finished painting, in which he points upwards with his whole arm raised, a motif anticipated in Nos. 97 and 99 as well as in a drawing in the Teylers Museum, Haarlem (inv. no. H. 13). Guercino further experimented with the gesture of Christ in another pen-and-wash drawing in the Royal Library, Windsor Castle (M & T, 1989, no. 80). St Teresa's hand-gestures also underwent several changes; No. 98 shows her hands clasped, as in the Haarlem drawing, rather than crossed over her breast as in the painting. She appears in the finalised pose in three drawings: a red chalk figure study in the Pinacoteca, Cento (M, *Disegni*, 1969, no. 138); a pen-and-wash drawing showing the saint and Christ together, from Lord Northwick's collection, formerly on the London art market (*Exhibition of Old Master Drawings*, exh. cat., London, Colnaghi's, June–July, 1971, no. 21, repr.); and a detail pen study for her head and shoulders in the Palazzo Rosso, Genoa (inv. no. 1736; Turner, 1990, p. 654, fig. 32).

The present drawing gives more of an idea of the whole composition than either of the other studies for the lower half of the altarpiece in this exhibition (Nos. 97 and 99). Two angels appear in the upper right corner (drawn to a much smaller scale than the principal figures below), and rays descend in the centre to denote the light of the heavenly apparition, though God the Father and the Holy Ghost are not included. Two other studies for the whole composition are the Haarlem drawing mentioned above and another in the Musée Turpin de Crissé at Angers (inv. no. MTC 5028; Huchard & Laing, 1977–8, no. 52, repr.).

The delicate application of pale grey wash in the present drawing is typical of Guercino's style in the 1630s.

99 Christ appearing to St Teresa

London, British Museum, inv. no. Ff. 2–134.

(For further details, see App. no. 20.)

A study for Guercino's altarpiece of this subject painted in 1634, for which see No. 97. The poses of the figures in No. 99 are similar to those in the finished work, except that St Teresa's hands are clasped instead of being crossed over her breast. Guercino was evidently uncertain of the position of Christ's head at this stage, as the significant pentiment beneath the figure's raised arm attests. In the painting the artist selected a more upright position for the head than either of the alternatives explored here. At the upper left of the drawing are rapid indications of two heads of angels and at the lower left what appears to be the pedestal of a column with a coat of arms on it.

100 God the Father with an Angel and three Putti

Pen and brown ink and brown wash. 202 × 298mm.

Windsor Castle, Royal Library, inv. no. 2785.

Provenance: Casa Gennari; King George III.

Literature: S, 1988, under no. 152; M & T, 1989, no. 81.

Mahon and Turner connected this drawing with the *Christ appearing to St Teresa* of 1634, discussed under No. 97. God the Father, resting his right hand on a globe, is close to the corresponding figure in the finished work; a pen-and-wash study for this figure alone, but in a pose more closely resembling his counterpart in the painting, is in the collection of Dr Manfredo Macioti, formerly of London. The two putti to the right of God the Father in No. 100 also feature in the painting, though more fully resolved. The putto with his arms raised on the left in the drawing is transferred to the top right edge of the altarpiece, his pose only slightly modified but in reverse. Meanwhile, the angel on the right of the drawing with one arm raised and half his chest exposed was moved to the left edge of the painting, beneath God's right hand. For another study of this figure, close in handling to No. 100 and much nearer to the painted solution, see No. 102. A composition drawing, in pen and ink, in the Teylers Museum, Haarlem (inv. no. H. 13), also shows the angel on the right, above St Teresa. These subtle reversals and modifications are typical of Guercino's preparatory method.

The somewhat sombre atmosphere of the altarpiece is anticipated in the graduated films of wash in No. 100, becoming quite dense in places.

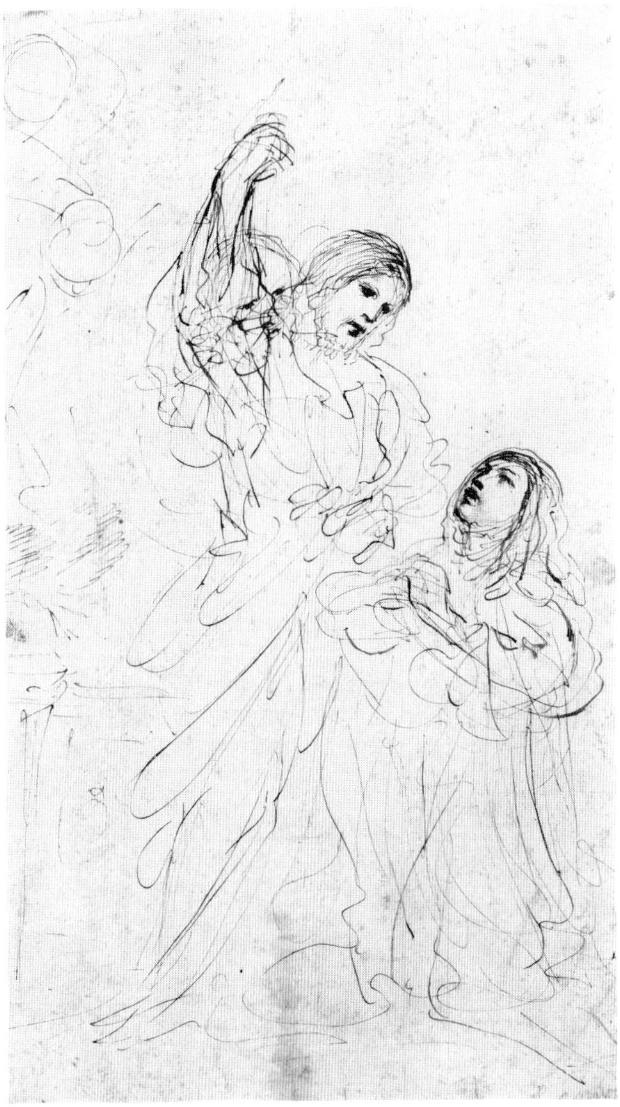

99

101 Three Putti among Clouds

Pen and brown ink and brown wash. 217 × 338mm; drawn on paper apparently from an account book.

Windsor Castle, Royal Library, inv. no. 2805.

Provenance: Casa Gennari; King George III.

Literature: S, 1988, under no. 152; M & T, 1989, no. 82.

Probably a study for the *Christ appearing to St Teresa* of 1634, for which see No. 97. None of the putti correspond directly with those in the painting, but there are definite echoes between the two groups of three, which are in reverse to each other. The putto on the left of the study, with the pentiment for his raised arms, is quite closely related to that in the top right-hand corner of the altarpiece while the others, one kneeling on one knee and his companion seen only to the waist, also share points in common with the pair in the picture. The three putti are again seen

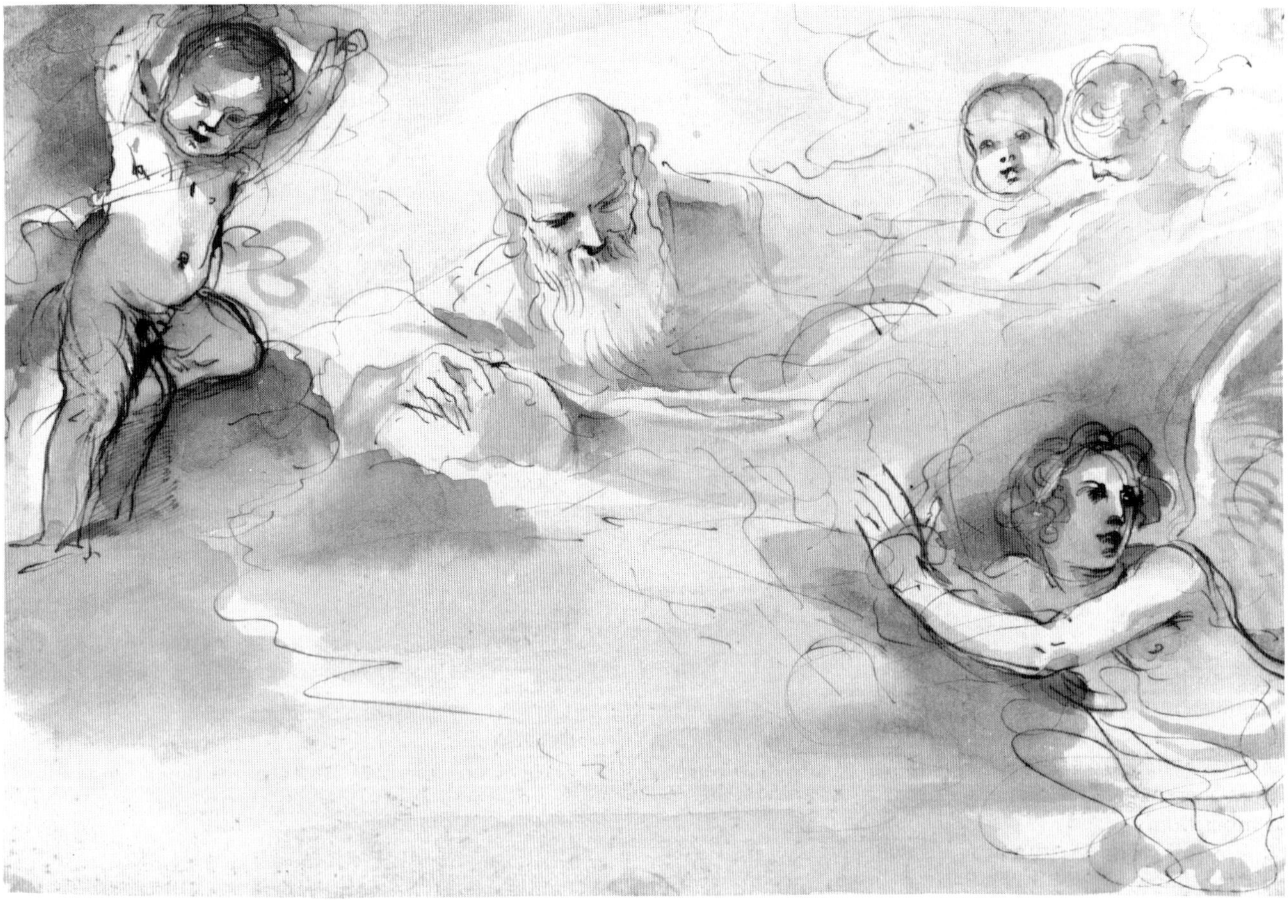

100

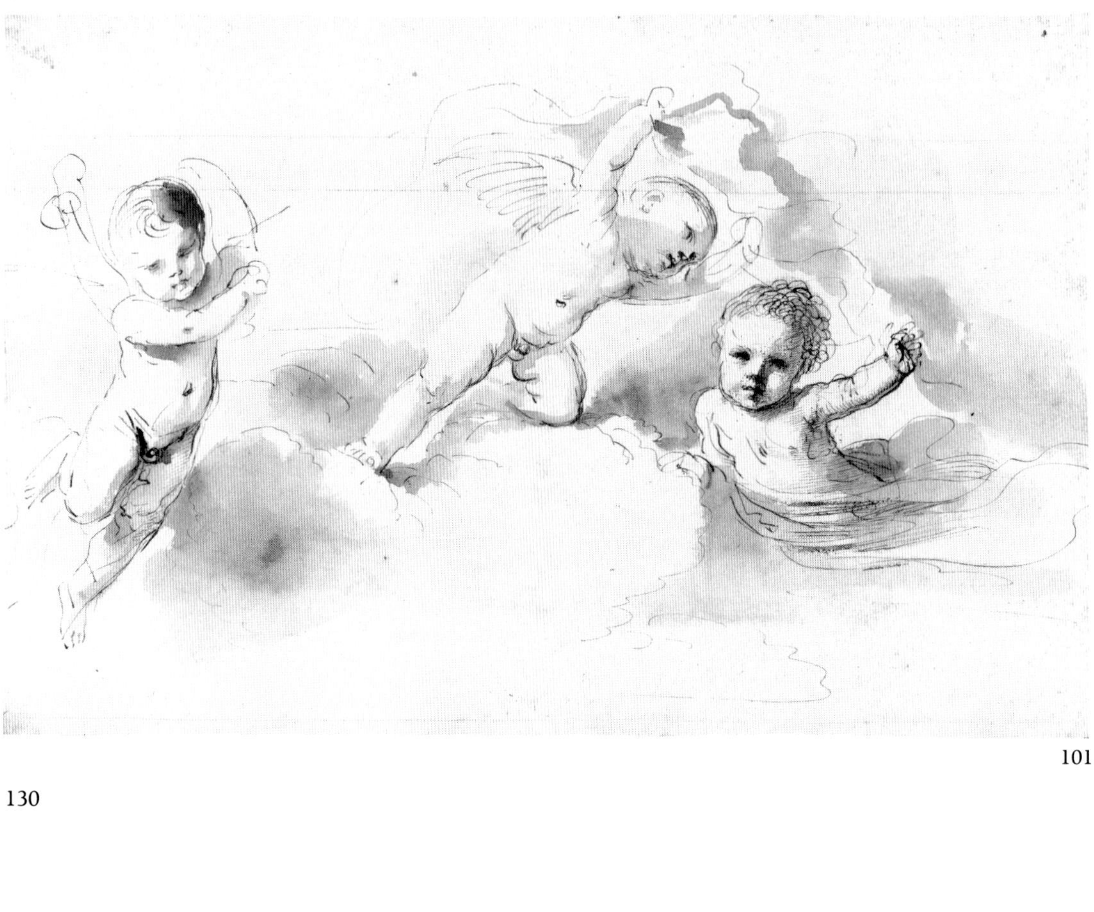

101

as a group, though in somewhat different poses and in a different arrangement, in a composition drawing in the Musée Turpin de Crissé, Angers (inv. no. MTC 5028; Huchard & Laing, 1977–8, no. 52, repr.). The half-length putto on the right of No. 101 appears on the left of the Angers drawing, his lower half obscured by Christ's cross. There is some analogy between the putto flying across the middle of either study, but in reverse.

102 An Angel

Pen and brown ink and brown wash. 257 × 201mm.

Oxford, Ashmolean Museum, KTP 875.

Provenance: Shrewsbury; Southesk; purchased 1946.

Literature: Parker, 1956, no. 875; M, *Disegni*, 1969, under nos. 137–8; Macandrew, 1980, p. 300; M & E, 1986, no. XIII; S, 1988, under no. 152; M & T, 1989, under nos. 78–82.

A study for the half-length figure of an angel in the upper left corner of Guercino's *Christ appearing to St Teresa* of 1634, for which see No. 97. The figure is similar to that in the painting except for the angle of the head, which is here turned further to the left. At one stage Guercino apparently planned to place this figure on the right of the altarpiece, above St Teresa, as can be seen in a composition drawing in the Teylers Museum, Haarlem (inv. no. H. 13); No. 102 must therefore have been made at a later moment in the composition's genesis.

A detail study for the head and shoulders of St Teresa has just come to light in the Palazzo Rosso, Genoa (inv. no. 1736; pen and brown ink on account-book paper, 195 × 156mm; repr. Turner, 1990, fig. 32 on p. 653, mistakenly captioned as in an exhibition at the Louvre). The Genoa study closely corresponds to the figure in the painting and, like the study of the head of the Madonna in the Fitzwilliam Museum, Cambridge (for which see under No. 92), it seems to have been drawn at a late stage in the preparatory work for the picture. Its function was to establish the exact expression and physiognomical type of the head, to which Guercino then closely adhered in the painting. Earlier in his career, such drawings would have been made in red chalk rather than pen and ink (see No. 50).

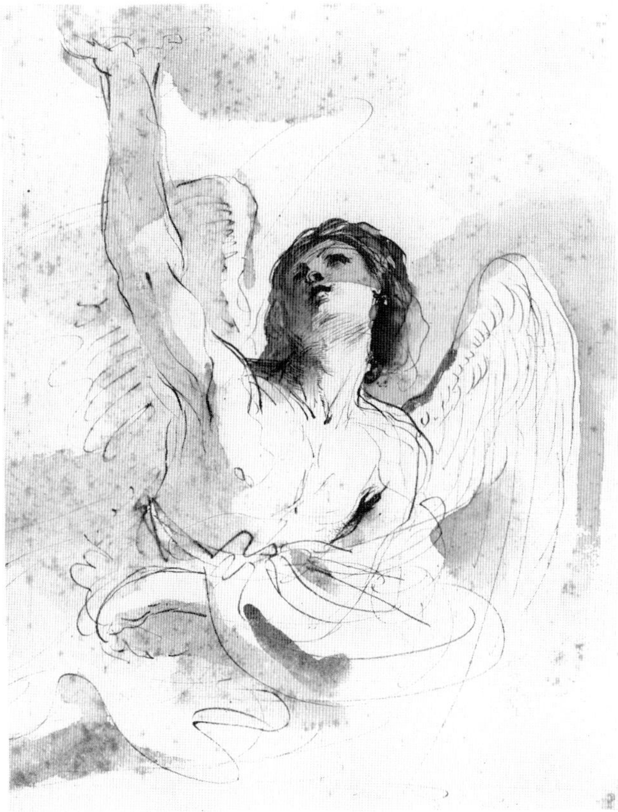

102

103 St Jerome reading a Book

Pen and brown ink and light brown wash. 261 × 381mm.

Private collection.

Provenance: Casa Gennari; Mr Bouverie; Mr Hervey; the Earls of Gainsborough.

Inscribed in brown ink in the bottom right corner: *C 4 S. Fio.*; such inscriptions are associable with a provenance from the Casa Gennari.

From its style, No. 103 would appear to date from the middle of the 1630s. The extensive use of the brush with wash, combined with a sparing, yet delicate use of the pen finds a parallel in a drawing of *Sisyphus*, datable 1636, in the collection of Robert and Bertina Suida Manning in New York (M & T, 1989, p. 49 and fig. 17), and the two drawings were probably made at about the same time. No. 103 is remarkable for its suggestion of bright sunlight, which is evoked by such details as the shadow of the saint's head cast onto the white pages of the open book propped up against the rock, or the reflection of light from his nude body and from his drapery, especially that lying on the ledge in the centre.

A drawing of an *Old bearded Man reclining among Rocks* in the Royal Library, Windsor Castle (M & T, 1989, no. 220), is similar in technique and is of much the same date.

104 Bearded old Man with a loose Drapery wrapped around his Shoulders

Pen and brown ink and light brown wash. 221 × 248mm.

Private collection.

Provenance: Casa Gennari; Mr Bouverie; Mr Hervey; the Earls of Gainsborough.

Like No. 103, this drawing apparently dates from around the middle of the 1630s. It too is largely drawn with the brush and wash, with only the finer details such as the facial

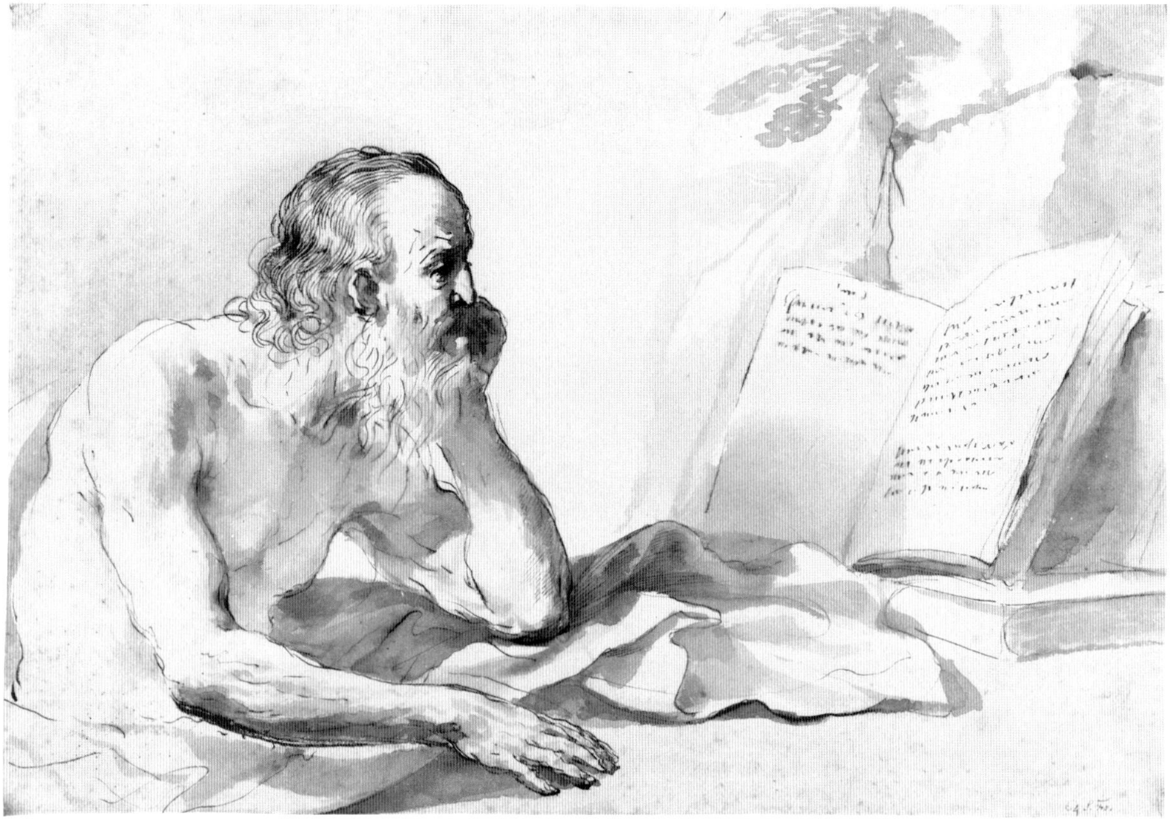

103

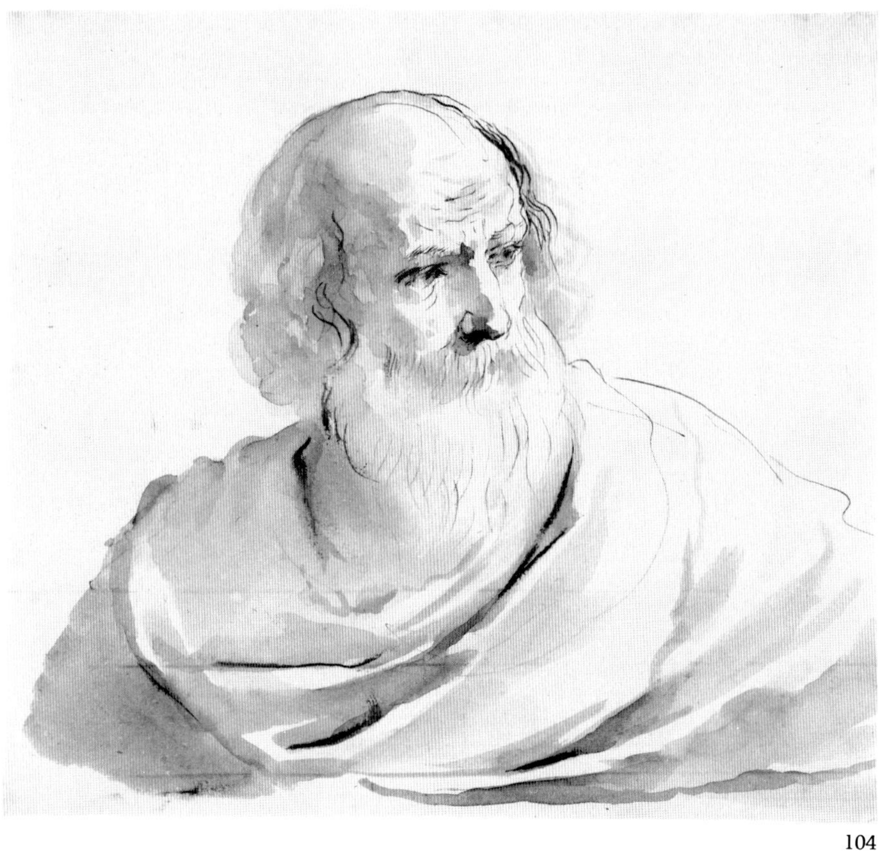

104

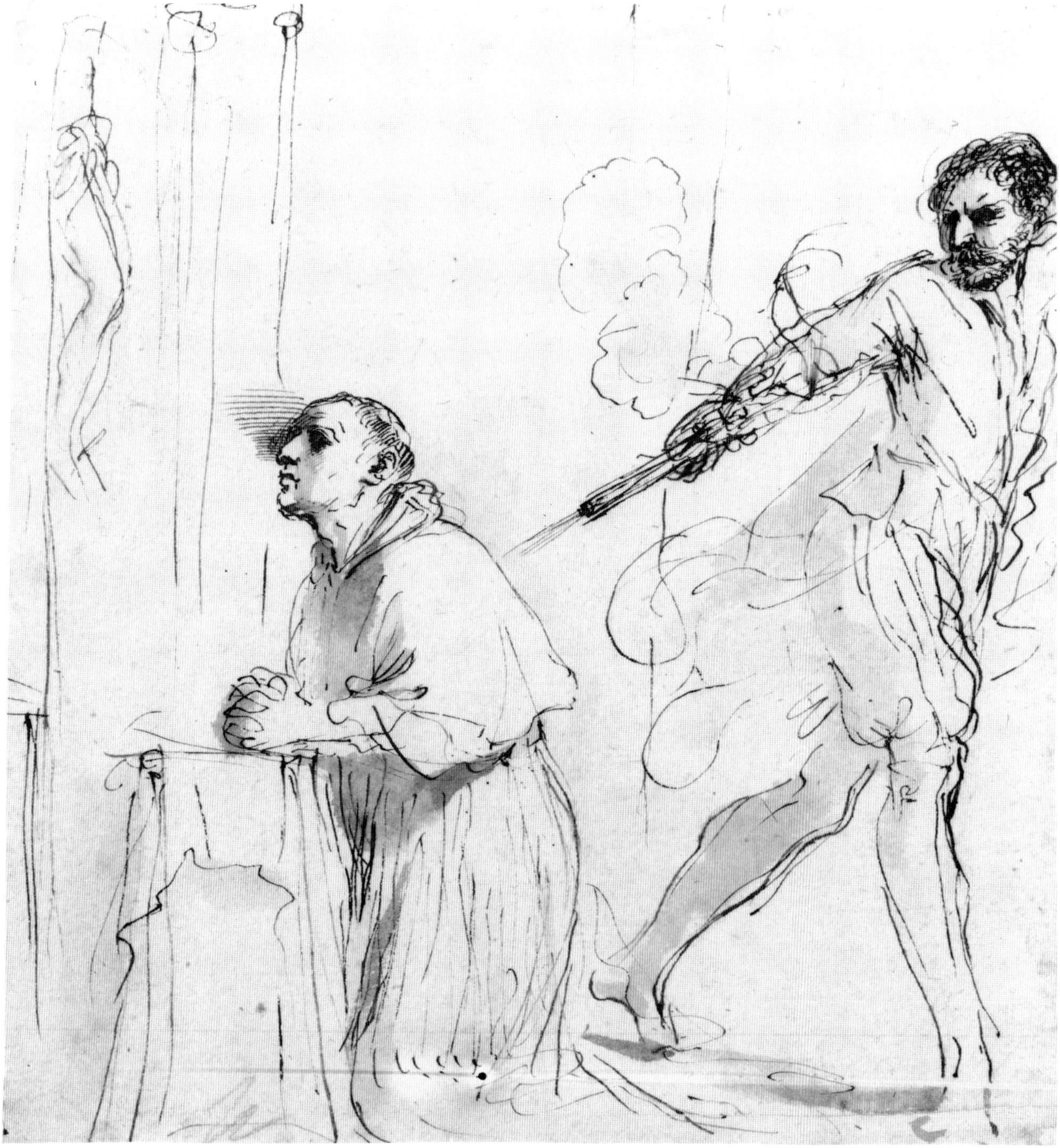

106

features, hair and beard picked out with touches of the pen. Apart from the example of the *Sisyphus* in the collection of Robert and Bertina Suida Manning in New York cited in the previous entry, a similarly liberated style of drawing is found in some of the studies for the *Christ appearing to St Teresa* of 1634 in the Musée Granet at Aix-en-Provence (e.g. Nos. 100–101).

The head compares well in type with that of Time in No. 105.

105 Allegory of the Toll of Death

(*see colour pl. 16*)

Pen and brown ink with touches of brown wash over faint traces of black chalk. 131 × 135mm.

Windsor Castle, Royal Library, inv. no. 2915.

Provenance: Casa Gennari; King George III.

Literature: B, 1988, no. 128; M & T, 1989, no. 83.

The meaning of the allegory is explicit enough: the aged figure of Time, with wings at his back and with an hourglass balanced on the top of his head, moves slowly but inexorably to the right on his crutches, while behind him, Death, in the form of a skeleton, pulls at the drapery of his victim, a terrified old woman, who turns to the left as if resisting him. As this miserable procession progresses, it tramples under foot the trappings of earthly power, both temporal and ecclesiastical – a papal tiara, a regal crown, a coronet, a mitre, a sceptre and a crozier.

No. 105 is a study, in reverse and to the same scale, for the title-page engraved by Francesco Curti (1610–90) for the book *Gabella della morte* by Don Antonio Mirandola, published by Monti and Zenero at Bologna in 1635 (Bertelà, 1973, no. 531; B, 1988, no. 127). The drawing shows no apparent sign of stylus work for the transfer of the design onto the copper-plate. Some erasures in the drawing indicate slight changes to the figures: for example, Time's left wing was first drawn just behind his head, and his right leg was first placed further forward; there are other slight pentiments for the figure of Death. Mirandola, who came from Bologna and was a close, life-long friend of Guercino, was then abbot of the church of S. Salvatore in Bologna, and Bagni has surmised that it may have been Mirandola who put the Bolognese engraver Francesco Curti in touch with Guercino (B, 1988, p. 90).

The state of the print reproduced by Bertelà is presumably later than that of the original title-page of 1635. Mirandola's title has been replaced by the following moral axiom: *GIUNGE COL TEMPO, AL FIN, L'ORRIBIL MORTE,/E MINISTRA DI DIO CIASCUNO AFFERRA*; and it is possible that prints taken from this state were intended as broadsheets.

106 St Charles Borromeo surviving the Shot of an Assassin

Pen and brown ink and brown wash, with traces of grey wash. 231 × 218mm.

Windsor Castle, Royal Library, inv. no. 2400.

Provenance: Casa Gennari; King George III.

Literature: Riccòmini, 1969, p. 39, under no. 53, repr.; M & T, 1989, no. 183.

This is a study made by Guercino almost certainly to assist his follower Antonio Bonfanti, called il Torricella (active in Ferrara in the 1620s and 1630s), in a commission for a lunette-shaped painting in the church of S. Carlo Borromeo at Ferrara (Riccòmini, 1969, pl. I). Another drawing by Guercino for this project is in the Teylers Museum, Haarlem (inv. no. H. 7; Riccòmini, 1969, p. 39, under no. 53, repr.). It is horizontal in format and shows the saint holding a crucifix rather than gazing up at the larger alternative attached to the wall in No. 106. Although the composition of the painting is more complex, showing the assassin kneeling among a gathering of five onlookers, there are enough parallels between the pose of the saint in both drawings and Bonfanti's lunette to warrant their connection.

Guercino had previously provided Bonfanti with at least one drawing for a painting of *Christ disputing with the Doctors* for the church of S. Francesco, Ferrara, which is datable before 1627 (Riccòmini, 1969, p. 38, no. 50). For a copy by Francesco Bartolozzi of one of Guercino's drawings for the latter commission, see App. no. 111.

107–108 Studies for *Sisyphus* (1636)

Lost

107 Sisyphus

Pen and brown ink. 232 × 192mm.

London, Courtauld Institute Galleries, Witt Collection, inv. no. 1366.

Provenance: Casa Gennari; Mr Bouverie; Mr Hervey; the Earls of Gainsborough (sale, Christie's, London, 27 July 1922, lot 81, with others, bt *Meatyard*); Sir Robert Witt.

Literature: Hammer, *et al.*, 1977, no. 33; M & T, 1989, under no. 84.

Numbered in graphite in the bottom left corner: *28* (for a discussion and further instances of sheets numbered in this way, see No. 10). On the *verso* of the drawing is a draft of a letter in the handwriting of Guercino's brother, Paolo Antonio Barbieri, to an unidentified correspondent, in which Paolo Antonio expresses his pleasure that Guercino's 'Abigaille' had met with the satisfaction of Cardinal Antonio Barberini. As Mahon and Turner pointed out (M & T, 1989, under no. 84), this is a reference to the large painting of *Abigail appeasing the Wrath of David by offering Gifts*, formerly at Bridgewater House but destroyed by fire in 1941 (for two drawings related to this picture, see App. nos. 31–2).

No painting of *Sisyphus* by Guercino survives, but the reference in the draft of a letter on the *verso* of No. 107 to the

Bridgewater House picture, which can be dated 1636, suggests that the drawing is connected with the only painting of this subject recorded in the artist's Account Book, namely that for which payment was received from Conte Girolamo Ranuzzi of Bologna on 28 October of the same year (*Libro dei Conti*, 1808, p. 78; 1841, p. 315). From a stylistic point of view, the drawing fits perfectly with this hypothesis. Guercino received 100 ducats for the picture, indicating almost certainly that the figure would have been whole length.

Sisyphus was the builder of Corinth, and as king he promoted navigation and commerce, though he was fraudulent, avaricious and deceitful. His wickedness during his lifetime was severely punished in the lower world, where he had to roll a huge marble block up a hill, but every time he reached the top, it rolled back down again.

The present drawing is unique among the series of five surviving preparatory drawings for this commission, since it shows the figure neither carrying the boulder on his back nor pushing it uphill. Drawings in the former category are discussed under No. 108. To the latter category belong a drawing in the collection of Robert and Bertina Suida Manning, New York (M & T, 1989, p. 50, fig. 17), which shows the figure also turned to the right, but half kneeling; and a double-sided sheet in black chalk in the Teylers Museum, Haarlem (inv. no. H. 29), mentioned by Carel van Tuyll in his review of M & T, 1989 (Van Tuyll, 1990, p. 217). The *recto* of the Haarlem study shows the figure, a beardless youth, with his head thrown back, stepping up with his left leg to the right. He supports the boulder with his left arm and pushes it with his right. The *verso* shows the figure from the rear, stepping to the right and supporting the rock on his left shoulder. In view of the fact that there is no record of the appearance of the finished work, it is difficult to determine a sequence for these studies.

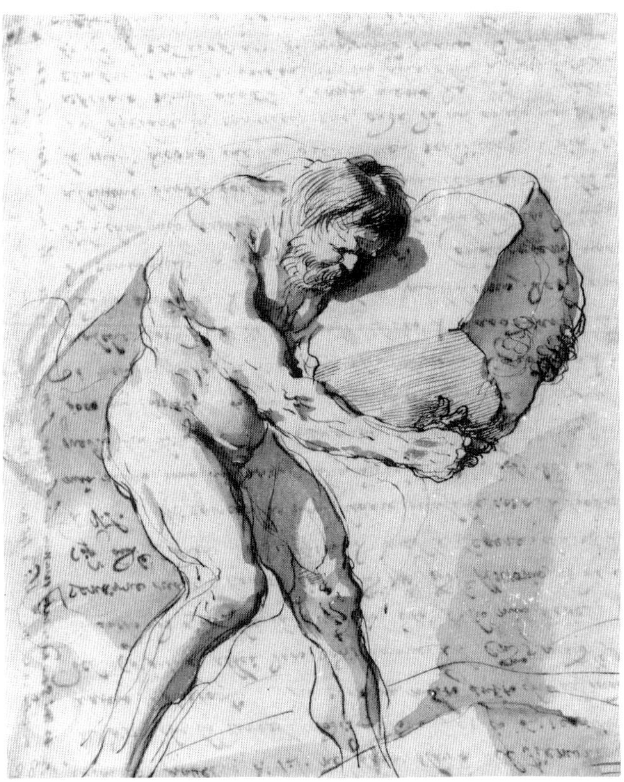

107

Dr David Stone has kindly pointed out a much-damaged pen-and-wash drawing of this subject, formerly on the New York art market (*Master Drawings*, exhibited at Herbert E. Feist Gallery, 11 October–30 November 1980, no. 16), showing Sisyphus pushing the rock up a cliff to the left, but looking down to the right over his left shoulder. We are unable to assess the quality of the drawing properly from the reproduction, but it is likely that it is a copy after a lost study by Guercino, rather than of the finished work.

No. 107 contains several pentiments, most notably for Sisyphus' left knee, which was once raised to bear the load of the rock, and for both hands. The figure most closely resembles that in a drawing formerly in the collection of Mr and Mrs Francis Avnet of New York (sale, Sotheby's, 27 March 1969, lot 14), particularly in the treatment of the head and the pentiments for the legs, except that there Sisyphus is represented with both arms raised to support the stone on his back.

108 Sisyphus

(*see colour pl. 16*)

Pen and brown ink and greyish wash, on light-buff paper. 266 × 198mm.

Windsor Castle, Royal Library, inv. no. 2882.

Provenance: Casa Gennari: King George III.

Literature: M & T, 1989, no. 84.

Like No. 107, this is most probably a preparatory study for the lost painting of *Sisyphus* recorded in Guercino's Account Book under the year 1636.

Of the four other sheets certainly by Guercino and connected with this commission, two also show the figure carrying the rock on his back, although in one of these, formerly on the London art market (sale, Christie's, 23 November 1971, lot 72), he is shown with his body facing the spectator, and in the other, formerly in the collection of Mr and Mrs Francis Avnet of New York (sale, Sotheby's, London, 27 March 1969, lot 14), he is turned to the right. This motif, showing Sisyphus with the burden resting on his shoulders, may possibly have been an early idea for the composition, as other drawings (discussed under No. 107) show him pushing the stone. However, Guercino appears to have returned to this arrangement to greater effect when preparing studies for the picture of *Atlas* (see Nos. 144–8), literally carrying the world on his shoulders; this was painted ten years later, in 1646, for Prince Don Lorenzo de' Medici and is now in the Museo Bardini, Florence (S, 1988, no. 230).

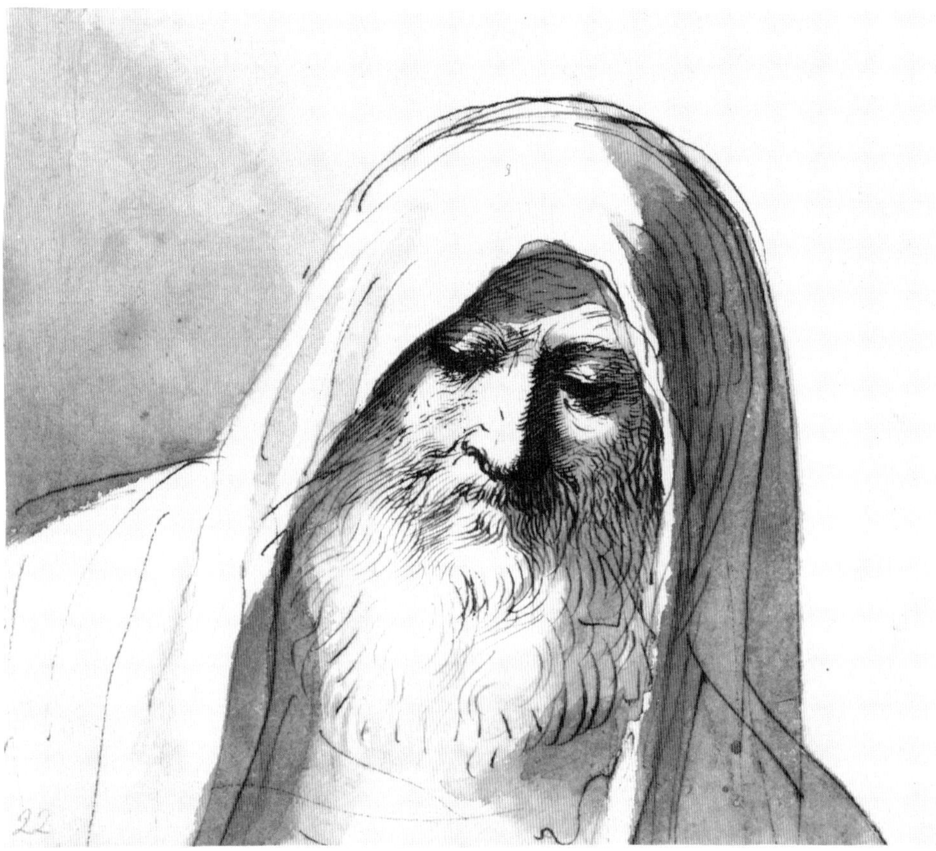

109

109 Head and Shoulders of a bearded Monk looking down

Pen and brown ink with light brown wash. 137 × 161mm.

Private collection.

Provenance: Casa Gennari; Mr Bouverie; Mr Hervey; the Earls of Gainsborough.

Numbered in graphite in the bottom left corner: *22* (for a discussion and further instances of sheets numbered in this way, see No. 10).

Datable from its style to the mid- to late 1630s.

110–111 Studies for the *Martyrdom of St Bartholomew* (1635–6)

Siena, S. Martino, repainted and damaged beyond recognition, but known from a contemporary copy in the church of S. Barnaba, Marino Laziale

110 The Martyrdom of St Bartholomew

(*see colour pl. 17*)

London, British Museum, inv. no. 1989–6–17–278.

(For other details, see App. no. 33.)

The drawing is in outstandingly good condition. It is a preparatory study for the *Martyrdom of St Bartholomew* of 1635–6, an altarpiece commissioned for the church of S. Martino in Siena (S, 1988, no. 158, where a contemporary copy of the now much-damaged original is reproduced). The picture was one of the more costly commissions received by the artist in the 1630s, amounting to 600 ducats (Malvasia, 1678, II, p. 370; 1841, II, p. 263).

This drawing and No. 111 belong to a group of four composition studies in which Guercino tried out a number of variations of this difficult subject. The other two are in the Pierpont Morgan Library, New York (inv. no. I, 101e; Stampfle & Bean, 1967, no. 41), and in the Art Museum, Princeton University, Princeton (inv. no. 48–734; Gibbons, 1977, no. 272). The New York drawing shows an early stage in the genesis of the composition when the saint was represented seated in front of a gallows, with both hands raised vertically above his head to the crossbar and with his legs splayed. As in No. 110, a crowd of onlookers, including the turbaned potentate, can be seen in the background on the right, while the classical architecture indicated above their heads finds an echo in the finished painting. In the Princeton drawing the saint is shown standing, tied to a post, with only one arm raised. At this stage, the poses of the executioners are even more compatible with those in the painted version; however, the background figures consist of a soldier keeping a crowd of curious onlookers at

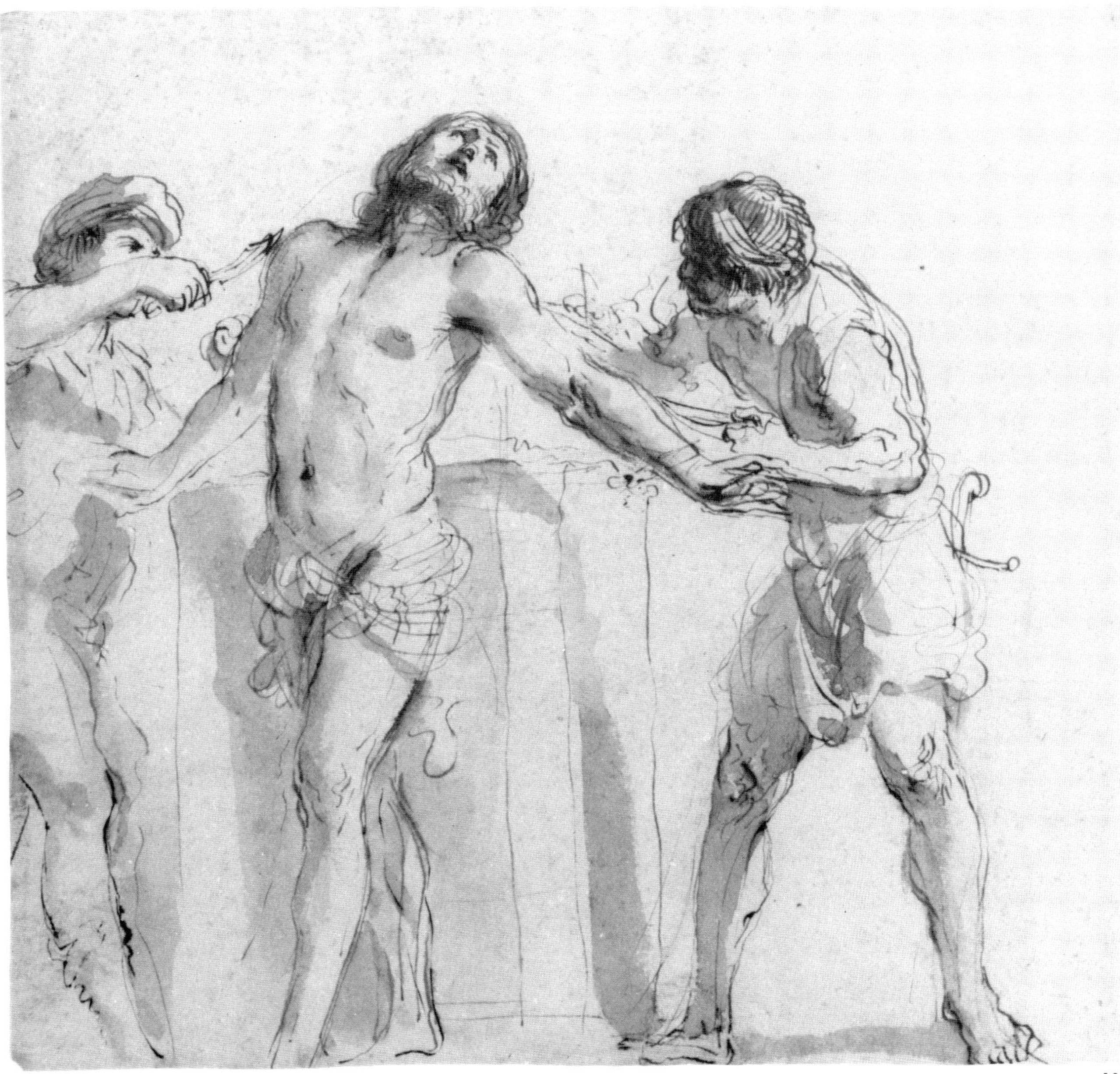

111

bay. No. 111, which concentrates on only the three central figures, shows the saint in a similar pose to that in No. 110, but with both feet on the ground. In view of the inventiveness of this series of composition drawings, the awkward, rather static poses ultimately adopted for this group of figures in the finished picture are disappointing.

Apart from App. no. 34 and the related drawings mentioned thereunder, further drawings for this composition are as follows: a drawing for the angel, identified by Mahon, in the Teylers Museum, Haarlem (inv. no. H. 48); a study for St Bartholomew with only one executioner, half length, in the possession of the Korda family, formerly in the collection of H. S. Reitlinger (his sale, Sotheby's, London, 9 December 1953, lot 53); and another also of the saint with one executioner, three-quarter length, in the Art Institute, Chicago (inv. no. 60.832; Joachim and McCullagh, 1979, no. 63).

111 Martyrdom of St Bartholomew

Pen and two different shades of brown ink, and grey and light brown wash. 234 × 256mm.

London, Courtauld Institute Galleries, Witt Collection, inv. no. 1337.

Provenance: Casa Gennari; Mr Bouverie; Mr Hervey; the Earls of Gainsborough (sale, Christie's, London, 27 July 1922, lot 81, with others, bt *Meatyard*); Sir Robert Witt.

Literature: Hammer, *et al.*, 1977, no. 25.

This is another study for the *Martyrdom of St Bartholomew*, for which see No. 110. Of the several surviving preparatory studies for the figure of the saint, No. 111 comes closest to the painted solution in terms of his pose, though in reverse. The executioners are also in poses similar to those adopted in the painting, though these have not been reversed. In the Courtauld drawing the face of the executioner on the left is boldly interrupted by his right hand wielding the knife, but in the painting this is clumsily avoided by the unconvincing repositioning of the figure's right arm. The end result is far more static, and indeed more awkward, than any of the preparatory studies. It is as though Guercino lost his nerve at the last minute and failed to follow through the courage of his own convictions as expressed with the fluency of his pen.

The sheet appears to have been cut, particularly on the left and at the bottom. In some passages where several pentiments occur, such as the right leg of the executioner on the left and, again, the right leg of St Bartholomew, the darker brown ink has been applied to clarify the drawing.

112 St Laurence distributing Alms

(*see colour pl. 18*)

London, British Museum, inv. no. 1910–2–12–3.

(For other details, see App. no. 28.)

This is a preliminary study for a composition of which the appearance is preserved in a pen-and-wash copy in the Fondazione Cini, Venice (inv. no. 31.140, from the Certani collection, Bologna), as was first pointed out by Mahon and Turner (1989, under no. 159). While the poses of St Laurence and several of the mendicants remain substantially unchanged between the two drawings, the Cini copy clearly records a relatively late stage in the composition since it includes the carefully constructed setting, in particular the classical loggia in the background (which is completely absent in No. 112).

The identity of the saint is by no means certain, but his short dalmatic confirms that he is a deacon. Interestingly, the Cini copy is paired in that collection with a copy, again after Guercino, of a scene also from the life of a deacon saint, namely St Stephen, showing the episode of his death by stoning. While it is not inconceivable that the same saint is depicted in both compositions, almsgiving is far more commonly associated with St Laurence than with St Stephen. The two Cini copies thus seem to record compositions that were conceived by Guercino at the same time and as a pair, each showing a scene from the life of a deacon saint. The two compositions may have been for pendant paintings, though no such commission is recorded; they may, on the other hand, have been intended as designs for a pair of prints, which were never carried out. There are two preliminary studies for the *Stoning of St Stephen*, one in the Royal Library, Windsor Castle (M & T, 1989, no. 159), and the other in Willumsen's Museum, Frederikssund, Denmark (inv. no. GS.397; Fischer, 1984, no. 44); a third drawing, formerly on the London art market and now in a private collection (sale, Christie's, 9 December 1982, lot 46, repr.), has also been associated with this composition.

Mahon and Turner, with whom Fischer agreed, were inclined to date both the *St Laurence distributing Alms* and the *Stoning of St Stephen* to the early 1620s. However, we now feel there are good stylistic grounds for dating both compositions in the second half of the 1630s. The figures are not as monumentally conceived as those encountered in Guercino's drawings of the early 1620s, such as those for the *St Petronilla* altarpiece (for which see Nos. 38–42). Furthermore, there are strong analogies both in the handling of the pen between the *St Laurence* and a drawing, undoubtedly from the 1630s, the *Martyrdom of St Bartholomew*, also in the British Museum (No.110), and in the fluid handling of the wash between the Windsor *Stoning of St Stephen* and another drawing from the later 1630s, the *Sisyphus*, also in the Royal Library, Windsor Castle (No. 108).

113 Madonna of the Rosary with Sts Dominic and Catherine

London, British Museum, inv. no. 1910–2–12–8.

(For other details, see App. no. 35.)

A study, with considerable variations, for the altarpiece of the subject painted in 1637 for the church of S. Domenico, Turin (S, 1988, no. 168). The painting differs most from this study in its more symmetrical composition, achieved by placing the figure of St Dominic further to the left, directly below the Madonna, facing inwards opposite St Catherine.

Another study of the subject, in pen and wash, perhaps made in connection with this painting, is in the Pierpont Morgan Library, New York (inv. no. IV, 167; Stampfle & Bean, 1967, no. 42). As in the British Museum sketch, the two saints are shown to the right of the Madonna, but in this instance St Dominic stands behind St Catherine on the right and the Madonna is seated on a throne rather than on clouds. While the setting is scarcely explored in the Morgan sketch, as it is in No. 113, the gestures of the two saints are extremely close to those adopted by Guercino in the finished painting (although St Dominic was eventually reversed); it is thus difficult to determine which was drawn first.

A further compositional sketch for this commission is recorded in a copy by Francesco Bartolozzi in the Albertina, Vienna (inv. no. 1377; Stix & Fröhlich-Bum, 1926, no. 440, repr. p. 192), after a lost drawing by Guercino. While the poses of the saints in Bartolozzi's copy are close to those adopted in the finished work, that of the Madonna and Child recalls a slightly later painting of the same subject, executed for the church of S. Marco, Osimo, in 1642 (S, 1988, no. 202). It seems probable that Guercino referred back to his ideas for the Turin composition when repeating the subject five years later.

Finally, another lost drawing for this composition is recorded in an etching by Adam Bartsch (*Recueil*, XXV,

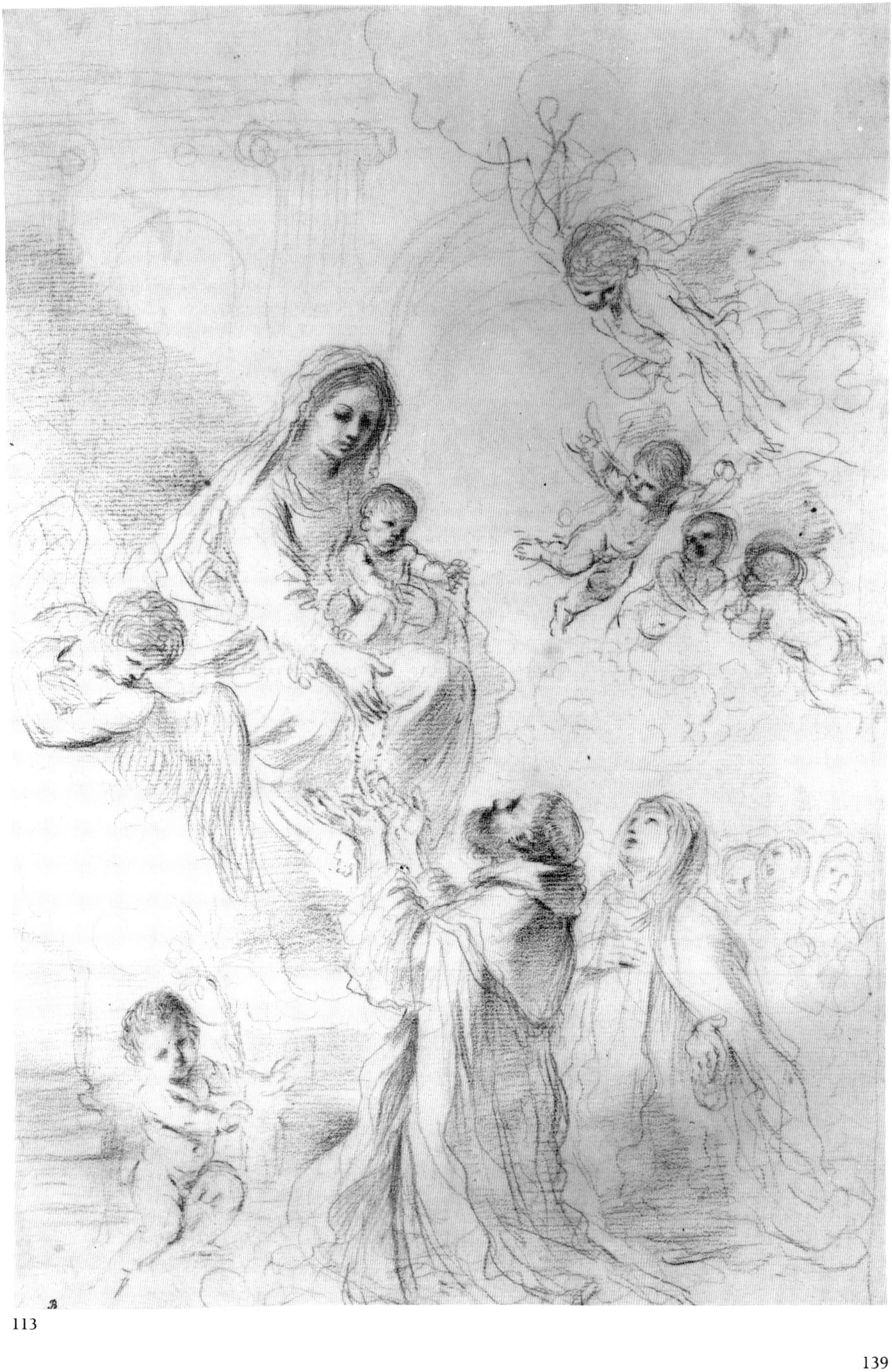

113

no. 963b). This shows St Dominic alone, kneeling to the right with his hands raised, having received the rosary, with the Madonna and Child and an angel above.

114–115 Studies for *Cato of Utica saying Farewell to his Son* (1637)

Marseille, Musée des Beaux-Arts

114 Cato of Utica saying Farewell to his Son

Pen and brown ink and brown wash. 125 × 188mm.

Mahon Collection, on loan to the Ashmolean Museum, Oxford, M & E, 27.

Provenance: Casa Gennari (the drawing is laid down on a fine Casa Gennari mount, for which see L *Suppl*, 2858c, and M, 1967, p. 20); Mr Bouverie; Mr Hervey; the Earls of Gainsborough; L. Franklyn; from whom purchased by Sir Denis Mahon in November 1953.

Literature: M, 1967, no. 25; M & E, 1986, no. 27; Loire, in Brejon & Volle, 1988–9, under no. 84; M & T, 1989, under no. 86.

This and No. 115 are studies for the painting *Cato of Utica saying Farewell to his Son*, completed in 1637 and now in the Musée des Beaux-Arts at Marseille (S, 1988, no. 165; Brejon & Volle, 1988–9, no. 84). The subject, which is represented only rarely, is taken from Plutarch (*Life of Cato of Utica*, lxxxvi) and shows Cato in his bedchamber saying farewell to his son before committing suicide. Cato was a Roman statesman and a stoic of uncompromising principle, who, at the time of the civil war, was Governor of Utica, near Carthage. He had sided with Pompey and refused to survive the Republic after its defeat in 46 BC. The dispassionate way in which he took his life with the sword seemed to exemplify the old Roman ideal of honour and integrity. It cannot be said that Guercino did full justice to his subject: in his treatment of it there is more of an air of a domestic genre scene than one of ancient history. No. 114 shows the two protagonists embracing. Cato's son was first drawn in profile: a pentiment for his head in this position is clearly visible behind his left shoulder. There are also indications of a different placing of his left arm.

The picture was commissioned in 1635 by the French patron Louis Phélypeaux de La Vrillière (1599–1681), Secretary of State to Louis XIII, as one of a series of ten large pictures of ancient subjects ordered from several artists to decorate the gallery of his mansion, or *hôtel*, in Paris (now the Banque de France in the rue Vivienne), which he built after receiving his appointment in 1629. La Vrillière later ordered three other pictures by Guercino for this same gallery: *Coriolanus entreated by his Mother* of 1643, now in the Musée des Beaux-Arts at Caen (S, 1988, no. 204; Brejon & Volle, 1988–9, no. 85); *Hersilia separating Romulus and Tatius* of 1645, now in the Louvre, Paris (S, 1988, no. 226; Brejon & Volle, 1988–9, no. 86; Loire, 1990, no. 9; see Nos. 141–2); and *Mucius Scaevola plunging his right Hand into the Flames*, now in the Palazzo Durazzo–Pallavicini at Genoa (S, 1988, no. 248), the precise date of which remains unknown. For reasons that remain obscure, the last-named picture was never delivered and stayed in the possession of the artist, in whose house it is recorded on his death in 1666. The decoration of the gallery of the Hôtel de La Vrillière remained intact until the French Revolution; shortly afterwards the pictures were split up and distributed between the Louvre and other French museums. Deprived of its proper context within a series of other pictures of ancient subjects, the true subject of the *Cato of Utica* was lost sight of in the nineteenth century, and it was for a long time thought to be a *Prodigal Son*.

The recent publication of the correspondence of Cardinal Bernardino Spada concerning Guido Reni's *Rape of Helen*, a picture that was itself eventually to form a part of this same decorative scheme, has caused the previously accepted view of the progress of the decoration to be somewhat modified (Dirani, 1982–3, pp. 83–94; see also No. 81). It was hitherto maintained that Reni's picture was the first of the group to arrive in France, in 1631; but, as Dirani has now demonstrated, it cannot have reached France before 1638, when it was still on sale in Rome. Guercino's *Cato* and Poussin's *Schoolmaster of the Falerii* were evidently the first in the series and were delivered sometime in 1637.

115 Cato of Utica saying Farewell to his Son, watched by two Spectators

Pen and brown ink and brown wash. 236 × 325mm.

Windsor Castle, Royal Library, inv. no. 2566.

Provenance: Casa Gennari; King George III.

Literature: M, 1967, under no. 25; M & E, 1986, under no. 27; Loire, in Brejon & Volle, 1988–9, under no. 84; M & T, 1989, no. 86.

A study for the *Cato of Utica saying Farewell to his Son*, for which see No. 114. It is a good example of Guercino's pen-and-wash technique, a medium to which he seems to have been especially attached in the middle of the 1630s and one in which he achieved remarkable mastery at this time (cf. Nos. 103, 104 and 112). In No. 115 Guercino has studied the figures in reverse to their eventual appearance in the finished picture, and, as in No. 114, Cato's son is still shown as a youth rather than as a fully grown young man, as he was finally to appear. In another, later study also at Windsor (M & T, 1989, no. 87), the two protagonists are reversed so that they appear in the same direction as in the finished work.

In MS. Inventory A, a late eighteenth-century inventory of the drawings at Windsor Castle, which was compiled during the reign of King George III, No. 115 was described as: 'The Prodigal Son receiv'd by his Father'. The picture itself was also at one time thought to represent this subject (see No. 114).

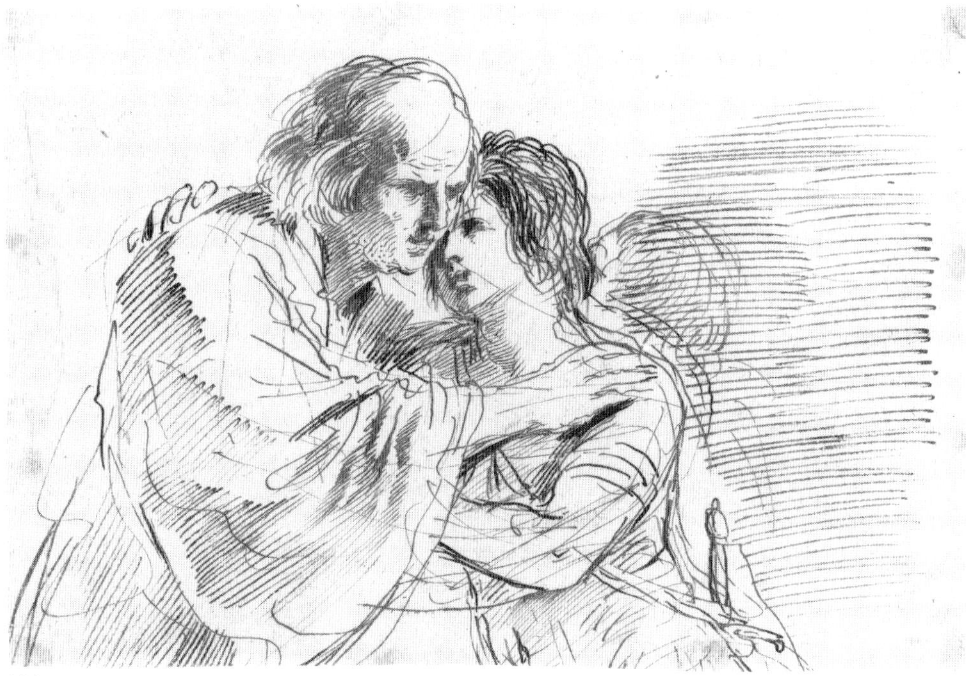

114

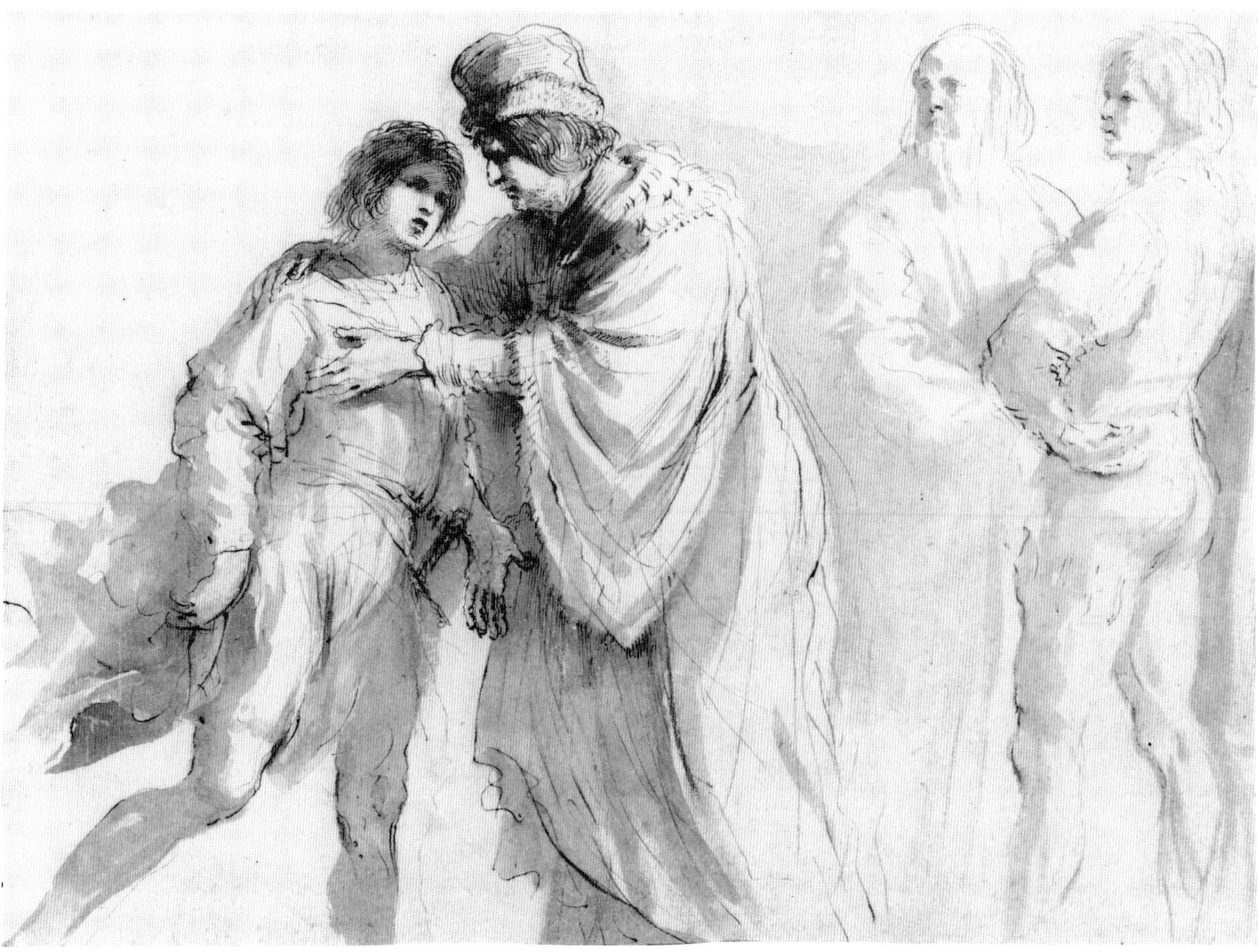

115

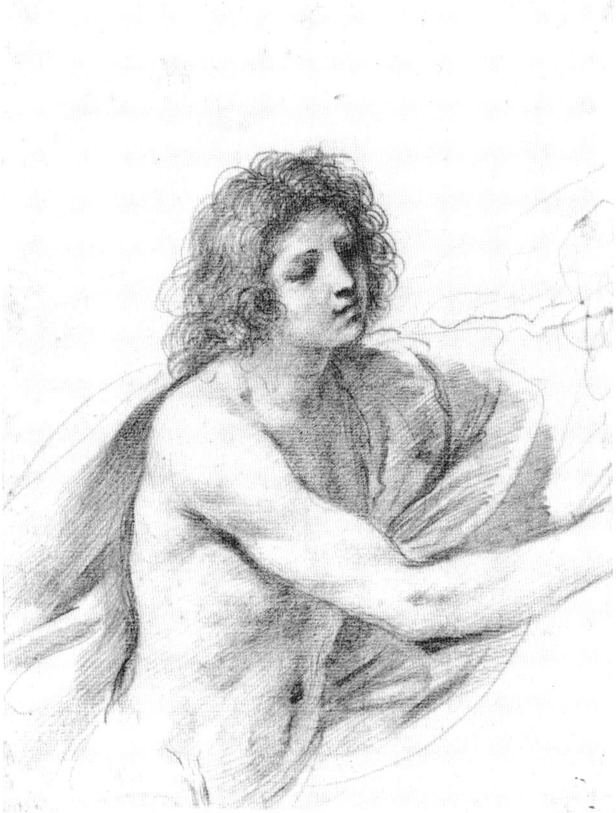

116

116 Youth with his Arms outstretched to the right

Red chalk. 265 × 207mm.

Windsor Castle, Royal Library, inv. no. 2842.

Provenance: Casa Gennari: King George III.

Literature: S, 1988, under no. 167; M & T, 1989, no. 91.

No. 116 is related to the figure of Apollo in a half-length picture of *Apollo flaying Marsyas*, which in 1984 was on the art market in Florence as 'School of Guercino' (S, 1988, no. 167). It is generally agreed that the ex-Florence picture records the appearance of an untraced original by Guercino of an 'Apollo, e Marsia due mezze figure', for which the master was paid on 18 December 1637 by a 'Sig. Saulo Guidotti' of Bologna (*Libro dei Conti*, 1808, p. 84; 1841, p. 317).

The drawing was almost certainly made from the life and corresponds reasonably closely to its painted counterpart, though the figure leans forwards more in the drawing and the position of his arms is slightly different.

117–119 Studies for *Salome, accompanied by a female Attendant, receiving the Head of St John the Baptist from an Executioner* (1637)

Rennes, Musée des Beaux-Arts

117–118 Studies for *Herodias watching as Salome receives the Head of St John the Baptist from an Executioner* (by a follower of Guercino)

Cento, Pinacoteca Civica

117 *Recto:* Two Women
Verso: A Woman wearing a Headdress

Red chalk. 249 × 187mm.

Windsor Castle, Royal Library, inv. no. 2789.

Provenance: Casa Gennari; King George III.

Literature: S, 1988, under no. 169; M & T, 1989, no. 89.

Mahon and Turner were the first to connect this double-sided sheet, together with two other drawings at Windsor (Nos. 118–19), with Guercino's painting of *Salome receiving the Head of St John the Baptist from an Executioner* of 1637, now in the Musée des Beaux-Arts, Rennes (S, 1989, no. 169; Loire, 1990, no. 6). Although the painting was commissioned by Lodovico Mastri of Bologna, a bid was made for it by Francesco I, Duke of Modena, when it was almost complete and it was diverted into his possession, Mastri being furnished with a much less expensive substitute at 80 ducats during the following year (for details of these transactions, see M & T, 1989, under nos. 88–90, and Loire, 1990, no. 6). The Duke's payment for his picture, at the equivalent of 180 ducats, was about 30 ducats higher than Guercino's normal tariff; the payment was delayed until 26 January 1639 (*Libro dei Conti*, 1808, p. 87; 1841, p. 318).

The relationship of Nos. 117–18 to Guercino's painting is complicated by their far greater resemblance to a workshop painting representing *Herodias watching as Salome receives the Head of St John the Baptist from an Executioner*. This variant, now in the Pinacoteca Civica at Cento (B, 1986, p. 202, fig. 95; M & T, 1989, p. 54, fig. 19), shows Salome's mother Herodias wearing the same distinctive headdress that features in Nos. 117 and 118. The former, in particular, has much in common with the Cento picture. The *recto* shows the figure of Salome in a similar pose to her counterpart in the painting, with her head turned to the left in the direction of her companion and her arms held out to the right, presumably to support the salver on which St John's head is about to be placed. The pose of the figure on the left, however, is far more animated than in the finished composition, as she apparently precipitates herself forward with her left hand raised in a gesture of surprise. The drawing on the *verso* seems to be a second attempt at this figure alone; she is shown with her arms crossed over her breast, in a

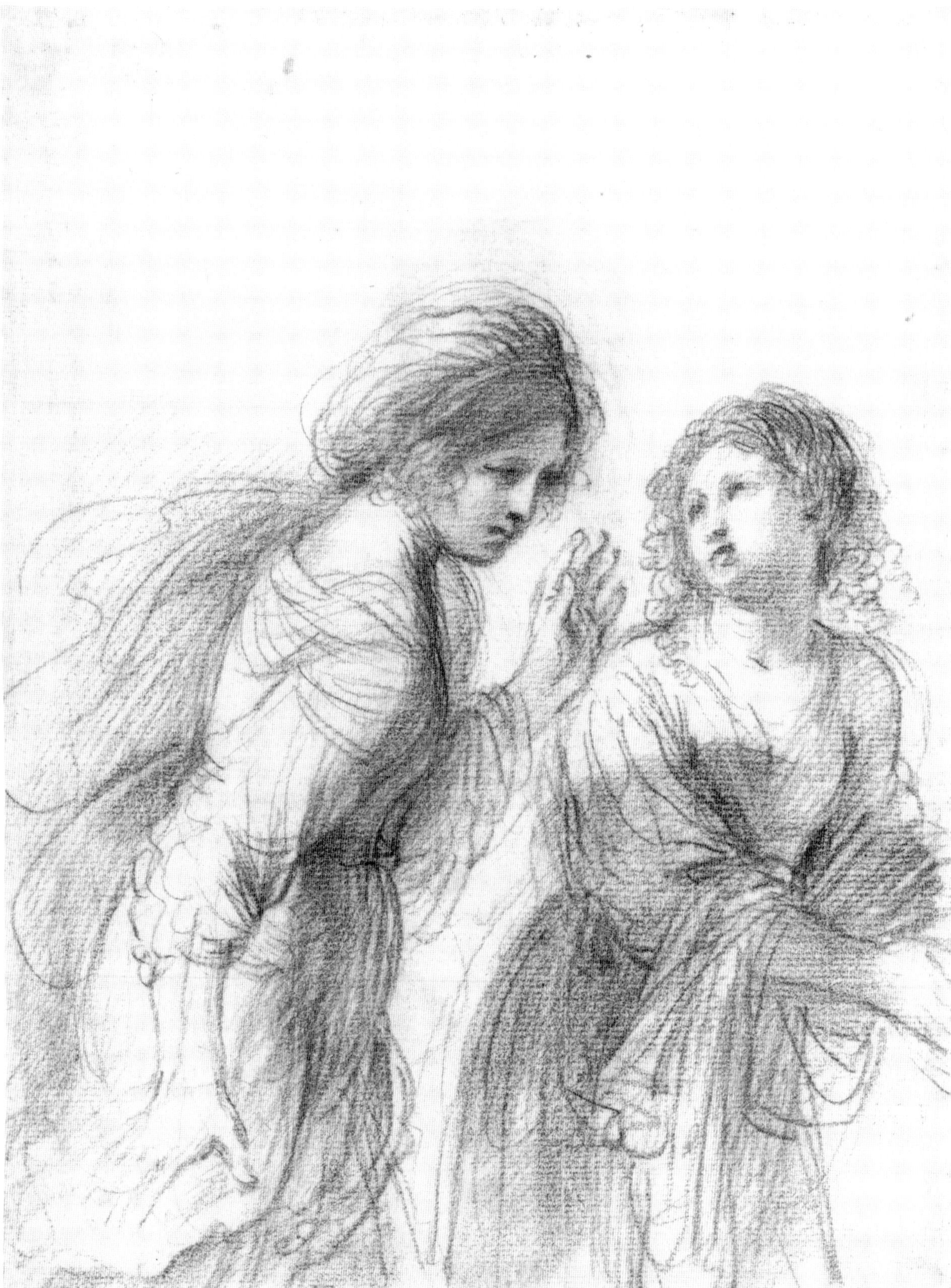

117

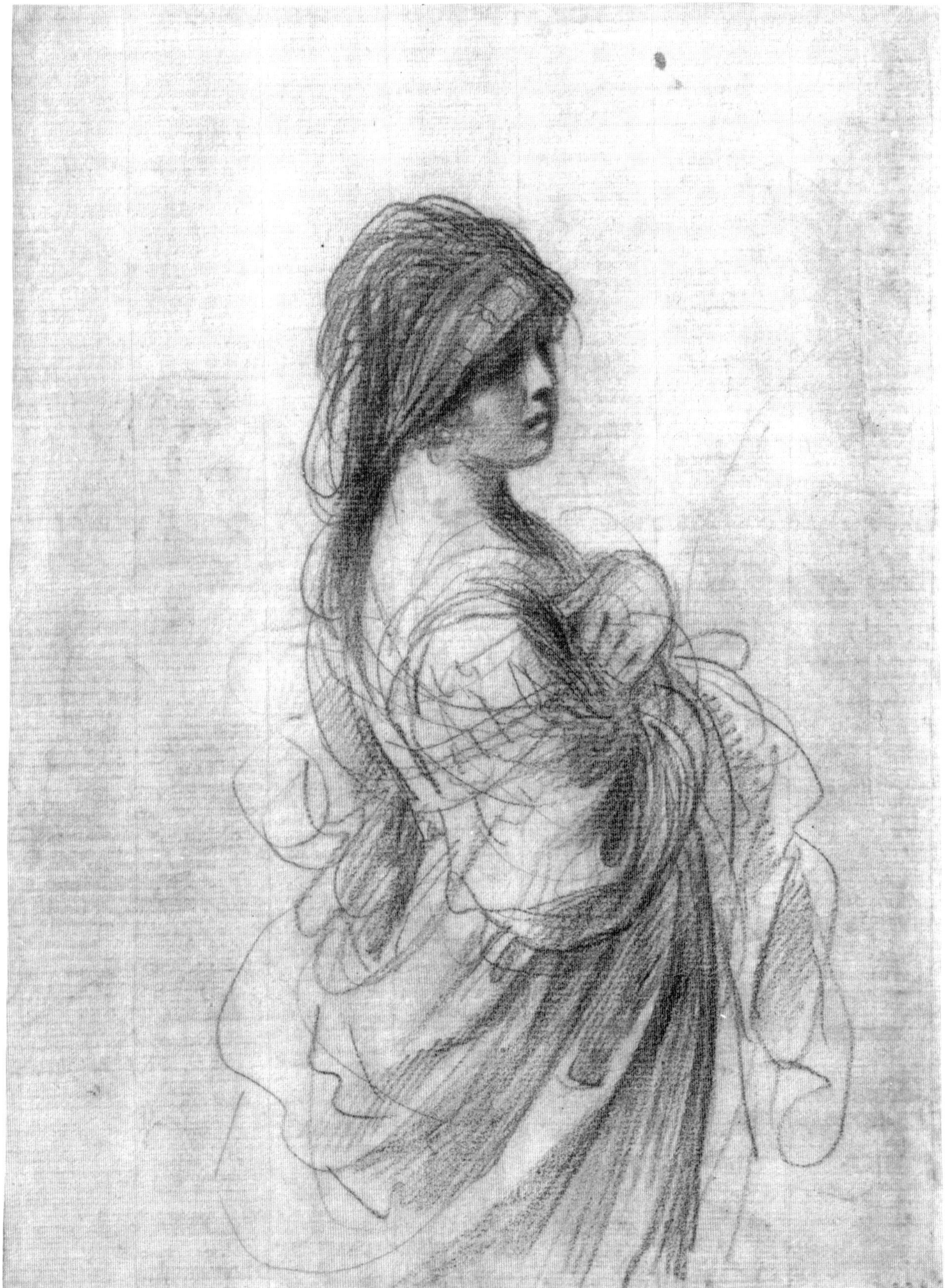

117 *verso*

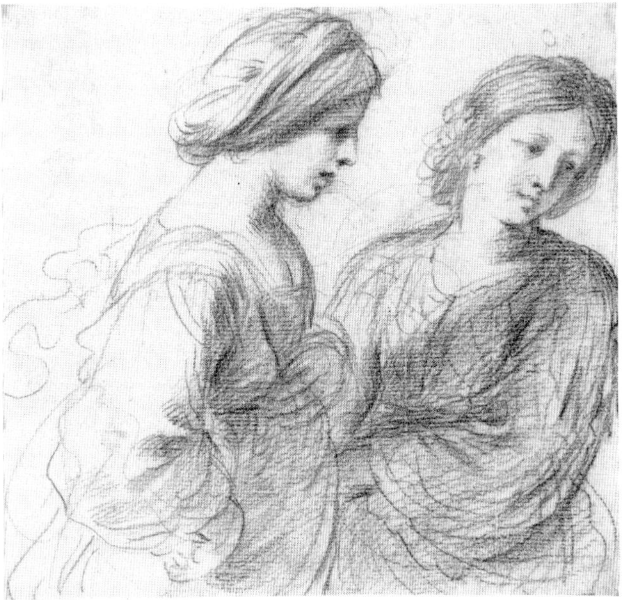

118

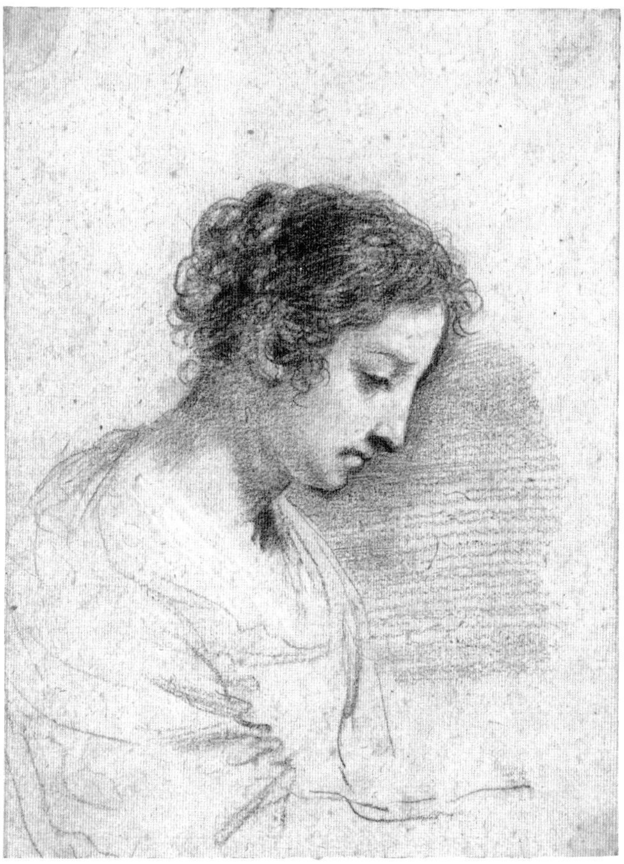

119

much calmer, more contemplative pose, again similar to that in the Cento painting.

Mahon and Turner suggested that Nos. 117–18 record an early idea for the Rennes picture which, although subsequently abandoned by Guercino himself, was later utilised by a member of his studio when a similar work was required.

118 Two Women looking downwards to the right

Red chalk. 170 × 180mm.

Windsor Castle, Royal Library, inv. no. 2686.

Provenance: Casa Gennari; King George III.

Literature: S, 1988, under no. 169; M & T, 1989, no. 90

Probably a study for Guercino's painting now in Rennes of *Salome receiving the Head of St John the Baptist from an Executioner* of 1637, for which see No. 117. There are certainly echoes in the painting of the two figures sketched in No. 118 (e.g. the profile pose for Salome and the folded arms for her companion). Like No. 117, however, the present study appears to have more in common with a closely related painting from Guercino's workshop, the *Herodias watching as Salome receives the Head of St John the Baptist from an Executioner*, now in the Pinacoteca Civica at Cento. Salome is in a pose very close to that of her counterpart in that picture, but in reverse, while Herodias is in profile to the right in both works, but with only one hand folded over her breast in the drawing.

119 Woman looking downwards

Red chalk, heightened with white, on buff paper. 230 × 171mm.

Windsor Castle, Royal Library, inv. no. 2635.

Provenance: Casa Gennari; King George III.

Literature: S, 1988, under no. 169; M & T, 1989, no. 88.

No. 119 seems to have been drawn from life and could afterwards have been used as a basis for the head of Salome in the picture of *Salome receiving the Head of St John the Baptist from an Executioner* of 1637, for which see No. 117. The study is drawn in red and white chalk on coarsely textured paper, a technique not unlike that used by Guercino for his studies of carefully arranged draperies, a large group of which is preserved in the Koenig-Fachsenfeld Collection, on deposit in the Staatsgalerie, Stuttgart (see also No. 93).

120 Cleopatra

(*see colour pl. 19*)

London, British Museum, inv. no. 1895–9–15–709.

(For other details, see App. no. 36.)

The style of the drawing suggests a date in the late 1630s. Guercino evidently painted three representations of this subject during this decade, only one of which survives, the painting commissioned by the Marchese Francesco Fiaschi (Malvasia, 1678, II, p. 372; 1841, II, p. 265; referred to in the Account Book under the date 21 December 1639, *Libro dei Conti*, 1808, pp. 90–91; 1841, p. 319) and now in a private collection in Ferrara (M, *Dipinti*, 1968, no. 70; S, 1988, no. 183). As Salerno has pointed out, another lost picture of Cleopatra is the subject of a small printed volume entitled *La Cleopatra, pittura dell'immortal pennello del Sig. Cav. G. F. Barbieri di Cento* (Forlì, 1638), which is dedicated to Alfonso Palettonio, Governor of Ferrara, who had been Governor of Cento the previous year. A third depiction of the subject, referred to on p. 3 of the Palettonio volume, is said to have been painted by Guercino for another patron, Conte Angelo degli Oddi of Perugia. Neither of these last two pictures is mentioned in either Malvasia's life of Guercino or the Account Book. Also mentioned in the volume is a *Cleopatra* in the process of being painted: in our opinion it is likely that this was the Fiaschi picture, rather than a fourth rendering of the subject.

Since there is no direct connection between the present drawing and the one extant painting of *Cleopatra* executed in the 1630s, it seems likely to us that it would have been made for one of the lost pictures.

A red chalk drawing of Cleopatra in the Ecole des Beaux-Arts, Paris (inv. no. 2695), has several points in common with No. 120 and may be a related drawing. Although the figure is seated, in full profile to the right, and more scantily clad, the position of the hands, details of the face and coiffure, and the technique of the drawing, with its dark background acting as a foil to the figure, all weigh in favour of such a connection.

121–123 Studies for the *Annunciation* (1638–9)

Milan, Ospedale Maggiore, SS. Annunziata

121 The Annunciation

Pen and brown ink and brown wash. 303 × 212mm.

London, Courtauld Institute Galleries, Witt Collection, inv. no. 1339.

Provenance: Casa Gennari; Mr Bouverie; Mr Hervey; the Earls of Gainsborough (sale, Christie's, London, 27 July 1922, lot 81, with others, bt *Meatyard*); Sir Robert Witt.

Literature: Hammer, *et al.*, 1977, no. 19; M & T, 1989, under nos. 94–7.

Almost certainly an early drawing for the altarpiece of this subject painted in 1638–9 for the high altar of the church of the SS. Annunziata in the Ospedale Maggiore, Milan, and still *in situ* (S, 1988, no. 177; see also M & T, 1989, no. 97 for a discussion of the preparatory drawings for this picture). The most important respect in which the study differs from the painting is that the angel is shown in mid-flight rather than kneeling on the ground before the Madonna as in the finished work. The diagonal thrust of the composition in No. 121 depends both upon the rapport between God the Father and the kneeling Madonna, who looks back up at him from below to the right; and upon the flying dove of the Holy Spirit, which occupies the space midway between them. It is further reinforced by the position of the angel, who flies forward to the left from behind the rays that descend from God the Father indicating the path down which the dove flies. The pentiment for the right arm of the angel, which was initially raised before being moved to a different position off the diagonal, seems to suggest that the artist was already attempting to mitigate somewhat the relentless emphasis on this axis. In a second composition drawing, in the Museum of Fine Arts, Budapest (inv. no. 2315; M & T, 1989, p. 58, fig. 21; Czére, 1989, no. 41), which is extremely close in technique and handling to No. 121, Guercino had already arrived at the more conventional compositional solution employed in the painting, with the angel and the Madonna kneeling on the ground, facing each other.

A study for God the Father and another for the winged putto immediately below him in the altarpiece are also in the Royal Library, Windsor Castle (M & T, 1989, nos. 96–7).

122 The Angel of the Annunciation

Pen and brown ink and brown wash. 236 × 159mm.

Windsor Castle, Royal Library, inv. no. 2794.

Provenance: Casa Gennari; King George III.

Literature: S, 1988, under no. 177; M & T, 1989, no. 94.

This and No. 123 are studies for the angel of the Annunciation in the altarpiece of that subject painted in 1638–9 for the church of the SS. Annunziata in the Ospedale Maggiore, Milan, for which see No. 121. Both drawings must have been made after Guercino had decided to place the angel on the ground, facing the Madonna, rather than flying above her, as in No. 121. In this drawing, Guercino seems to have been preoccupied with the gestures of the angel, making three attempts at the right hand and two attempts at the left, which is shown both raised and resting on his knee while holding the lily.

123 The Angel of the Annunciation

Pen and brown ink and slight traces of brown wash. 248 × 202mm.

Windsor Castle, Royal Library, inv. no. 2801.

Provenance: Casa Gennari; King George III.

Literature: S, 1988, under no. 177; M & T, 1989, no. 95.

This and No. 122 are studies for the angel of the Annunciation in the altarpiece of that subject painted in 1638–9 for the church of the SS. Annunziata in the Ospedale Maggiore, Milan, for which see No. 121. The present drawing is slightly closer to the finished work, although there the angel actually kneels on one knee, whereas in No. 123 he seems still to be moving forward, with a greater sense of urgency. The composition study in the Museum of Fine Arts,

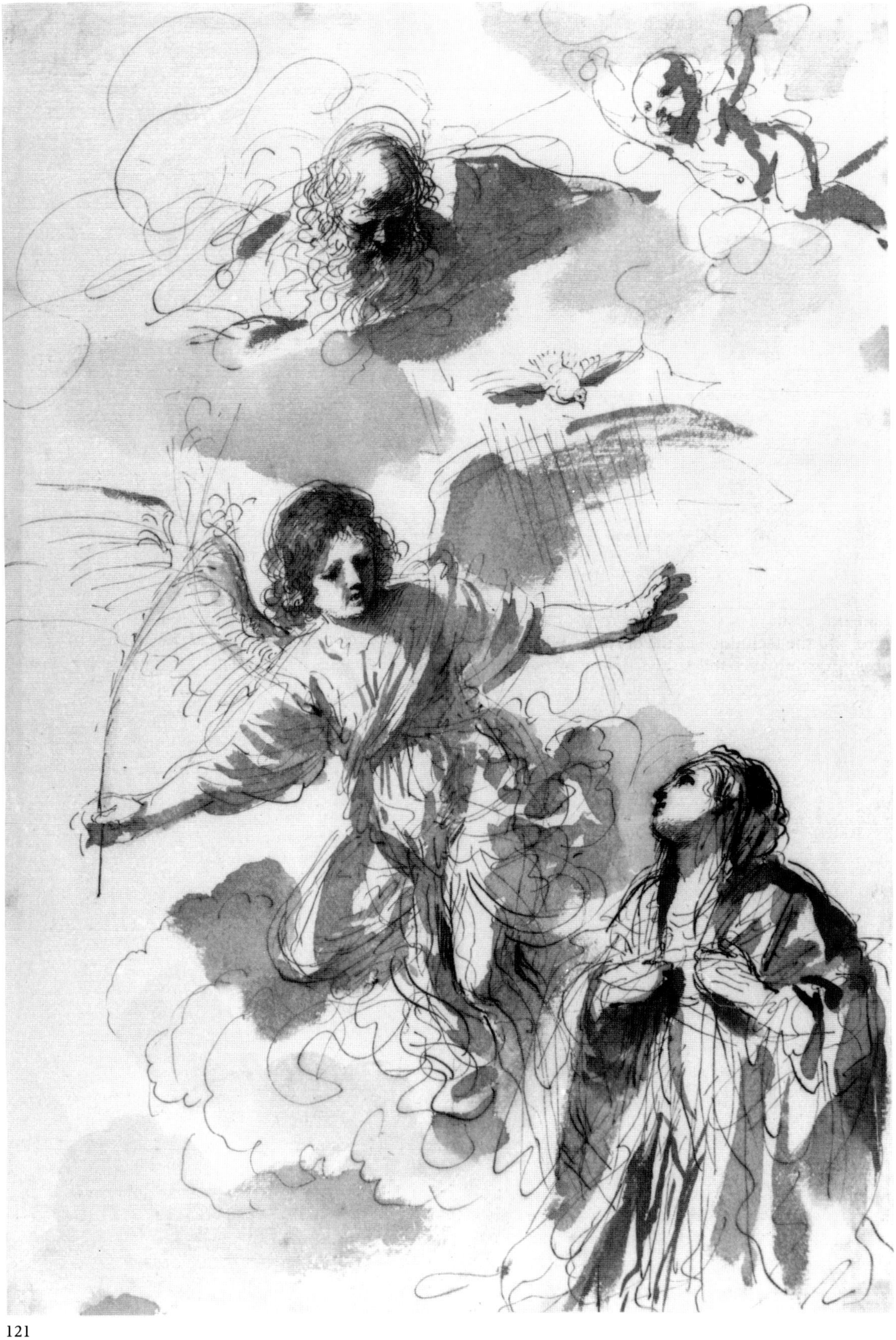

121

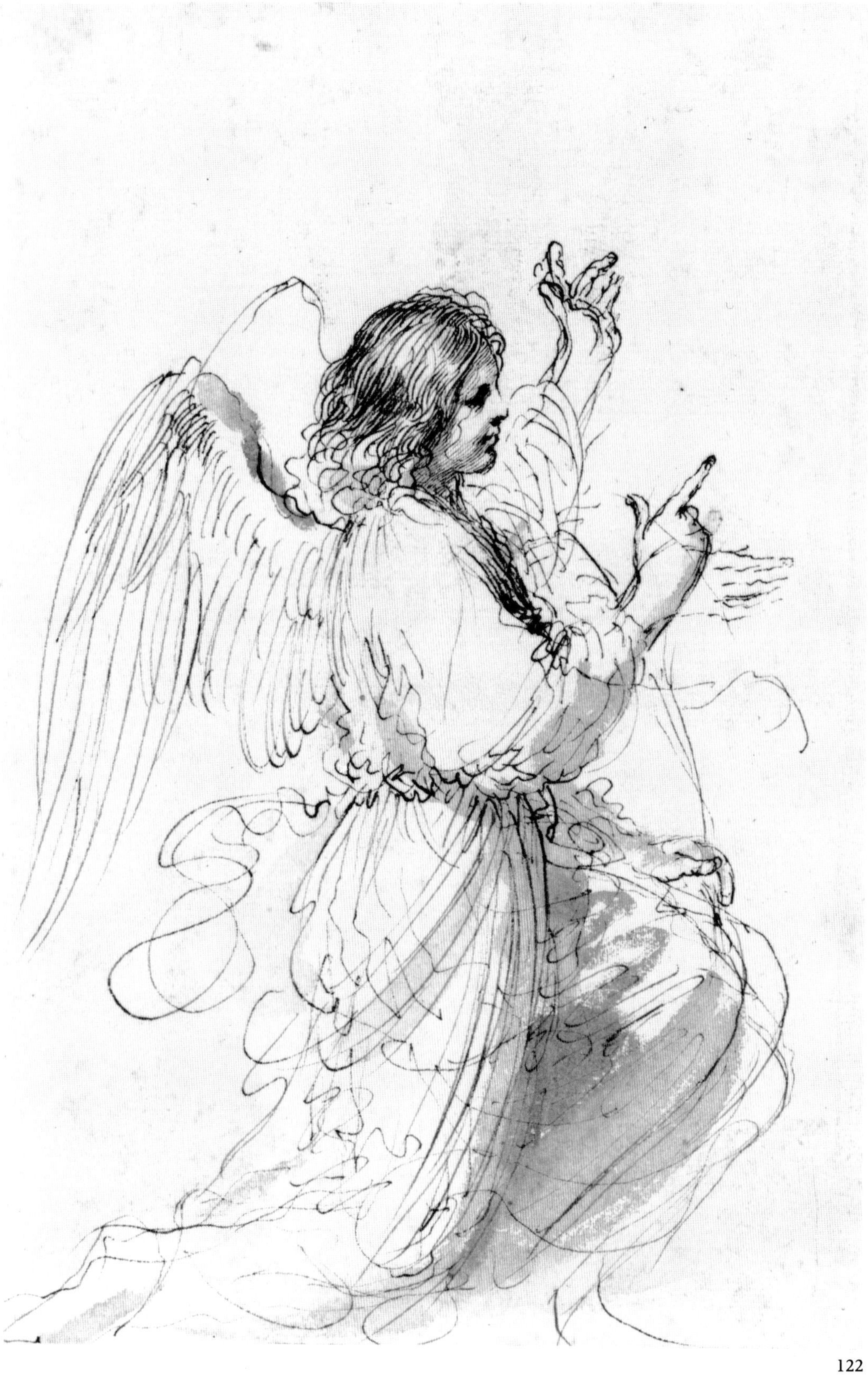

122

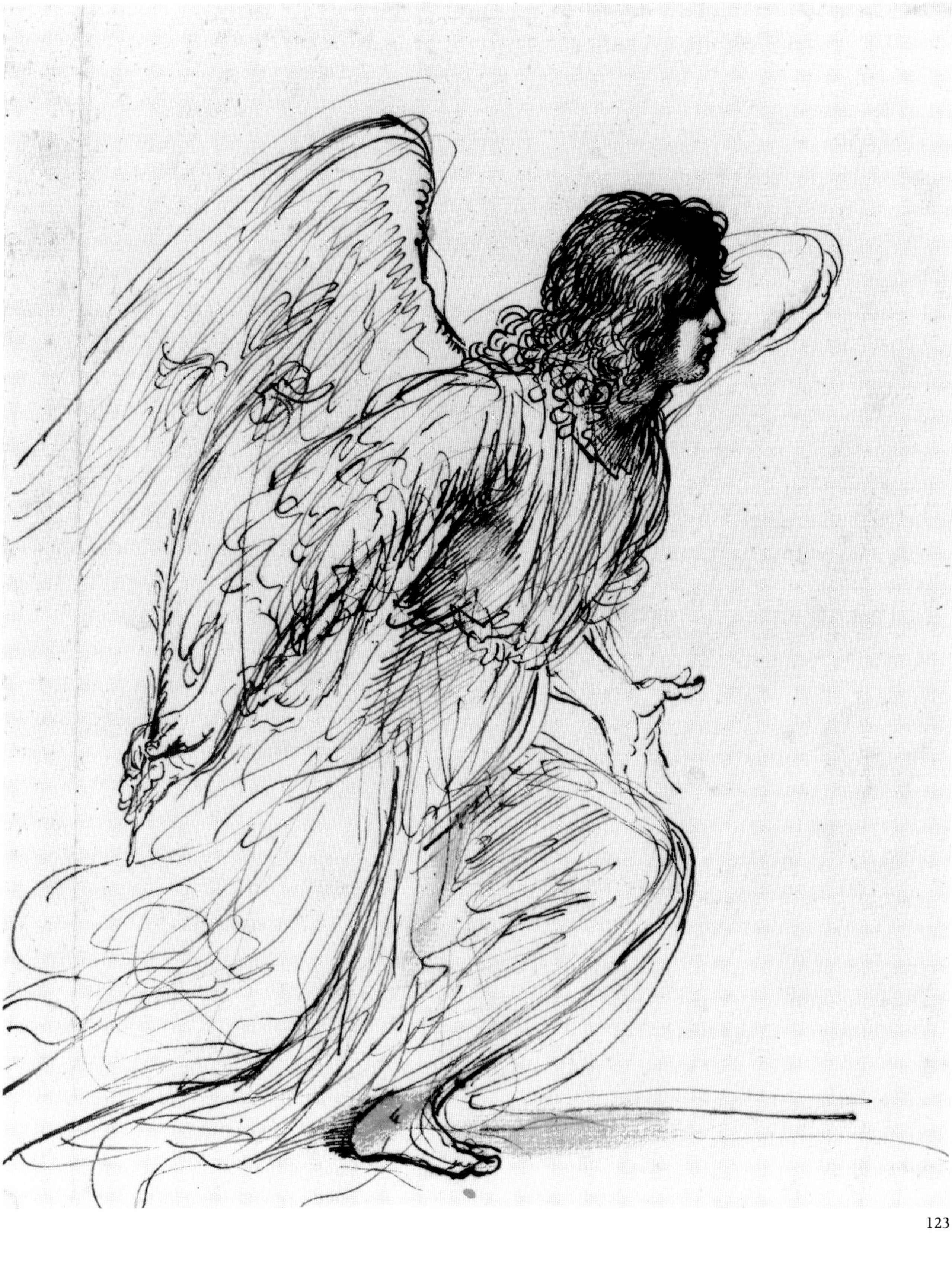

123

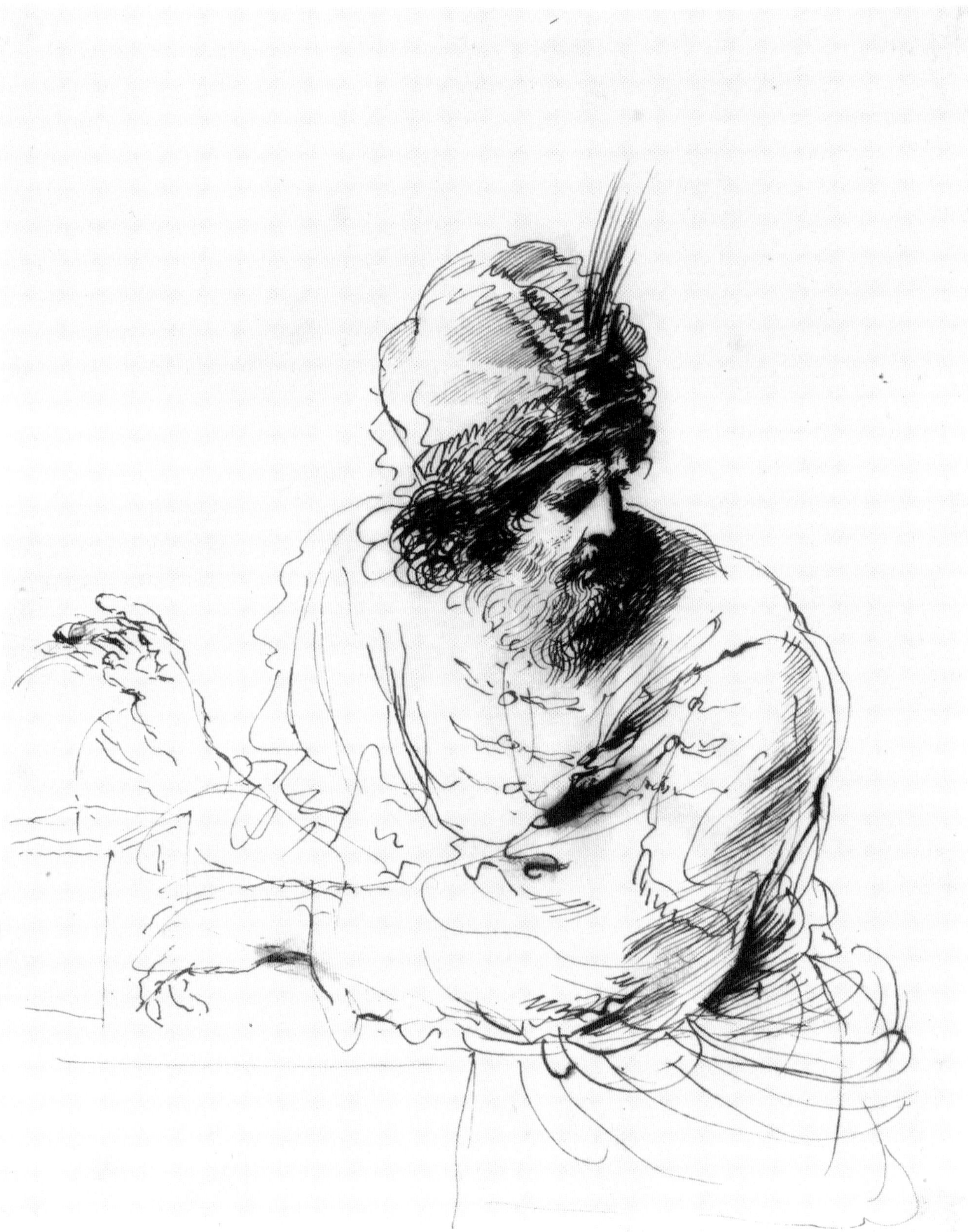

124

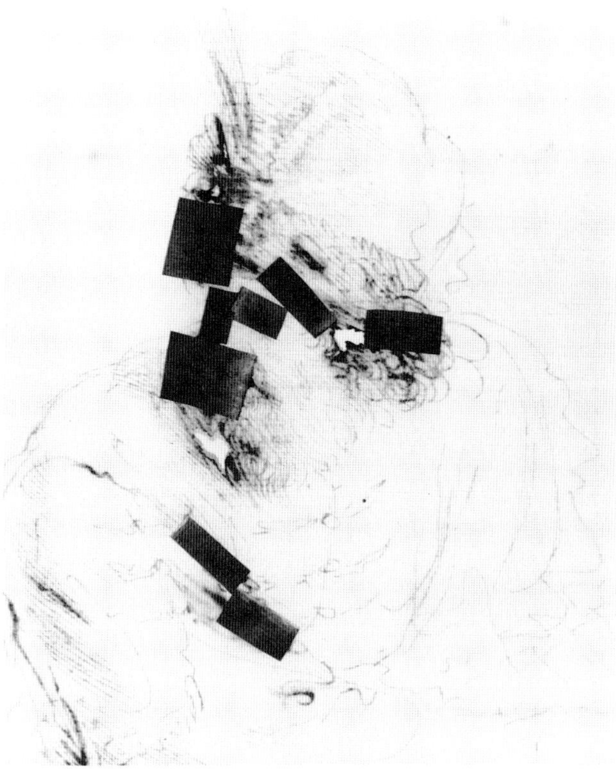

124 *verso*

Budapest (inv. no. 2315; Czére, 1990, no. 41), probably drawn after No. 123, shows the angel in very much the same pose, except that he is more upright, as in the painting.

124 Half-length Figure of a bearded Man wearing a fur-trimmed Hat with a Plume

London, British Museum, inv. no. 1987–7–25–47.

(For other details, see App. no. 49.)

The identity of the figure is not immediately apparent. He is clad in exotic attire and appears to be furtively removing something from the casket. The drawing may date to the 1630s or 1640s.

125 St George and the Dragon

Red chalk. 288 × 209mm.

Mahon Collection, on loan to the Ashmolean Museum, Oxford, M & E, 28.

Provenance: C. L. Chute, The Vyne, Basingstoke (sale, Sotheby's, London, 22 June 1949, lot 1, one of a folio volume of 28 drawings by Guercino, bt *Wilson*); R. E. A. Wilson; from whom purchased by Sir Denis Mahon on 8 February 1950.

Literature: M, 1967, no. 38; M, *Disegni*, 1969, no. 143; Tan Bunzl, 1972, no. 68; M & E, 1986, no. 28.

Under the year 1639 Malvasia recorded a painting of this subject as follows: 'Un s. Giorgio grande al naturale per il P. D. Angelo Torre Abbate Ferrarese' (Malvasia, 1678, II, p. 372; 1841, II, p. 264). Payments for the only *St George* to be cited in the Account Book are noted on 5 February 1637 and 14 October 1639 (*Libro dei Conti*, 1808, pp. 80 and 90; 1841, pp. 315 and 319); these are from the same patron and are clearly for the very same picture. The sum paid, 125 ducats, confirms Malvasia's statement that this was a large, life-size composition. A picture belonging to the Pinacoteca Nazionale, Bologna, and now on deposit at the Palazzo della Prefettura of that same city (S, 1988, no. 182) was identified by Mahon (1967, no. 38, and *Disegni*, 1969, no. 143) as a copy of the painting Guercino was commissioned to paint in 1637. In the painted composition, St George is mounted on a horse that rears up towards the right as he leans down to the left to strike the dragon with his lance, which breaks in the middle as he does so; the dragon, transfixed in the mouth by the other end of the lance, writhes on the ground in the bottom left, as the princess flees to the left behind the horse.

Although the drawing shows a subsequent moment to that represented in the picture, with the saint dismounted and about to despatch the wounded dragon with his sword, there can be no doubt, as Mahon was the first to point out, that it is related to this same composition, but to an earlier phase in its evolution. A pen drawing in the Uffizi, Florence

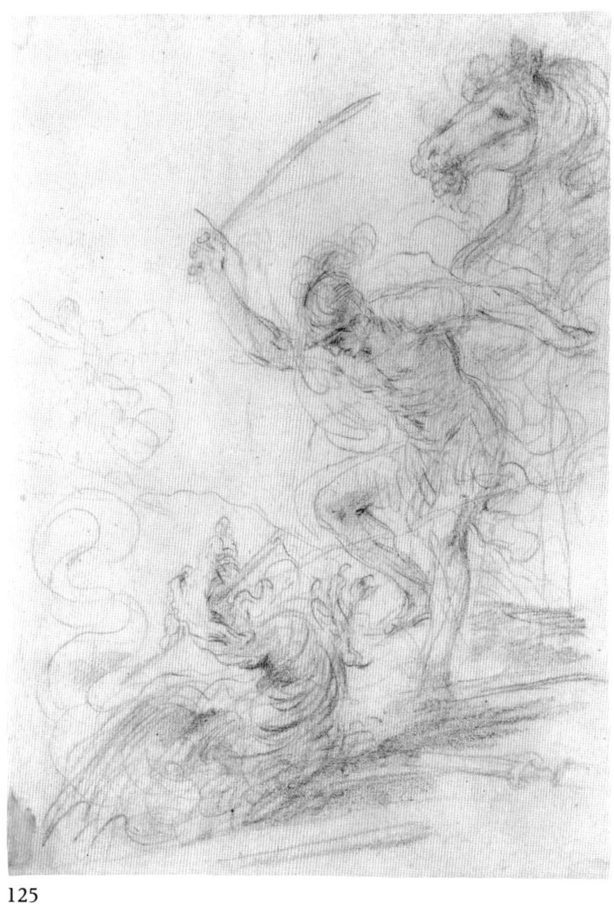

125

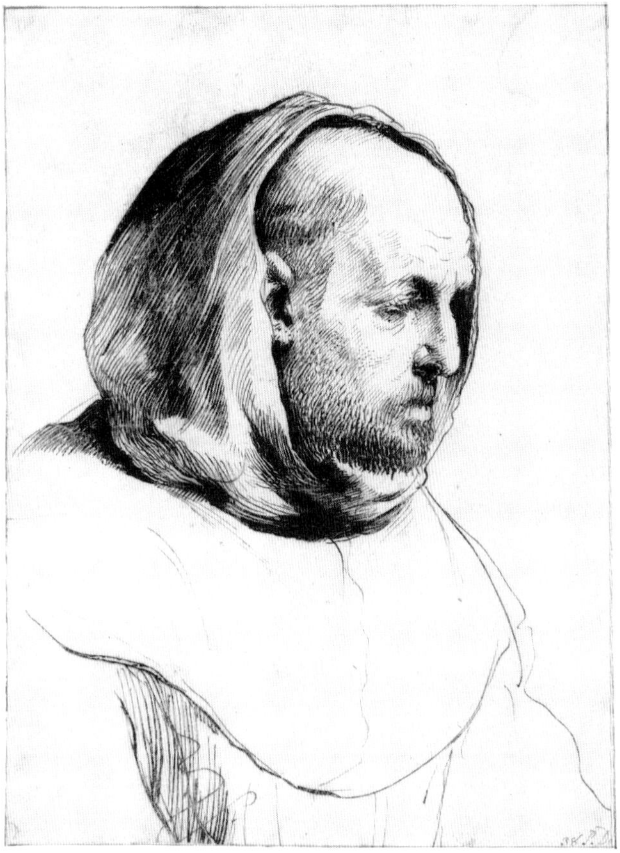

126

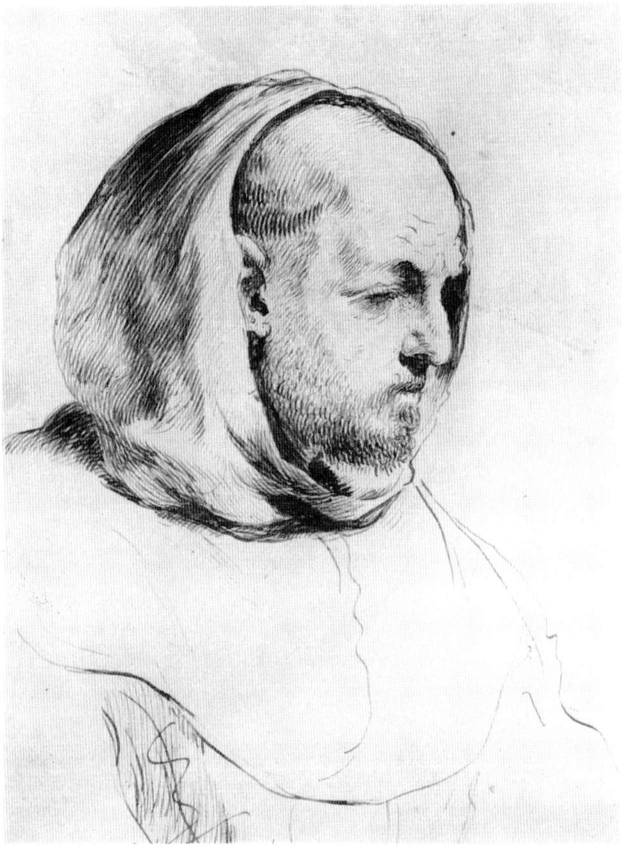

Fig. 19 Sir Joshua Reynolds after Guercino, *Head of a Monk wearing a Cowl*. Pen and brown ink, 250 × 200 mm (formerly Christie's, London). See No. 126

(inv. no. 3659–S; Roli, 1972, p. 56), showing St George walking towards the dragon and about to draw his sword, is also clearly related to No. 125 and may even have been drawn before it. A coarsely retouched offset in the Royal Library at Windsor Castle (M & T, 1989, no. 634) records another preparatory drawing, now untraced, for this same composition, but at an advanced stage in the evolution of the design. It corresponds fairly closely to the finished composition, except in reverse (Guercino's original drawing would therefore have been in the same sense as his picture).

126 Head of a Monk in profile, wearing a Cowl

Pen and brown ink. 239 × 181mm.

Private collection.

Provenance: Casa Gennari; Mr Bouverie; Mr Hervey; the Earls of Gainsborough.

Literature: Turner, 1984, p. 211f., fig. 3.

Inscribed in pen and brown ink in the bottom right corner: *38 P. Do.* (Such inscriptions are associable with a provenance from the Casa Gennari.)

The purpose of this impressive, finished study remains unknown, though, from its style, it appears to have been drawn around 1640. In type it resembles a small group of carefully executed, detailed studies of heads, which were made at the end of the preparatory process and served as models for the artist when he painted the corresponding passage. Two such examples, also drawn in pen, are the *Study for the Head of Semiramis* in the Ecole des Beaux-Arts, Paris (inv. no. 151; Loire, 1990, no. 34; Turner, 1990, pp. 653f., and fig. 31), for the painting of *Semiramis at her Toilet* of 1624 in the Museum of Fine Arts, Boston (S, 1988, no. 102), and the *Study for the Head of St Teresa* in the Palazzo Rosso, Genoa (inv. no. 1736; Turner, 1990, p. 654, and fig. 32), for the altarpiece of *Christ appearing to St Teresa* of 1634 in the Musée Granet, Aix-en-Provence (S, 1988, no. 152). For a drawing of this type in red chalk, see No. 50.

No. 126 was the subject of a remarkably faithful repetition by the English painter Sir Joshua Reynolds (1723–92), who made several pen-and-ink copies after drawings by Guercino (two others are discussed under App. nos. 46 and 48, and a third, attributable to Reynolds, under No. 127). It is easy to see why Reynolds would have been attracted to the present fine example of Guercino's draughtsmanship. His copy, drawn to a slightly larger scale than the original,

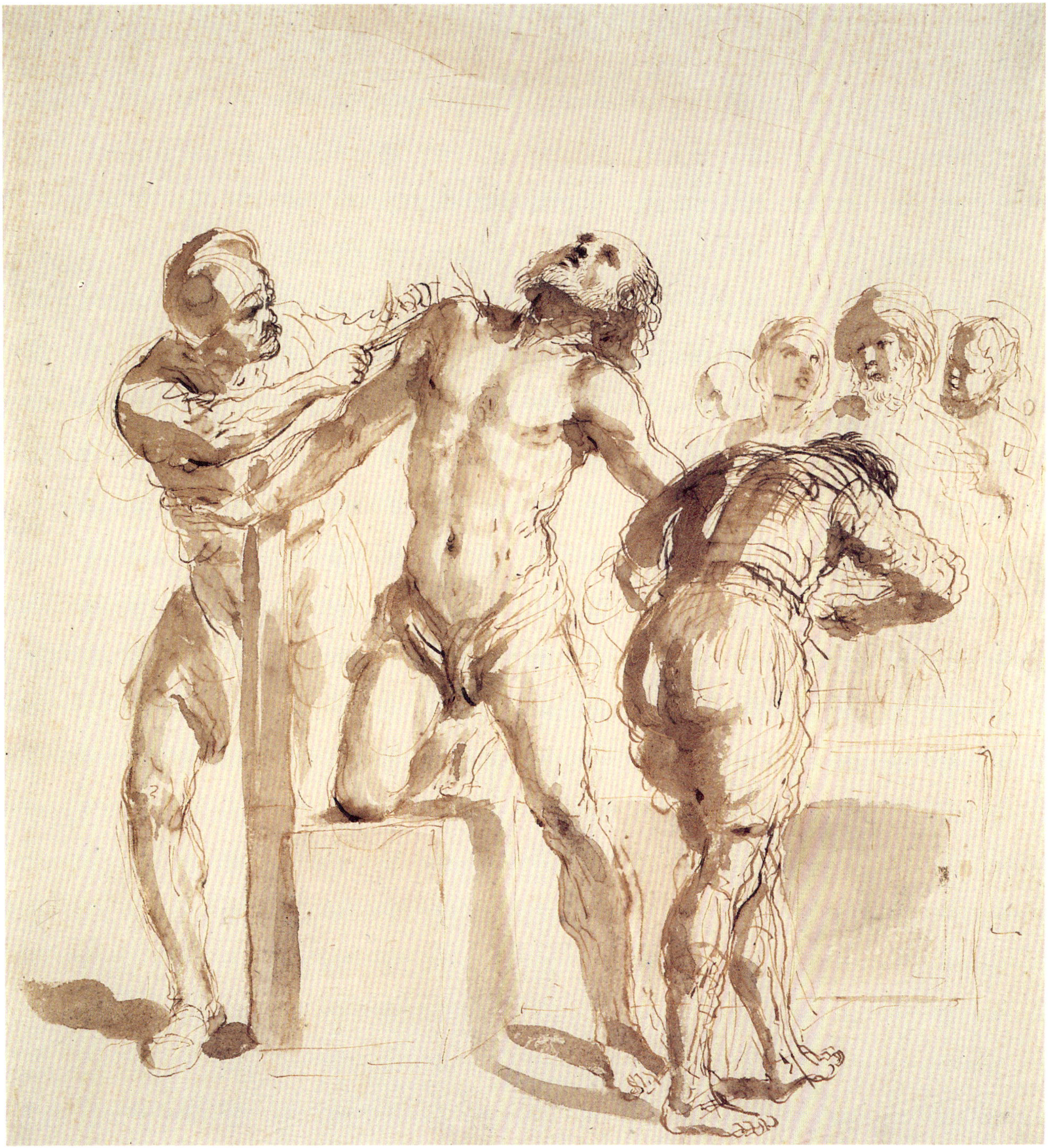

110 *The Martyrdom of St Bartholomew*. London, British Museum (see also App. no. 33)

PLATE 18

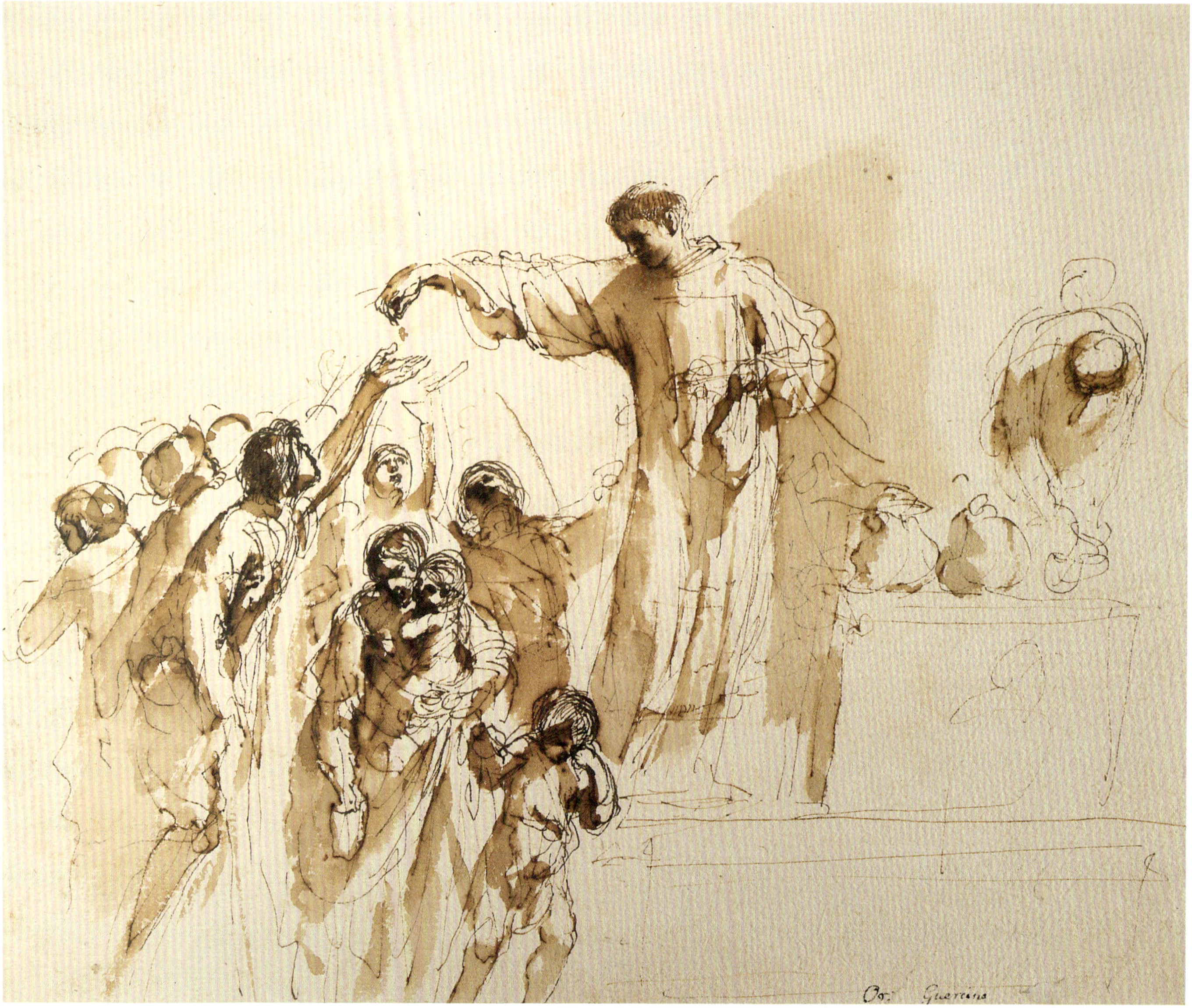

112 *St Laurence distributing Alms*. London, British Museum (see also App. no. 28)

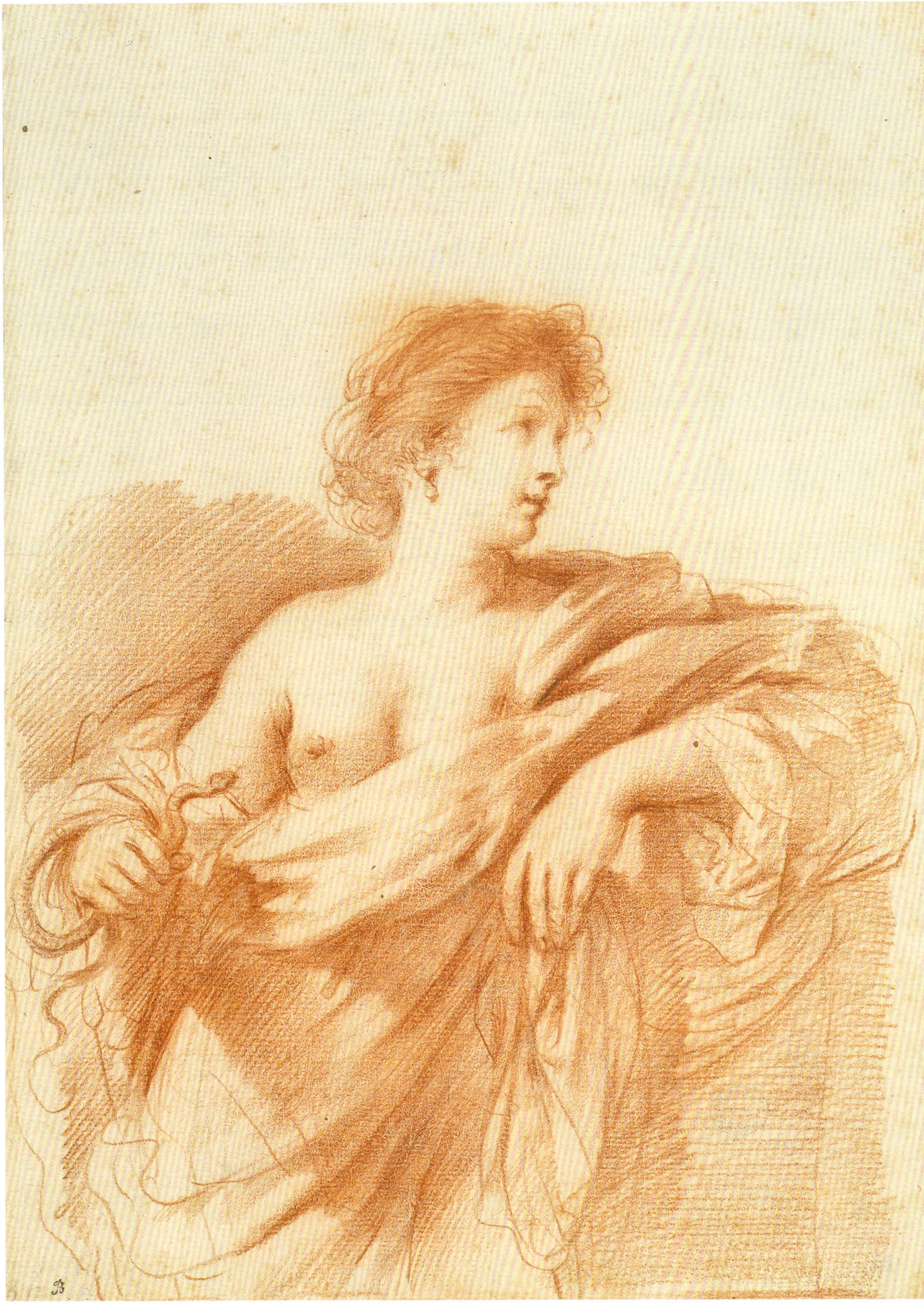

120 *Cleopatra*. London, British Museum (see also App. no. 36)

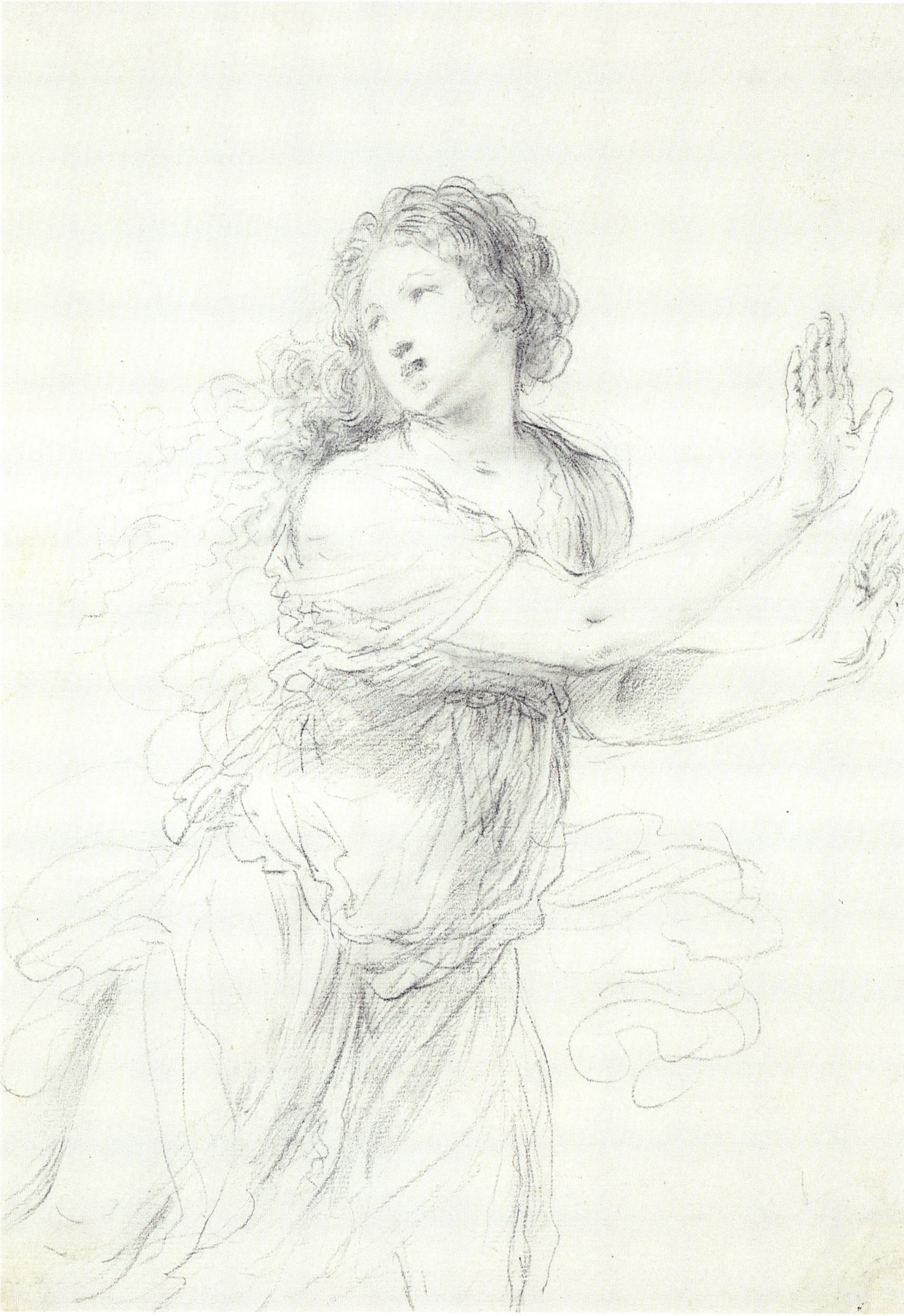

142 *Study for a Figure of Hersilia*. Windsor Castle, Royal Library

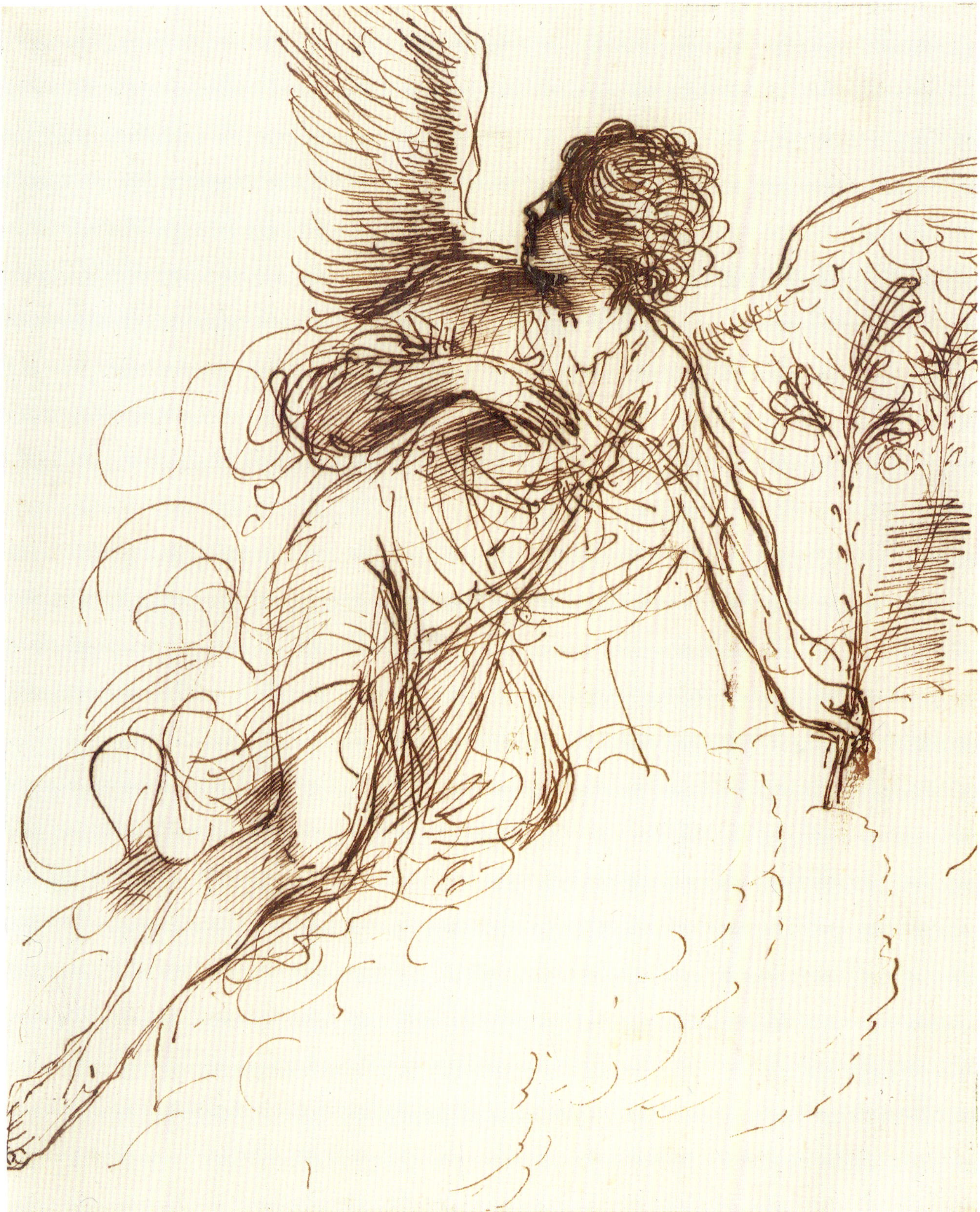

149 *The Angel of the Annunciation*. Windsor Castle, Royal Library

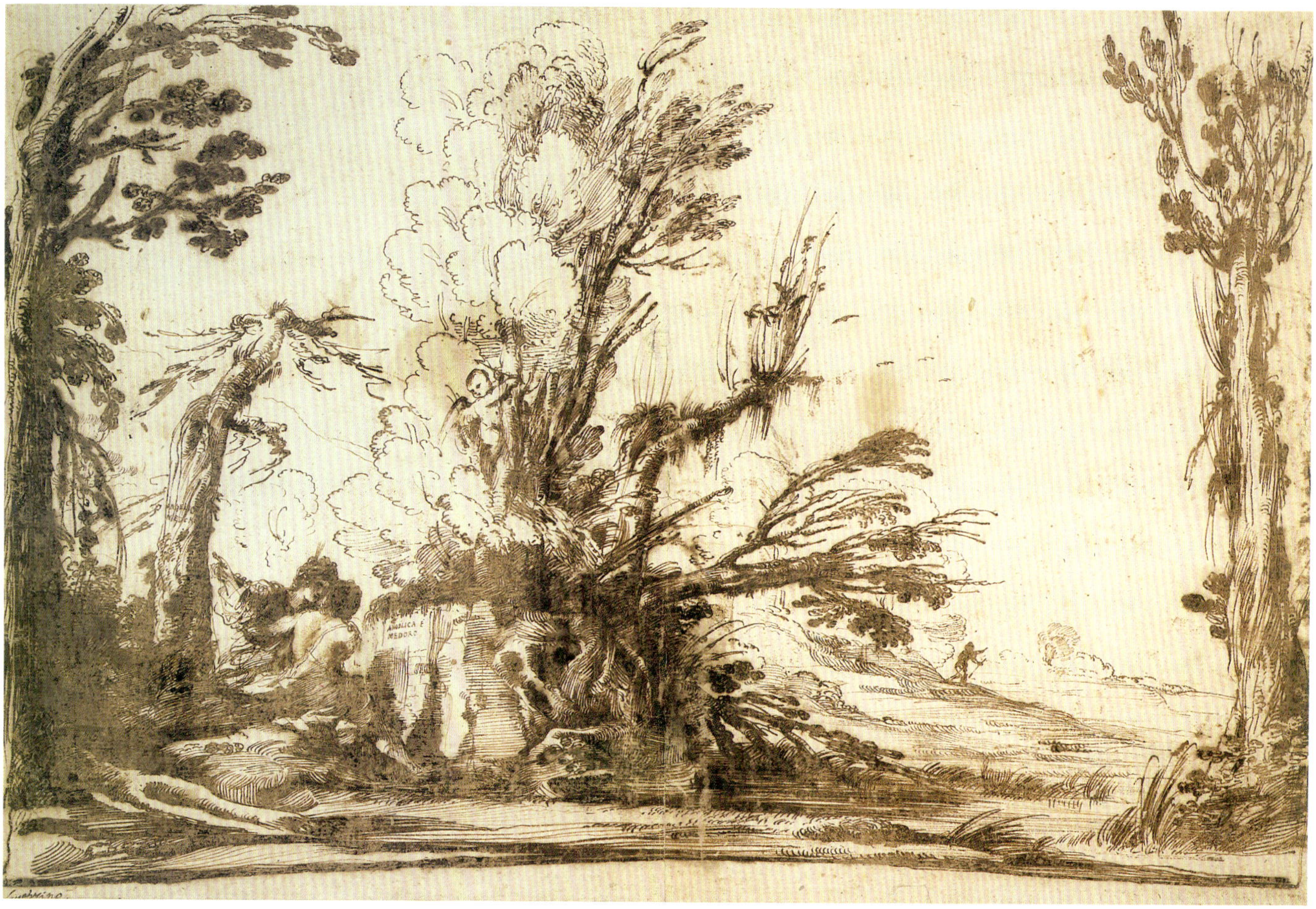

164 *Landscape with Angelica and Medoro*. London, British Museum (see also App. no. 57)

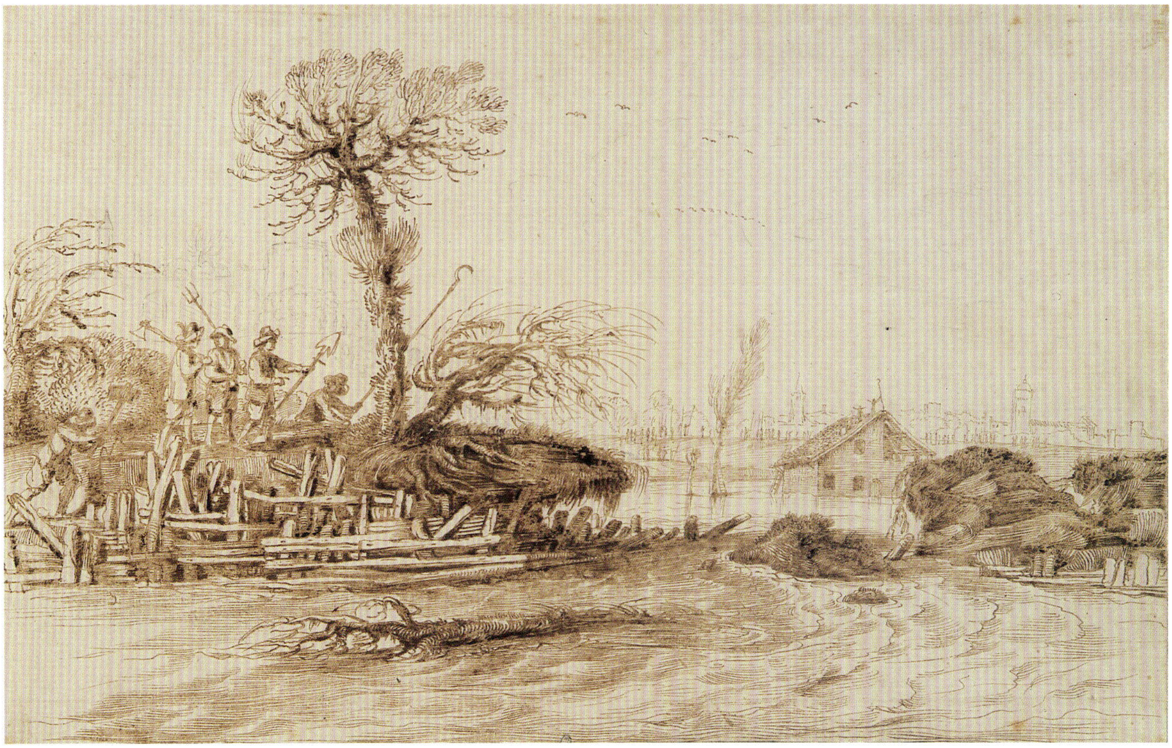

166 *Landscape with a River flooding its Banks*. Devonshire Collection, Chatsworth

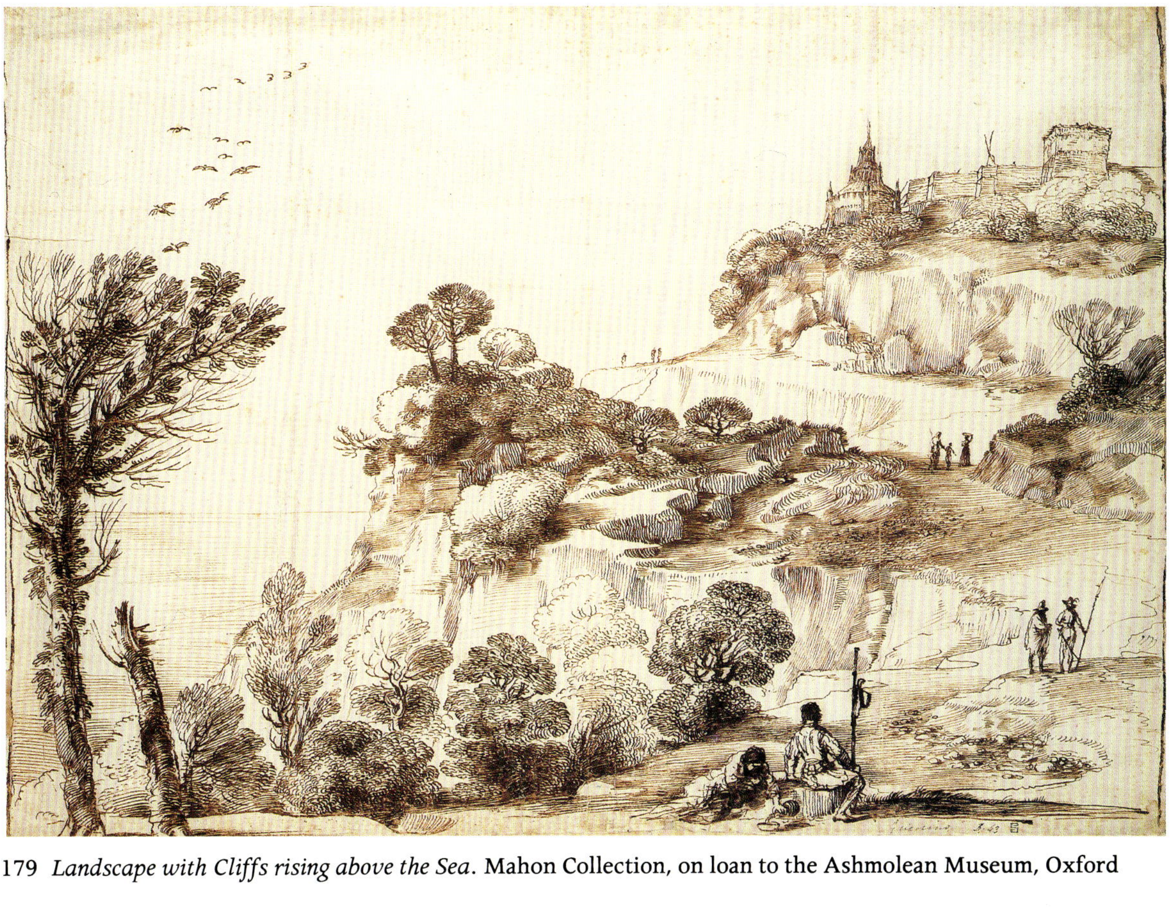

179 *Landscape with Cliffs rising above the Sea*. Mahon Collection, on loan to the Ashmolean Museum, Oxford

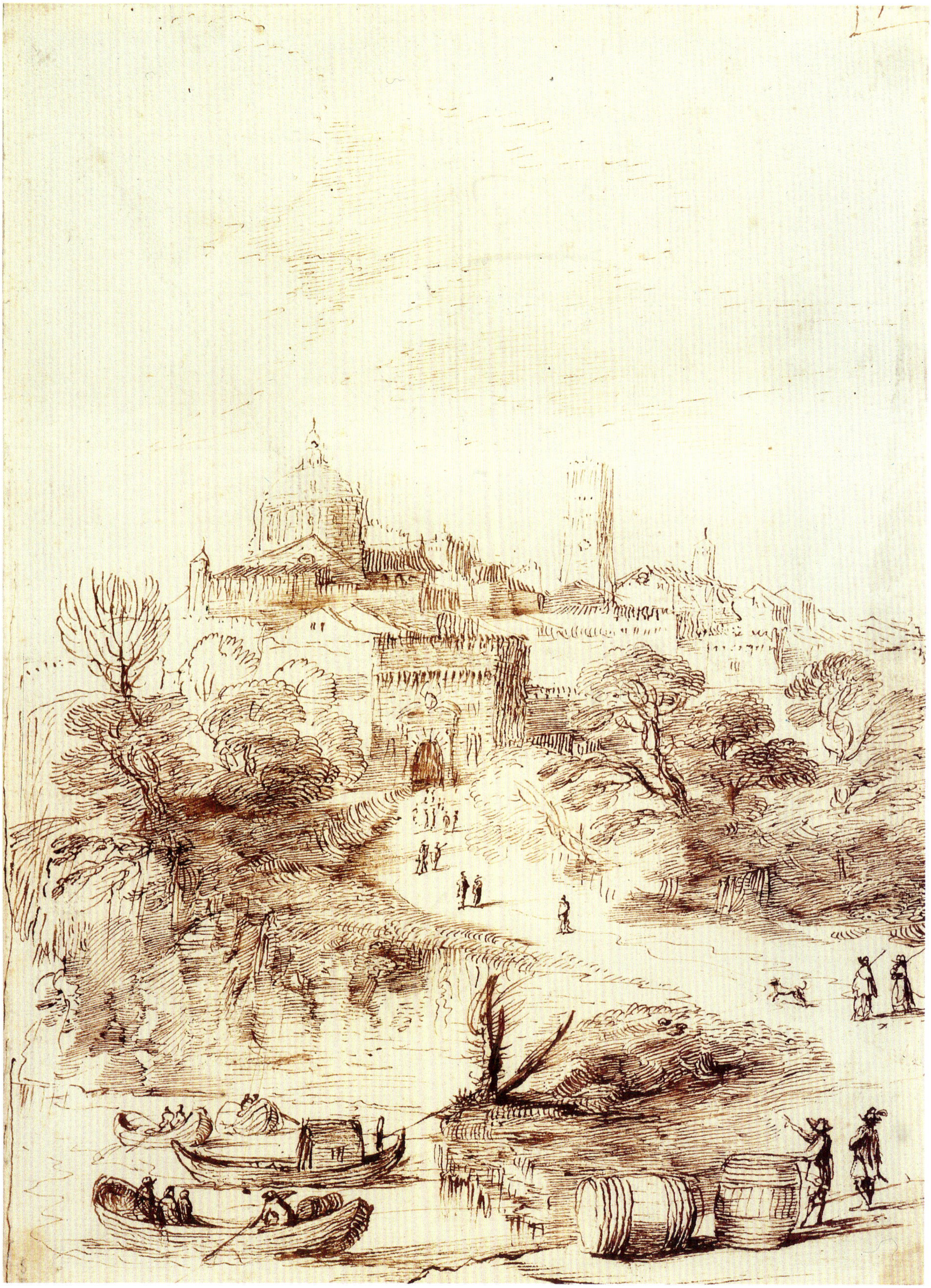

180 *Landscape with a winding Road leading up to the Gate of a Town.* Windsor Castle, Royal Library

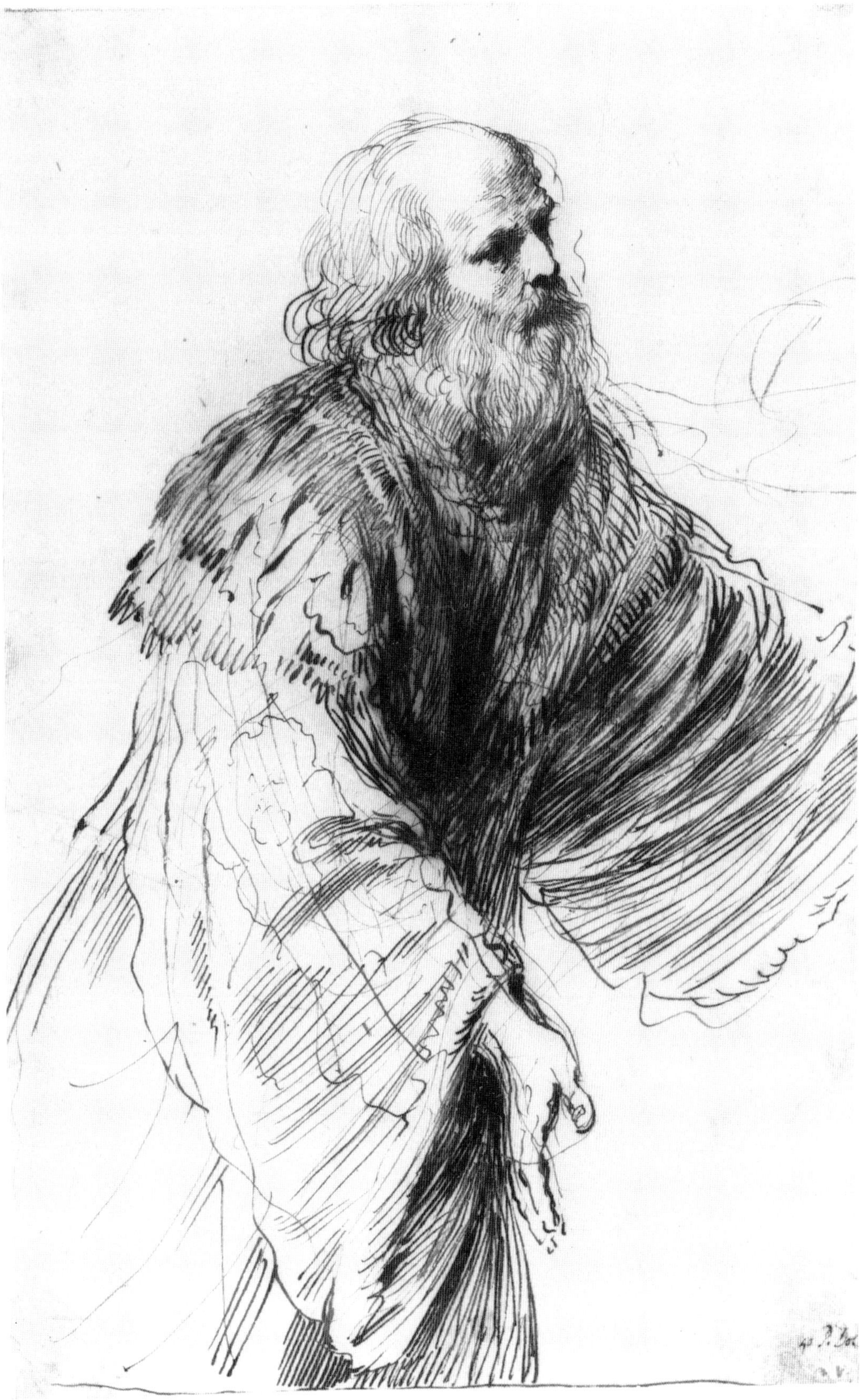

127

was formerly on the London art market (Christie's, 16 July 1974, lot 32; pen and brown ink, 250 × 200mm; see Fig. 19). A label attached to the backing of Reynolds's drawing is inscribed as follows: 'This drawing is by Sr Joshua Reynolds while Pupil to M. Hudson/it was bought at the Sale of M. Hudsons Drawings & has his mark at the right hand corner. G. Baker wishes Dr. Westrop may think it worth his acceptance/13 Decem. 99/Purchased with 2 others of Sir Joshua at a Sale of Dr Westrops collection by King Lochée May 25 1809. Mr. G. Baker of St. Pauls Ch Yard (the buyer) at the same time presented it to me. W. A.'. (The collection mark of Hudson mentioned in the inscription is not visible in the Figure here reproduced.) Sir Joshua's activity as a copyist of Guercino's drawings is discussed in greater detail in the Introduction, pp. 22–3).

127 Bearded Man, with his Arms held open in a Gesture of Greeting

Pen and brown ink. 258 × 165mm.

Private collection.

Provenance: Casa Gennari (the drawing is laid down on a fine Casa Gennari mount, for which see L *Suppl*, 2858c, and M, 1967, p. 20); Mr Bouverie; Mr Hervey; the Earls of Gainsborough.

Inscribed in brown ink in the bottom right corner: *40 P. Dol/3 v* (such inscriptions are associable with a provenance from the Casa Gennari).

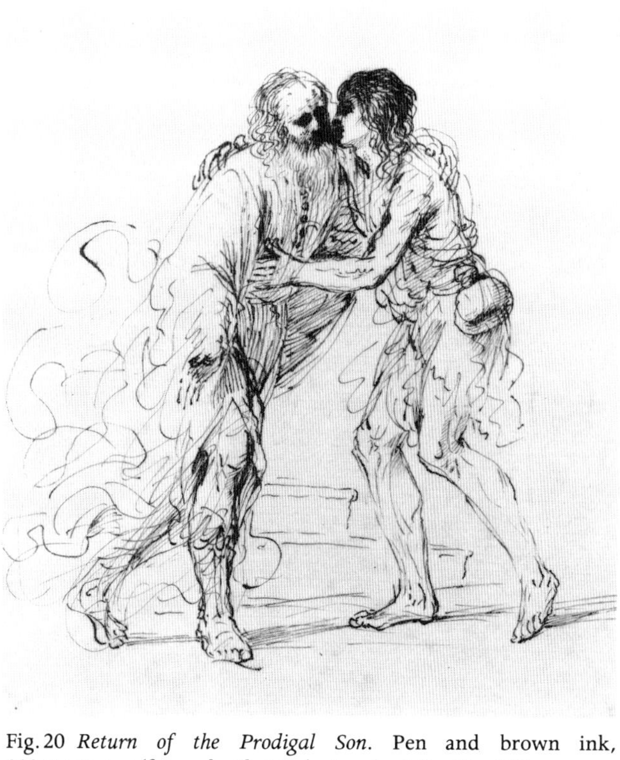

Fig. 20 *Return of the Prodigal Son*. Pen and brown ink, 203 × 176 mm (formerly Christie's, London). See No. 127

The figure in No. 127 may be related to that of the father in a composition study of the *Return of the Prodigal Son*, with full-length figures, formerly on the London art market (sale, Christie's, 9 December 1982, lot 45, pen and brown ink, 203 × 176mm; see Fig. 20). Although the old man in the ex-Christie's drawing lacks the fur cape seen in No. 127, he wears a similarly long robe with loose-fitting sleeves, his right arm is held in roughly the same position and he is bare-headed. From their style, both drawings appear to date from around 1640, or shortly afterwards. Indeed, in some respects the ex-Christie's drawing compares well in handling with No. 131, datable 1641, particularly in the swirling lines that make up the back of the father's robe, which correspond closely with a similar passage in No. 131.

According to Malvasia, Guercino painted two different pictures of the *Return of the Prodigal Son* in 1642: 'Al sig. Principe Tadeo Barberini un figliuol Prodigo, donato à Papa Urbano VIII. Al Padre Massoni un figliuol Prodigo' (Malvasia, 1678, II, p. 373; 1841, II, p. 265). These two works are also mentioned in the Account Book, where they are both described as half lengths: the first, commissioned by Prince Taddeo Barberini, was paid for on 21 June, the second, ordered by Padre D. Gregorio Maffone, on 20 October (*Libro dei Conti*, 1808, pp. 101–2; 1841, p. 323). Unfortunately, both pictures are untraced, and no copies or engravings after them exist recording their appearance.

No. 127 and the ex-Christie's drawing (even though it is of whole-length figures) may have been conceived with one or other of these half-length pictures in mind. It can be demonstrated that No. 127 was intended for a half-length composition: the roughly drawn, horizontal line at the bottom edge of the sheet indicates the lower extremity of the figure. This 'bottom line' is a device found elsewhere in Guercino's drawings for marking the base of a given composition (see, for example, Nos. 49, 79, 136, 145, 147 and 148). The earlier study for the whole composition, with this same figure full-length, may have been made either because one or other of the two patrons initially favoured a full-length picture or because the artist simply wished to gauge the position of the upper part of the legs of the two half-length figures, something he could best do by first drawing the entire figure.

Although in the 1650s Guercino returned to the subject of the Prodigal Son in two pictures that show marked analogies with the composition studied in No. 127 and the ex-Christie's drawing (see S, 1988, nos. 278 and 310), we do not believe that the two drawings considered here – given their style so strongly suggestive of the 1640s – bear a direct relationship to the two later pictures.

Dr David Stone has kindly brought to our attention a pen-and-ink copy of No. 127 in a private collection in Massachusetts, USA, which, judging from a photograph, may be attributable to Sir Joshua Reynolds, whose copies after drawings by Guercino formerly in the Bouverie collection are discussed in the Introduction and under No. 126 and App. nos. 46 and 48.

5 The 1640s (Nos. 128–152)

At the death of his rival Guido Reni in 1642, Guercino transferred his studio from Cento to Bologna, taking over as the city's leading painter. At first he lived in the palace of Conte Filippo Aldrovandi. Then in 1644 he bought a house in the Parish of S. Nicolò degli Albari, in the street now known as Via S. Alò (no. 3), which he later enlarged by the purchase in 1659 of the adjacent property – this was the house that later came to be known by the name of the painter's heirs, as the Casa Gennari. The tireless activity that characterised Guercino's work of the 1630s continued unabated. From his new studio in Bologna there flowed a stream of altarpieces and easel pictures, their cool, classical style more than ever recalling the language of the pictures of his now deceased rival.

Among the more prestigious commissions that followed his transfer from Cento to Bologna were three further canvases for his Parisian patron Louis Phélypeaux de La Vrillière, the *Coriolanus*, painted in 1643, the *Hersilia separating Romulus and Tatius*, painted in 1645 (see Nos. 141–2), and the *Mucius Scaevola plunging his right Hand into the Flames*, which, for unknown reasons, was never actually delivered to the patron. The succession of altarpieces that continued to emerge from Guercino's studio includes the *Finding of the True Cross*, executed in 1644 for the church of S. Lazzaro dei Mendicanti in Venice (see Nos. 136–7); the *Flagellation of Christ*, painted in the same year for the Beregani family of Vicenza (see No. 135); and the *All Saints in Glory*, painted in 1645–7 for the high altar of the church of the Sacre Stimmate at Modena (see App. no. 47). The production of smaller easel pictures still amounted to a substantial proportion of his output, a good example being the *Atlas* painted in 1646 for Prince Don Lorenzo de' Medici (see Nos. 144–8).

The drawings in this decade, especially those in pen and ink, are surprisingly uninhibited compared with the disciplined finish of the pictures for which many are preparatory. Characteristic of the pen drawings of this moment is an almost heavy-handed line, accompanied by equally emphatic passages of cross hatching; this expressionistic manner, which is almost deliberately unpleasing in appearance, is well shown in the study for the *Annunciation* in the church of S. Maria Maggiore at Pieve di Cento (No. 149). The pen or pen-and-wash studies for the *Atlas* show a similarly fiery, almost impatient touch that verges on coarseness (Nos. 145–8), though two of them (Nos. 146 and 148) are drawn more painstakingly. Although he did not abandon the use of red chalk in the 1640s (see No. 137), Guercino does seem to have employed black chalk more than he had done for many years (see Nos. 142 and 144).

128–129 Studies for the *Madonna of the Rosary with Sts Dominic and Catherine of Siena* (*c.*1640–43)

Osimo, S. Marco

128 Madonna seated among Clouds

Pen and brown ink. 224 × 173mm.

Windsor Castle, Royal Library, inv. no. 2851.

Provenance: Casa Gennari; King George III.

Literature: M & T, 1989, no. 98.

This good example of Guercino's free drawing with the pen is probably an early study for the figure of the Madonna in the altarpiece of the *Madonna of the Rosary with Sts Dominic and Catherine of Siena*, painted in *c.*1640–43 for the church of S. Marco at Osimo (S, 1988, no. 202). Work on the preparation of the picture seems to have lasted a few years. At the outset the patrons evidently asked Guercino to supply them with preparatory drawings in order to give them an idea of the appearance of his composition (see No. 129). Furthermore, there is a record of a visit made to Guercino's studio at Cento by a certain Camillo Talleoni before 20 October 1640 'mentre il quadro era in esecuzione' (Zampetti, 1967, p. 27, n. 19); it is possible, however, that Guercino was at work on the drawings for this picture rather

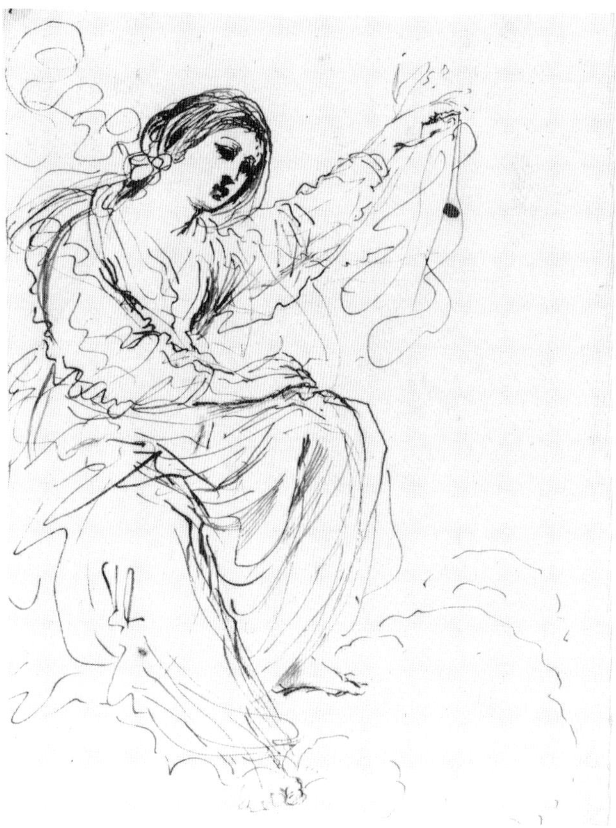

128

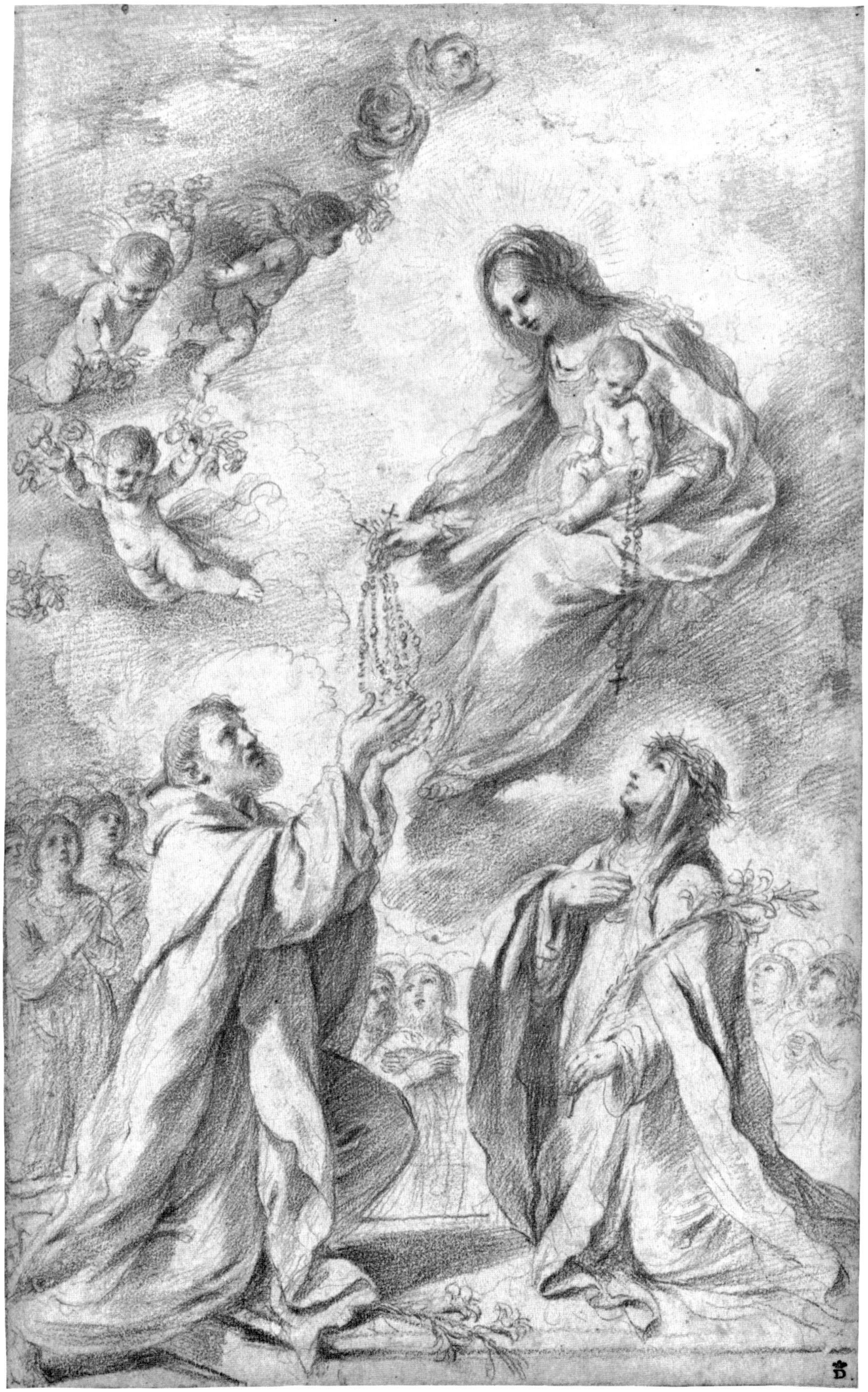

129

than on the picture itself when this visit took place (see M & T, 1989, no. 98).

In No. 128 the Madonna holds aloft in her left hand what appears to be string, but this is evidently intended for the rosary. Presumably only at a later stage in the evolution of the design was it decided to show the Christ Child on the Madonna's lap.

Two other drawings for the putti in the composition were, at different times, formerly on the London art market (see M & T, 1989, under no. 98).

129 The Madonna of the Rosary, with Sts Dominic and Catherine of Siena

Red chalk. 334 × 215mm.

Chatsworth, inv. no. 515.

Provenance: William Cavendish, 2nd Duke of Devonshire (L 718); thence by descent.

Literature: M, *Disegni*, 1969, under no. 145; Jaffé, 1987, no. 41; S, 1988, under no. 202; M & T, 1989, under nos. 98 and 643.

Like No. 128, this is a study for the altarpiece in S. Marco at Osimo. It is an especially fine example of Guercino's finished composition studies in red chalk, of which only comparatively few survive. In the picture the two saints occupy roughly the same corresponding positions, but the Madonna and Child are shown seated to the left and looking towards the right, directly in reverse to their appearance in the drawing.

According to a document in the Archive of the Propaganda Fide in Rome, in June 1640 Guercino was already under consideration as the artist to paint the altarpiece in the Cappella del Rosario (see M & T, 1989, no. 98). The document states that Guercino should furnish drawings ('vulgo disegni') of the proposed altarpiece for the approval of the congregation. It is probable that No. 129, or drawings associated with it, may have been prepared by the artist as a presentation study for the patrons.

For an accurate copy of No. 129, drawn by the early eighteenth-century Irish painter and collector Hugh Howard, see App. no. 109.

130 Angelica and Medoro

Pen and brown ink and brown wash. 259 × 381mm.

Mahon Collection, on loan to the Ashmolean Museum, Oxford, M & E, 30.

Provenance: Thomas Jenkins, Rome, by 1764; Max de Beer; from whom purchased by Sir Denis Mahon on 3 June 1964.

Literature: M, 1967, no. 26; M, *Disegni*, 1969, no. 159; M & E, 1986, no. 30.

Inscribed on the tree to the right of Medoro: *ANGELICA E MEDOR*.

The scene is from Ariosto's epic *Orlando furioso* (XIX, 36); it depicts Angelica with her Moorish lover and eventual husband Medoro, carving their names in the bark of a tree. It was the discovery of such inscriptions attesting their love that provoked the jealous rage of the Christian hero Orlando, a rival suitor.

Unlike No. 164, *Landscape with Angelica and Medoro*, which was almost certainly drawn as a composition in its

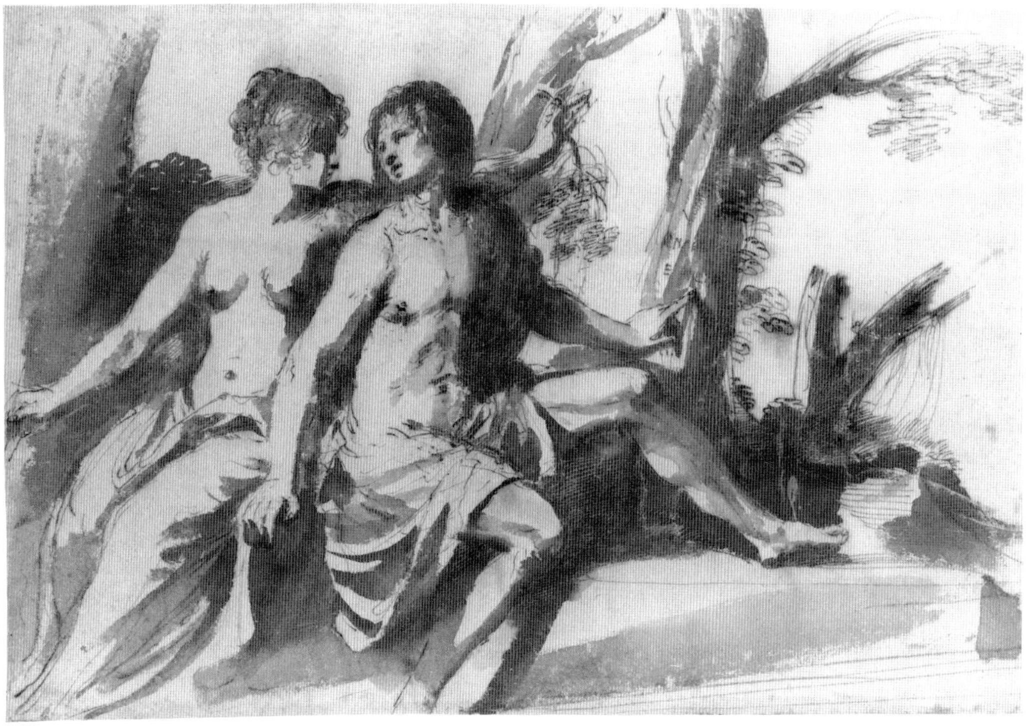

130

own right, the present drawing appears to have been made as a study for a painting, though no such work has been traced. Mahon (1969) pointed out that Guercino's Account Book records payments for two large paintings of the story in 1642 and 1647 (*Libro dei Conti*, 1808, pp. 102 and 117; 1841, pp. 323 and 328). The first of these was paid for by the Comunità di Cento and given to Cardinal Ginetti, Legate of Ferrara, and the second was commissioned by one of Guercino's influential French patrons, César, Sieur du Plessin-Praslin, Duc de Choiseul and Maréchal de France. Although a date in the 1640s seems appropriate for the drawing on the grounds of style, there is not enough evidence to determine for which of the two commissions it could have been preparatory. Mahon (in M & E, 1986), citing the similarity in handling to other drawings of 1646–7, preferred a connection with the later commission.

There are several important differences between No. 130 and the photograph reproduced by Salerno (1988, no. 245) of an untraced painting apparently by Guercino of this same subject. This lost painting is likely, according to Mahon, to be identical with the picture commissioned for Cardinal Ginetti in 1642, which seems to have been sold from the Hope collection at Christie's, London, on 20 July 1917, together with two other pictures by Guercino with a Ginetti provenance (see M, *Dipinti*, 1968, pp. 104f.). Assuming that the picture reproduced by Salerno is the ex-Ginetti version of the subject, then No. 130 is indeed less likely to have been drawn in that connection.

No. 130 was etched in reverse by Giovanni Ottaviani while in the collection of Thomas Jenkins and was included in the series of prints after Guercino's drawings gathered together in Piranesi's *Raccolta*, published in 1764. (For further particulars, see M, *Disegni*, 1969, no. 159.)

131 The Guardian Angel

Pen and brown ink. 258 × 175mm.

Royal Library, Windsor Castle, inv. no. 2685.

Provenance: Casa Gennari; King George III.

Literature: S, 1988, under no. 196; M & T, 1989, no. 101.

No. 131 is for the picture of the same subject formerly in S. Agostino at Fano and now on deposit at the Museo Civico Malatestiano (S, 1988, no. 196). This is the only painting of a 'sant'Angelo Custode' recorded in the Account Book. Payment for it was received on 12 October 1641 (*Libro dei Conti*, 1808, p. 98; 1841, p. 322), a date entirely consistent with the present drawing's style. The painting differs from the preparatory drawing in several ways: in the finished work the putto is kneeling on one knee on a block at the right and the body of the angel is turned towards him as he holds him with both hands; both figures look upwards to the left, but the angel no longer points in that direction.

Mahon and Turner noted two drawings by an indifferent follower of Guercino, also in the Royal Library at Windsor (M & T, 1989, nos. 432–3), that may reflect other studies by the master for this composition.

132–134 Studies for *Cupid restraining the enraged Mars* (?c.1640)

Lost but known from a print by Giacomo Giovannini

132 Cupid restraining Mars

Pen and brown ink. 227 × 188mm; damaged and patched in the areas of greatest dark.

London, Courtauld Institute Galleries, Witt Collection, inv. no. 1349.

Provenance: Casa Gennari (the drawing is laid down on a fine Casa Gennari mount, for which see L *Suppl*, 2858c, and M, 1967, p. 20); Mr Bouverie; Mr Hervey; the Earls of Gainsborough (sale, Christie's, London, 27 July 1922, lot 81, with others, bt *Meatyard*); Sir Robert Witt.

Literature: Horton, 1960, pp. 7ff., fig. 5; Hammer, *et al.*, 1977, no. 36; M & T, 1989, under nos. 55 and 661.

The condition of the drawing bears many of the features of those once kept in albums in the Casa Gennari, in particular in the losses and paste stains evident in two of the four corners, which presumably date from the time the drawing was removed from its album (see M & T, 1989, p. xxi). There are also paste stains at regular intervals along the four edges. These are a consequence of the usual method of attaching the sheet onto the Casa Gennari mount by means of small, thin paper tabs along the edges (see App. no. 49). The damage caused by the corrosive action of the iron-gall ink in the areas of greatest dark has been made good by eleven small rectangular slips of paper attached to the *verso*, in a manner characteristic of early repairs to other drawings by Guercino in the Casa Gennari.

Numbered in graphite in the bottom left corner of the drawing: *11* (for a discussion and further instances of sheets numbered in this way, see No. 10).

The drawing is a study for the lost painting of *Cupid restraining the engraged Mars*, which Malsavia recorded as being in Guercino's house at the time of his death (Malvasia, 1678, II, p. 384; 1841, II, p. 273: 'Marte furibondo ritenuto da un Amorino'). The appearance of the picture, showing Mars full-length, is preserved in an engraving by Giacomo Giovannini (1667–1717), which is inscribed: *Marte pronto p[er] combattere tratenuto dal Genio allato. Gio: Fran.*[co] *Barbieri da Cento dipin:* (S, 1988, no. 364). The date of the composition is not known, though judging from the style of the preparatory drawings we are inclined to situate it about 1640.

No. 132 is similar to the finished composition in the pose of Cupid, but differs substantially from it in the dynamic attitude and billowing drapery of Mars. Contributing to the drawing's dramatic effect is Guercino's rapid and aggressive penwork, so heavy in places that the acid content of the iron-gall ink quickly bit through and destroyed the paper in several of the deeper darks. This effect is also enhanced by the numerous pentiments, most spectacularly evident in the artist's five different attempts to find a suitable axis for the sword. Of the other studies for this composition, No. 132 most closely resembles one, also in pen and ink, in the Allen Memorial Art Museum, Oberlin, Ohio (inv. no. 58.154;

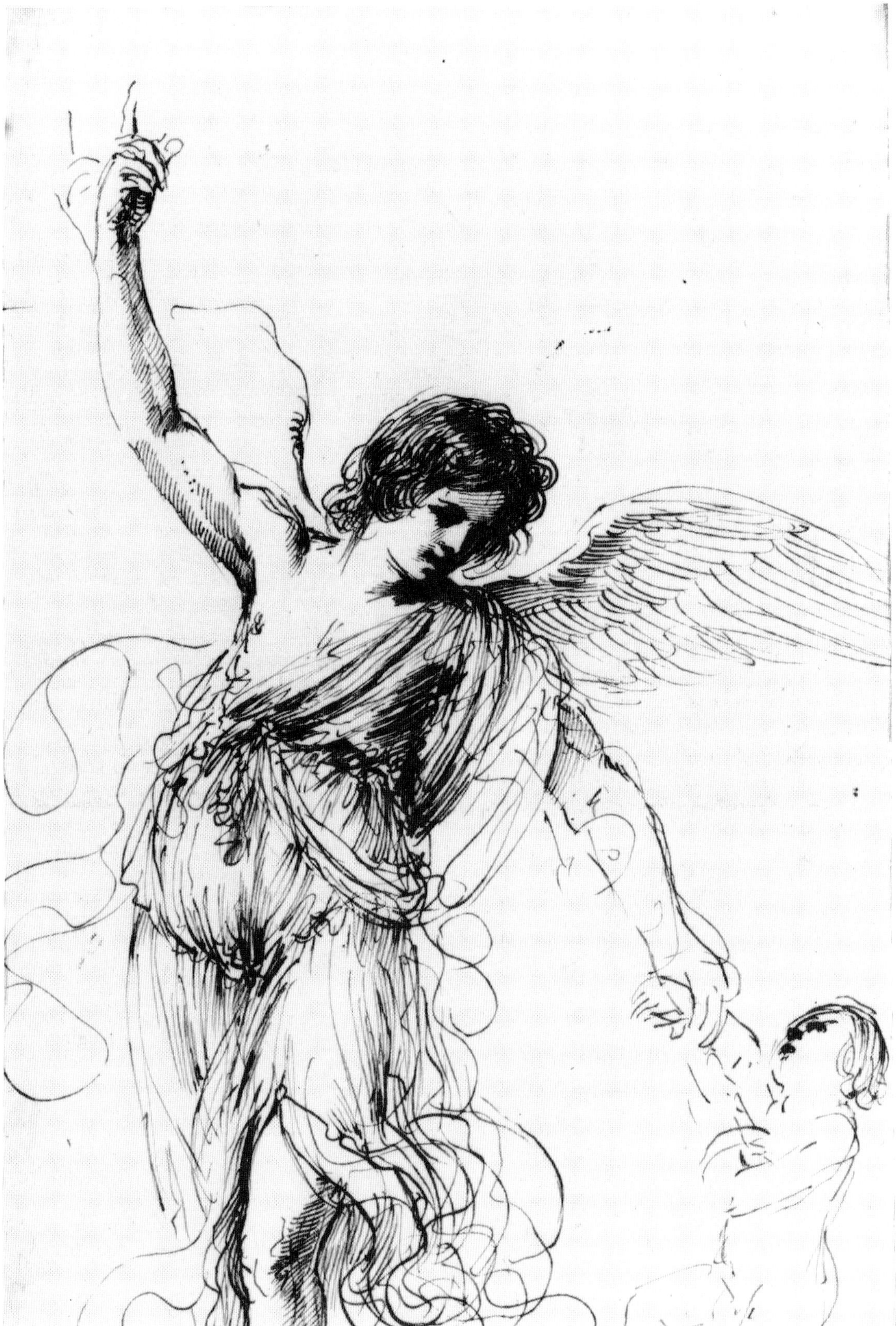

131

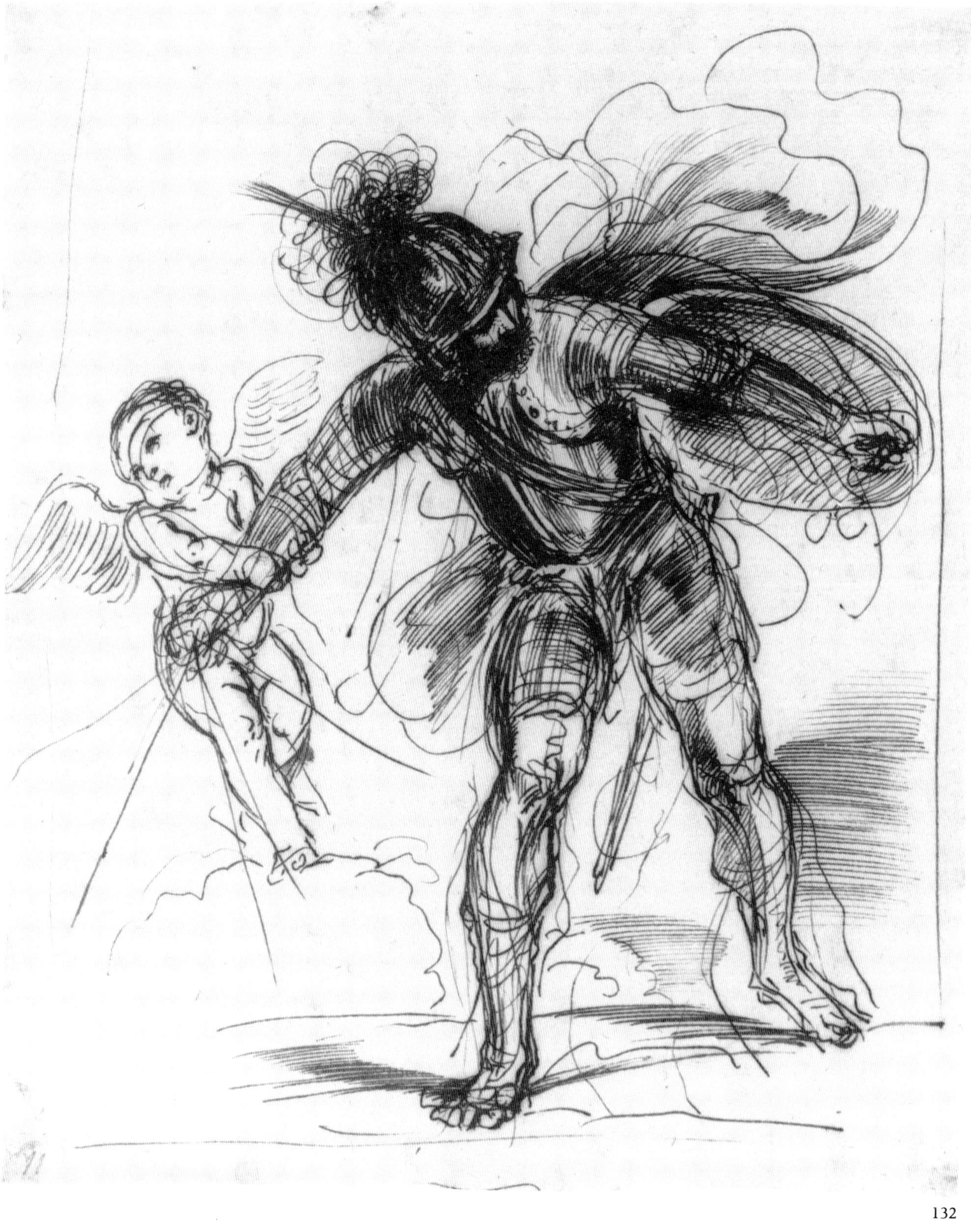

132

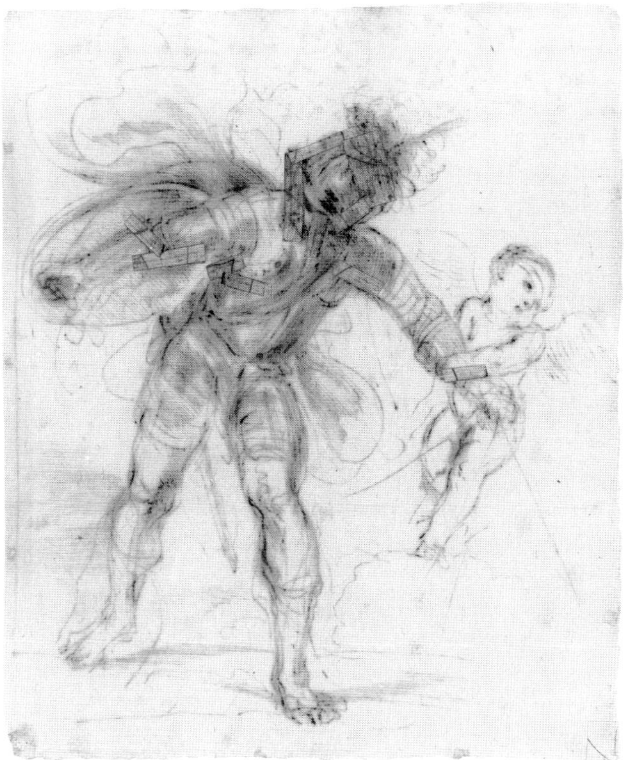

132 *verso*

Horton, 1960, p. 4, fig. 1; Stechow, 1976, no. 160), which shows Cupid in a similar pose and Mars in a slightly different, but still flamboyant, attitude. Cupid's pose in both sheets echoes that of the finished composition in which his body is on a diagonal axis leaning away from Mars and his head is also turned away: he is also represented standing on a cloud as in the finished composition instead of on the more prosaic block shown in No. 133.

A drawing of *Cupid* in the Museum of Fine Arts, Boston (inv. no. 1891.161; Macandrew, 1983, no. 133), may be a copy after a lost study by Guercino for the same commission. It shows the putto turned to the right, tugging at a man's forearm in the clenched hand of which is a sword. A coarsely retouched offset of this or another closely related drawing is in the Royal Library, Windsor Castle (M & T, 1989, no. 716).

133 Cupid restraining Mars

London, British Museum, inv. no. Ff. 2–135.

(For other details, see App. no. 38.)

The drawing is a study for the lost painting of *Cupid restraining the enraged Mars*, for which see No. 132.

No. 133 diverges most from the composition recorded in Giacomo Giovannini's print in the pose of Cupid. By contrast, the pose of Mars resembles that of the print and is repeated with little variation in two drawings of Mars alone, one, in red chalk, in the Städelsches Kunstinstitut, Frankfurt (inv. no. 6895; M & T, 1989, p. 193, fig. 35), and the other, in pen and ink, now in the collection of David Koetser at Zurich (sold earlier at Sotheby's, London, 22 July 1953, lot 7, from the collection of the Earls of Gainsborough). A retouched offset of the Frankfurt drawing is in the Royal Library, Windsor Castle (M & T, 1989, no. 661), and another offset in the same collection (no. 662) records another red chalk drawing (the whereabouts of which are unknown) of the same figure of Mars, this time in half length.

134 Study for a Warrior in profile to the right

Pen, point of the brush and brown wash. 254 × 159mm.

Private collection.

Provenance: Casa Gennari; Mr Bouverie (L 325); Mr Hervey; the Earls of Gainsborough; T. S. R. Boase.

In the freedom of its technique of brush and brown wash, with only occasional touches of the pen, No. 134 resembles

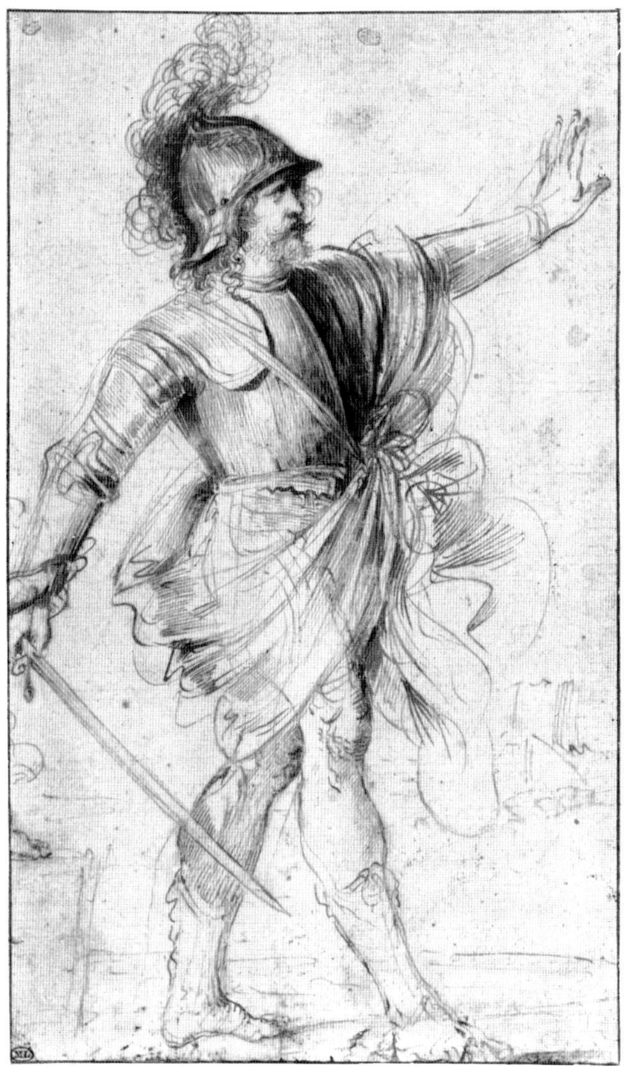

Fig. 21 By or after Guercino, *The enraged Mars*. Pen and brown ink, 165 × 142 mm (Paris, Louvre, inv. no. 6893). See No. 134

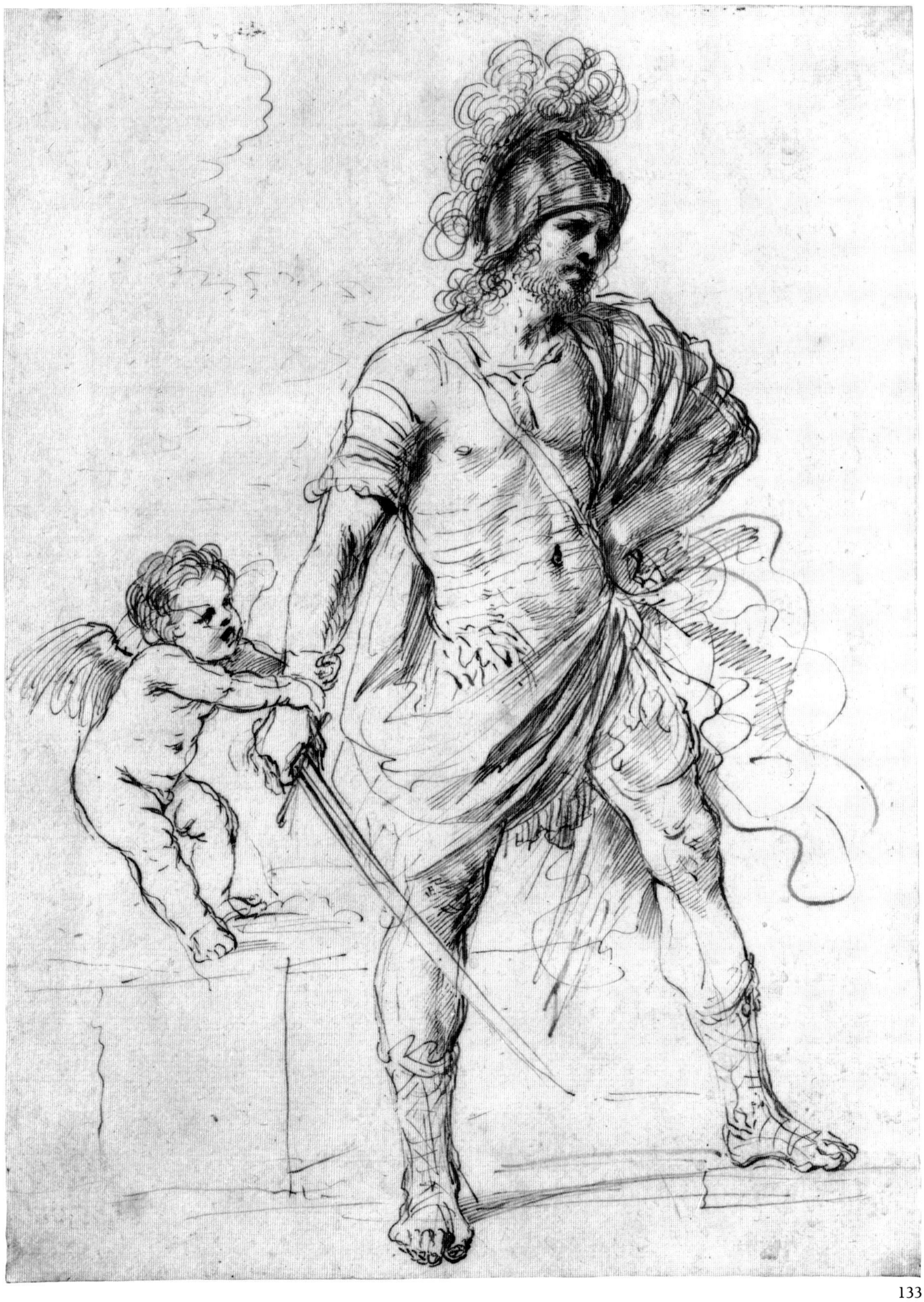

133

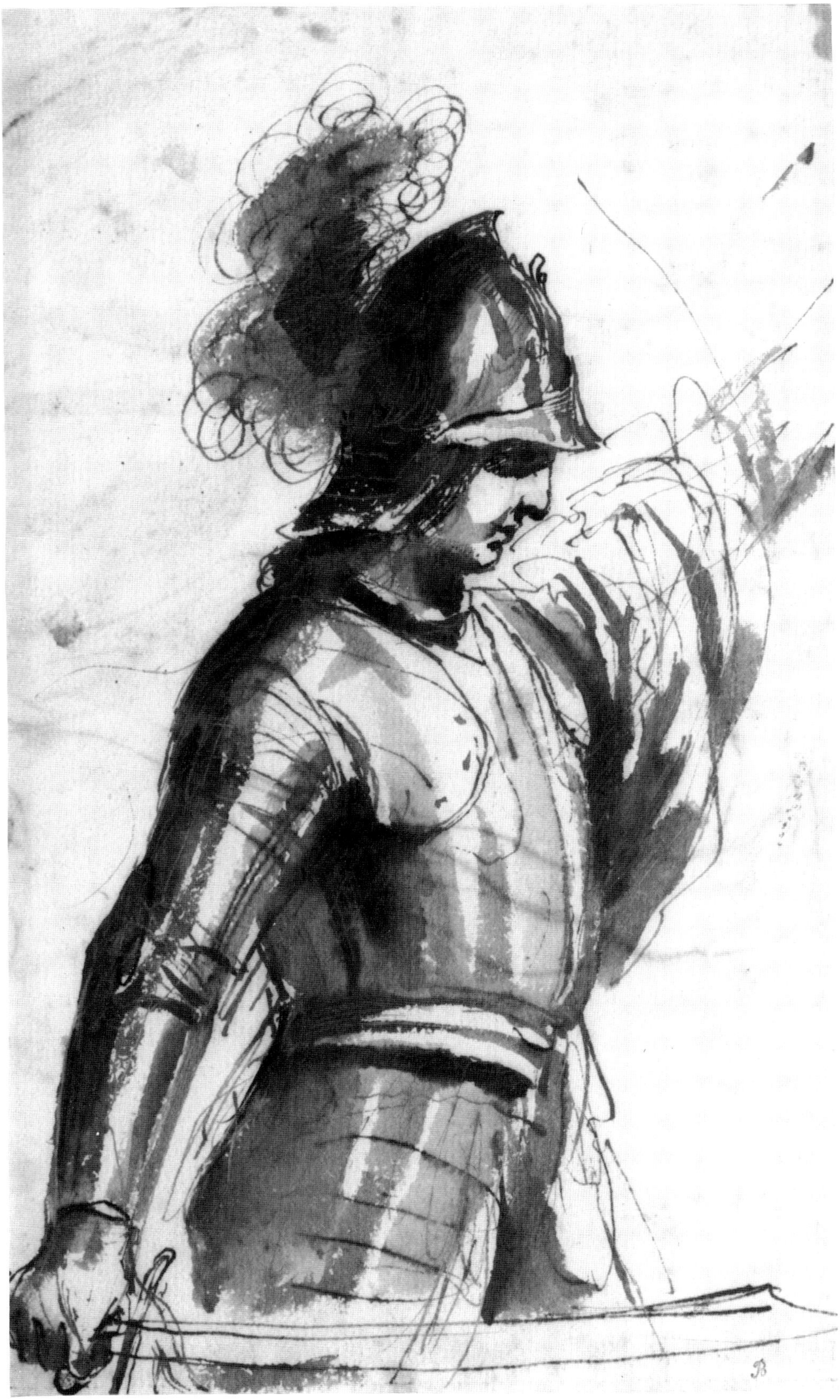

134

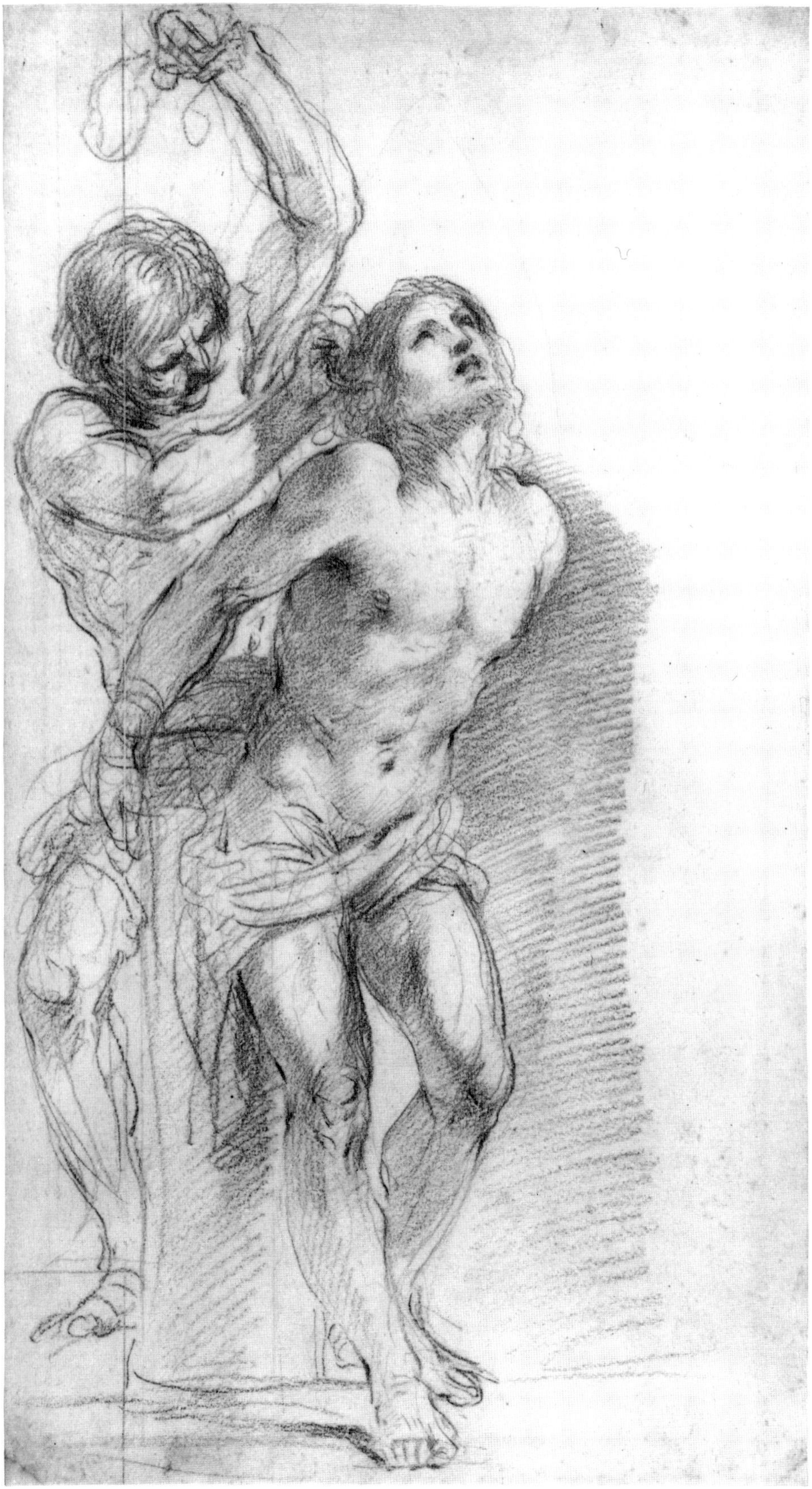

135

the treatment of No. 141, a study for the *Hersilia separating Romulus and Tatius* of 1645, now in the Louvre, Paris. Although it is possible that the figure in No. 134 could be a study for the warrior on the left of that composition, an hypothesis supported by the similarity in the position of his right arm with the sword held horizontally to the ground, his raised left arm casts doubt on such a connection.

Alternatively, the figure might be intended for a Mars – shown beardless perhaps on account of being studied from a studio model – and the drawing could be another study for the lost painting of *Cupid restraining the enraged Mars*, for which see No. 132. No. 134 relates closely to a pen-and-ink drawing of Mars, full-length, by or after Guercino in the Louvre, Paris (inv. no. 6893, 165 × 142mm; see Fig. 21), which was brought to our attention by Stéphane Loire. The presence in the Louvre drawing of Cupid (though largely curtailed by the left edge of the sheet) clinches the warrior's identity, and though the putto is not present in No. 134, we feel that similarities in both pose and style between the drawings are compelling enough to warrant their connection.

For a copy by Robert Shipster after a drawing extremely similar to that in the Louvre, but omitting Cupid, see App. no. 116.

135 Flagellation of Christ

Red chalk. 360 × 203mm; drawn on paper apparently from an account book.

Oxford, Ashmolean Museum, KTP 863.

Provenance: C. L. Chute, The Vyne, Basingstoke (sale, Sotheby's, London, 22 June 1949, lot 1); R. E. A. Wilson.

Literature: Parker, 1956, no. 863; M, *Disegni*, 1969, no. 151; Macandrew, 1983, p. 299; M & E, 1986, no. XIV; S, 1988, under no. 213.

This magnificent drawing is a study for the altarpiece of the *Flagellation of Christ*, now in the Museum of Fine Arts, Budapest (S, 1988, no. 213). It was paid for in 1644 by the Beregani family of Vicenza (*Libro dei Conti*, 1808, p. 107; 1841, p. 325) and is mentioned in an early guide to the pictures of Vicenza as being in the church of S. Biagio Nuovo (Boschini, 1676, p. 96); Salerno (S, 1988, no. 213) is incorrect in saying that Boschini cited it as once being in the church of S. Bartolomeo, Vicenza. The picture and the circumstances of its commission have been discussed in a recent study of the history of the church of S. Biagio Nuovo (Dirani, 1988, pp. 10, 32–7, and 61–2).

The drawing shows the artist's confident handling of red chalk at its very best, and the violence of the subject is made only too clear. Whereas the figure of Christ in No. 135 is fairly close to his counterpart in the painting, the flagellator is very different. He is brought round from behind Christ to stand parallel with the picture plane, where he takes up so static a pose that the spectator almost loses sight of the brutality of his action.

As Mahon pointed out (1969), another drawing for the composition, also in red chalk, is in the Palazzo Rosso, Genoa (inv. no. 1698; Roli, 1972, pp. 31f. and pl. 58).

136–137 Studies for the *Finding of the True Cross* (1644)

Venice, S. Lazzaro dei Mendicanti

136 St Helen finding the True Cross

Pen and brown ink and slight touches of brown wash. 240 × 152mm.

Windsor Castle, Royal Library, inv. no. 2681.

Provenance: Casa Gennari; King George III.

Literature: M, *Disegni*, 1969, no. 150; S, 1988, under no. 209; M & T, 1989, no. 110.

Nos. 136–7 are studies for the now much repainted altarpiece of the *Finding of the True Cross*, executed in 1644 for the second chapel on the left of the church of S. Lazzaro dei Mendicanti in Venice (S, 1988, no. 209). According to Malvasia, Guido Reni had earlier refused the commission (1678, II, p. 75; 1841, II, p. 54): this must have been just before Reni's death in 1642.

St Helen, the mother of Constantine the Great, discovered the True Cross in the Holy Land. A man by the name of Judas, who knew of its whereabouts on Golgotha, outside Jerusalem, revealed where it could be found only after lengthy and painful persuasion. The genuineness of the Cross was confirmed by a miracle that occurred immediately after it was unearthed: a corpse was brought into contact with it and was immediately restored to life. The drawing shows both the miracle and St Helen's prayer of thanksgiving. In the finished picture it was only the saint's prayer in gratitude in front of the Cross that was represented.

The composition of No. 136 is far more dynamic than that of the finished work. In the drawing the Cross divides the space diagonally in two and the miracle of the resurrection of the corpse is featured as an event of at least equal importance to St Helen's wonderment; in the upper part of the composition an angel enhances the sense of movement, and its energetic pose is taken up by the gravediggers below who are raising the Cross. At one point Guercino evidently thought of emphasising the steep angle of the Cross still further by showing in the right background a crowd of figures carrying another cross, which leans diagonally in the opposite direction to that in the foreground, and beyond them a city on a hilltop (presumably Jerusalem). He evidently thought better of it and cancelled the whole passage with dark hatching. Apart from the fact that such considerable changes were made, the rapidity of execution of No. 136 also indicates that it was an early idea in the evolution of the composition.

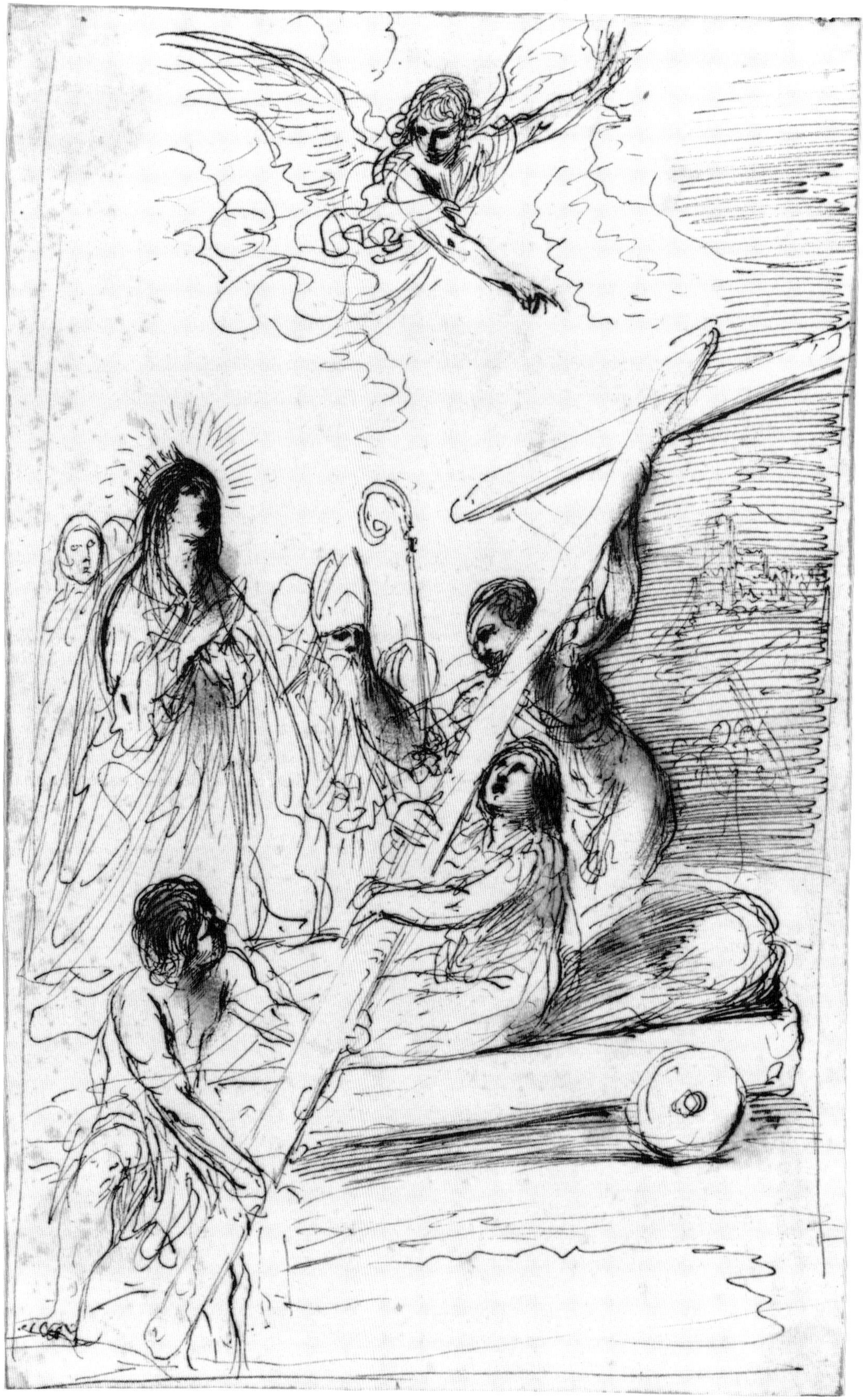

136

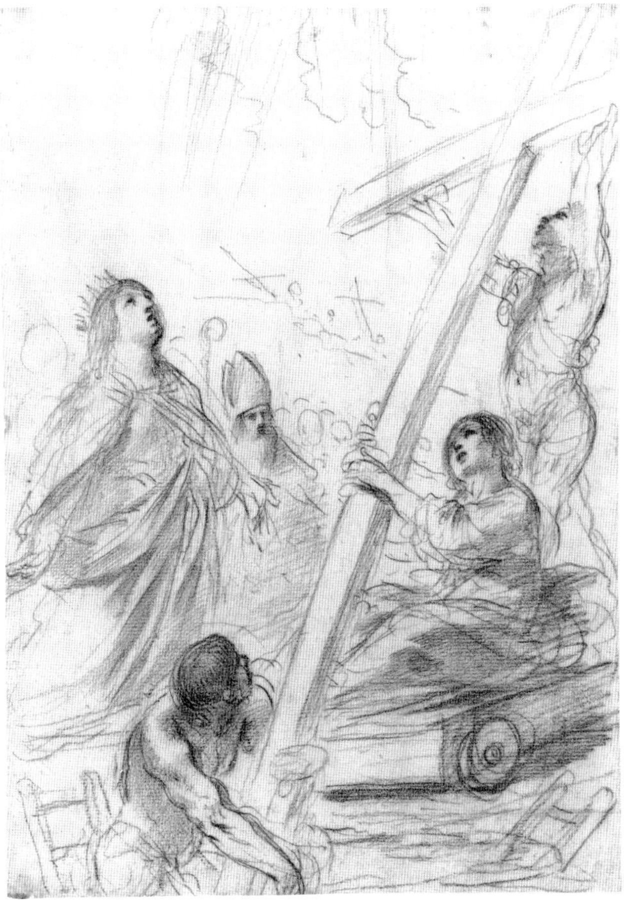

137

137 St Helen finding the True Cross

Red chalk. 300 × 204mm.

Windsor Castle, Royal Library, inv. no. 2788.

Provenance: Casa Gennari; King George III.

Literature: M, *Disegni*, 1969, under no. 150; S, 1988, under no. 209; M & T, 1989, no. 111.

A study for the *Finding of the True Cross*, for which see No. 136. Like that drawing, the present sheet also features the miracle of the corpse. The scale of the figures in relation to the overall space of the composition is greater than in No. 136, though the presentation of the story is, with a few obvious variations, much the same. In the slight enlargement of the proportions of the figures the drawing comes closer to the finished picture.

It remains unclear, however, why Guercino should have switched to red chalk to draw this second composition study. Perhaps having established the essential form of the composition in pen-and-wash studies, he was concerned in this sheet with defining the subject's chiaroscuro more precisely, an exercise he was able to do more accurately with red chalk. It is illuminating, nonetheless, to compare Guercino's treatment of the same subject in different media.

Other preparatory drawings for the altarpiece, both composition studies (including two with the miracle of the corpse) and studies for individual figures within it are discussed by Mahon and Turner (1989, under nos. 110–11).

138 Two Studies of the Crucified Christ

Red chalk. 298 × 219mm.

Mahon Collection, on loan to the Ashmolean Museum, Oxford, M & E, 29.

Provenance: C. L. Chute, The Vyne, Basingstoke (sale, Sotheby's, London, 22 June 1949, lot 1, one of a folio volume of 28 drawings by Guercino, bt *Wilson*); R. E. A. Wilson; from whom purchased by Sir Denis Mahon on 11 July 1949.

Literature: M, 1967, no. 27; M, *Disegni*, 1969, no. 149; Hammer, *et al.*, 1977, no. 27; M & E, 1986, no. 29; S, 1988, under nos. 220–23.

A preparatory study for the *Crucifixion with the Madonna, the Magdalen and St John the Evangelist* (S, 1988, no. 220), an altarpiece painted by Guercino, along with three ceiling canvases depicting *God the Father, St John the Baptist* and *St Francis* (S, 1988, nos. 221–3), for his family chapel in the Chiesa del Rosario at Cento. The first mass was held in the chapel in 1645, and expenditure for its construction and embellishment is recorded in the Account Book under the years 1642 and 1645 (*Libro dei Conti*, 1808, pp. 103 and 111; 1841, pp. 323 and 326). Mahon (1967) plausibly suggested that the altarpiece was executed towards the end of this period, in 1644–5.

The central study on this impressive sheet is particularly close to the figure of Christ in the finished work, both in pose and illumination, despite being the first of the two attempts at the figure. Guercino appears to have been particularly concerned with the torso, since the extremities of the limbs are left unfinished.

Curiously, for such a personally significant project, only one other drawing has been connected (M, *Disegni*, 1969, under no. 149) with the Rosario chapel decorations, namely a study for the drapery of St John the Evangelist in the Koenig–Fachsenfeld Collection now on deposit in the Staatsgalerie, Stuttgart (inv. no. Barbieri 31; Thiem, 1979, p. 417, no. 24, who expressed some doubts about the connection; M & E, 1986, under no. 29, where Mahon gave reasons for endorsing his original idea).

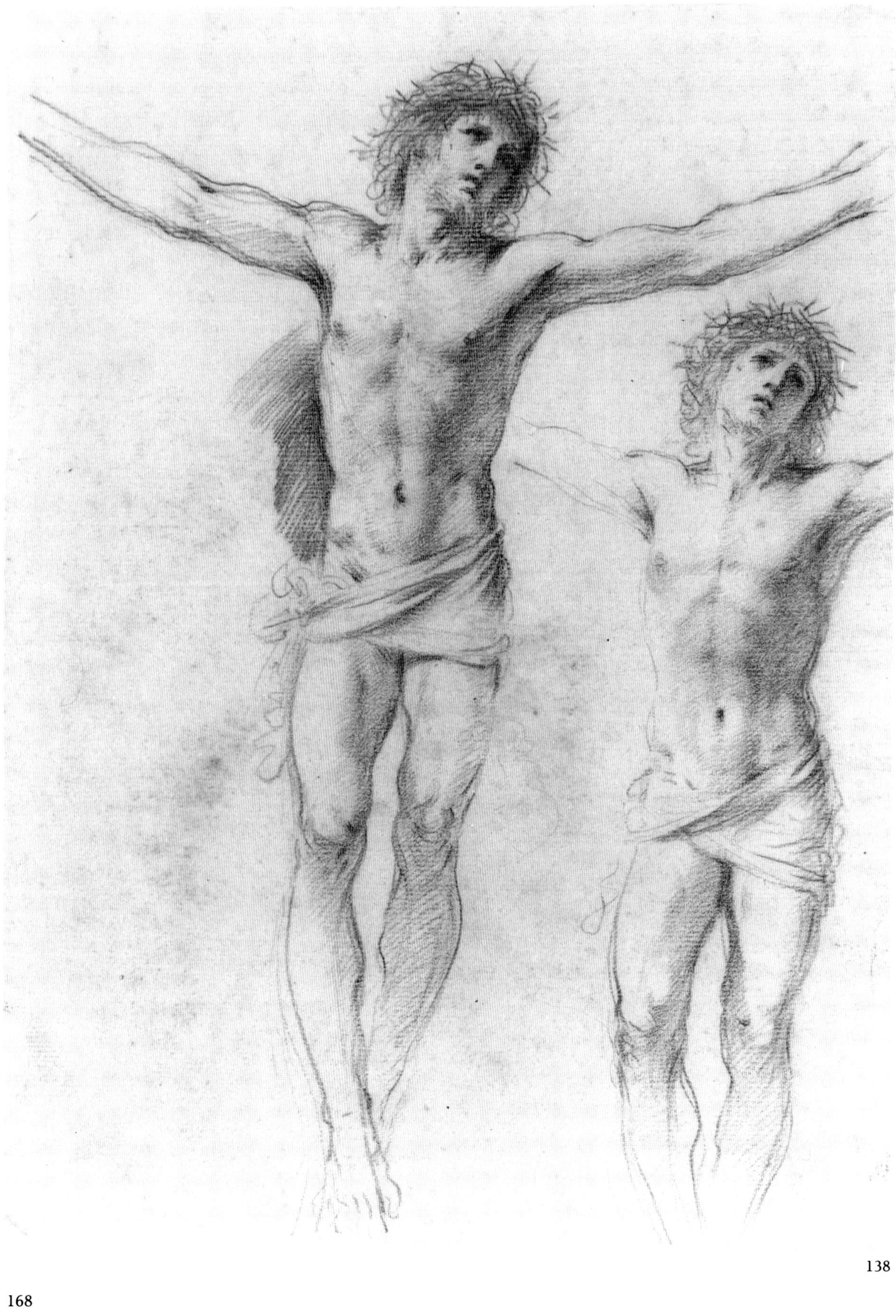

138

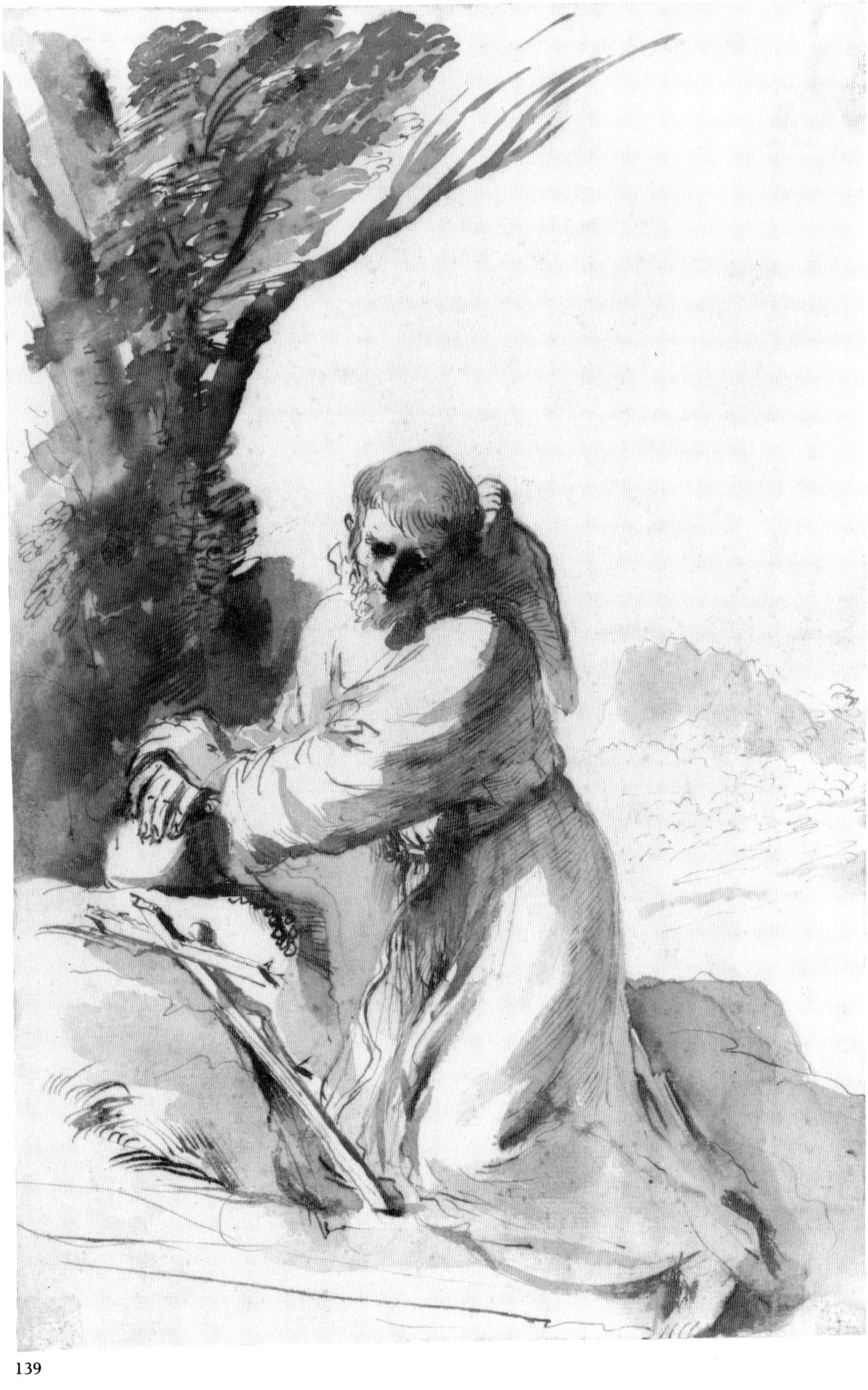

139

139 St Francis meditating in a Landscape

Pen and brown ink and brown wash. 280 × 185mm.

Windsor Castle, Royal Library, inv. no. 2582.

Provenance: Casa Gennari; King George III.

Literature: M, 1947, pp. 17–18 and fig. 3; M, 1951, p. 58, no. xii; M, *Disegni*, 1969, no. 152; Byam Shaw, 1983, pp. 357f., fig. 96; Roberts, 1986, no. 94; S, 1988, under no. 224; M & T, 1989, no. 113.

A study for the altarpiece of this subject painted in 1645 for the church of S. Giovanni in Monte in Bologna (S, 1988, no. 224). The drawing is unusual in anticipating the finished painting so fully, and particularly in showing the figure already integrated in the landscape setting. Guercino more frequently studied his figures in isolation or out of context, before synthesising all the elements of a given composition on canvas. In No. 139 even the illumination has been satisfactorily worked out and there are only minor discrepancies between it and the painting, most notably the absence in the drawing of St Francis's companion in the background. The saturated wash used for the tree in the left background of the drawing creates a bold contrast against the white of the paper, a contrast that is echoed in the painting by the sombre tree trunk silhouetted against the dusky sky at the upper left.

There is a copy by Bartolozzi of this drawing in the Lugt Collection, Paris (inv. no. 1066; M, *Disegni*, 1969, under no. 152; Byam Shaw, 1983, no. 359, pl. 407), and an etching by T. Bislinger after a lost drawing by Guercino that may have been connected with this composition (M & T, 1989, under no. 113).

140 Head of an Ecclesiastic in profile to the right

Pen and brown ink and brown wash, with some smudging. 121 × 262mm.

Private collection.

Provenance: Casa Gennari; Mr Bouverie; Mr Hervey; the Earls of Gainsborough.

The broadness of touch and unusually large scale of No. 140 strike an unfamiliar note at first sight. But the amusing

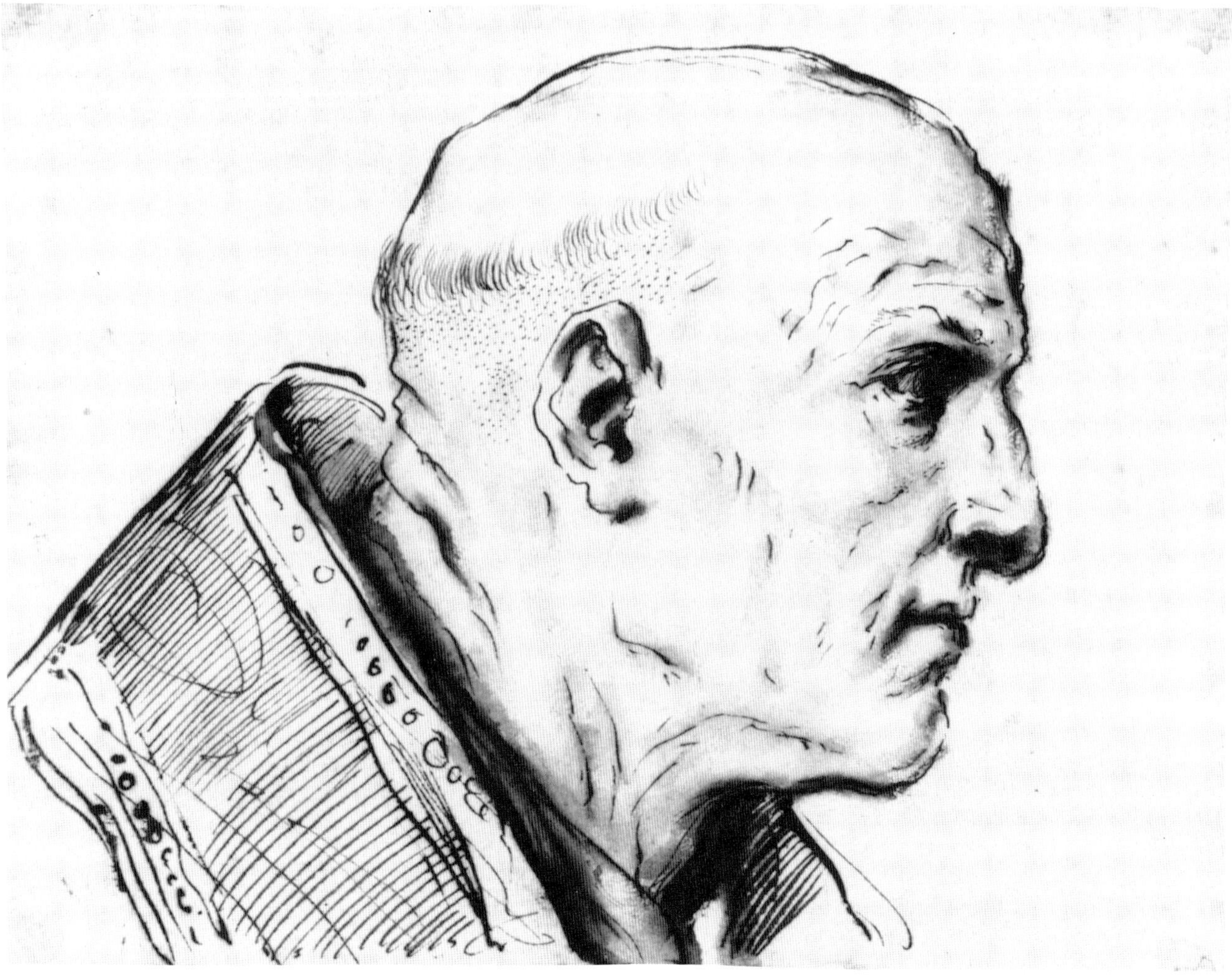

140

contrast between the small tufts of hair at the back of the man's head and the stubble beneath is entirely typical of Guercino's acute visual wit. Other passages also reveal his hand, for example the hatching in the collar of the cope and the touches of wash in the wrinkly flesh.

In our opinion the drawing may be dated from its style in the middle of the 1640s. It seems to belong to a small group of drawings of detailed studies of heads which the artist made towards the end of the preparatory process for his pictures and which served as models when he painted the corresponding passage (for further examples, see Nos. 50 and 126). Unfortunately, we have not been able to find an exact counterpart in Guercino's painted work, though there exist a number of roughly similar heads, for example that in reverse of the priest in the *Circumcision* of 1646 in the Musée at Lyon (S, 1988, no. 233).

Visible through the paper in the area of the man's collar are some small dark patches stuck onto the back of the sheet repairing the holes in the paper caused by the erosion of the iron-gall ink. These patches, almost certainly applied to the drawings before *c.*1740 when they left the possession of the artist's heirs, are of the same type as those referred to under Nos. 124 (App. no. 49) and 132 and are associable with drawings with a Casa Gennari provenance.

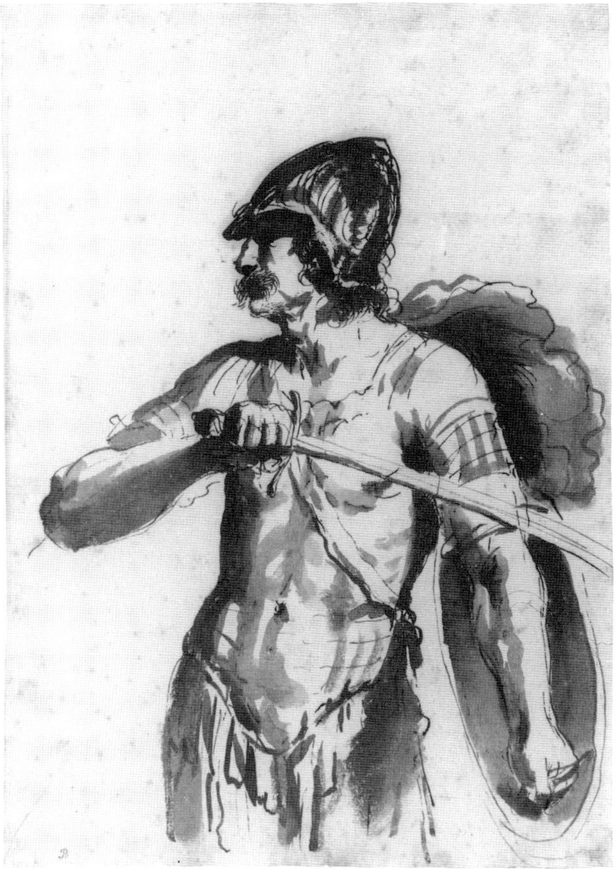

141

141–142 Studies for *Hersilia separating Romulus and Tatius* (1645)

Paris, Louvre

141 A Warrior

Pen, point of the brush and brown wash. 265 × 194mm.

London, Courtauld Institute Galleries, Witt Collection, inv. no. 1368.

Provenance: Casa Gennari (the drawing retains its Casa Gennari mount, for which see L *Suppl*, 2858c, and M, 1967, p. 20); Mr Bouverie (L 325); Mr Hervey; the Earls of Gainsborough (sale, Christie's, London, 27 July 1922, lot 81, with others, bt *Meatyard*); Sir Robert Witt.

Literature: Horton, 1960, p. 9, fig. 6; Hammer, *et al.*, 1977, no. 31; Loire, in Brejon & Volle, 1988–9, under no. 86; M & T, 1989, under nos. 115 and 138; Loire, 1990, under no. 9.

Much of No. 141 has been carried out using the point of the brush, making the tonal contrasts rather marked, particularly in the face, as if to convey the effect of bright sunlight. It is probably a study for the leader on the right of Guercino's painting representing *Hersilia separating Romulus and Tatius*, now in the Louvre, Paris (S, 1988, no. 226; Loire, in Brejon & Volle, 1988–9, no. 86; Loire, 1990, no. 9). This work was painted in 1645 for Louis Phélypeaux de La Vrillière as one of a series of pictures decorating the gallery of his mansion in Paris, the Hôtel de La Vrillière. (For Guercino's other pictures in this series, see Nos. 114–15.)

Besides the similarity between the armour of the figure in the drawing and that of the leader on the right in the painting, it is the manner in which the sword is held back across his chest, and the presence of the shield, that lend support to the connection. The warrior in the drawing differs from that in the painted work by holding his shield back rather than thrusting it forward to fend off Hersilia. The painted figure is far more wooden, a fact not helped by the unfortunate foreshortening of the sword-bearing arm, with which Guercino appears to have had no problems in the drawing. (For other drawings related to the *Hersilia separating Romulus and Tatius*, see No. 142; Loire, in Brejon & Volle, 1988–9, under no. 86; and M & T, 1989, under no. 115.) See also No. 134.

142 Study for a Figure of Hersilia

(*see colour pl. 20*)

Black chalk, with some stumping. 280 × 201mm.

Windsor Castle, Royal Library, inv. no. 2854.

Provenance: Casa Gennari; King George III.

Literature: S, 1988, under no. 226; Loire, in Brejon & Volle, 1988–9, p. 247, under no. 86; M & T, 1989, no. 115; Loire, 1990, under no. 9.

As Mahon and Turner were the first to point out, this beautiful drawing is a preparatory study for the figure of Hersilia in the *Hersilia separating Romulus and Tatius*, for which see No. 141. The figure is shown running forward, and the suggestion of movement is enhanced by the attractive *contrapposto* of her body, her fluttering garment and windswept hair. The stumping or smudging of the chalk gives an added refinement, especially in the flesh and hair.

The correspondence in pose between the drawn and painted figures is remarkably close, though in the painting the artist has omitted the small piece of drapery that billows out in front of Hersilia's body to allow for the view of the background with the fighting armies. Another small difference is that in the drawing Hersilia's left hand is shown with the palm facing outwards, like her right hand, while in the picture it grips the wrist of one of the soldiers in armour to stay his sword. Besides omitting to show how Hersilia's left hand would connect with the figure on the right, there is also nothing in the drawing to show in which area it was going to be covered by the shield of the soldier on the left. The absence of such contextual indications shows the extent to which Guercino, having already worked out the positions of the main figures within a given composition, went on to study them in isolation from each other.

For another example of Guercino's use of black chalk in the later part of his career, see No. 156.

143 Samson and Delilah

Pen and brown ink. 200 × 240mm.

Holkham Hall, Popham & Lloyd, 150.

Provenance: 1st Earl of Leicester; thence by descent.

Literature: Whitfield, 1977, no. 47; Popham & Lloyd, 1986, no. 150; S, 1988, under no. 288; M & T, 1989, under no. 649.

The subject of the present drawing is aptly summarised in the Account Book, where payment for the related picture is recorded under 31 March 1646: 'due mezze figure di

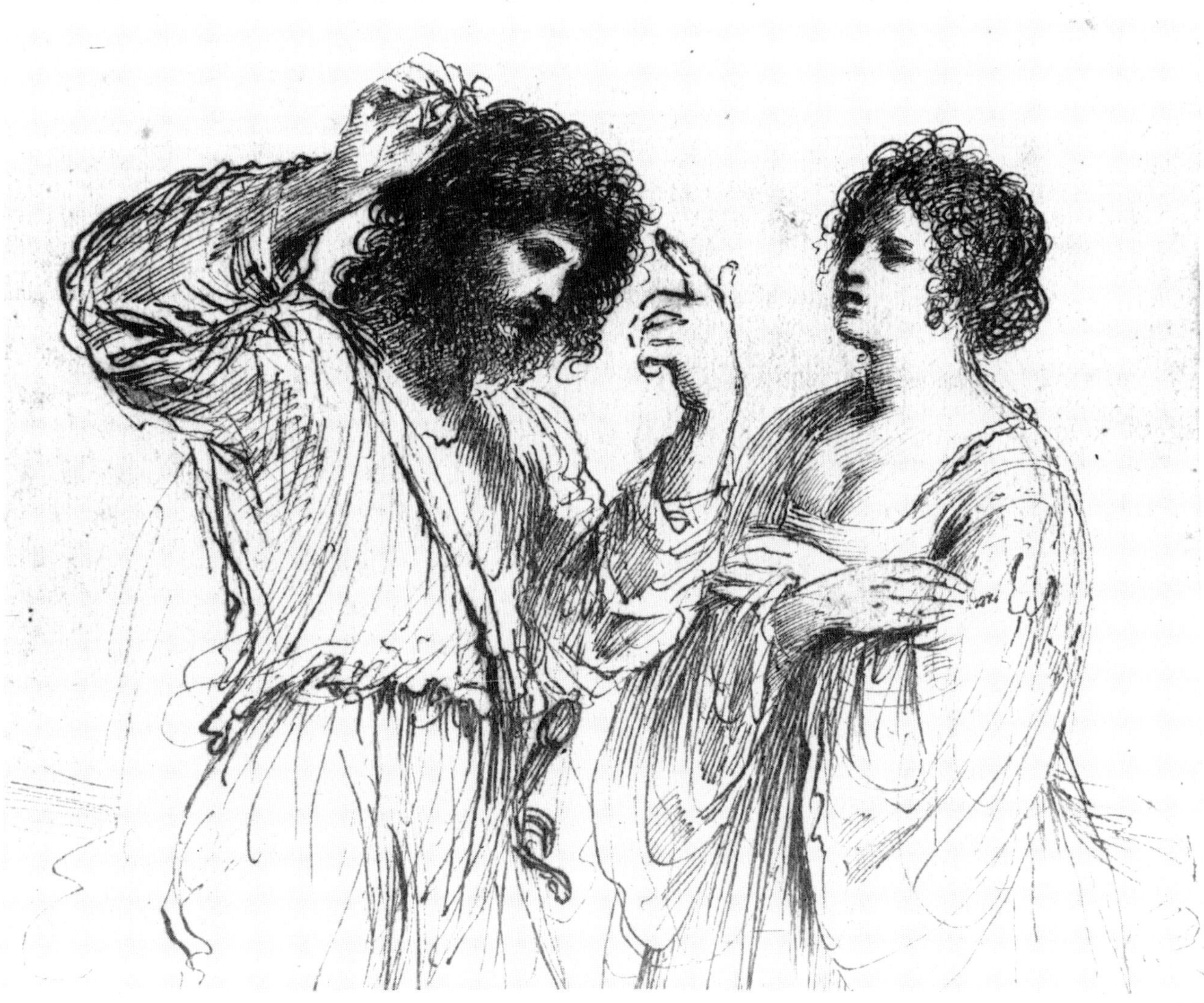

143

Sansone, e Dalida, quando le mostrò che ne'capeli stava posta la forza sua' (*Libro dei Conti*, 1808, p. 112; 1841, p. 326). The picture, which was painted for Cardinal Lelio Falconieri, Legate of Bologna, was formerly on the London art market (sale, Sotheby's, 21 March 1973, lot 118, repr.) and is now in the collection of Edward Goodstein, Atherton, California (S, 1988, no. 228). Its pendant, the *Saul and David*, painted in the same year for the same patron, is now in the Galleria Nazionale d'Arte Antica in Rome (S, 1988, no. 228bis).

As Mahon pointed out (in the 1973 sale catalogue), Malvasia's list of Guercino's commissions describes a somewhat different subject, namely Delilah showing Samson his already shorn locks, a later moment in the story which would have required more figures, in the form of Philistines, to pin Samson down (Malvasia, 1678, II, p. 375; 1841, II, p. 266). Malvasia also specified that Falconieri originally ordered two large pendant paintings ('Due quadri grandi compagni'), whereas the two that were actually made were half lengths, as the Account Book records. Since it was Guercino's practice to price his paintings according to the number of figures they contained and to charge considerably less for half-length figures, it seems likely that Falconieri modified the scope of the commission, in terms of size as well as subject, in order to keep costs down. By showing the earlier moment in the story of Samson and Delilah, the artist was able to confine himself to two figures only.

At the time the drawing was made, it had already been established that the composition was to be half length. The study is in reverse to the finished work, with Samson on the left and Delilah on the right. Samson's position is almost identical to that in the painting except that he is not shown wearing armour, and his sword is worn on his inner hip. A pentiment for the sash from which the sheathed sword is suspended shows that Guercino originally intended it to hang on the outer hip as in the painting. Delilah's pose was originally more demure, with both hands crossed over her breast, in contrast to the gesture of surprise she makes in the painting.

144–148 Studies for *Atlas* (1646)

Florence, Museo Bardini

144 Atlas standing, turned towards the right

Black chalk, partly oiled. 247 × 180mm.

Windsor Castle, Royal Library, inv. no. 2705.

Provenance: Casa Gennari; King George III.

Literature: M & T, 1989, no. 117.

This and Nos. 145–8 are studies for the half-length picture of *Atlas* in the Museo Bardini in Florence (S, 1988, no. 230; M & T, 1989, p. 68, fig. 22). This picture is almost certainly identical with the one cited in Guercino's Account Book on 30 April 1646 and paid for by Prince Don Lorenzo de' Medici (*Libro dei Conti*, 1808, p. 113; 1841, p. 326). An *Atlas* by Guercino does not, however, feature in the inventory of Don Lorenzo's effects drawn up in 1649 following his death in the previous year, so it is probable that the picture was commissioned as a gift rather than as an addition to the Prince's own collection.

The Florentine dealer Stefano Bardini (1836–1922), who bequeathed much of his collection to his native city, appears to have bought the *Atlas* from the Capponi family of Florence, in whose palace it is recorded in the nineteenth century. From this same family Bardini also bought a second half-length picture by Guercino of *Hercules*, which had been commissioned from the artist by another member of the Medici family, Cardinal Giovan Carlo, some two years earlier. It is not impossible that both pictures were ordered at much the same time, as gifts to the then head of the Capponi family, whose heirs much later sold them to Bardini.

Whatever the original destination of the *Atlas*, an exceptional series of preparatory drawings survives for it at the Royal Library at Windsor Castle, all of which are included here. Most of them seem to have been drawn from life, presumably from the same model. Guercino apparently considered almost every possible permutation for the pose, studying it in opposite directions simultaneously; but the precise sequence of the drawings cannot, alas, be convincingly reconstructed. The survival of the group should not be taken as evidence that Guercino had any great difficulty with this particular picture, but rather as witness to the extraordinary care that he took in composing any given work. There is every reason to believe that when inventing a composition he tested his ideas to much the same extent: all that we know of his working method points to this conclusion. It is nonetheless true that the inherently improbable subject of an old man balancing what is in effect a large ball on the back of his shoulders might have presented a more troublesome figure than usual.

No. 144 is the only drawing from the group to be drawn in chalk, unusually in black chalk. Of all the studies it is the most likely to have been made from the life (see No. 4), although it is hard to see how the other more rapidly drawn studies in pen were not also made in front of the model. The figure in No. 144 is shown turned to the right, almost in profile, and lit from above and from the left. Somewhat awkwardly perhaps, both arms are placed on the same side of the globe, which balances precariously on the figure's neck and back. The cast of Atlas's features is surprisingly close to that of his counterpart in the painting, and the artist seems already to be veering towards the idea adopted there of showing only one of Atlas's hands, the other being largely concealed by the globe – a solution that undoubtedly saved Guercino a little time and effort.

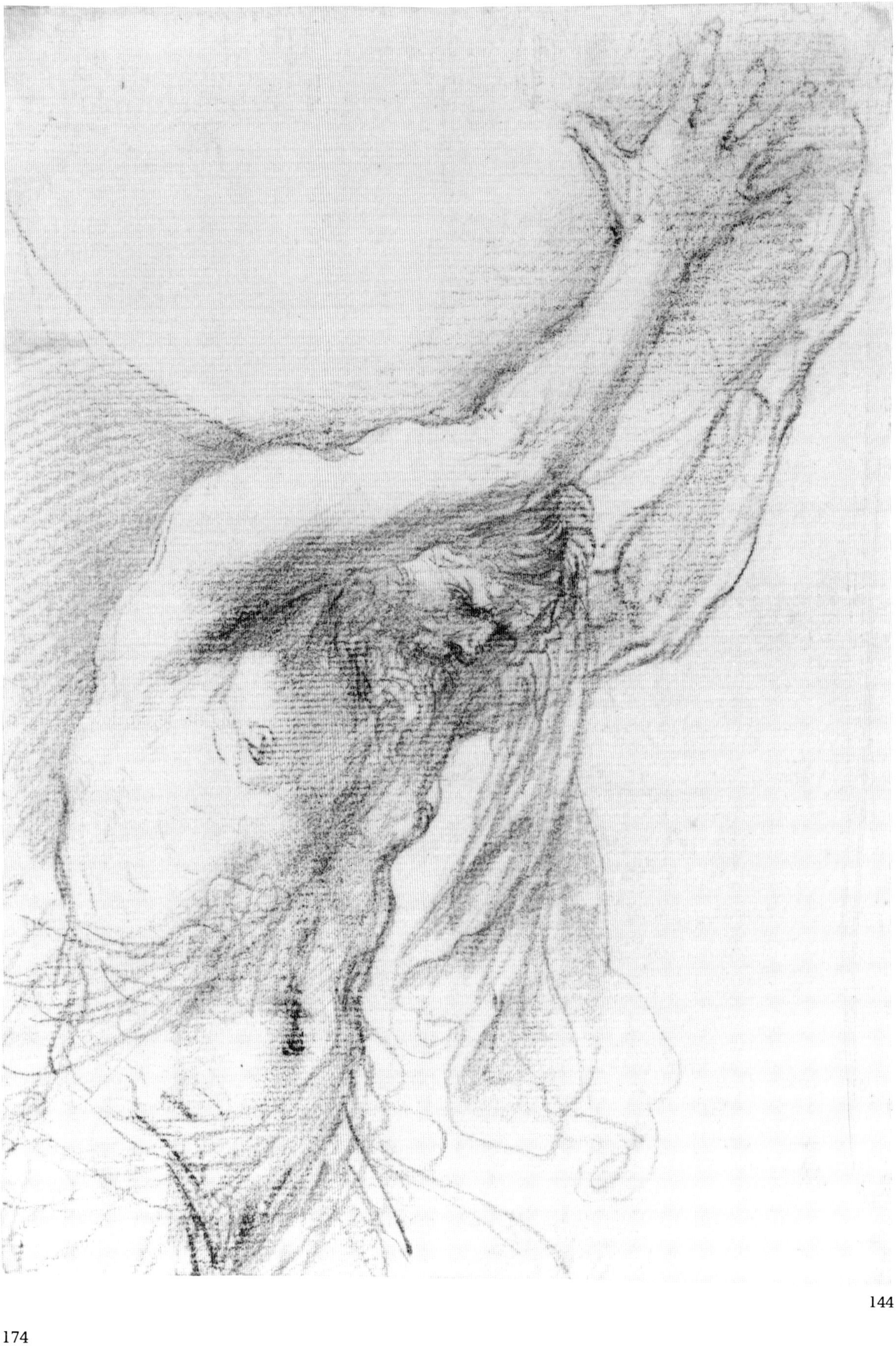

144

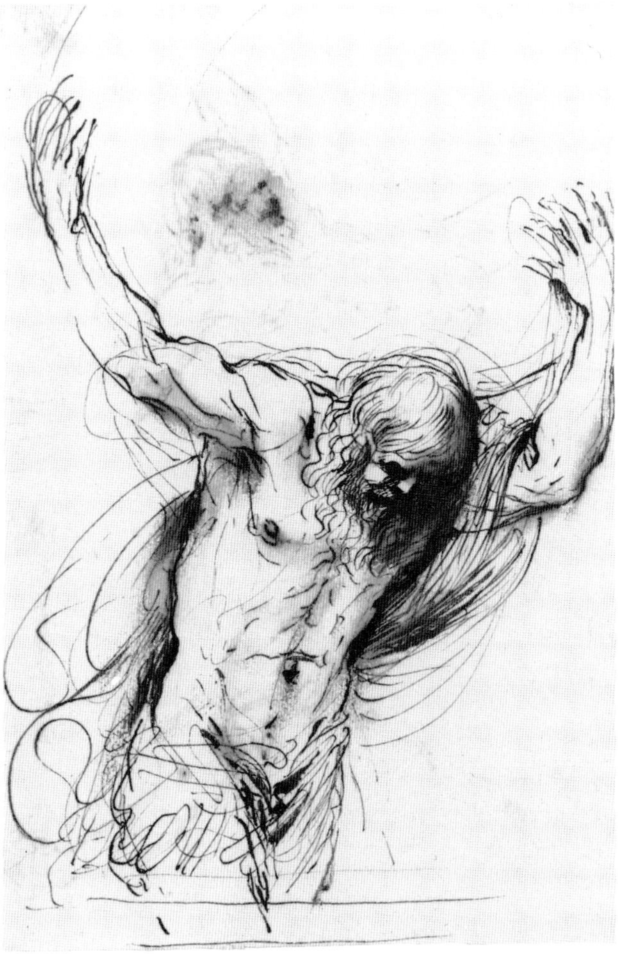

145

145 Atlas standing, turned slightly towards the right

Pen and brown ink and brown wash. 211 × 141mm.

Windsor Castle, Royal Library, inv. no. 2815.

Provenance: Casa Gennari; King George III.

Literature: M & T, 1989, no. 118 and p. 177.

Showing through the paper at the top of the sheet is part of another study for the same figure drawn on the *verso* in pen and brown ink.

In the *recto* study the pose of Atlas is roughly the same as that in the painting: in both the drawn and painted figures the arms are raised and held widely apart to steady the globe, which is supported on the shoulders and back. The lighting is also similar in both works. In the drawing, however, the drapery is disposed differently, and the figure's left hand is placed in front of the globe so that the hand is fully visible. Also worthy of note is the pentiment for the right arm, showing it in a buttress-like position – bent at the elbow, with the right hand placed flat on the small of the back.

Like No. 144, the present study was almost certainly made from the live model, who would have been drawn standing rather than seated even though he was not to be shown full length. The partial indication of the position of the legs of Atlas in the painting is important to suggest the balance of the figure. As he leans forward under the strain of his burden, it was necessary to show that the extra weight was being compensated for by his stance. The lines at the bottom of the sheet therefore show the artist deciding how much of the figure's legs should be shown in the composition – there being no point in drawing the legs below the upper

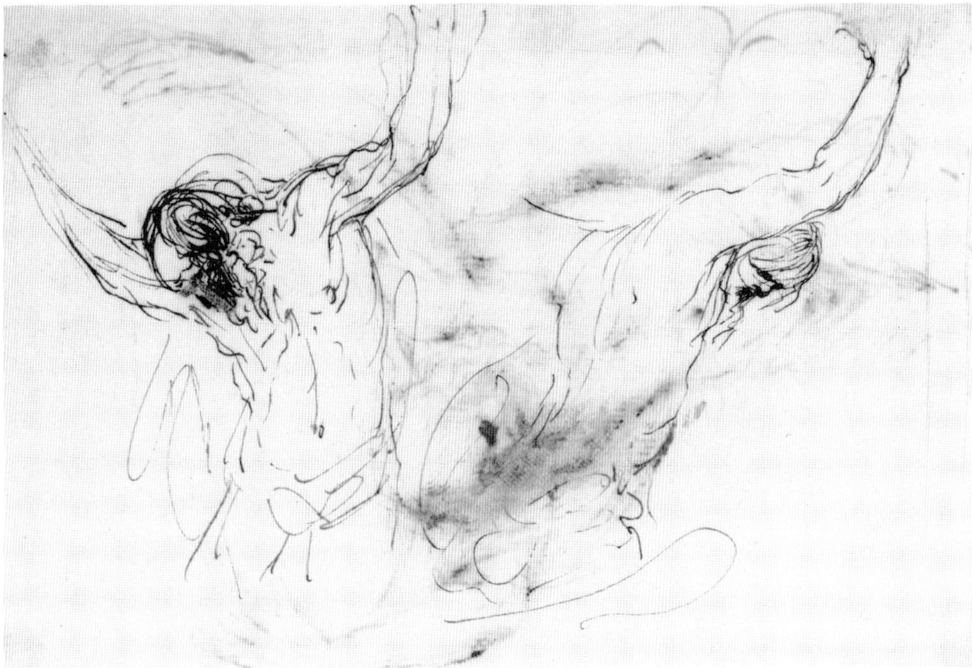

145 *verso*

thigh. It is significant too that at this early stage of his ideas Guercino modified the position of this lower 'limit' three times. The demarcation of such a 'limit' in his working drawings, indicating the boundary of a given composition at the bottom, top or side, is a device found quite frequently (see Nos. 56, 147 and 148).

With the sheet turned at right angles, Guercino made two rapid studies of the figure on the *verso*. In the study on the left Atlas is turned to the left, with his head bent down to the left; and in that on the right he is in profile to the right with his back turned slightly towards the spectator, with only his right arm visible. It should not come as a surprise that Guercino reversed the figure in the left-hand study, since it was frequently his practice to study a composition in opposite directions. The figure was also studied in reverse in Nos. 147 and 148.

146 Atlas standing, turned slightly towards the right

Pen and brown ink. 208 × 200mm.

Windsor Castle, Royal Library, inv. no. 2850.

Provenance: Casa Gennari; King George III.

Literature: M & T, 1989, no. 119.

Perhaps more so than any of the other studies for Atlas, the figure in No. 146 gives the appearance of walking forwards. In lighting and to some extent in pose, it differs in many respects from the painted solution, for which see No. 144. Compared with No. 145 *recto*, the execution of No. 146, in pen and brown ink alone, is painstaking, almost pedantic – a quality it shares somewhat with No. 148.

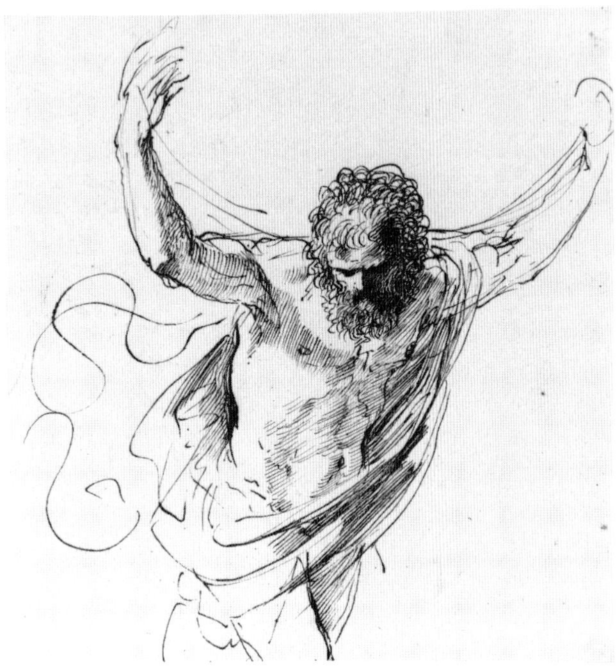

146

147 Atlas standing, turned slightly towards the left

Pen and brown ink with brown wash. 241 × 192mm.

Windsor Castle, Royal Library, inv. no. 2716.

Provenance: Casa Gennari; King George III.

Literature: M & T, 1989, no. 120 and p. 177.

Like No. 148 and one of the studies on the *verso* of No. 145, the present drawing shows Atlas in reverse to his painted counterpart, as though the artist had still not decided whether to show him facing left or right. In spite of the difference in direction, the correspondence is surprisingly close, except that the figure stands more erect in the drawing.

Guercino evidently found the switching of directions of a given figure refreshing to his creative powers. Gauging the appearance in reverse of a given study in red chalk could be easily achieved by offsetting (or counterproofing). This simple process of reproduction merely required the original drawing to be dampened and then pressed or 'squeezed' onto another sheet of paper; the image thereby obtained (the offset or counterproof) was reversed from that of the drawing from which it had been taken. For Guercino to study the image of a pen-and-ink or pen-and-wash drawing in reverse was also simple enough, because of his frequent use of thin paper for drawings of this type. He could judge them by simply turning the sheet over and holding it up to the light; the transparency of the sheet allowed the reversed image to be seen clearly. It is possible that the present drawing could have been derived from No. 145 *recto*, but with the sheet turned the other way round so that the *recto* faced the light. When one or other of these two drawings is reversed in relation to the other, the two solutions seem extraordinarily close.

The cursorily drawn right hand in the version of the figure studied in No. 147 seems to indicate that Guercino intended this hand to come behind the globe, as in No. 148, and as the left hand does in the painting. The upper and lower limits of the composition have also been clearly delineated, each by a horizontal line, that at the bottom emphasised by an area of wash just below it. For Guercino's habit of marking the boundaries of his compositions in this way, see No. 145.

148 Atlas standing, turned slightly towards the left

Pen and brown ink with some slight touches of brown wash. 202 × 178mm.

Windsor Castle, Royal Library, inv. no. 2808.

Provenance: Casa Gennari; King George III.

Literature: M & T, 1989, no. 121.

Like No. 147 and one of the studies on the *verso* of No. 145, this drawing shows Atlas in reverse to the painted figure. Though in the opposite direction, the closeness of the correspondence is striking and is plainer even than that

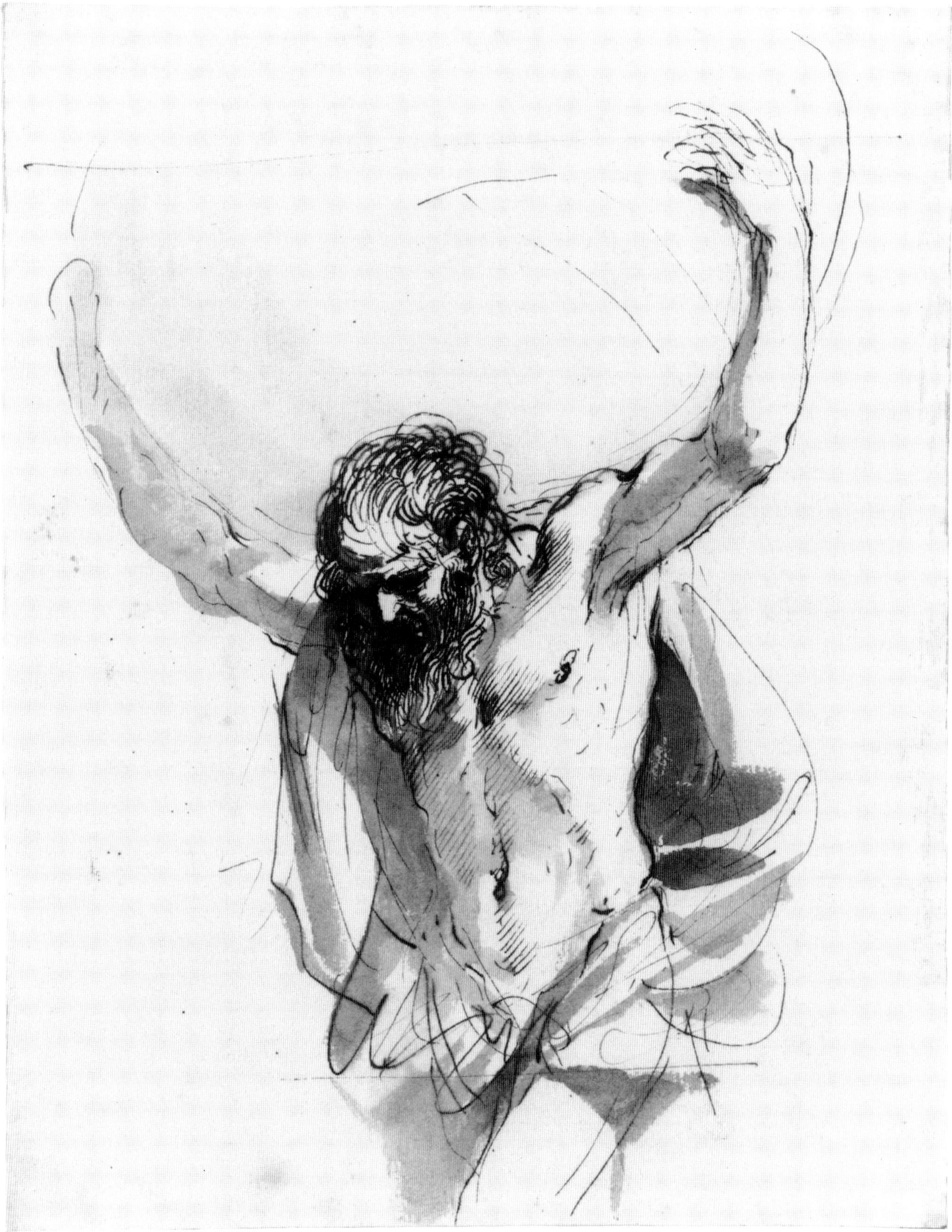

147

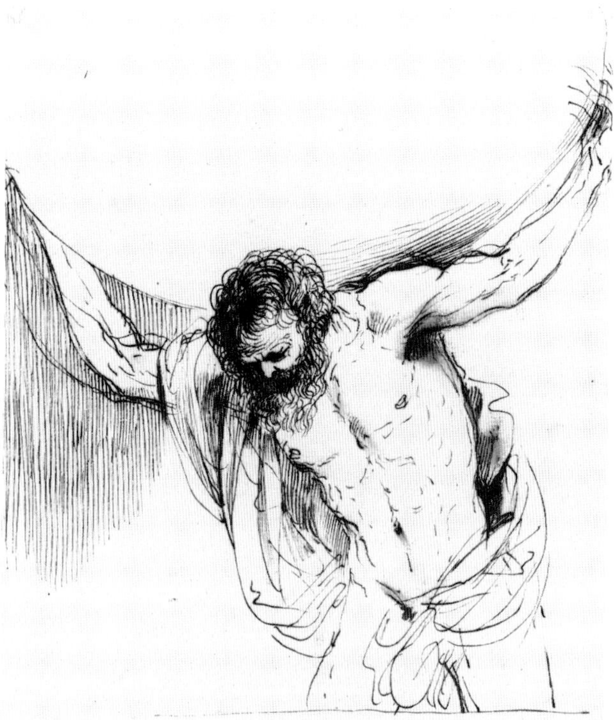

148

between No. 147 and the picture. The correlation may be seen in such details as the disposition of the drapery around the body; the hand concealed behind the globe; the pose of the figure, with the torso bent and the head jutting forward; and the arc formed by the leaning torso and the forward-moving leg.

The bottom of the composition has been indicated by a horizontal line (for this same device, see also Nos. 145 and 147). It is probable that the curve of the globe was drawn with the assistance of compasses; in the other studies it seems to have been drawn free-hand.

149 The Angel of the Annunciation

(*see colour pl. 21*)

Pen and brown ink. 229 × 190mm.

Windsor Castle, Royal Library, inv. no. 2841.

Provenance: Casa Gennari; King George III.

Literature: Byam Shaw, 1983, under no. 349, n. 3; S, 1988, under no. 232; M & T, 1989, no. 122.

A study for the angel in the *Annunciation* in S. Maria Maggiore at Pieve di Cento, for which payment was received in 1646 (S, 1988, no. 232). The pose of the angel is very similar to that in the finished work, except that the gestures of either hand are transposed in the painting, so that he holds the lily in his right hand while his left is held to his breast. This working drawing is notable for its rapid pen-work; in his search for a satisfactory position for the arms and a contour for the legs, the artist seems not to have been concerned with the precise delineation of the drapery (one can easily discern the figure's naked form beneath its tunic). There are several pentiments for the angel's left arm, including perhaps the two lines between the finalised position for the arm and the left knee, and another variation showing it bent to meet the right arm at the breast. This last observation may shed some light on the question of whether a pen drawing in the Lugt Collection, Paris, representing God the Father and the angel (inv. no. 1201; Byam Shaw, 1983, no. 349), is connected with the Pieve di Cento altarpiece or with another very similar one commissioned for the church of S. Filippo Neri at Forlì and now in the Pinacoteca Comunale there (S, 1988, no. 250); payment for the Forlì altarpiece was received two years later in 1648. It has always been acknowledged that the Lugt drawing is strikingly similar in handling to No. 149 and other pen drawings connected with the Pieve di Cento altarpiece, such as one for the Madonna reading, in the Royal Library, Windsor Castle (M & T, 1989, no. 123), and a study for the head and shoulders of the angel in the Teylers Museum at Haarlem (inv. no. H. 46). Furthermore, the pose of the angel in the Lugt drawing is very similar to that in No. 149 and, to a large extent, that in the finished work. However, in the Lugt drawing the angel, although flying in the opposite direction with his legs to the left, has his arms crossed, very much as they are in the Forlì *Annunciation* and in four drawings preparatory to that work (see No. 152). On account of this shared motif, the Lugt drawing has usually been associated with the later of the two altarpieces. But the pentiment for the angel's left arm in No. 149, bent over his breast to meet the right, proves that Guercino had considered the motif for the earlier project; it thus surely removes any lingering doubts as to the connection of the Lugt drawing with the Pieve di Cento commission.

Also related to the Pieve di Cento picture is a drawing in red chalk for the head of the angel in the Uffizi, Florence (inv no. 3636-S; see Marangoni, 1959, pl. 46, where it is associated with the Forlì altarpiece).

150 St Bruno

Red chalk. 195 × 170mm.

London, Victoria and Albert Museum, inv. no. D.999–1900.

Provenance: Emily Frances Dalton; bequeathed to the Museum in 1900.

Literature: M, *Disegni*, 1969, no. 160; Ward-Jackson, 1980, no. 716; S, 1988, under no. 241.

A study for the figure of the saint in the *Madonna and Child with St Bruno*, which Guercino painted in 1647 for the Certosa at Bologna and which is now in the Pinacoteca Nazionale in that city (S, 1988, no. 241). The moment the commission was first issued by the Certosi is recorded in the eye-witness account of Francesco Scannelli (see M, *Dipinti*, 1968, under no. 82). According to Scannelli (1657, p. 74), Guercino turned down their request to complete a composition by Guido Reni that had been left unfinished

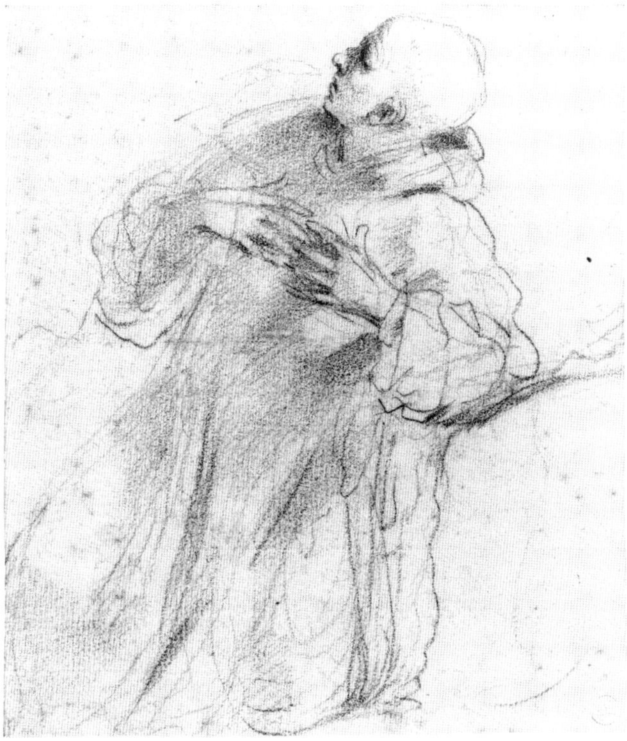

150

at his death in 1642; instead he insisted on being allowed to paint his own picture from scratch.

The drawing is the only one related to this composition that has so far come to light. It shows an early idea for the figure of St Bruno, who is represented leaning back, propping himself up on a block with one elbow and twisting round to look upwards to the left. Greater decorum is observed in the painting, where the figure kneels in an upright pose, though, as in the drawing, he still gazes upwards in the same direction (towards the apparition of the Madonna and Child), his fingers spread out upon his chest.

There is a remarkable similarity between the saint's pose and that of the angel in No. 149, a preparatory study for the Pieve di Cento *Annunciation* of the previous year (1646). The dramatic twist of the head to the left and the bent left knee compare particularly well, and the saint's almost interlocking fingers find an echo in the pentiment for the angel's left arm which was at first joined with the other at the figure's breast. Guercino frequently returned to ideas and motifs with which he had experimented in the past, often – as in this case – as a starting point from which to develop an entirely new and different composition or pose.

151 'Ecce Homo'

Red chalk. 193 × 187mm.

Private collection.

Provenance: sale, Sotheby's, New York, 13 January 1989, lot 49.

This is a study for the *'Ecce Homo'* painted in 1647 for the Marchese Tanari and now in the Staatliche Gemäldesammlungen, Munich (S, 1988, no. 246); the picture is, in fact, on view at the Staatsgalerie Schleissheim, an outstation of the Bayerische Staatsgemäldesammlungen.

The most notable difference between No. 151 and the finished picture is that in the latter the bearded dignitary wearing a turban, presumably intended to represent Pontius Pilate, is shown on the left of the composition rather than on the right. The figure of Christ, on the other hand, corresponds closely to his painted equivalent, except that in No. 151 he lacks the reed in his right hand and his drapery does not cover his left shoulder. In the drawing Pilate reaches behind Christ's body with his right hand, in which he holds one end of the drapery, as if he were about to wrap it around the 'King of the Jews'. This almost tender gesture was rejected in the finished work; but Guercino retained the idea of showing Pilate holding one end of Christ's robe and shifted him to the left-hand side of the composition, where he raises it, somewhat contemptuously, with his right hand. Just discernible behind Christ's head in the top left of the drawing is the glove of the soldier in armour who, in the picture, stands on the right and pushes back the crowned head of Christ so that his face is better revealed.

A red chalk drawing at Windsor Castle (M & T, 1989, no. 126) shows all three protagonists in roughly the same corresponding positions as they appear in the painting, but with many variations in detail. An offset also at Windsor (M & T, 1989, no. 655) records an untraced drawing by Guercino showing the composition with the lateral figures again in the same relationship as they appear in the painting.

A School drawing in the Albertina, Vienna (inv. no. 2327; Wickhoff, 1891, p. cccii, SB 385), shows the soldier and the potentate reversed from their counterparts in the painting, and therefore in the same relationship as in No. 151.

152 An Angel in flight

Red chalk. 275 × 272mm.

Mahon Collection, on loan to the Ashmolean Museum, Oxford, M & E, 31.

Provenance: (?)Casa Gennari (on account of the old mount, which is similar to that of No. 196, which bears a characteristic inscription indicative of such a provenance); Mr Bouverie; Mr Hervey; the Earls of Gainsborough (probably sale, Christie's, London, 27 July 1922); Capt. H. S. Reitlinger (sale, Sotheby's, London, 9 December 1953, lot 49), purchased by Sir Denis Mahon.

Literature: M, 1967, no. 28; M, *Disegni*, 1969, no. 161; Byam Shaw, 1983, under no. 349, n. 3; M & E, 1986, no. 31; M & T, 1989, under nos. 122–3.

Numbered in graphite on the old mount, below the bottom left

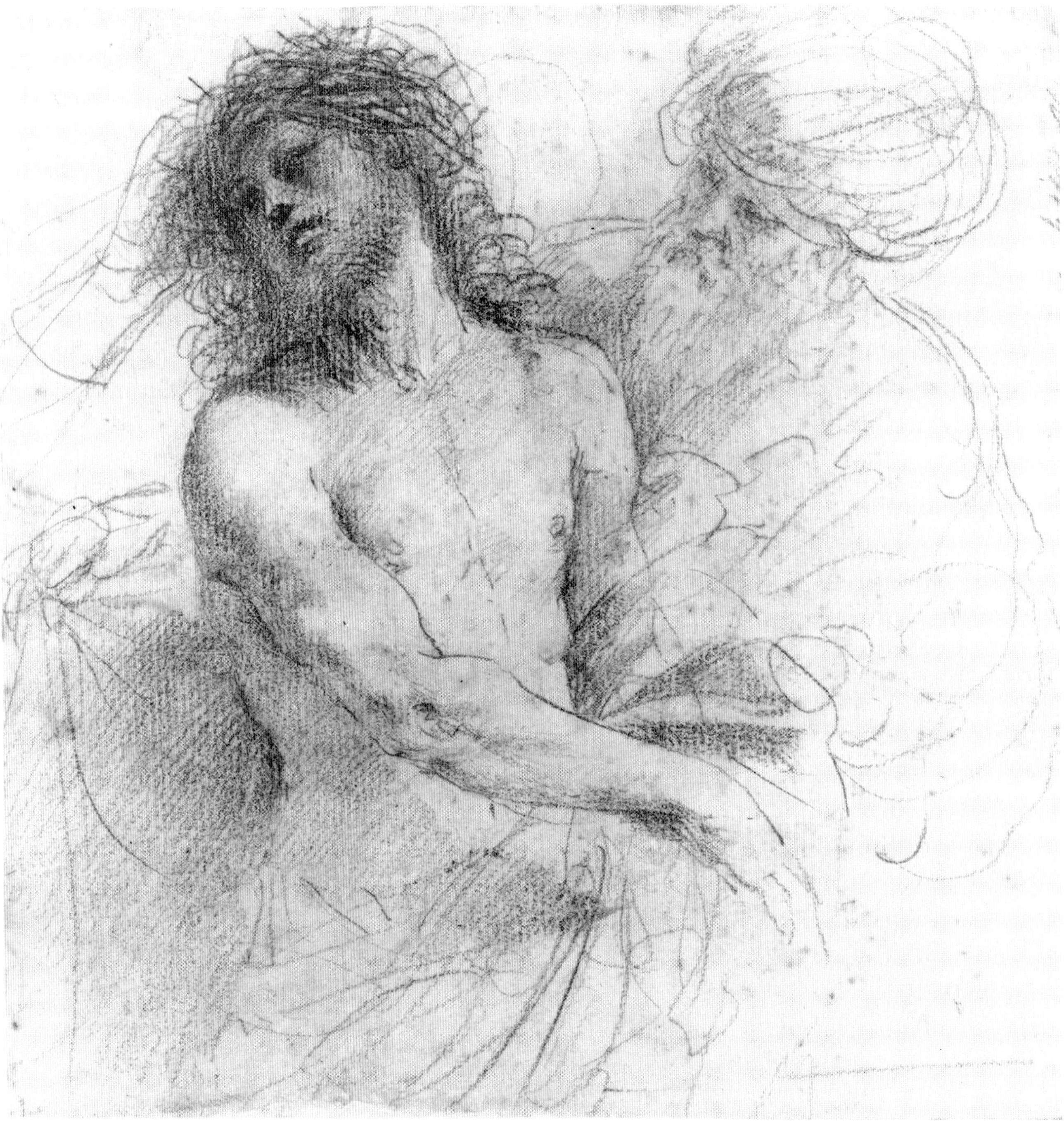

151

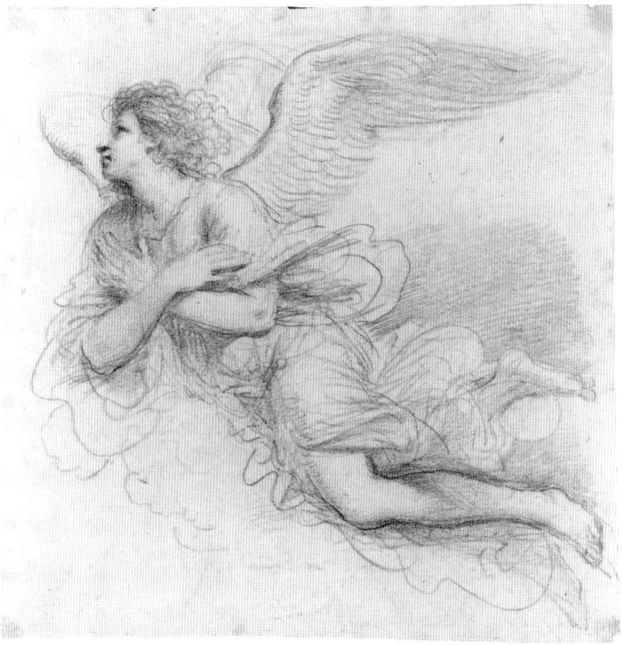

152

corner of the drawing: *5* (for a discussion and further instances of sheets numbered in this way, see No. 10).

A study for the angel in the *Annunciation*, painted for the church of S. Filippo Neri at Forlì and now in the Pinacoteca Comunale at Forlì (S, 1988, no. 250). Guercino was paid for the commission in 1648 (*Libro dei Conti*, 1808, pp. 118f.; 1841, p. 329). The figure in the drawing corresponds closely with the angel in the picture both in terms of the pose and the arrangement of the drapery, except that the lily is absent.

Several drawings for this altarpiece exist (for which see S, 1988, under no. 250, and M & T, 1989, under nos. 122–3). A much more summary red chalk study for the head and shoulders of the angel with God the Father is in the Teylers Museum, Haarlem (inv. no. H. 49), together with another in the same collection for the head and shoulders of the angel alone in black chalk (inv. no. H. 70). A more elaborate red chalk study, again for the head and shoulders of the angel, is in the Albertina, Vienna (inv. no. B.228), and a study for God the Father, also in red chalk, is in the National Gallery of Scotland, Edinburgh (inv. no. D.3122). For a study of the three putti above and behind the angel in the British Museum, see App. no. 52. Finally, see No. 149 for two drawings formerly associated with the Forlì commission but in fact almost certainly for a very similar altarpiece painted by Guercino two years earlier for the church of S. Maria Maggiore at Pieve di Cento.

The hypothesis that No. 152 must have a Casa Gennari provenance is corroborated by its condition, in particular the losses at the corners which imply that the drawing may once have been kept in one of the albums belonging to the artist's heirs (see M & T, 1989, p. xxi).

6 The late Period, 1650–66 (Nos. 153–63)

One of the high points of the painter's later life was the visit paid to him in his studio in Bologna by Queen Christina of Sweden on her way to Rome, who 'volle toccargli la mano, come quella che avea operato maraviglie' (Malvasia, 1678, II, p. 384; 1841, II, p. 273). Far fewer drawings survive for this period than any other, the 1660s being particularly poorly represented. This is curious in view of the fact that Guercino's painted output was still considerable, especially in the 1650s, as Malvasia and the Account Book attest. In view of his advancing years, it is not improbable that Guercino drew less, delegating more of the preparatory work to students. In a letter to one of his regular patrons, Don Antonio Ruffo, dated 15 February 1650, Guercino actually states that his doctors had forbidden him from drawing altogether owing to a pain in his chest and that he was having to resort to sketching out his ideas with a piece of chalk attached to the end of a cane directly onto canvas: 'bisogna ch'assolutamente me n'astenga si ben però con mio gran disgusto, la onde i disegni di Quadri che ora faccio mi conviene farli su l'istess'opra col gesso in appo di una canna e quelli pochi ch'appresso a me mi ritrovavo li ho distribuiti alli miei che alle volte me ne addimandavano' (Ruffo, 1916, p. 98). Several of his own drawings contain configurations or motifs reminiscent of the work of the Gennari, such as the putti in Nos. 156–7, 159 and 160, suggesting a close working relationship with his nephews. Many of these late drawings are hesitant and lack the characteristic *brio* of earlier studies. Broken contours and lines of fluctuating intensity are a particular feature of Guercino's draughtsmanship in this period, perhaps indicative of the unsteady hand and failing sight of old age (see Nos. 156–8).

153 Lot and his Daughters

Pen and brown ink. 238 × 198mm.

Oxford, Ashmolean Museum, KTP 869.

Provenance: Casa Gennari; Mr Bouverie; Mr Hervey; the Earls of Gainsborough (sale, Christie's, London, 27 July 1922, lot 81, with others, bt *Meatyard*); Sir Robert Witt (L *Suppl*, 2228b); from whom purchased 1944.

Literature: Parker, 1956, no. 869; Bottari 1966, pl. LX; Macandrew, 1980, p. 299; M & E, 1986, no. XVII.

Numbered in graphite in the bottom left corner of the drawing: *46* (for a discussion and further instances of sheets numbered in this way, see No. 10).

Lot took refuge with his two daughters in a cave, after the destruction of Sodom and Gomorrah and the transformation of his wife into a pillar of salt. Believing themselves to be the only inhabitants left on earth, the daughters plied their father with wine until he was drunk, and then slept with him in turn, each conceiving a child in order to perpetuate the human race.

According to Malvasia (1678, II, pp. 378–9; 1841, II,

p. 269), Guercino painted three versions of this subject in 1650–51. All three were destined for the same patron, the artist's friend Girolamo Panesi (Malvasia's citation of the name as *Pavese* is apparently a misreading as the manuscript Account Book gives it as *Panessi*). As it happened, the first two pictures were diverted to other more influential clients. The first was given to the Commendatore Giovanni Battista Manzini, who in turn gave it to the Duke of Modena whose favours he sought and for which he was rewarded with a marquisate on the Duke's territory (for Manzini, see S, 1988, under no. 210). There is no mention of this commission in the Account Book. The picture is now in the Staatliche Gemäldegalerie, Dresden (S, 1988, no. 275).

Guercino embarked on a second painting of this subject for Panesi in 1651, but this suffered much the same fate as the first. This time it was the Archduchess of Mantua who saw the work in the artist's studio and determined to have it. This painting is now in the Louvre, Paris (S, 1988, no. 284; Loire, 1990, no. 15). It was consigned to the Archduchess the same year it was painted, according to a letter from Guercino to Duke Carlo II Gonzaga of 9 September, but nevertheless the artist was not rewarded for his flexibility over the deal until 23 December 1657, when he was at last remunerated (*Libro dei Conti*, 1808, p. 145; 1841, p. 338).

Panesi finally received his picture at the third attempt, as recorded by Malvasia under the year 1651: 'Onde fece un altro Lot differente dagli altri due al sig. Girolamo Pavese, e si mandò a Roma' (Malvasia, 1678, II, p. 379; 1841, II, p. 269). Once again Guercino's fee was considerably delayed and is not recorded in the Account Book until 20 October 1656 (*Libro dei Conti*, 1808, p. 142; 1841, p. 337). For this third composition, see S, 1988, no. 296.

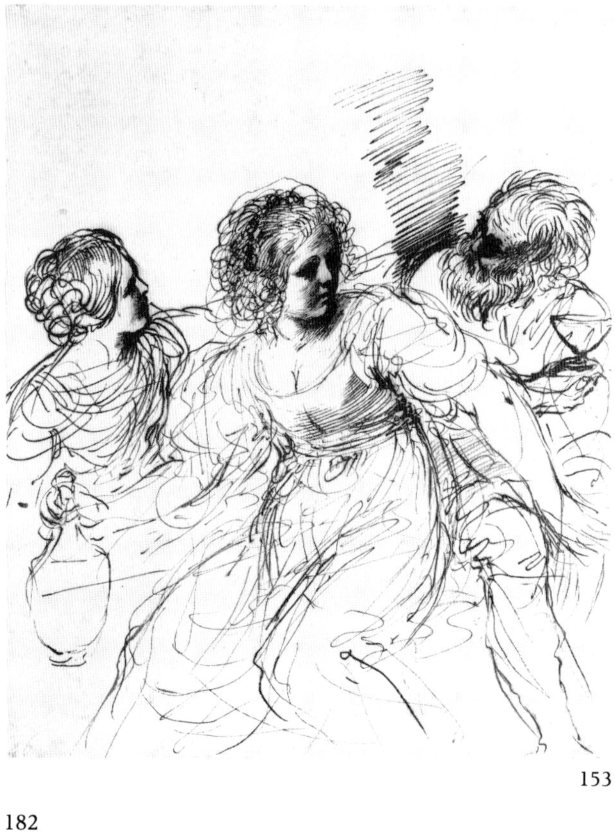

153

154 Flying Putto

Red chalk. 205 × 289mm.

London, Courtauld Institute Galleries, Witt Collection, inv. no. 1861.

Provenance: Casa Gennari (the drawing retains its fine Casa Gennari mount, ruled with red ink, for which see L *Suppl*, 2858c, and M, 1967, p. 20); Mr Bouverie (L 325); Mr Hervey; the Earls of Gainsborough (sale, Christie's, London, 27 July 1922, lot 82 or 83, with others, bt *Meatyard*); Sir Robert Witt, who (according to Courtauld records) bought the drawing from 'Oriolo, Florence'.

Literature: Hammer, *et al.*, 1977, no. 41.

Putti in similar poses appear frequently in Guercino's work of the late 1640s and the 1650s. A particularly good comparison, in reverse, is the *amorino* in the painting of *Mars and Cupid* of 1649, now in the Art Museum, Cincinnati, Ohio (S, 1988, no. 257), or the putto on the right, bearing the crown, in the *St Francesca Romana* of 1656–7, now in the Galleria Sabauda, Turin (S, 1988, no. 315). The style of the drawing points to a date in the 1650s, but it is not possible on the evidence available to connect it with any specific commission.

The drawing is a good example of Guercino's more finished studies in red chalk, a medium he adopted increasingly towards the end of his career.

155 The Angel appearing to Hagar and Ishmael

Red chalk. 186 × 261mm.

Mahon Collection, on loan to the Ashmolean Museum, Oxford, M & E, 33.

Provenance: Mrs Austen; Holcroft family; from whom acquired by Sir Denis Mahon in 1948.

Literature: M, 1967, no. 29; M, *Disegni*, 1969, no. 166; M & E, 1986, no. 33; S, 1988, under no. 299.

Ishmael was the illegitimate first son of Abraham; his mother was Hagar, the handmaiden of Abraham's wife Sarah. When Sarah eventually bore Abraham another son, Isaac, Ishmael taunted his young half-brother and Sarah asked Abraham to banish the boy and his mother. Abraham carried out her wishes, sending the pair into the desert with only bread and water for sustenance. When they had drunk the last of the water, Hagar laid her son out under a bush to die and was sitting weeping nearby when an angel visited her and revealed a well in the vicinity, thereby saving them.

The drawing is a study for the picture of the same subject painted in 1652 for Pandolfo Saccini of Siena (Malvasia, 1678, II, p. 379; 1841, II, p. 269), for which Guercino received payment on 17 March 1653 (*Libro dei Conti*, 1808,

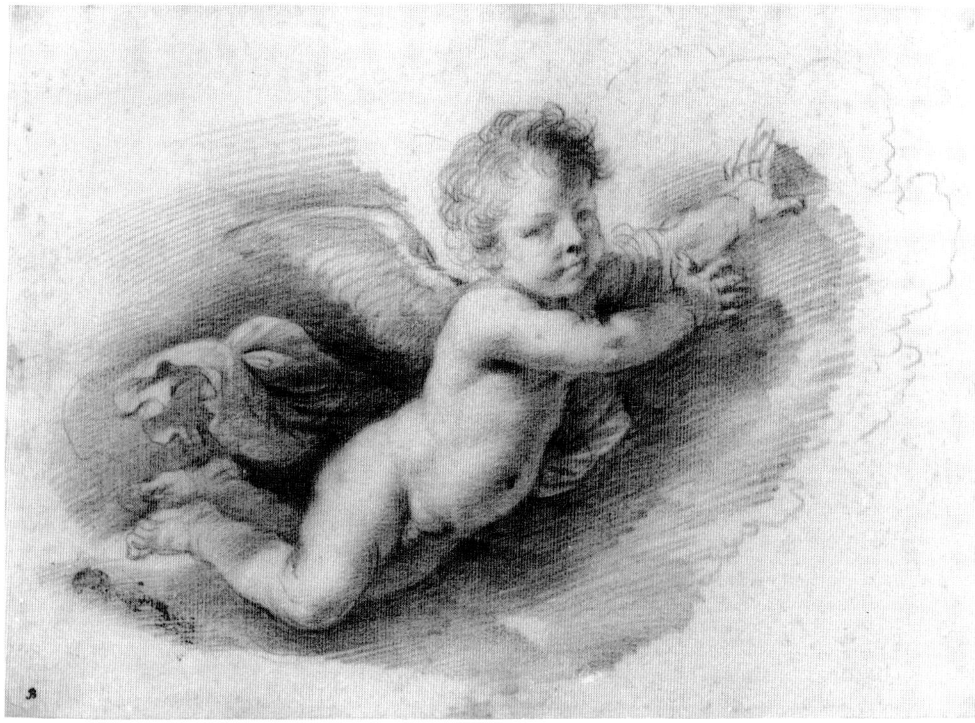

154

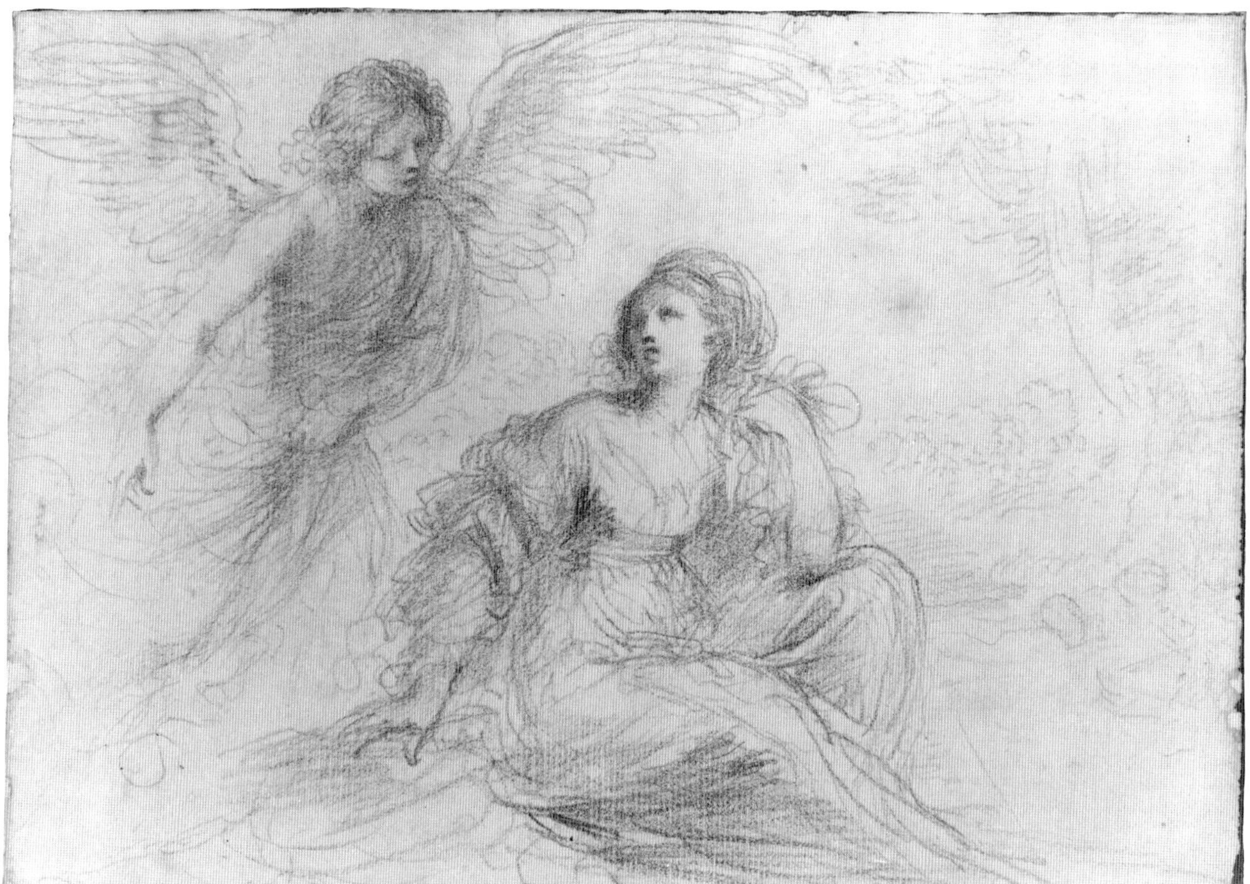

155

p. 134; 1841, p. 334, where the name is given as *Paccini*, but Mahon, 1967, p. 54, noted that this is a misreading of the manuscript of the Account Book). The painting is now in the collection of Sir Denis Mahon, London (S, 1988, no. 299).

There are few discrepancies between No. 155 and the painting, which it resembles particularly closely in the poses of the two principal figures, the details of Hagar's costume and the general outline of the landscape background. It is not immediately clear whether the angel in the study, whose lower legs are denoted only by calligraphic marks, is walking, as he is in an earlier drawing for this composition in the Museum Boymans–van Beuningen, Rotterdam (inv. no. I. 423; M, *Disegni*, 1969, no. 165), or flying as in the finished painting. No. 155 clearly represents a transitional stage, when Guercino was still undecided about this point. Although anticipating the finished composition fairly fully, No. 155 nevertheless lacks certain narrative props, such as the empty water pitcher lying on its side to the left of Hagar and the natural spring to which the angel points (this last detail does feature in the Rotterdam study). The only other significant difference is the position of Hagar's right hand, which, in the drawing, rests on the ground behind her, while in the painting it rests on her thigh and clasps the end of her sash.

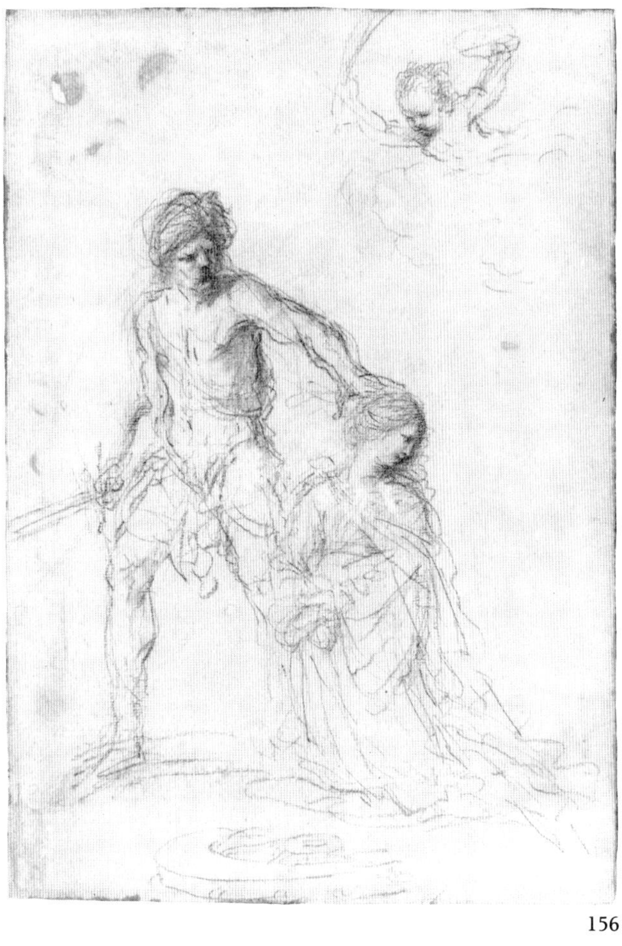

156

156 The Martyrdom of St Catherine

Black chalk. 260 × 185mm.

Mahon Collection, on loan to the Ashmolean Museum, Oxford, M & E, no. 34.

Provenance: sale, Christie's, London, 9 May 1958, lot 49, purchased by Sir Denis Mahon.

Literature: M, 1967, no. 30; M, *Disegni*, 1969, no. 167; Roli, 1972, p. 33 and pl. 64; M & E, 1986, no. 34; S, 1988, under no. 305.

A study for the picture of 1654 now in the Hermitage at Leningrad (S, 1988, no. 305). It was commissioned by the 'Communità [*sic*] di Cento' as a gift for Cardinal Alderano Cibo, Legate of Ferrara (Malvasia, 1678, II, p. 379; 1841, II, p. 270). The composition of the drawing is much the same as that of the picture, except that in the latter the putto who is holding the crown and laurel wreath is differently posed and is brought a little closer to the centre of the upper part of the composition; the executioner's right leg is straight rather than bent at the knee; and the broken wheel leans against the base of a column on the left of the composition rather than lying on its side in the middle foreground.

Guercino seems to have used black chalk only rarely, especially in the later part of his career, even though he achieved effects of great delicacy with the medium. No very convincing explanation as to why this was so can be put forth. For another drawing in this same technique, see No. 142.

157 Abraham expelling Hagar and Ishmael

Red chalk. 280 × 208mm.

Windsor Castle, Royal Library, inv. no. 2318.

Provenance: Casa Gennari; King George III.

Literature: S, 1988, under no. 327; M & T, 1989, no. 130.

Mahon and Turner (1989) related this late drawing to the only commission for an *Expulsion of Hagar* recorded in the Account Book (*Libro dei Conti*, 1808, pp. 145f. and 148; 1841, pp. 338–9) which corresponds to the only surviving painted treatment of the subject, the half-length composition in the Brera, Milan (S, 1988, no. 327). The painting was commissioned in 1657 by the 'Comunità' of Cento as a gift for the Legate of Ferrara, Cardinal Lorenzo Imperiali, and was delivered in 1658. For an analysis of the six recorded payments under the years 1657–8, see S, 1988, and M & T, 1989.

No. 157 differs most strikingly from the painted work in its vertical format, which allows the figures to be represented full length, and in the exclusion of the fourth figure of Sarah, who is included in the painting. The documents reveal that the modifications Guercino eventually made to this initial idea were governed almost exclusively by the economics of the commission rather than as a result of aesthetic choices (see M & T, 1989). It seems that the Comunità had a threshold of 180 ducats, or 225 *scudi*, above which they could not spend. According to Guercino's system of pricing his paintings by the number and length

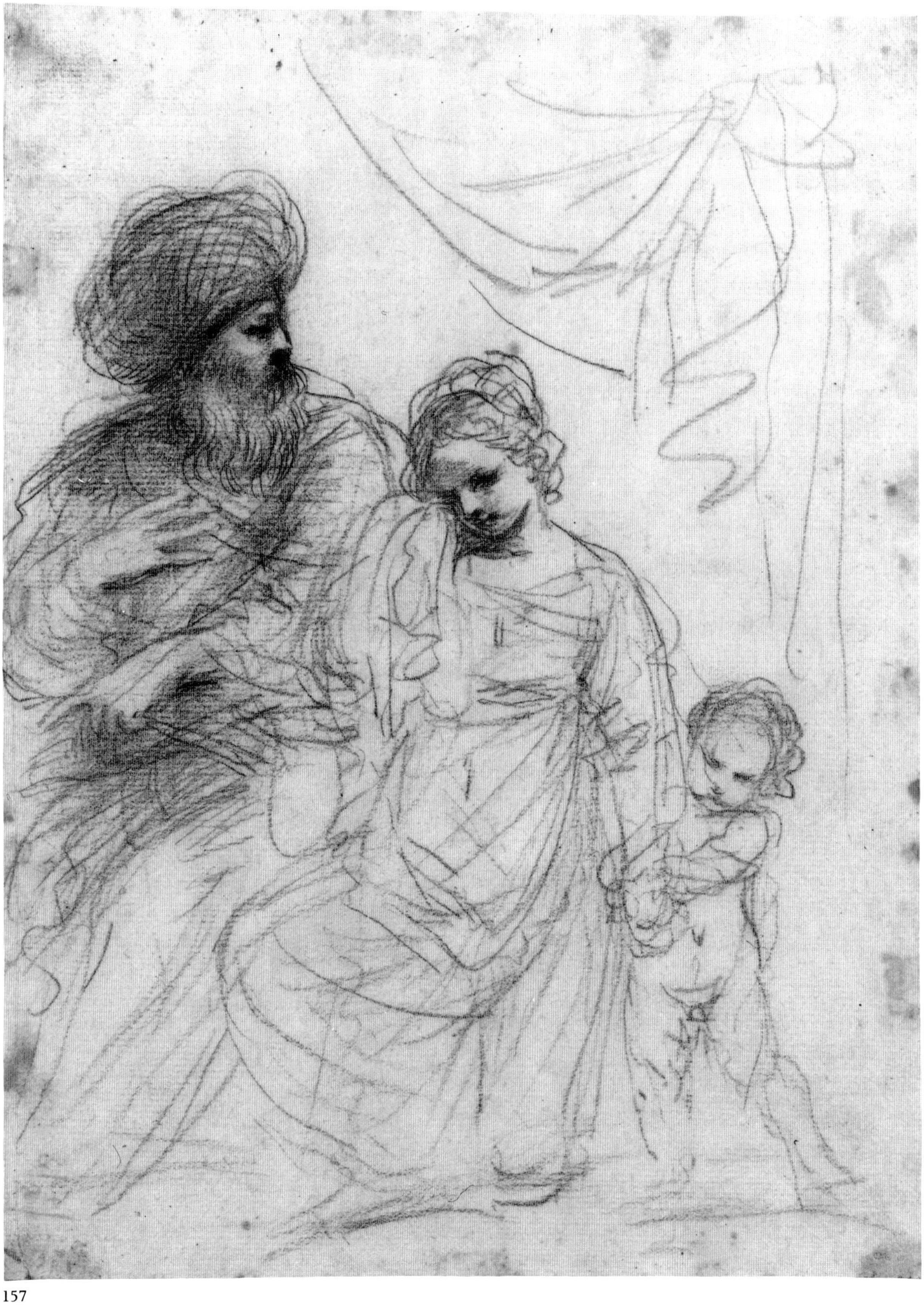

157

of the figures they contained, his initial idea of showing the two adults and one child full length, as represented in No. 157, would have pushed the budget established by the Comunità beyond its limit. Another red chalk drawing in the Public Library, Museum and Art Gallery, Folkestone (inv. no. F 3644.34; M & T, 1989, under no. 130, repr. fig. 23) must have been made after No. 157, for it shows half-length figures of both Abraham and Hagar, who is holding the infant Ishmael. Mahon and Turner calculated that this somewhat concise rendering of the subject fell short by 30 ducats of the allocated 180 ducats; thus the head and shoulders of Sarah would have been included in the finished work to make up the full price. For another drawing possibly related to this commission, see M & T, 1989, no. 230.

The Folkestone drawing is highly reminiscent, in the juxtaposition and pose of the figures, of the *Return of the Prodigal Son*, also a half-length composition, made slightly earlier than the *Expulsion of Hagar* at the request of Girolamo Boncompagni, Archbishop of Bologna, in 1654–5; it is now in the Timken Art Gallery, San Diego (S, 1988, no. 310). This appears to be another instance of Guercino returning, possibly unconsciously, to configurations he had used in the past to launch a new idea, although he invariably modified it in the course of the new composition's development.

158–159 Studies for *St Teresa receiving a Necklace from the Madonna in the Presence of St Joseph, her Patron* (1660–61)

Bologna, S. Gabriele delle Monache Carmelitane Scalze

158 The Madonna, St Teresa and St Joseph

Pen and brown ink and brown wash. 271 × 201mm.

Mahon Collection, on loan to the Ashmolean Museum, Oxford, M & E, 35.

Provenance: Casa Gennari; Mr Bouverie; Mr Hervey; the Earls of Gainsborough (sale, Christie's, London, 27 July 1922, lot 81, with others, bt *Meatyard*); Sir Robert Witt (L *Suppl*, 2228b, partially erased); D. Giese; from whom purchased by Sir Denis Mahon in 1937.

Literature: M, 1967, no. 31; M & E, 1986, no. 35; S, 1988, under no. 338.

This and No. 159 are studies for an altarpiece depicting *St Teresa receiving a Necklace from the Madonna in the Presence of St Joseph, her Patron*, destined for the church of S. Gabriele delle Monache Carmelitane Scalze in Bologna (S, 1988, no. 338), for which Guercino received payment on 21 March 1661 (*Libro dei Conti*, 1808, p. 153; 1841, p. 341). The drawing shows the three figures, isolated from their surroundings, in the same relationship to each other as in the painting but in slightly different poses. Although Guercino's style naturally developed throughout his career, his working practices varied little and he seems often to have returned to motifs he had used before. The pose of St Teresa in No. 158, kneeling in three-quarters profile to the left, is reminiscent, for example, of that of the same figure in an altarpiece of nearly thirty years earlier, the *Christ appearing to St Teresa*, for which see Nos. 97–102. The technique is similar to those preparatory drawings too, with its broken pen lines and pale films of wash (cf. in particular, No. 98). The late style of the present drawing and of No. 159 is, however, notably less robust and the facial features of the figures are much smaller and closely set in the middle of their faces.

Another drawing for this composition was formerly on the London art market (sale, Sotheby's, 15 June 1983, lot 56, repr.). A beautiful drapery study for the mantle of the Madonna is in the Koenig-Fachsenfeld collection, on deposit at the Staatsgalerie, Stuttgart (inv. no. III/78; Thiem, 1979, pp. 412–13, 415, n. 26, p. 417, no. 22, repr. pl. 32a). The drawing, like other red chalk studies of its type, was taken from the life, and its model was seated on a bench in preparation for the Madonna's position in the painting, seated on clouds. A second sheet in the same collection at Stuttgart (inv. no. Barbieri 32; M, *Disegni*, 1969, no. 173) has red chalk drapery studies on both sides, the *recto* for St Joseph and the *verso* for the Madonna. Based on this double-sided sheet, Mahon has suggested that at one stage Guercino considered transposing the figures of the Madonna and St Joseph (see M, *Disegni*, 1969, under nos. 172–3).

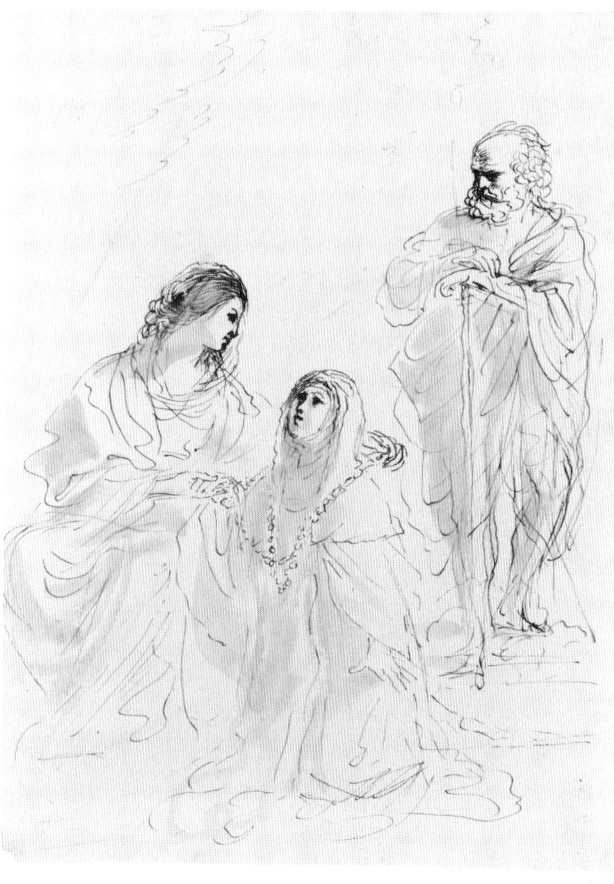

158

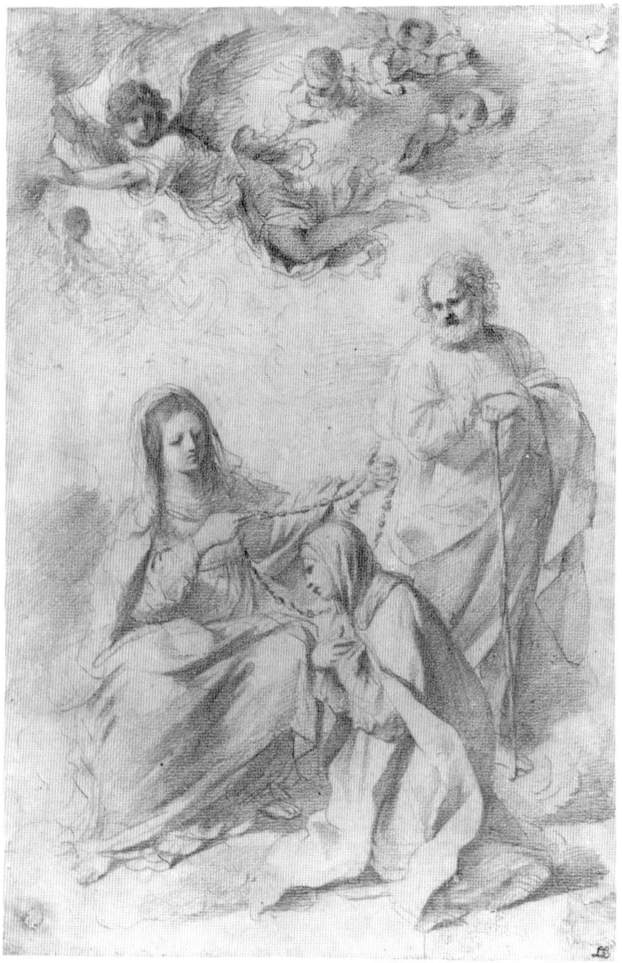

159

mentioned under No. 158, which, despite certain obvious discrepancies, are much closer in detail to the finished painting.

160 *Recto*: The Madonna and Child with the Blessed Bernardo Tolomei receiving the Rule of his Order
Verso: Two Studies of the Infant Christ

Red chalk. 312 × 212mm.

Windsor Castle, Royal Library, inv. no. 2380.

Provenance: Casa Gennari; King George III.

Literature: M, 1951, p. 58, no. xiv; M, *Disegni*, 1969, no. 174; S, 1988, under no. 339; M & T, 1989, no. 133.

A study for the altarpiece, now destroyed, painted in 1661 for S. Michele in Bosco in Bologna, the appearance of which is preserved in a copy by a member of Guercino's Studio in the church of the Madonna del Pilastrello at Lendinara (S, 1988, no. 339; M & T, 1989, p. 76, fig. 25). Another, later copy by Jacopo Alessandro Calvi (1740–1815) now decorates the altar formerly occupied by Guercino's original, but, for rather complicated reasons, this is a less accurate

159 The Madonna, St Teresa and St Joseph, with an Angel and Putti above

Two shades of red chalk. 417 × 274mm.

Mahon Collection, on loan to the Ashmolean Museum, Oxford, M & E, 36.

Provenance: Lionel Lucas (L *Suppl*, 1733a); Claude Lucas (sale, Christie's, 9 December 1949, lot 79), purchased pseudonymously by Sir Denis Mahon.

Literature: M, 1967, no. 32; M, *Disegni*, 1969, under nos. 172–3; M & E, 1986, no. 36.

A study for *St Teresa receiving a Necklace from the Madonna in the Presence of St Joseph, her Patron* of 1660–61, for which see No. 158. The drawing is more elaborate than No. 158, showing in the sky above the three main protagonists an angel and three putti, with music-making angels in the background, all executed in a darker coloured chalk. In the finished painting, only two putti are shown, the more modest solution perhaps reflecting the limitations of the patrons' purse, as Mahon (1967) suggested. No. 159 may therefore have been an informal presentation drawing; it was certainly executed before the red chalk drapery studies

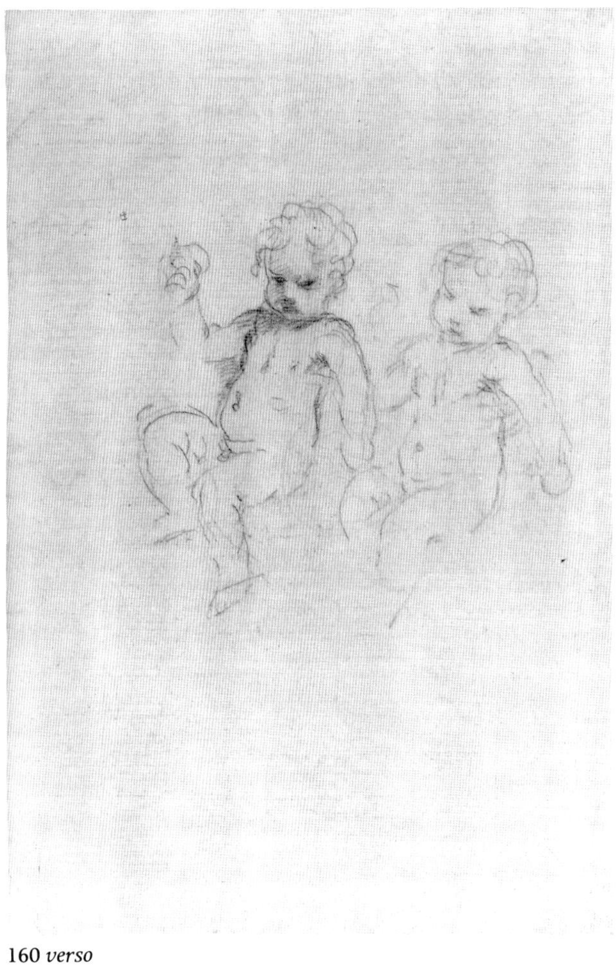

160 *verso*

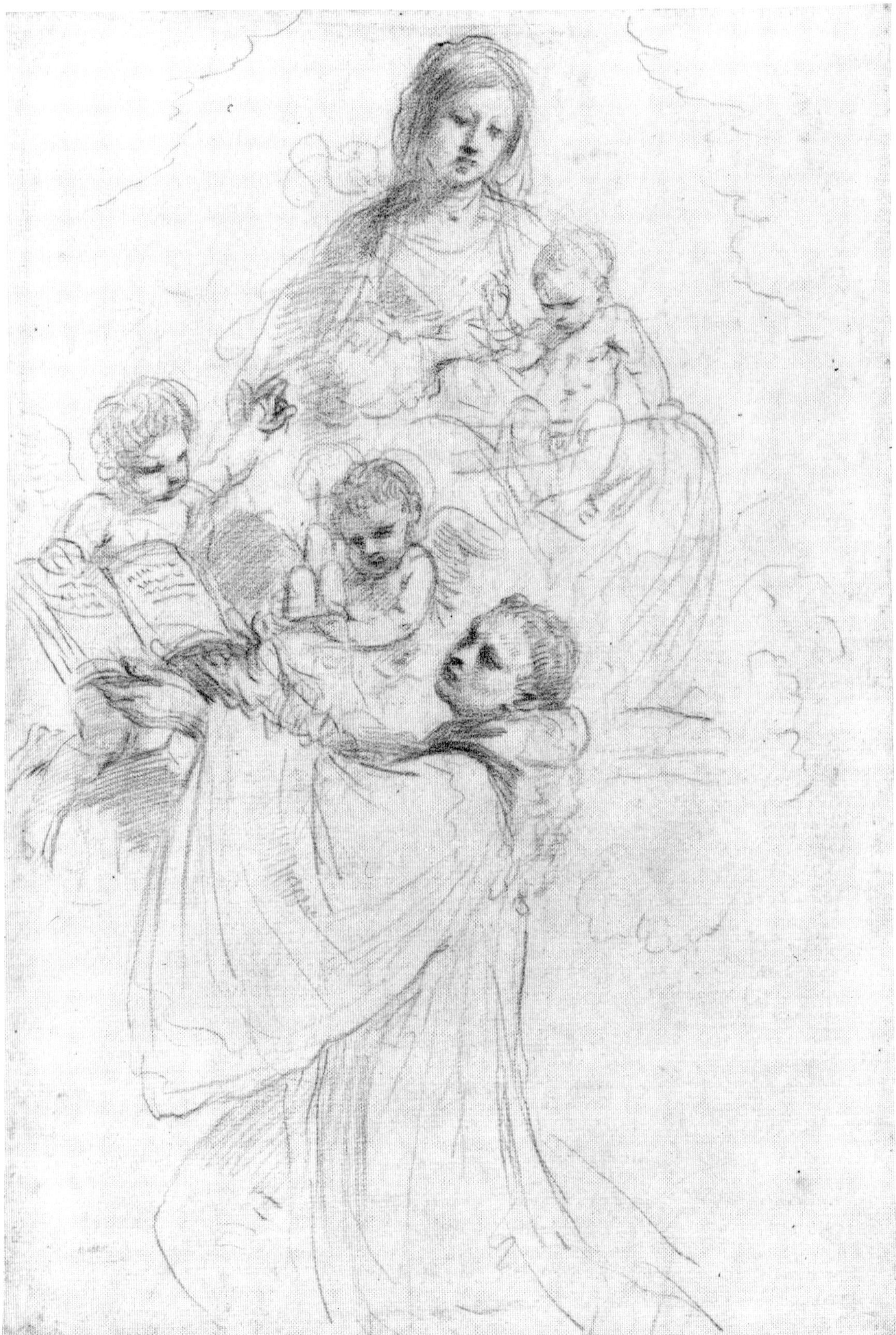

160

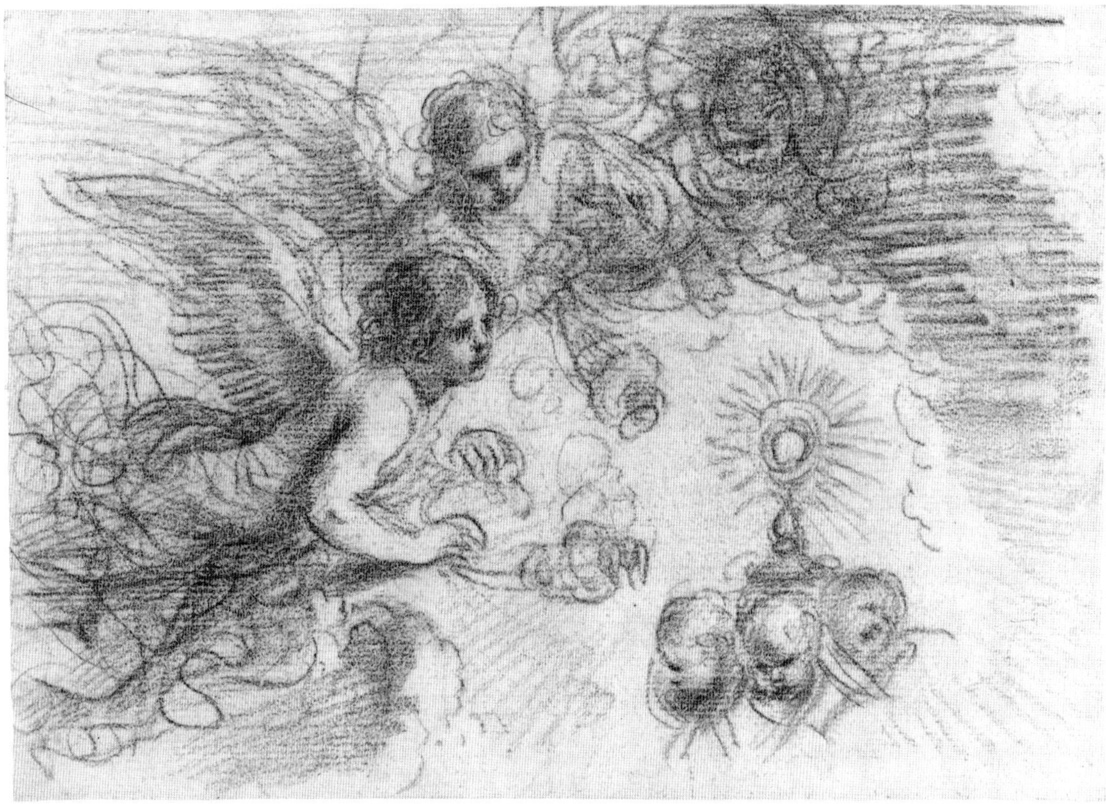

161

rendering of the original composition (see M & T, 1989, no. 133).

Since the Lendinara picture must be an accurate record of Guercino's finished picture, it is clear that many further changes occurred between No. 160 and the master's finished compositional idea. In the end it was a winged angel, not a small putto, who hands the book of his rule to Beato Bernardo, and the Madonna, not the other putto, who holds out the emblem of the three hills surmounted by a cross. Only one putto and two winged putti heads appeared in the finished composition, and they were relegated to a more decorative role in the top right of the picture.

No. 160 has been recently lifted to reveal two studies in red chalk for the figure of the seated Christ Child on the *verso*. One can understand with hindsight Guercino's desire to make further attempts to resolve the pose of this important figure, for in the composition study on the *recto* the Child is not only perhaps a little too diminutive compared with the two putti attending to Beato Bernardo, but he looks downwards with an almost cross expression on his face. The decision to give the Christ Child greater prominence may well have coincided with that of dismissing the two attendant putti. Of the two studies on the *verso*, it would seem that Guercino first drew the one on the left, since of the two it is the more completely drawn and occupies the centre of the sheet. In pose this first study seems largely to echo that of the Christ Child on the *recto*, except that his head is shown more erect. In fact the more faintly drawn second study on the right, where the right arm seems no longer to be raised in blessing, is closer to the pose of the Child that was in the end adopted.

161–162 Studies for *St Thomas Aquinas writing the Hymn in Honour of the Holy Sacrament* (1662–3)

Bologna, S. Domenico

161 Two Angels among Clouds, each waving an Incense-burner near a Monstrance

Red chalk. 151 × 250mm.

Windsor Castle, Royal Library, inv. no. 2892.

Provenance: Casa Gennari; King George III.

Literature: M, *Disegni*, 1969, under no. 175; Ward-Jackson, 1980, no. 717; S, 1988, under no. 342; M & T, 1989, no. 134.

A good example of Guercino's late style. The tremulousness of touch is striking, especially when compared with the sureness of hand in drawings of this same medium, for example No. 135, done when Guercino was at the height of his powers.

This is a study for the large altarpiece of *St Thomas Aquinas writing the Hymn in Honour of the Holy Sacrament*, the most important work of the artist's final years, painted in 1662–3 for the church of S. Domenico in Bologna (S, 1988, no. 342). In the picture only one winged angel with a censer appears and the monstrance is replaced by a chalice, as in No. 162. The drawing indeed seems a little crowded in the upper centre, where the second winged angel appears to impinge upon a winged putto head which has been cancelled by the heavy shading of the cloud on the right.

Two other drawings at Windsor of putti were related by Mahon and Turner to this same altarpiece (M & T, 1989, nos. 135 and 136).

162 Flying Angel offering Incense to the Host

Red chalk. 213 × 206mm.

London, Victoria and Albert Museum, inv. no. E.4263–1915.

Provenance: W. H. Hammond.

Literature: M, *Disegni*, 1969, no. 175; Ward-Jackson, 1980, no. 717; S, 1988, under no. 342; M & T, 1989, under nos. 134–6.

For the altarpiece of *St Thomas Aquinas writing the Hymn in Honour of the Holy Sacrament*, for which see No. 161. Although only a slight study when compared with No. 161, the present drawing seems to come closer to the solution of the picture. The way the incense-burner is swung forward resembles that of the winged angel painted in the top left corner, and the monstrance shown in No. 161 has been replaced by a chalice with the Host, as in the picture.

Perhaps even more than the previous drawing, No. 162 shows the unsteadiness of the master's hand.

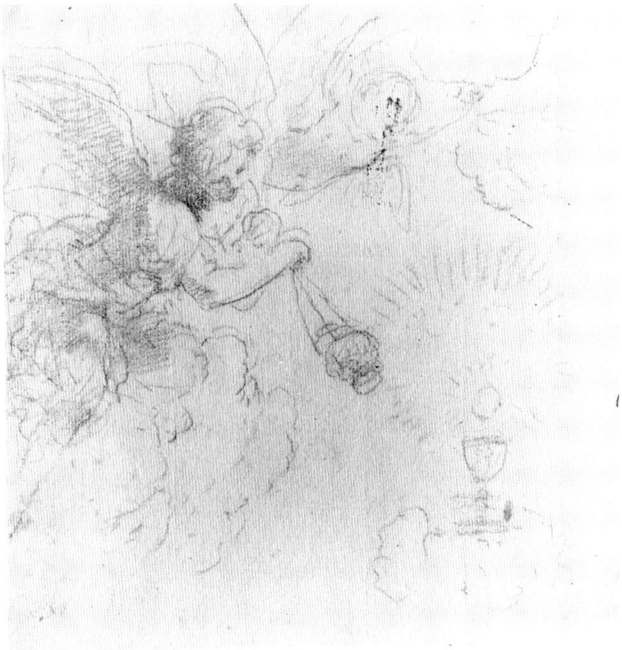

162

163 The Madonna enthroned in an Interior, adored by two Suppliants

Red chalk. 282 × 195mm.

Windsor Castle, Royal Library, inv. no. 2465.

Provenance: Casa Gennari: King George III.

Literature: M & T, 1989, no. 236.

On the *verso* is a rapid study for the right sleeve and hand of the Madonna.

The subject is not easy to decipher. The Madonna is seated on a throne, with (?)St Joseph on her left and (?)a kneeling angel on her right who holds a board with an inkstand on it. The Madonna seems to be proffering a scroll or piece of paper to the bearded suppliant, apparently a pilgrim, who kneels with a woman in the right foreground. Other pilgrims may be seen in the doorway on the right waiting to be presented to the Madonna.

No picture corresponding in subject to No. 163 is recorded either by Malvasia or in the *Libro dei Conti*. The style of drawing is that of Guercino's very last years and its loose, almost impressionistic handling compares well with that of the *St John the Baptist drinking Water from a Spring*, also at Windsor (M & T, 1989, no. 137), which, according to an inscription, probably in the hand of Guercino's nephew and heir Benedetto Gennari (1633–1715), was the last drawing made by the master.

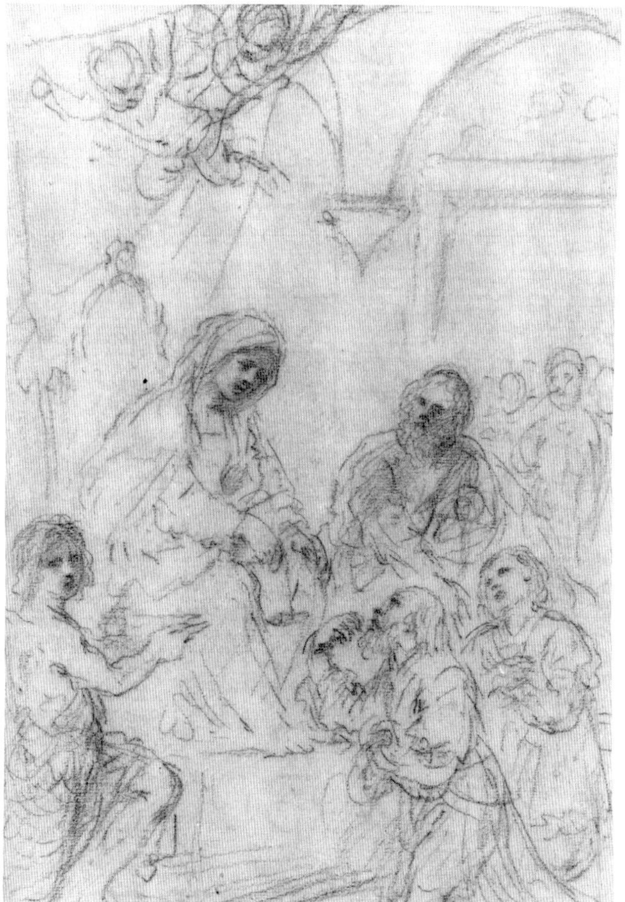

163

II Landscapes (Nos. 164–82)

Guercino made numerous landscape drawings, yet the motivation behind this prolific output and its ultimate purpose remain obscure. Guercino rarely painted pure landscapes (though there are a few notable examples both in fresco and on canvas among his early works: S, 1988, nos. 19, 20, 24 E-H, 28, 30, 51, 83), and usually the backgrounds of his history subjects are devoid of landscape details. It is therefore impossible to assign to any of these drawings a preparatory function. They were apparently made as ends in themselves, probably for the artist's own personal satisfaction and for the amusement of his friends.

Guercino's landscape drawings are executed almost exclusively in pen and ink. Only occasionally did he venture into the more atmospheric but less precise technique of pen and wash (e.g. No. 182) so favoured by Claude Lorrain (1600–82) and other Northern painters. The landscapes differ markedly from the artist's working studies for history paintings in their meticulous execution, concern for detail and highly finished appearance. Guercino nonetheless succeeded in achieving spectacular effects of light and space. While the figure studies often appear to have been hastily executed, one after another, with many pentiments, cancellations and reversals as Guercino searched for a satisfactory pose or configuration, he seems to have found no difficulty in committing his landscape compositions smoothly to the paper; somehow he was able to avoid corrections and alternatives, working carefully in a sustained and systematic effort to bring each part of the drawing to a similar degree of finish, almost in the manner of a painting or a presentation drawing. This is particularly true of the drawings that seem to have been made in the 1630s, such as Nos. 179–81. Although their confident execution belies the fact, the balanced and well-ordered compositions of such drawings plainly indicate that the artist was not working on the spot. To evoke such convincing panoramas at the first attempt, Guercino must have seen the general shape of a given composition in his mind's eye before setting pen to paper. He appears frequently to have facilitated the genesis of a given landscape by having recourse to a fund of favourite motifs such as windswept trees and round towers, just as he habitually drew on stock poses and motifs (often unconsciously) for use in all sorts of different contexts in his figure and genre drawings. Another technique Guercino frequently used to bring his landscapes to life was the clever distribution within each composition of figures performing various appropriately rural activities, which arrest the eye between the spaces and vistas he had created. Despite working so frequently from the imagination, Guercino could not fail to be influenced by the Emilian environment that was his home for most of his life, and his drawings contain frequent echoes of, for example, the River Reno and the plains around Cento.

Only one drawing in this selection (No. 164) provides the setting for a specific subject, namely, the courtship of Angelica and Medoro. A few others accommodate, with a degree of pathetic fallacy, dramatic events such as a river in flood and a funeral procession (Nos. 166 and 168), which punctuate the otherwise monotonous course of country life. Even when a landscape records no particular event, some narrative element is usually subtly introduced by the agency of Guercino's animated cast of country folk going about their business, negotiating over merchandise, making music, strolling, riding and conversing.

Guercino's landscapes are difficult to date, being unconnected with documented paintings; indeed, only one of the following group is securely dated, thanks to the year inscribed on the *verso* (No. 180). Nevertheless, some stylistic progression can be discerned, the earlier drawings being more dramatic and rather broader in execution, with greater chiaroscuro contrasts (Nos. 164, 169), while the later ones, as described above, concentrate more on space and structure. The ordering of the nineteen landscape drawings that follow is therefore not strictly chronological, but their arrangement approximately charts the progression between these two poles.

164 Landscape with Angelica and Medoro

(*see colour pl. 22*)

London, British Museum, inv. no. Pp. 4–63.

(For other details, see App. no. 57.)

A particularly fine example of the painter's landscape drawings. The subject is taken from Ariosto's *Orlando furioso* (XIX, 36). It was unusual for Guercino to animate his landscape drawings with literary protagonists such as these, and indeed it is only the inscriptions and the presence of Cupid that distinguish the figures from those that normally people his landscape scenes. The drawing appears to date from the early 1620s, possibly when the artist was in Rome (1621–3).

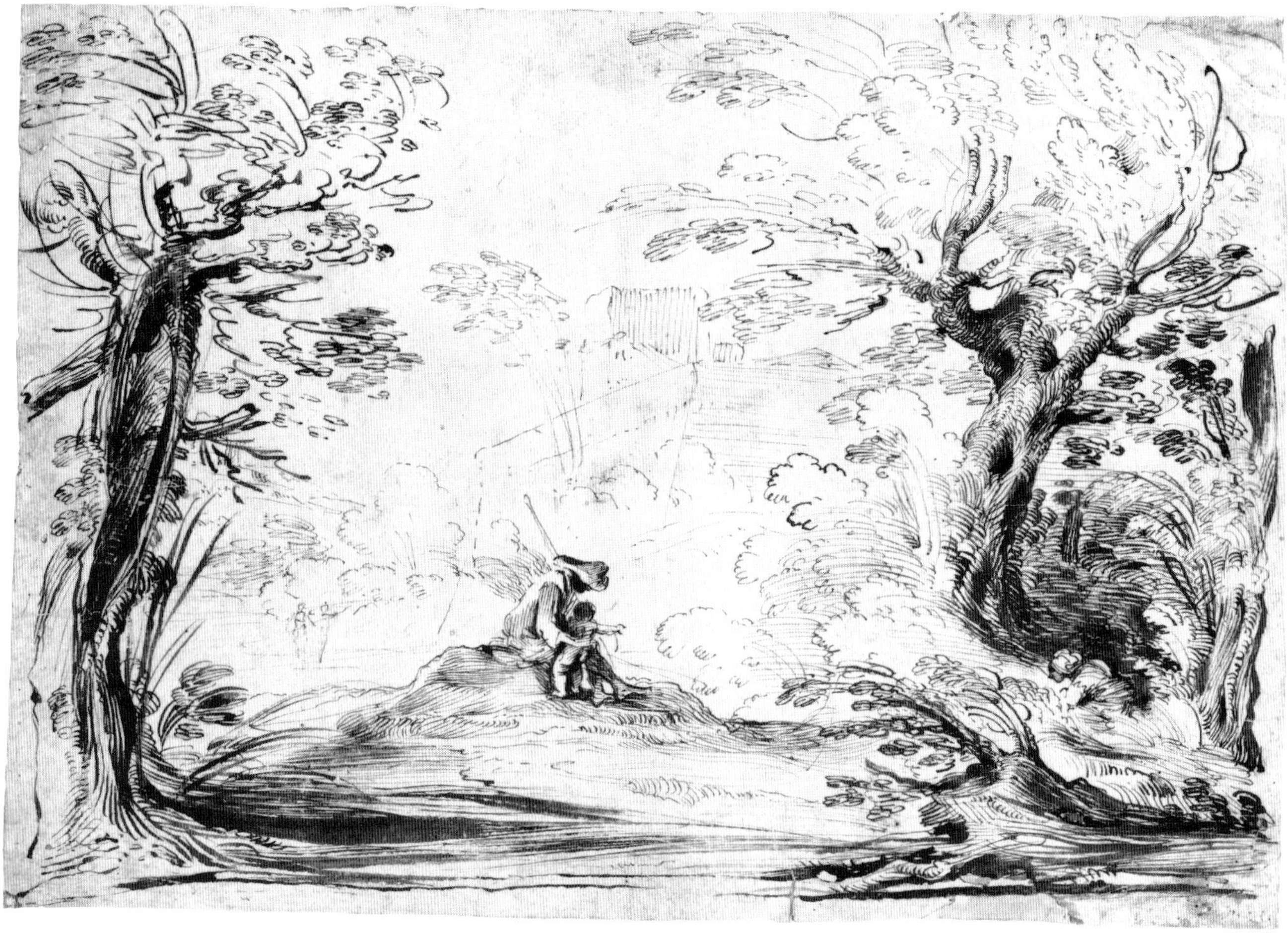

165

165 Landscape with a Man seated on a Hummock in the centre accompanied by a small Boy

London, British Museum, inv. no. Ff. 2–142.

(For other details, see App. no. 59.)

A good example of Guercino's landscape style. The subject, with the woman crouching in the undergrowth on the right and the man with the naked infant in the centre, remains enigmatic.

166 Landscape with a River flooding its Banks

(*see colour pl. 23*)

Pen and brown ink and some brown wash; some black chalk in the top left, indicating an arched wall with a tower in the distance (perhaps not by Guercino). 263 × 423mm.

Chatsworth, inv. no. 544.

Provenance: probably Benedetto Gennari; William Cavendish, 1st Duke of Devonshire; thence by descent.

Literature: Popham, 1962–3, no. 30; M, 1969, no. 196; Roli, 1972, pl. 52; B, 1985, no. 116; Penny, 1987, p. 542f.; Bora, 1988, under no. 58; M & T, 1989, under no. 246.

Mahon (1969) hinted that the river could be the Reno, which flows near Cento and which flooded its banks in 1635. Bagni (1985) went further to claim that the view was probably of this event and was taken from Pieve di Cento, the town on the opposite bank from Guercino's birthplace. In his view, the buildings seen in the background on the right are of Cento itself. Whether or not the scene is as specific as Bagni supposed, it certainly provided Guercino with a dramatic subject. The rushing movement of the flood waters is enhanced by the floating tree-trunk and the frantic efforts of the men on the bank to repair its broken sides. The sense of drama is further heightened by such details as the two figures standing stranded on the roof of the building in the distance on the right, waving their arms to attract attention.

No. 166 is one of a group of fourteen landscape drawings, which, until recently, was preserved intact at Chatsworth. In the present exhibition there are four others from this same group: two others still at Chatsworth (Nos. 167–8), one now in the Fitzwilliam Museum, Cambridge (No. 169), and one now in the Ashmolean Museum, Oxford (No. 170). The other nine drawings from the group are still at

Chatsworth: inv. nos. 528, 531–2, 535–8, 540 and 545. The Chatsworth landscape drawings have been discussed often, notably by Mahon (M, *Disegni*, 1969, pp. 182–5, and nos. 192, 195–6 and 206–8), Bagni (1985, *passim*, in which the reproductions of the material are particularly useful) and Mahon and Turner (1989, under no. 246).

At some point in the period 1672–4 Guercino's nephew Cesare Gennari must have sent the fourteen landscape drawings, together with some other material, from Bologna to his brother Benedetto, who was then in Paris, in order for them to be engraved by Jean Pesne (1623–1700). Once the fourteen copper-plates had been completed by Pesne, who reversed the designs, they were sent to Bologna for Cesare to provide the series with a frontispiece based on his own design. This was engraved by the Bolognese artist Gioseffo Roli (1645–1727) with the title: *Frontespicio a Paesi, Dissegni del Cav. Gio: Fran.co Barbieri intagliati da Gio: Penna in Parigi.* Cesare's original drawing for the frontispiece, formerly in the collection of the Bolognese engraver Clemente Nicoli, is now in the Courtauld Institute Galleries, London (inv. no. 567; B, 1985, no. 38; M & T, 1989, under no. 246). The frontispiece also included Benedetto and Cesare's dedication of *questi pochi fogli, capricci del gia' Caval.re Gio. Fran.co Barbieri nostro Zio* to Francesco II d'Este, Duke of Modena, a portrait bust of whom also appears. The original drawings must then have been sent from France to England, where Benedetto was then living. He must have sold them, probably to the 4th Earl of Devonshire, later the 1st Duke, before 1689, the year he hurriedly left England following the flight of his patron King James II. The drawings certainly did not return to Bologna, since they are not mentioned in the inventory of the Casa Gennari drawn up in 1719 (for which see Introduction, p. 20), which does, however, include the copper-plates of Pesne and the copper-plate of Roli's frontispiece.

No. 166 was engraved in reverse as no. 11 in Pesne's series of fourteen prints (B, 1985, no. 117). The black chalk addition in the left background of the drawing, showing an arched wall with a tower, is included in Pesne's engraving.

The fourteen drawings in the series have certain features in common: they are finished compositions in their own right, in a horizontal format; they are in pen and brown ink or pen and brown ink and brown wash; and they are mostly drawn in Guercino's meticulous, engraver-like style, a careful drawing technique which he seems to have reserved for his landscape drawings. In spite of these similarities, there are many differences between them. For example, they do not all seem to have been drawn in the same period: in the the opinion of Mahon (M, *Disegni*, 1969, no. 192), No. 169 is an early drawing, carried out before the painter's visit to Rome in 1621, while others seem to date from the 1630s. It would therefore be incorrect to imagine that Guercino himself conceived all fourteen *en serie*, though clearly he must have seen some of them as groups. Although all of them are in horizontal format, this was the standard shape of most landscape drawings, including others by Guercino from Chatsworth (e.g., ex-Chatsworth inv. no. 534, sold at Christie's, London, 3 July 1984, lot 20, and now in the Staatsgalerie at Stuttgart), which were not engraved by Pesne, but which must have entered the collection at the same time as the fourteen considered here. That they are not all contemporaneous is also borne out by their variation in theme. Some show figures in serene enjoyment of the out-of-doors (e.g., No. 167), while the present drawing shows humanity struggling with the elements and attempting to avert imminent natural disaster. No. 168 is alone in not including any figures; it concentrates purely on nature, on the gnarled tree to the right and the lions sporting themselves in the foreground to the left.

167 Landscape with a Building with a round Tower and on the right a broken Column

Pen and brown ink, and some traces of brown wash. 251 × 416mm.

Chatsworth, inv. no. 533.

Provenance: probably Benedetto Gennari; William Cavendish, 1st Duke of Devonshire; thence by descent.

Literature: Popham, 1962–3, no. 29; M, 1969, no. 208; B, 1985, no. 121; M & T, 1989, under no. 246.

Engraved in reverse as no. 12 in Pesne's series of fourteen prints (B, 1985, no. 122), for which see No. 166. As Bagni pointed out, the broken column on the right of the drawing has been substituted on the left of Pesne's print by a tree.

168 Landscape with two Lions in the left Foreground

Pen and brown ink. 258 × 425mm.

Chatsworth, inv. no. 526.

Provenance: probably Benedetto Gennari; William Cavendish, 1st Duke of Devonshire; thence by descent.

Literature: B, 1985, no. 129; M & T, 1989, under no. 246.

Engraved in reverse as no. 13 in Pesne's series of fourteen prints (B, 1985, no. 130), for which see No. 166.

169 Landscape with a Funeral Procession

Pen and brown ink and brown wash. 233 × 402mm.

Cambridge, Fitzwilliam Museum, inv. no. PD.1–87 (ex-Chatsworth inv. no. 546).

Provenance: probably Benedetto Gennari; William Cavendish, 1st Duke of Devonshire; thence by descent; sold from Chatsworth to the Fitzwilliam Museum in 1987.

Literature: M, *Disegni*, 1969, no. 192; B, 1985, no. 69; Penny, 1987, p. 542; M & T, 1989, under no. 246 and note.

Engraved in reverse as no. 5 in Pesne's series of fourteen prints (B, 1985, no. 70), for which see No. 166.

Mahon (1969) was inclined to date the drawing in Guercino's early period, before the artist's departure for Rome in 1621, a point of view that we share. Indeed, there are parallels in the pen-and-wash technique between No. 169 and a figure drawing of this same period, No. 18, which

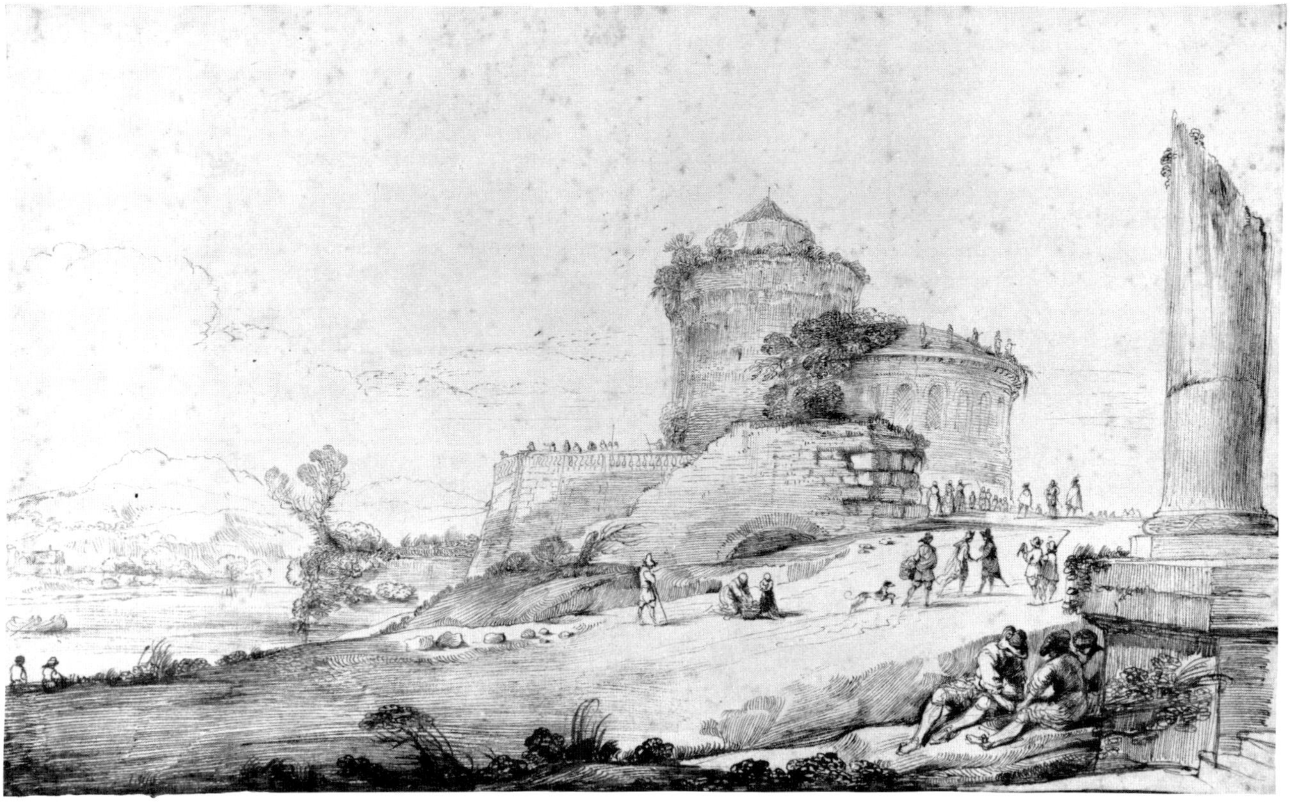

167

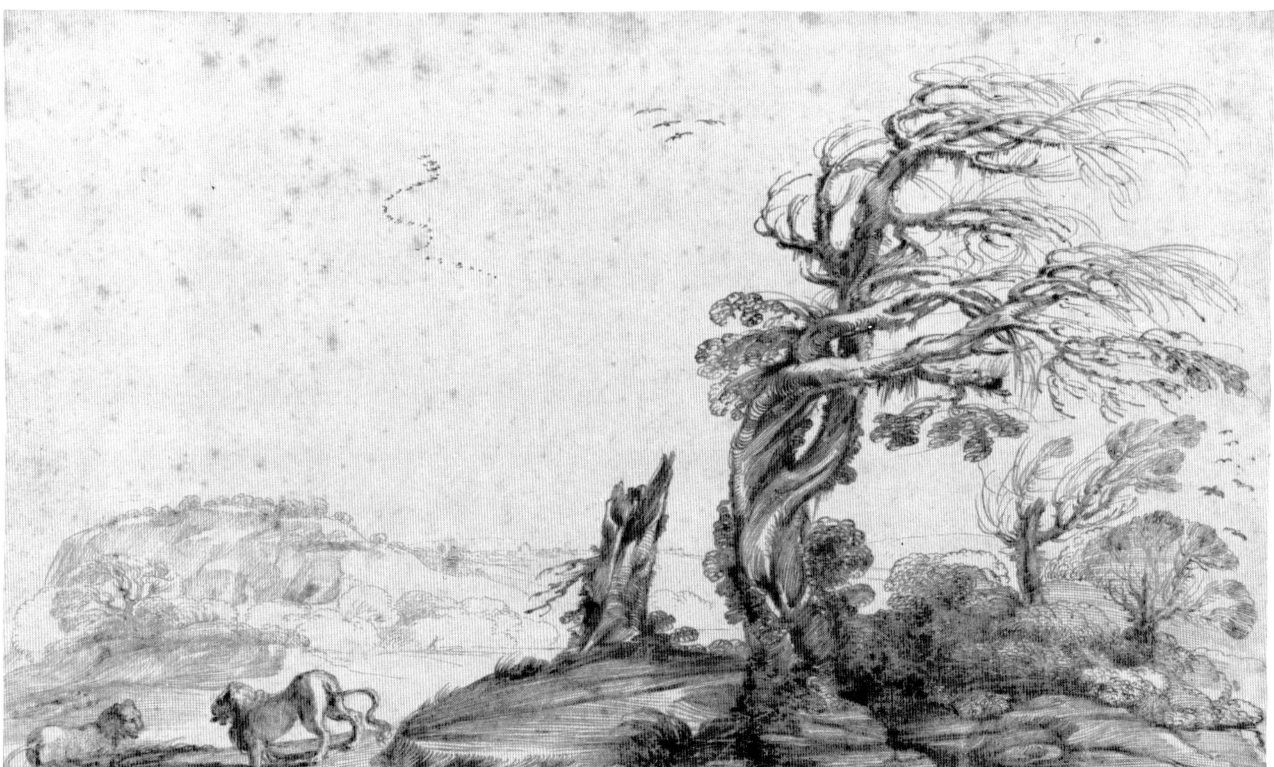

168

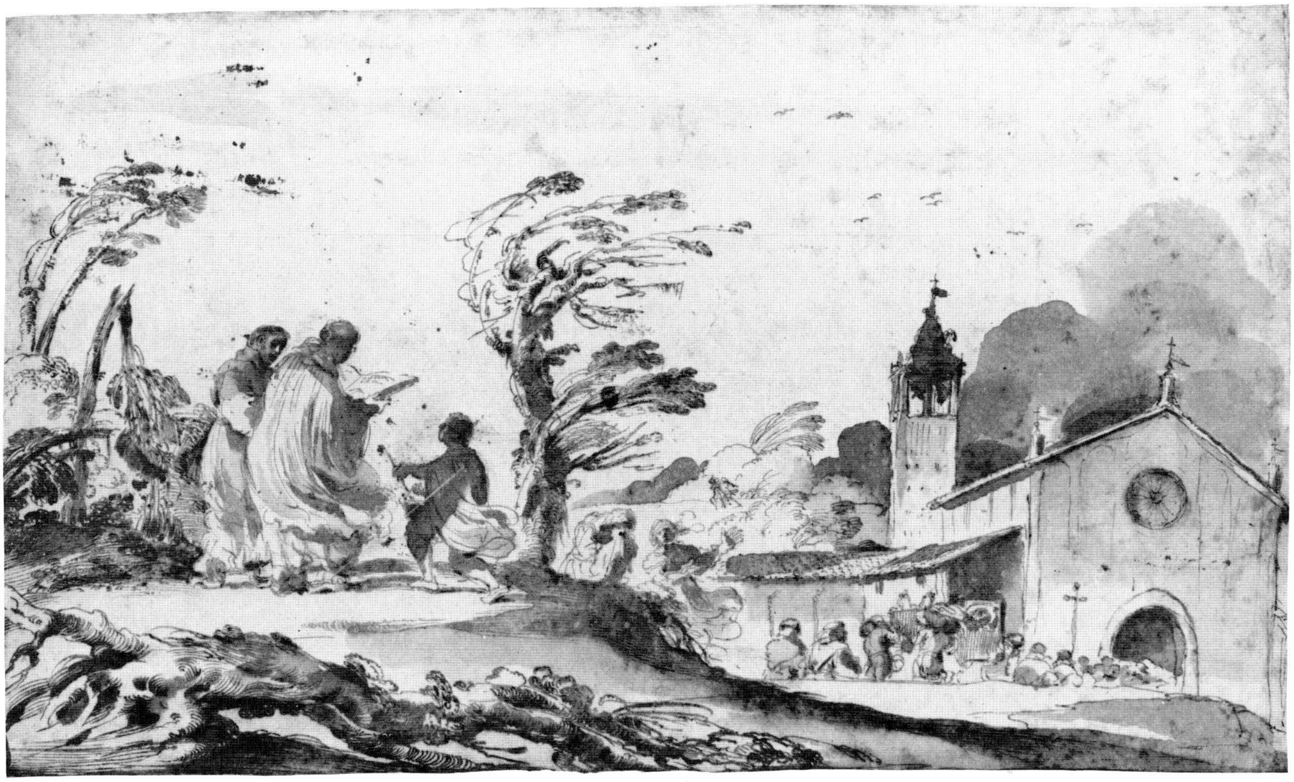

169

is unquestionably datable 1620. The similarities are most apparent in the artist's treatment of tree trunks and foliage.

Bagni (1985) has claimed that No. 169 was probably taken from the river-bank of the River Reno at Pieve di Cento, at the beginning of the lane leading to the church ('dalla sponda di Pieve di Cento del fiume Reno, all'inizio del viottolo che portava alla chiesa'). He went on to suggest that the tree in the centre of No. 169 might be that visible, bottom centre, on the bank of the River Reno, near to the church of S. Francesco, in the map of Cento and its environs of 1643 by Bartolomeo Lucatelli (B, 1985, p. 55, fig. 36). We are not convinced by this hypothesis, since many of the trees in this map seem to have served mostly as decoration and need not necessarily have corresponded with actual trees in those positions in the seventeenth century. Moreover, the tree in Guercino's drawing is highly stylised.

In his review of Bagni's book, Nicholas Penny justifiably questioned the view that certain of Guercino's landscape drawings can be interpreted as being strictly accurate topographically. As evidence against such 'realism', he emphasised the compositional harmony of No. 169, with its single dramatic thread: 'the foreground priest, monk and acolyte with their garments billowing, and the figures entering the Church with the uncovered coffin, have that air of near burlesque which we associate with Venetian eighteenth-century drawings of popular ceremonies, while the dramatic grief of the women in the centre seems continuous with the agitation of the trees and clouds'. Though some of the details, for example the church, might well show some dependence on buildings in Guercino's native town of Cento, we agree with Penny that, rather than being an accurate representation of a specific place, the way in which No. 169 is composed is of Guercino's own invention, like the other landscapes from the Chatsworth series (Nos. 166–70).

That the composition originated in the artist's imagination is further suggested by the artificial placing of the tree trunk as a *repoussoir* in the left foreground, the dramatic silhouetting of the two priests accompanied by an acolyte in the middle ground on the left, and the rhythmical movement of the figures downwards and to the right to the open door in the church. It is characteristic of this relatively early stage of his career that Guercino has not neglected the detail of the corpse lying on the bier, the uncovered feet of which are directed towards the spectator as it is carried by the mourners head-first into the church.

170 Landscape with a Horseman and two armed Men

Pen and brown ink, with some touches of brown wash; some black chalk on the left, indicating part of a tree (perhaps not by Guercino). 258 × 423mm.

Oxford, Ashmolean Museum, inv. no. 873B (ex-Chatsworth inv. no. 530).

Provenance: probably Benedetto Gennari; William Cavendish, 1st

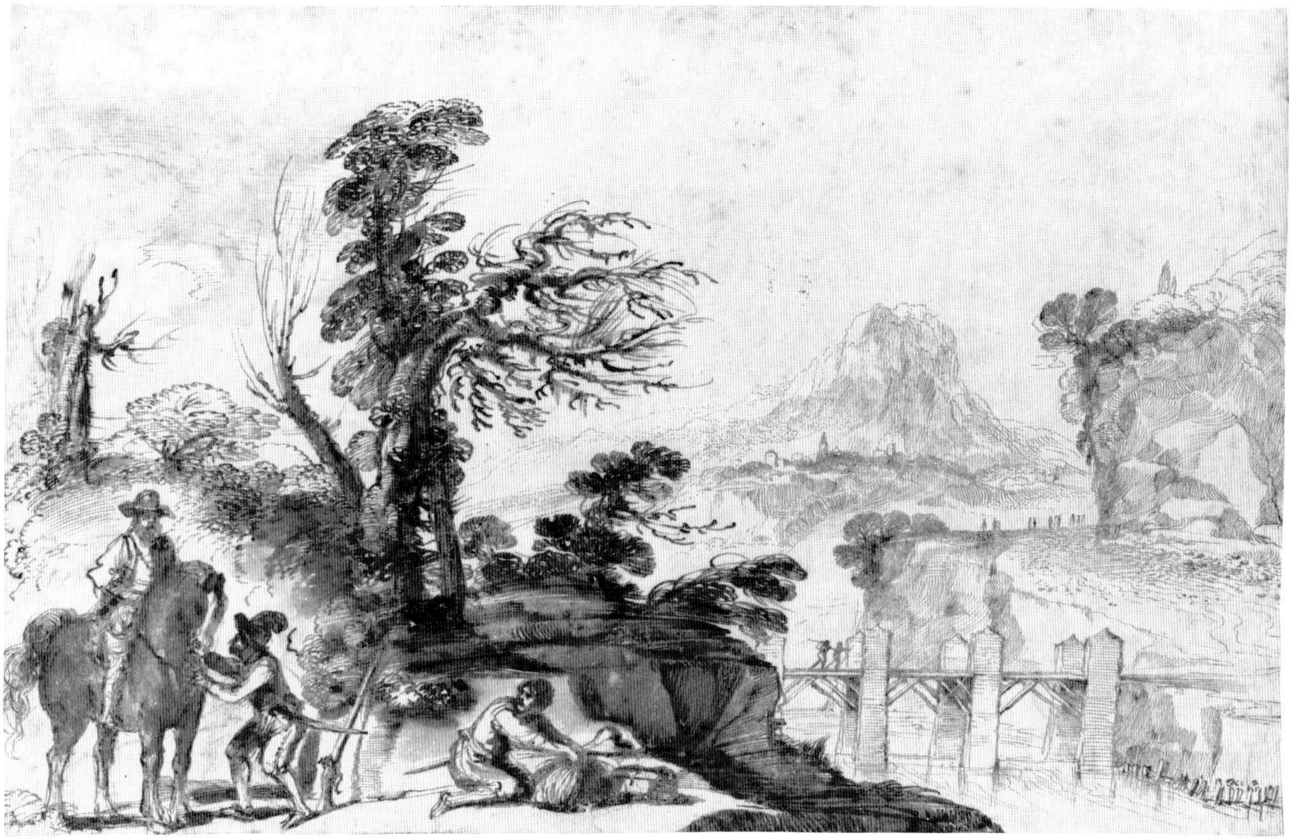

170

Duke of Devonshire; thence by descent; sold from Chatsworth to the Ashmolean Museum in 1987.

Literature: M, *Disegni*, 1969, no. 195; B, 1985, no. 102; Penny, 1987, p. 543; M & T, 1989, under no. 246 and note.

Engraved in reverse as no. 9 in Pesne's series of fourteen prints (B, 1985, no. 103), for which see No. 166. The black chalk addition to the tree on the left of the drawing was included in Pesne's engraving.

171 Landscape with the Sun seen low behind a Church

Pen and brown ink. 167 × 249mm.

Windsor Castle, Royal Library, inv. no. 2771.

Provenance: Casa Gennari; King George III.

Literature: B, 1985, no. 19; M & T, 1989, no. 256.

The sun is only rarely represented in Guercino's drawings of landscape, or, for that matter, in those of other artists of the seventeenth-century Bolognese School. A precedent exists, however, in Annibale Carracci's beautiful pen drawing of a *Landscape with the setting Sun* in the British Museum (inv. no. 1972–7–22–13; Turner, 1980, no. 3), in which the sun shines weakly through clouds much in the same way as it does in No. 171. In No. 171 Guercino juxtaposes the natural forms of the dark tree and boulders in the foreground with the open road in sunlight at the side and the noble architecture of the church behind.

172 Landscape with a Man on Horseback and Boats on a River

Pen and brown ink and some touches of brown wash. 330 × 407mm.

Nottingham Castle, City Museum and Art Gallery, inv. no. 91.144.

Provenance: Lady Galway (L *Suppl*, 1969c bis).

Literature: B, 1985, no. 4.

No. 172 includes most of the different ingredients from which Guercino's landscape drawings are typically composed. The eye happily wanders from detail to detail, as absorbed by the scene as the figure of a man, with his back to the spectator, who leans against the wall in the bottom left corner gazing into the distance. Besides the varied natural features of the river, the mountainous background and the plain leading up the hill on the right, there is the miscellany of buildings, including the artist's favourite round tower, and the rich array of human activity. This last ranges from the figure at the window top left to the man hurrying on horseback with his companion bottom right, and from the men in the boats on the river in the centre to the soldiers standing on the opposite bank in front of the tower.

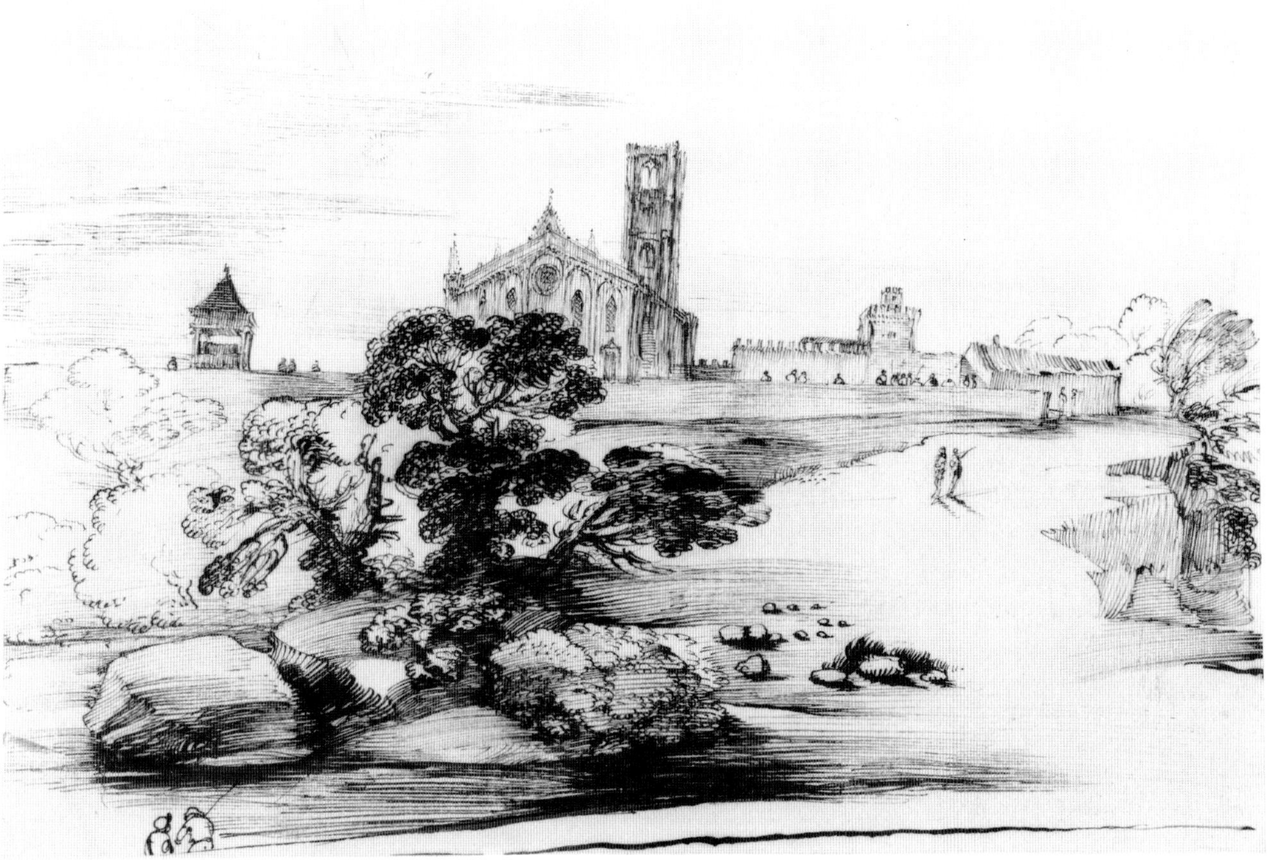

171

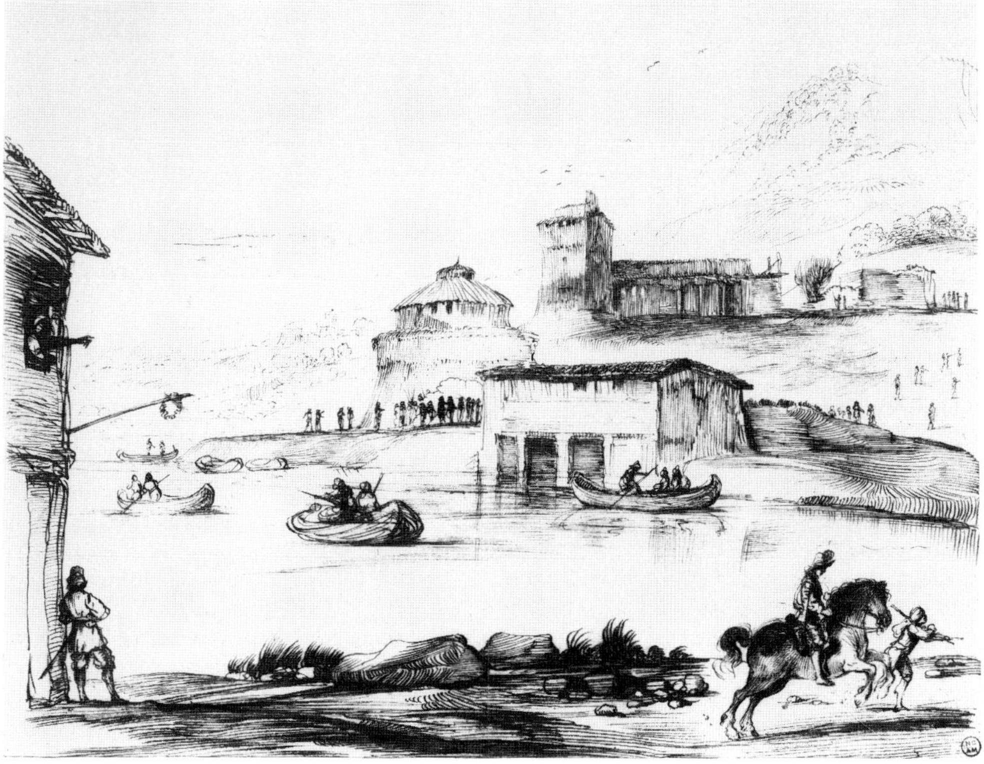

172

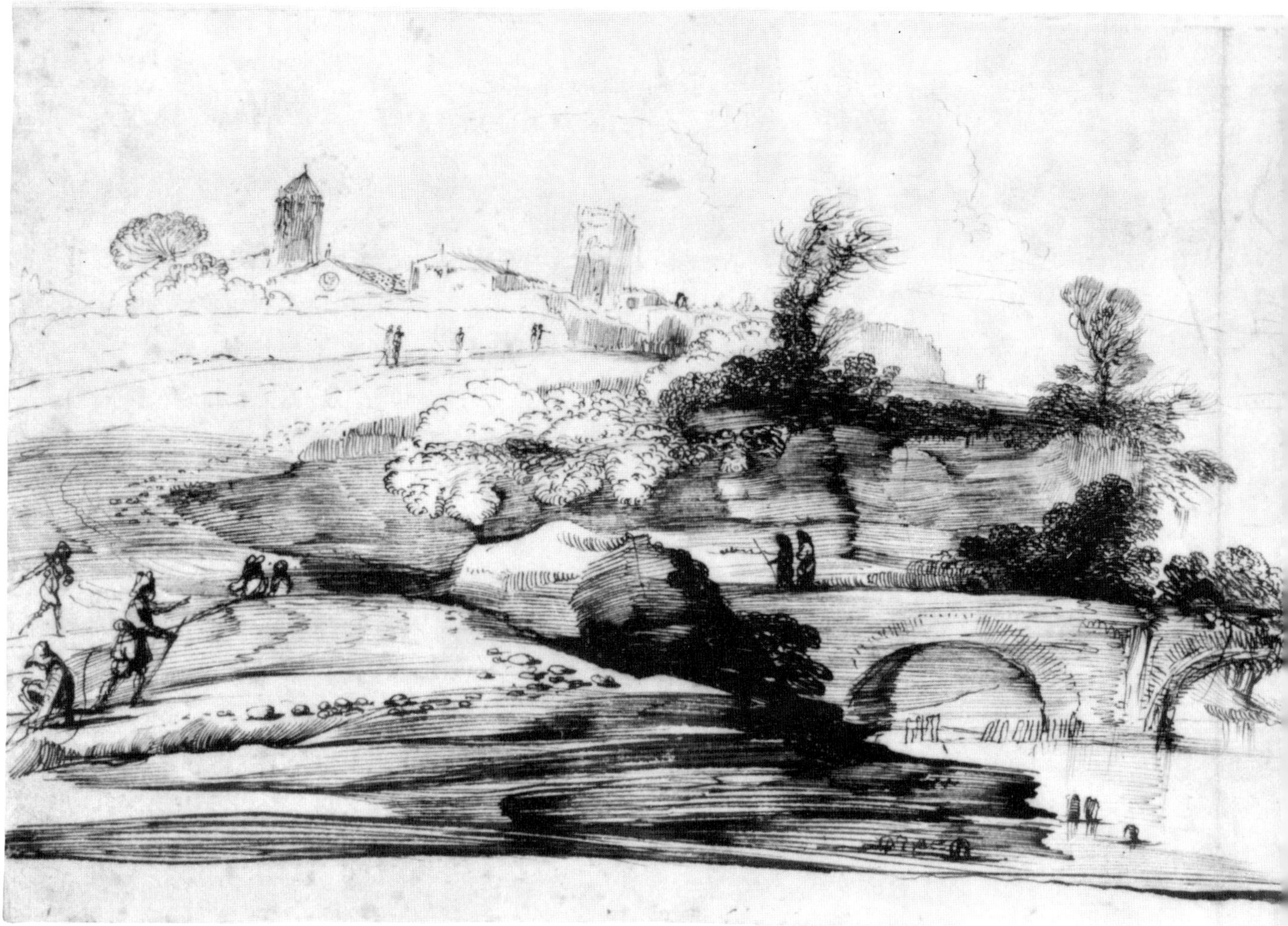

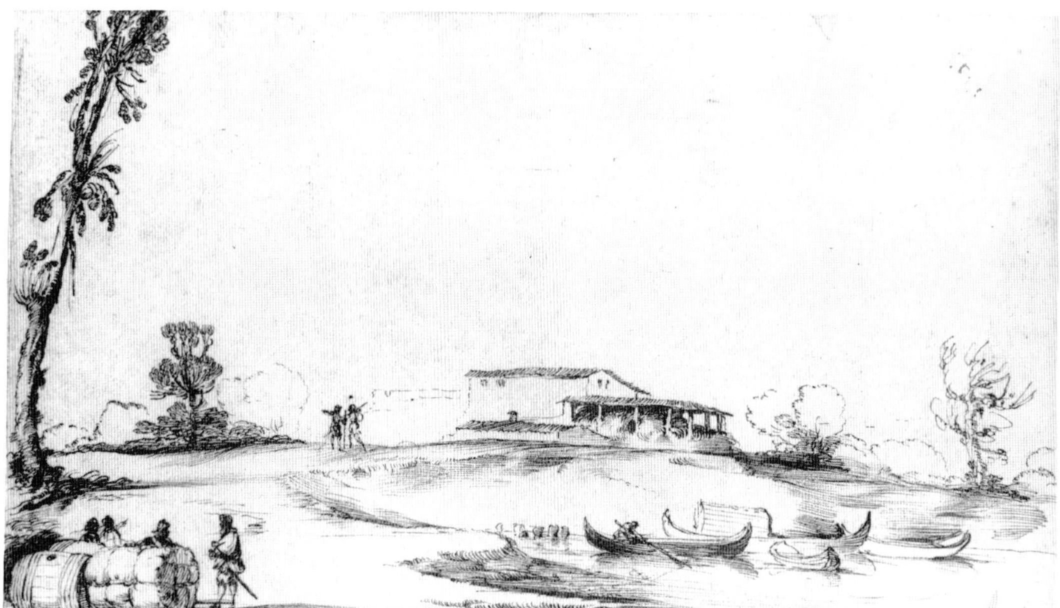

173

198

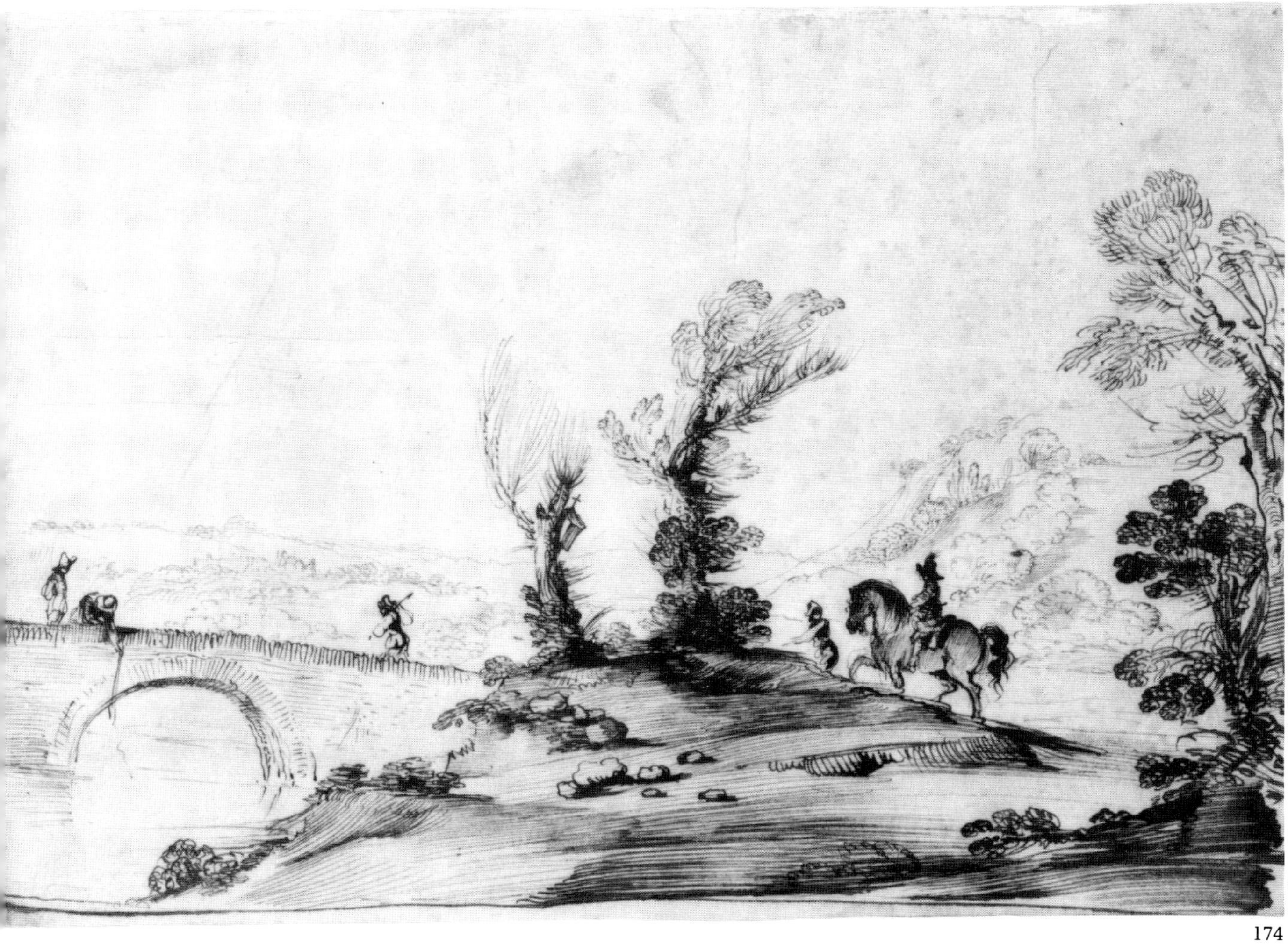

174

173 Landscape with Boats on a River and Merchandise on the Shore

Pen and brown ink. 198 × 344mm.

Holkham Hall, Popham & Lloyd, 148.

Provenance: 1st Earl of Leicester; thence by descent.

Literature: Whitfield, 1977, no. 48; B, 1985, no. 23; Popham & Lloyd, 1986, no. 148.

The flat terrain of the landscape is reminiscent of that surrounding Guercino's native town of Cento. Bagni (1985) has suggested that the distant building is the furnace or kiln that still exists today on the banks of the River Reno, just outside Cento, though it seems equally possible that it may be a barn attached to a farmhouse and containing straw. Guercino frequently introduced into his landscape drawings a narrative element, such as the figures in conversation beside the merchandise in the left foreground.

App. no. 100 is a copy of No. 173.

174 Landscape with a three-arched Bridge over a River

Pen and brown ink. 197 × 598mm.

Windsor Castle, Royal Library, inv. no. 2717.

Provenance: Casa Gennari; King George III.

Literature: B, 1985, no. 3; M & T, 1989, no. 240.

The unusually long format of this sheet is a rarity among Guercino's landscape compositions. In setting himself the difficult task of filling the space, the artist has responded with characteristic ingenuity: the orchestration of the scene depends for its coherence on the bridge that runs parallel to the composition's plane and links together the two sides divided by the river at the centre. In scanning the whole, the eye inevitably fixes on the figures scattered about the landscape, variously engaged in different tasks.

It seems doubtful that there was any ulterior purpose for the drawing, other than as an exercise in its own right undertaken for the artist's own amusement. This conclusion seems borne out by its remarkably fine condition, a result of its preservation first in the albums of the artist's drawings

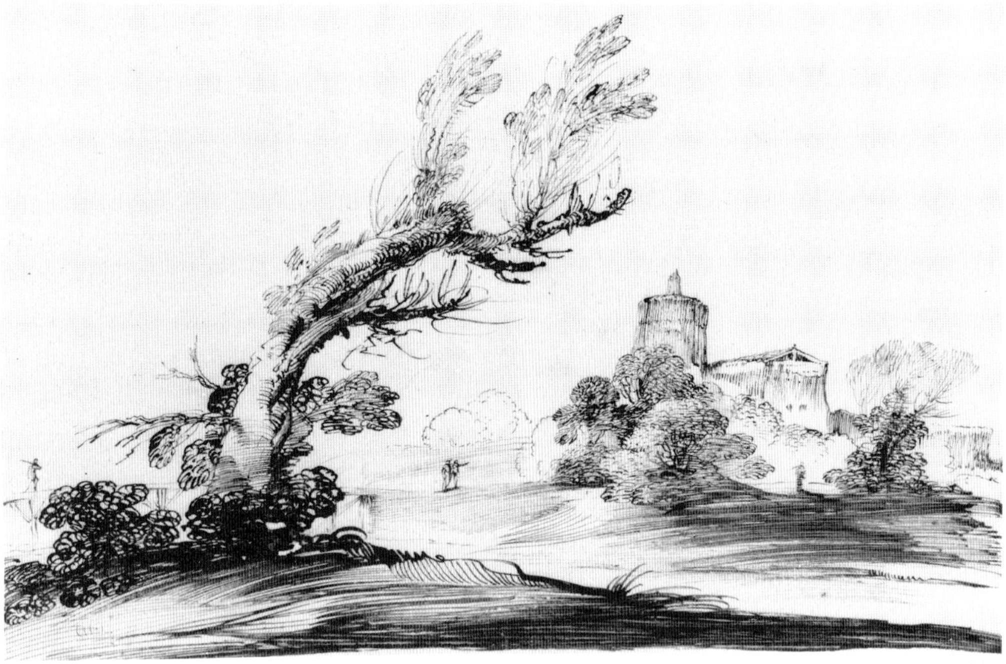

175

in the Casa Gennari and afterwards in those of the Royal Library, Windsor Castle (it was eventually mounted early in this century). Had the drawing once served as an over-door or as the decoration over some piece of furniture, as its unusual shape might suggest, its condition would not be as impressive as it is today.

175 Landscape with a windswept Tree and Buildings in the Distance

Pen and brown ink. 161 × 252mm.

Windsor Castle, Royal Library, inv. no. 2767.

Provenance: Casa Gennari; King George III.

Literature: M & T, 1989, no. 254.

No. 175 well demonstrates the artist's favourite, but contrasting methods of drawing ground and foliage in his landscape drawings. The typically drawn bank is made up of heavy dark lines, which are closely hatched and parallel to each other, while the foliage of the trees is represented by his universal shorthand of tightly drawn circular scribbles.

176 Landscape with a Tree and a round Tower

Pen and brown ink. 230 × 392mm.

Windsor Castle, Royal Library, inv. no. 2769.

Provenance: Casa Gennari; King George III.

Literature: Thiem, 1982, no. 24; M & T, 1989, no. 253.

A fine example of Guercino's landscape drawing.

177 Landscape with a River and a Church with a tall Spire

Pen and brown ink, and some occasional touches of the brush. 239 × 418mm.

Windsor Castle, Royal Library, inv. no. 2768.

Provenance: Casa Gennari; King George III.

Literature: Popham, 1938b, no. 453; M, *Disegni*, 1969, no. 203; M & T, 1989, no. 255.

Guercino conveyed great depth in his landscapes with relatively few marks, by means of a subtle gradation of tone. In the present example the composition is anchored by the carefully defined tree in the right foreground, drawn with the nib heavily laden with ink. The artist's touch becomes progressively lighter with each successive plane, culminating in the furthest horizon where the discontinuous outline of the mountains is almost invisible.

There are always interesting details to be noted in Guercino's landscapes, in this case, for example, the section of bridge under construction or in repair, supported by wooden scaffolding.

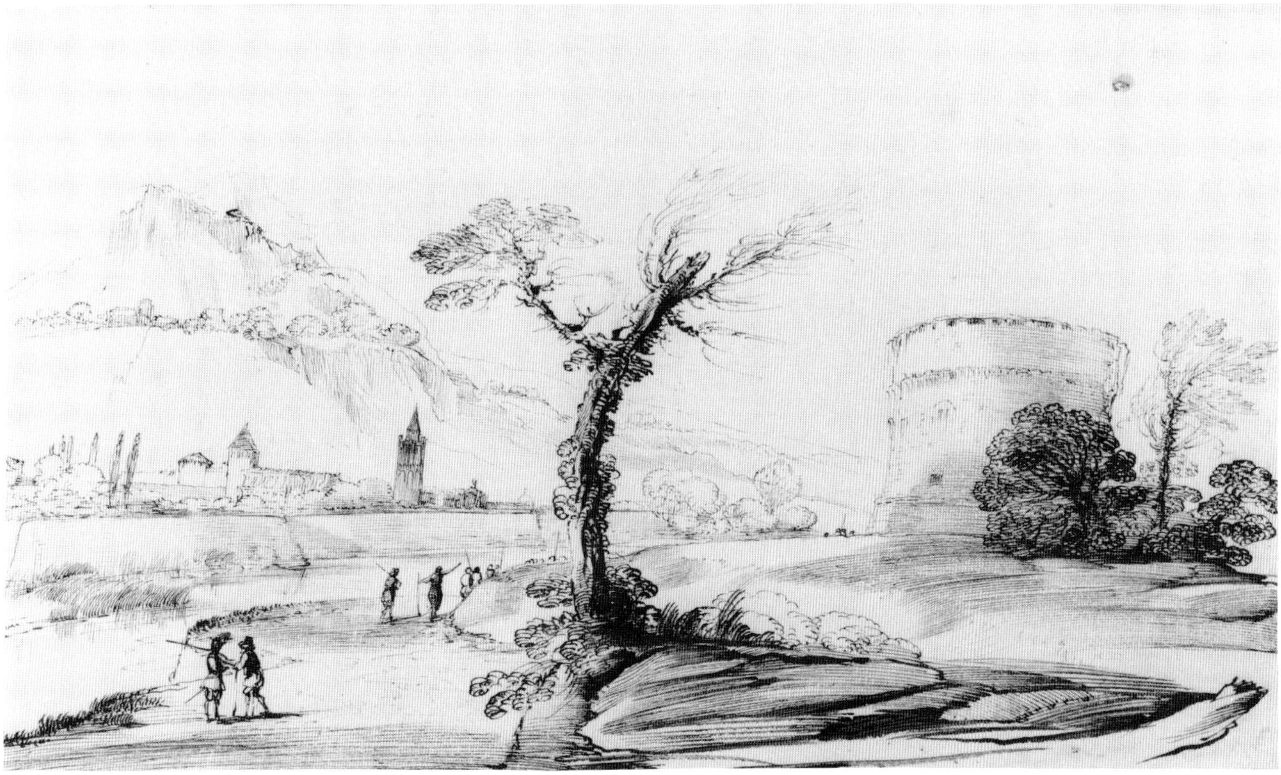

176

177

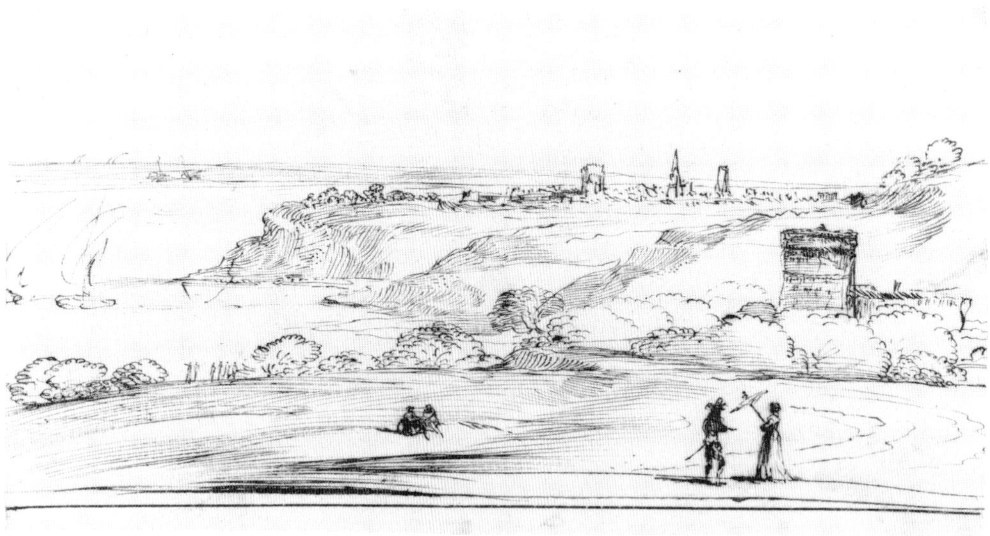

178

178 Coastal Landscape

Pen and brown ink. 148 × 281mm.

Windsor Castle, Royal Library, inv. no. 2723.

Provenance: Casa Gennari; King George III.

Literature: Mahon, 1951, p. 56, n. 2; Bottari, 1966, pl. L; M, *Disegni*, 1969, no. 201; M & T, 1989, no. 238.

Guercino frequently included stretches of water in his landscapes, but these are usually rivers or lakes, rather than the sea as in this example. This is probably a reflection of his native surroundings in land-locked Emilia.

The drawing, which must have been rapidly executed, represents a break with the artist's more precise style. The loose handling of the town in the distance, composed of little more than a series of dots and dashes, effectively evokes the hazy atmosphere of a day apparently hot enough to warrant a parasol.

179 Landscape with Cliffs rising above the Sea and a Fortress on the Hilltop to the right

(*see colour pl. 23*)

Pen and brown ink. 309 × 443mm.

Mahon Collection, on loan to the Ashmolean Museum, Oxford, M & E, 43.

Provenance: Anton Schmid (L *Suppl*, 2330b); P. & D. Colnaghi; from whom purchased by Sir Denis Mahon in 1955.

Literature: M, 1967, no. 46; M, *Disegni*, 1969, no. 205; Tan Bunzl, 1972, no. 70; M & E, 1986, no. 43.

Mahon (1967) has suggested that this, along with several other landscape drawings made in the same rather precise style, may have been influenced by the landscape drawings of Northern artists, of which Guercino may have had a collection. The drawing is indeed wonderfully controlled, with vertical, horizontal and oblique hatching juxtaposed to create a variety of different textures.

180 *verso*

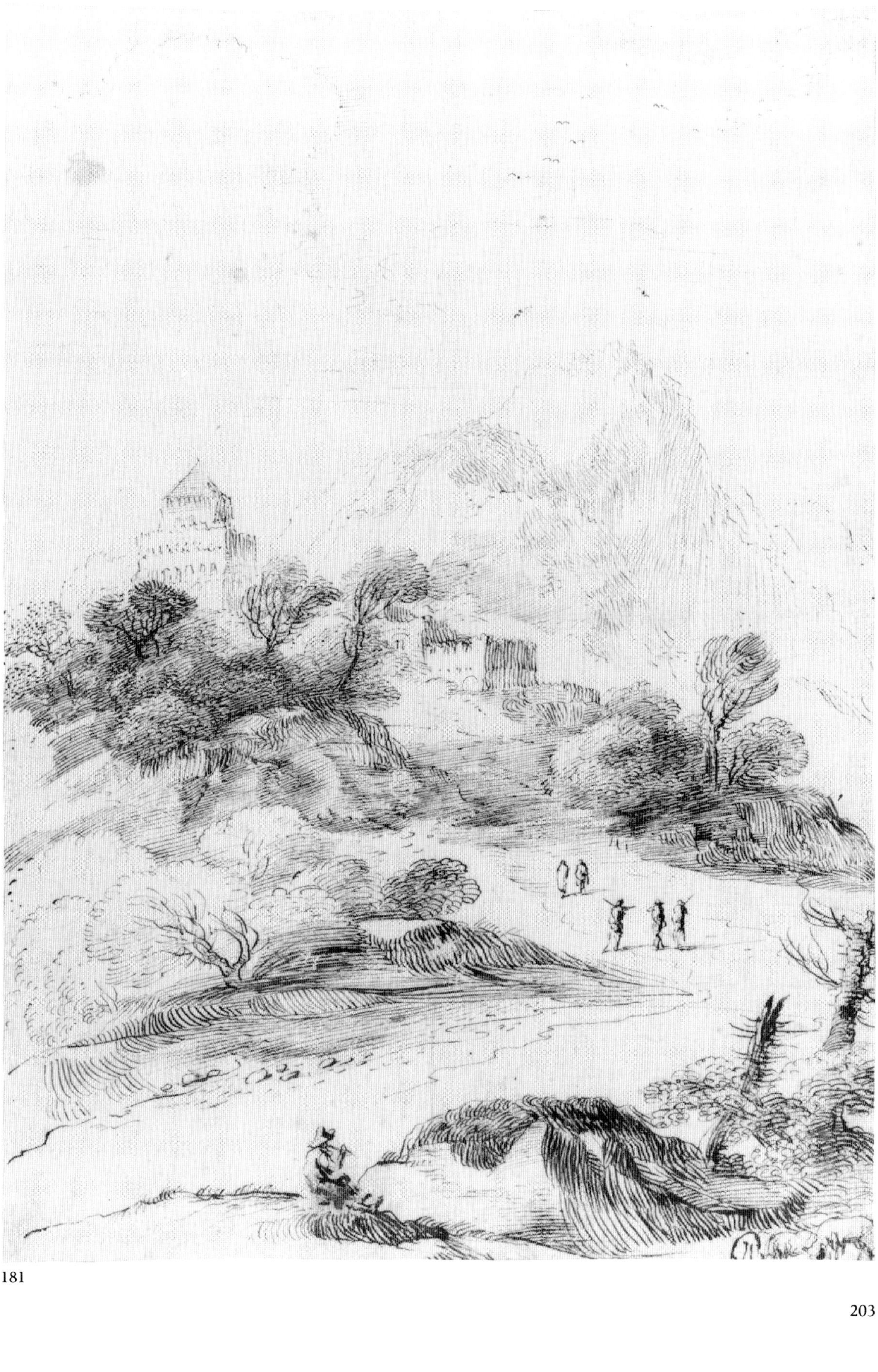

181

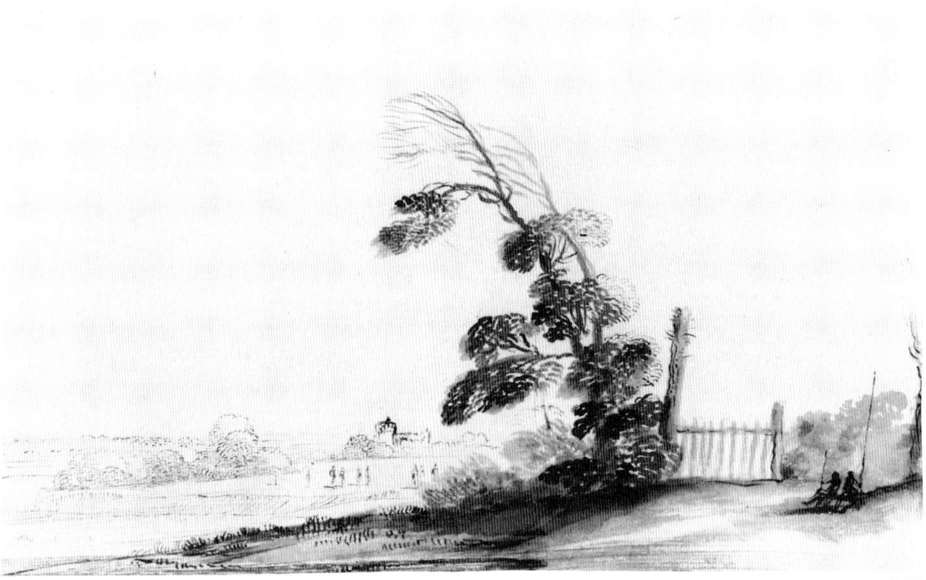

182

180 Landscape with a winding Road leading up to the Gate of a Town

(*see colour pl. 24*)

Pen and brown ink. 286 × 212mm.

Windsor Castle, Royal Library, inv. no. 2762.

Provenance: Casa Gennari; King George III.

Literature: M, *Disegni*, 1969, no. 204; Roberts, 1986, p. 123; M & T, 1989, no. 247.

Inscribed on the *recto* in the top right corner of the sheet in ink (cut by the top edge): possibly *12* (or *72*). Inscribed on the *verso* at the top of the sheet in pen: *1635*; and in the centre: *Sono in tutte Carte numero 32 / che fanno 32 disegni / Opera del Sig:r Gio: Francesco Barbieri / da Cento* (discussed by M & T, 1989).

If the inscribed date on this sheet is correct, it provides a rare touchstone for Guercino's work in this genre, which is otherwise very hard to date. Like No. 181 and one other landscape drawing in the Royal Library, Windsor Castle (M & T, 1989, no. 248), No. 180 is unusual in its upright format; this Guercino exploited to good effect (particularly in the two drawings exhibited here), showing a path winding up a hill. The extraordinarily dynamic quality of the present landscape derives principally from Guercino's decision to eschew the precision of straight lines in favour of short, flicking penstrokes, constantly varied in their thickness and direction.

181 Mountainous Landscape with five Figures on a winding Road

Pen and brown ink. 286 × 205mm.

Windsor Castle, Royal Library, inv. no. 2761.

Provenance: Casa Gennari; King George III.

Literature: Thiem, 1982, no. 23, repr.; M & T, 1989, no. 249.

Probably executed at about the same time as No. 180, in the mid-1630s. The vertical format is used to even greater effect here to encompass the mountains looming in the background. Guercino often placed spectator figures in the foreground of his landscapes, and in this instance a pastoral note is introduced by the seated shepherd piping while his sheep graze in the bottom right corner.

182 Landscape with a Tree rising in the centre Foreground

Pen and point of the brush and wash. 159 × 262mm.

Windsor Castle, Royal Library, inv. no. 2765.

Provenance: Casa Gennari; King George III.

Literature: M & T, 1989, no. 263.

Unlike the vast majority of Guercino's landscape drawings, which are executed exclusively in pen and ink, No. 182 has extensive brushwork in the foreground.

Two landscape drawings executed almost entirely in brush and wash, with only occasional touches of pen and brown ink, were formerly in the collection of the English collector, Archibald Russell (for whom see Introduction, p. 27). One, now in the Pierpont Morgan Library, New York, was formerly in the collection of Janos Scholz (Stampfle & Bean, 1967, no. 50); the other was formerly in the collection of John Nicholas Brown, Providence, Rhode Island (B, 1985, no. 34).

III Genre, Capricci and Caricatures (Nos. 183–216)

The drawings in this section appear to have been made for the amusement of the artist and his friends, almost as a tribute to his own ingenuity and wit. Like the landscapes, they were not preparatory to any painted work. With extraordinary economy of means Guercino recorded his acute observations of the people and events of everyday provincial life, filtered by a sharp perception of the comic. His biographer, Malvasia, chronicled the artist's compassionate nature, his empathy for the poor and needy, his humility and his curiosity in his surroundings, and many of these qualities emerge in these informal sketches. Guercino tended to acknowledge the pathos of his subjects, while at the same time highlighting the comic or incongruous aspects of their situation. Often one enjoys a sense of collusion with the artist, who frequently presents his subjects with their backs turned so that the spectator can relish, unchallenged, some joke at their expense (see Nos. 186–91, 197, 203, 215–16). Guercino's sensitive appraisal of the most mundane human situations together with a distinct penchant for the absurd gives his work a surprisingly timeless flavour.

The genre drawings in Section 1 (Nos. 183–98) show scenes from daily life and concentrate, with few exceptions, upon the local *contadini*, for whom Guercino clearly felt considerable affection. His interest in the events and activities of the rural community of his home town was noted by another of his biographers, Giovanni Battista Passeri, who reported having seen 'alcuni disegni di sua [mano], balli, feste, e sponsalizi costumati nella sua Rocca di Cento, imitando l'idee, il portamento e le sembianze di quei rusticani, e di quelle foretane del Paese, li quali, per verità, erano curiosi, e bene imitati' (Hess, 1934, p. 347). Two fine sheets depicting an open-air theatre and an entertainment in a tavern (Nos. 185–6) admirably bring to life the kind of public spectacle that must have taken place in a small town like Cento, the social mix among the audience affording Guercino ample material for comic contrasts and amusing details. The genre drawings, focusing as they do on everyday subjects, are not exclusively humorous in intent. Some simply capture an intimate moment and were almost certainly drawn from the life, such as No. 183, showing two women conversing, and No. 192, representing a girl looking at a landscape drawing. In other domestic scenes gentle fun is poked at the protagonists for their actions (No. 184) or poses (Nos. 190–91), while elsewhere again it is the subject's appearance that is the butt of the artist's humour (Nos. 195–6). Guercino's drawing in this vein was clearly influenced by the example of Annibale Carracci, who was one of the first Italian artists to regard mundane, low-life scenes and characters as a legitimate subject for art.

Section 2 (Nos. 199–205) contains those drawings sometimes classed as *capricci*, that is fantastical subjects in which the humour and exaggeration already evident in the genre drawings is stretched beyond all plausibility, further demonstrating Guercino's considerable powers of invention. Thus we witness curious hybrid monsters (No. 199); characters engaged in mysterious antics and rituals (Nos. 200–201); nymphs surprised by a satyr (No. 203); and a witch (No. 204). One of the most horrifying of the *capricci* (No. 205) represents the allegorical figure of Death, in the form of a skeleton, visiting a family of *contadini*, an image that almost certainly reflects the outbreak of a virulent plague in Cento in 1630–31.

Section 3 (Nos. 206–16) contains a group of Guercino's caricature drawings, a genre in which he was prolific. No social rank escaped the satirising powers of his pen, as the following selection – which includes peasants, merchants, gentlefolk and the clergy – well demonstrates. Only one of these caricatures, that of Guercino's friend Fra Bonaventura Bisi (No. 206), is of a named contemporary. It is likely that other drawings of this sort also represent particular individuals, yet despite their anonymity today, one can still relish the exaggerated portrayal of their features and attitudes. Guercino probably made whole series of caricatures, of the type afterwards collected in albums such as that in the Art Museum, Princeton University (inv. no. 48–1290–1319; Gibbons, 1977, nos. 276–305). One favourite formula was the profile view, most often used to emphasise some physical defect such as a jutting jaw (Nos. 208, 212) or drooping lips (No. 239), his choice of physiognomic types fitting into a tradition going back to Leonardo da Vinci (1452–1519), whose treatise Guercino proudly possessed. Sometimes he caricatured whole groups, often with brutal realism, such as the unruly mob of peasants in No. 215; elsewhere, the arrangement of a given group may be highly contrived, as in the descending scale of urchins in No. 216.

Guercino displayed great ingenuity not only in his choice (and consequent dissection) of subject, for the drawings are also virtuoso pieces from a stylistic point of view. At times he would evoke his subjects with only a few clever marks (Nos. 211, 214), while others were brought to life by a dense web of pen strokes (No. 210) or subtle shades of wash (No. 216). The caricatures were clearly intended as showpieces and are admirable demonstrations of the artist's wit and versatility. However, it is important not to lose sight of their relevance for Guercino's work as a painter, representing as they do a further insight into his interest in human expression and physiognomy.

1 Genre (Nos. 183–98)

183 Two Women conversing

(*see colour pl. 25*)

Red chalk, partly stumped, on discoloured paper. 279 × 384mm.

Oxford, Ashmolean Museum, KTP 864.

Provenance: Philippe Mercier (inscribed on the *verso*, in Richardson's hand: *Given me by Mr. Mercier, 1724*); Jonathan Richardson Sr (L 2184; sale, Cock, London, 5 February 1746 (old style), lot 52, *£4–5–6*); Blomberg; William A. Worsley; sale, Sotheby's, London, 20 July 1932, lot 82 (as Mercier), bt with 9 others; H. S. Reitlinger (L *Suppl*, 2274a; sale, Sotheby's, London, 27 January 1954, lot 172 (as Mercier), bt *Colnaghi, £10–0–0*).

Literature: Parker, 1956, no. 864; M, *Disegni*, 1969, no. 223; Sutton & Garlick, 1969–70, no. 52; Macandrew, 1980, p. 299; M & E, 1986, no. XXI.

An extremely unusual example of a study from the life in red chalk that is neither preparatory to a painting nor laced with the humour characteristic of the majority of Guercino's genre drawings. Although doubts have in the past been raised as to Guercino's authorship, the drawing is undoubtedly an early work by him, sharing many of the distinguishing features of his academic studies from the nude in oiled charcoal, such as No. 16. This is particularly true of the exaggerated chiaroscuro and the blocked-out background; moreover, the somewhat knobbly left hand of the woman on the right in the present drawing is very similar in treatment to the right hand of the youth in No. 16. Like the 'academy' studies, No. 183 must have been executed before Guercino left for Rome in 1621.

184 Woman pulling out a young Girl's Tooth

Pen and brown ink. 238 × 277mm.

Oxford, Ashmolean Museum, KTP 868.

Provenance: Uvedale Price (sale, Sotheby's, London, 3 May 1854, lot 93, bt *Rodd, £0–18–0*); Christie-Miller.

Literature: Parker, 1956, no. 868; Bottari, 1966, pl. LXI; Macandrew, 1980, p. 299; M & E, 1986, no. XVI.

The scene has been interpreted as a domestic quarrel, but the thread running from the end of the distaff held by the woman on the left into the other's mouth seems to indicate that the latter's tooth is being extracted. The woman holds her young companion's head steady with one hand as she prepares to tug with the other. Her 'patient' still grasps an implement for hooking and unhooking the pan over the fire and in her distress pulls on the other woman's hair or headdress.

No. 184 surely dates from an early moment in Guercino's career, either just prior to his departure for Rome in 1621 or at the beginning of his stay there. The technique of the sketch, in which form is suggested by means of contoured parallel hatchings (see particularly the young girl's raised right hand), is reminiscent of Guercino's early drawings for prints, such as No. 31 engraved by Pasqualini in 1621. The technique may also be compared with that of No. 36.

185 Tavern Scene

(*see colour pl. 25*)

Pen and brown ink and brown wash. 210 × 395mm.

Oxford, Ashmolean Museum, KTP 861.

Provenance: Neyman; sale, Paris, June 1776, lot 330 (not in Lugt's *Catalogue des ventes*); purchased 1948.

Literature: Parker & Byam Shaw, 1953, no. 134; Parker, 1956, no. 861; Bottari, 1966, pl. XXXIII; M, *Disegni*, 1969, no. 214; Macandrew, 1980, pp. 298–9; B, 1984, pl. 23; M & E, 1986, no. III.

Inscribed on the rat-catcher's placard: *PER FAR MORIR I RATTI*; and beneath the cutpurse at the left edge in the centre: *[G]UARDA IL LADRO CH AROBA LA SCHARSELA*.

Etched in the same sense by Baron D. Vivant-Denon (the etching is signed in reverse: *Denon Scul. 1788*). An impression is in the British Museum (U.4–156). A copy of No. 185, bearing the mark of the Habich collection, formerly belonged to Mr H. M. Calmann and was given by him to Prisco Bagni of Milan.

Nos. 185–6 both represent exceptionally animated scenes, packed with amusing details, of local life in a provincial town such as Cento. They were surely made before Guercino departed for Rome in 1621. The type of entertainment in hand is uncertain, but the audience seems to consist of a mixture of gentlefolk, peasants and, in the background left, carnivalesque characters. Apart from the central encounter between a finely dressed man and a woman of more modest rank, the floor is empty and the assembled company themselves become the spectacle. This is also true of No. 186, in which the centre stage is empty but for two rabbits.

186 A theatrical Performance in the open Air

(*see colour pl. 26*)

London, British Museum, inv. no. 1937–10–8–1.

(For other details, see App. no. 62.)

This is a typical example of Guercino's studies of genre subjects and is similar in treatment to No. 185. It is amusing to observe the variety of posture and activity of the different members of the audience, seen from behind. The gentlefolk are seated on chairs, their heads ranged in a rhythmical row, behind which a more unruly selection of youths and peasants crane their necks to get a view of the stage. To this end, one figure, to the right of centre, stands half on a bench and half on a box, and another, at the far right, carries a boy on his shoulders. At the very back of the audience, a man in a curious feathered headdress attracts the attention of a dog with a rod and line, distracting two youths from the spectacle. One cannot help wondering at the nature of the play, with its elaborate stagecraft and the pair of rabbits, apparently its principal players.

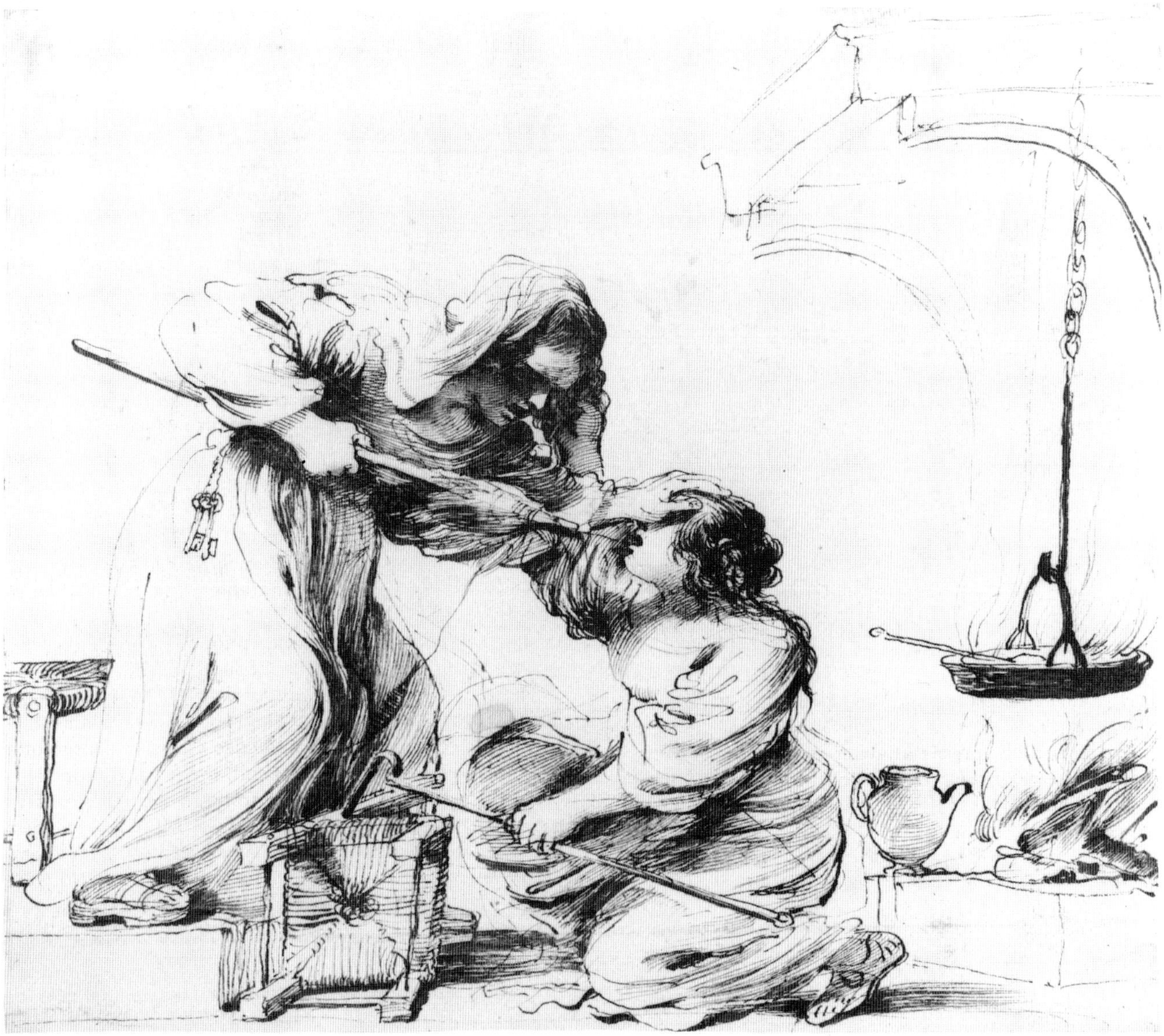

184

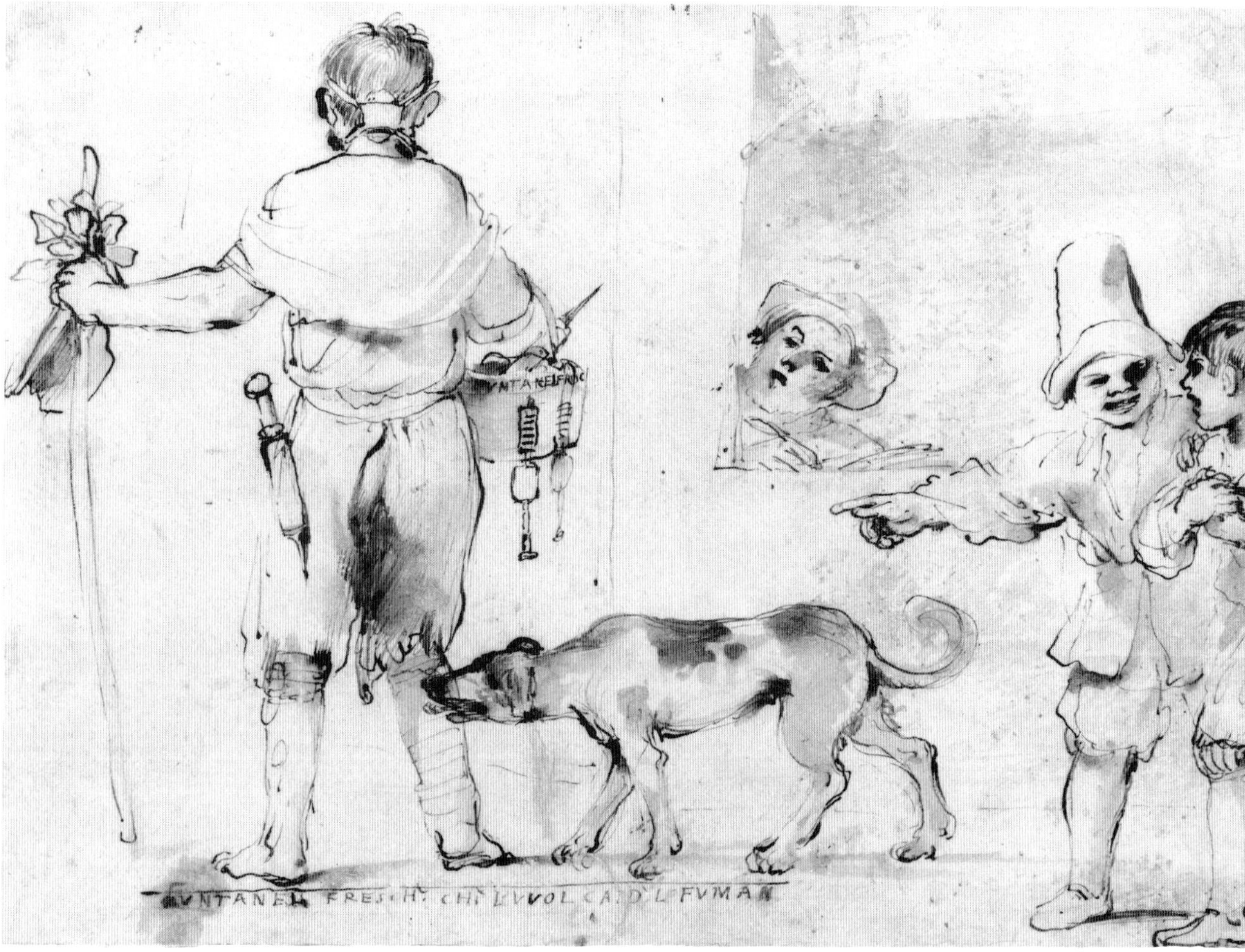

187

187 Street Scene with a Vendor

Pen and blackish-brown ink and grey wash. 207 × 281mm.

Windsor Castle, Royal Library, inv. no. 2474.

Provenance: Casa Gennari; King George III.

Literature: M & T, 1989, no. 278.

Inscribed in blackish-brown ink at the bottom of the sheet, presumably in the artist's hand: *FVNTANEL FRESCH'. CHÌ L' VVOL CA[L]D' L' FVMAN*; and on the basket carried by the vendor: *FVNTANELFRESC*.

The inscription, apparently written in Bolognese dialect, helps to identify the unusual subject. In this dialect *'Funtanèla d[e]la goùla'* or *'fontanella'* means that part of the chicken where the gullet commences, and the two objects hanging from the vendor's basket do appear to be chicken gizzards with windpipes, which the vendor advertises as 'fresh', 'warm' and 'steaming'. In the past, chicken's blood was used as a cauterising agent, and the boy on the right, directed towards the vendor by his companion, clasps his hands together as if one of them had been cut. Presumably also pertaining to the vendor's general services as a quack are the leaves (probably herbs) that he holds with his hat and stick in his left hand and the two clyster pipes that appear respectively in his basket and at his belt.

Although a seller of remedies, the young vendor strikes a notably unhygienic figure. He is barefooted (the two boys on the right are both shod); one leg has open sores while a dog licks the other bandaged one; strings tied round his head hold in place a dressing that protects a wound at the back of his neck; and his trousers hang awkwardly open at the back, in which area the paper has been crudely gouged and then heavily tinted, as if to suggest excrement. The contradiction between his appearance and his mission provokes both the curiosity of the man seated at his work at the window and the amusement of the boy with the hat, about to entrust his companion into the vendor's doubtful care.

On stylistic grounds, the drawing has been dated to 1618–19.

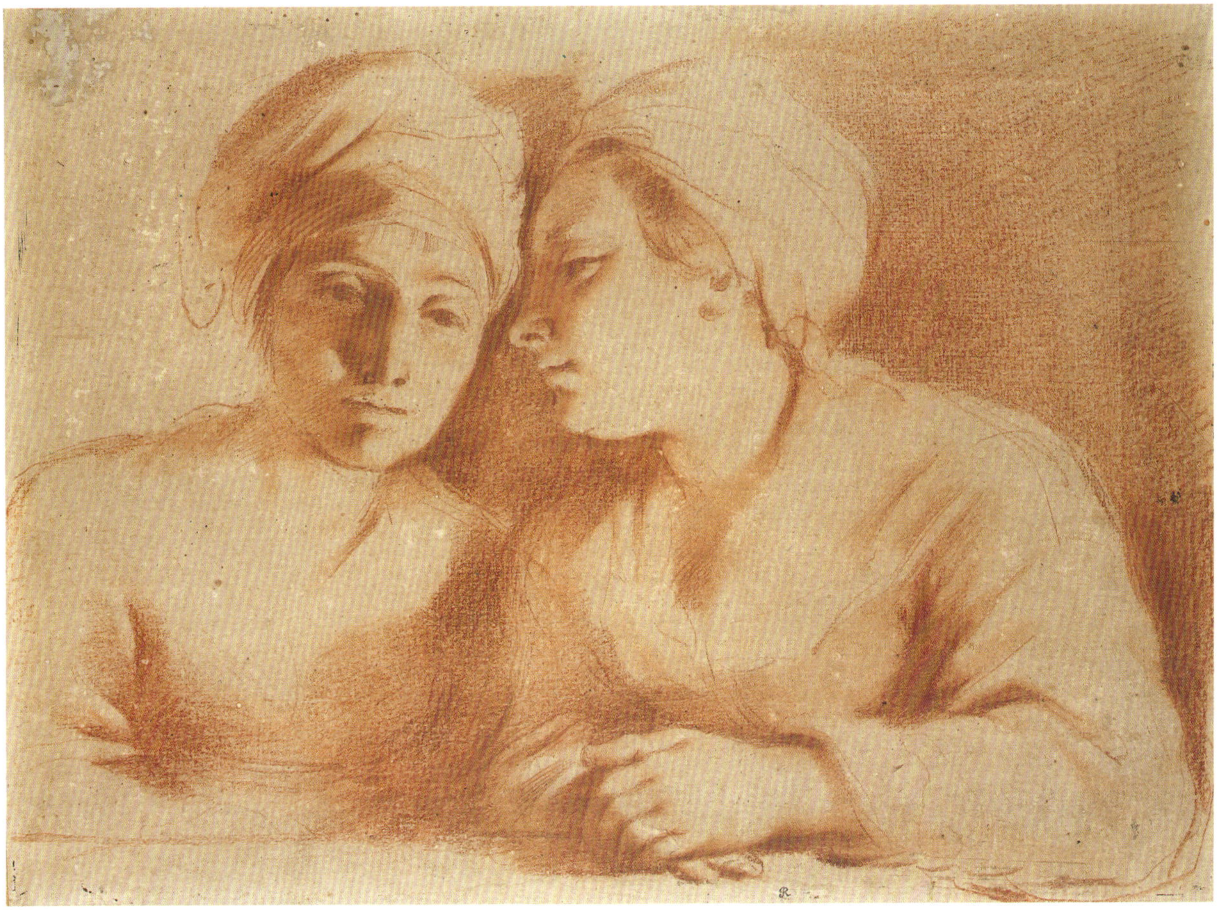

183 *Two Women conversing*. Oxford, Ashmolean Museum

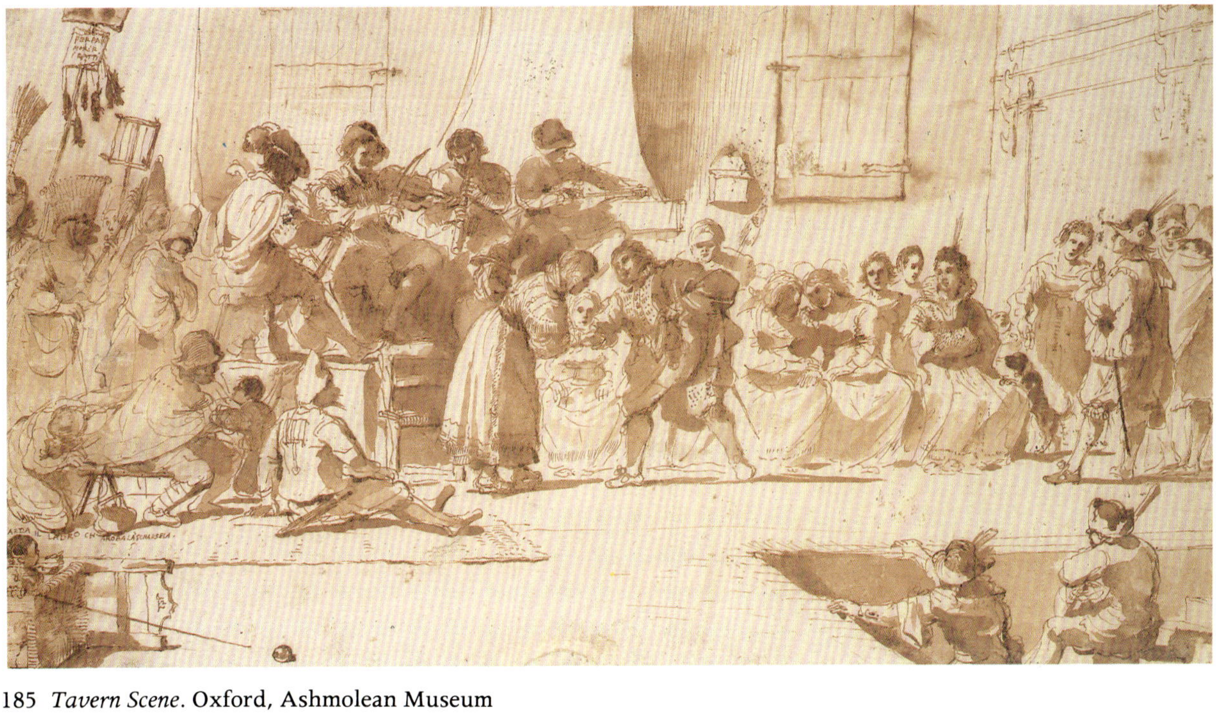

185 *Tavern Scene*. Oxford, Ashmolean Museum

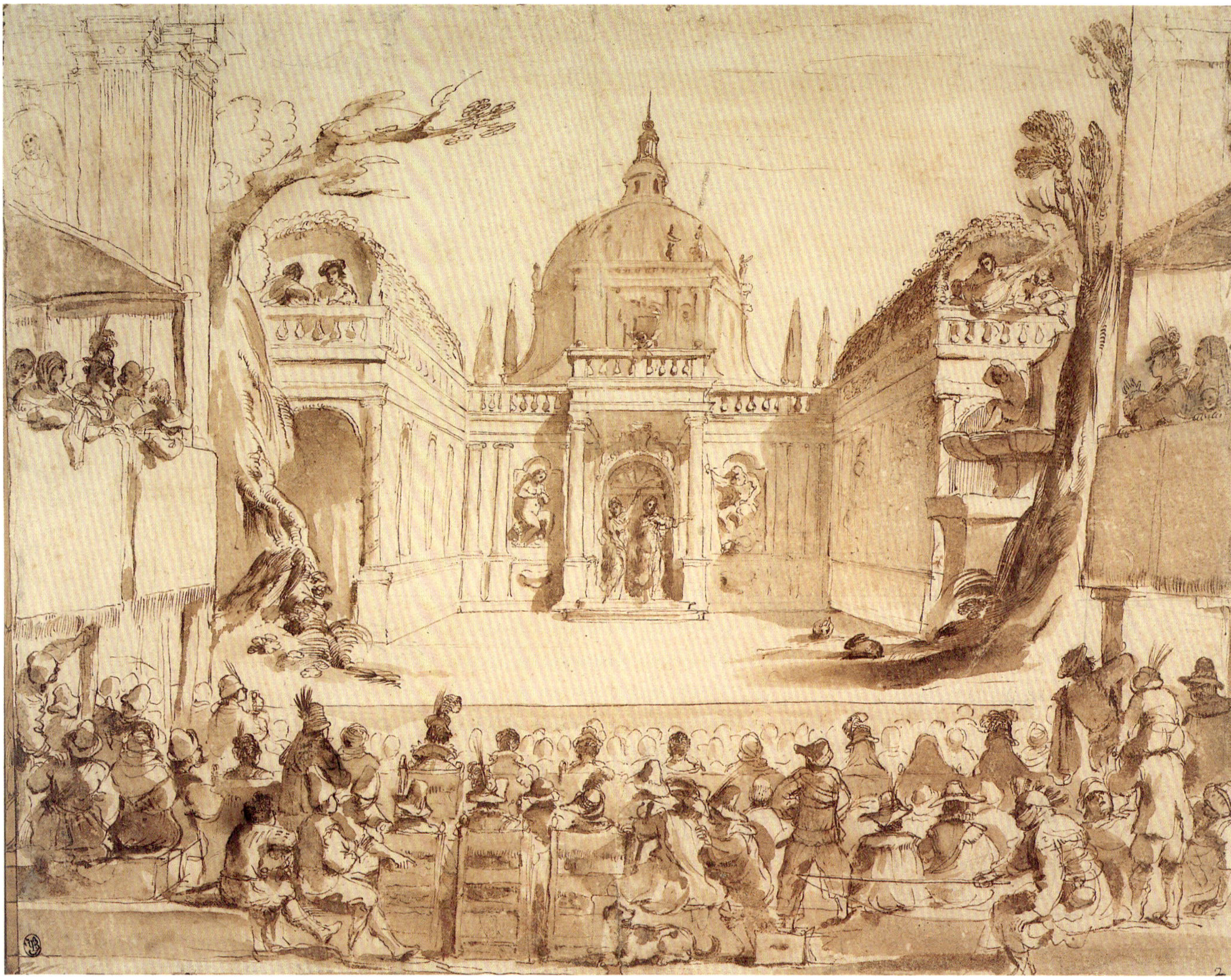

186 *A theatrical Performance in the open Air*. London, British Museum (see also App. no. 62)

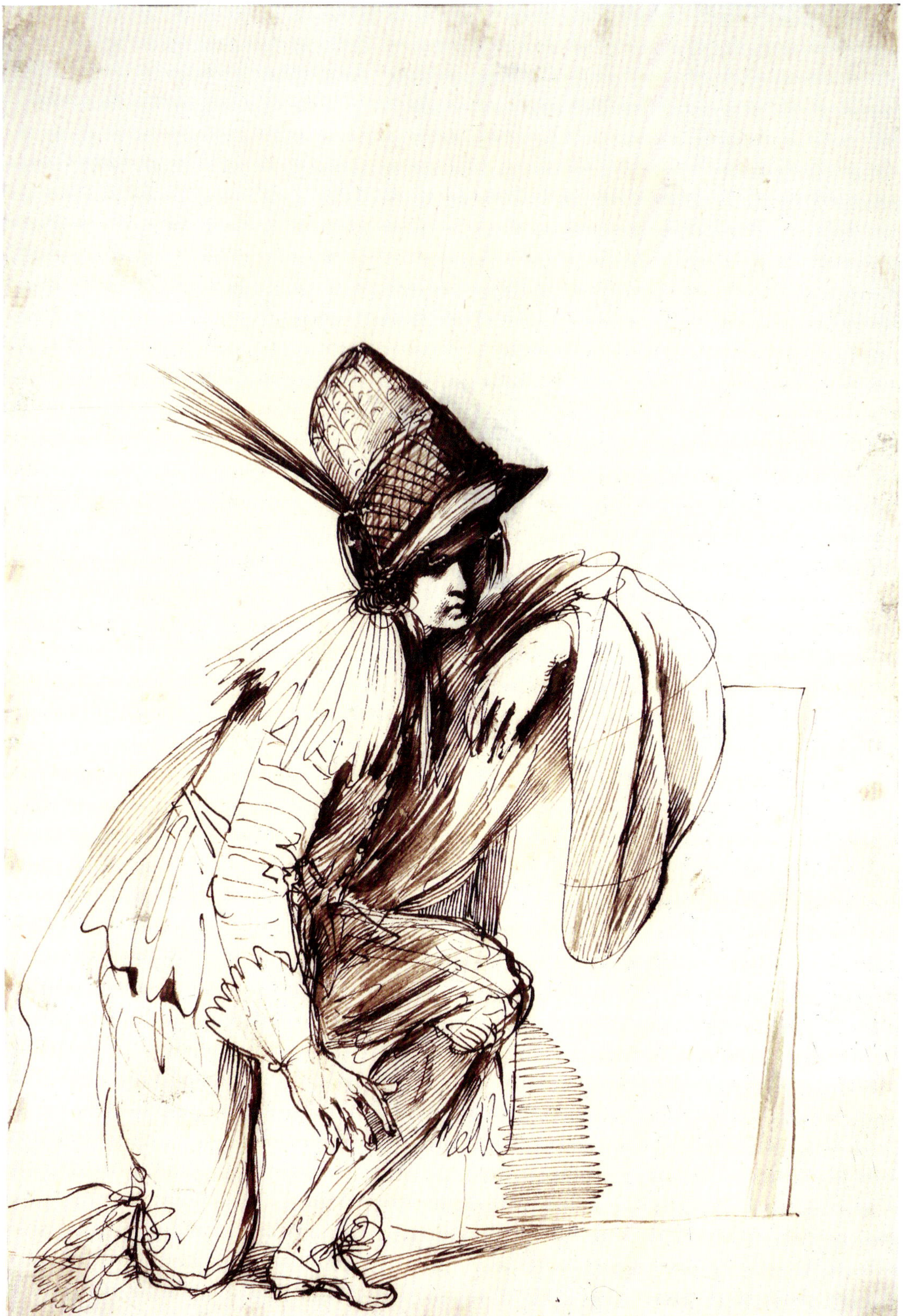

194 *Kneeling Youth wearing a tall Hat with a Feather*. Mahon Collection, on loan to the Ashmolean Museum, Oxford

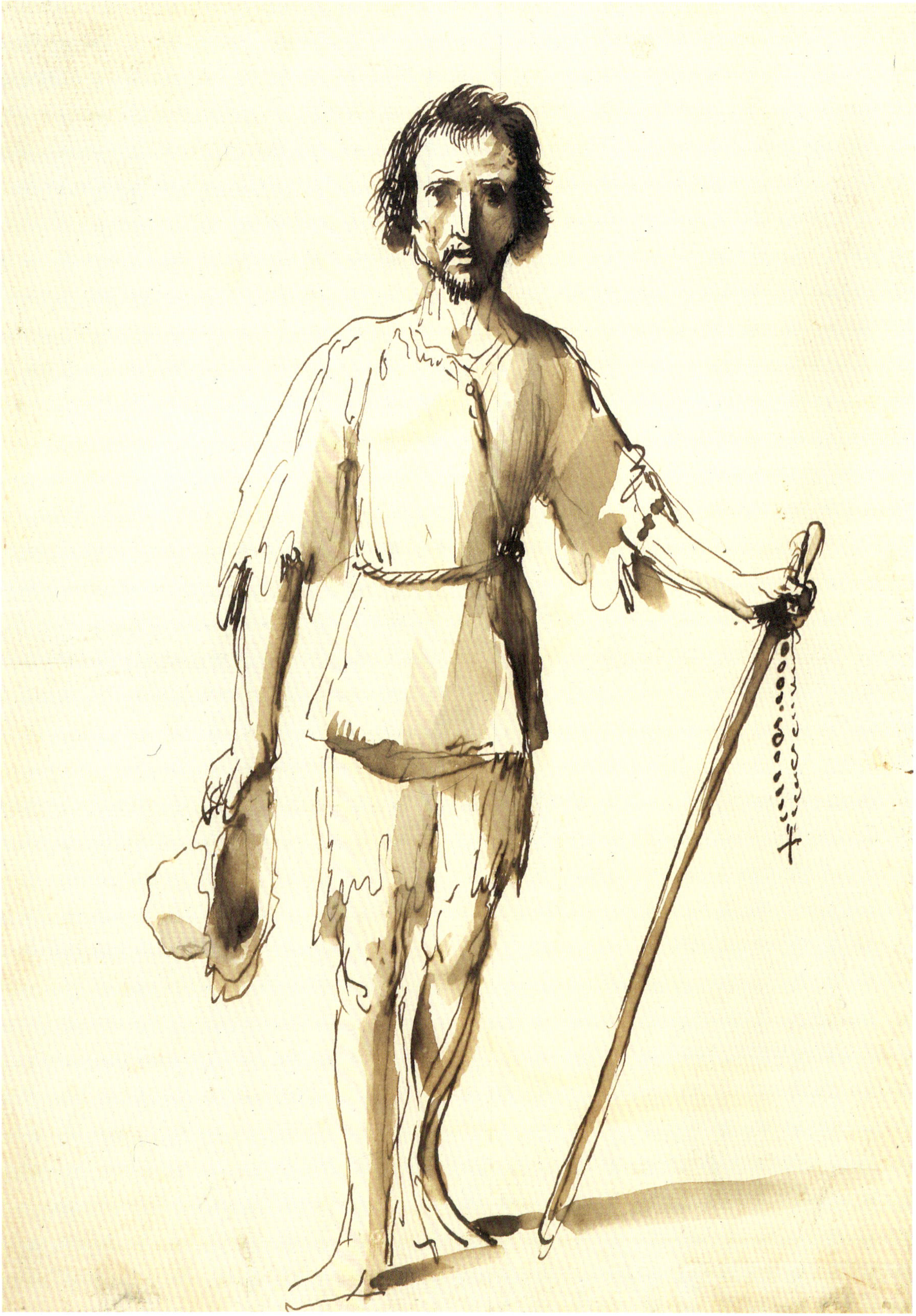

195 *Standing Beggar*. Windsor Castle, Royal Library

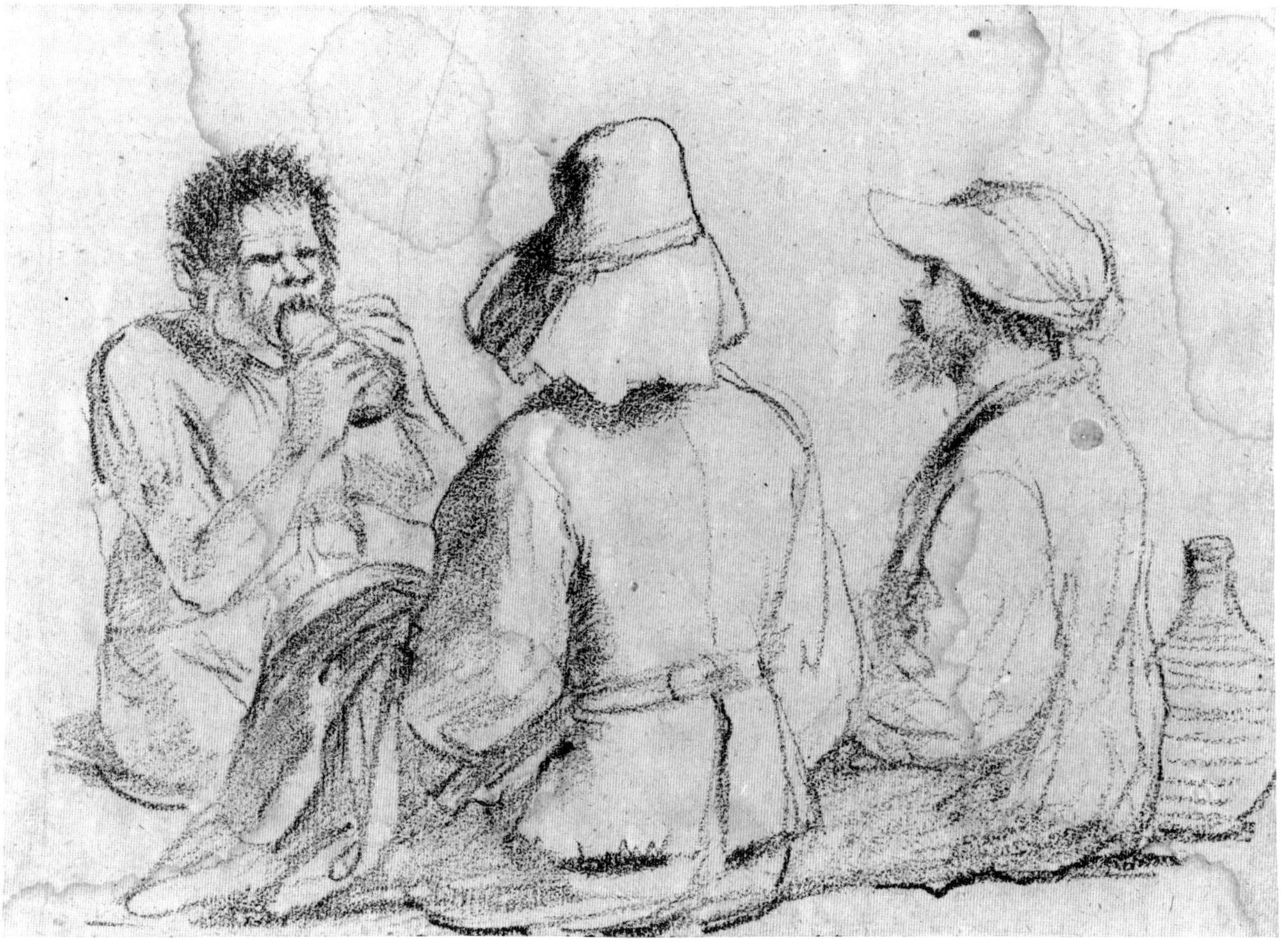

188

188 Three Peasants picnicking

Oiled black chalk or charcoal on tinted paper faded to a buff colour and much stained. 244 × 343mm.

Windsor Castle, Royal Library, inv. no. 2902.

Provenance: Casa Gennari; King George III.

Literature: M, *Disegni*, 1969, no. 231; Roli, 1972, pl. 51; M & T, 1989, no. 277 and p. 110.

From its style, the drawing appears to date from towards the end of Guercino's pre-Roman period, around 1619–20.

The unhesitatingly confident touch of this wonderful drawing suggests that it was made from life, probably out in the open. The latter claim is supported by the impression of bright sunlight striking the hat of the man seated in the middle with his back turned. At first, the subject seems straightforward enough: the artist has happened by chance upon a group of peasants pausing from their labours for rest and refreshment and has drawn them as he saw them, portraying one perhaps a little unflatteringly as he bites at a loaf of bread held in both hands. Roli, however, was inclined to see a further, more 'human' significance in the scene. In his view 'a poor devil with bristly hair and a face like a monkey is fed, given drink and reclothed through the mercy of the two peasants seated at his side'. The interpretation is not implausible: certainly the man on the left seems a little different from his companions, both of whom are more fully clothed and sport hats (though the appearance of the man in the centre with his back turned cannot of course be properly judged). It is also true that the man in the centre holds a garment over his lap, while the man seated on the right next to the flask does not himself take drink.

As the old stains on the sheet bear witness (recently some of these were removed with restoration), the drawing used to hang framed on the upper floor of the Gennari family's country villa, the Casino di Bel Poggio, located outside Bologna in the Comune di S. Silvestro, outside the gate of S. Stefano (B, 1985, p. 17, n. 16). In the inventory of the property of the Gennari family, dated 31 October 1719, in the Archivio Notarile at Bologna (carte del Notaio Camillo Casanova; fascicule H, sheet 28 of the inventory), it is described as follows: 'Nella Quarta Camera, con Finestre a Sera e Tramont.a . . . Un Dissegno di trè Figure di Villani, che mangiano fatto di Carbone, Mano del Guerz.' (for other drawings by Guercino mentioned in this same inventory, see App. no. 5). When listed in the late eighteenth-century

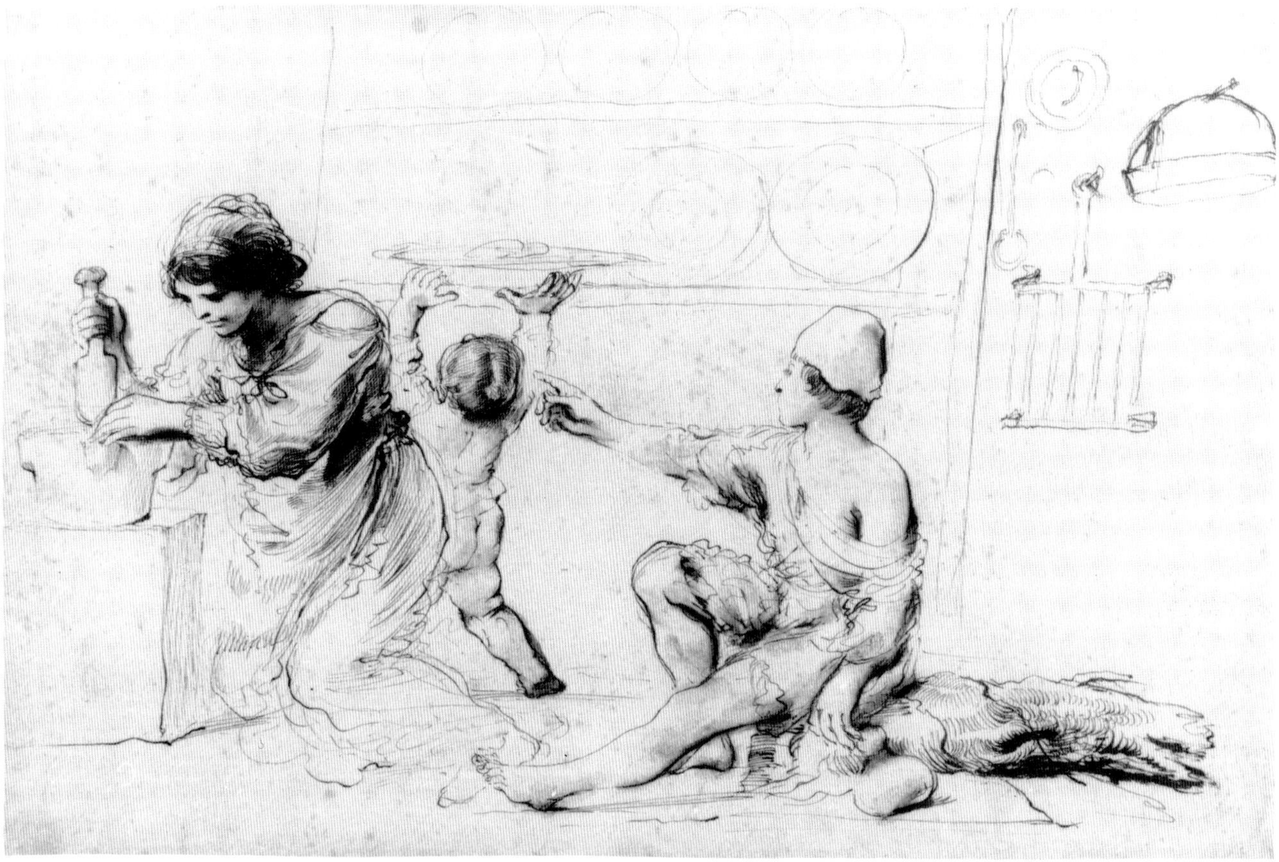

189

inventory of the drawings at Windsor Castle (known as MS. Inventory A), which was compiled during the reign of King George III, it was referred to simply as: 'Three clowns regaling themselves'.

189 Interior of a Kitchen

Pen and brown wash, the wash smudged in parts. 260 × 403mm.

London, Courtauld Institute Galleries, Witt Collection, inv. no. 1347.

Provenance: Casa Gennari; Mr Bouverie; Mr Hervey; the Earls of Gainsborough (sale, Christie's, London, 27 July 1922, lot 81, with others, bt *Meatyard*); Sir Robert Witt.

Literature: M, *Disegni*, 1969, no. 216; Hammer, *et al.*, 1977, no. 46.

Numbered in graphite in the bottom left corner: *3*, or possibly *5* (for a discussion and further instances of sheets numbered in this way, see No. 10).

The drawing may date from the early or mid-1620s. The pen-and-ink drawing of the woman's drapery compares well with that in a composition study in the Royal Library, Windsor Castle, the *Holy Family with Sts John the Baptist and Anne* (No. 31), which was engraved by G. B. Pasqualini in 1621.

As so often with Guercino's drawings of genre subjects, the viewer is left to speculate on what precisely is occurring. While the mother is conscientiously working at her pestle and mortar, behind her back a conspiracy seems to be taking place involving the young rustic seated on a log, apparently directing the proceedings, and the bare-bottomed infant who reaches for the platter of food, which it seems he is about to drop.

190 Baker's Shop

Pen and brown ink. 177 × 265mm.

London, Courtauld Institute Galleries, Witt Collection, inv. no. 1342.

Provenance: Casa Gennari; Mr Bouverie; Mr Hervey; the Earls of Gainsborough (sale, Christie's, London, 27 July 1922, lot 81, with others, bt *Meatyard*); Sir Robert Witt.

Literature: M, *Disegni*, 1969, no. 215; Hammer, *et al.*, 1977, no. 47.

The women appear to be kneading dough to make rolls such as those arranged in rows at the left and in the oven. The scene has been drawn at an angle, establishing a rather low viewpoint for the spectator. As a result, while we observe the shoulders of the women hunched expressively over their toil, we also cannot avoid the view up their skirts, for Guercino has humorously drawn attention to the trio's

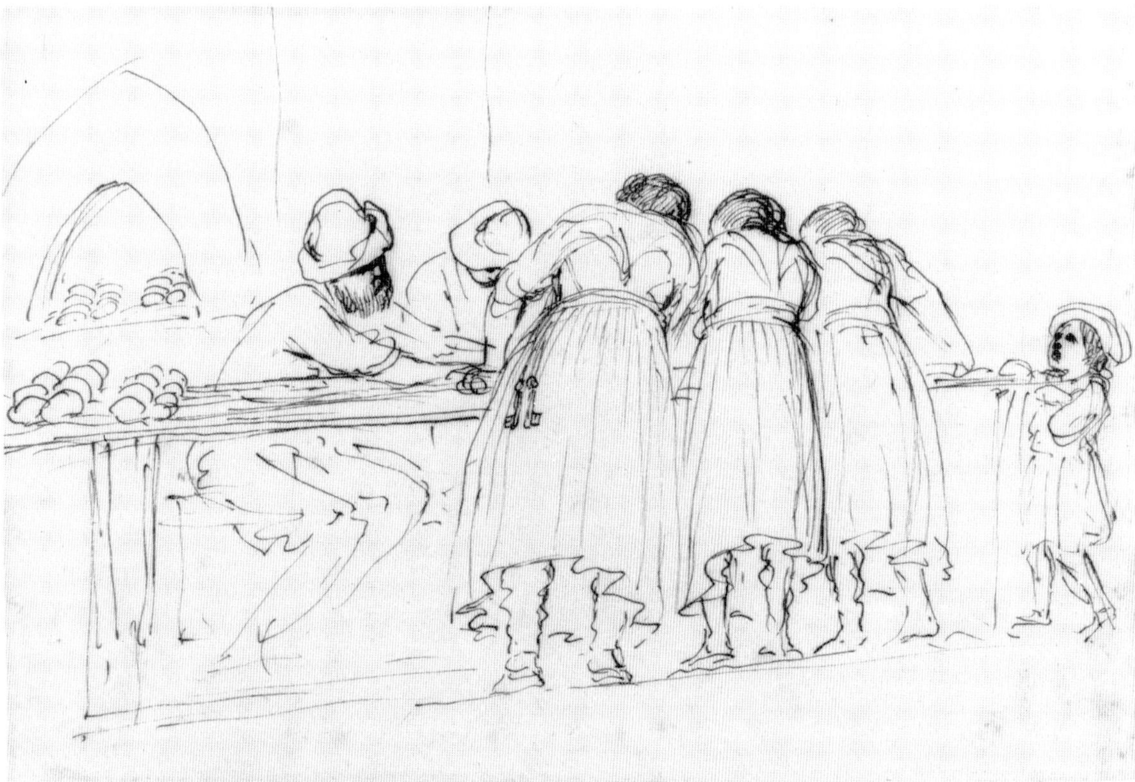

190

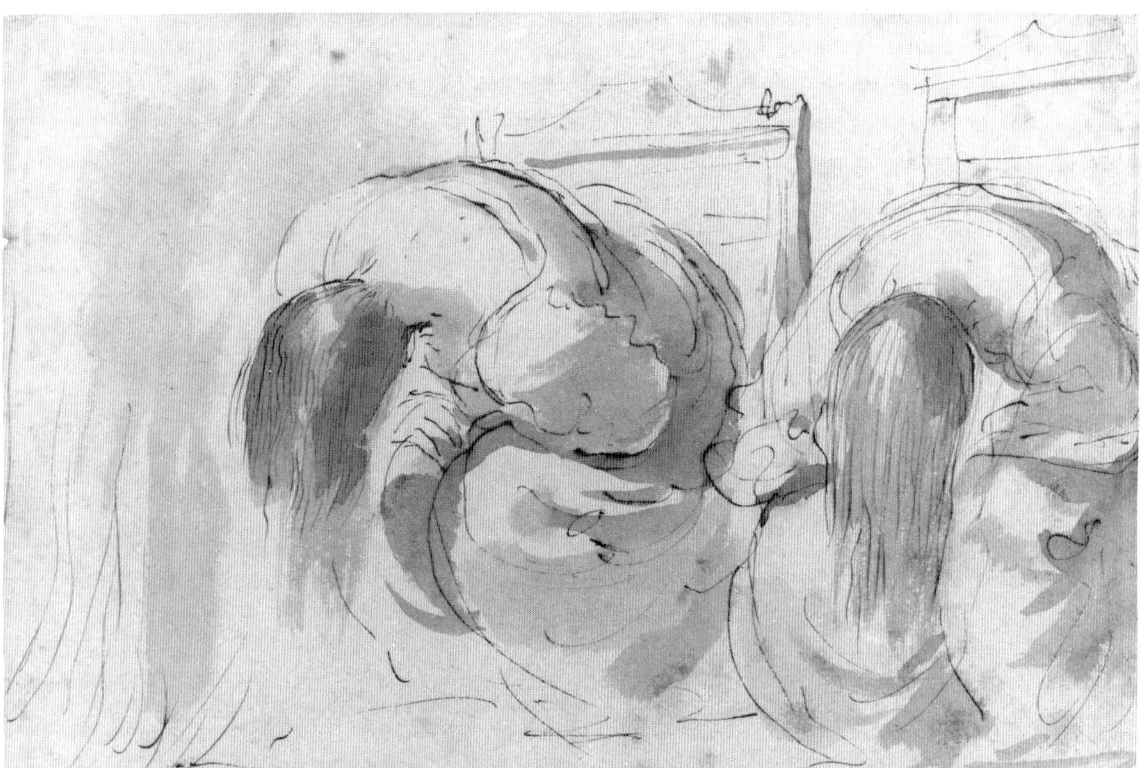

191

ill-fitting stockings wrinkling about their calves. Also typical of Guercino's human touch is the inclusion in the scene of the small boy at the right who watches the proceedings with acute interest, doubtless in the hope of gaining a *panino* for himself. The drawing may date from the 1630s.

For two damaged drawings very close in style, see App. nos. 79 and 80.

191 Two seated Women drying their Hair in front of a Fire

Pen and brown ink and brown wash. 189 × 262mm.

London, Courtauld Institute Galleries, Witt Collection, inv. no. 1359.

Provenance: Casa Gennari; Mr Bouverie; Mr Hervey; the Earls of Gainsborough (sale, Christie's, London, 27 July 1922, lot 81, with others, bt *Meatyard*); Sir Robert Witt.

Literature: M, *Disegni*, 1969, no. 217; Hammer, *et al.*, 1977, no. 48.

Guercino has typically captured in this sheet a small event from everyday life in all its intimacy. The style, with its predominant use of wash, is reminiscent of his drawings of the 1630s (e.g. Nos. 100 and 101). The treatment of the hair is particularly subtle, with the artist using a dark patchy wash, contrasted with areas of white, to describe the wet hair over the skull and a very lightly loaded brush to denote the wispy ends of the hairs in the process of drying.

The possibility that this is a study of one woman from two slightly different angles is ruled out by a drawing related to it by Mahon (1969) in the collection of Signora Valentina Latini of Jesi, which shows a slightly different arrangement of the two women, seated one behind the other.

192 Girl looking at a Drawing of a Landscape

Pen and brown ink. 179 × 191mm.

Private collection.

Provenance: (?)Casa Gennari (an old inscription, similar to others on drawings from the Casa Gennari, shows through the sheet, top left, from the *verso*: *15* [. . .]); Sir Charles Greville (L 549); Earl of Warwick (L 2600).

From its style the drawing seems to date from the 1620s and may be compared in its high degree of finish with a

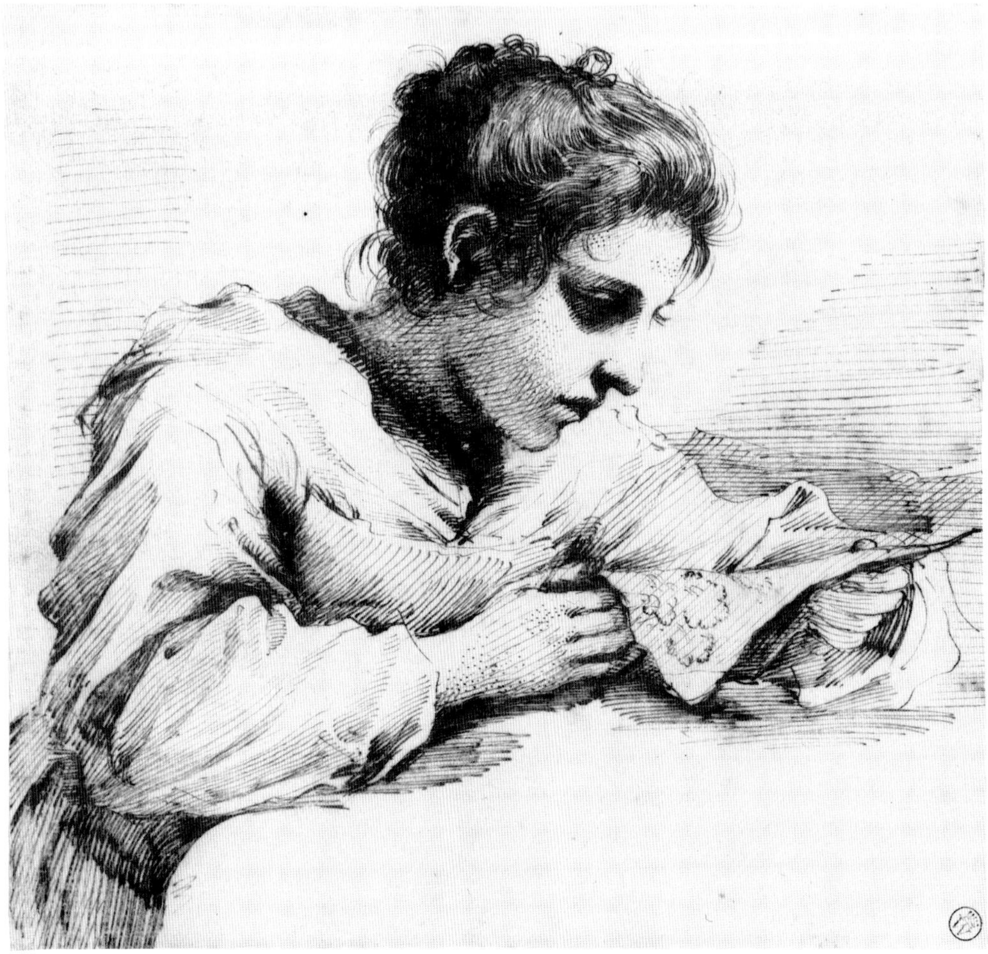

192

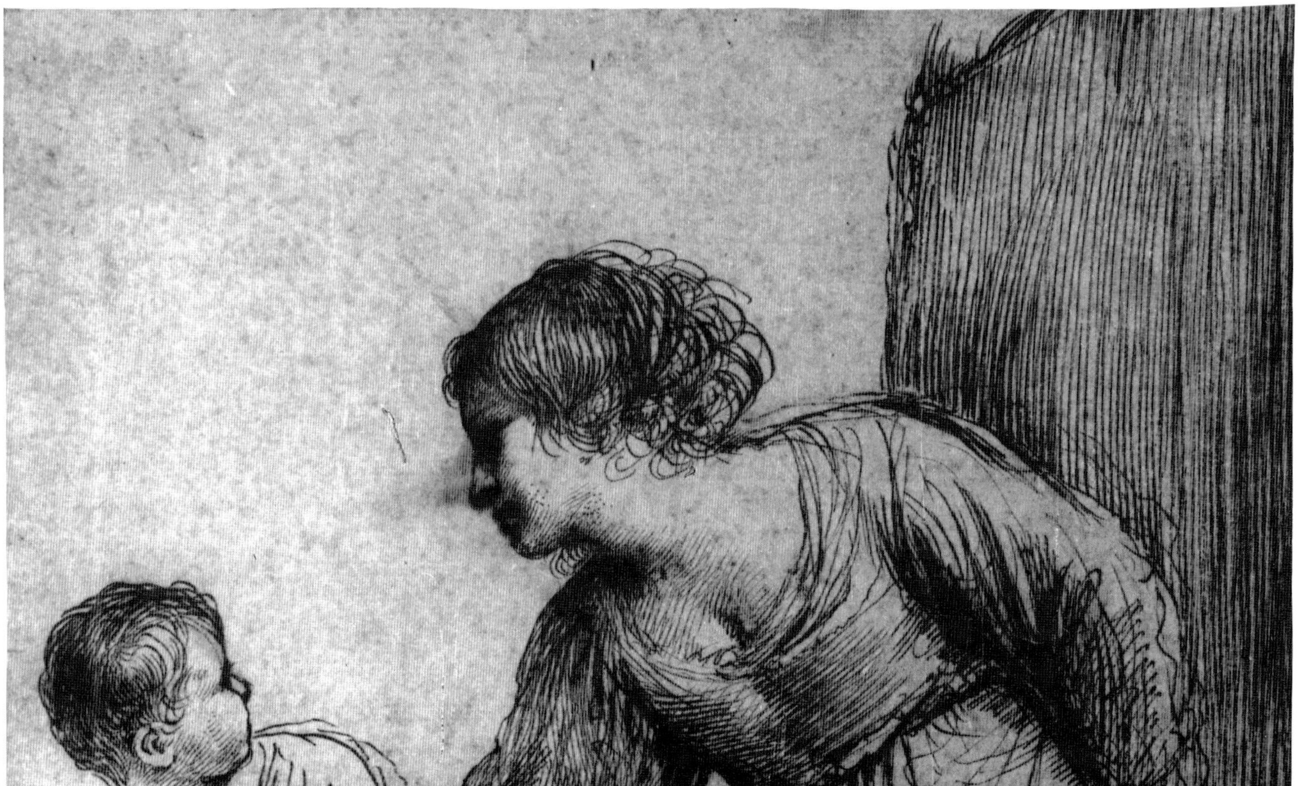

193

drawing of the *Holy Family* of 1621 in the Royal Library, Windsor Castle (No. 31). It falls into a class of 'fancy subjects', a type of subject-matter (distinct from either genre or caricature) that Guercino explored in several series of drawings, many of which were subsequently engraved as exemplars intended for the instruction of beginners. A drawing of a girl reading from a book, similar to No. 192, was engraved by Oliviero Gatti in 1619 (Bertelà, 1973, no. 670) in a series of such prints (see No. 21). Two similarly 'fancy' studies, one of a *Woman wearing a Turban* and the other of a *Woman wearing a loose Mob-cap*, are in the Royal Library, Windsor Castle (M & T, 1989, nos. 400–401), though both are clearly later in date (perhaps from the late 1630s or the early 1640s).

The sheet held by the girl in No. 192 was originally drawn standing erect, so that the spectator could see it only from the back. Guercino later decided to show one corner flopping down to reveal a landscape as the subject of her perusal.

193 Woman and Child with a Bucket

Pen and brown ink. 266 × 233mm.

Holkham Hall, Popham & Lloyd, 149.

Provenance: 1st Earl of Leicester; thence by descent.

Literature: Popham, 1938b, no. 459; Popham 1948, no. 18; Whitfield, 1977, no. 51, repr.; Popham & Lloyd, 1986, no. 149.

The drawing appears to date from the mid-1640s and compares well in its untidy, somewhat scratchy penwork with another drawing at Holkham, the *Samson and Delilah* of 1646 (No. 143) and a drawing in the Royal Library, Windsor Castle, *Semiramis at her Toilet receiving a Messenger* of 1645 (M & T, 1989, no. 114). The exact nature of the scene, with the infant pointing into the bucket and the woman hiding one hand behind her back, remains a mystery.

194 Kneeling Youth wearing a tall Hat with a Feather

(*see colour pl. 27*)

Pen and brown ink. 294 × 205mm.

Mahon Collection, on loan to the Ashmolean Museum, Oxford, M & E, 42.

Provenance: Casa Gennari (the drawing retains its fine Casa Gennari mount, for which see L *Suppl*, 2858c, and M, 1967, p. 20); Mr Bouverie; Mr Hervey; the Earls of Gainsborough (sale, Sotheby's, London, 22 July 1953, lot 5), purchased by Sir Denis Mahon.

Literature: M, 1967, no. 44; M, *Disegni*, 1969, no. 224; Roli, 1972, pl. 62; M & E, 1986, no. 42.

Inscribed in black ink in the bottom left corner of the old mount: *35 S. Fo.*, a numbering system associable with the Casa Gennari. Numbered in graphite below the bottom left corner of the drawing: *25* (for a discussion and further instances of sheets numbered in this way, see No. 10).

Mahon dated this beautiful drawing in the first half of the artist's late period, that is between 1635 and 1650. In our view it is likely that it was drawn sometime in the middle of the 1640s, since it compares especially well with drawings such as Nos. 146 and 148 and a drawing of the *Circumcision*, in the Royal Library, Windsor Castle – all three datable 1646 or shortly before.

According to Mahon, an old, possibly eighteenth-century copy of the drawing was formerly in the collection of Dan Fellows Platt of New Jersey.

195 Standing Beggar

(*see colour pl. 28*)

Pen and brown ink and brown wash. 267 × 192mm.

Windsor Castle, Royal Library, inv. no. 2913.

Provenance: Casa Gennari; King George III.

Literature: M & T, 1989, no. 289.

The technique of this drawing is outstanding, particularly in the subtle passages of wash. A gentle humour is at work in the contrast between the beggar's elegant pose (more suited, for example, to a halbardier) and his scruffy appearance.

For the possible dating of this drawing, see No. 196.

196 Standing Man holding a Stick in his left Hand

Pen and brown ink and brown wash. 279 × 192mm.

Mahon Collection, on loan to the Ashmolean Museum, Oxford, M & E, 45.

Provenance: Casa Gennari (on account of the pen inscription on the old mount); Mr Bouverie; Mr Hervey; the Earls of Gainsborough (probably sale, Christie's, London, 27 July 1922); Capt. H. S. Reitlinger (sale, Sotheby's, London, 9 December 1953, lot 55), purchased pseudonymously by Sir Denis Mahon.

Literature: M, 1967, no. 43; M, *Disegni*, 1969, no. 227; Hammer, *et al.*, 1977, no. 50; M & E, 1986, no. 45.

Inscribed in pen in the bottom left corner of the old mount: *33 N° S. T. Fo.*; and in graphite below the bottom left corner of the drawing: *56* (for a discussion and further instances of sheets numbered in this way, see No. 10).

The subject of this portrait caricature stands in very much the same pose as the beggar in No. 195. The two drawings provide an amusing contrast, though they do not appear to have been conceived as a pair. Nevertheless, the comparison points up nicely the hyperbole of each, for the one is as short and fat as the other is tall and thin; and whereas a piece of rope is all that keeps the beggar's trousers up and prevents his shirt from flapping loosely about his waist, the last few buttons on the jacket of the gentleman in the present drawing remain unfastened on account of his ample midriff.

Both drawings probably date from the mid-1620s.

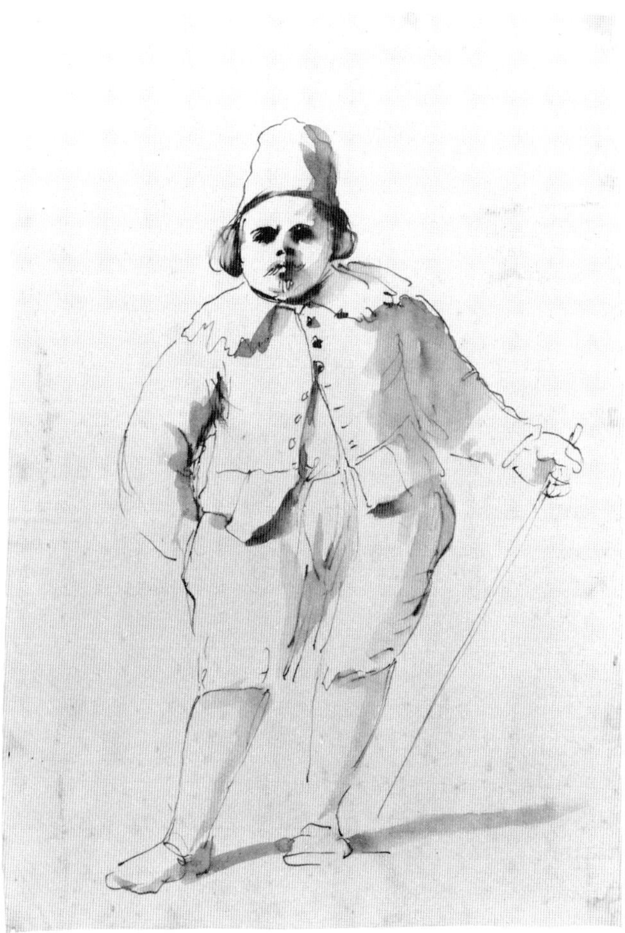

196

197 Girl carrying a sleeping nude Baby

Pen and brown ink and dark brown wash. 190 × 148mm.

Windsor Castle, Royal Library, inv. no. 2912.

Provenance: Casa Gennari; King George III.

Literature: M & T, 1989, no. 287.

Blocked in with a few broad strokes of the brush, the dark shadows evoke the bright light of midday. The quick pace of the girl, emphasised by the angle of the shadow she casts on the ground, is well contrasted with the stillness of the sleeping infant on her back, whose head lolls back to provide a counterbalance to the general movement to the right.

From its style, the drawing would appear to date from the middle of the 1640s.

198 Four Youths singing, watched by an old Man

(see colour pl. 29)

Pen and brown ink and brown wash. 266 × 381mm.

Windsor Castle, Royal Library, inv. no. 2515.

Provenance: Casa Gennari; King George III.

Literature: Thiem, 1982, no. 18; M & T, 1989, no. 280.

Four singers are grouped around a table, watched by an old man, presumably their instructor. To suggest further the atmosphere of a music room, a trumpet, lute and violin have been included on the left. On the table stands an inkpot with two quill pens, towards which the youth on the left reaches with his right hand, as if about to write on the score lying on the table in front of him. He points at this score with his left hand, and the page indeed appears incomplete at the bottom. The drawing is unusually elaborate and was almost certainly made as an end in itself rather than as a study for a picture. The foxing and the fading of some of the wash suggest that it was once framed and exposed to light for a long period, probably when it was in the possession of the Gennari family.

In MS. Inventory A, an inventory of the drawings at Windsor Castle compiled at the end of the eighteenth century during the reign of King George III, this drawing is referred to as 'The large Concert'. The subject of the 'Concert' is a common one in Emilian painting of the seventeenth and eighteenth centuries. Its antecedents go back to the sixteenth century, to the work of such painters as Nicolò dell'Abate (1509–71). In this example, however, Guercino has departed from the usual Emilian prototypes and has given instead a notably Caravaggesque flavour to the representation. The youth wearing an elaborate cap with a plume recalls some of the young *bravi* in the paintings of Caravaggio (1573–1610), as do, to a rather lesser extent, the other three youths. It may be accidental, but it is also worth pointing out the distant echoes in composition between Guercino's 'Concert' and Caravaggio's famous *Calling of St Matthew* in the church of S. Luigi dei Francesi in Rome.

Although the drawing has been dated from 'the second half of the 1620s or the beginning of the 1630s' (M & T, 1989, no. 280), it seems to us that a comparison between it and No. 115, datable 1635, is especially telling, particularly in the similarity in the application of the wash. A counterpart to the old man standing on the right in the present drawing is found in one of the spectators standing on the right in No. 115.

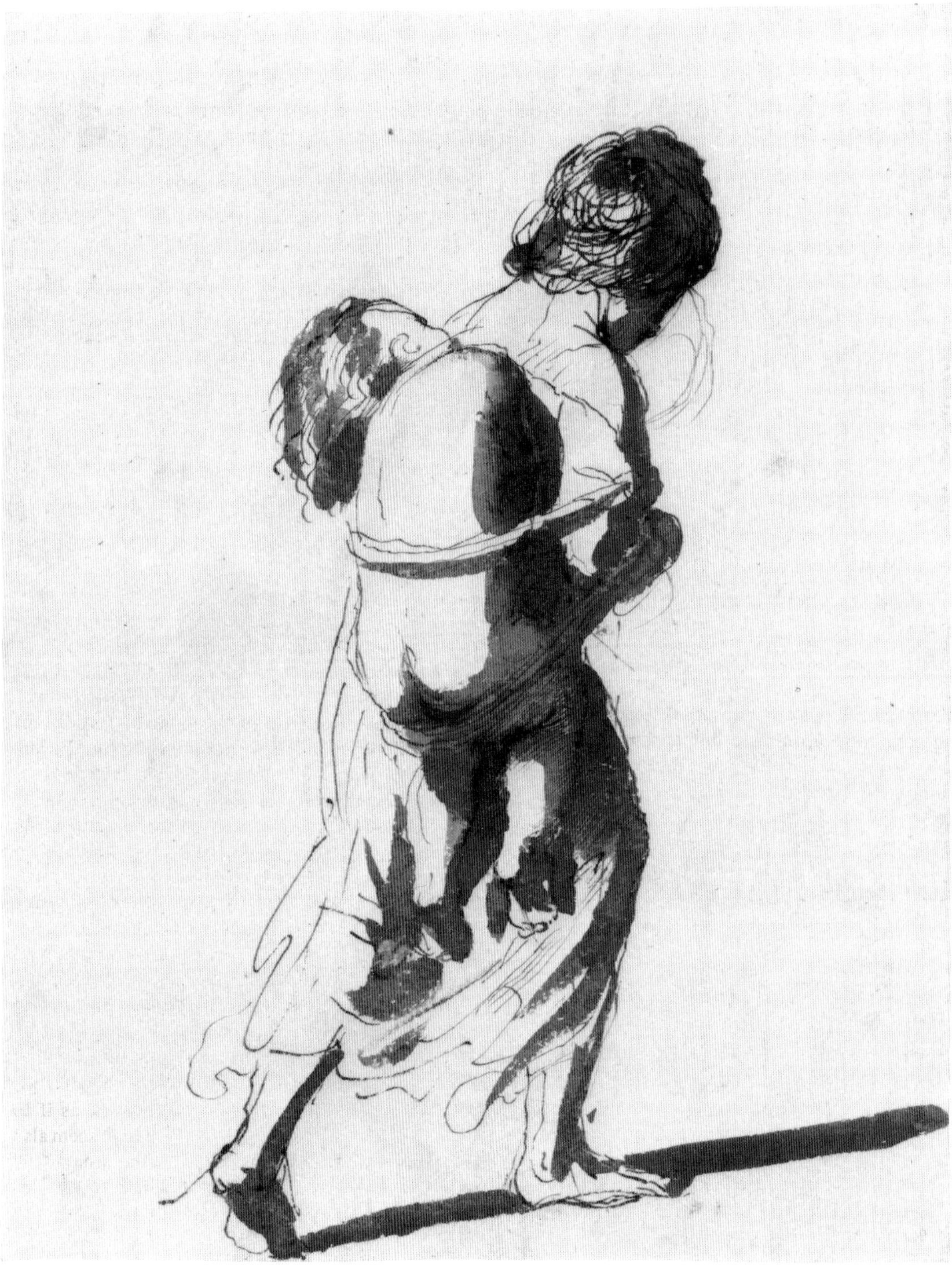

197

2 Capricci (Nos. 199–205)

199 Man fleeing from a monstrous Animal

(*see colour pl. 29*)

Pen and brown ink and brown wash. 150 × 222mm.

Liverpool, Walker Art Gallery, inv. no. 9213.

Provenance: Earl Spencer (L 1530); W. Roscoe; W. Dyce; Sir J. C. Robinson (L 1433 and L *Suppl*, 2141b); J. Malcolm; by whom given to the Hon. A. E. Gathorne-Hardy between 1869 and 1876; by descent to the Hon. Robert Gathorne-Hardy; acquired directly from the Gathorne-Hardy Estate in 1977 by the Walker Art Gallery, Liverpool.

Literature: Robinson, 1869, no. 288; Gathorne-Hardy, 1902, no. 21; Colnaghi, 1971, no. 33; Morris & Hopkinson, 1977, text vol., pp. 253–4, pl. vol., p. 347; M & T, 1989, under no. 324.

A good example of a class of drawing generally referred to as '*capricci*', from the Italian word *capriccio*, meaning flight of fancy, caprice or whim. In these studies Guercino displayed with pride his imaginative invention, indulging it deliberately in order to amuse the viewer. In this drawing a man gapes in surprise at the grotesque, cockerel-like creature, strutting by, high up on the bank in front of him. Scrutiny of the bizarre animal inevitably raises at least a smile on the part of the onlooker. The body is composed of a human foot, with toes instead of a tail; the legs resemble those of a fowl, though the foot of one is a human hand; the head is also vaguely humanoid, but it has the ears of a dog and its chin and mouth are concealed by fleshy lobes, rather like the wattles of a cock. The finer details are as alarming, for example the bristles at the top of the creature's head and the fine long hairs that make up its brows.

A similar creature is represented in a drawing in the Royal Library at Windsor Castle (M & T, 1989, no. 324). The head of this animal is a cross between those of a dog and a monkey and its body is that of a plucked bird (though the wings are still feathered), but instead of a tail it terminates in a human foot, as in the Liverpool drawing.

The Liverpool drawing appears on stylistic grounds to date from the middle or late 1620s.

200 Caricature of a Man emptying a Pot of Liquid onto the Head of a kneeling Soldier

Pen and brown ink and brown wash. 183 × 270mm.

Chatsworth, inv. no. 513.

Provenance: (?)William Cavendish, 2nd Duke of Devonshire; thence by descent.

Literature: Popham, 1962–3, no. 28; Bottari, 1966, pl. XXXIV; M, *Disegni*, 1969, no. 241.

Showing through the paper from the *verso*, at the left, is an inscription, and, just above the back of the soldier, a diagrammatic sketch of a woman and a man holding hands. Both inscription and sketch were made with the sheet turned at right angles.

To the left of the centre kneels a soldier on a slab, holding one of his gauntlets in his right hand and with his left pulling at the hilt of his sword, which juts back behind him. On the left, a man leans over the soldier and empties liquid from a pot over his head. On the right is a standing man wearing a loose-fitting costume and an outlandish hat, in the band of which are tucked various instruments; he draws a dagger from its sheath with his left hand.

Popham was the first to connect the esoteric subject of this drawing with the *Commedia dell'arte*, a type of comedy developed in Italy in the sixteenth century and still widespread there in the seventeenth and eighteenth centuries, which was characterised by improvisation from a standard plot outline and by the use of stock characters. Whether or not this identification is correct, the pouring ritual represented in this drawing has something in common with a similar rite enacted by even more bizarre characters in No. 201.

201 Symbolic or magical Subject

Pen and brown ink and brown wash. 176 × 188mm.

Windsor Castle, Royal Library, inv. no. 2760.

Provenance: Casa Gennari; King George III.

Literature: Thiem, 1982, no. 21; M & T, 1989, no. 319.

The precise significance of the subject remains elusive. In the centre a fantastic, composite figure squats on the ground, with its head made up of three faces. Two are in profile, one middle-aged and the other youthful (on the left and right respectively), while the one in the middle is of an old bearded man seen full face. The ears of the two heads in profile double as the eyes of the old man. Behind the figure is a large upright slab supported by two devils. One of the devils pours liquid from a jug into a funnel, the conical part of which rests like a cap upon each of the two heads in profile, while the narrow tube end makes up the nose of the old man. The liquid collects into a large flask placed at the bottom centre between the figure's legs. The second devil, half kneeling to the left, extends his right hand to stroke the chin of the middle-aged face.

As the drawing progressed, Guercino slightly modified his ideas. In place of the flask he first drew a pair of arms extending downwards and crossing at the wrists, as if to protect the composite figure's private parts, which seem also to have been drawn and then cancelled in the area at the base of the flask. When the flask was put in, a third arm, holding the flask in place, was also drawn on the right. The pentiment near the thigh and lower leg of the devil on the left is hard to interpret.

Although the symbolism of the pouring ritual enacted in the present drawing has defied the explanation of a number of experts consulted on the matter, it seems to us that some sort of fertility rite or rejuvenating ceremony is taking place. Equally self-evident is the allusion to the three ages of man in the central figure. Nevertheless, there must be some specific magical ritual in the recesses of popular seventeenth-century Emilian culture to which Guercino was alluding in

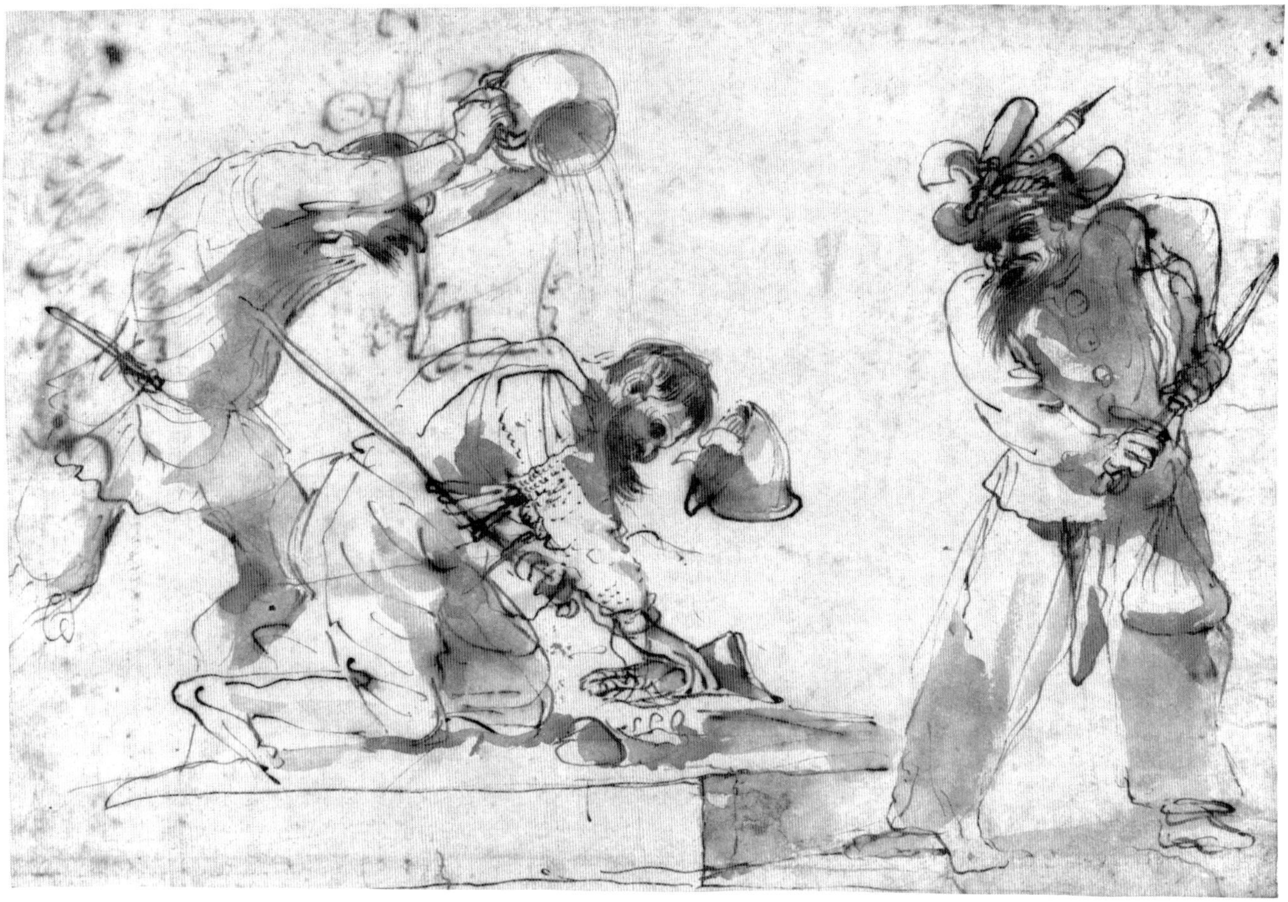

200

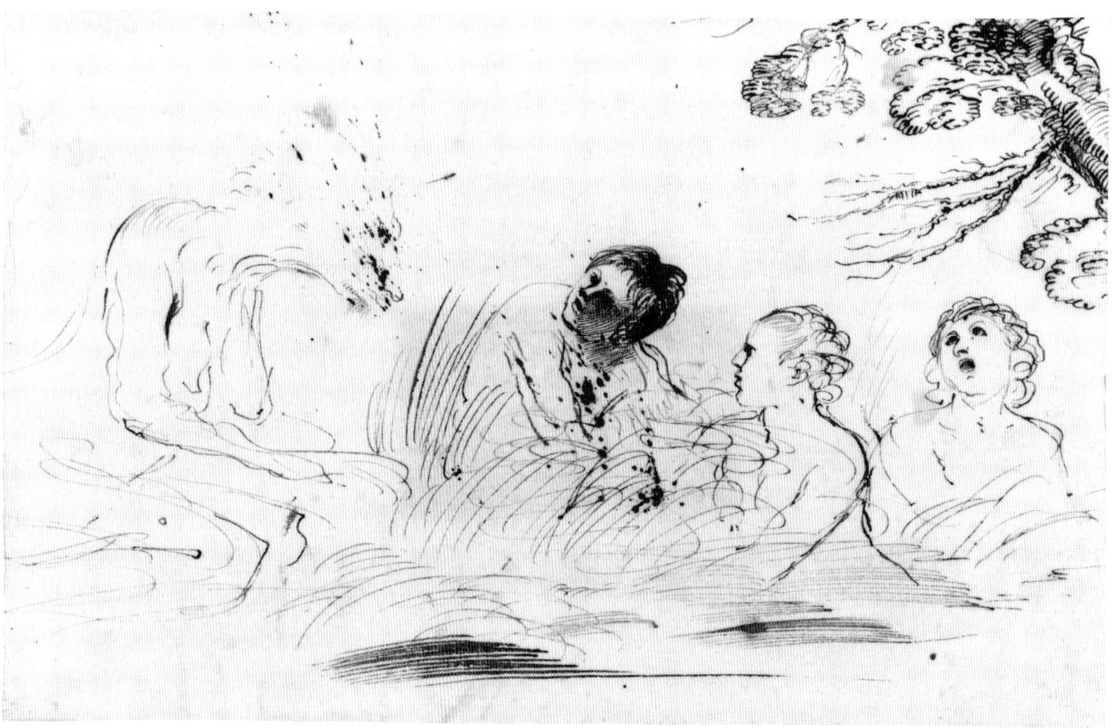

202

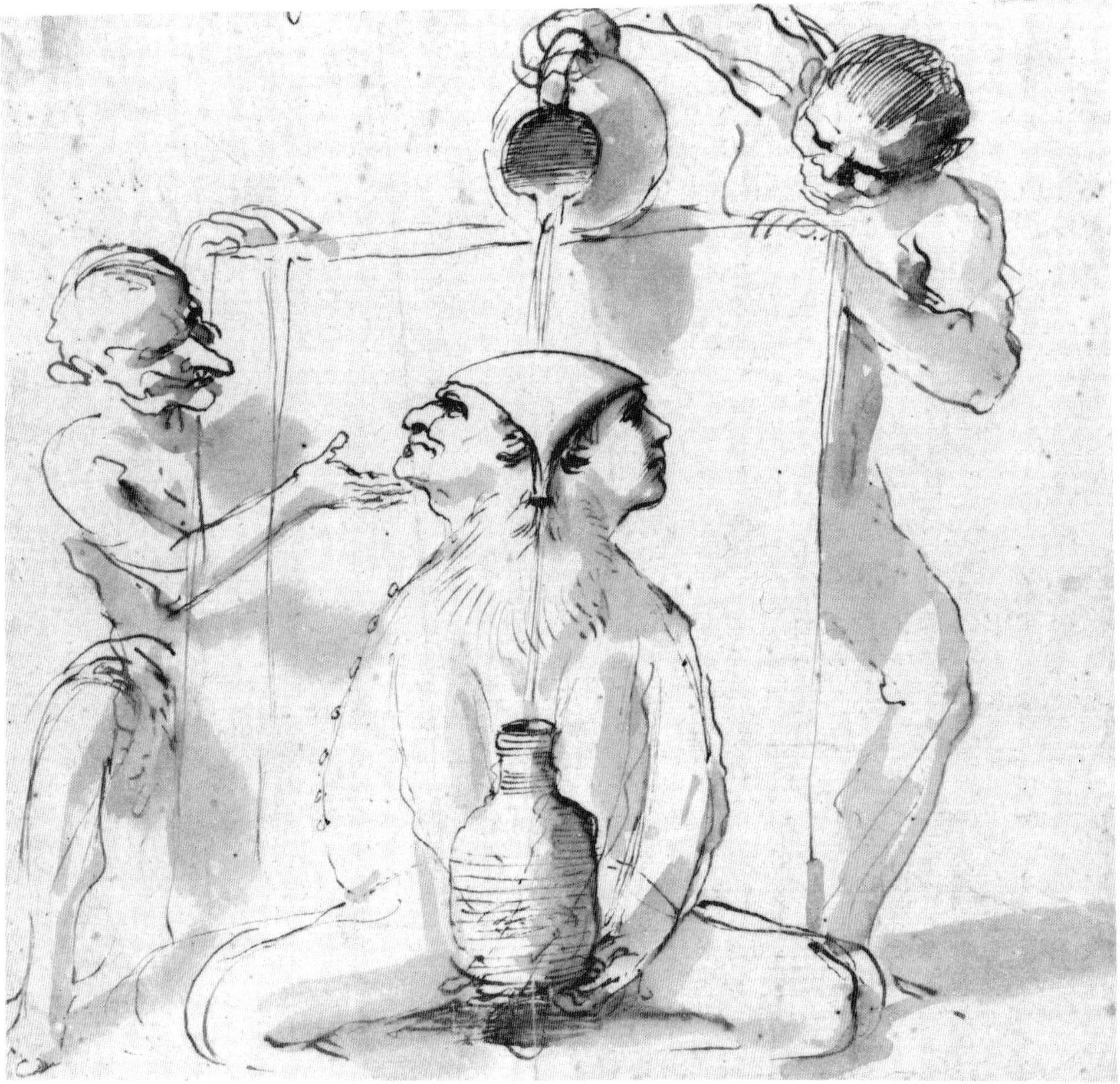

201

this representation but which remains to be identified. If at times Guercino's world and humanitarian interests seem near our own, there are moments, such as this, when they seem far distant indeed.

202 Three Bathers surprised by a Monster

Pen and black ink. 162 × 257mm.

Windsor Castle, Royal Library, inv. no. 2477.

Provenance: Casa Gennari; King George III.

Literature: M & T, 1989, no. 318.

The starting point for this spirited drawing seems to have been the random blobs of ink splashed across the paper which the artist has then exploited in a bravura demonstration of his imaginative fertility. From some of the blobs he has constructed the muzzle and head of the monster, touching in with the pen only the whiskers at its chin, the hair at the back of its head, and the diminutive snout and brow. The horrified bathers thrash around in the water at the sight of this freak bearing down on them, their confusion enhanced by further blobs of ink and a tangle of lines also drawn at random.

The style suggests a date in the 1620s.

203 Two Nymphs and a Satyr

(*see colour pl. 30*)

Pen and brown ink and brown wash. 203 × 137mm.

London, Courtauld Institute Galleries, Witt Collection, inv. no. 1346.

Provenance: Casa Gennari (the sheet retains its fine Casa Gennari mount, for which see L *Suppl*, 2858c; Fig. 4 in the Introduction; and M, 1967, p. 20); Mr Bouverie; Mr Hervey; the Earls of Gainsborough (sale, Christie's, London, 27 July 1922, lot 81, with others, bt *Meatyard*); Sir Robert Witt.

Literature: Russell, 1923, p. 21, pl. VIII; Marangoni, 1959, p. 13; M, *Disegni*, 1969, no. 245; Hammer, *et al.*, 1977, no. 40.

The sheet is remarkable for the freshness of its condition. The drawing is also notable for its bold chiaroscuro effects; for instance, the total absence of modelling in the back of the nymph nearest the spectator – giving the impression that she is bathed in very strong sunlight – does not result in any erosion or flattening of her form.

The drawing may be dated in the mid-1620s.

204 Witch wearing a high cylindrical Hat

Pen and brown ink and brown wash. 195 × 170mm.

Windsor Castle, Royal Library, inv. no. 2657.

Provenance: Casa Gennari; King George III.

Literature: M & T, 1989, no. 339.

The distinctive hat was evidently an afterthought, since a pentiment beneath it reveals that the figure's head was originally covered with a simple drapery. The scene of *diavoleria*

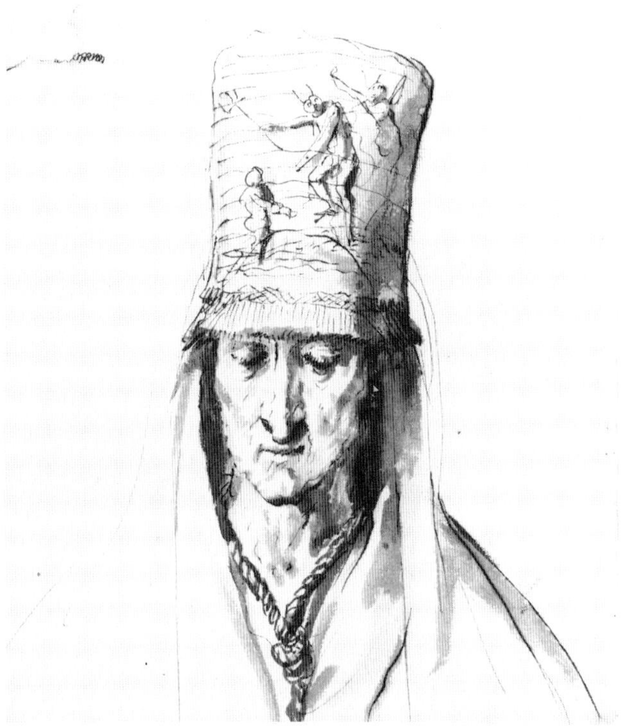

204

on the hat is hard to read, but it seems to represent two horned demons bearing down on a nude figure who is either kneeling or standing up to his knees in water. The significance of this image and the implications of the rope about the witch's neck remain obscure, ominous though they certainly seem.

205 Death visiting a peasant Family

Pen and brown ink and brown wash. 292 × 272mm.

Private collection.

Provenance: D. Vivant-Denon; sale, Christie's, London, 26 March 1974, lot 116.

The drawing was etched in reverse by Baron D. Vivant-Denon (Weigel, 1865, pp. 282–3, no. 3341), and the etching appears as plate CCI in the catalogue of the Denon collection (Pineux-Duval, 1829, II, pl. 206; an impression is in the Department, inv. no. 1856–2–9–822).

No. 205 is a moving representation of Death visiting a peasant family. The hour has come for a woman, the mother of seven, and her three babies who lie on the family bed by her side, as Death in the form of a skeleton approaches from the left. Her arms are raised dramatically towards heaven, as though she were begging for a reprieve (the family's faith is attested by the cross above the bed). In the left foreground, her husband sits dejectedly on a stool by the hearth, his head in his hands, as four older children clamour for attention.

The drawing may be dated in the early 1630s on stylistic

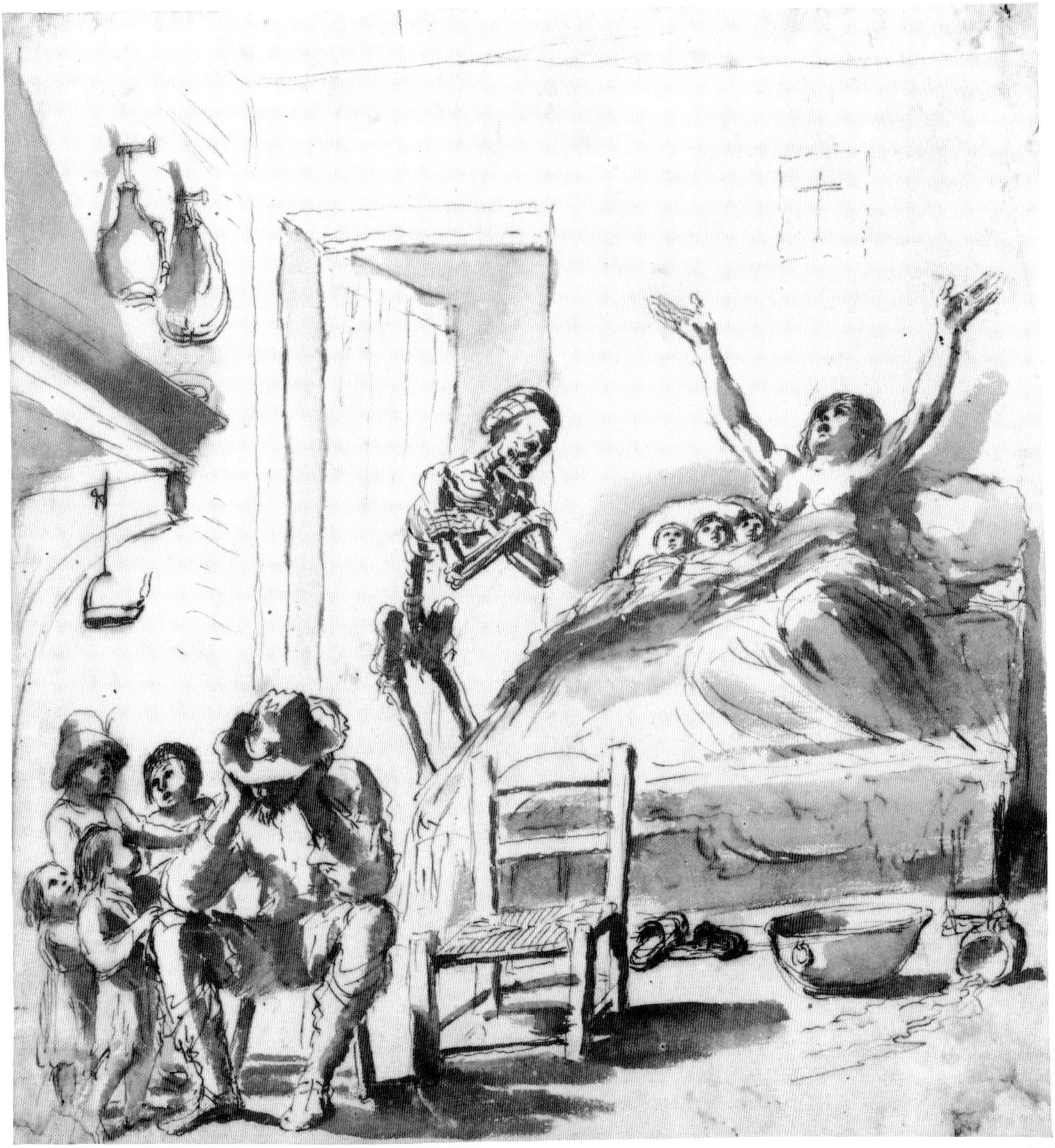

205

grounds. The woman's imminent death may have been occasioned by the birth of the triplets who lie in the bed beside her. It is also possible that the subject could be a reflection of the devastating plague, often referred to as the Great Plague of Milan, which spread through northern Italy in 1630, hitting Cento in the latter part of the year. The plague was described by a contemporary, Giuseppe Ripamonti (*J. Ripamontii* [. . .] *de peste quae fuit anno 1630 libri v.*, Milan, 1641) and was the subject of Alessandro Manzoni's classic *I promessi sposi*. During the epidemic, Guercino made drawings, which were engraved by Giovanni Battista Pasqualini for widespread, popular consumption, such as a *lasciapassare*, showing St Blaise and St Michael vanquishing the devil, which was used on 10 June 1630 and states that Cento was free of the plague (B, 1988, pl. 118); and a prayer to St Antony of Padua, showing him interceding against the plague (B, 1988, pl. 120), both dated 1630. Pasqualini's involvement in projects such as these acquires a particular poignancy in view of the fact that he himself died of the plague on 18 March 1631. For another drawing of a plague-related subject, see No. 75.

The pose of the woman is reminiscent of that frequently employed by Guercino for the Magdalen beneath the cross, as in several drawings for the Reggio *Crucifixion*, cited under No. 51. The child who rests his hand on his father's right knee in No. 205 bears a distinct resemblance to figures in two other genre drawings in this catalogue which also appear to date from the 1630s: the child on the right (in reverse) in the Courtauld Institute *Baker's Shop* (No. 190); and the three boys reaching for a morsel in a drawing in the British Museum (App. no. 79).

3 Caricatures (Nos. 206–16)

206 Caricature of Fra Bonaventura Bisi

Pen and brown ink. 198 × 237mm.

Oxford, Ashmolean Museum, KTP 870.

Provenance: Sir Karl Parker, by whom presented.

Literature: Parker, 1956, no. 870; M, *Disegni*, 1969, no. 230; Roli, 1972, pp. 29f., pl. 50; Galleni, 1975, pp. 80–82; Macandrew, 1980, p. 299; M & E, 1986, no. XVIII; Southorn, 1988, pl. 47; M & T, 1989, under no. 436.

The drawing is inscribed in Guercino's hand at the top of the sheet: *MA COME P[ER] GRATIA COME*, and *CHAPIRA, OTTO HORE E MEZZ' AL BISO CHE VADI A LETTO/ CHE DOMATINA E IL PRIMO DI DI QUARESIMA BISO PREDICARE.*

As Galleni was the first to observe, the sitter in this caricature portrait is Guercino's friend Fra Bonaventura Bisi (1612–59). The identification was suggested by the word play on Bisi's name found in the inscription. Galleni pointed out that Bisi was a miniaturist and an engraver, who from this activity earned himself the nickname 'Padre pittorino'; he is best known, however, as the adviser to the Este and Medici families on the acquisition of works of art.

In 1657–8 Guercino gave Bisi two of his pictures, probably intended as a pair, each showing a putto carrying symbolic emblems (see M & T, 1989, under no. 436). As gifts they do not, of course, feature in the *Libro dei Conti*, but they are nonetheless described by Malvasia: in one picture the putto held a 'testa di morte' and in the other the 'instrumenti della passione' (Malvasia, 1678, II, pp. 380f.; 1841, II, p. 270).

A drawing by Guercino of an ecclesiastic in profile to the left in the Art Museum, Princeton University (inv. no. 48–1308; Gibbons, 1977, no. 294, as School of Guercino), almost certainly also represents Fra Bonaventura, on account of many analogies with No. 206.

207 Bearded Man wearing a large Hat

Red chalk. 271 × 205mm.

Windsor Castle, Royal Library, inv. no. 2826.

Provenance: Casa Gennari; King George III.

Literature: M & T, 1989, no. 307.

The caricature is less one of physiognomy than of expression, the figure's pronounced scowl and fancy hat being all that distinguishes him from the type Guercino used for his more mature saints such as St Joseph.

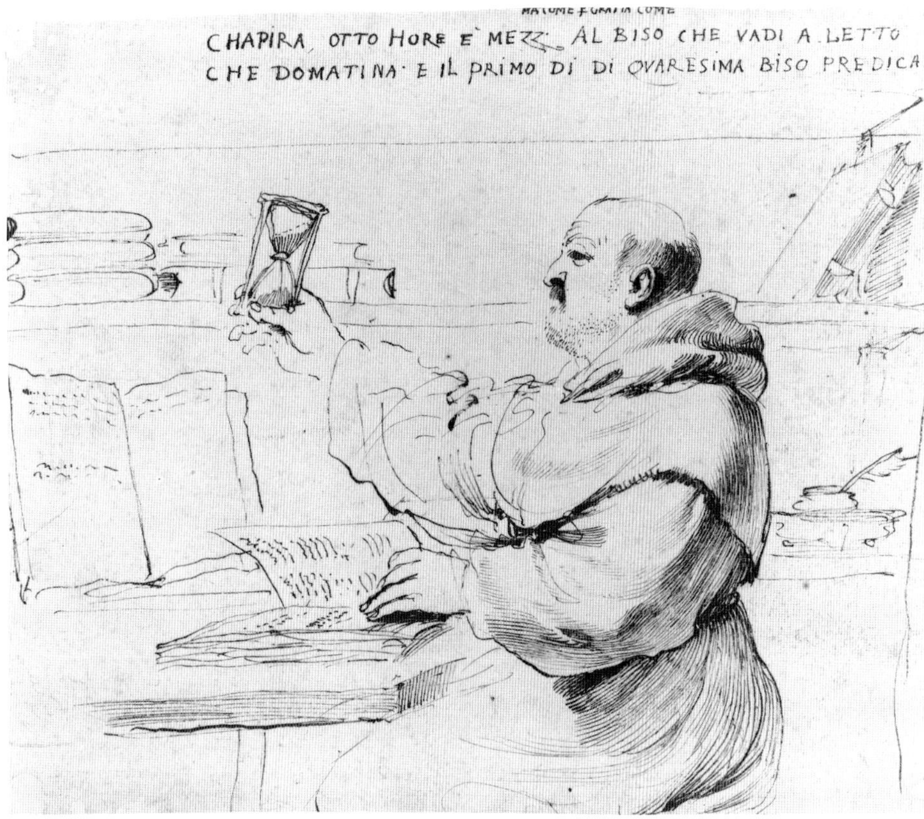

206

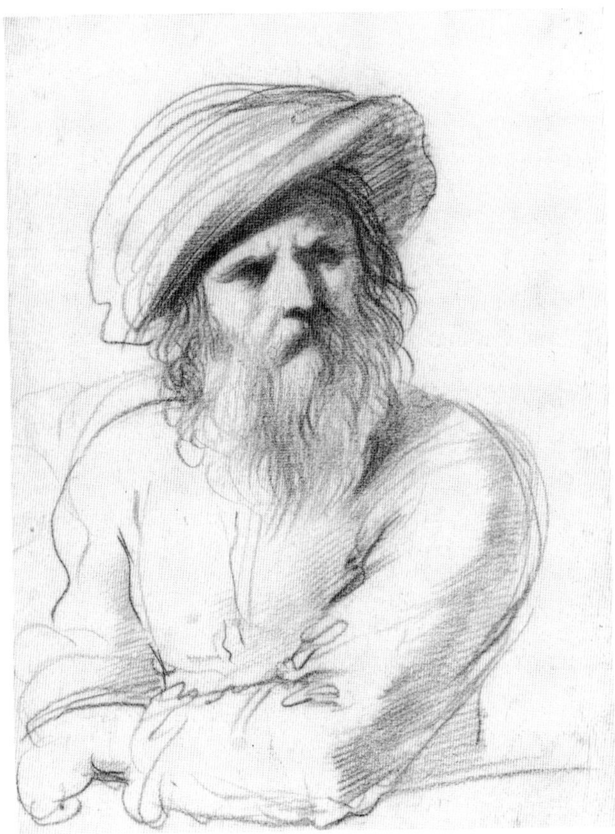

207

208 Caricature of an old Man with a Pair of Spectacles stuck over his Ear

(*see colour pl. 31*)

London, British Museum, inv. no. Pp. 4–58.

(For other details, see App. no. 65.)

Much of the humour of this sketch resides in Guercino's incongruous use of the noble profile portrait formula to depict a grotesque subject, while simultaneously exposing the sitter's comic storage facility for spectacles, behind the ear.

The drawing may date from around the middle of the 1630s.

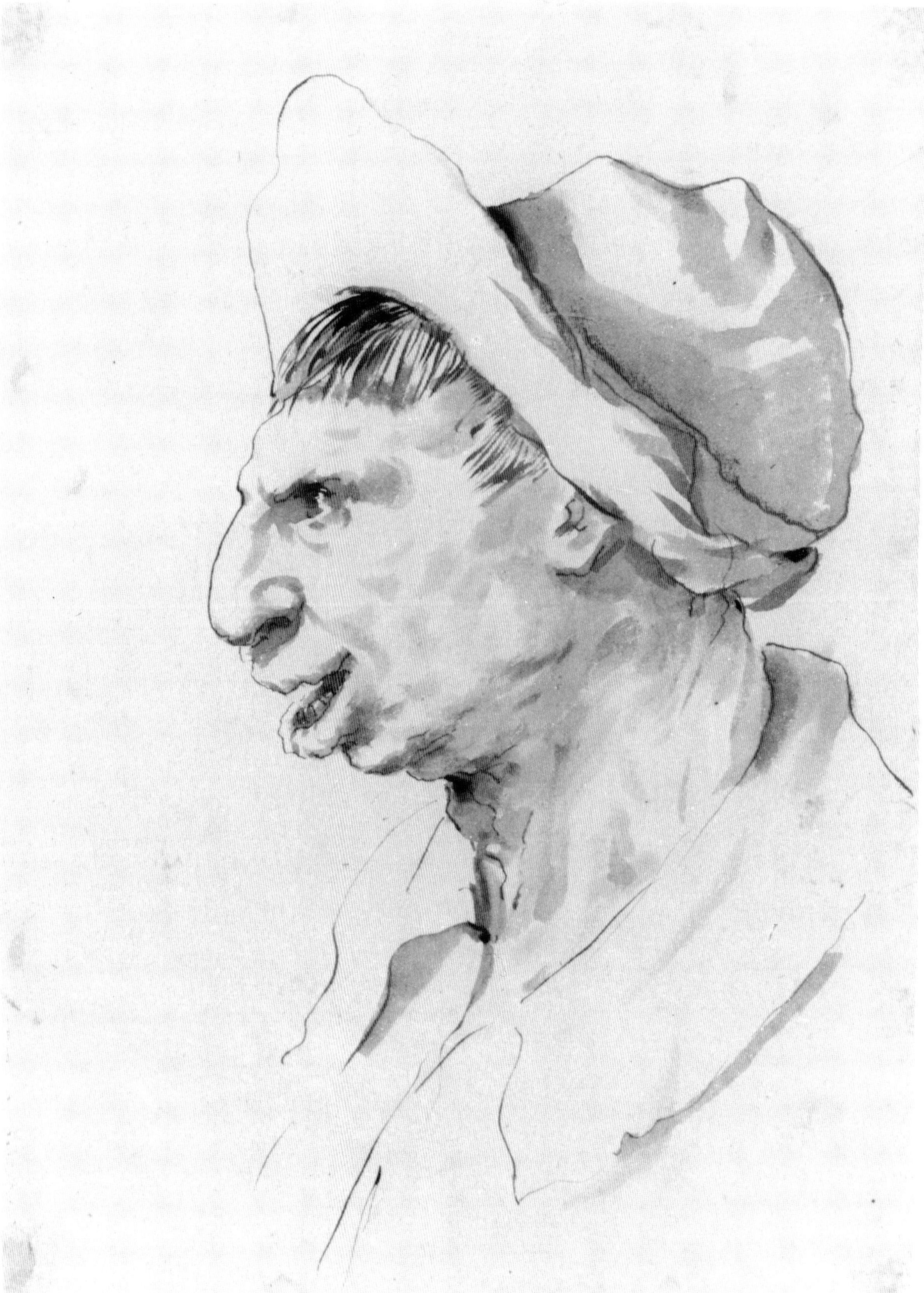

209

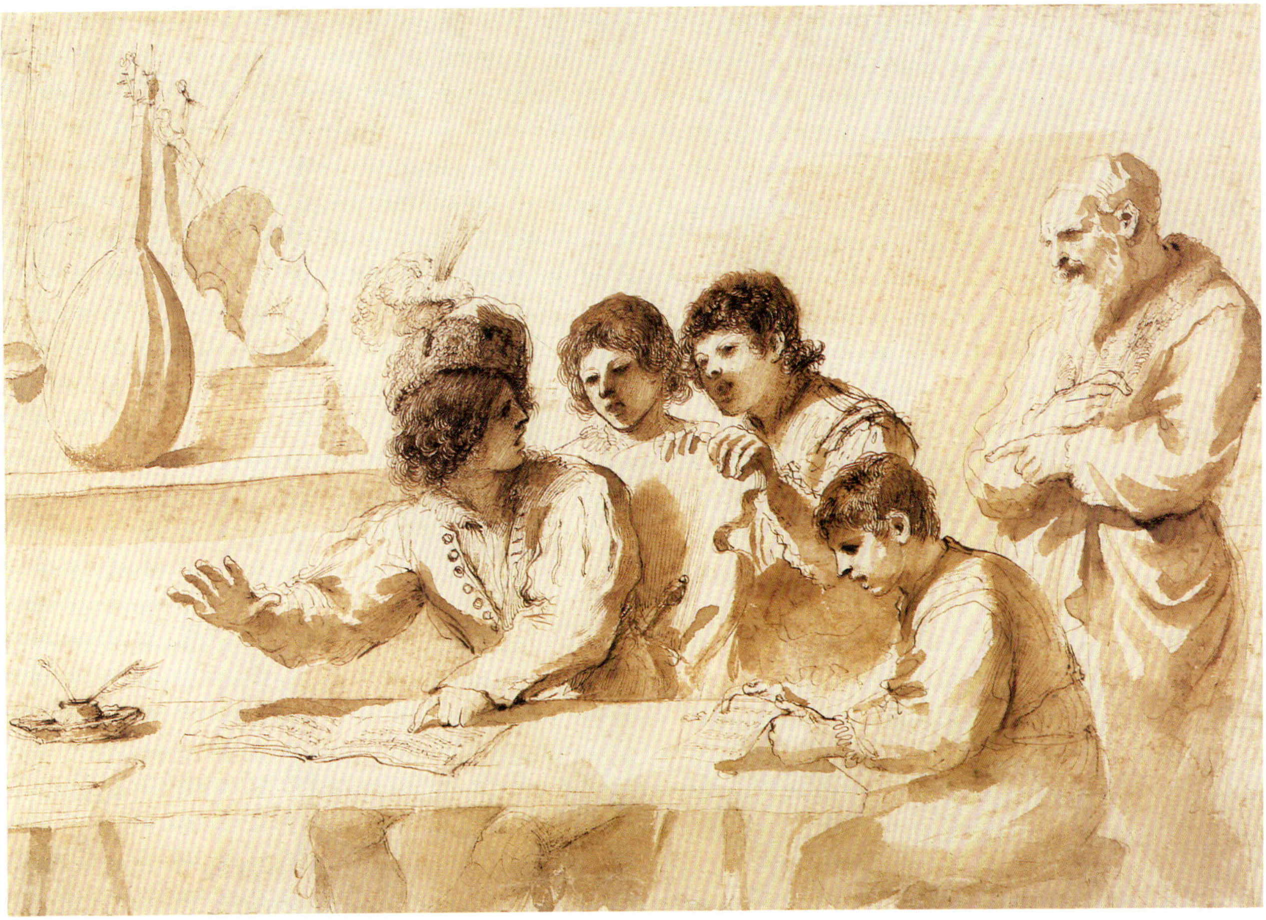

198 (above)
Four Youths singing, watched by an Old Man.
Windsor Castle, Royal Library

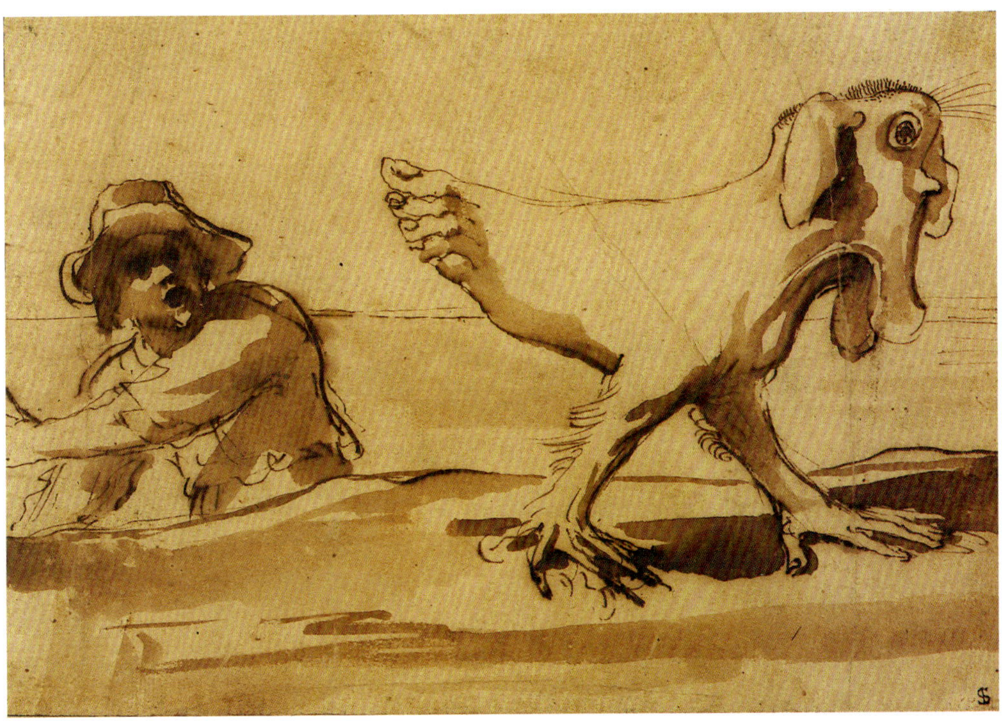

199 (right)
Man fleeing from a monstrous Animal.
Liverpool, Walker Art Gallery

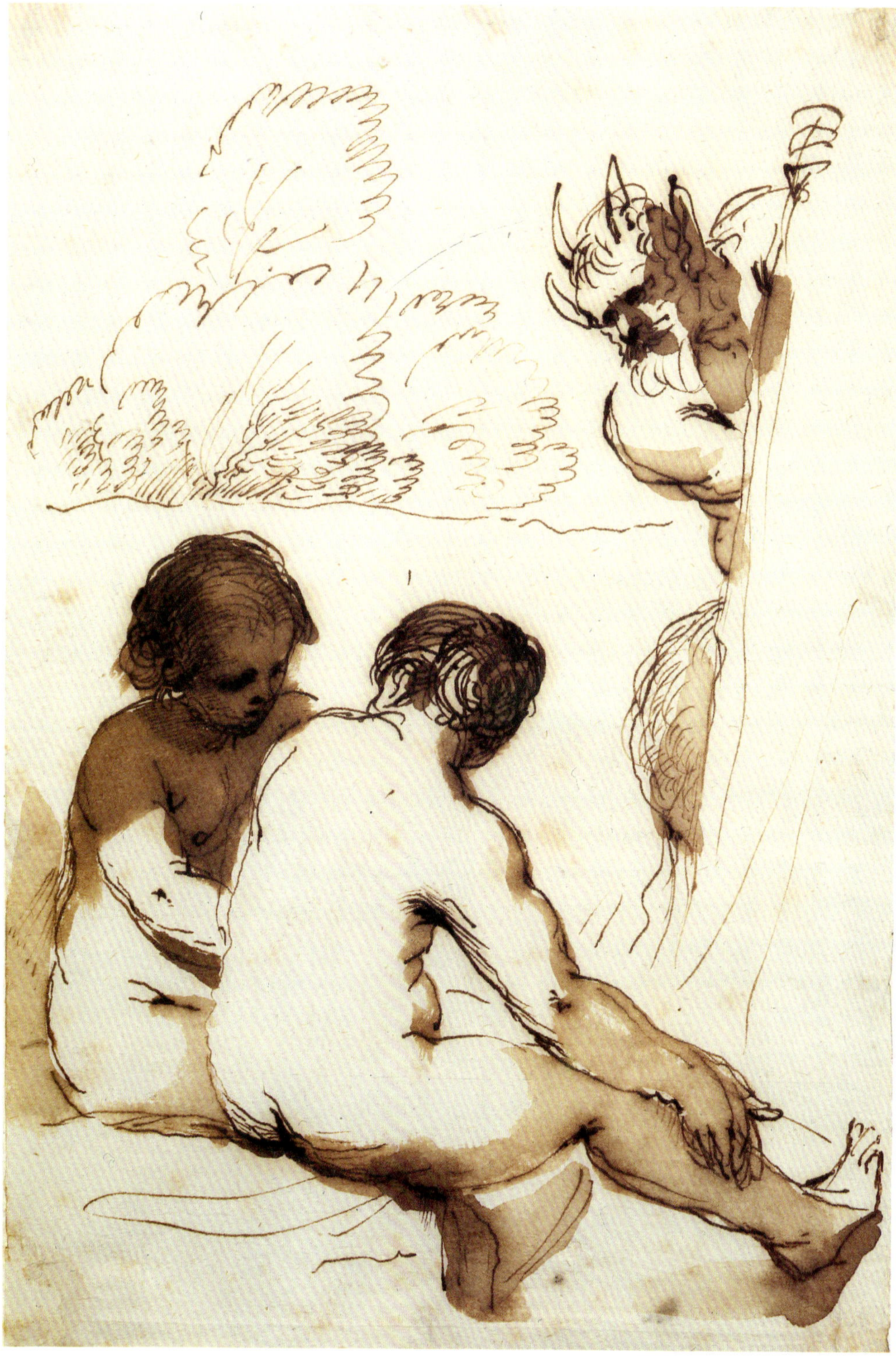

203 *Two Nymphs and a Satyr*. London, Courtauld Institute Galleries

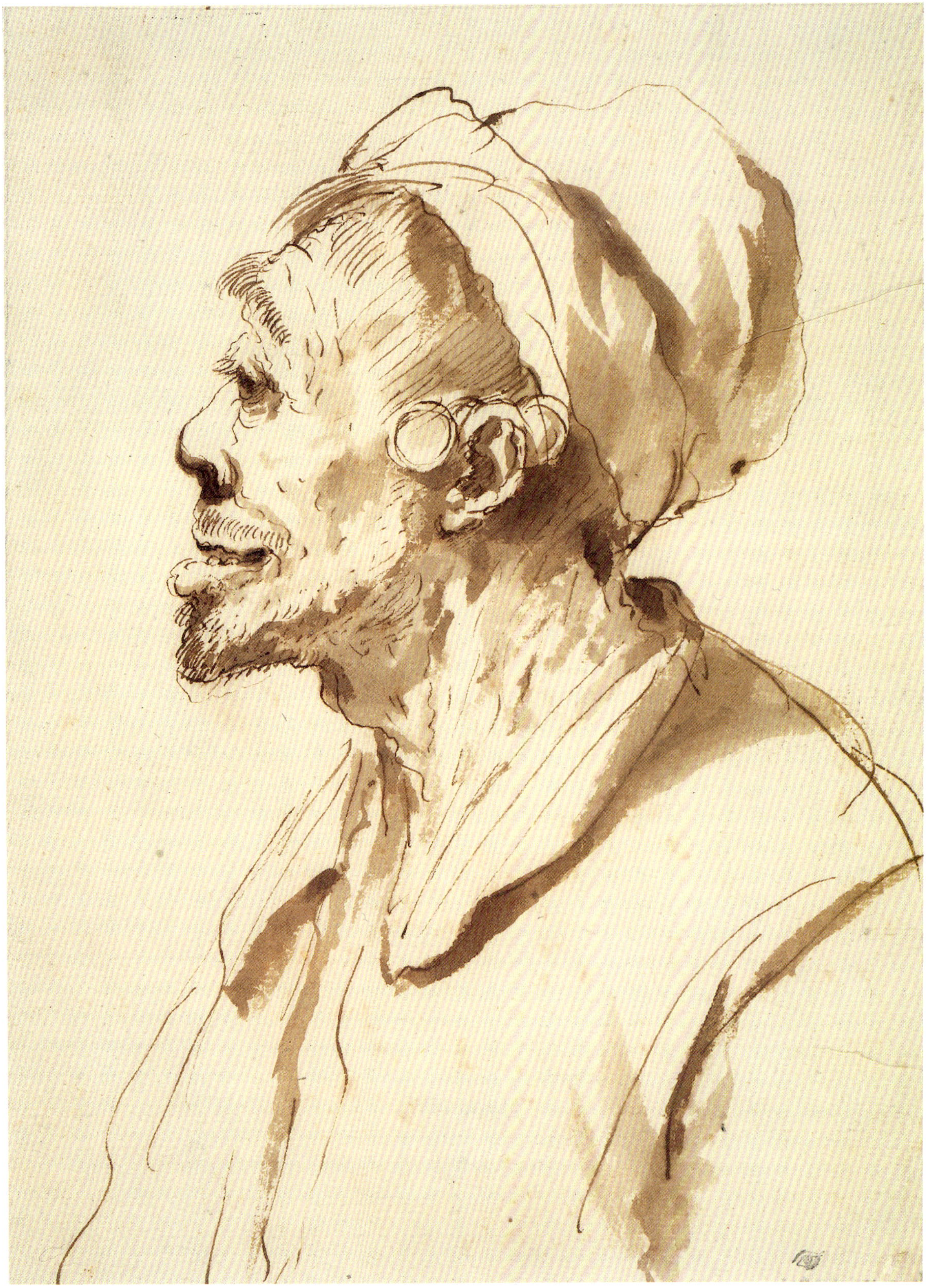

208 *Caricature of an old Man with a Pair of Spectacles stuck over his Ear*. London, British Museum (see also App. no. 65)

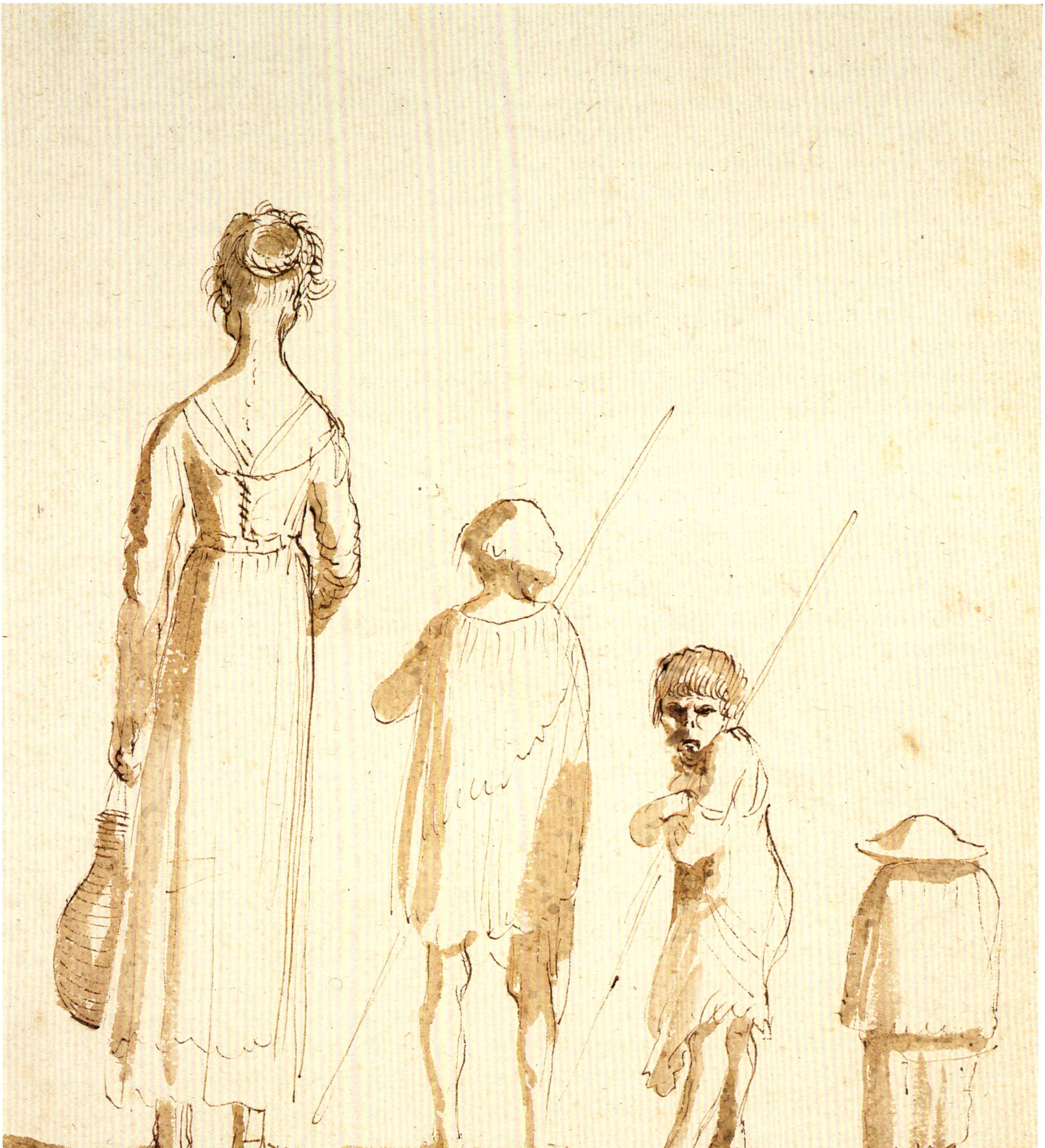

216 *Caricature of four Children standing*. London, British Museum (see also App. no. 63)

209 Head of a Peasant in profile to the left

Pen and brown ink and brown wash. 289 × 211mm.

Private collection.

Provenance: Casa Gennari; Mr Bouverie; Mr Hervey; the Earls of Gainsborough (sale, Christie's, London, 27 July 1922, lot 85, with others); E. Parsons and Sons; from whom acquired by A. P. Oppé on 5 August 1922.

Literature: Parker & Byam Shaw, 1953, no. 149; Scott-Elliot, 1958, no. 285; M, *Disegni*, 1969, no. 234.

One of Guercino's many and varied profile caricatures of peasant types. The artist retained his delicacy of touch even when making humorous drawings, here using the thinnest veils of wash to denote sagging pouches of skin about the figure's jowls.

Judging from its style, the drawing was probably made in the middle of the 1630s.

210 Elderly Man wearing a Ruff

Pen and brown ink. 311 × 226mm.

Windsor Castle, Royal Library, inv. no. 2831.

Provenance: Casa Gennari; King George III.

Literature: M & T, 1989, no. 334.

A splendid example of Guercino's pen technique, the variety of textures achieved being more reminiscent of his landscape studies. The peasant classes were not the only target of the artist's wit and often the local dignitaries and gentlefolk of Cento came in for the same treatment. In the present caricature an ironic contrast is set up between the subject's handsome attire and his aging features and unkempt hair and beard.

211 Group of Peasants

Pen and brown ink. 203 × 186mm.

Private collection.

Provenance: Casa Gennari; Mr Bouverie; Mr Hervey; the Earls of Gainsborough (sale, Christie's, London, 27 July 1922, lot 85, with others); E. Parsons and Sons; from whom acquired by A. P. Oppé on 5 August 1922.

Literature: Russell, 1923, p. 21, pl. IV; Scott-Elliot, 1958, no. 280.

These three wonderfully individual caricatures make up a curiously detached group, owing to the strange aloofness that seems to exist between them. The viewer's attention is focused on the old woman wearing a straw hat, with her single thick eyebrow and moustache, snub nose and puffy eyes. She holds a child in swaddling-clothes to her breast, conceivably suckling it. Her relationship to the man and woman on the right, staring stonily in different directions, is not explained.

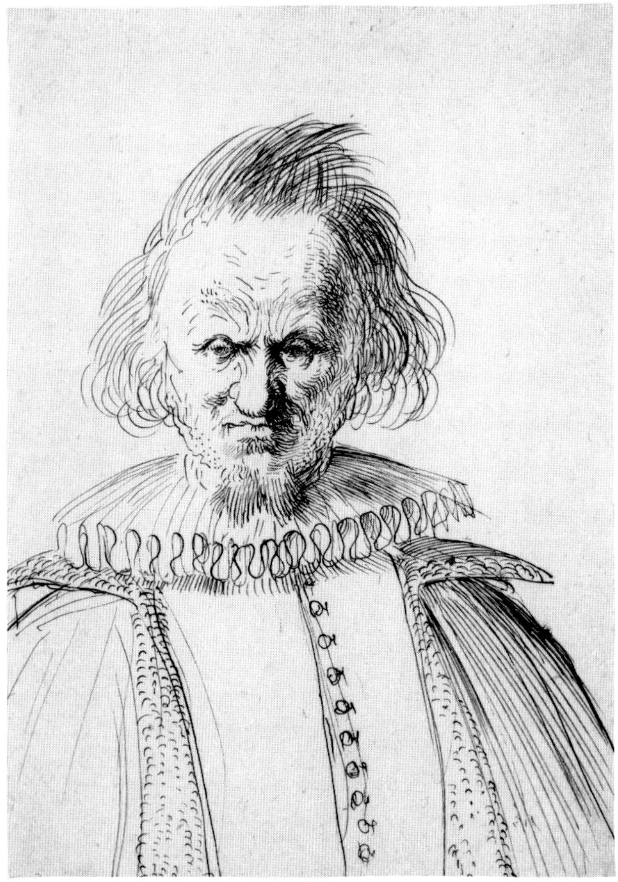

210

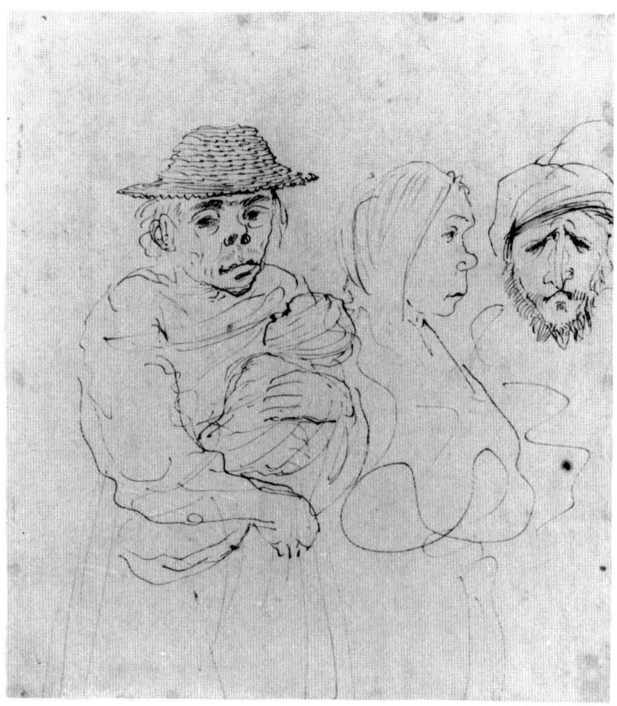

211

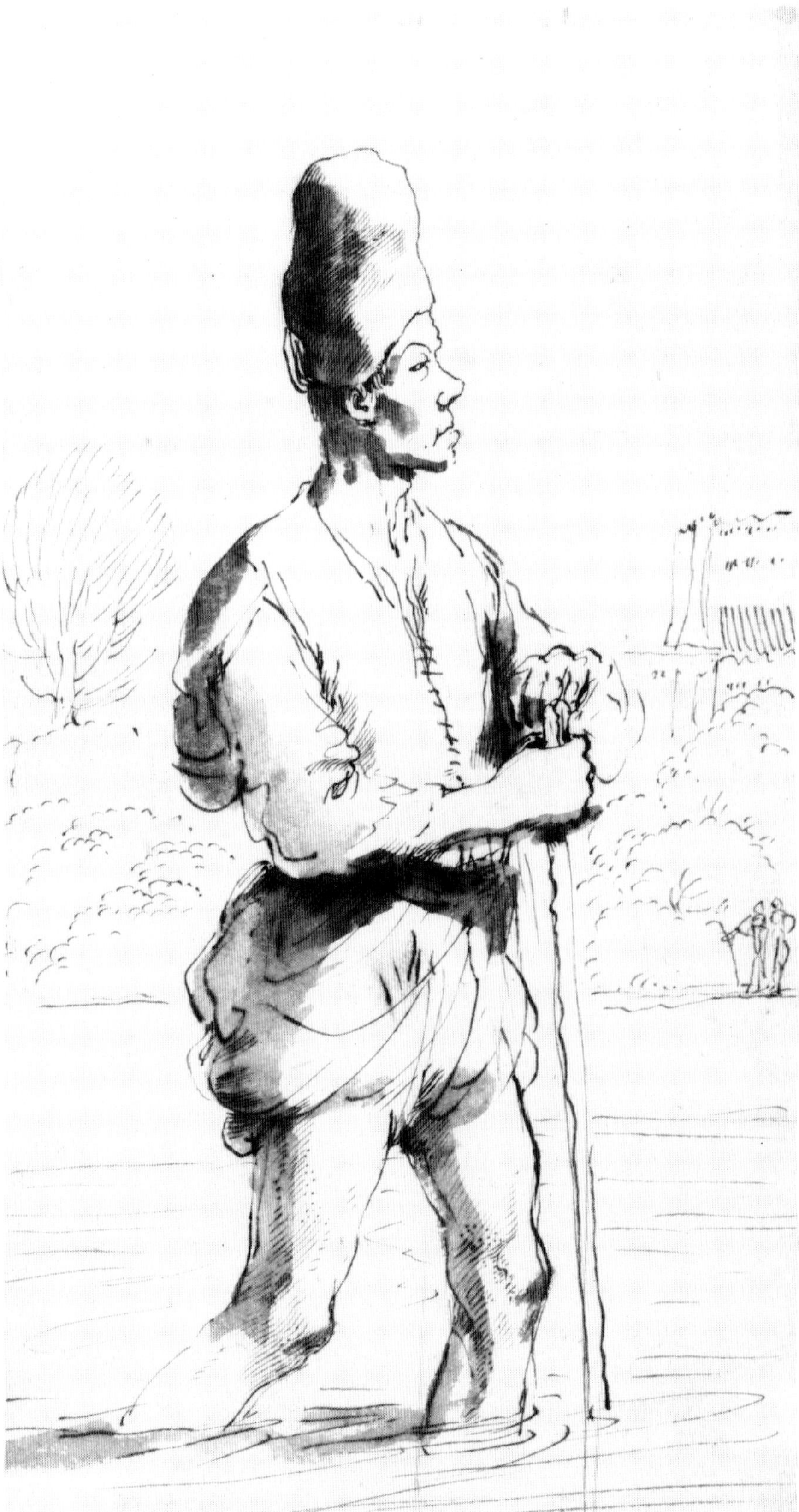

212

212 Caricature of a young Man in a tall Hat wading through a River

Pen and brown ink and brown wash. 230 × 123mm.

Private collection.

Provenance: Casa Gennari; Mr Bouverie; Mr Hervey; the Earls of Gainsborough.

Datable from its style to the 1630s. The sense of the out-of-doors is conveyed not just by the landscape setting but by the feeling of the strong midday light, suggested by the pronounced contrasts of light and dark in the figure. The spectator's gaze inevitably concentrates upon the absurd haughtiness of the youth's expression and his extraordinary hat.

The figure is probably a wayfarer fording a river.

213 Old Friar

Pen and brown ink. 223 × 201mm.

Windsor Castle, Royal Library, inv. no. 2655.

Provenance: Casa Gennari; King George III.

Literature: M & T, 1989, no. 329.

A real 'warts and all' portrait. The friar's professional status, attested by his cowl, is completely undermined by his dissolute and degenerate physical appearance.

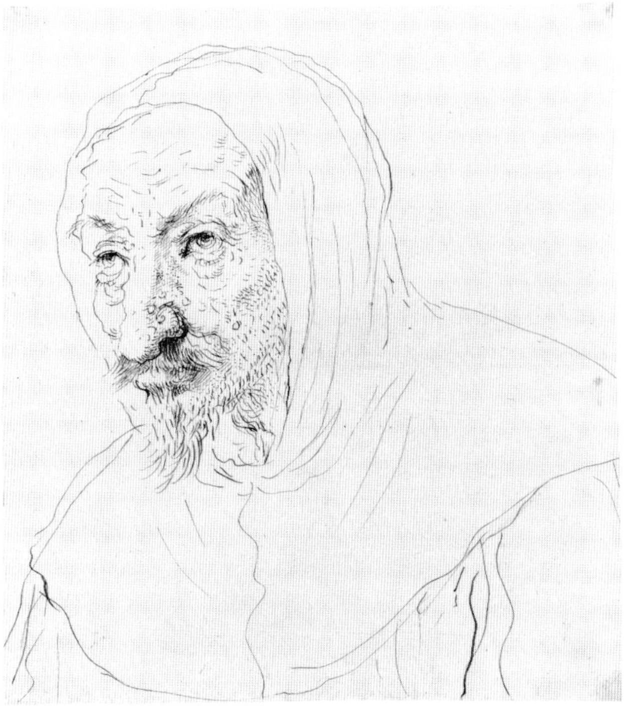

213

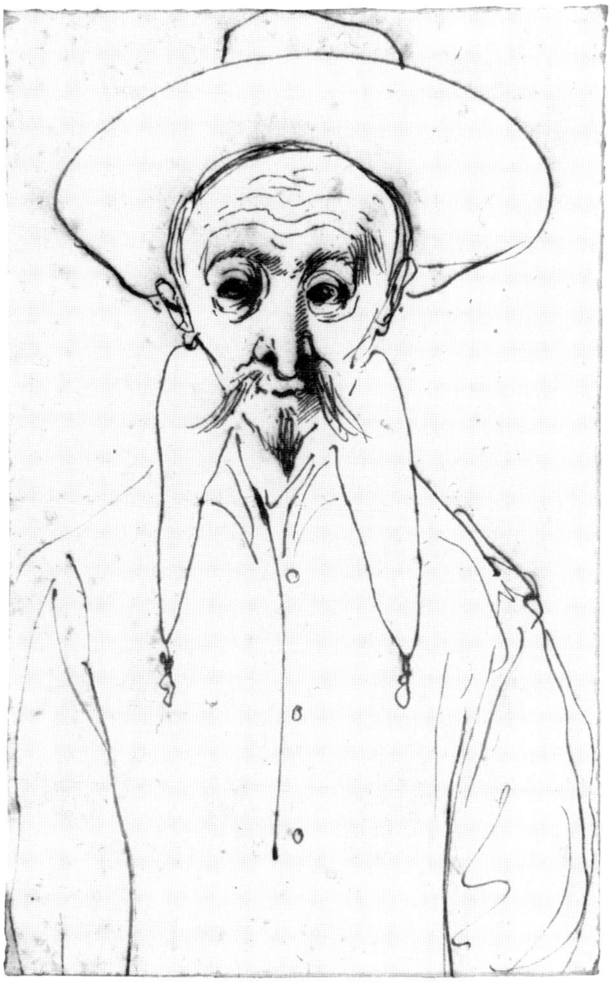

214

214 Caricature of a Man wearing a Hat and a Jacket with long Lapels

Pen and brown ink on faded blue paper. 225 × 145mm; losses in the sitter's right eye and both nostrils made up.

Edinburgh, National Gallery of Scotland, inv. no. D 4897.

Provenance: Prof. Gertrude Bing, by whom bequeathed in 1965.

Literature: Andrews, 1968, p. 61, fig. 437; M, *Disegni*, 1969, no. 237.

The drawing was formerly ascribed to Mola until it was reattributed to Guercino by Mahon, who pointed out the striking similarities between it and other caricature drawings by the master (e.g. M & T, 1989, nos. 326–8). In our view the more emphatic line, together with the use of blue paper, point rather to Mola's authorship. This exhibition provides an opportunity to compare No. 214 with Guercino's undoubtedly authentic caricature drawings.

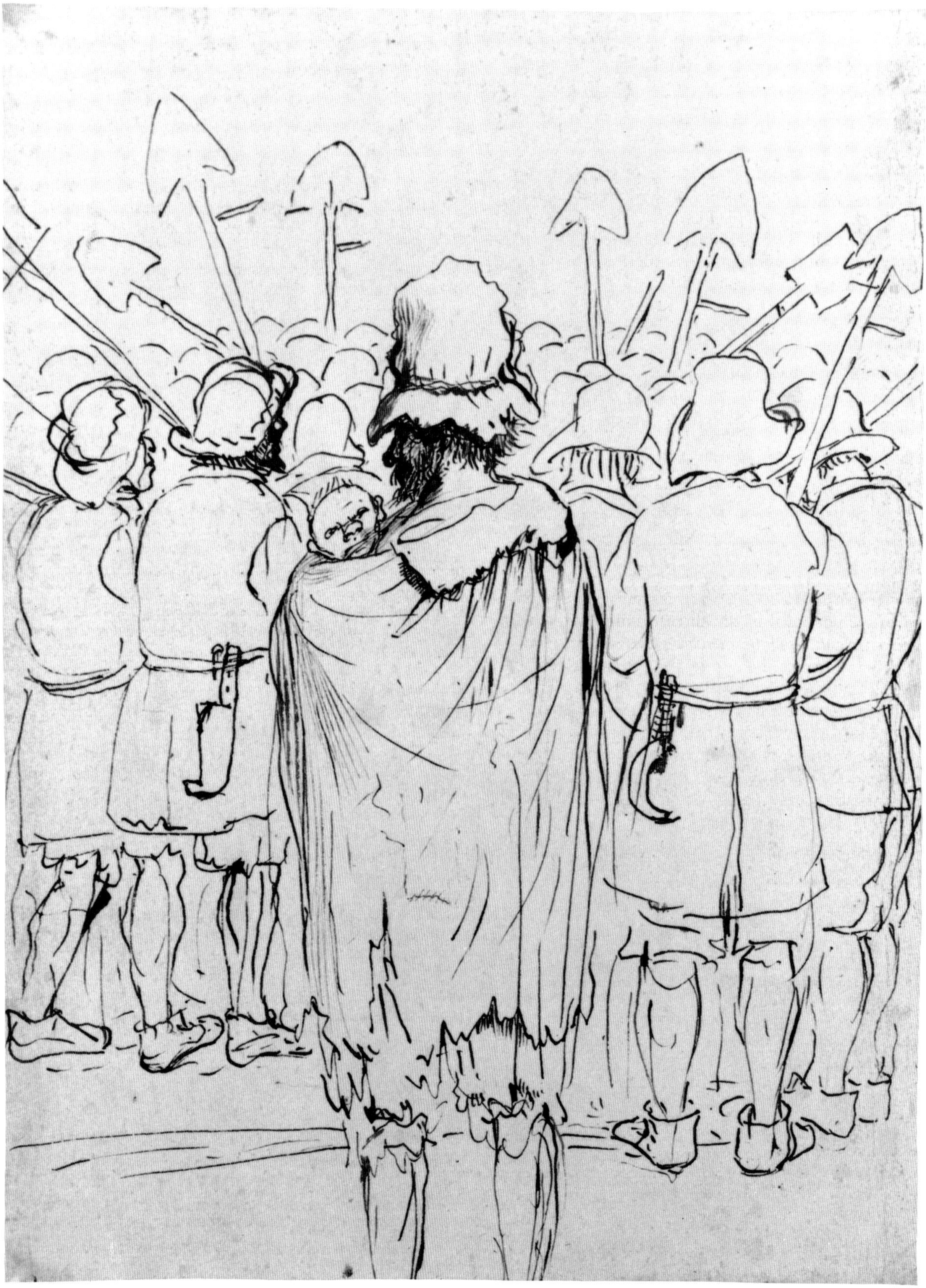

215

215 A Crowd of Peasants, many carrying Spades on their Shoulders

Pen and brown ink. 315 × 234mm.

Windsor Castle, Royal Library, inv. no. 2833.

Provenance: Casa Gennari; King George III.

Literature: M & T, 1989, no. 282.

Guercino had a great talent for drawing people from the back without relinquishing anything of their personality and expressiveness, as Nos. 215–16 attest. The spectator's amusement is here challenged only by the gaze of the ugly little snub-nosed baby looking out over the shoulder of the peasant in the foreground, apparently mocking us in our turn.

In MS. Inventory A, a late eighteenth-century inventory of the drawings at Windsor Castle, which was compiled during the reign of King George III, this drawing was referred to as: 'A Groupe of Clowns with Spades and Bills going to Labour'.

216 Caricature of four Children standing

(see colour pl. 32)

London, British Museum, inv. no. Ff. 2–140.

(For other details, see App. no. 63.)

Much may be deduced about Guercino's sense of humour from the abrupt portrayal of the three urchins with their backs rudely turned, and the menacing scowl of the only one who peers round at the spectator. The artist characterises them by their attire as well as by the exaggeration of some of their physical defects, such as the scrawny neck and prominent cheeks of the girl and the complete absence of a neck in the smallest member of the group on the right.

Guercino has suggested strong sunlight with great economy of means, breaking up the regularity of the group with the subtle play of the shadows. He has further varied their regimented poses by the tilt of the rods held by the urchins in the centre.

217 Album from the Collections of Mr Bouverie, Mr Hervey and the Earls of Gainsborough, entitled on the Spine 'ORIG/DEL/GUER/CINO'

The boards, which measure 385 × 306mm, are bound in white vellum and are decorated by a tooled gilt border; at the edges are four pairs of green silk tapes for tying the volume closed. Some of the blank pages of the album, between which the drawings were tipped in loose, carry a watermark of a hunting horn within a shield surmounted by a crown which is almost identical to that of a paper recorded in Schuttern, Schwarzwald, in 1747 (Piccard, 1979, VII, p. 277, no. 236; Heawood, 1950, pls. 344–9, reproduces a group of similar watermarks which he associates with papers used mostly in London and Amsterdam in a period roughly between 1676 and 1730).

Private collection.

Provenance: Mr Bouverie; Mr Hervey; the Earls of Gainsborough.

Besides the title *ORIG/DEL/GUER/CINO* stamped on the leather label stuck near the top of the spine, the front board is also inscribed in brown ink, vertically across the front, as follows: *Rembrant* [*sic*], which is crossed out and immediately followed by *Guercino*. Attached to the inside of the front cover is a sheet of paper with a list of names of Italian artists (frequently misspelt) each followed by a number, presumably referring to the number of drawings by the artist then contained within the album; the list is in two columns and is inscribed in light brown ink in what appears to be a mid- to late eighteenth-century English hand (perhaps that of John Bouverie; see the Introduction, pp. 22ff). The list is headed *Portfolio 16*, and is as follows: [in the first column] *Donato Creti – 4/Piola – 6/Pietro in Bologna – 1/Fr: Trevisano – 2/Vanni di Siena – 1/Calatese – 1* [perhaps intended for 'Calabrese', the nickname of Mattia Preti]/*Mecarino B. da Siena – 1* [Domenico Beccafumi]/*Santo Bartoli – 1/Gio. Francesco Rustici – 1/Gourdains – 1* [either Jacob Jordaens or, more probably, since he was an Italian, Luca Giordano]/*Giuseppe & c: & c: – 1*; *P. Farinati – 1/Pietro Sorri Sanese – 1/Sig. S. Pignoni – 1/D. da Corona – 1/Cigoli – 3/Veranisse – 1*[Veronese]/*M:r Guglielmo – 2* [probably Guglielmo Cortese was here intended]/*C: d: Bologna – 1/Crogel – 1/C. Stafano Altoni – 1* [perhaps Cristofano Allori]/*Cambiasi – 2/L: Feii lano – 1*; [in the second column] *Tiziano – 1/Pietro Parrogini – 1* [perhaps Pietro Perugino]/*Jaco' Colloni – 1/Angiolo de Vossi – 1/del Primatici – 1/Sioli – 1/ Manino Devase – 1/Maturino – 1/S. Pesaro –1* [Simone Cantarini]/*Sg.r Francesco – 1*; [at the bottom of the second column is the total] *47*. Inscriptions in an identical hand sometimes occur on drawings with a Bouverie/Hervey/Earls of Gainsborough provenance, for example on the mount of a drawing presently attributed to Giovanni Antonio Burrini, but given by the scribe to *Piola* (with Thomas Williams Fine Art Ltd., London, in the summer of 1990).

Dr Mirjam Foot of the British Library has kindly informed us that the binding and characteristic tooling of the album are English, in her opinion of *c*.1700. Thus, even though it has an Italian inscription on its spine, it could not have been one of the 'Dieci Libri di dissegni' that Malvasia mentioned in his life of Guercino as having been left in the Master's studio at his death (1678, II, p. 385; 1841, II, p. 273). What may well be the same series of seventeenth-century Italian albums – though eleven rather than ten are cited – is mentioned in the 1719 inventory of the Casa

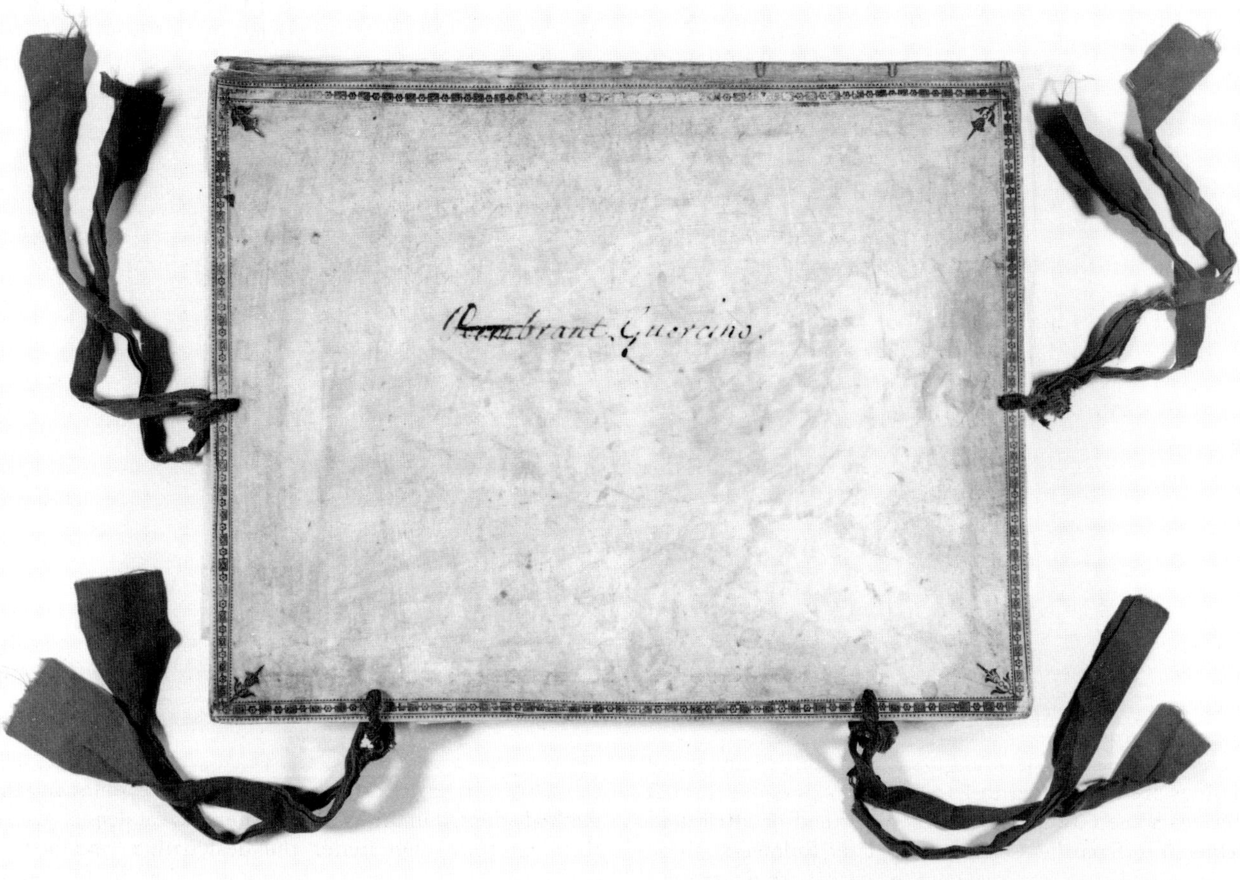

217 (front board)

Gennari: of these five were imperial and three royal, and the first six albums were said to have been bound in red leather, trimmed with gilt and with silk cords of different colour attached to the spine to act as dividers (M & T, 1989, pp. xviiiff.).

A date of *c.*1700 for No. 217 conflicts with what little was previously known about the acquisition of the Bouverie collection of drawings by Guercino, which was hitherto assumed to have been purchased in Italy and brought to England nearer the middle of the eighteenth century or even as late as the late 1760s (for further details, see Introduction, pp. 21–6). What is certain is that No. 217 was one of the 'about twelve volumes' containing 'the finest collection of Guercino's drawings in England', which by at least 1820 were said to be in the possession of Mr Hervey of Welbeck Street, London, and which he had inherited from a Mr Bouverie (Reveley, 1820, p. 77; see also Mahon's discussion of this report, 1968, pp. 348f.).

It is not known what happened to the drawings by various Italian artists listed on the inside front cover, how they came to be inside an album of drawings by Guercino (who is not mentioned at all on the list, though he could conceivably be the last-named artist, *'Sg.r Francesco'* by whom there was one drawing), nor why they were subsequently replaced again by Guercino drawings.

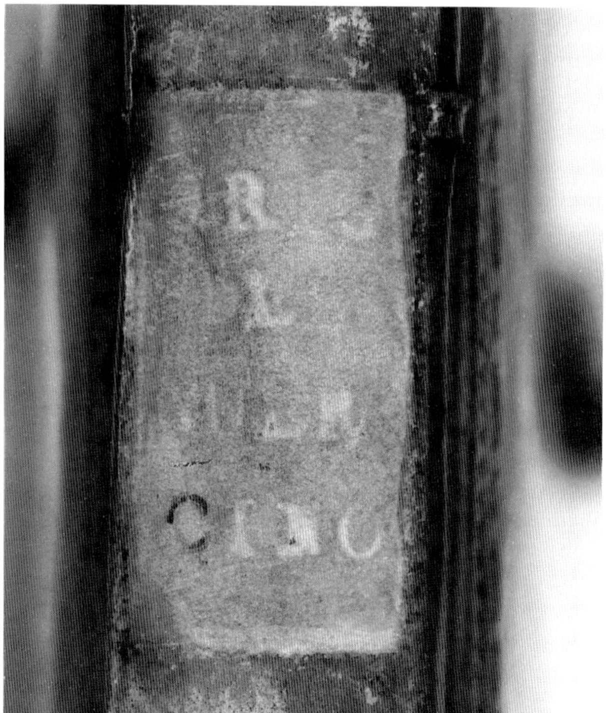

217 (spine label)

Appendix: Drawings by Guercino, his School and his Followers, in the British Museum

The following Appendix comprises a catalogue of the drawings in the British Museum by Guercino, his School, and his later followers. Given the special interest in Guercino prompted by the fourth centenary year of the artist's birth and the coherence of the British Museum group, never before published in its entirety, it was thought appropriate to catalogue these drawings ahead of the permanent catalogue of the seventeenth-century drawings of the Bolognese School in the British Museum, in which they were to have appeared and for which no definite publication date has yet been fixed. Although far smaller than the collection of the artist's drawings in the Royal Library, Windsor Castle (which numbers well over 350 autograph sheets), but only slightly less numerous than that in the Ashmolean Museum, Oxford (which, together with the drawings from the Mahon Collection, now on permanent loan there, numbers some 72), the collection of 65 drawings by Guercino in the British Museum is remarkably fine and well illustrates the many different aspects of his draughtsmanship. The autograph drawings are catalogued in Part I of the Appendix. Part II describes some 60 drawings, either ascribed or attributed to Guercino, from his School or by later followers; these have inevitably accumulated over the years with the growth of the collection and allow his autograph drawings to be studied in a wider context.

In cataloguing these drawings, we have used, with slight variations, the system employed in previous volumes in the series of catalogues dealing with Italian drawings from the Department of Prints and Drawings (for explanations the reader is referred to the preface of A. E. Popham and Philip Pouncey, *Italian Drawings in the Department of Prints and Drawings in the British Museum: The fourteenth and fifteenth Centuries*, London, 1950, vol. I, pp. vi–vii). For the 17 drawings by Guercino from the British Museum included in the Exhibition, a reproduction and much of the discursive part of the entry will be found in the foregoing text of the Exhibition Catalogue, to which the reader will be referred from the Appendix where appropriate. Details of provenance, literature, and other more incidental particulars for these same 17 drawings remain in the Appendix. Because of the limitations on the number of reproductions to be included in the Appendix, only about a third of the drawings are illustrated. Nonetheless, most of the more important autograph drawings are reproduced, together with a good sample from the School drawings and drawings by followers.

The autograph drawings in Part I are divided into three sections: studies for history subjects (App. nos. 1–56); landscapes (App. nos. 57–61); and genre and caricatures (App. nos. 62–5). The first section is by far the largest and is arranged in chronological order. Many of the drawings can be connected with pictures, the dates of which are known more or less exactly. (For the fortunate circumstances of Malvasia's extensive list of Guercino's commissions in his life of the painter and the survival of the Account Book kept in Guercino's studio from 1629 onwards to record the payments received for these commissions, see Introduction.) Around these fixed points we have disposed, by analogy of style, the figure drawings to which no date can be attached. The smaller groups of landscape, genre and caricature drawings are arranged by type, since such drawings are much less easy to date on stylistic grounds than the more characteristic figure studies, though it is often possible to distinguish whether a given example is from the early, middle or late period of the artist's career.

The first section of Part II contains 15 drawings (App. nos. 66–80) about which we did not feel sufficiently certain to include them in Part I among the autograph drawings. Such is the doubt surrounding some drawings occupying the grey area between the artist's certain studies and those by members of his School that we have, following the method adopted in the Windsor Guercino catalogue, placed them on their own under the designation 'ascribed to Guercino'. Then come two drawings in the rare technique of oiled charcoal (App. nos. 81–2), traditionally attributed to Cavedone, which we have preferred to give, with strong reservations, to Guercino because of their marked resemblance to the artist's studies from the nude drawn in this same medium (e.g. Nos. 4 and 16). The third section of Part II, the drawings of the School of Guercino (App. nos. 83–94), is little more than a catch-all for that heterogeneous mass of Guercinesque material that is too inferior to be given to his better followers, Benedetto and Cesare Gennari, let alone to the master himself. The great majority of these drawings remain in the unmounted series, being of too poor quality to merit being placed in the collection among the main series of mounted drawings. Likewise almost solely of documentary value are the drawings grouped in the next section (4), containing copies after Guercino by anonymous artists, mostly active in the late seventeenth century and the early eighteenth, and presumed copies (App. nos. 95–107): these are without exception unmounted.

Of far greater interest are the copies after Guercino by late seventeenth-century and eighteenth-century named artists of all schools (Part II, section 5, Nos. 108–17), most of which are to be found in the mounted series. These begin with the drawing by the Flemish painter Livio Mehus (1630–91), who was for long active in Italy. This sheet (App. no. 108) well demonstrates the already lively interest taken in Guercino's drawings by contemporary artists outside his immediate circle; unusually in this instance the copy is of some of his caricatures. An even more remarkable example of the understanding of Guercino's graphic style is shown in the copy (App. no. 109) by the Irish painter and collector Hugh Howard (1675–1738) after a red chalk drawing of the *Madonna of the Rosary* (No. 129); then, as now, the original was in the collection of the Dukes of Devonshire, having possibly been acquired as one of a group directly from the artist's nephew Benedetto Gennari (1633–1715), who had been employed by the 4th Earl (afterwards 1st Duke) of Devonshire during his stay in England from 1675 to 1689. Howard, in his turn, worked for the 2nd Duke of Devonshire, who shared his keen interest in collecting Old Master drawings, and it is likely that he came upon this particular drawing by Guercino while in the Duke's employ. The lack of a good copy after Guercino by Sir Joshua Reynolds (1723–92), whose numerous imitations of the master's work are discussed elsewhere (see Introduction, Nos. 126–7 and App. nos. 46 and 48), is a sad gap in the Department's collection.

Without doubt, the ablest copyist of Guercino's drawings was the Florentine-born engraver Francesco Bartolozzi (1727–1815). In 1764 he settled in England, having been commissioned by the Royal Librarian, Richard Dalton, to engrave many items among the outstanding collection of drawings by Guercino that Dalton had acquired for King George III (see M & T, 1989, p. xxx, n. 44). Although some of his drawn copies after Guercino are related to engravings for which they must have been preparatory, the majority was not engraved: they were presumably either made as ends in themselves or drawn with the intention that they should be published in a work that was eventually abandoned. It is also possible that some of them were made as records of drawings to be considered for possible purchase by George III. One such example of a Bartolozzi copy unrelated to a print is App. no. 111, after a drawing by Guercino now in the J. Paul Getty Museum, Malibu, California; the copy in the British Museum reveals the engraver's extraordinary capacity to mimic Guercino's style, albeit with a prettiness not found in the original.

Sections 6 and 7 of Part II contain the handful of drawings that can be associated with some degree of confidence with two members of the Gennari family, Guercino's nephew Cesare Gennari (1637–88) and his great-great-nephew Carlo Gennari (1716–90). The drawings of the Gennari remain extremely hard to pin down. Four drawings are here catalogued under the name of Cesare, some with more certainty than others (App. nos. 118–21); only one under the name of Carlo (App. no. 122).

The last section (8) contains the four drawings in the collection that are by the 'Faker' of Guercino, probably a Bolognese artist active in the second half of the eighteenth century (App. nos. 123–6).

In spite of the great vogue for Guercino in England in the eighteenth century, only a single drawing undoubtedly by the master found its way into the British Museum in the first forty-five years, following its foundation in 1753. There are many and varied reasons for this state of affairs, one of them being their rarity on the English art market throughout most of the eighteenth century. By 1770, the two largest *blocs* of the artist's drawings, accounting for a very sizeable proportion of his entire surviving output, were firmly located in the hands of English owners – King George III and a certain Mr Bouverie (see Introduction). Although several of the finest drawings in King George III's collection had been lavishly published in two volumes of engravings by Bartolozzi, making Guercino's drawings seem all the more tantalising to collectors of the day, good specimens of his work were all too scarce in the sale-rooms. Thus Sir Hans Sloane's founding bequest of 1753 of a remarkable series of collections, among them some highly important Old Master drawings, seems not to have included a single drawing by Guercino himself, though it did number two drawings after him (App. nos. 102 and 105). The first drawing actually by Guercino to enter the collection arrived sixteen years later in 1769 through another bequest, that of William Fawkener (dates unknown). Fawkener's collection of Old Master drawings was comparatively small, numbering less than 400 sheets, but was rich in drawings of the Italian Baroque. His one drawing by Guercino, *Standing nude Infant* (App. no. 27), resided unnoticed and in poor condition among the unmounted drawings until 1980; it has subsequently been identified as a study for the small boy in the picture of *St Augustine in Meditation* of 1635, now in the Prado, Madrid. Fawkener's bequest also included three still problematic 'Guercinos' which may turn out to be by the artist himself but which we have, for the moment, preferred to catalogue as only ascribed to him (App. nos. 75–7). All four drawings are laid down on characteristic Fawkener mounts.

The situation was dramatically transformed in 1799 through the bequest of the carefully chosen and extensive collection of Old Master prints and drawings of all schools that had belonged to the Rev. Clayton Mordaunt Cracherode (1730–99). Cracherode had excellent taste, and his collection of drawings by Guercino contained some of the best of the comparatively few that would then have been available to him. There are no less than twelve fine autograph sheets, including particularly good landscapes and caricatures (App. nos. 4, 20, 23, 38, 42, 44–5, 58–60, and 63–4). Cracherode seems to have been attracted to the artist's rapid studies in pen or pen and wash, as well as to more finished studies in the same medium. Insofar as it has been possible to ascertain, Cracherode acquired these drawings from a number of different sources. Most – though it is only possible to demonstrate this in two cases (App. nos. 38 and 45) – would seem to have come originally from the sizeable group of drawings bought by the dealer William Kent directly from the Casa Gennari and then sold by him in London at the so-called 'Luti' sale (Langford's, London, 8–11 December 1762). It is unlikely that Cracherode bought the drawings himself at the sale, since his name does not appear among those of the buyers in the annotated copy of the sale catalogue in the library of P. & D. Colnaghi, London. Nor, it seems, did he begin buying in earnest until the 1780s and 1790s, following his inheritance in 1773 of a large fortune.

Two of Cracherode's Guercinos changed hands three times between other collectors in England before entering his possession: one (App. no. 42) belonging first to Jonathan Richardson, Sr (1665–1745), then Joannes Michiel Rysbrack (1693–1770) and then John Barnard (d.1784); the other (App. no. 60) belonging also first to Jonathan Richardson, then to the engraver and early collector of drawings Arthur Pond (*c*.1735–58), and after, to Sir Joshua Reynolds (1723–92). No less than three of Cracherode's Guercino drawings, all landscapes, had at one time belonged to Arthur Pond (App. nos. 58–60).

An even more spectacular collection of Old Master drawings, also including many of the Italian School, entered the Museum in 1824 with the magnificent bequest of the collections of Richard Payne Knight (1750–1824). Of the seven drawings called Guercino from this collection, all are still accepted as autograph here (App. nos. 5, 7, 24, 41, 52, 57 and 65); an eighth drawing (App. no. 72), which Payne Knight believed to be by the artist's nephew Benedetto Gennari, is tentatively ascribed to Guercino. The seven drawings form a well-balanced group, comprising landscapes and caricatures as well as figure studies, but with a distinct preference for highly finished drawings in pen and ink alone in an engraver-like technique (e.g., App. nos. 5, 41, 52 and 57). Like many of Cracherode's drawings, Payne Knight had acquired his Guercinos from English sales, for example those of Nathaniel Hone and H. C. Jennings. But at least two had been in Continental collections shortly before they entered his possession, one (App. no. 24) in the collection of the famous engraver and architect Giovanni Battista Piranesi (1720–78) and the other (App. no. 7) in that of the minor Bolognese painter Antonio Beccadelli (1718–1803). It is possible that others by Guercino may also have found their way into his collection from abroad.

The much-lamented catastrophic failure of the British Museum to purchase in 1830 the vast collection of Old Master drawings formed by the portrait painter Sir Thomas Lawrence (1769–1830) deprived the Museum of a significant series of drawings by Guercino. Thirty drawings by the master are listed in the manuscript *Inventory of the Collection of Drawings by Old Masters formed by Sir Thomas Lawrence, P.R.A., drawn up while the Collection was still in his House*, of which a typescript is in the library of the Department of Prints and Drawings (shelfmark N. 6. 33). In spite of what was undoubtedly a large number of drawings by the artist, it was by Lawrence's standards relatively modest in comparison with the remarkable series of drawings by Michelangelo, Raphael, Parmigianino and the Carracci. It seems reasonable to claim that Lawrence did not prize Guercino's drawings as highly as those by the earlier Italian draughtsmen. The Museum possesses only one drawing generally accepted as by Guercino from the Lawrence collection, that of *Cupid* (App. no. 51), though it does not bear Lawrence's collector's mark. Robinson's claim that the drawing had belonged to Lawrence seems to be borne out by the entry for the sixteenth drawing by Guercino in the *Inventory*: *A Flying Cupid, pen*. For two other drawings by Guercino from Lawrence's collection, one in the Ashmolean Museum, Oxford, and the other on loan to the Ashmolean from the Mahon Collection see Nos. 20 and 17 respectively.

By the early nineteenth century Guercino's reputation, along with that of many other Italian Baroque painters, was beginning to be eclipsed, in favour of the earlier Italian masters of the Renaissance whose drawings were appearing on the market as a result of the great social and political changes in Europe in the wake of the French Revolution and the Napoleonic Wars. Ironically, it was shortly afterwards, when enthusiasm for Guercino's drawings had reached something of a nadir, that a large batch of them was released onto the market. This occurred when the 1st Earl of Gainsborough apparently decided to sell a portion of the 'Bouverie collection' of Old Master drawings, which he had inherited and which included a large group of drawings by Guercino. It seems almost certain that all of the drawings in the sale had the characteristic *B* stamp of the Bouverie collection applied to them (L 325). Of the items offered for sale on this occasion (Christie's, London, 20 July 1859), 116 were presented as by Guercino, just over one third of the total. Perhaps it was the great quantity of drawings offered, many in the same technique of red chalk, as much as the scant popularity of Guercino himself at that time, that made this part of the sale something of a failure: twenty-three out of forty-seven lots of drawings were bought in (the name of 'Hogarth' as a buyer alongside the low-priced lots was almost certainly used as a code for bought in), and many of those drawings that did sell fetched poor prices.

Once again the Museum was slow to see its opportunity. Tiffin, the dealer who habitually acted for the Museum during this period, bought a mere six lots at the sale, just two of which (lots 58–9) were acquired on commission by the Museum. These two lots contained five drawings in all, only two of which turn out to be autograph (App. nos. 39 and 56), and cost the then princely sum of one guinea. Of the remaining three, two are indifferent School works (App. nos. 85 and 89), while the third (inv. no. 1859-8-6-69) is a good autograph study by the minor Bolognese painter Giovanni Battista Caccioli (1623–75), a follower of Domenico Maria Canuti (1620–84).

Fortunately, other drawings from the 1859 'Bouverie' sale did subsequently find their way into the British Museum. Among the eight drawings certainly by Guercino that entered the collection thirty-six years later with the purchase of the magnificent collection of prints and drawings that had belonged to John Malcolm of Poltalloch (1805–93), there were no less than four from the 1859 sale, among the best of the group (App. nos. 9, 25, 26 and 36). These four had been acquired at the sale by or on behalf of the expert connoisseur and collector of Old Master drawings Sir J. C. Robinson. Among them was one of the star lots, no. 54, the *Charity, with an old Man*, for which Tiffin had then paid 3 guineas. This is one of the finest drawings in pen and wash by Guercino in existence (No. 54, otherwise App. no. 9). The four had passed into Malcolm's possession when Robinson sold much of his own collection of drawings to him in 1860.

It is important to recall that the groups of drawings by Guercino that entered the Museum with the collections of

Fawkener, Cracherode, Payne Knight and Malcolm were each no more than a tiny section of a much larger collection, in which, as much as possible, the range of drawings by the best artists of the different European schools of painting were represented according to the tastes and means of the collector concerned. Malcolm's collection was brought together at great cost and, perhaps a little self-consciously, with a deliberately scientific purpose. Quantity was eschewed for quality, as the collector acquired the best available specimens of Old Master drawings almost regardless of price. In the Italian School, Malcolm's interests, and those of his adviser Robinson, were in the Renaissance rather than the Baroque, which was given merely a token representation. In its combination of exclusivity and comprehensiveness, Malcolm's method typified a new style of collecting that emerged at the end of the nineteenth century and has had a number of successors in the twentieth.

The bequest of George Salting (1835–1909) brought to the Museum a further series of drawings by Guercino, part of an extensive collection of Old Master drawings and prints of the highest quality. Two of the Guercinos had earlier been sold in the 1859 'Bouverie' sale (App. nos. 35 and 40), though one other may well also have come from this source, since it too shows evidence of having once been in the Casa Gennari collection (App. no. 28). Salting, a man of great wealth and impressively wide interests, devoted his life to collecting. His first love was Chinese porcelain but he also accumulated a large collection of paintings and drawings (though it is said that these had less attraction for him). In the same year as his bequest to the British Museum, he left to the National Gallery 192 paintings of all schools.

In 1943 Eric Hamilton Rose (1872–1947), formerly of Leweston Manor, Sherborne, Dorset, the Founder and Vice President of the Mining Corporation of Canada, presented a group of no less than eleven autograph drawings by Guercino (App. nos. 18–19, 31–2, 37, 46–8, 53–4 and 61). It also included five others, four of which we have preferred to ascribe to the master (App. nos. 70–71, 73–4 and 95). These were among a large collection of Old Master drawings, English watercolours and prints given to the Department at the same time. The group of drawings by Guercino is noteworthy, because, with four exceptions (App. nos. 18, 31, 32 and 48), they were for many years almost completely overlooked, having been stored loose in a brown envelope marked 'School Drawings' in a wrapper with the rest of the unmounted drawings placed under the artist's name. Since 1980 they have been mounted and placed with the autograph drawings of Guercino, with only one exception (App. no. 95). As one and almost certainly a second of the drawings from the Eric Rose gift was copied by Sir Joshua Reynolds (App. nos. 48 and 46), there can be little doubt that practically the whole group belonged at one time to the Bouverie collection. One of the drawings (App. no. 73), however, was etched by Zocchi and was thus presumably one of the 'Kent' group of drawings by Guercino. It is conceivable that this could have strayed into the Bouverie collection sometime in the second half of the eighteenth century and was then absorbed into the main group that had been purchased probably via Forni and later passed into the possession of the 1st Earl of Gainsborough. The Rose drawings were probably part of one of five lots (nos. 81–5) each containing scores of drawings by different masters included in a subsequent sale of a later Earl of Gainsborough at Christie's, London, 27 July 1922. While it is true that none of the Rose drawings is a first-rate finished composition drawing, they fill an important gap in the collection by representing for the first time Guercino's working drawings in pen and ink. Very little is known about Eric Rose himself, other than what is recorded in a short note appended to a family history by him, entitled *History of the Family de Ros, de Rose, Rose of Kilravock*, Frome and London, 1939.

Among more recent gifts should be mentioned App. no. 16, bequeathed by Mr and Mrs A. Nussbaum. Even more notable are App. nos. 49 and 50, both formerly from the collection of the Earls of Gainsborough and the latter mounted on a characteristic Casa Gennari mount; these form part of the gift from Sir Denis Mahon of an interesting group of Guercinesque drawings presented in 1986–7 to mark his gratitude to the Director and Trustees for allowing the cataloguing of the fine series of Guercino and Guercinesque drawings at the Royal Library, Windsor Castle, to take place at the British Museum, in collaboration with Nicholas Turner. Other drawings from this group in the present catalogue are App. nos. 79–80, 113, 115–17, 119 and 123.

With the exception of the two drawings bought directly by the Museum at the 1859 'Bouverie' sale (App. nos. 39 and 56), two others bought in 1893 at the sale of Heneage Finch, 5th Earl of Aylesford (App. nos. 29 and 30), and those that came to the Museum with the Malcolm collection, all of the drawings discussed hitherto were bequeathed to the Museum. By contrast, in the twentieth century, acquisition by purchase has become the principal means by which the Museum collects. When in 1919, 1920 and 1922 (see Introduction) unparalleled opportunities to buy still more drawings by the master occurred – at about 1 guinea each, or less – it was presumably thought unnecessary to expand further what by then was rated to be a good collection of his drawings. Several years later, in 1937, the Museum did make an important purchase of a Guercino drawing, the magnificent, large-scale *Theatrical Performance in the open Air* (No. 186, otherwise App. no. 62), bought with funds raised from the sale of duplicate prints from the Malcolm collection. Recent purchases have included App. no. 3, an early black chalk study, which helps supplement the rather meagre representation of Guercino's early, pre-Roman style of drawing (before 1621); App. no. 17, the only drapery study by Guercino to have survived outside the large group of such studies in the Staatsgalerie, Stuttgart, on deposit from the Koenig–Fachsenfeld Collection; and App. no. 33, the magnificent composition study of *The Martyrdom of St Bartholomew*, purchased with the help of funds bequeathed to the Museum by the late Mrs V. J. Playfair.

I Drawings by Guercino (App. nos. 1–65)

1 Studies for History Subjects (App. nos. 1–56)

1 Return of the Prodigal Son

He kneels to the left, just left of centre, with his back to the spectator, at the bottom of a flight of steps; his head and arms are raised in the direction of his father who hastens down the stairs at the left with his arms also outstretched in greeting; on the right are two onlookers watching the reunion from behind a balustrade.

Pen and brown ink and brown wash, much faded; retouched in places with black chalk. 198 × 267mm.

1873–5–10–3535. Not illustrated.

Provenance: J. H. Anderdon, by whom presented.

Literature: M, *Disegni*, 1969, under no. 25; M & T, 1989, under no. 2.

One of a group of studies for a painting of this subject executed in 1617 for Cardinal Alessandro Ludovisi, then Archbishop of Bologna and afterwards Pope Gregory XV. The painting, now in the Galleria Sabauda, Turin (S, 1988, no. 33), was extensively repainted after the serious damage it sustained when in store in the Second World War. A list of other drawings related to the picture can be found in M & T, 1989, under no. 2.

2 *Recto*: Studies for a kneeling St Francis *Verso*: Landscape; two cancelled small-scale Studies of a kneeling St Francis; calligraphic Exercises

On the *recto*, the figure on the left kneels, with his body facing the spectator, his hands crossed over his breast and his right hand pointing upwards to the right while his head looks downwards to the left; the figure on the right kneels in profile to the right, with both arms raised in supplication. The *verso* includes a landscape of two trees and a building and two studies of the kneeling St Francis with his arms raised to shoulder level, one sketch more summarily drawn than the other but both crossed out; pen trials or calligraphic swirls occupy most of the upper part of the sheet.

Pen and brown ink. 133 × 188mm.

1946–7–13–721. Illustrated in main Catalogue (No. 9).

Provenance: (?)L. Gori (the idiosyncratic π-shaped *n* sometimes being associated with this collector); (?)S. Woodburn; Phillipps-Fenwick; presented anonymously.

Literature: Turner, 1981, pp. 164ff.; S, 1988, under no. 40.

Inscribed on the *recto* in brown ink, a quarter of the way down the sheet, in the artist's hand: *Avendo*; in dark brown ink, at the bottom, right of centre, in another hand: *Lodovico Carazzi*; and in black ink in the top left corner: π. 456.. The sheet was previously placed among the unmounted drawings of Ludovico Carracci.

For the main discussion of this drawing, see No. 9.

3 Head of a Warrior wearing a Helmet

He is bearded, in three-quarters profile to the right.

Black chalk, with some slight touches of white chalk, on buff paper. 192 × 144mm; made up with a narrow strip of paper at the left edge.

1979–10–6–84. Not illustrated.

Provenance: R. Joseph, from whom purchased.

Literature: Turner, 1980, no. 43; S, 1988, under no. 42; M & T, 1989, under no. 148.

The drawing had been attributed in the past to both Pietro Faccini (1562–1602) and Giacomo Cavedone (1577–1660). As Mario di Giampaolo was the first to observe, it is in fact a study for the soldier in armour seen on the left of the fresco *St Roch thrown into Prison*, painted in 1618 in the Oratorio di S. Rocco in Bologna (S, 1988, no. 42). In the fresco the soldier holds a staff in his right hand: what may be a rough indication of the right hand appears in the drawing at the bottom right, though there is no trace of the spear. The left edge of the sheet, before the addition of the strip of paper, corresponds with the left edge of the fresco.

Two drawings with studies for the whole composition survive: a double-sided sheet in the collection of Mortimer Brandt, New York (M, *Disegni*, 1969, no. 28), the *verso* of which shows the composition with the same soldier standing on the right with his back to the spectator; and a second drawing in the Louvre, Paris (inv. no. 6880; Bottari, 1966, pl. XII; Loire, 1990, p. 92, no. 25), in which the design is far closer to the finished result, with the soldier now standing on the left, facing the spectator, just behind the jailer who forces the saint through the prison door.

A drawing of what appears to be the head of the same soldier, which has been silhouetted and laid down onto another sheet of paper, is in the Nationalmuseum, Stockholm (inv. no. NMH 1142/1863), placed with the drawings of Guercino and his School: it is hard to judge the status of this drawing, though it seems not to be an original study.

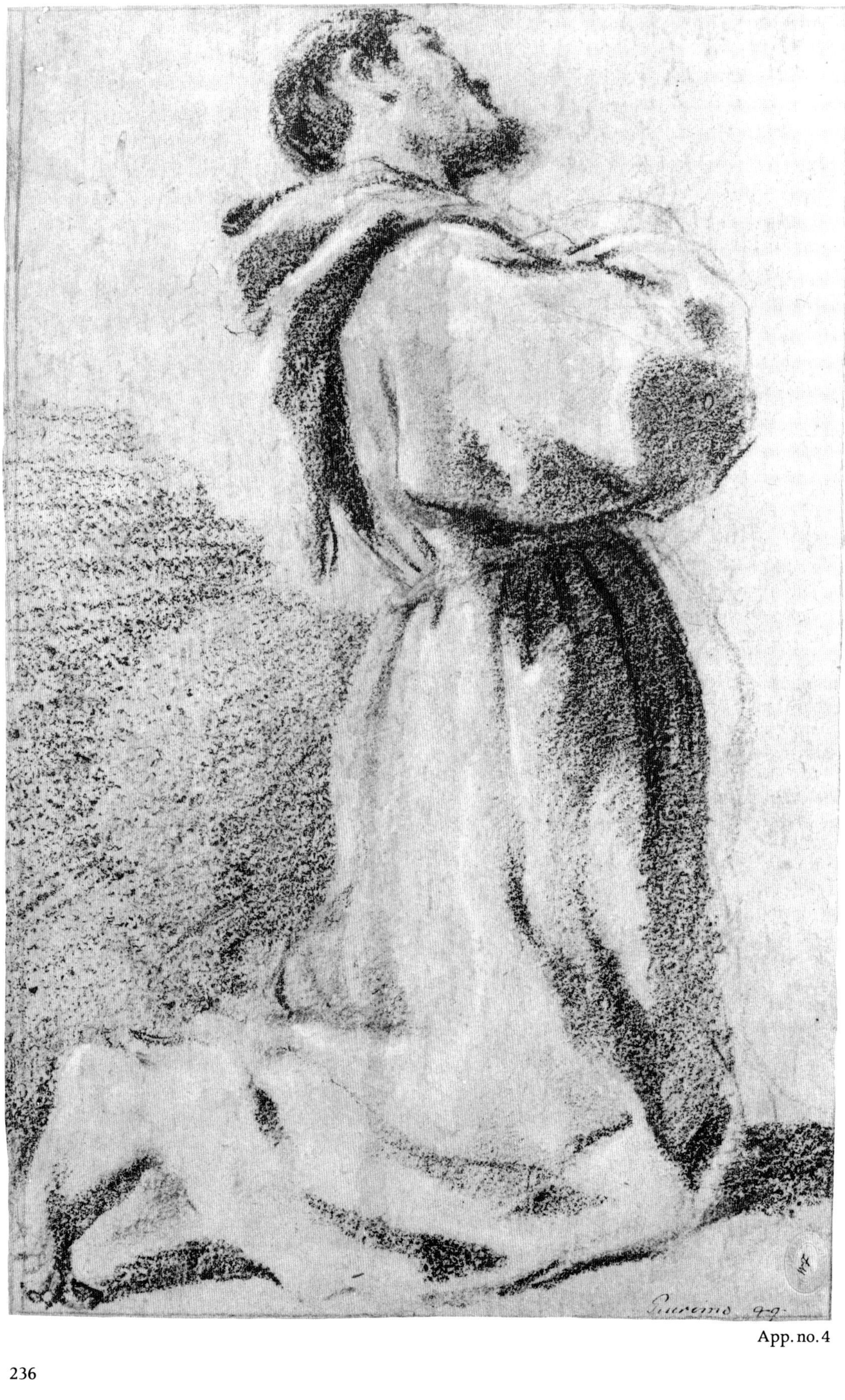

App. no. 4

4 Friar kneeling

He kneels in profile to the right and looks upwards, his arms crossed on his breast.

Oiled charcoal over black chalk, heightened with white chalk, on blue (faded) paper; at each edge is a ruled red line, drawn twice at the left edge. 397 × 255mm.

Ff. 2–133

Provenance: Rev. C. M. Cracherode Bequest, 1799 (the drawing has the Cracherode stamp (L 298) with the initials *W F* (William Fawkener) written inside it in error).

Literature: M, 1967, pp. 58–9, under no. 34; M, *Disegni*, 1969, under no. 7; M & E, 1986, p. 3, under no. 1.

Inscribed in brown ink in the bottom right corner: *Guercino 49*.

In a note on the mount, now erased, K. T. Parker tentatively attributed the drawing to the Bolognese painter Pietro Faccini. A. E. Popham, according to Departmental records, supported the traditional identification, with the rider 'but possibly Cavedone (not Faccini)', as if he were certain that Parker's idea was wrong, but was not yet wholly convinced of Guercino's authorship.

Another drawing of a kneeling friar in profile to the right, also in black chalk, is in the collection of Sir Denis Mahon (No. 1). Mahon identified the figure in his drawing as St Francis and connected it with that saint in the *Madonna and Child with Sts Francis, Antony Abbot and Bovo* executed in Guercino's workshop for the church of S. Sebastiano at Renazzo di Cento (S, 1988, no. 9), one of three altarpieces Guercino painted for this church early in his career; Mahon is now inclined to redate this picture *c*.1616–17. More tentatively, he suggested that App. no. 4 might be for the same commission. However, although it has always been accepted that the two drawings were at least of the same date if not necessarily for the same commission, the British Museum study appears to us to have been made at a later moment, possibly from the second half of the second decade. This slight discrepancy in style could conceivably be explained by the fact that the Renazzo altarpiece cited above, along with two others also made for the church in that village (S, 1988, nos. 6 and 11), probably took a longer period to deliver than one would normally expect. Guercino's career was just taking off at this stage, with more prestigious but time-consuming projects on the horizon; yet he was still saddled with what he might then have considered routine local commissions, such as the decoration of the Casa Pannini. It is therefore likely that the young artist's attention was increasingly diverted away from his provincial commissions, a fact that may explain the presence of studio hands in two of the three Renazzo pictures. Yet even if the altarpiece with St Bovo took as much as two or three years to deliver, the style of the British Museum drawing seems to us to be somewhat later.

Several other compositions that include the figure of a kneeling friar survive from Guercino's early career: the *Madonna and Child with Sts Joseph, Augustine, Louis and Francis and a Child Donor* of 1616 (S, 1988, no. 27); the *Madonna del Carmine with Sts Albert and Francis and another Franciscan* of 1618 (S, 1988, no. 38); the *Sts Francis and Louis of France kneeling in Adoration* of 1618 (S, 1988, no. 40); and the *Sts Bernardino of Siena and Francis of Assisi with the Madonna of Loreto* of 1618 (S, 1988, no. 44); one might point out that App. no. 4 closely resembles the figure of St Bernardino in this latter painting, though in reverse and with a small beard. Finally, a drawing showing two kneeling friars (one with features in common with the Mahon drawing, the other with App. no. 4) has recently come to light in Perugia and is discussed under No. 1. In short, since this was an absolutely stock pose for a popular patron saint, there does not seem to be enough evidence to conclude with any certainty for which picture the present drawing was made.

5 Madonna and Child with St Anne

St Anne is seated, turned to the left, on a low ledge; the naked Christ Child stands on tiptoe in profile to the left on the ledge in front of her, and she supports him under the arm with her left hand; the Madonna is seated on a chair at the left with her knees very slightly to the left and the upper half of her body inclined to the right, as she leans towards the Christ Child while resting her head against her mother's cheek.

Pen and brown ink. 293 × 255mm; damaged and repaired in the darks.

Pp. 4–62. Illustrated in main Catalogue (No. 36).

Provenance: Casa Gennari; H. C. Jennings (L 2771); R. Payne Knight Bequest, 1824.

Literature: Mariette, 1851–3, vol. 1, p. 63; Marangoni, 1920, fig. 45; Marangoni, 1959, no. 51, repr.; M, 1967, p. 12 and n. 26.

The Casa Gennari inventory of 31 October 1719 mentions this as one of the few drawings that were not kept in albums but instead hung, framed, on the wall: *Un disegno a Penna d'una Madona S. Anna, e Bambino con Cornice dorata e Vetro del Guerzino Segnato n.º 73 L Cento* (fascicule G, sheet 8, item 73). For two other drawings in the British Museum also described in the inventory, see App. nos. 7 and 9. While still in the Casa Gennari, the drawing was etched in reverse by Francesco Bartolozzi (1727–1815), with the inscription beneath: *De Pinacotheca Gennariorum Equitis I. F. Barberii Centensis Nepotum Bononiae* (Calabi, 1928, no. 2113). The print was included in Piranesi's *Raccolta* of 1764 and was one of three in the volume by Bartolozzi after drawings by Guercino from the Casa Gennari. All of Bartolozzi's prints in this series must have been made before 1762 since they were already known to the art amateur Giampietro Zanotti (1674–1765), who spoke of them in a letter to Monsignor Giovanni Bottari (1689–1775) dated 20 August 1762. (For further details see M & T, 1989, p. xxix and n. 43.) A red chalk copy, also in reverse and probably after Bartolozzi's print, is in the Fondazione Cini, Venice (inv. no. 31.142).

The drawing has been cut down on the left and probably also at the bottom. This had already occurred by some time around the middle of the eighteenth century since Bartolozzi's print records the format of the sheet as it survives today.

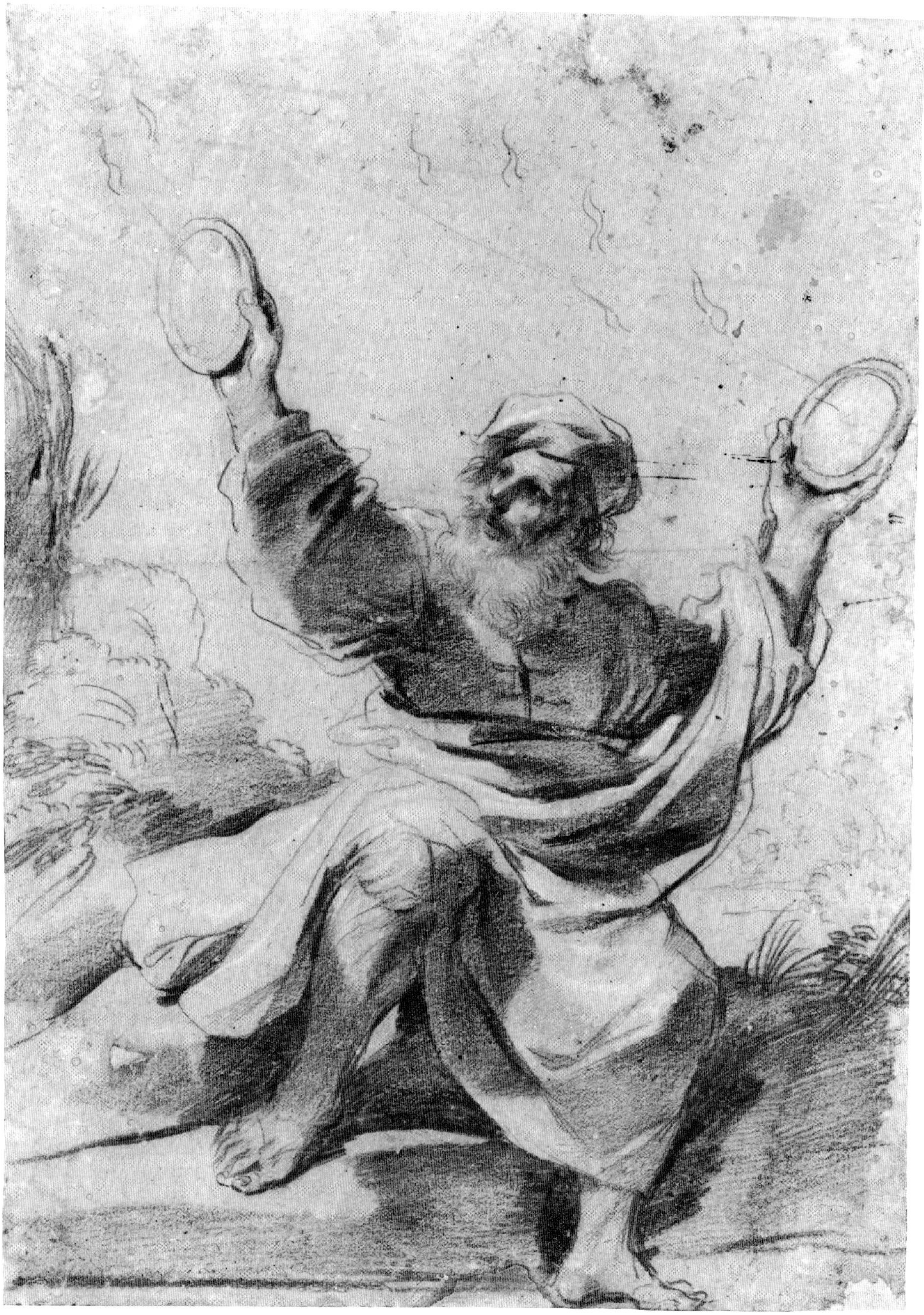

App. no. 7

Mahon has kindly drawn our attention to a drawing by the so-called 'Faker', in the Museo Correr, Venice (inv. no. Classe III, 371; B, 1990, no. 114), which, being in reverse, is clearly based on Bartolozzi's print after App. no. 5. The 'Faker' has eliminated the figure of St Anne altogether and has situated the remaining two figures in a simple outdoor setting, denoted by a tree in the left background. For another example of the 'Faker's' work based on a print after Guercino in Piranesi's *Raccolta*, see App. no. 24.

For the main discussion of this drawing, see No. 36.

6 Head of a Girl looking to the front

She leans slightly to the right; her right hand is visible in the bottom left corner.

Red chalk. 132 × 130mm; the paper much wormed; repaired and retouched in parts.

1873–5–10–3534. Not illustrated.

Provenance: J. H. Anderdon, by whom presented.

Inscribed in black ink along the bottom of the old mount: *Giovanni Francesco Barbieri, called Guercino*; and in the bottom left corner of the same, in graphite, the number 5. On the back of the mount, in the bottom centre, in black ink but in a different hand, is another inscription: *Guercino*. Another inscription, also on the back of the mount, in pencil, and in the hand of J. A. Gere, is as follows: *Genuine Guercino, surely?*.

The head could conceivably be that of a youth. From its style, the drawing may date from Guercino's Roman period, 1621–3, or possibly a year or two earlier.

7 Archimedes deflecting the Rays of the Sun

He is seated on the ground with his body facing the spectator and with his head raised to the left; he holds up a round mirror in each hand, from which are reflected rays that burst into small tongues of flame.

Red chalk, heightened with some touches of white. 364 × 260mm; some damages and repairs throughout, the paper discoloured light brown.

Pp. 4–60

Provenance: Casa Gennari; A. Beccadelli; R. Payne Knight Bequest, 1824.

Engraved in the same sense by Clemente Nicoli (*fl.* 1786) in a volume of prints entitled *Dissegni d'eccellenti pittori italiani incisi di maniere diverse da Clemente Nicoli*, Bologna, 1786; an impression of the print is in the Bibliothèque Nationale, Paris (Bd. 35, no. 91). An inscription on the print records that the drawing was in the collection of Antonio Beccadelli (1718–1803), who was a minor Bolognese painter.

Antony Griffiths first pointed out that the figure is Archimedes, who constructed various engines of war for Hiero in the defence of Syracuse against Marcellus and is reputed to have burnt the Roman ships by deflecting the sun's rays.

It is conceivable that the drawing is that described in an entry in the 1719 Casa Gennari inventory as follows: *Un dissegno d'un'Archimede a Lapis Rosso del Guerz; con Cornice Nera, et Oro, valutato L quindici* (fascicule H, sheet 19, item 204). This section lists all the drawings that hung at the family's country villa at Bel Poggio, in the *comune* of S. Silvestro, outside the Porta di S. Stefano. Very few drawings described in the inventory can be matched with Guercino drawings that survive today. For two other drawings in the British Museum also described in the inventory, see App. nos. 5 and 9. For four drawings at Windsor, also apparently described in the inventory, see M & T, 1989, p. xix, n. 17. (The 1719 inventory is discussed by M & T, 1989, pp. xviiiff.)

The style of App. no. 7 suggests that of Guercino's drawings of his Roman period (1621–3). The pose of Archimedes recalls that of *Gloria*, in the ceiling fresco painted in *c.*1621 in the Palazzo Lancellotti in Rome (S, 1988, no. 84). It is also reminiscent of that of Jeremiah in two preparatory drawings for this figure in the fresco in the cupola of Piacenza Cathedral of 1626–7: one in the Mahon Collection, on loan to the Ashmolean Museum, Oxford (No. 60); and another in an Italian private collection (B, 1983, no. 32).

8 Woman holding a Drapery over her Head

She is naked, seated to the right and raises her arms above her head, as if about to put on a shift.

Pen and brown ink and brown wash. 256 × 207mm; the paper probably from an account book.

1910–2–12–5

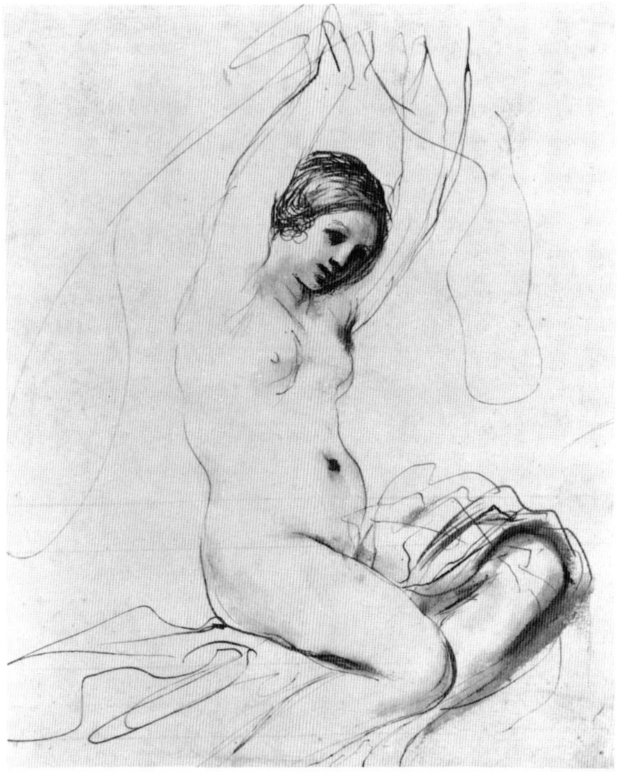

App. no. 8

Provenance: G. Salting Bequest, 1910.

Literature: Vasari Society, 1st ser., VII (1911–12), 12, repr.; Russell, 1923, p. 54, pl. XV; Meder, 1919, p. 41, fig. 16; Leporini, 1925, p. 68, no. 203, repr.; Marangoni, 1959, pl. 17; Bottari, 1966, p. 4, pl. XX; M, *Disegni*, 1969, no. 219; M & T, 1989, under nos. 26–8.

This drawing has been discussed in connection with a painting of the *Toilet of Venus*, now in the Goethe Academy, Renaissance, California (S, 1988, no. 93; see M & T, 1989, p. 16, under nos. 26–8). The relationship rests on a comparison with the figure of Venus in a preparatory drawing, undoubtedly for the *Toilet of Venus*, formerly in the Kunsthalle at Bremen but lost the Second World War (inv. no. 09/697; repr. Marangoni, 1959, pl. 10). Although the position of the figure is different in the ex-Bremen drawing, in both studies she is shown with a garment or towel over her head. A connection between the British Museum drawing and the painting cannot be further demonstrated.

9 Charity, with an old Man

(*see colour pl. 12*)

Charity is seated on the ground in the centre, almost in profile to the right; one child, to whom she bends her head, stands at her side to the right within her embrace; immediately to the left of Charity are two more children; one, on the left, holds an amphora in both hands, but turns to the right in the direction of the other, who leans diagonally towards him, with both hands over his head; the old man, wearing a turban, looks on from the right.

Pen and brown ink and brown wash. 268 × 417mm; some abrasion and slight general discoloration.

1895–9–15–706

Provenance: Casa Gennari; Mr Bouverie (L 325); Mr Hervey; 1st Earl of Gainsborough (anonymous sale, Christie's, London, 20 July 1859, lot 54, bt *Tiffin, £3–3–0*); J. C. Robinson; J. Malcolm.

Literature: Robinson, 1869, no. 254 (as *Repose in Egypt*); Robinson, 1876, no. 266 (as *The Virgin, seated, with the Infant Saviour*); M, *Disegni*, 1969, no. 185; M & T, 1989, p. 48, under nos. 78–82.

The subject, which Robinson, in the first edition of the Malcolm catalogue (1869, p. 103, no. 254), understandably identified as a *Repose in Egypt*, is unusual in the inclusion of the turbaned man on the right whose iconographical significance is unclear, and who indeed might easily be mistaken for Joseph.

The poses of the two full-length putti recur in other drawings datable to this period or a little later, a good instance of Guercino's characteristic reworking of ideas: the putto with his arms raised, for example, recurs scarcely modified, but in reverse, in a drawing of two putti, in the Royal Library, Windsor Castle (M & T, 1989, no. 51), for the *Martyrdom of St Laurence* of *c.*1628; Mahon and Turner noted this same motif in another, slightly later drawing at Windsor (M & T, 1989, no. 81; see No. 100) which is datable 1634 on account of its connection with the *Christ appearing to St Teresa* of that year. The standing putto with the amphora reappears in an almost identical pose, but with wings and supporting a Baroque cartouche, in a drawing in the Ashmolean Museum, Oxford (see No. 66), which we have dated near the Piacenza frescoes of 1626–7.

A red chalk copy of the group of Charity and the three children but omitting the old man (except for a few scant indications of his turban) was sold at Sotheby's, London, 8 December 1920, in the anonymous [Benno Geiger] sale; this drawing, possibly the second item in lot 149, was said to have come from the Grahl Collection, Leipzig (photo, Witt Library). A second, more feeble copy, also in red chalk and omitting the old man, is in the Fitzwilliam Museum, Cambridge (inv. no. PD. 17–1956).

As Mahon pointed out, App. no. 9 was first described in an entry in the 1719 Casa Gennari inventory as follows: *Un Simile* [i.e., *un disegno*] *d'Acquarella d'una Carità con Puttini ed' un Vecchio, in Cornice dorata e lastra Seg.*[to] *n.*[o] *43. del Guerzino L Novanta* (fascicule G, sheet 5, item 43). The provenance of the drawing subsequent to its ownership by Guercino's heirs has been admirably described by Mahon (*Disegni*, 1969, no. 185). Very few drawings described in the inventory can be matched with Guercino's surviving studies: for other examples see App. nos. 5 and 7.

For further discussion of this drawing, see No. 54.

10 A Woman seized by Soldiers being rescued by a Youth

The young woman is on the left, her hands bound in front of her with a rope which is held at either end by two soldiers, one behind her holding a torch and the other on the right gripping a sword; the youth charges at the latter, brandishing his sword over his head; two other soldiers are behind, to the right.

Pen and brown ink and brown wash, somewhat faded. 276 × 377mm; the sheet has sustained damage, possibly as a result of having once been hung on the wall, and has then been partly repaired.

1895–9–15–711

Provenance: J. Malcolm.

Literature: Robinson, 1869, no. 261; Robinson, 1876, no. 271; M, *Disegni*, 1969, no. 186; Châtelet, 1970, under no. 46.

The subject of the nocturnal scene in the drawing remains to be identified. Mahon (*Disegni*, 1969, no. 186) dated the drawing *c.*1624–8 and suggested the possibility that it was intended as a design for a painting, now untraced.

Another drawing of the same composition but at a different stage is in the Musée des Beaux-Arts, Lille (Châtelet, 1970, no. 46); it differs from the British Museum study in a number of details. Before entering the collection of Jean-Baptiste Wicar (whence it passed to the Palais des Beaux-Arts, Lille), it belonged to Thomas Jenkins (1722–98), an English collector who lived in Rome. While in his possession it was etched in the same sense by Giovanni Ottaviani (1735–1808) with the inscription *Ex Collectione Tomae Ienkins Pictoris Angli*; the print is included in Piranesi's *Raccolta* of 1764. As Mahon rightly pointed out, Robinson was mistaken in believing that the print was after the British Museum drawing.

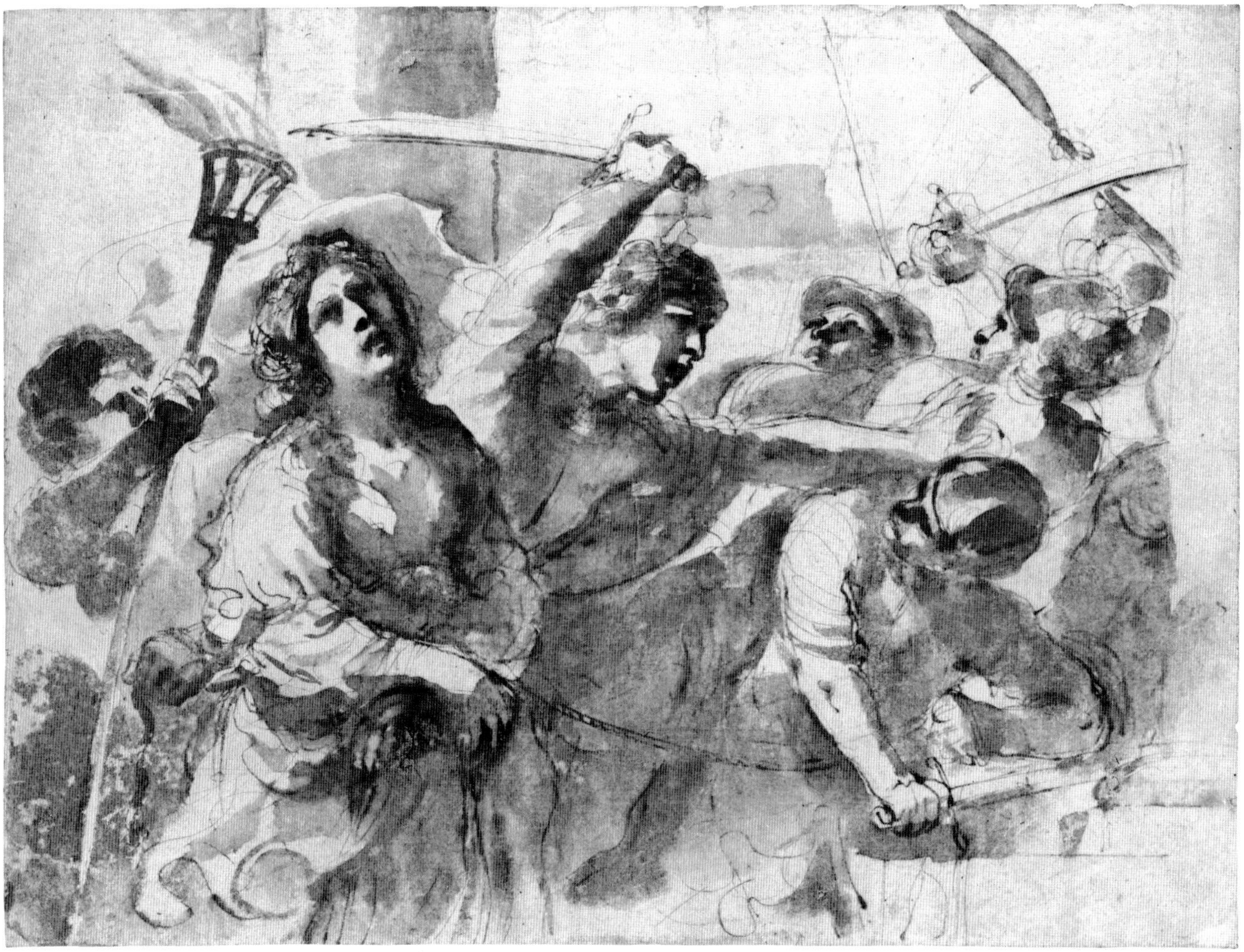

App. no. 10

What is perhaps a related composition to that of the British Museum and Lille drawings is recorded in a drawing now in a Parisian private collection, a copy of which was, in 1927, in the collection of the Abbé Thuélin, Paris (photo, Witt Library, London). In this second composition a woman is led away to the left by a soldier and another man, and as she leaves she looks to the right and points at a second soldier who clasps his hands and returns her gaze as he moves away from her to the right. The scene is not, however, nocturnal, nor does a young man intervene in an attempt to rescue the woman, who herself is not bound. It is therefore possible that another subject may be represented.

11 Kneeling Woman (?Mary Magdalen)

She is in profile to the right looking up, her hands clasped; she wears a shawl over her head.

Pen and brown ink and light brown wash. 255 × 172mm; the paper abraded, with losses in the darks. Hatched indentations are evident along several of the lines, although the reason for this remains obscure. The top right corner cut away diagonally and made up.

1895–9–15–713

Provenance: J. C. Robinson; J. Malcolm.

Literature: Robinson, 1869, no. 262; Robinson, 1876, no. 273.

Probably a study for the Magdalen in the altarpiece of the *Crucifixion* for the church of the Madonna della Ghiara in Reggio Emilia of 1624–5 (see Nos. 51–2), though the two figures differ in important respects, notably in pose: in the painting the Magdalen stands and supports the fainting Virgin. In the treatment of the figure's head, the painted work and the British Museum sketch have much in common. In both, the head is upturned and in profile to the right and the wash strokes of the drawing appear to anticipate the play of light about the figure's features in the painting.

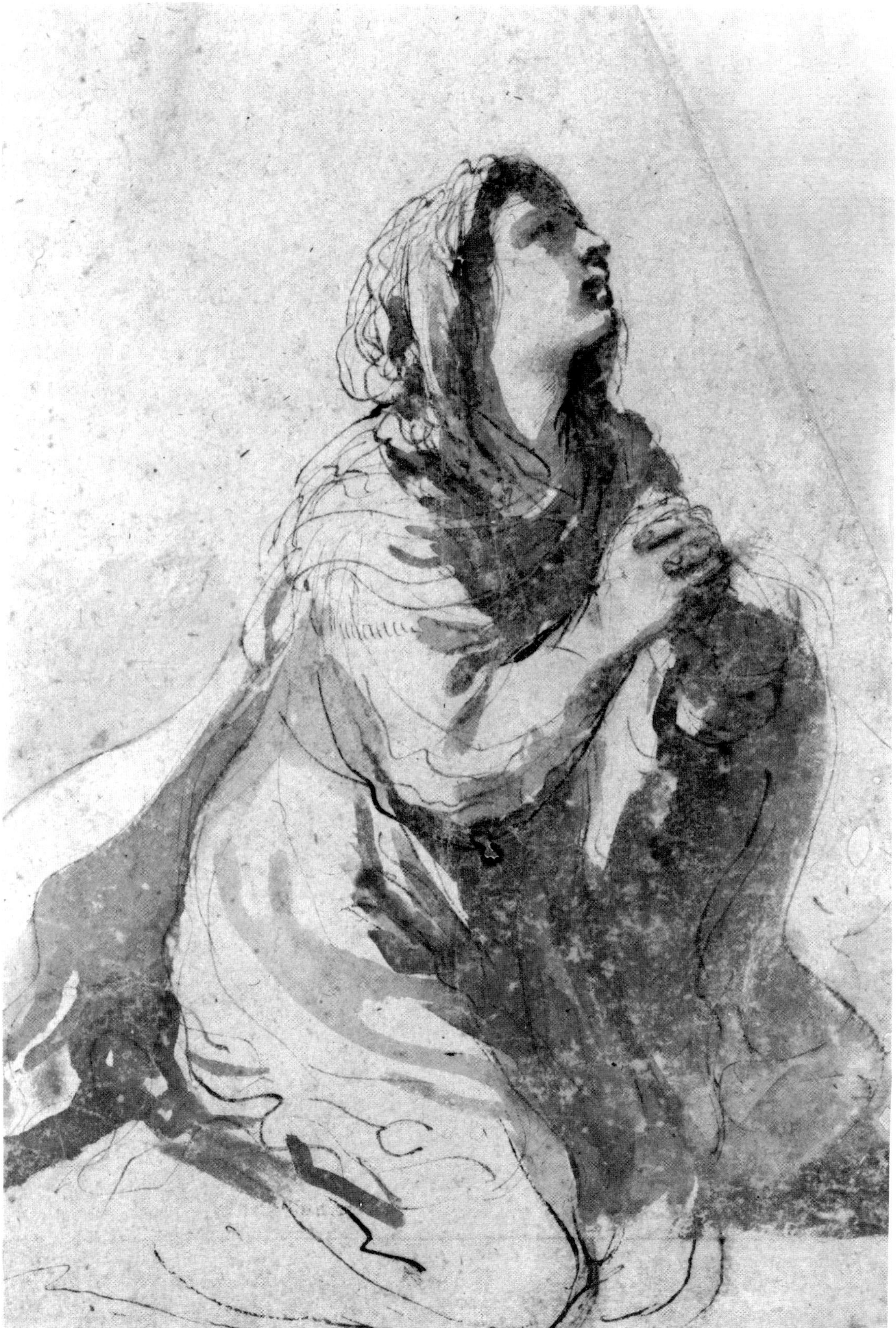

App. no. 11

In the finished work the Magdalen is depicted bare-headed, but in several of the numerous other preparatory drawings for this project, her hair is covered with a veil. She is shown thus in two drawings at Windsor (No. 52 and M & T, 1989, no. 33, under which appears a full discussion of the other drawings connected with this project) and in one in the Gabinetto Nazionale delle Stampe, Rome (inv. no. F.N. 120; M, *Disegni*, 1969, no. 95).

In these preparatory drawings, Guercino explored a wide range of poses and gestures for the figures, sometimes reversing them as he proceeded. The Magdalen, in particular, was subject to several transformations, both at the left and at the right of the composition. That Guercino indeed toyed with the idea of a kneeling Magdalen for the Ghiara composition is established by the fact that she is shown thus in other preparatory drawings, one in the Teylers Museum, Haarlem (inv. no. H. 3; M, *Disegni*, 1969, no. 94), and another in the Lugt Collection, Institut Néerlandais, Paris (inv. no. 5076; M, *Disegni*, 1969, no. 93; Byam Shaw, 1983, no. 343). In the Lugt sheet, there are five different studies of the Magdalen and that in the bottom right corner shows her in a pose roughly corresponding with App. no. 11, but in reverse. Having experimented with the kneeling attitude for the Magdalen, Guercino ultimately employed it for St John in the painting. An interesting drawing at Windsor (M & T, 1989, no. 32; see No. 52) appears to encapsulate a moment of transition when ideas incorporated in the single figure of the British Museum study were separated out into two distinct figures (the Magdalen, with her head raised in a very similar attitude to App. no. 11, and St John, who adopts the kneeling pose).

The motif of the clasped hands further connects the British Museum drawing to others in this group, namely the Lugt sheet once again, where it occurs in three out of the five figure studies; another drawing in the Teylers Museum, Haarlem (inv. no. H. 20; M, *Disegni*, 1969, no. 92); and again in one of the group of Windsor drawings (M & T, 1989, no. 30). The same motif is sometimes adopted for St John the Evangelist (e.g. Teylers Museum, Haarlem, inv. no. H. 3; M, *Disegni*, 1969, no. 94), although it is nowhere used in the finished painting. This free flow of motifs between protagonists in the preparatory stages was typical of Guercino's working method.

A pen-and-wash drawing in the Civica Pinacoteca Tosio-Martinengo, Brescia (Nicodemi, 1921, no. 199, repr.), of a female figure kneeling in profile to the left, also with her head covered, may be a study for the same figure of the Magdalen as that in App. no. 11. The two drawings have many common points of style and, indeed, of composition. It must be said that the Magdalen does not appear to be pointing so emphatically in any other study for this composition, but, on the other hand, the sheet in the Lugt collection shows the artist experimenting with a wide range of gestures for this figure, including at least one study which shows her indicating something with one arm outstretched.

12 Head and Shoulders of an Angel

He is in profile to the left, looking down.

Pen and brown ink and brown wash. 85 × 131mm.

1954–6–10–7. Not illustrated.

Provenance: Sir Joshua Reynolds (L 2364); Lady Lucas (sale, Sotheby's, London, 29 June 1926, lot 43, with 2 others, bt *Campbell, £3-0-0*); Campbell Dodgson Bequest.

Inscribed in brown ink in the bottom centre of the old mount: *Guercino*. On the back of the mount, in blue ink, in (?)Campbell Dodgson's hand, is the inscription: *Reynolds Collection. / From the collection of Lady Lucas. / Sold at Sotheby's, 29 June 1926. Lot 43.*

The drawing appears on stylistic grounds to date from the mid-1620s. The figure bears some resemblance to the angel on the right of the *Magdalen and two Angels* of 1622 in the Pinacoteca Vaticana, Rome (S, 1988, no. 88), though this seems too early for the style of the drawing.

13 St Gregory

He is seen head and shoulders, with his head turned slightly to the right, but with his eyes directed towards the spectator; he wears a *camauro* on his head and a cope on his shoulders.

Red chalk with stumping. 238 × 200mm.

1847–3–6–10. Not illustrated.

Provenance: J. Richardson, Sr (L 2184); J. Thane (L 2461).

The style suggests the period between Guercino's Roman visit of 1621–3 and his work on the Piacenza frescoes of 1626–7. The stumping in the cope is particularly reminiscent of this phase in the development of the artist's red chalk studies. Such passages are to be found in the sheet of studies of putti in the Royal Library, Windsor Castle (M & T, 1989, no. 35; see No. 53) for the painting of *St Gregory the Great with Sts Ignatius Loyola and Francis Xavier* of *c.*1625–6 in the collection of Sir Denis Mahon, London (S, 1988, no. 112). The head is not altogether unlike that of St Gregory in that picture, in spite of the difference of pose. Indeed the British Museum drawing could conceivably be a rejected study for the picture.

14 Reclining Putto

He leans to the left, supporting himself on his right elbow; he looks downwards towards the left, while his left arm is raised to support what appears to be a drapery, the end of which billows out in front of him.

Red chalk. 153 × 208mm.

1952–1–21–41. Not illustrated.

Provenance: Lord James Cavendish; L. Colling-Mudge. From an album purchased with the help of a generous contribution from the National Art-Collections Fund.

Literature: Turner, 1980, no. 44; B, 1983, no. 75; M & T, 1989, under nos. 38–45 and no. 613.

A study for one of the swag-bearing putti in one of the coloured sections (as opposed to those in *grisaille*) of the frieze running immediately above the arcade in the drum of the cupola of Piacenza Cathedral, which Guercino decorated in 1627; the putto is that in the centre of a group of three in the section of frieze situated below the compartment of the vault with the Prophet Isaiah, painted by Morazzone. A preparatory drawing for the putto on the right in this group is also in the Department (see App. no. 15). As in App. no. 15, the drapery was replaced in the finished work by a swag of fruit and foliage.

Two offsets, one (retouched) in the Royal Library, Windsor Castle (M & T, 1989, no. 613), and the other in the Kunstmuseum, Düsseldorf (inv. no. FP 10415), must have been taken from a drawing close to, but not identical with App. no. 14.

15 Putto kneeling and pulling at a Drapery

He kneels to the right, his back turned towards the spectator, and pulls at the drapery with his left arm.

Red chalk and some stumping, damaged and retouched.
116 × 164mm.

1952–1–21–45. Not illustrated.

Provenance: Lord James Cavendish; L. Colling-Mudge. From an album purchased with the help of a generous contribution from the National Art-Collections Fund.

Literature: Turner, 1980, under no. 44; B, 1983, no. 76; M & T, 1989, under no. 612.

A study for a figure in the same section of the frieze of putti as that described in App. no. 14; the putto in question is furthest right of the group of three in this section (repr. B, 1983, figs. 60 and 73). In the painted work, the drapery is replaced by a swag of fruit and foliage.

An offset of the drawing is in the Royal Library at Windsor Castle (M & T, 1989, no. 612). A study for the putto immediately to the left of that shown in the present drawing is also in the Department (App. no. 14).

16 Damon and Pythias

On the left Damon kneels on the ground while an executioner prepares to behead him; in the centre, seated on a throne, is the tyrant Dionysius the Younger with two attendants; he turns to his left, raising his left hand in surprise, to see Pythias at his side kneeling and gesturing to himself in an act of submission; behind Pythias stands another figure.

Pen and brown ink with blue-grey wash. 205 × 308mm.

1969–9–20–17. Illustrated in main Catalogue (No. 83).

Provenance: Mr and Mrs A. Nussbaum, by whom bequeathed.

Literature: Turner, 1980, no. 45; S, 1988, under no. 138; Southorn, 1988, pl. 87; M & T, 1989, under no. 70.

On the *verso* of the drawing, in brown ink, is the following draft of a letter, which seems to be in neither the hand of Guercino nor that of his brother, Paolo Antonio Barbieri: *Ill.mo et R.mo Sig.r / Hò consignato Il Quadro del San Mateo nelle mani / del Sig.r Dottor Bianchi qual tiene ordine / dà* [*sua Sig*]*ria Ill.ma di mandare il d.to quadro á Rom*[*a*] */ qual lo potrá vedere, sé sara di suo gusto / né haveró molto contento, e lá prego insieme a / scusarmi della pocha consideratione fatta*. There are also faint studies in pen, which the artist has abandoned: one, below the draft letter, is possibly of a figure with its hands clasped; another, to the right of the draft, consists of a series of parallel lines possibly denoting architecture.

The draft letter refers to a picture of a *St Matthew* which was sent to Rome, on approval, to an unknown patron, under the aegis of a certain Dottor Bianchi. There is no mention of any picture of this subject in the Account Book between the date of the first entry on 4 January 1629 and the final payment for the *Damon and Pythias* in 1632. The only *St Matthew* recorded by Malvasia before this latter date was executed in 1615, far too early, and not apparently destined for Rome (Malvasia, 1678, II, p. 362; 1841, II, p. 258). A number of paintings of this subject do survive from the period before 1632 but only one, the *St Matthew and the Angel*, dated *c.*1622 by Mahon (M, *Dipinti*, 1968, no. 50) and now in the Pinacoteca Capitolina, Rome (S, 1988, no. 89), has a Roman provenance. It seems unlikely, but not impossible, that Guercino would have kept the draft letter for ten years before using it to draw on.

For the main discussion of this drawing, see No. 83.

17 Study for the Drapery of a Madonna in a Visitation

The figure is seen from the waist down, in profile to the right; some of the drapery is gathered in her right hand.

Red chalk, heightened with white chalk, on buff-coloured paper. 350 × 241mm.

1986–6–21–14. Illustrated in main Catalogue (No. 93).

Provenance: (?)Casa Gennari; (?)F. Giusti; A. Maggiori (L *Suppl*, 3005b); sale, Sotheby's, London, 22 October 1984, lot 132 (as Roman, 17th Century).

Literature: Turner, 1987, pp. 6–7; S, 1988, under no. 140; M & T, 1989, pp. xiii-xiv, n. 2, and p. 39, under nos. 62–8.

Inscribed in brown ink in the centre of the *verso*, near the top: *A. Maggiori compró / a Bologna il giorno 10. / d'Ap*[*ri*]*le del 1792*. Another inscription on the *verso*, lower down, has been cancelled out with brown ink, probably by the author of the first inscription (i.e., Maggiori). Although mostly illegible, the first line seems to be an old attribution to Andrea Sirani.

Apart from this example, the only drapery studies by Guercino to have survived are the large group in the Staatsgalerie at Stuttgart, on deposit from the Koenig–Fachsenfeld Collection. (For a discussion of this group, see M, *Disegni*, 1969, p. 14 and nos. 39, 75, 99–100, 105, 108–11, 131, 146–8, 153–4, 156–7, 162–3 and 173; and, more recently, Thiem, 1979, pp. 401–17.) In the Casa Gennari inventory of 1719, a group of these drapery studies is mentioned among the miscellaneous loose sheets subdivided into categories and listed under the letter E, after the description of the albums of drawings: *Panegiamenti Studiati dal vero lo maggior parte del Sud.º S. Cavagl.re, cioè N. 136*. Mahon (*Disegni*, 1969, p. 14) observed that Guercino's studies of draperies remained in the Casa Gennari until the end of the eighteenth century, when they were sold by Carlo Gennari

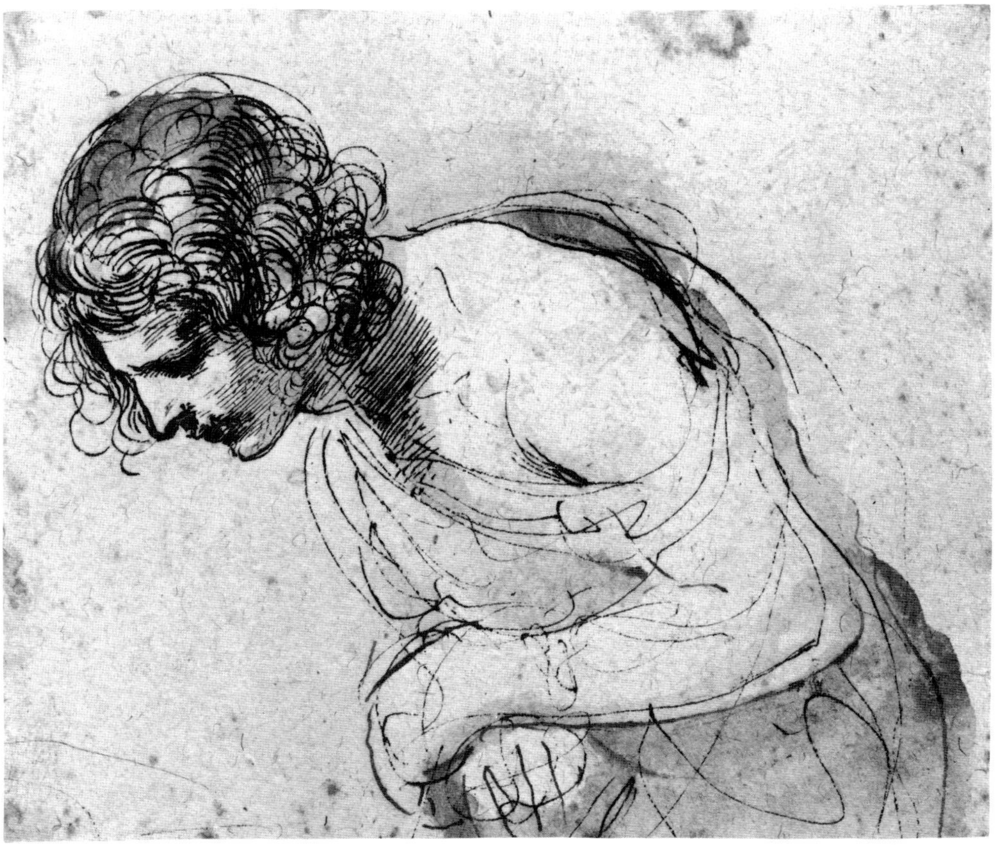

App. no. 18

(1716–90) to the Bolognese painter Francesco Giusti (1752–1828): the drawings that had belonged to Giusti were acquired in 1899 by Franz Freiherr Koenig-Fachsenfeld and are now on deposit in the Staatsgalerie, Stuttgart. The British Museum drawing was purchased by Alessandro Maggiori of Faenza in Bologna in 1792, possibly from Giusti, although there is no specific evidence to support this claim.

The drapery studies are invariably drawn to this same large scale, on poor-quality, light brown paper, with the artist often combining red and white chalk.

For the main discussion of this drawing, see No. 93.

18 Half-length Study of a Man bending to the left: St John about to be beheaded

He is in profile to the left, his left shoulder is bare and his hands are crossed over his waist.

Pen and two shades of brown ink and brown and greyish wash on rough, buff-coloured paper. 116 × 141mm.

1943–11–13–20

Provenance: Eric Rose, by whom presented.

Literature: M, *Disegni*, 1969, under nos. 127–31; S, 1988, under no. 139.

A study for the figure of St John in the *Martyrdom of Sts John and Paul, with the Madonna and Child above* (S, 1988, no. 139) of 1632, now in the Musée des Augustins, Toulouse (for which see No. 85). Popham, in a note in the Departmental register, pointed out the connection as early as 1939: 'Appears to be for the head of a saint in the *Decapitation of the Baptist* at Windsor, engr. by Bartolozzi', i.e., the print dated 1794 by Bartolozzi (Calabi, 1928, no. 2191; two impressions are in the Department, inv. nos. 1873–7–12–414 and S. 5–39), which records a preparatory drawing for the Toulouse picture; the drawing on which Bartolozzi's print is based is not, as Popham supposed, in the Royal Library but is untraced; nor is the figure represented St John the Baptist. (The St John in this drawing was a Roman official who was executed with his companion St Paul under Julian the Apostate.)

As noted under Nos. 85–8, Guercino experimented with several different ideas for the pose of St John. In the present drawing the pose of the figure is close to that of the saint in the painting and therefore must have been made towards the end of the series of studies.

It may be noted in passing that the slightly coarse buff-coloured paper is also found in other pen drawings for this picture and its pendant, for example two in the Royal Library, Windsor Castle (Nos. 85 and 91), both likewise made after the final pose of the figures in the composition had been more or less settled.

19 Youth leading a Woman by the Hand

The youth, holding a spear upright in his left hand, takes the woman's left hand in his right and looks back at her as he runs towards the right; the woman strides forward in the same direction, her head in profile to the right; she carries a spear in her right hand (which is cut off by the left edge of the paper).

Pen and brown ink. 189 × 194mm.

1943–11–13–22

Provenance: Eric Rose, by whom presented.

Inscribed in pencil in an early nineteenth-century hand in the bottom right corner: *Guercino.* (Identical inscriptions appear on the following Guercino and Guercino School drawings with a provenance from the collection of Eric Rose: App. nos. 31 (the inscription now erased), 46, 47, 48, 53, 54 and 74.) An inscription on the *verso* of App. no. 19, which we are unable to decipher, shows through the paper near the bottom right corner, above and to the left of the previous inscription.

The identity of the female warrior remains unclear. We are inclined to date the drawing on stylistic grounds to the early 1630s by analogy with a drawing in the Teylers Museum, Haarlem, for the figures of St Matthew and the Angel (inv. no. H. 22; M & T, 1989, p. 40 and fig. 13). Mahon and Turner have related the Haarlem drawing to a lost altarpiece

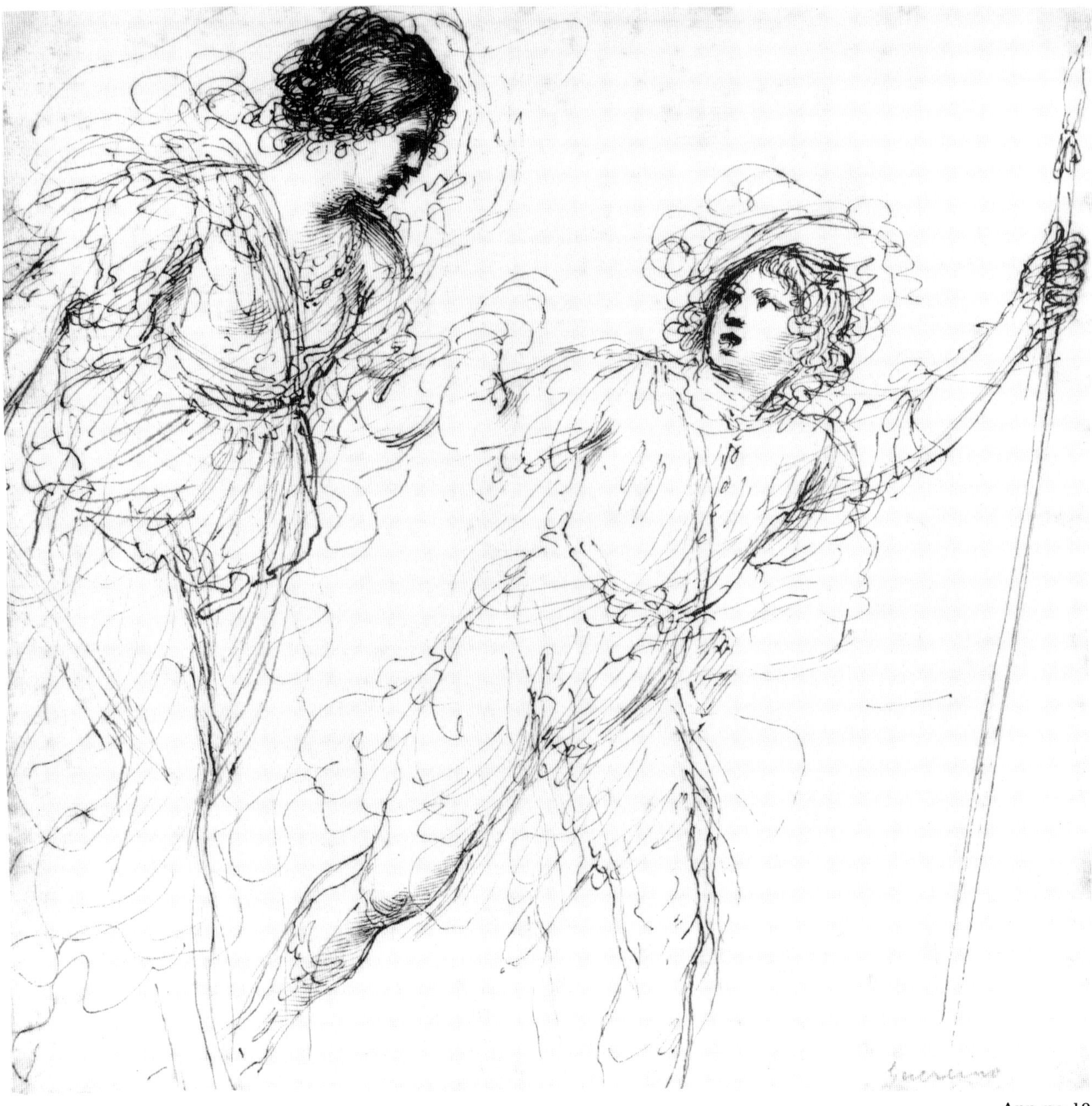

App. no. 19

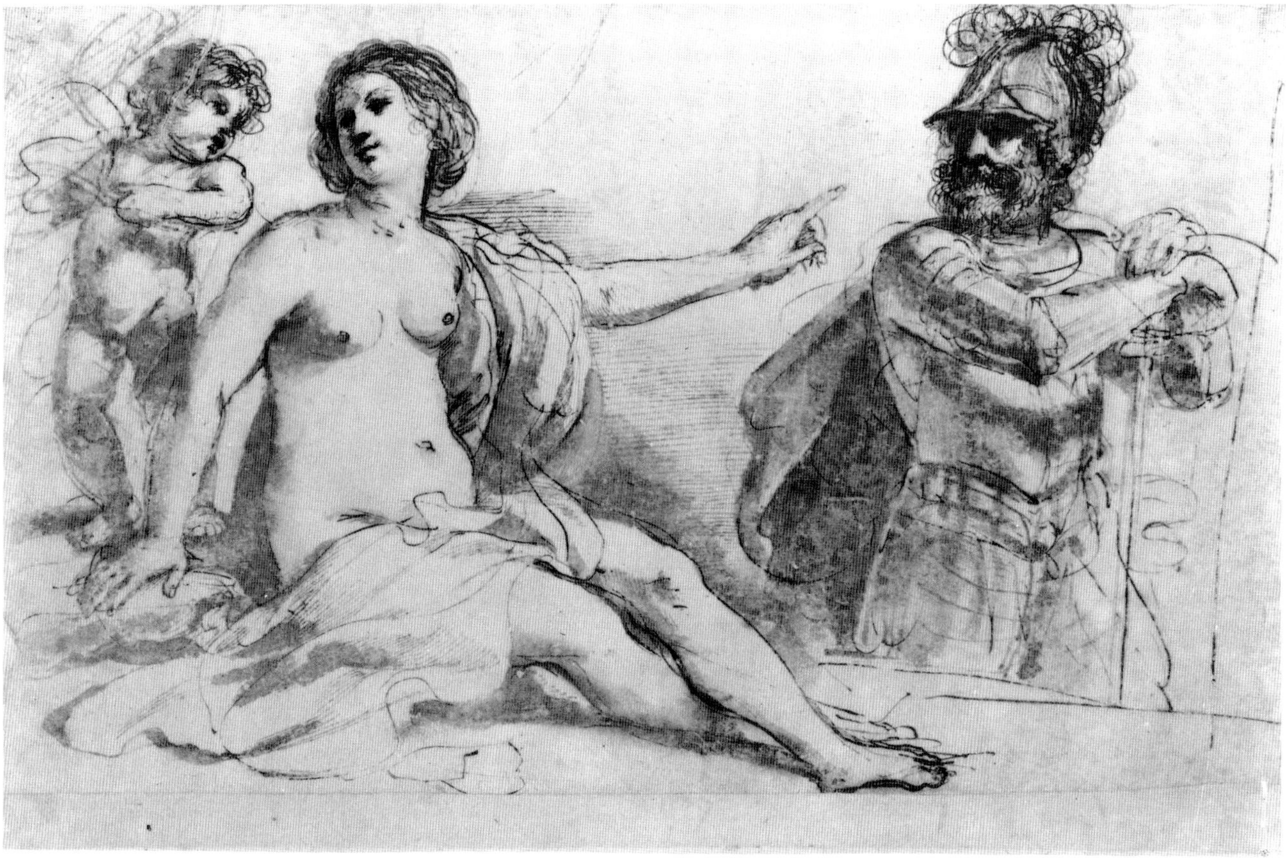

App. no. 21

of the *Madonna and Child with Sts Matthew and Andrew Corsini*, which was commissioned for Brescia in 1633 and delivered in 1634.

20 Christ appearing to St Teresa

Christ stands in the centre with his legs apart and with his right arm raised, pointing upwards; he looks down at St Teresa who kneels on the right, with her hands clasped, and reciprocates his gaze.

Pen and brown ink. 353 × 203mm; the paper probably from an account book.

Ff. 2–134. Illustrated in the main Catalogue (No. 99).

Provenance: Rev. C. M. Cracherode Bequest, 1799.

Literature: M, *Disegni*, 1969, under no. 138; Turner, 1980, no. 46; M & T, 1989, under nos. 78–82.

An indecipherable inscription in pencil appears in the bottom right corner.

For the main discussion of this drawing, see No. 99.

21 Venus, Mars and Cupid

Venus, naked except for a drapery thrown over her left shoulder and falling over her loins, is seated on the left; she points with her left hand to Mars, who is on the right, in complete armour and plumed helmet; he is seen only to the waist, resting both hands on the hilt of his propped-up sword; to the left of Venus stands Cupid, towards whom she turns her head.

Pen and brown ink and light brown wash, faded, and then re-inforced, probably by Guercino himself, in pen with a darker shade of brown ink. 207 × 343mm, excluding the strip added at the bottom; much abraded and the lighter ink and wash faded.

1910–2–12–4

Provenance: G. Salting Bequest, 1910.

Literature: M & T, 1989, under no. 77.

A study for the *Venus, Mars and Cupid*, paid for on behalf of the Duke of Modena in January 1634 and now in the Galleria Estense at Modena (S, 1988, no. 151; for various other studies for this composition, see M & T, 1989, under no. 77). In addition to the preparatory studies previously published, there is a red chalk study for the figure of Mars alone in the Palazzo Rosso, Genoa (inv. no. 1705; 280 × 193mm).

In total, four composition studies are known, two being autograph, one a School work, and one a lost original, which is recorded in an engraving. Apart from the British Museum drawing, these are: a pen-and-ink drawing, formerly in the Chute collection at The Vyne, Basingstoke, and now in the Ratjen Collection, Vaduz (Schaar, 1977, repr. p. 155); a red chalk Studio copy (after a lost drawing), formerly on the London art market (Christie's, London, 30 March 1971, lot 133, repr.), and finally a drawing by Guercino, the present whereabouts of which are unknown, but which was formerly in the collection of Thomas Jenkins and is known from the etching (possibly not reversed) by Giovanni Ottaviani (an impression is in the Department, shelfmark 189* b. 1, no. 134). Of these, only the Studio copy shows the figures disposed in the same relationship to each other as those in the painting, with Venus on the right, Mars on the left, and Cupid in between them, though their individual poses still differ. In all the other examples, including App. no. 21, Venus is seated on the left, with her legs extending to the right, which would imply that Guercino decided to reverse the design at a relatively late stage in the composition's genesis.

App. no. 21 appears to be one of the earliest in the series of composition studies, together with the rather similar drawing recorded in Ottaviani's etching. In both of these, the psychological interplay is confined to the figures within the composition with none of the figures looking out at the spectator; a strong emphasis is placed instead on the link between Venus and Mars, by means of Venus' outstretched arm (in the British Museum drawing she points at Mars, whereas in Ottaviani's print, she actually grasps the peak of his helmet). In both the remaining drawings, the spectator's participation is enlisted in different ways: in the Vaduz sketch, Cupid points in the direction of the spectator as Venus checks the sharpness of his dart; and in the Studio copy, Venus looks out at the viewer as Cupid sinks his dart into a heart. Both these ideas anticipate the more emphatic conceit of the painting, in which Venus both looks and points at the spectator, indicating to Cupid his target; and Cupid, his bow drawn and pointing in our direction, fixes us with a determined gaze.

A rapid pen sketch in the Gabinetto Nazionale, Rome (inv. no. FN 119 (22556); not referred to by M & T, 1989), representing Venus suckling Cupid with the figures of Mars and Time, has several points in common with the composition of App. no. 21 and its related drawings. Again, Venus reclines with her head to the left and her legs to the right and a curtain falls behind her, away to the left, to reveal Mars standing in a similar pose with both hands resting on the end of his propped-up sword. Indeed, were it not for the inclusion of the figure of Time, one would be tempted, on the grounds of both composition and style, to connect this drawing with the Modena picture. Although the figure of Time appears in none of the composition drawings discussed above, it is possible that Guercino at one time contemplated including such a figure, as he had previously done in the picture of *Venus, Mars, Cupid and Time*, at Dunham Massey (National Trust), Cheshire (S, 1988, no. 109).

22 Woman standing and pointing to the left

Her body is turned slightly to the left, but her head leans back to the right; she wears a flowing garment and some of her drapery billows out behind her to the right.

Pen and brown ink, with some point of the brush, for example in her left forearm and hand. 227 × 148mm.

1910–2–12–9. Not illustrated.

Provenance: G. Salting Bequest, 1910.

According to the Departmental register, the figure was identified (presumably on the old mount) as: *the angel leading Lot and his family out of Sodom*. No inscription, however, survives with the drawing.

Although no painting of this exact subject is known, the iconography suggested in the lost inscription seems plausible enough.

A similarly posed figure sometimes occurs in Guercino's work, for example in the following instances: in the distance in the *Rest on the Flight into Egypt*, a copy of which is in the Martin d'Arcy Gallery of Art, Loyola University, Chicago (S, 1988, no. 153); the *St Michael* in S. Nicola, Fabriano (S, 1988, no. 216); and the angel in the *Calling of the Blessed Luigi Gonzaga*, in the Metropolitan Museum of Art, New York (S, 1988, no. 276).

23 King David

He is represented half length, apparently seated, holding his harp to his left shoulder; he is looking up to the left and places his right hand on his chest.

Pen and brown ink and pale brown wash. 222 × 211mm.

Ff. 2–136

Provenance: Rev. C. M. Cracherode Bequest, 1799.

Literature: Popham & Lloyd, 1986, under no. 144.

Inscribed in dark brown ink in the bottom right corner: *Guercin*.

Another three-quarter-length study for the same composition, drawn in a very similar technique but showing a substantially different interpretation of the figure, who is standing rather than seated, is in the collection of Viscount Coke at Holkham Hall (Popham & Lloyd, 1986, no. 144). Since the Holkham drawing has many more pentiments, it is possible that it may have been drawn first.

No commission for a three-quarter-length King David with his harp is recorded either in Malvasia or in the Account Book. Nonetheless the drawings may perhaps be dated in the mid-1630s, by analogy with such drawings as the *Sisyphus* in the Royal Library, Windsor Castle (No. 108), and a drawing of *St Jerome* in a private collection (No. 103), in which liberal passages of wash also appear.

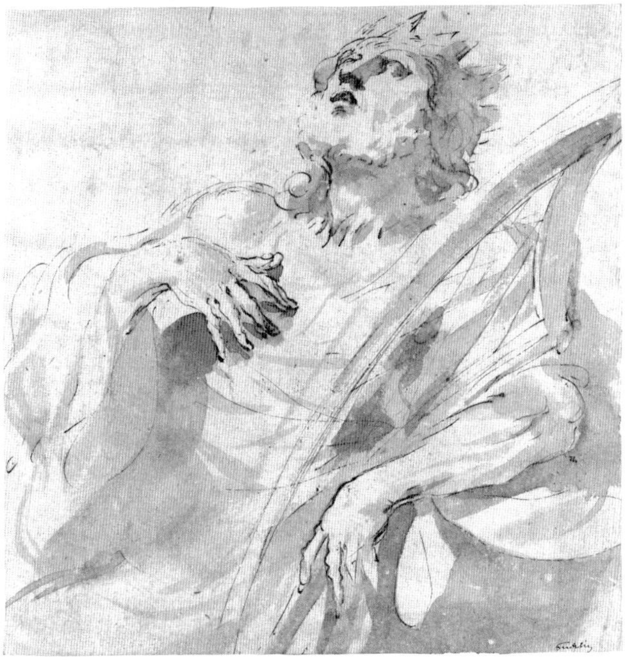

App. no. 23

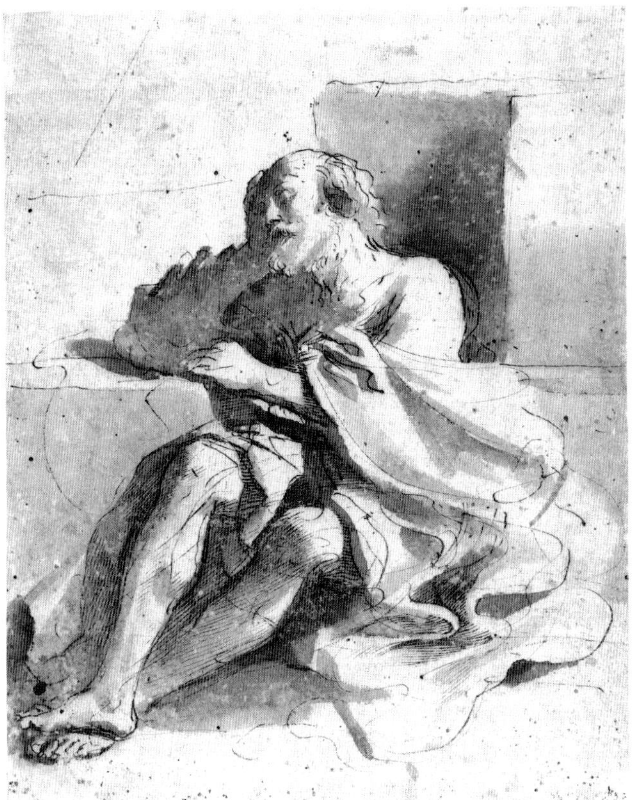

App. no. 24

24 Old Man asleep

He is seated on the ground, leaning his elbow on a ledge and supporting his head in his right hand; his legs are extended to the left with his right foot resting on his left; some of his drapery tumbles from the crook of his left arm towards the right; behind him is a large block.

Pen and brown ink and brown wash on buff paper. 249 × 198mm; the drawing has damages such as fading and fly-blow, consistent with it having once been framed and exposed to light.

Pp. 4–59

Provenance: G. B. Piranesi; R. Payne Knight Bequest, 1824.

As Mahon was the first to point out (note on the back of the old mount, May 1979), the drawing was etched in the same sense, with some additions, by Giovanni Battista Piranesi (1720–78), apparently when it was in Piranesi's own collection; the print was included in Piranesi's *Raccolta* of 1764. The Department's copy of this volume does not contain an impression of the print (repr. Bettagno, 1978, no. 308). The etching is inscribed in the bottom margin: *Apud Equitem Johannem Baptistam Piranesi* and shows the image extended at both top and bottom, and slightly to the sides. As is not entirely unexpected in a man of Piranesi's imagination, some extra properties have been added, namely what appears to be a column above the block on the right and a step at the bottom with a boulder and part of a tree stump in the foreground on the right. That the drawing engraved is indeed App. no. 24 can be demonstrated by Piranesi's faithful reproduction of random pentiments, particularly the lines passing over the ledge to the left of the figure and some pentiments for the legs.

From its style, the drawing seems to date from the 1630s (cf. Nos. 86, 92 and 100). The figure resembles to some extent (though in reverse) that of St Joseph in a composition of the *Rest on the Flight into Egypt* of 1634–5, known from a copy in the Martin d'Arcy Gallery of Art, Loyola University, Chicago (S, 1988, no. 153), though we would not go so far as to claim that this drawing is a study for that composition.

A similar figure, again in reverse, appears in *The Angel Raphael proposing their Journey to Tobias in the Presence of Tobias's Parents*, a drawing ascribed to Guercino in the Royal Library, Windsor Castle (M & T, 1989, no. 359). The Windsor drawing may reflect a lost painting of the late 1620s, a date that would not radically conflict with the style of App. no. 24. Although the pose of Tobit in the Windsor drawing is not identical with that of the figure in the present sketch, the way he rests his head on his hand is particularly close and details such as the rectilinear drapery about both figures' knees, the depiction of the feet, and the blocks in the background of both drawings suggest a possible link. However, the figure in the British Museum sketch does not appear to be blind, as Tobias's father should be, but asleep. Thus any connection with this lost composition must remain tentative.

Mahon has kindly drawn our attention to a drawing of this same figure by the so-called 'Faker', in the Biblioteca Reale, Turin (inv. no. 16122–IIC; B, 1990, no. 45). Being in reverse, it would seem that the 'Faker' had access to Piranesi's print, rather than to the drawing itself. The artist has scarcely altered the figure, but has placed it in a simple landscape setting. (For another example of the 'Faker's' work based on a print after Guercino in Piranesi's *Raccolta*, see App. no. 5.)

25 Winged Figure carrying Torches

She is flying to the right, carrying a torch in either hand; she looks up to the left.

Red chalk, heightened with white chalk, on blue (faded) paper. 277 × 217mm.

1895–9–15–704

Provenance: Casa Gennari; Mr Bouverie (L 325); Mr Hervey; 1st Earl of Gainsborough (anonymous sale, Christie's, London, 20 July 1859, lot unknown; see below); J. C. Robinson; J. Malcolm.

Literature: Robinson, 1869, no. 251; Robinson, 1876, no. 263.

The figure is Canens, who melted and then vanished into thin air grieving for her husband, Picus, King of the Ausonians, after he was transformed into a bird by the sorceress Circe. The story is related in Ovid's *Metamorphoses* (XIV, 416–34). As Bagni has pointed out to us, Antonio Tempesta (1555–1630), in his illustrated edition of the *Metamorphoses* (title-page dated 1606), used the same iconography to depict Canens (Bartsch, 1808–21, XVII, p. 151, no. 774; Bartsch, 1983a, p. 78, no. 774 [151]).

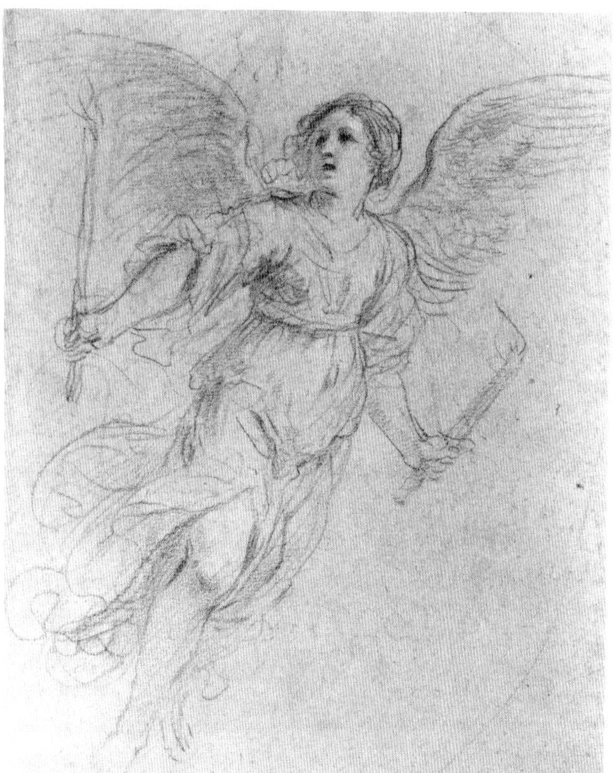

App. no. 25

At one time Guercino intended the composition to be oval, as is apparent from the curved lines in the lower and upper right-hand corners of the sheet. The allusion to flames might imply that the design was made for the decoration of a chimney-breast, though no such commission is known. From its style, the drawing may date from the mid-1630s.

Another drawing in red chalk, but on white paper, recently on the London art market (Sotheby's, London, 18 November 1982, lot 8, repr.), shows the figure without wings, and in a different pose. In the British Museum drawing, Guercino rejected a more dynamic pose for the figure, with the right arm raised (see the pentiment beneath her right wing), in favour of a symmetrical solution which more satisfactorily fills the pictorial field.

It is not possible to specify the lot number of the Christie's sale of 20 July 1859 of the 'Bouverie collection' under which this drawing was sold. The large group of Guercino drawings was divided up into forty-eight lots, each containing several items, with often only one drawing singled out in the description of the lot. However, it is likely that all the drawings by Guercino with the Bouverie stamp were included in that sale. As Mahon has argued (M, *Disegni*, 1969, p. 174), the stamp was probably applied shortly before the 1859 sale, since many other drawings by Guercino with a Bouverie, Hervey and 1st Earl of Gainsborough provenance which were not put up for sale at that time do not have the same stamp (examples in the British Museum are App. nos. 33, 49 and 50). It should be noted, however, that one drawing in the Museum, which was certainly among those in the 1859 sale, does not bear the Bouverie stamp (App. no. 85). This is surely an exception. The drawing is little more than a scrap, and was evidently deemed of such insignificance as not to warrant stamping.

26 Putto with an Amphora

He is seated to the front, looking up to the left; his right arm is across his body and his right hand rests on the amphora.

Red chalk. 255 × 186mm.

1895–9–15–705. Not illustrated.

Provenance: Casa Gennari; Mr Bouverie (L 325); Mr Hervey; 1st Earl of Gainsborough (anonymous sale, Christie's, London, 20 July 1859, lot unknown; see App. no. 25); J. C. Robinson; J. Malcolm.

Literature: Robinson 1869, no. 252; Robinson, 1876, no. 264; M & T, 1989, under no. 821.

The drawing may perhaps date in the 1630s or 1640s. A retouched offset from App. no. 26 is in the Royal Library, Windsor Castle (M & T, 1989, no. 821).

Like App. nos. 9, 25 and 36, this was one of the drawings acquired by Robinson at the Christie's 'Bouverie collection' sale of 1859 and then sold to Malcolm, probably in 1860 (see L 1489 and M, *Disegni*, 1969, p. 174).

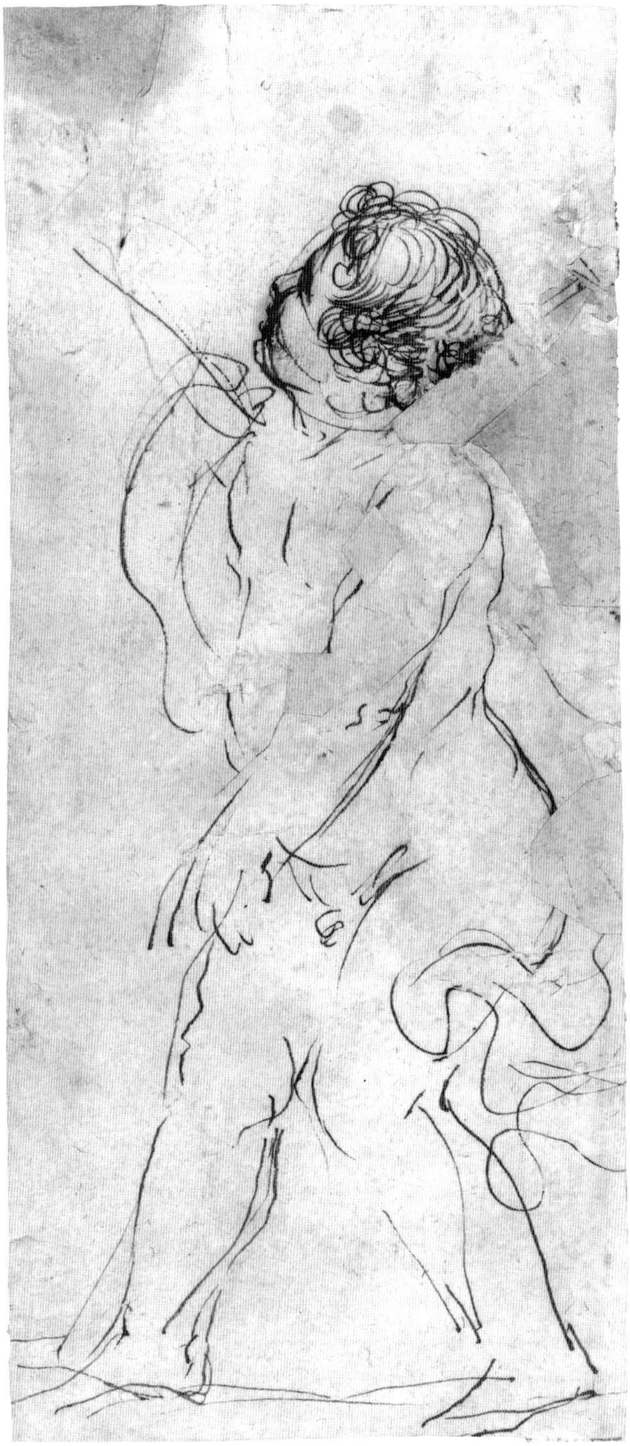

App. no. 27

27 Standing nude Infant

He is in profile to the left and looks upwards; the top of his raised right arm is covered by a drapery which falls the other side of his body to just behind his left leg; with his left hand he points to the ground.

Pen and light brown ink on greyish paper. 252 × 112mm; the sheet is very thin and has been creased from being badly laid down onto a backing; there are many other damages, including ineptly applied patches concealing losses in the original sheet.

5212–66

Provenance: W. Fawkener Bequest, 1769.

On the back of the old mount, in the centre, is an inscription in brown ink, in an old hand: *Guercino da Cento.*

A study for the small boy in the *St Augustine in Meditation* of 1635 (the final payment was received on 16 January 1636), painted for Abbot Peretti of Naples and now in the Prado, Madrid (S, 1988, no. 157). A study in red and white chalks for the figure of St Augustine in the same picture is in the Staatsgalerie, Stuttgart (Koenig–Fachsenfeld Collection, inv. no. III/34; Thiem, 1979, p. 416, no. 11, repr. pl. 22).

The picture represents the encounter between St Augustine, meditating on the sea shore, and a boy in the act of scooping water from the sea into a sand pit with a shell. Upon enquiry, St Augustine discovered that the boy was attempting the impossible task of emptying the sea; he interpreted the incident as a symbol of the unfathomable mystery of God. The pose of the figure in App. no. 27 is very close to that of the child in the painting, in which he looks up at the saint, pointing to the sea with his right hand and to the sand pit with his left.

A reproduction of a drawing of this subject, showing both the saint and the boy, is in the Witt Library (the drawing was formerly on the art market in Paris: sale, Drouot, 11 December 1930, lot 20, repr.); the quality of the original is hard to assess from the photograph, but it seems to be an autograph study. Dr David Stone has kindly pointed out to us that this drawing is now in the Nelson–Atkins Museum of Art, Kansas City.

28 St Laurence distributing Alms

(*see colour pl. 18*)

The saint stands on a platform in the centre and takes coins from a bag of money, which he distributes to a group of poor men and women below on the left; among them is a woman carrying a child and leading a small boy, crying; to the right of St Laurence is a table on which a man is placing bags of money.

Pen and brown ink and brown wash. 226 × 275mm.

1910–2–12–3

Provenance: Casa Gennari (similar inscriptions to the one that appears here in the bottom right, consisting of an upper case letter followed by a lower case letter, are found on drawings with this same provenance: e.g. M & T, 1989, nos. 140, 197, 360 and 481); G. Salting Bequest, 1910.

Literature: Vasari Society, 1st ser., VIII (1912–13), 9 (repr.); Fischer, 1984, under no. 44, pl. 36; M & T, 1989, under no. 159.

Inscribed in brown ink along the bottom edge, to the right: *Or: Guercino.*

For the main discussion of this drawing, see No. 112.

29 Man's left Leg

The thigh is partly covered by drapery.

Pen and brown ink. 227 × 189mm; damaged and repaired.

1893–7–31–3. Not illustrated.

30 Man's left Leg wearing a Shoe

The leg is clad in breeches and a stocking, and a ribbon is tied in a bow behind the knee.

Pen and brown ink. 236 × 151mm.

1893–7–31–4. Not illustrated.

Provenance (for both): Earl of Aylesford (sale, Christie's, London, 18 July 1893, lot 238, with 7 others, bt *Colnaghi* commissioned).

These two studies were perhaps made as exercises in drawing rather than for figures within a specific picture or pictures. They were presumably always preserved together, possibly even as part of a larger series. In some respects they recall the series of designs (including disembodied limbs, legs and other parts of the body) that Guercino made in 1618 for the instruction of novice draughtsmen (see Nos. 20–21). From their style, however, they seem to date from the late 1630s.

In the Casa Gennari inventory of 1719, a group of such drawings of limbs is mentioned among the miscellaneous loose sheets subdivided into categories and listed under the letter F, after the description of the albums of drawings: *Diversi Dissegni di Mani, Braccia, Gambe, e Piedi, parte del Sud. Guerzino, e qualchedun ancora de Carazzi N. 199. in tutto valutati – 24:1 –*. It is possible that the two British Museum drawings once belonged to this group.

31 Three-quarter-length Study for the Figure of David

His body faces forward but he leans slightly to the left, standing with his legs apart, his left arm on his hip and his right arm extended downwards; his head, which is clad in a helmet, is turned in profile to the right.

Pen and brown ink. 219 × 166mm.

1943–11–13–15

Provenance: Eric Rose, by whom presented.

Literature: M, *Disegni*, 1969, under nos. 139–40.

From a photograph in the Department's records, reproduced here, it appears that two old pencil inscriptions once written on the drawing in different hands have been erased, probably when the drawing was mounted. These were as follows: in the bottom left corner, between the figure's right arm and leg: *Guercino*; and, in the bottom right corner: *Study* [. . .] / *David* (for another inscription in this hand, see App. no. 37). (The first inscription is also found on other drawings in the collection presented by Eric Rose; see App. no. 19.)

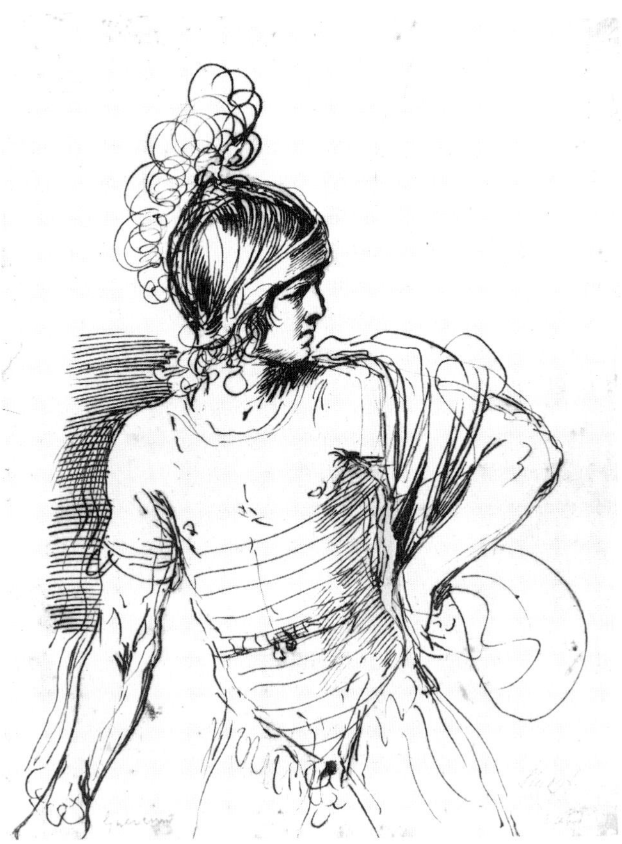

App. no. 31

In 1636 Guercino painted a large-scale, full-length composition of *Abigail appeasing the Wrath of David by offering Gifts* for Cardinal Antonio Barberini: the picture, one of the most prestigious commissions of that decade, passed from the Barberini to Cardinal Mazarin and thence into the Orléans collection and eventually into that of the Earls of Ellesmere at Bridgewater House, London, where it was destroyed in an air raid in 1941; its appearance is preserved in an old photograph (S, 1988, no. 161). Although preparatory drawings for the picture formerly at Bridgewater House have been discussed together (M, *Disegni*, 1969, under nos. 139–40) with studies for another composition of this same subject, half length and painted earlier, in *c.*1625–7 (S, 1988, no. 116; original also lost, but well recorded in various copies), they are clearly not all for the same project. Three of the drawings from the group are undoubtedly for the earlier composition and were identified independently by Meijer and van Tuyll (1983, no. 55) and Mahon and Turner (1989, no. 48).

Besides App. no. 31, which will be discussed below, it is worth listing here those drawings that we believe to be for the painting formerly at Bridgewater House (including those already cited by Mahon).

1. Genoa, Palazzo Rosso, inv. no. 5803, *Three-quarter-length Study of a Man holding a Staff in both Hands*, pen and brown ink, 285 × 172mm (for the halberdier standing immediately to the right of King David).

2. Haarlem, Teylers Museum, inv. no. H. 73, *Study for Abigail placating David with Gifts* (M, *Disegni*, 1969, no. 139).

3. Haarlem, Teylers Museum, inv. no. H. 33, *Study for the Head of David* (M, *Disegni*, 1969, no. 140).

4. London, British Museum, inv. no. 1943–11–13–9, *Head and Shoulders of a helmeted Warrior* (App. no. 32).

5. Formerly Munich, Herbert List collection, *Abigail with two Attendants and a Pack-mule* (see M, *Disegni*, 1969, p. 135, under nos. 139–40; the drawing is reproduced in Katrin Bellinger, *Master Drawings*, exh. cat., London, Harari & Johns, 26 June to 11 July 1990).

6. Oxford, Mahon Collection, on loan to the Ashmolean Museum, *Three-quarter-length Study for the Figure of David* (M, *Disegni*, 1969, under nos. 139–40; M & E, 1986, no. 26).

7. Vienna, Albertina, inv. no. 2161, *Study of Attendants unloading Sheep from a Pack-mule* (placed with the drawings of Annibale Carracci but attributed to Guercino by Dr Ann Sutherland Harris, according to a note on the mount).

8. Vienna, Albertina, inv. no. 2364, *Study for Abigail placating David* (M & E, 1986, under no. 26).

Although of different types, all nine drawings are stylistically homogeneous. A characteristic of them is a fine system of pen hatching and a notably classical cast to the features of the figures.

In the Haarlem and Albertina composition studies, and in the Mahon drawing, the figure, dressed in armour and wearing a helmet, is posed with his left hand on his hip and part of his cloak wrapped around his left shoulder; his right arm is directed downwards, a gesture explained by the Haarlem and Albertina drawings in which the figure appears holding a staff. All these features appear in the present study.

As noted in the Departmental register by John Gere, A. E. Popham supposed App. no. 31 to be a study related to another drawing in the British Museum, No. 133, which is now generally accepted as a study for a lost painting of *Cupid restraining the enraged Mars*, the date of which is unknown. As pointed out under No. 132, the picture's appearance is preserved in the form of an engraving by Giacomo Giovannini and, furthermore, several drawings document the evolution of Guercino's ideas for the composition. The pose of the figure in the present drawing agrees in almost every respect with that of Mars in the print, and there are also notable parallels between it and the figure of Mars in the related studies. However, in the print and in all the preparatory drawings for the *Cupid restraining the*

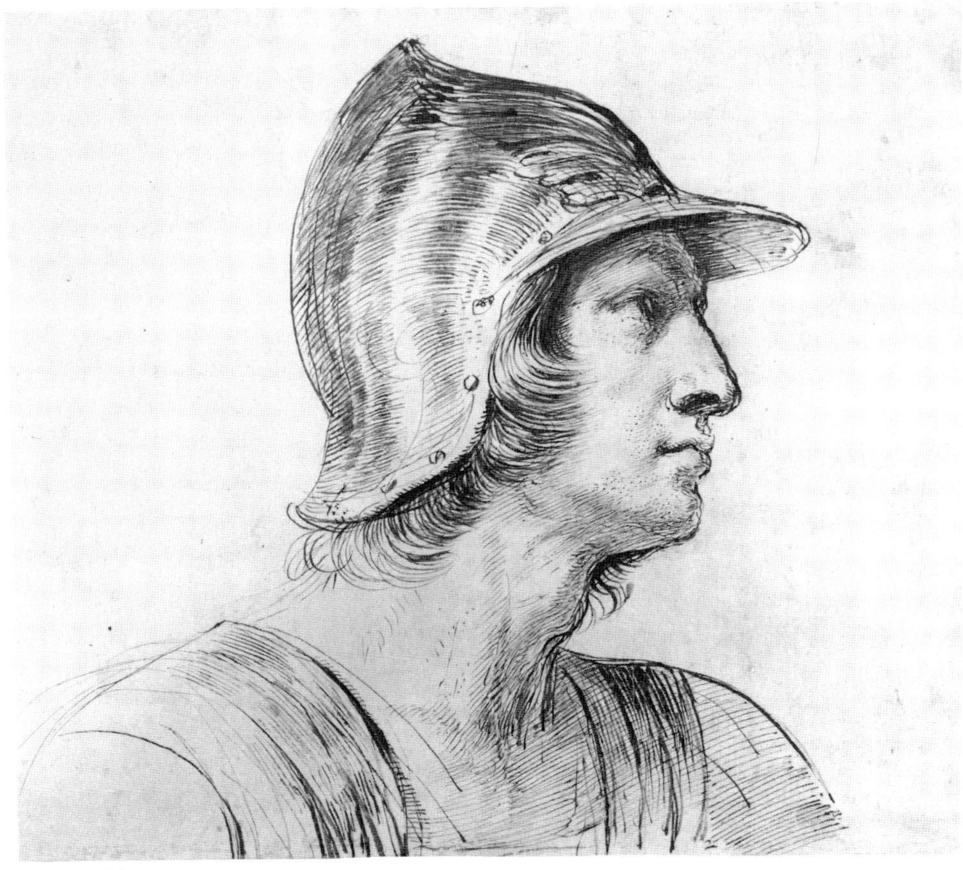

App. no. 32

enraged Mars, Mars is shown bearded, with a sash tied diagonally across his chest. These differences encourage one to support Mahon's identification of App. no. 31 as a study for the ex-Bridgewater House painting.

32 Head and Shoulders of a helmeted Warrior

He is in profile to the right and looks slightly upwards.

Pen and brown ink. 256 × 299mm.

1943–11–13–9

Provenance: Eric Rose, by whom presented.

Probably a preparatory study for the head of David in the painting, formerly at Bridgewater House and now destroyed, of *Abigail appeasing the Wrath of David by offering Gifts*, executed in 1636 for Cardinal Antonio Barberini, for which see App. no. 31.

Although it is all too easy to dismiss this rather unattractive drawing as a School work, there is no denying that it shares many of the stylistic features found in Guercino's other preparatory drawings for this commission. Its careful, almost laboured handling certainly sets it apart from most of Guercino's other drawings from the late 1630s in this medium, where his touch is much freer; but its highly-wrought appearance may be explained by its function. The drawing was probably made as a finished study in its own right for one of the most important details in the painting; the artist would most often have executed this type of drawing in red chalk immediately before putting brush to canvas, but examples of this class of drawing have only rarely survived. One is the *Head of God the Father* in the Museum of Fine Arts, Budapest (inv. no. 2323; Czére, 1989, no. 37); another, the *Head of a young Man* in the Royal Library, Windsor Castle (M & T, 1989, no. 128, as S. Luigi Gonzaga, but identified as St Laurence in this Catalogue; see No. 50). One might point out, on the other hand, the parallels between App. no. 32 and two smaller-scale pen drawings, also at Windsor, with detailed studies for the head of Alexander, for a lost composition of *Alexander and Hephaestion* of 1631 (No. 80 in this Catalogue and M & T, 1989, no. 59).

Militating against the connection of this drawing with the ex-Bridgewater House picture is the fact that the figure in the sketch looks upwards, whereas David gazes down at the kneeling Abigail in the two composition sketches, in the Teylers Museum, Haarlem, and in the Albertina, Vienna, respectively, as well as in the finished painting. However, in the only other study for the head and shoulders of David, that in Haarlem (inv. no. H. 33; M, *Disegni*, 1969, no. 140), the figure is also shown with his head erect, looking straight ahead of him.

33 The Martyrdom of St Bartholomew

(*see colour pl. 17*)

The saint stands in the centre of the composition with his right knee bent under him on a block and his right hand tied to a post; an executioner on the left cuts into his right shoulder with a knife, while a second executioner, with his back turned, bends over his left forearm; in the background on the right are a potentate and three other spectators.

Pen and brown ink and brown wash. 249 × 236mm.

1989–6–17–278

Provenance: Casa Gennari (the drawing is laid down on a fine Casa Gennari mount, for which see L *Suppl*, 2858c, and M, 1967, p. 20); Mr Bouverie; Mr Hervey; 1st Earl of Gainsborough; thence by descent. Purchased with funds bequeathed by the late Mrs V. J. Playfair.

For the main discussion of this drawing, see No. 110.

34 (?)St Bartholomew

He stands over half length with his body turned slightly to the left, his arms held apart and his head looking up to the right; he wears a loincloth.

Pen and brown ink. 206 × 164mm.

1895–9–15–703

Provenance: Sir J. St Aubyn (L 1534); J. C. Robinson; J. Malcolm.

Literature: Robinson, 1869, no. 250; Robinson, 1876, no. 262.

Although Robinson considered this to be a study for a St

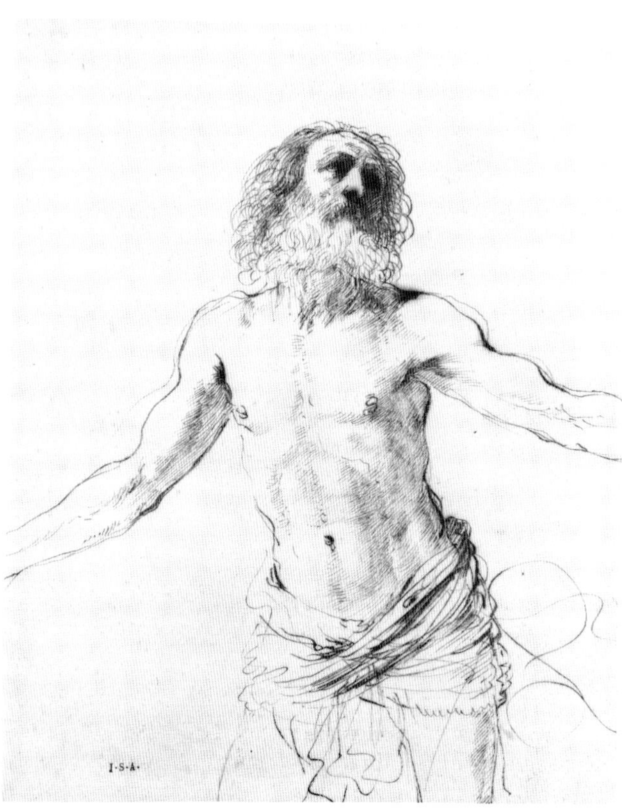

App. no. 34

Jerome, there are good reasons for supposing that the figure was intended as a St Bartholomew for the altarpiece discussed under No. 110. The pose of the figure in App. no. 34 most closely resembles that of St Bartholomew in two of the composition drawings for this altarpiece, Nos. 110 and 111, as well as in two other figure studies for the saint, one in red chalk in the Steiner collection, Larchmont, New York (Oberhuber, 1977, no. 18, where it is identified as perhaps for a *Raising of Lazarus*), and the other in pen and brown wash formerly in a private collection, Dorset (sale, Sotheby's, London, 17 April 1980, lot 146, repr.). In all five drawings the saint is represented with a squarish beard, his head tilted back and his arms outstretched; a cloth is wrapped about his loins; and his torso is illuminated in much the same way, though not always from the same direction.

35 Madonna of the Rosary with Sts Dominic and Catherine

The Madonna is seated on a cloud, with the Christ Child on her lap, just left of centre and turned three-quarters to the right; with her right hand she passes a rosary to St Dominic who kneels, turned to the left, below her; behind him is St Catherine, also kneeling and gazing upwards at the Christ Child, who extends a rosary to her; in the bottom left-hand corner is a putto holding a lily and behind St Catherine are indications of a crowd of onlookers; two angels and three putti appear in the sky; the whole composition is framed by classical architecture.

Red chalk. 410 × 280mm.

1910–2–12–8. Illustrated in the main Catalogue (No. 129).

Provenance: Casa Gennari; Mr Bouverie (L 325); Mr Hervey; 1st Earl of Gainsborough (anonymous sale, Christie's, London, 20 July 1859, lot 69, bt singly *Graves, £1–0–0*); G. Salting Bequest, 1910.

Literature: Stampfle & Bean, 1967, under no. 42; M, *Disegni*, 1969, no. 141; Roli, 1972, no. 55.

For the main discussion of this drawing, see No. 129.

36 Cleopatra

(*see colour pl. 19*)

She stands three-quarter length with her body facing the spectator but with her head turned almost in profile to the right, looking upwards; she rests her left arm on a block and in her right hand she holds an asp which makes towards her bared right breast.

Red chalk. 292 × 215mm.

1895–9–15–709

Provenance: Casa Gennari; Mr Bouverie (L 325); Mr Hervey; 1st Earl of Gainsborough (anonymous sale, Christie's, London, 20 July 1859, lot 66, with 2 others, bt *Smith, £0–13–0*; see below); J. C. Robinson; J. Malcolm.

Literature: Robinson, 1869, no. 259; Robinson, 1876, no. 269.

It is clear from the annotated copy of the 1859 Christie's sale catalogue in the Library of P. & D. Colnaghi's, London, a xerox of which is in the Library of the Department (shelf-mark A. 6. 32), that Robinson was the purchaser of only one of the lots of red chalk drawings by Guercino. This was lot 72 containing four drawings, of which none of the three listed represented Cleopatra. While it is possible that the fourth drawing in this lot was App. no. 36, this seems unlikely since a drawing of such distinction would surely have merited description. On the other hand, lot 66, purchased by 'Smith', contained three drawings: *'The Holy Family*; and two studies for *Cleopatra'*. Robinson probably acquired his drawing from 'Smith' after the sale, since he often negotiated swaps or purchases with other buyers immediately after the sales he attended.

For the main discussion of this drawing, see No. 120.

37 Half-length Study of Cleopatra

Her body faces forward, slightly to the left, but her head is turned upwards and to the right; her left arm, with a drapery wrapped around the top of it, lies across the front of her body and in her right hand she holds the asp which makes towards her bared breast.

Pen and brown ink. 163 × 175mm.

1943–11–13–17. Not illustrated.

Provenance: Eric Rose, by whom presented.

Inscribed in pencil in the bottom right corner: *Study for the Sibilla Cum[ea]*. (The handwriting is the same as that which formerly appeared in the second of two inscriptions in the bottom right corner of App. no. 31.)

We at first doubted whether this drawing was by Guercino on account of the extensive and over-emphatic hatching in the background and over the figure's left forearm. Nonetheless, similar, less prominent passages of shading with the pen occur in his other drawings (e.g., App. no. 31), and the rest of the study seemed so characteristic that it would have been perverse to exclude it on these grounds alone. Furthermore, comparison with the red chalk drawing of Cleopatra in the British Museum (App. no. 36) reveals so many parallels in handling as to rule out any remaining doubts in our minds. It seems that Guercino was simply using his pen in the manner he normally reserved for chalk drawings, and, in the background on the left, resorting to a favourite trick of blanking out redundant lines of the underdrawing with close hatching.

It is perhaps no accident that the two British Museum drawings share further features in common. These include the artist's concentration upon the contrast between the pale flesh of the bared right shoulder and the dark background against which it is silhouetted; the swathe of drapery descending over the left upper arm; and a distinct resemblance between the facial types and, to some extent, the coiffure of the two figures. These points of similarity would seem to confirm that the two drawings belong to roughly the same period.

App. nos. 36 and 37, although extremely close to each other in many ways, were probably not conceived with the same picture in mind. We know that Guercino painted several renderings of Cleopatra in the second half of the

1630s, only one of which has survived, namely that painted in 1639 for Marchese Francesco Fiaschi of Ferrara and now in a private collection there (S, 1988, no. 183). The present drawing resembles the Ferrara painting in some respects (particularly in the angle of the figure's upturned head), but it does not match so well in style with the one preparatory drawing undoubtedly for this picture in the Uffizi, Florence (inv. no. 1626-F; M, *Disegni*, 1969, no. 144).

38 Cupid restraining Mars

Mars stands with his legs apart and his body turned slightly to the right; his cloak, cast over his left shoulder and about his loins, is held in place by his left hand resting on his hip; in his right hand he holds a sword and Cupid, who stands on a block on the left, restrains his arm with both hands.

Pen and brown ink. 272 × 199mm.

Ff. 2–135. Illustrated in main Catalogue (No. 133).

Provenance: Casa Gennari; probably William Kent (?his sale, Langford's, London, 8–11 December 1762, lot unknown; see M & T, 1989, p. xxviii); Rev. C. M. Cracherode Bequest, 1799.

Literature: Stechow, 1976, under no. 160; Turner, 1982, p. 162; M & T, 1989, under no. 661.

Etched in reverse by the Florentine engraver Giuseppe Zocchi (1711–67), presumably shortly after William Kent's acquisition of the drawing from the Casa Gennari, probably in the late 1750s. Kent's activities are known, among other sources, from the *Abecedario* of the well-known connoisseur Mariette who, in discussing the passion of English collectors for the drawings of Guercino, mentions a 'M. Kent', who commissioned Zocchi to make facsimile etchings of some of them; these same drawings and their relative copper-plates by Zocchi were subsequently sold in London, in 1762, in the 'Luti' sale (so-called because it contained a large portion of the collection Kent had acquired in 1759 from Benedetto Luti; for further discussion, see M, 1967, pp. 10–11, M & T, 1989, pp. xxviii–xxix, and the Introduction to this Catalogue). An impression of Zocchi's etching after App. no. 38 is also in the Department (189* b. 1, no. 102).

A copy after a Guercino drawing by Robert Shipster (App. no. 116) appears to record a lost study for the figure of Mars connected with this same composition.

For the main discussion of this drawing, see No. 133.

39 Christ Child seated on the Madonna's Lap

He is seated on his mother's knee with his legs to the right, looking down to the left and stretching out both arms; he is held across the chest in the Madonna's hands; her head does not appear and her body is only partly indicated.

Red chalk with occasional touches of white chalk on blue paper. 236 × 253mm.

1859–8–6–71

Provenance: Casa Gennari; Mr Bouverie (L 325); Mr Hervey; 1st Earl of Gainsborough (anonymous sale, Christie's, London, 20 July 1859, lot 59, bt with one other, together with lot 58, *Tiffin, £1–1–0*).

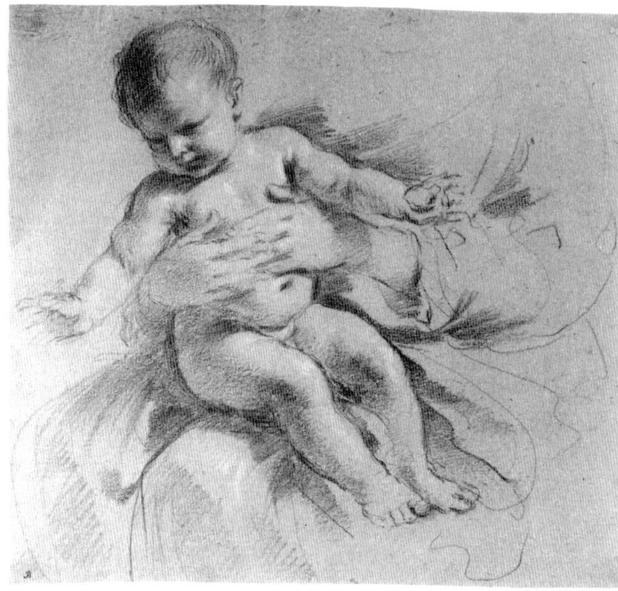

App. no. 39

Literature: S, 1988, p. 409, under no. 353.

A study, closely corresponding with the finished result, for a painting formerly on the London art market, the present whereabouts of which are unknown (S, 1988, no. 353). In the painting the Madonna and Child are seated among clouds and the Child opens his arms to catch a dove which flies up towards them (the dove is omitted in the drawing but its position in the painting roughly corresponds with that of the Madonna's right knee). The picture is dated by Salerno in the 1640s, but it might conceivably be somewhat earlier. The drawing's connection with this composition was independently recognised by Pouncey when the picture was sold in 1962 (sale, Sotheby's, London, 28 November 1962, lot 118).

In type the drawing, with its technique of red chalk, heightened with white, on tinted paper, suggests the class of drapery studies and detailed studies of limbs, etc., which make up the magnificent group of drawings by Guercino in the Koenig-Fachsenfeld Collection, on deposit in the Staatsgalerie, Stuttgart (see especially App. no. 17).

40 Figure seated by a Rock

He is seen from behind seated on a square block and resting both hands on another, larger block; he has a cloak draped over his left shoulder, leaving his back bare.

Red chalk. 220 × 191mm.

1910–2–12–6. Not illustrated.

Provenance: Casa Gennari; Mr Bouverie (L 325); Mr Hervey; 1st Earl of Gainsborough (anonymous sale, Christie's, London, 20 July 1859, lot unknown; see App. no. 25); G. Salting Bequest, 1910.

To judge from the brawny upper arm, the model seems to be male. This enigmatic figure does not apparently occur in any of Guercino's surviving pictures.

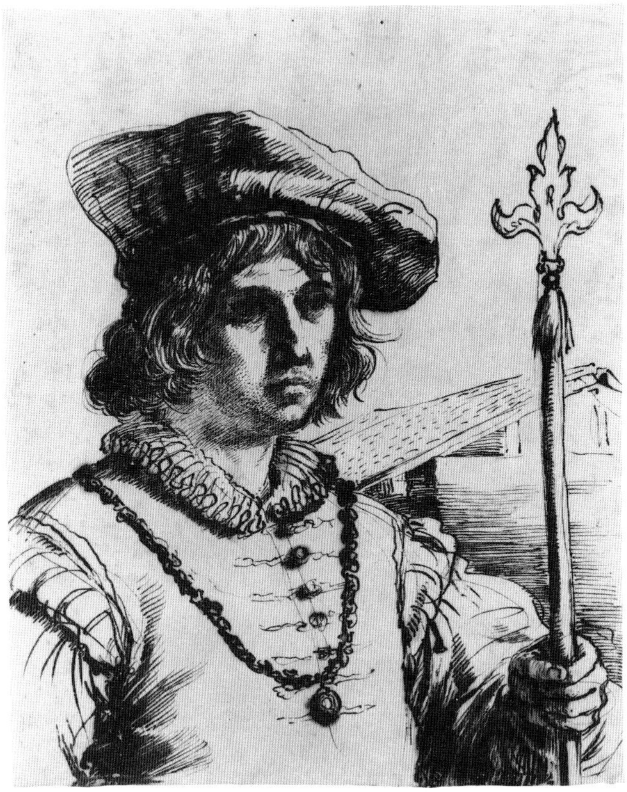

App. no. 41

41 Head and Shoulders of a Youth holding a Halberd

He is turned three-quarters to the right and wears a beret, a ruff and a chain; in his left hand he holds the halberd, which has a decorative blade.

Pen and dark brown ink. 238 × 188mm; damaged and repaired in the areas of greatest dark.

Pp. 4–61

Provenance: R. Payne Knight Bequest, 1824.

Literature: B, 1988, p. 119, repr.

The old mount on which this drawing was once laid down was inscribed: *Cav. Gio Francesco Barbieri detto Il Guercino.*

An unsigned engraving in reverse, inscribed in the lower left: *1640/cento,* was made from this drawing. An impression of the print is in the collection (inv. no. 1970–1–31–13) and is placed with the drawing. The engraver must be Giovanni Francesco Mucci (1621–65), a nephew and pupil of Guercino, who was active in Cento (see B, 1988, p. 119, where the engraving is published as by Muccio).

Judging from its style, the drawing did not precede the print by any great length of time. Indeed, it is highly reminiscent of the artist's work of the 1630s.

42 St Francis contemplating a Crucifix

He is over half length and stands in profile to the right, resting his chin on his left hand and gazing at the crucifix on an altar in front of him; his right hand, which holds a rosary, rests on a skull.

Red chalk. 180 × 147mm.

Ff. 2–129. Not illustrated.

Provenance: J. Richardson, Sr (L 2184); J. M. Rysbrack; J. Barnard (L 1419); Rev. C. M. Cracherode Bequest, 1799.

Literature: Ryskamp, et al., 1979, under no. 119; M & T, 1989, under no. 678.

The drawing was engraved in the same sense by W. W. Ryland in 1763, while in the collection of J. M. Rysbrack, and is included in Rogers (1778, unpaginated; a copy is in the Department, shelfmark 163 c. 26, in which the print is numbered 99). From its style, the drawing would appear to date from *c.*1640.

The lines at the bottom of the sheet seem to indicate that the composition was intended as a half length. A similar compositional drawing, in the Palazzo Rosso, Genoa (inv. no. 985, black chalk heightened with white, 223 × 195mm), shows the saint with his hands clasped together at his chin and without the skull. Like App. no. 42, the Genoa study was also for a half-length picture, since its confines have also been established, in this instance at both top and bottom. A difference between the two drawings, however, is that the hood of the figure in the Genoese sketch is pulled up further over its head.

A similar treatment of the saint kneeling in contemplation of the crucifix, in which, however, he is shown full length and facing to the left, occurs in two studies, one formerly on the London art market (Christie's, 25 June 1974, lot 47, repr.), and the other in the collection of HRH Queen Beatrix of the Netherlands (Ryskamp, *et al.*, 1979, no. 119).

A coarsely retouched offset, possibly of App. no. 42 or a closely related drawing, is in the Royal Library, Windsor Castle (M & T, 1989, no. 678).

43 St Onuphrius in the Wilderness

He is naked except for some leaves round his loins, is seated on a hummock in profile to the right and reads from a book lying on a rock in front of him.

Red chalk, faded from having been offset. 292 × 195mm.

1910–2–12–7. Not illustrated.

Provenance: G. Salting Bequest, 1910.

Literature: M & T, 1989, under nos. 218 and 702.

It seems likely that the saint in question is Onuphrius on account of the girdle of leaves about his loins, as distinct from St Paul the Hermit who wears a more substantial shroud of woven palm leaves (see App. no. 44).

A stylistically similar drawing, also in red chalk, in the Royal Library, Windsor Castle (M & T, 1989, no. 218), shows a kneeling hermit saint, his hair and beard still more abundant, clad in a similar girdle. They may well have been drawn in the same connection since they apparently date from the same period, around the 1640s or possibly the 1650s. Retouched offsets of both drawings are also at Windsor, two having been taken from App. no. 43 (M & T, 1989, nos. 702 and 703) and one from the Windsor drawing (M & T, 1989, no. 704).

A pen-and-wash drawing of this subject, but identified as St Jerome, was formerly on the New York art market (sale, Parke Bernet, 22 October 1970, lot 5, repr., where a provenance of the drawing from the Earl of Gainsborough is given).

44 Hermit Saint (?St Paul)

He is represented standing, facing the spectator, in front of an arched recess; his right hand, in which he holds a rosary, rests on a Tau-cross, and his left hand is raised with the palm outwards; he wears only a primitive garment over his right shoulder and round his loins.

Red chalk. 270 × 133mm (including a strip about 15mm wide added at the bottom).

Ff. 2–131

Provenance: (?)Casa Gennari; (?)P. Crozat (?his number *23*, inscribed in ink in the bottom right corner); Rev. C. M. Cracherode Bequest, 1799.

Inscribed in brown ink in the bottom right corner: *guarchino*; and below, also in brown ink but in a different hand, what appears to be the number *23*. On the *verso*, visible through the sheet (which has been laid down), is a capital *T*, inscribed in ink, in the top left corner. Letters of this sort are sometimes to be found on the backs of drawings with a Casa Gennari provenance.

The saint is almost certainly St Paul the Hermit, who is shown with the same attributes (a stick and a rosary) in the altarpiece *St Augustine with Sts John the Baptist and Paul the Hermit* of 1637–8 in S. Agostino, Rome (S, 1988, no. 170). Apart from this picture, for which payment was received on 2 January 1637 and 7 May 1638 (*Libro dei Conti*, 1808, pp. 79 and 84f.; 1841, pp. 315 and 317), the Account Book mentions only two other commissions for a St Paul the Hermit, the first under 15 October 1631 (*Libro dei Conti*, 1808, pp. 63–4; 1841, p. 309) and the second under 20 December 1663 (*Libro dei Conti*, 1808, p. 157; 1841, p. 342). App. no. 44 is clearly not connected with the S. Agostino picture. Nor, would it seem, can one associate it with the others mentioned in the Account Book, these being too early and too late respectively, and most probably both half lengths (priced at 46 and 75 *scudi*).

A pen-and-wash drawing in the Royal Museum, Copenhagen (inv. no. VII GIL/23, 11132), almost certainly a study for the same composition as that shown in App. no. 44, also shows the saint before an arched recess, but at half length and resting with his right elbow and his left hand on the end of the stick. The Copenhagen sketch appears to have been cut down and it is possible that it originally showed the figure full length. The style of the British Museum and Copenhagen drawings points to a date in the 1630s or 1640s.

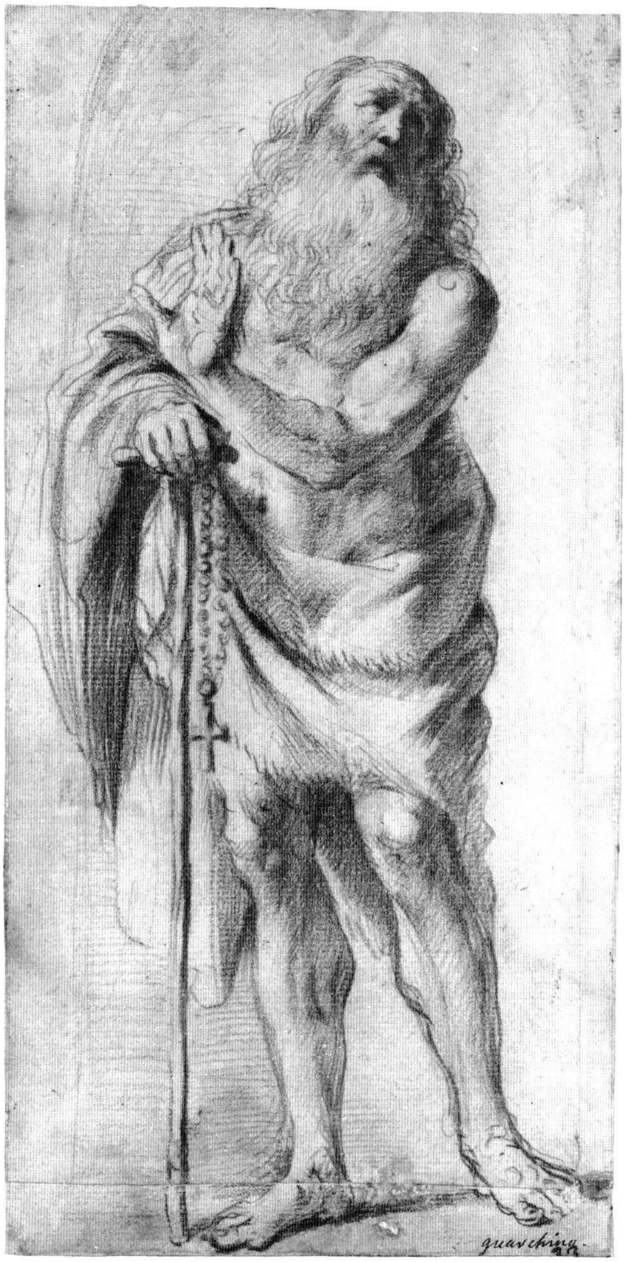

App. no. 44

45 St Peter denying Christ

St Peter, on the left and facing left, warms both hands at a fire of sticks on a raised hearth; he turns back to the right to speak to the serving woman, whose head is in profile to the left; her arms are crossed over her chest and she points to the right with her right hand; behind is a soldier with a halberd.

Pen and brown ink and light brown wash. 254 × 200mm; the drawing, which was previously laid down on canvas, is much abraded.

Ff. 2–137

Provenance: Casa Gennari; probably William Kent (?his sale, Langford's, London, 8–11 December 1762, lot unknown; see M & T, 1989, p. xxviii); J. Barnard (L 1420); Rev. C. M. Cracherode Bequest, 1799.

Literature: Turner, 1982, p. 162; S, 1988, under no. 231.

According to Popham (note in the Departmental files), the backing of the drawing, now covered by the mount, has an inscription in Barnard's hand.

Etched in reverse by Giuseppe Zocchi; an impression of the print is also in the collection (189* b. 1, no. 103). (For a discussion of the provenance of the small group of Guercino drawings etched by Zocchi, see App. no. 38.)

The condition of the sheet is deplorable, making it extremely difficult to judge the quality of the drawing; we believe, however, that it is a damaged original rather than a School drawing. The surface abrasions seem to have resulted from the fact that the paper was once laid down onto canvas, a method of displaying drawings that was extensively employed in the Casa Gennari (see M & T, 1989, pp. xviii–xx).

In our opinion, the drawing is a preparatory study for the painting of this subject commissioned by Cardinal Mazarin and now in a private collection (sale, Sotheby's, London, 11 December 1985, lot 8; S, 1988, no. 231), for which Guercino received payment in 1641. The drawing differs from the finished painting in several respects, perhaps the most important being that the composition is treated in a vertical format, with only two half-length figures and a head, rather than horizontally with three half-length figures as in the painted composition. Guercino's method of pricing his paintings was according to the length of each figure to be painted and it would seem that in App. no. 45 the artist was perhaps considering a slightly cheaper version of the subject than was eventually carried out.

The drawing is close in style to those made by Guercino for the altarpiece of *All Saints in Glory* of 1645–7 (S, 1988, no. 239). One of these preparatory sketches, *A Pope and a bearded Saint conversing*, in the Royal Library, Windsor Castle (M & T, 1989, no. 116) – even though it is a more rapid study for a figure group rather than a finished composition study – compares particularly well with App. no. 45, both in the morphology of the faces and in the manner of their juxtaposition.

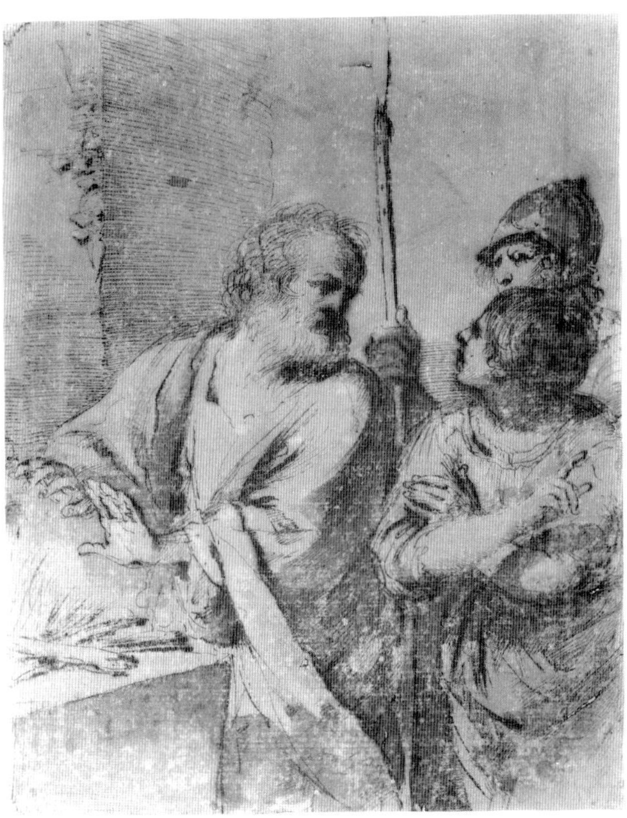

App. no. 45

46 Head of an old Man

He is bearded and looks upwards, slightly to the right; his lips are parted, as if to speak or cry out.

Pen and brown ink. 146 × 139mm.

1943–11–13–18

Provenance: (?)Casa Gennari; (?)Mr Bouverie; (?)Mr Hervey; (?)Earls of Gainsborough; Eric Rose, by whom presented.

Inscribed in pencil in the bottom right-hand corner: *Guercino*. (For similar inscriptions on drawings by Guercino and his School from the collection of Eric Rose, see App. no. 19.) What appears to be an analogous inscription in ink and in a different hand shows through at the top right from the *verso*.

In the drawing the artist has been exercised by the study of hair of different colour and profusion and has succeeded in his objective. At first sight, the head recalls those of Guercino's hermit saints, though the cape worn over the figure's shoulders shows that he must belong to some monastic order. There are indeed points in common between the drawing and the figure of St Romuald in an altarpiece of 1640–41, now in the Istituto di Belle Arti, Ravenna (S, 1988, no. 193), in which the saint wears the habit of the Camaldolese order. The style of the drawing is consistent with this dating and it is therefore possible that it may be a study for the Ravenna picture. Salerno (1988, in a note on the drawings, under no. 193) referred to a red chalk study for the figure of St Romuald, which was sold in Vienna in 1917 (reproduction in the Witt Library, under Guercino). A comparison of the head of the saint in the drawing formerly in Vienna with that of App. no. 46 in our view

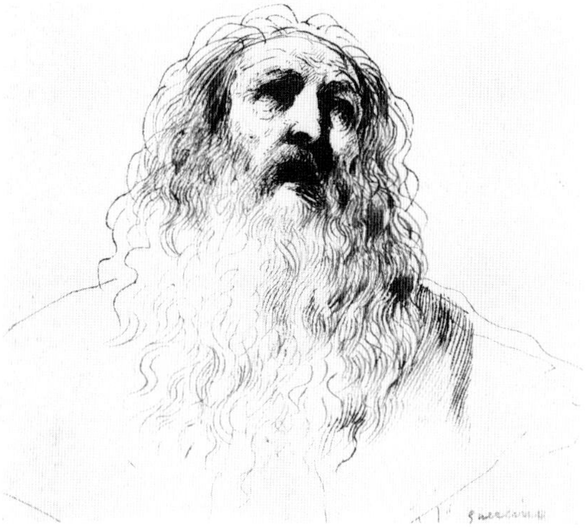

App. no. 46

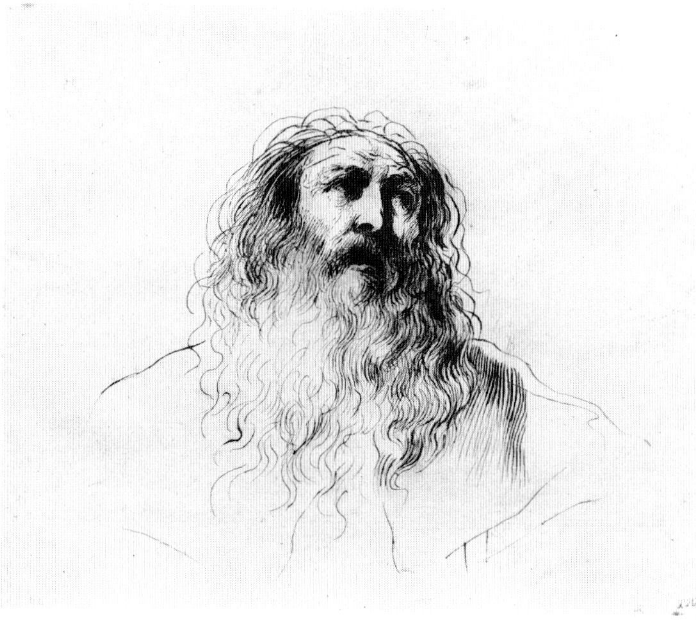

Fig. 22 Sir Joshua Reynolds after Guercino, *Head of an old Man*. Pen and brown ink, 165 × 194 mm (Budapest, Museum of Fine Arts, inv. no. 2480). See App. no. 46

reinforces the connection of the latter with the Ravenna picture.

An accurate pen-and-ink copy of App. no. 46 is in the Museum of Fine Arts, Budapest (inv. no. 2480, 165 × 194mm; see Fig. 22) and may be attributed to Sir Joshua Reynolds. The Budapest drawing was once in the collection of Thomas Hudson, the master of Reynolds, and Hudson's stamp (L 2432) appears in the bottom right of the drawing. Hudson seems to have owned a number of copies after Guercino drawn by Reynolds; what is almost certainly another example, also with Hudson's stamp in the bottom right corner, was formerly on the London art market (pen and brown ink, 142 × 180mm) and is copied from a drawing in the Art Museum, Princeton University, Princeton (inv. no. 48–712; Gibbons, 1977, no. 259). Another drawing among the group of pen-and-ink studies presented to the Museum by Eric Rose in 1943 was copied by Reynolds (see App. no. 48).

47 Priest reading

He is seated in profile to the left and wears a cap and a voluminous robe.

Pen and point of the brush and brown ink. 156 × 184mm.

1943–11–13–13

Provenance: Eric Rose, by whom presented.

Inscribed in the bottom left corner, in pencil: *Guercino*. (For similar inscriptions on drawings by Guercino and his School from the collection of Eric Rose, see App. no. 19.)

The figure's pose is reminiscent of that of St Gregory in the pen-and-ink drawing *A Pope and a bearded Saint conversing* in the Royal Library, Windsor Castle (M & T, 1989, no. 116), a connection strengthened by the striking stylistic harmony between the two drawings. This can be seen, for example, in the parallel hatching in the folds of the drapery in both and in the way the ink has been applied with the point of the brush in some of the features of the face. The Windsor drawing is a preparatory study for the *All Saints in Glory* of 1645–7 (S, 1988, no. 239), formerly in the church of the Sacre Stigmate at Modena and now in the Musée des Augustins at Toulouse. The British Museum sketch was probably drawn at an early stage in the composition, before the figures of St Gregory and St Jerome were transposed and shown standing, instead of seated, and before they had been relegated to the second plane, behind the kneeling St Sebastian. The drawing may have been taken from the life, the model only approximating in his dress the papal regalia.

48 Half-length Figure of St Gregory, seated on a Throne

His body faces forward and he looks upwards to the left; his right hand rests on the arm of his throne.

Pen and brown ink. 148 × 174mm; damaged and repaired in some of the darks.

1943–11–13–12

Provenance: (?)Casa Gennari; (?)Mr Bouverie; (?)Mr Hervey; (?)Earls of Gainsborough; Eric Rose, by whom presented.

Literature: M, 1967, under no. 12; M, *Disegni*, 1969, under no. 102; Byam Shaw, 1983, under no. 355; M & E, 1986, under no. 14.

A photograph of the drawing before conservation, held among

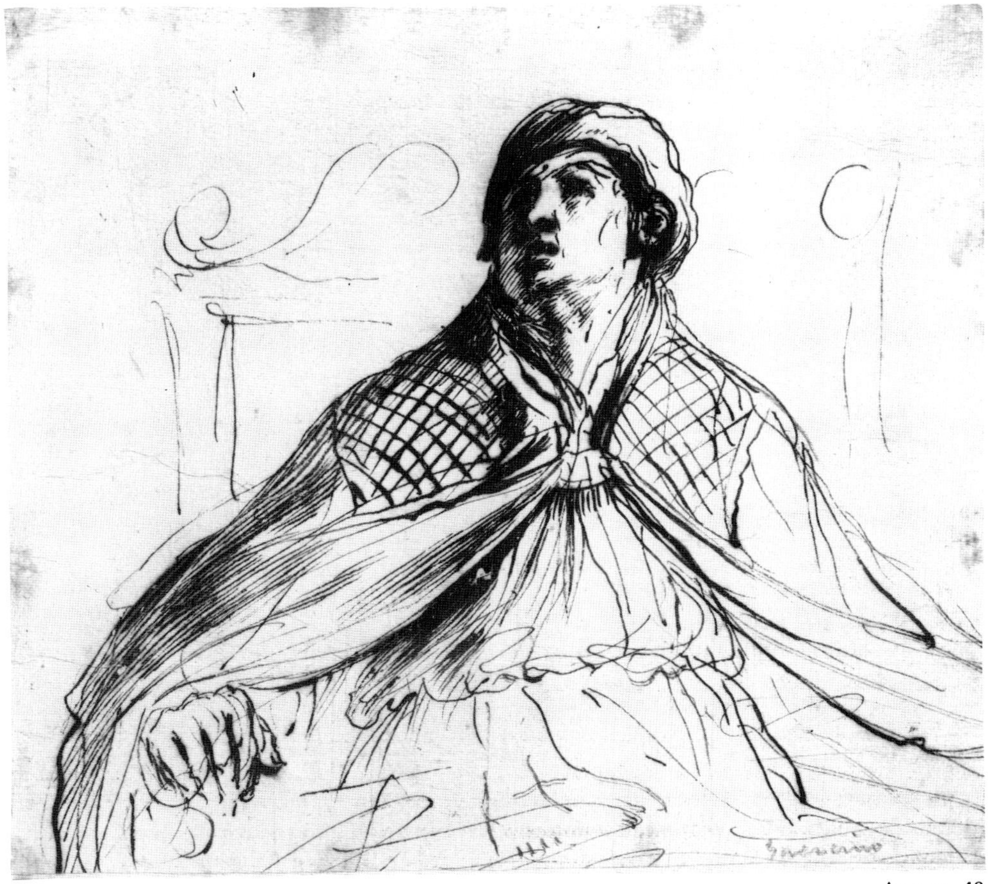

App. no. 48

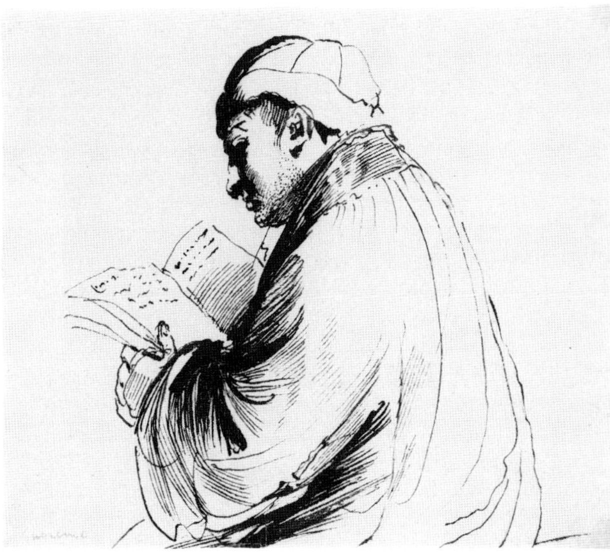

App. no. 47

the Departmental records and reproduced here, reveals that it once bore an early nineteenth-century inscription, presumably in pencil, in the bottom right corner: *Guercino*. (For similar inscriptions on drawings by Guercino and his School from the collection of Eric Rose, see App. no. 19.)

Mahon connected this drawing with a painting in his own collection, the *St Gregory the Great with Sts Ignatius Loyola and Francis Xavier* of *c*.1625–6 (S, 1988, no. 112). Certainly the pose of the saint in the drawing is similar to that of the figure in the picture, but the direction of the lighting is different and there are some discrepancies of detail, such as the absence in the drawing of the book in the saint's lap. Indeed the pen-and-ink style is more in keeping with Guercino's practice of the 1640s (see, for example, the study for the figure of *St Cecilia* in the Royal Library, Windsor Castle; M & T, 1989, no. 105).

A copy of App. no. 48 by Sir Joshua Reynolds, one of three pen-and-ink drawings said to be by Reynolds after Guercino, was formerly on the London art market (sale, Christie's, 20 November 1979, one item (repr.) in lot 5; the three drawings were included in an extra-illustrated copy of Edmund Malone's *Testimonies to the Genius and Memory of Sir Joshua Reynolds*, 1762) and is now in an English private collection. The Reynolds copy (which is illustrated by Byam Shaw, 1983, p. 490, fig. 94) is inscribed in pencil at the bottom: *Drawn by Sir Joshua Reynolds, from Guercino*. Interestingly, another drawing from the small group of mostly pen-and-ink studies presented to the Museum in 1943 by Eric Rose seems also to have been copied by Sir Joshua Reynolds. The copy was in the collection of his master Thomas Hudson and is now in the Museum of Fine Arts, Budapest (see App. no. 46 and Fig. 22). It was apparently Hudson who was responsible for encouraging Reynolds to copy the drawings of Guercino (see No. 126).

Of the many drawings by Guercino copied by Sir Joshua, several can be shown to have been in the Bouverie collection. This led Mahon (1967, under no. 45; *Disegni*, 1969, under no. 225) to suggest that the copies may have been drawn after the originals had passed into the collection of the Hon. Edward Bouverie, portraits of whose wife Reynolds had painted (see Introduction). The existence of Reynolds's copy after App. no. 48 might presuppose that the latter was also once in the Bouverie collection.

49 Half-length Figure of a bearded Man wearing a fur-trimmed Hat with a Plume

His body is turned to the left as he reaches to open a casket on a table or block on the left; he looks to the right, over his left shoulder, as he does so.

Pen and brown ink with some very slight touches of wash, smudged. 250 × 206mm; several losses in the darks, once repaired with patches, have been infilled.

1987–7–25–47. Illustrated in main Catalogue (No. 124).

Provenance: Casa Gennari (as indicated by inscription); Mr Bouverie; Mr Hervey; 1st Earl of Gainsborough (as indicated by pencil number on the mount, just beneath the bottom left corner of the drawing); Sir Denis Mahon, by whom presented.

Literature: Donnithorne, 1988, p. 19; Turner, 1988, p. 35, repr.; M & T, 1989, p. xxi, note 17.

The old mount is inscribed in brown ink, in an eighteenth-century hand, in the bottom left corner: *9 N° T. T. Fo.* (the coded number is similar to others sometimes found on drawings by Guercino with a Casa Gennari provenance, e.g., Nos. 10, 46 and 96). Numbered in graphite, in a nineteenth-century hand, just beneath the bottom left corner of the drawing: *55*; and in green ball point, in a modern hand, in the bottom right-hand corner: *5668D*.

The condition of the drawing bears all the hallmarks of those kept in albums in the Casa Gennari; in particular, it has losses at the corners (now made up) and traces of paste stains in the four corners (these have been mostly removed by the restoration of the drawing; for a discussion of these quirks of condition, see M & T, 1989, p. xxi). Furthermore, the holes in the darks caused by the action of the iron-gall ink were originally made good by small rectangular slips of paper, tinted blackish brown, almost certainly with iron-gall ink, and glued to the back of the sheet in a manner characteristic of the early repairs to the drawings by Guercino in the Casa Gennari (e.g., No. 132 and App. no. 64). These patches were removed in the course of the recent restoration of the drawing but had caused local staining on the old backing. One might conclude that the drawing, along with many others, was roughly torn from the Casa Gennari albums, presumably with a view to its sale; after having been crudely repaired in the manner described above and the damaged corners having also been made up with white paper slips, the sheet was laid down onto its present mid-eighteenth-century support by means of thirteen small, thin paper tabs. The mending of the holes in the drawing indicates that the substantial damage to the paper resulting from the acidic action of the iron-gall ink had occurred within the first hundred years or so of the drawing's existence. We are grateful to Mr Alan Donnithorne of the Western Pictorial Art Section of the Department of Conservation in the British Museum, who carried out the restoration of the drawing, for his help in compiling this entry.

For further discussion of this drawing, see No. 124.

50 Warrior wearing a plumed Helmet

He is seen just over half length, striding in profile to the left; in his left hand he holds the end of a scabbard, while with his right he draws his sword.

Pen and brown ink with some black chalk. 249 × 183mm.

1986–6–21–1

Provenance: Casa Gennari (the drawing has a Casa Gennari mount and is inscribed bottom left *17 P. Dol.*); Mr Bouverie; Mr Hervey; the Earls of Gainsborough (sale, Sotheby's, London, 22 July 1953, lot 5, with 2 others); Sir Denis Mahon, by whom presented.

Literature: Turner, 1987, p. 9; Turner, 1988, p. 35.

The black chalk underdrawing does not correspond with the penwork of the figure and may have been drawn as part of another preliminary sketch which the artist then abandoned.

This is perhaps a study for one of the protagonists in the *Hersilia separating Romulus and Tatius* in the Louvre, painted in 1645 for Louis de La Vrillière as one of a series of paintings to decorate the gallery of his *hôtel* in Paris (Stéphane Loire in Brejon & Volle, 1988–9, no. 86; S, 1988, no. 226). For other drawings connected with this commission, see Nos. 141–2. Some doubt about Guercino's authorship of App. no. 50 arises from the unrestrained quality of the draughtsmanship, particularly apparent in the plume and in the hair emerging from beneath the soldier's helmet; but although it is tempting to exclude Guercino's name on the grounds of such lack of control, there are good reasons for thinking that the drawing may indeed be by him. One is that it occupies a pivotal place in the evolution of the poses of the two principal soldiers. Whereas the position of the crooked right arm holding the sword relates to the soldier on the right, the figure's profile, with the light catching his nose and cheek and with his eye cast in deep shadow by the helmet, point to a resemblance, in reverse, to the principal soldier on the left. The link with the soldier on the left is further established by the strong harmony in style between the British Museum drawing and a drawing of the head and shoulders of a warrior in profile to the right and four separate studies for his head, formerly on the New York art market (Colnaghi's, exh. cat., 7 May to 9 June 1984, no. 16, repr.) which is undoubtedly a study for this latter figure.

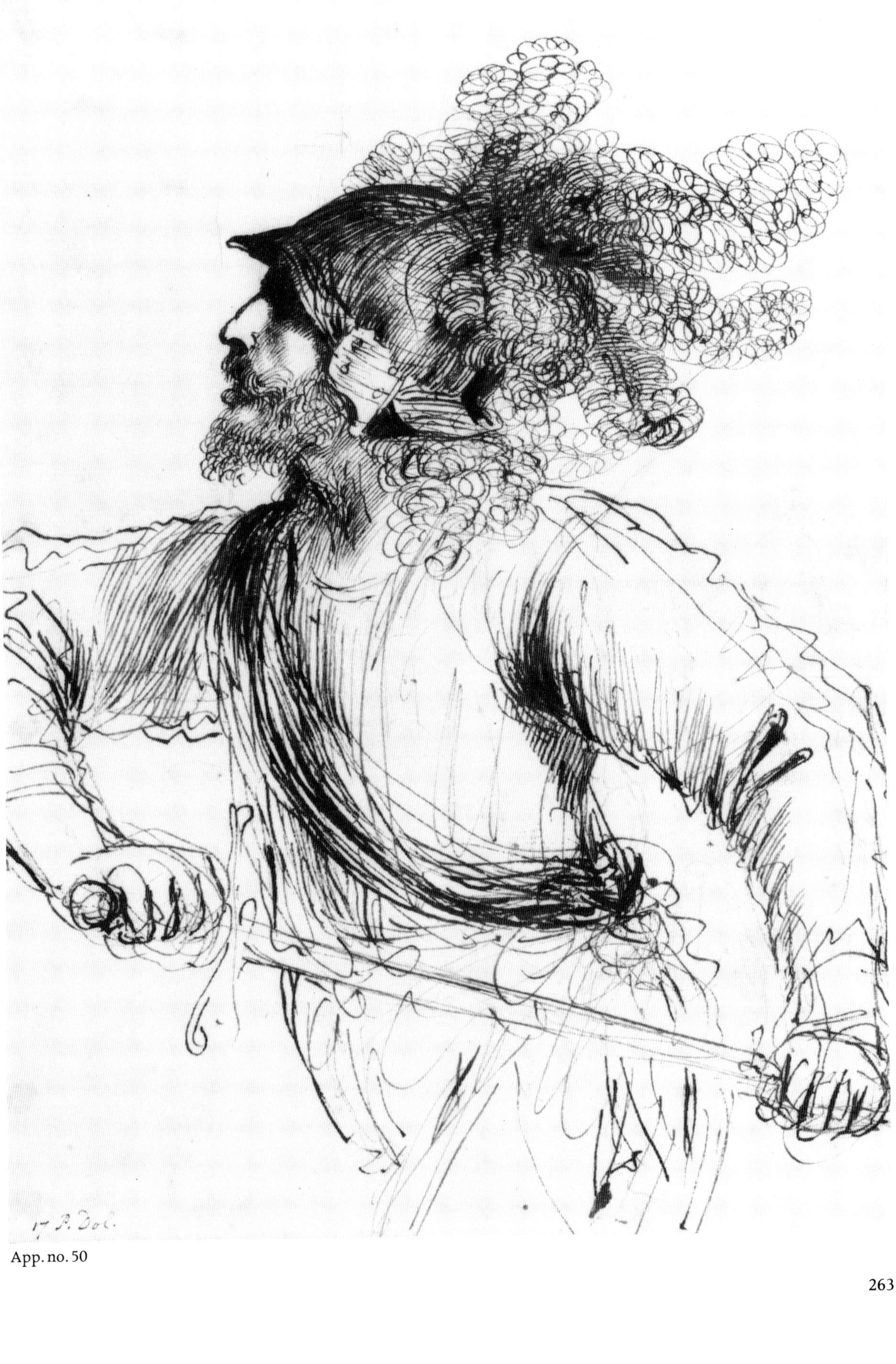

App. no. 50

A second study for the soldier on the left from the semi-nude model, almost certainly from the life, and thus presumably made at an early stage in the genesis of the figure, was formerly on the London art market (sale, Sotheby's, 4 July 1977, lot 121).

It is worth mentioning two further drawings, whose relationship to the finished work is less clear. The first, in pen and wash, in the Lugt Collection, Institut Néerlandais, Paris, is of a soldier striding to his right and drawing his sword (inv. no. 522; Byam Shaw, 1983, no. 340). There are many points of similarity between this drawing and App. no. 50, though the figure is reversed and drawn with far greater restraint. The second drawing, in red chalk, in the Museum of Fine Arts, Budapest (inv. no. 2316; Czére, 1989, no. 39), shows a bearded warrior, also with his head, though not his body, in profile to the left and apparently drawing a sword. This too has points in common with App. no. 50, though less obviously with the finished work.

Stéphane Loire (in a letter to the Department) suggested that the figure depicted in App. no. 50 might be Mars, on account of the design of the helmet with its flamboyant plume (see the series of drawings for Guercino's lost painting of *Cupid restraining the enraged Mars*, Nos. 132–4 and App. nos. 38 and 116), but we find his identification less compelling.

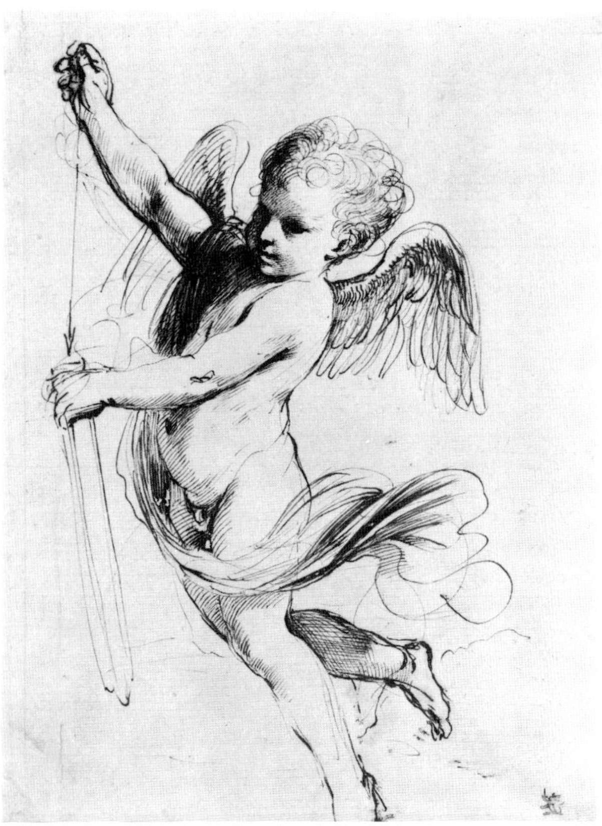

App. no. 51

51 Cupid

He is represented flying to the left and drawing an arrow from his quiver with his right hand.

Pen and brown ink. 262 × 199mm.

1895–9–15–707

Provenance: Sir T. Lawrence (according to Robinson, 1876, and see above, p. 233); G. Leembruggen (sale, Amsterdam, 5 March 1866, lot 878, £2–5–6); W. Mayor (L 2799; not mentioned in the catalogues of his collection of 1871, 1874, and 1875 referred to by L); J. C. Robinson; J. Malcolm.

Literature: Robinson, 1876, no. 267; M & T, 1989, under no. 715.

This drawing cannot, for the moment, be associated with any known painting. The subject may have been Cupid alone with his quiver, as here represented, or, conceivably, Venus and Cupid, as, for example, in the fresco painted by Guercino for Count Filippo Aldrovandi in 1632 and now in the Accademia di San Luca, Rome (S, 1988, no. 144). From its style, the drawing would appear to date from the mid-1640s. Pentiments for the figure's right leg reveal that the artist originally drew him kneeling, probably on a stone, presumably before adding the billowing drapery denoting flight.

A crudely retouched offset of a standing Cupid, with his body turned to the left, drawing an arrow from a quiver, is in the Royal Library, Windsor Castle (M & T, 1989, no. 715). The original drawing from which it was offset would have shown the figure in the reverse sense from App. no. 51. A lost drawing by Guercino closely related to App. no. 51 is recorded in an etching by Giuseppe Zocchi, an impression of which is preserved in the collection (189* b. 1, no. 131). It differs from the present drawing in that the block of stone is fully drawn, the quiver now rests firmly on it, a tree stump appears on the left and Cupid looks over his left shoulder at the spectator; in addition, his bow lies on the ground in the bottom right corner. The drawing was probably once in the collection of the English dealer William Kent, for whose activity see M, *Disegni*, 1969, pp. 10–11, M & T, 1989, pp. xxviii–ix, and Introduction and App. no. 38.

App. no. 51 is mentioned only in the 1876 edition of Robinson, presumably having been acquired from Mayor after the first edition of 1869, and possibly at the time of Mayor's death in 1874, despite not being mentioned in any of the catalogues of the latter's collection. Both editions of Robinson record a red chalk drawing of a *Flying Amorino* with a Bouverie provenance, but such a drawing was not to be found when the Malcolm collection was acquired by the Museum in 1895. There is a note to this effect in the register but there are no further clues as to the drawing's appearance or whereabouts.

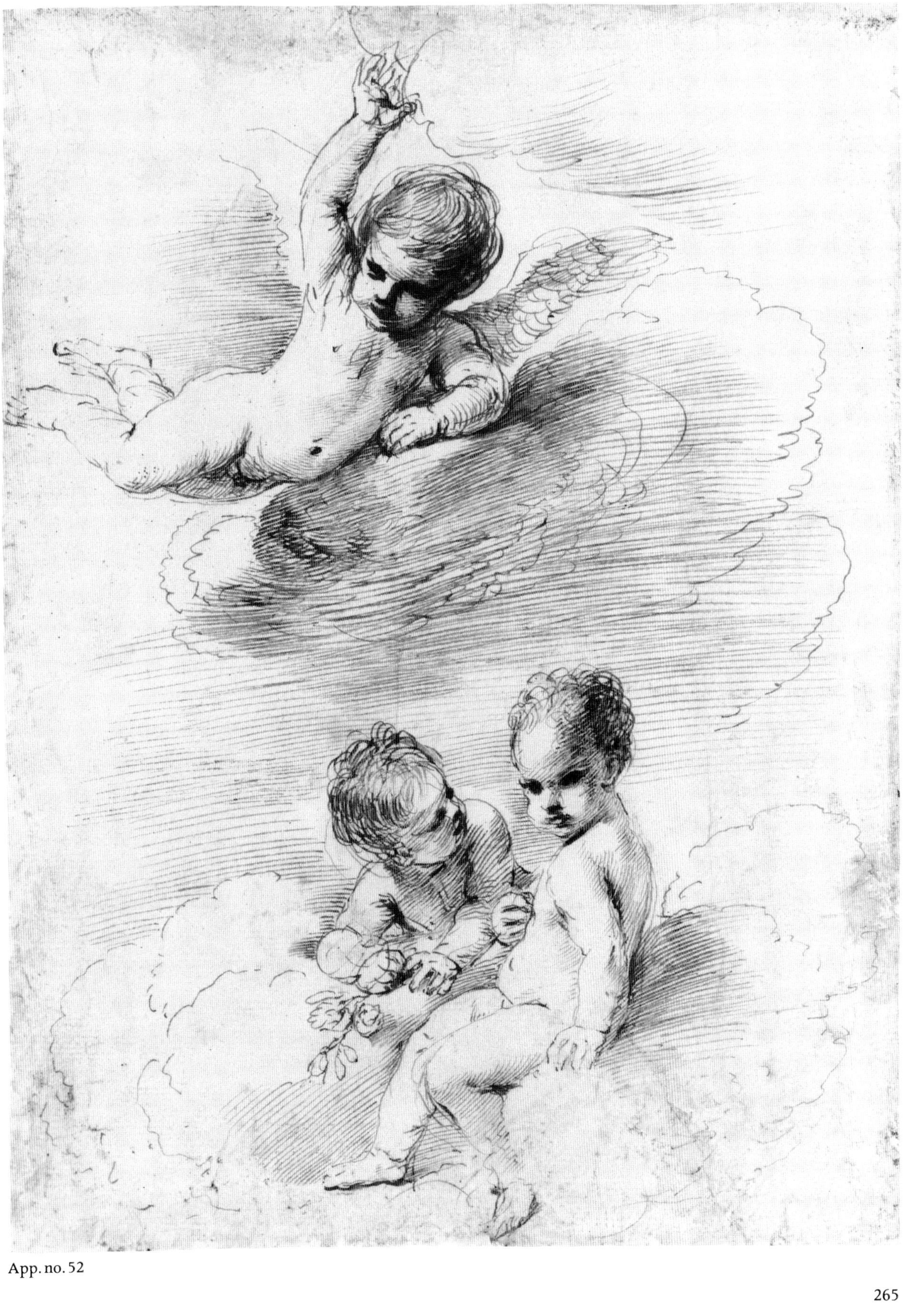

App. no. 52

52 Three nude Putti in Clouds, one with Wings

The winged putto is at the top, his left arm resting on a cloud and his right arm raised, with his legs extended behind him; the other putti are below him, one seated to the right on a cloud with his body turned to the left but with his face directed towards the spectator; the other, on the left, only partly visible behind his companion, leans forward with both arms resting on a cloud, looking into the face of the first; in one hand he holds a twig of blossoms.

Pen and brown ink. 254 × 187mm.

Pp. 4–57

Provenance: R. Payne Knight Bequest, 1824.

As A. E. Popham was the first to point out (note in Departmental records), this is a study for three of the putti in the clouds surrounding God the Father and the Angel Gabriel in the altarpiece of the *Annunciation* executed in 1648 and now in the Pinacoteca Comunale at Forlì (S, 1988, no. 250). Although it seems that Guercino made the drawing as a coherent study in itself, with the figures carefully composed in relation to each other against a background of clouds, the space treated as a whole, and with its own unified system of lighting, he later came to regard it as two separate studies for figures to be seen apart from each other. In the finished picture the flying putto appears at the very top, in the middle, while the pair of putti are placed on their own at the side, behind the wing of the full-size figure of the Angel Gabriel. Guercino made only minor changes to the poses of the individual putti in the painting, and he omitted the flower held by one of the putti in the pair at the bottom of the sheet.

Other drawings for the Forlì *Annunciation* are discussed under No. 152.

53 Head and Shoulders of a Youth

He is seen full face and has bushy hair with a fringe.

Pen and brown ink. 216 × 141mm.

1943–11–13–19. Not illustrated.

Provenance: Eric Rose, by whom presented.

Inscribed in pencil in the bottom right corner: *Guercino*. (For similar inscriptions on drawings by Guercino and his School from the collection of Eric Rose, see App. no. 19.)

In style the drawing compares well with another from the group presented by Eric Rose, App. no. 54, which in our view is by Guercino; it may, like that drawing, date from the 1650s. The youth can be compared with the acolyte holding a candle who stands behind the priest's left shoulder in the *Purification of the Virgin* in S. Maria della Pietà dei Teatini, Ferrara, of 1654 (S, 1988, no. 311): the style of the hair and the rounded features of the face are particularly similar, though the figure in the drawing is lit from the left and not from the right.

54 Study of a Youth in a broad-brimmed Hat holding a Stick

He is just over half length, turned three-quarters to the right, but with his head facing the spectator; he rests his right hand on his hip and his left arm is extended, his left hand holding the end of a stick.

Pen and brown ink. 238 × 198mm.

1943–11–13–21. Not illustrated.

Provenance: Eric Rose, by whom presented.

Inscribed in pencil in the bottom right corner: *Guercino*. (For similar inscriptions on drawings by Guercino and his School from the collection of Eric Rose, see App. no. 19.)

The drawing may possibly date from the 1650s. The light, broken touches which suggest the form of the left arm may be compared with similar passages in a drawing in the Boymans–van Beuningen Museum, Rotterdam (inv. no. I.423; M, *Disegni*, 1969, no. 165), which is a preparatory study for the *Hagar and Ishmael* of 1653 in the Mahon Collection (S, 1988, no. 299).

55 Youth in Profile, half length

His body faces forward but his head is turned in profile to the left; he has long hair and his jerkin is unbuttoned except at the top.

Red chalk. 187 × 159mm.

1953–4–11–48

Provenance: E. H. W. Meyerstein, by whom bequeathed.

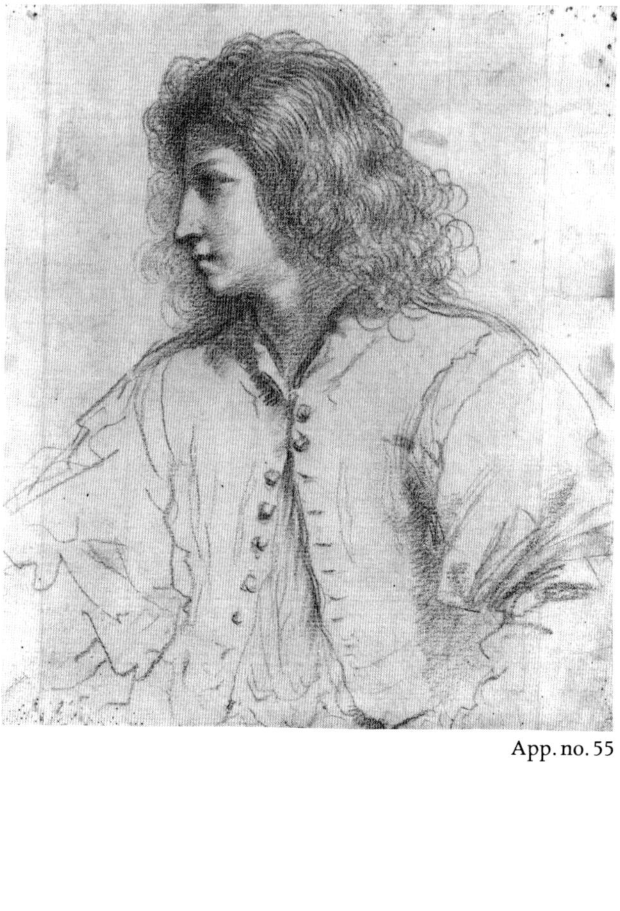

App. no. 55

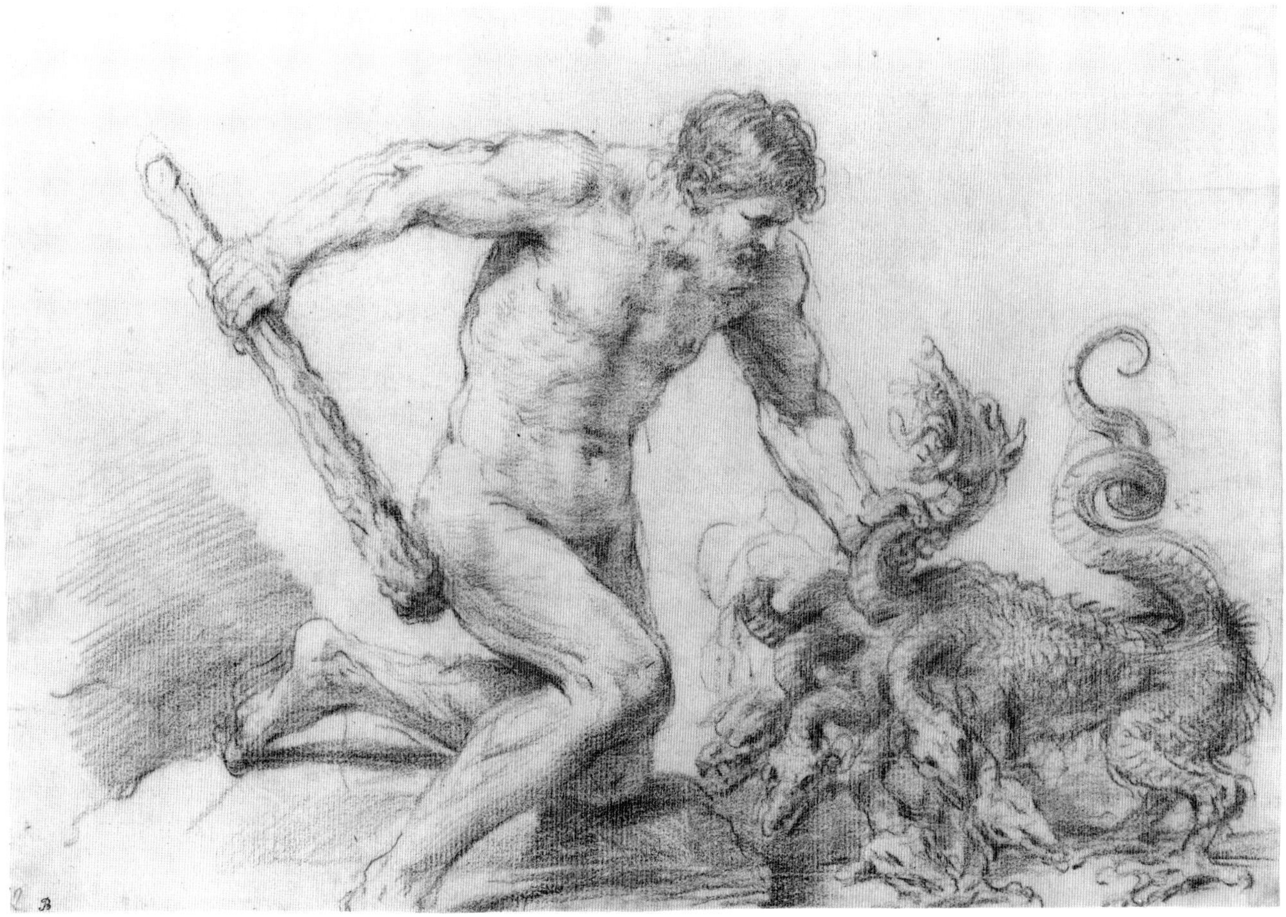

App. no. 56

Similar youthful types in classicising profile are most frequently found in Guercino's painted work of the 1640s and 1650s. Two good comparisons are the Madonna in the *Purification of the Virgin* in S. Maria della Pietà dei Teatini, Ferrara, of 1654 (S, 1988, no. 311) and the figure of Samson in *Samson bringing the Combs of Honey to his Parents* in the M. H. de Young Memorial Museum, San Francisco, of 1657 (S, 1988, no. 326).

56 Hercules and the Hydra

He is represented turned to the right, kneeling on his left knee and seizing the Hydra by one of its heads with his left hand while preparing to strike it with a club which he holds in his right.

Red chalk. 211 × 311mm.

1859–8–6–67

Provenance: Casa Gennari; Mr Bouverie (L 325); Mr Hervey; 1st Earl of Gainsborough (anonymous sale, Christie's, London, 20 July 1859, lot 58, bt with 2 others, together with lot 59, *Tiffin, £1–1–0*).

Literature: BM *Repr.*, II (1891), no. 19; Russell, 1923, p. 50.

Numbered in graphite in the bottom left corner [*?1*]*2*. A similar pencil numbering appears on many drawings with a Bouverie and Earls of Gainsborough provenance, see under No. 10 in the main Catalogue.

Guercino is recorded as having painted the subject of Hercules slaying the Hydra twice in his career, once at the beginning and again at the end (Malvasia, 1678, II, pp. 363 and 382; 1841, II, pp. 258 and 271): in 1618 he painted the façade of the Palazzo Tanari with a fresco, now lost, showing the figure as a feigned sculpture in a niche, the appearance of which can be deduced from several surviving preparatory studies (see M, *Disegni*, 1969, no. 29); he painted it a second time on the commission of the 'Marchese di Marzera', 'Ambasciatore di Spagna che risiede a Venezia' in 1659, for which no corresponding painting survives (*Libro dei Conti*, 1808, pp. 149f.; 1841, p. 339). The total payment of 124 *scudi* for this second commission suggests that this too was a full-length composition.

To judge from its style, App. no. 56 may well date from the 1640s or 1650s, some two or three decades after the Tanari commission, from which it also differs in showing the figure in a horizontal rather than a vertical format. On the other hand, the style does not seem late enough to justify a conclusive relationship with the 1659 commission, though it would be rash to rule out such a connection altogether.

Another composition of the same subject by Guercino is also recorded in an undated engraving by Francesco Curti (1610–90), the frontispiece to a volume of engravings by the same printmaker of figure subjects after Guercino dedicated to Marchese Francesco Montecuccoli and aimed at instructing the beginner in drawing (repr. B, 1988, p. 90; see also App. no. 99). From the type of subjects included and their treatment, the volume would seem to date from around 1640 or shortly thereafter. In the frontispiece, Hercules holds the burning torch above his head with both hands, thrusting it down upon the cringing Hydra. There are, however, some general resemblances between the frontispiece and App. no. 56, namely their horizontal format and the strong diagonal of the man's pose contrasted with the ornamental treatment of the beast.

A double-sided drawing in red chalk for the Hydra, almost certainly for the animal in the present drawing, is in the Palazzo Rosso, Genoa (inv. no. 1685; 253 × 205mm). A pen-and-wash drawing, also in a horizontal format, in the Gabinetto Nazionale delle Stampe, Rome (inv. no. FN 101 (20029), cited in M, *Disegni*, 1969, p. 59, under no. 29), at first sight bears a striking resemblance to the British Museum drawing. The superficial formal relationship is not, however, borne out by the drawing's style which is much closer to the artist's drawings of around 1620 than to those of the 1640s and 1650s. We have been unable to agree on the purpose of the Rome drawing, though we are inclined to favour its connection with the Palazzo Tanari commission.

For the application of the Bouverie stamp (L 325) to drawings in the 1859 Gainsborough sale, see App. no. 25.

2 Landscapes (App. nos. 57–61)

57 Landscape with Angelica and Medoro

(*see colour pl. 22*)

The composition is bounded on either side by a single tree; on the left a man and woman sit embracing, the woman pointing at a tree stump behind them to the left, on which is carved the inscription *Angelica e Medoro*; in the centre rises a clump of trees out of ruined masonry or rock on which the same inscription *Angelica e Medoro* is cut; Cupid appears clinging to one of the trees and looks at the couple while holding one of his arrows in his right hand; to the right is marshy ground and a distant prospect with a wayfarer.

Pen and brown ink. 307 × 462mm; somewhat abraded in parts, and other miscellaneous damages.

Pp. 4–63

Provenance: R. Payne Knight Bequest, 1824.

Literature: Klingsor, XII, 1931, p. 355, fig. 17; Bottari, 1966, p. 5 and pl. XXX; M, *Disegni*, 1969, under no. 159; Clarke & Penny, 1982, no. 141; Bartrum, 1984, no. 36.

Inscribed in brown ink in the bottom left corner: *Guercino.*

Guercino painted two representations of this subject, in 1642 and 1647 respectively (both untraced; see M, *Disegni*, 1969, p. 150; S, 1988, no. 245). A drawing in the Uffizi, Florence (inv. no. 3704-S; Gernsheim, photo no. 4089), appears to be a copy after a different composition of this subject, vertical in format, and with the figures seated at the right instead of at the left. Like App. no. 57, this composition is also datable to the artist's early period.

A drawing in the Mahon Collection, on loan to the Ashmolean Museum, Oxford (No. 130), which has been dated to the 1640s, shows Angelica and Medoro seated beside some tree trunks, one of which bears the carved inscription to which Medoro points. This study has little in common with App. no. 57 beyond its subject, concentrating as it does on the figures and not elaborating the background into a full landscape.

For the main discussion of this drawing, see No. 164.

58 Landscape with a Bridge and a Fortress

On a knoll to the right is a partly dead tree; to the right of this are two men walking, and to the left two other men sitting on the ground; on the extreme left is a round bastion with a river at its base crossed by a trestle bridge and behind, in the centre and to the right, are other buildings.

Pen and dark brown ink. 183 × 268mm.

Ff. 2–144. Not illustrated.

Provenance: R. Houlditch (L 2214); A. Pond; Rev. C. M. Cracherode Bequest, 1799.

According to Departmental records, the back of the old mount is inscribed with the year *1736*, the date of Houlditch's death. (It is probably the date at which Pond acquired the drawing, and the inscription may conceivably be in Pond's hand. Pond died in 1758, two years before the sale of 'The genuine, entire and valuable

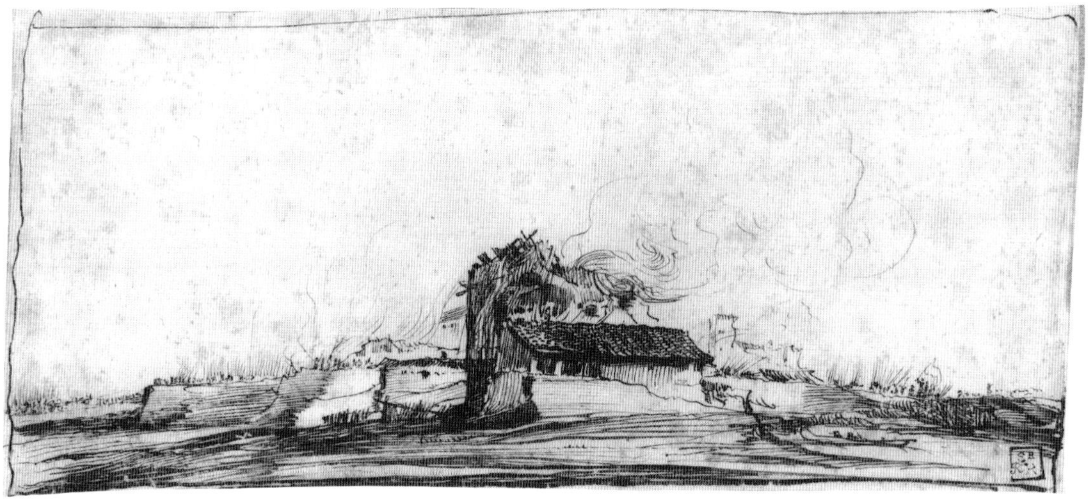

App. no. 60

collection of drawings' from Houlditch's collection on 12 February 1760, and the two following evenings.)

Etched in reverse by Charles Knapton, as one of a series of prints after Old Master drawings issued by him and Arthur Pond, with the inscription: *E Museo Arthuri Pond* (Weigel, 1865, no. 3436; Hake, 1922, p. 342, no. 32). For other drawings etched in this same series, see App. nos. 59 and 93.

59 Landscape with a Man seated on a Hummock in the centre, accompanied by a small Boy

The landscape is closed on the left by a hollow tree; on the right are two other trees, between which a woman crouches, while a fallen tree lies in the right foreground; in the background is a large building.

Pen and brown ink. 210 × 310mm.

Ff. 2–142. Illustrated in main Catalogue (No. 165).

Provenance: A. Pond; J. Barnard (L 1419; his initials and inscription *No. 331* $12\frac{1}{4}$ *by* $8\frac{1}{2}$. *Engraved by Mr. Pond, & out of his collection* on back of mount); Rev. C. M. Cracherode Bequest, 1799.

Literature: M, *Disegni*, 1969, no. 197; Lippincott, 1983, fig. 17a; M & T, 1989, p. 107, under no. 246; Czére, 1989, under no. 45.

Etched in reverse by Charles Knapton in 1735 (Weigel, 1865, no. 4139; Hake, 1922, p. 342, no. 39), with the inscription *E Musæo Dn̄i Arthuri Pond*. As Mahon has pointed out (*Disegni*, 1969, p. 192), Barnard was mistaken in saying that Pond, rather than Knapton, engraved the drawing. For other drawings etched in this same series, see App. nos. 58 and 93.

A feeble copy after this subject, in pen and brown wash, is in the Hessisches Landesmuseum, Darmstadt (inv. no. AE 1680; 206 × 305mm).

For further discussion of this drawing, see No. 165.

60 Attack on a walled Town

A tower in the centre, against which a long penthouse is built, is in flames; troops with lances converge on the town from left and right; in the extreme left the besiegers are firing a cannon into the fort.

Pen and brown ink (the freely drawn pen lines surrounding the composition are by Guercino). 131 × 298mm.

Ff. 2–145

Provenance: Penny; J. Richardson, Sr (L 2184: sale, Cock, London, 23 January 1746–7, lot 42, bt with 2 others *£2–11–6*); A. Pond; Sir J. Reynolds (L 2364); Rev. C. M. Cracherode Bequest, 1799.

Literature: Bartrum, 1984, no. 38; B, 1985, p. 46, no. 28.

On the back of the Richardson mount (now laid down) are the inscriptions: *J. Richardson Given me by Mr. Penny Jan: 1743*; and *the* 2^{d} *night Lot 42*; and finally, in black chalk, *true A Pond*.

Bagni suggested that the town is probably Cento and that the view was taken from the Pieve di Cento bank of the River Reno.

61 Landscape with two Fishermen

In the foreground is a bank with two trees between which, at the edge of the bank, are two men with fishing rods; a stretch of water can be seen on the left extending to its other shore from which a mountain rises.

Pen and brown ink. 158 × 190mm.

1943–11–13–23. Not illustrated.

Provenance: Eric Rose, by whom presented.

Inscribed in brown ink in the bottom right corner: *Guercin*[o].

3 Genre and Caricatures (App. nos. 62–65)

62 A theatrical Performance in the open Air

(see colour pl. 26)

The stage, which is seen from the centre of the auditorium, is contained on either side by natural trees and, in front of them, flanking walls articulated with giant pilasters; the scenery consists of closed colonnades round three sides of a square; in the centre, facing the audience, is a portico in front of the closed door of which are two figures; on either side of the portico are statues in niches; above is a central dome; the numerous members of the audience occupy the raised boxes to right and left or stand or sit in front of the stage, on which appear, to the right, two rabbits.

Pen and brown ink and brown wash with some black chalk. 360 × 465mm.

1937–10–8–1 (Malcolm Add. 160: purchased with proceeds from the sale of duplicate prints from the Malcolm Collection)

Provenance: (?)P. Crozat (?his number 2, inscribed in ink in the bottom right corner); A. Beurdeley (L 421; sale, Féral et Paulme, Paris, 8–10 June 1920, lot 62); A. W. M. Mensing (sale, Frederick Muller & Cie, Amsterdam, 27–29 April 1937, lot 243); Walter Gernsheim (exh. cat., *Exhibition of Drawings of the Bolognese School*, London, 1937, no. 28), from whom purchased.

Literature: Popham, 1938a, pp. 25–6, pl. x; Ragghianti, 1938, p. xxi, fig. 6; Sutton, 1967, p. 90, fig. 3; M, *Disegni*, 1969, no. 213; Roli, 1972, no. 16; Rowlands, 1984, no. 31; B, 1984, p. 23, fig. 22.

On the back of the old mount is a (?)nineteenth-century inscription in brown ink: *Le moment de Representention* [sic] *d'une Piece dans Le Teatre De Parme/a La plume Lavè de Bistre*. In pencil, above: *N.° d'achat 62* (this is evidently a reference to the lot number of the drawing in the Beurdeley sale). An inscription on the front of the old mount, bottom left, is concealed by the 'window' of the present solid mount. A pencil inscription above this, just below the drawing's bottom edge, has been erased and is no longer decipherable.

Mahon connected the drawing with a passage in Giuseppe Maria Pannini, *Compendiosi Ragguagli d'alcune attioni seguite nella Nobilissima Patria di Cento* (Bologna, per Giacomo Monti, 1655), which he quoted from a manuscript copy in the Archivio Comunale at Cento (MS. no. 175); it reads as follows: *L'Anno seguente* [after the description of a performance given in 1620] *per non lasciar la Gioventù in abbandono all'ozio, comparvero sù la scena i figliuoli d'Aminta Pastorale del Pellizari che fecero pomposa mostra sù i labri dei Recitanti, e resero via più riguardevole il fabbricato Teatro: ma perche il Sig: Fabri ambiva d'erigere un Tempio alla Virtù, in cui la Gioventù più risvegliata, con operosi progressi, per la strada di lodevoli operazioni animosamente s'incaminasse, quindi nacque, che si cominciarono introdurre in quello si i Musici, come i Pittori, de quali era Capo il Sigr. Cavaliere Gio. Francesco Barbieri, che al presente sotto il Cielo Italiano, colla vivacità de' colori anima esquisitamente le tele, mercando* [?] *in un medesimo tempo lode a stesso, e grido alla Patria*. This passage certainly throws light on Guercino's involvement in the theatre when he was a young man and still based at Cento, though it should be stressed that the theatrical performance represented in this drawing is not necessarily one of those described in Pannini's account. The style of the drawing in any case points to an early period of Guercino's career. Mahon dated the drawing before 1621. A drawing in a similar style and of much the same subject matter is in the Ashmolean Museum, Oxford (see No. 185).

According to Malvasia, Guercino had already had contacts with a Sig. Fabri in 1616 (Malvasia, 1678, II, p. 362; 1841, II, p. 258): in that year he had put at Guercino's disposal two rooms for the painter's *Accademia del nudo*. This would seem to confirm Pannini's anecdote about Guercino's involvement in Fabri's theatrical activities.

The nineteenth-century inscription on the back of the drawing identifies the subject as a spectacle in the theatre at Parma. This seems no more than a fanciful identification based on the knowledge that a famous old theatre exists in Parma.

For a further discussion of the drawing, see No. 186.

63 Caricature of four Children standing

(see colour pl. 32)

They stand in descending order of size, all except one with their backs turned; tallest, on the left, is a girl holding a *fiasco* in her left hand; next to her is a boy dressed in a shirt reaching to above the knees who holds a staff; next to him, also holding a staff, is a smaller boy, who looks over his left shoulder to scowl at the spectator; and finally, on the right, is a small child wearing a flat cap.

Pen and light brown ink and light brown wash. 276 × 248mm.

Ff. 2–140

Provenance: Rev. C. M. Cracherode Bequest, 1799.

Literature: Ragghianti, 1938, p. xxvii, fig. 13; M, *Disegni*, 1969, no. 232.

For the main discussion of this drawing, see No. 216.

64 Caricature of a Lady and Gentleman

Seen to below the waist, they face each other, in profile, the man on the left and the woman on the right; he places his left hand on his chest and clasps her right.

Pen and light brown ink. 254 × 200mm; apart from three old, eighteenth-century patches on the back of the sheet concealing holes in the paper (for the application of which, see App. no. 49), the drawing is in exceptionally good condition.

Ff. 2–139

Provenance: Rev. C. M. Cracherode Bequest, 1799.

A pen-and-ink drawing of the head and shoulders of a man in profile to the right in the Brera, Milan (inv. no. 33; Emiliani, 1959, no. 84, repr.), is evidently a study for the gentleman on the left of App. no. 64. In the Milan study he is wearing a more ornate collar, with what appears to be a cloak over one shoulder, and his left hand is held slightly further up his chest.

In this humorous representation of a genteel couple, Guercino used the profile view to emphasise the physiognomic characteristics of the pair, in particular the gentleman's double chin, scarcely disguised by his small beard, and the lady's exaggeratedly high forehead and pointed chin. The couple seem to be greeting each other, though it is possible that they are exchanging vows.

65 Caricature of an old Man with a Pair of Spectacles stuck over his Ear

(*see colour pl. 31*)

He is in profile to the left and wears a cap.

Pen and brown ink and light brown wash. 215 × 160mm.

Pp. 4–58

Provenance: Casa Gennari; probably William Kent (?his sale, Langford's, London, 8–11 December 1762, lot unknown; see M & T, 1989, p. xxviii); N. Hone (L 2793); R. Payne Knight Bequest, 1824.

Literature: M, *Disegni*, 1969, no. 233; Turner, 1982, p. 162.

Etched in reverse by Giuseppe Zocchi (Weigel, 1865, no. 3319); an impression of the print is in the collection (189* b. 1, no. 106). Zocchi was commissioned to make facsimile etchings of this and other Guercino drawings from the Casa Gennari by William Kent (see also App. no. 38).

Hone bought several drawings from Kent's collection at the so-called 'Luti' sale at Langford's on 8–11 December 1762, as emerges from the annotated copy of the catalogue in the library of P. & D. Colnaghi, London. These included four Guercinos etched by Zocchi (lots 34, 57 (2) and 61, of the second night's sale). Besides App. no. 65, Hone's purchases that evening would also have included App. no. 72.

For a further discussion of the drawing, see No. 208.

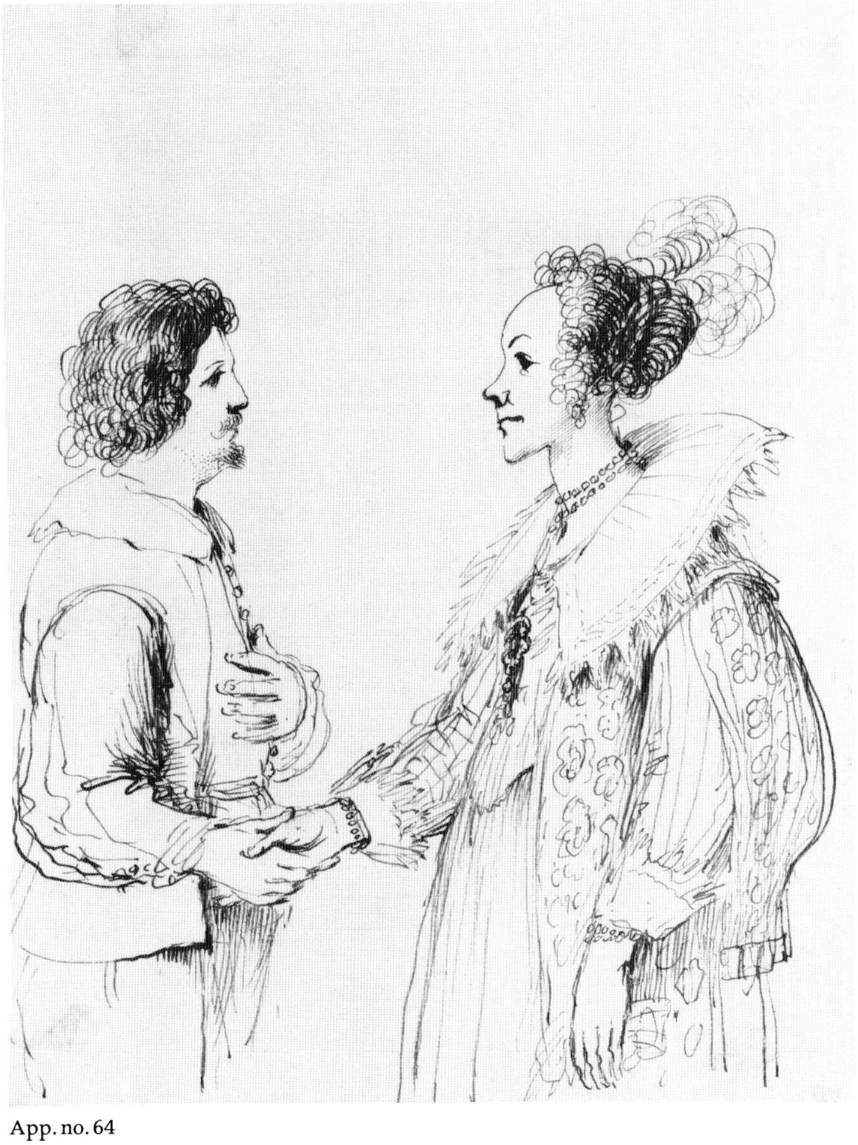

App. no. 64

II Drawings by Guercino's School and by his Followers (App. nos. 66–126)

1 Drawings ascribed to Guercino (App. nos. 66–80)

66 Head of a Youth looking to the right

He is in three-quarters profile to the right.

Oiled charcoal, heightened with white chalk, on blue-grey paper. 356 × 261mm.

5211–20

Provenance: W. Fawkener Bequest, 1769.

Inscribed in brown ink in an old hand in the bottom centre of the old, Fawkener mount: *Guercino*. Popham (in a pencil note on the mount) suggested a tentative attribution to the Bolognese painter Pietro Faccini (1562–1602).

The drawing is surely Bolognese and seems to us to have more in common with Guercino's style than with that of his more eccentric precursor Faccini. As discussed under App. no. 81, Guercino was in the habit of making large-scale studies from the life in oiled charcoal in the years preceding, and perhaps during, his visit to Rome in 1621–3. In the modelling of the face, the treatment of the hair and the sharp contrast between light and dark, seen at the contour of the youth's left forehead and cheek, this drawing is not dissimilar to such studies. The technique also compares well with Guercino's drawing style in its luminosity, especially apparent in the model's neck and shirt and in the shadow of his right cheek. Indeed the touch in these passages might even suggest Guercino's own hand. Against this, however, is the unpleasing structure of the head with its over-prominent brow and sightless eyes, failings that seem to speak against his authorship. A possible explanation for the unnatural appearance of the head, as suggested to us by Mahon, is that the artist used a cast, possibly after an antique bust, as the point of departure for his drawing. We thus remain undecided about the status of App. no. 66, though we are inclined to favour the opinion that it could be by Guercino himself. If so, it would date from an early period, *c.*1618.

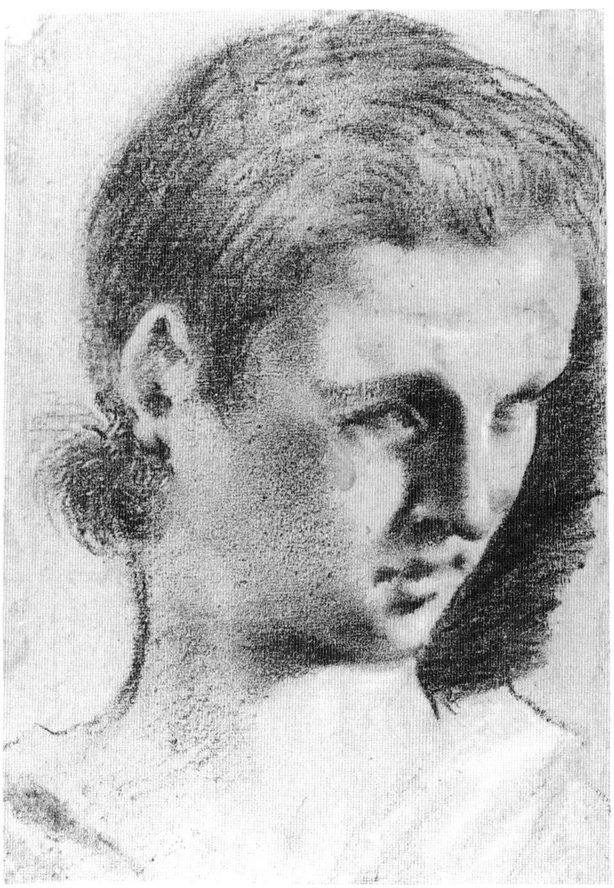

App. no. 66

67 Head of a Man wearing a Turban

He is in profile to the right and has a large moustache.

Pen and brown ink. 108 × 93mm; two holes by the figure's mouth and neck have been patched.

1952–1–21–42. Not illustrated.

Provenance: Lord James Cavendish; L. Colling-Mudge. From an album purchased with the help of a generous contribution from the National Art-Collections Fund.

On the *verso*, in the bottom left corner, visible through the backing, is a pen-and-ink sketch of a (?)woman's head, looking upwards to the right.

The drawing on the *recto* was engraved in reverse, with the head of a bearded man as its pendant, in one of a series of prints ascribed to Francesco Curti (Bertelà, 1973, no. 544).

68 Woman in Profile to the left

She is half length.

Pen and brown ink. 125 × 74mm; the upper corners cut away.

1952–1–21–43. Not illustrated.

Provenance: Lord James Cavendish; L. Colling-Mudge. From an album purchased with the help of a generous contribution from the National Art-Collections Fund.

Like App. no. 69, this may be associable with the drawings that Guercino gave Curti to engrave, though no print is known.

A pen-and-ink drawing of notably inferior quality, in the Fondazione Horne, Uffizi, Florence (inv. no. 5584; Gernsheim, photo no. 115026), represents a similar figure to that shown in App. no. 68, but in reverse, with slight variations in the woman's coiffure and attire.

69 Bearded Man in Armour

He stands half length, in profile to the left, holding a spear in his left hand and raising, in his right, an unidentified object which is partly cut away by the top left corner of the drawing; he wears a plumed helmet.

Pen, point of the brush and brown ink. 142 × 156mm; a horizontal hole below the figure's chin has been repaired.

1952–1–21–44. Not illustrated.

Provenance: Lord James Cavendish; L. Colling-Mudge. From an album purchased with the help of a generous contribution from the National Art-Collections Fund.

Visible through the old backing, on the right-hand side of the *verso*, is a pen-and-ink drawing of a man's head in profile to the left.

In type and style, the drawing belongs to those (e.g., App. no. 67), which Curti engraved in his series of prints after drawings by Guercino. However, no print directly corresponding with this subject is known.

70 Soldier wearing a plumed Helmet

He is half length and bearded; his body is turned to the left and his arms are extended downwards in that direction while his head is turned to the right.

Pen and brush and brown ink. 191 × 161mm; the paper has been badly holed in the areas of greatest dark; these damages have been repaired and retouched.

1943–11–13–16. Not illustrated.

Provenance: Eric Rose, by whom presented.

Although the drawing is boldly handled, we feel uncertain as to whether or not it is by Guercino.

71 Hermit Saint contemplating a Cross

He is bearded, half length, with his body facing the spectator but with his head turned in profile to the right; his left arm, partly covered by a drapery, rests on a support, possibly a skull, and his right arm passes in front of his body to grasp a fold of this same drapery; behind is the base of the cross, up at which he gazes.

Pen and brown ink. 228 × 203mm.

1943–11–13–11. Not illustrated.

Provenance: Eric Rose, by whom presented.

The drawing may date from the 1630s or 1640s.

72 Head and Shoulders of an old Man wearing a fur-trimmed Hat

He is in profile to the left with his arms across his chest.

Pen and brown ink. 202 × 168mm.

Pp. 5–130. Not illustrated.

Provenance: (?)Casa Gennari; (?)William Kent (?his sale, Langford's, London, 8–11 December 1762, lot unknown: see M & T, 1989, p. xxviii); N. Hone (L 2793); R. Payne Knight Bequest, 1824.

Literature: Turner, 1982, p. 162.

Inscribed in grey-black ink in the bottom centre of the old mount: *GENARI Nipote di GUERCINO*. The drawing was attributed to Benedetto Gennari when in the Payne Knight collection and entered the Museum under this name.

The drawing was etched in reverse by Giuseppe Zocchi (1711–67), presumably on the commission of William Kent, for whom see M, 1967, pp. 10–11, M & T, 1989, pp. xxviii–xxix, and the Introduction to this Catalogue. An impression of Zocchi's etching is in the Department (189* b. 1, no. 107; Weigel, 1865, no. 3312). A similar drawing of a young man in a much taller fur-trimmed hat, again in profile to the left and etched by Zocchi (189* b. 1, no. 105), is also in the British Museum (App. no. 73).

Since the so-called 'Luti' sale at Langford's, Covent Garden, on 8–11 December 1762 included copper-plates by Zocchi along with the corresponding original drawings by Guercino, it seems likely that the two British Museum drawings, together with their related plates, were among the items exported to London by Kent and sold at this sale.

The old attribution to Gennari of the present drawing – probably Benedetto was intended rather than Cesare, whose graphic style seems to be different from this – not only postdates the time when the drawing was in the Casa Gennari but also the 1762 sale, since all of the drawings accompanied by corresponding copper-plates by Zocchi were attributed to Guercino himself. Two drawings by '*Gennari*, nephew of *Guercino*' sold on the third night (Friday 10 December, lot 40) to a Mr Bernard (according to a copy of the catalogue in the library of P. & D. Colnaghi, London) must be ruled out for this reason. The drawing must have been one of the four Guercinos purchased at the sale by Hone (whose mark it bears), along with No. 208 (for details of Hone's purchases, see App. no. 65).

Although extremely close in style to Guercino, the penmanship of App. no. 72 is less fluent than his, and we remain uncertain about attributing it to him in full. App. no. 73 is surely by this same hand. The possibility that both may be by one of the Gennari should not be dismissed.

73 Head and Shoulders of a Youth wearing a tall fur-trimmed Hat

He is in profile to the left and has long hair; his right hand, holding a fold of the drapery which passes over his right shoulder, rests on his chest.

Pen and brown ink. 202 × 168mm.

1943–11–13–10

Provenance: (?)Casa Gennari; (?)William Kent; Eric Rose, by whom presented.

Literature: Turner, 1982, p. 162.

The drawing was etched in reverse by Giuseppe Zocchi and an impression is in the Department (189* b. 1, no. 105; Weigel, 1865, no. 3294). For a discussion of the drawing's provenance and the question of its attribution see App. no. 72.

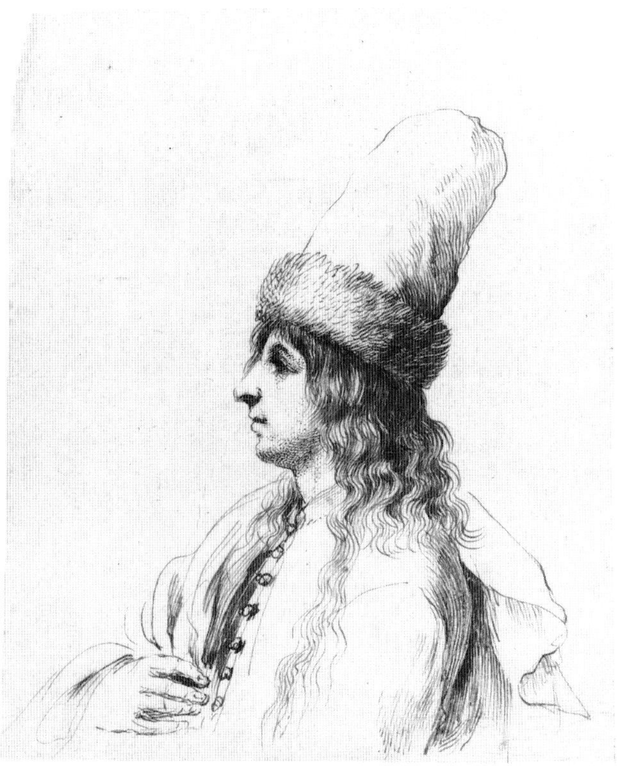

App. no. 73

74 Head and Shoulders of a Youth

He is profile to the right and has curly hair.

Pen and brown ink. 165 × 161mm.

1943–11–13–14. Not illustrated.

Provenance: Eric Rose, by whom presented.

Inscribed in graphite in the bottom right corner: *Guercino*. (For similar inscriptions on drawings by Guercino and his School from the collection of Eric Rose, see App. no. 19.)

The pose of the figure is not unlike that of the retouched figure of the youthful shepherd in a drawing in the Royal Library, Windsor Castle (M & T, 1989, no. 352), though that figure is bare-chested and somewhat older. Mahon and Turner tentatively related the autograph underdrawing of the Windsor sheet to Guercino's *Adoration of the Shepherds*, one of the frescoes he executed in Piacenza Cathedral in 1626–7. App. no. 74, however, may date from the 1640s.

In the British Museum sketch, the artist has set himself the difficult task of meticulously drawing the figure's full head of hair with its profusion of curls. Two drawings also at Windsor (M & T, 1989, nos. 395 and 396) show a similar fascination for the depiction of hair, but in spite of the clear analogies between these three studies, their authorship remains problematic.

75 Aged King in Supplication

He is bearded, just over three-quarter length, and appears to be kneeling; he gazes upwards to the left and holds out his left hand in supplication, while in his right he proffers an unidentifiable object, probably a heart; he wears a gown and an ermine cape over which hangs a chain.

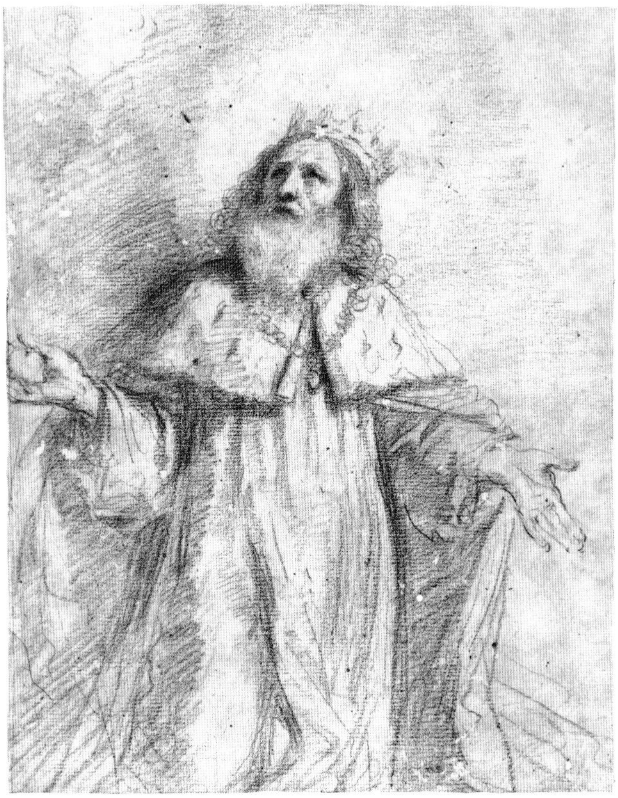

App. no. 75

Red chalk. 231 × 185mm; the sheet, which is discoloured from exposure to light and is slightly damaged, has been partly repaired with patches added at the back.

5210–68

Provenance: W. Fawkener Bequest, 1769.

Inscribed along the bottom of the old mount, slightly to the right, in pencil: *Guercin[o]*. On the *verso* of the drawing, in the centre, visible through the mount, is an inscription in ink: *Guercino da [Cen]to*.

The damage to the sheet is consistent with that of many of the drawings that were preserved in frames on the walls in the Casa Gennari and the family's villa at Bel Poggio (see M & T, 1989, pp. xviii ff., and the Introduction to this Catalogue).

The figure appears to be kneeling and may possibly be identified as King David. The pose and the execution suggest Guercino's style of the late 1650s and early 1660s. In our opinion, the drawing is of sufficient quality to be by Guercino himself. However, knowledge of Guercino's late style of drawing is still so patchy that it is hard to be certain which drawings are his and which are by his nephews Benedetto and Cesare Gennari. Thus we have not placed App. no. 75 with the autograph drawings in the first section of the Appendix, since there is no further evidence, other than that of style, to justify an attribution to the master.

76 Nude Woman partly draped

She is seated with her body turned slightly to the right and with her head raised to the left; a drapery lies across her lap and only partly covers her left arm, which is raised; in her left hand she holds an unidentifiable object.

Black chalk on buff-coloured paper. 250 × 180mm.

5210–73. Not illustrated.

Provenance: W. Fawkener Bequest, 1769.

On the *verso* of the sheet, in the centre, visible through the old mount, is the number *14*, inscribed in ink; and in the bottom left-hand corner the number (?)*5*, also in ink. Inscribed in the bottom centre of the mount, in brown ink: *Guercino*.

The woman appears to be holding something, perhaps flowers, in the drapery on her lap and has taken up one of them in her left hand. The style suggests Guercino's late period, that is of the late 1650s or early 1660s. We believe the drawing may well be by Guercino himself, but for the reasons given in the last paragraph of App. no. 75, we have preferred to keep it in the section of drawings ascribed to him.

77 Standing Child, almost nude

His body is turned slightly to the right as he appears to step in that direction; he raises his right arm as if pointing to the right and a thin drapery hangs loosely about his body.

Red chalk on white paper discoloured light brown. 211 × 138mm; the sheet appears to have once been laid down on canvas.

5210–74. Not illustrated.

Provenance: W. Fawkener Bequest, 1769.

Visible through the backing, near the bottom right edge of the *verso* of the sheet, is a pen inscription: *Guercin[o]*. The front of the old mount is inscribed in brown ink in the top centre: *Guercino fece 42*.

The drawing may be compared in type with the *Seated Christ Child with the Cross*, a School drawing, datable 1657, in the Royal Library, Windsor Castle (M & T, 1989, no. 436), and it may also have been drawn at about that date. We believe the drawing may well be by Guercino himself, but for the reasons given in the last paragraph of App. no. 75, we have preferred to keep it in the section of drawings ascribed to him.

The faintly drawn lines, just to the right of the child's chest, may have been intended as a frond or some other object held by him.

78 Landscape with a Tree in the centre Foreground

To the left of the tree, in the middle distance, are three people gathered on a bank giving onto an expanse of water; in the background, to the right, two people stand before a house which is surrounded by trees and bushes.

Pen and brown ink. 179 × 263mm.

1946–7–13–1318. *Recto* not illustrated.

Provenance: Sir T. Lawrence (L 2445); S. Woodburn (sale, Christie's, London, 7 June 1860, lot 667, bt with 19 others *Sir T. Phillips, £1–10–0*); Phillipps-Fenwick; presented anonymously.

Literature: Popham, 1935, p. 146, no. 2.

Inscribed in brown ink on the *verso* near the top: *Guercin[o]*.

On the *verso* (the sheet having been turned upside-down) there is a sketch of an erect penis in profile to the left, in close proximity with a female pudendum, hastily drawn, which it is apparently about to penetrate. Above, on the right, are two further erect male members, this time represented ideogrammatically.

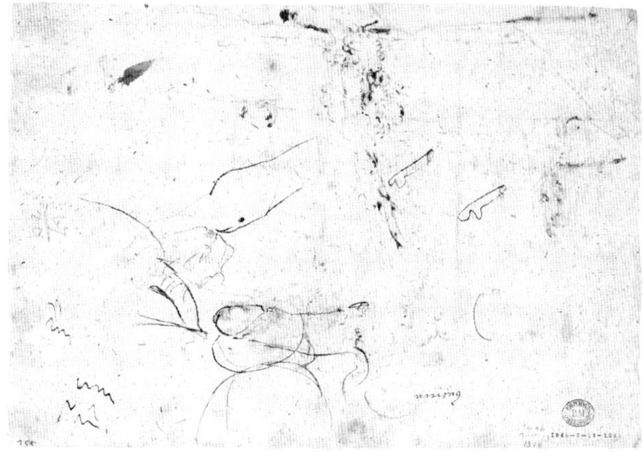

App. no. 78 *verso*

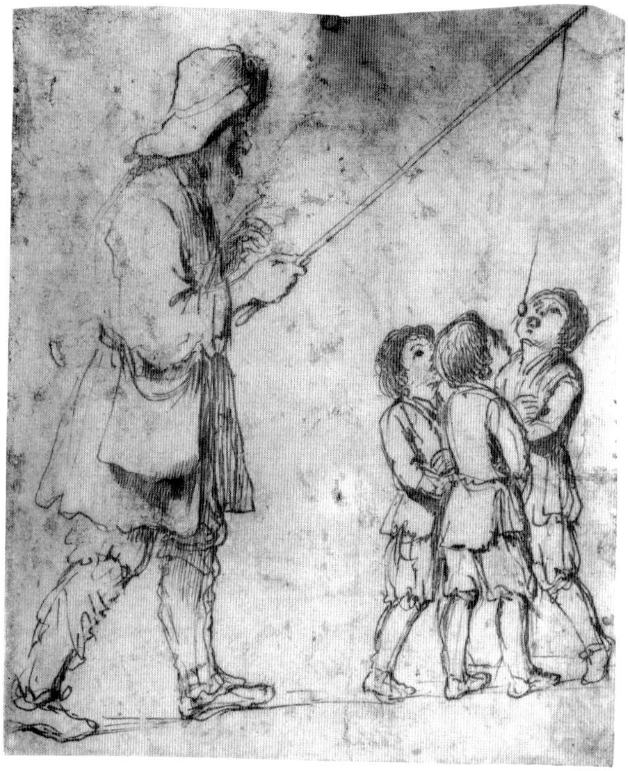

App. no. 79

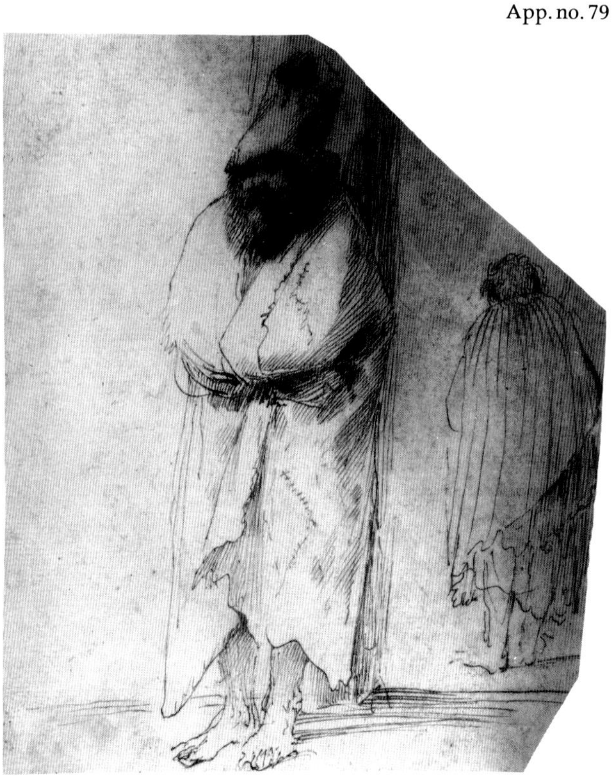

App. no. 80

79 Man and three Boys playing with a Rod

The man stands on the left and holds the rod in his right hand so that the line, at the end of which is a morsel, dangles over the children who raise their heads, mouths agape, to catch it.

Pen and brown ink. 194 × 164mm

1986–6–21–5

Provenance: Sir Denis Mahon, by whom presented.

See App. no. 80 for a discussion of the drawing.

80 Two Beggars

One stands in front of a post; he wears a tall hat torn at the top, and huddles inside a ragged, much-patched drape; in the background on the right is another hunched figure with his back turned.

Pen and brown ink. 188 × 160mm; cut irregularly at the top and right (for the damage to the sheet, see below).

1986–6–21–6

Provenance: Sir Denis Mahon, by whom presented.

On the *verso* are some lines ruled vertically, to the right, which suggest that the sheet may be a page from an account book; pen trials are on the left.

App. nos. 79 and 80 come from the same 'sketchbook', which at some point in its history was burnt. This explains (a) the brown marks on the sheets with this provenance and (b) their sometimes irregular shape, where the most damaged parts have been trimmed away. Other leaves from this 'sketchbook' were formerly in the collection of E. Schapiro and now belong to M. Jacques Fryszman, Boulogne-Billancourt, Paris.

App. nos. 79 and 80 come close in style and technique to Guercino's drawing of a *Baker's Shop* in the Courtauld Institute Galleries, London (No. 190). A particularly good comparison can be made between the little boy standing on the right in the Courtauld drawing and the three boys reaching for the morsel with their mouths in App. no. 79. A date in the 1630s for the Courtauld drawing seems likely by analogy with the style of, for example, some of the drawings for the St Bartholomew altarpiece of 1636 (S, 1988, no. 158), particularly one in the Art Museum, Princeton (inv. no. 48–734; Gibbons, 1977, no. 272).

The two British Museum drawings were presented as School drawings although an attribution to Guercino himself might be considered; they are accordingly classed here among the ascribed drawings.

2 Drawings attributed to Guercino (App. nos. 81–82)

81 Head of a Youth

His head is turned towards the spectator, with his body (which is not seen) apparently facing right; his left hand is visible, resting on something at shoulder level.

Oiled charcoal, touched in places with white chalk, on rough, buff-coloured paper. 402 × 276mm; the top corners cut away and made up.

1946–7–13–83

Provenance: William Young Ottley (sale, T. Philipe, London, 8 June 1814, lot 366 (as Cavedone), bt *Clarke Edinb, £2–10–0*); Sir T. Lawrence (L 2445); S. Woodburn (sale, Christie's, London, 4 June 1860, lot 213 (as Cavedone), bt with 2 others *Sir T. Phillipps, £0–4–0*); Phillipps-Fenwick; presented anonymously.

Literature: Popham, 1935, p. 134, no. 2 (as Cavedone).

Inscribed in pencil along the bottom left edge: *Jacopo Cavedone, Pittore.*

In spite of Popham's endorsement of the traditional attribution to Cavedone of this sheet and App. no. 82 (Popham 1935, p. 135, under no. 3), comparable drawings on this grand scale – they are over life size – in oiled charcoal, and treated in this way do not exist in Cavedone's *oeuvre*. Both in terms of style and figure type App. no. 81 seems to us in particular to be more compatible with the early work of Guercino, who made several large studies from the nude model, often using the same oiled charcoal medium on rough, granular, tinted paper; the technique seems to have been intended to create the effect of reflected light within deep shadow as well as to suggest the texture of flesh (e.g., M & T, 1989, nos. 148, 149 and 150). Such drawings have been dated to his pre-Roman period, and these two heads would be of approximately the same date or a little later. The youth, with his broad face, flattish nose and pointed chin, resembles Guercino's youthful types of the 1620s, of which a good example is the angel pointing to the Christ Child and looking out at the spectator in the *Adoration of the Shepherds* (S, 1988, no. 114 H), one of the frescoes in the cupola at Piacenza Cathedral, decorated in 1627. Such a date, however, seems too late for the present drawing. A youthful type with a similar fringe and facial features is depicted in another drawing by Guercino in the British Museum, App. no. 6, which we have dated around the artist's Roman period or a year or two earlier.

In spite of the several good reasons for giving this pair of drawings to Guercino rather than Cavedone, we nonetheless remain uneasy about the attribution largely on account of the slight coarseness of quality in both, but particularly App. no. 82.

An indifferent copy of App. no. 81, in black chalk, is in the Weld Collection at Lulworth Manor, attributed to the Bolognese School (inv. no. 53; Witt neg. no. 504/28/16).

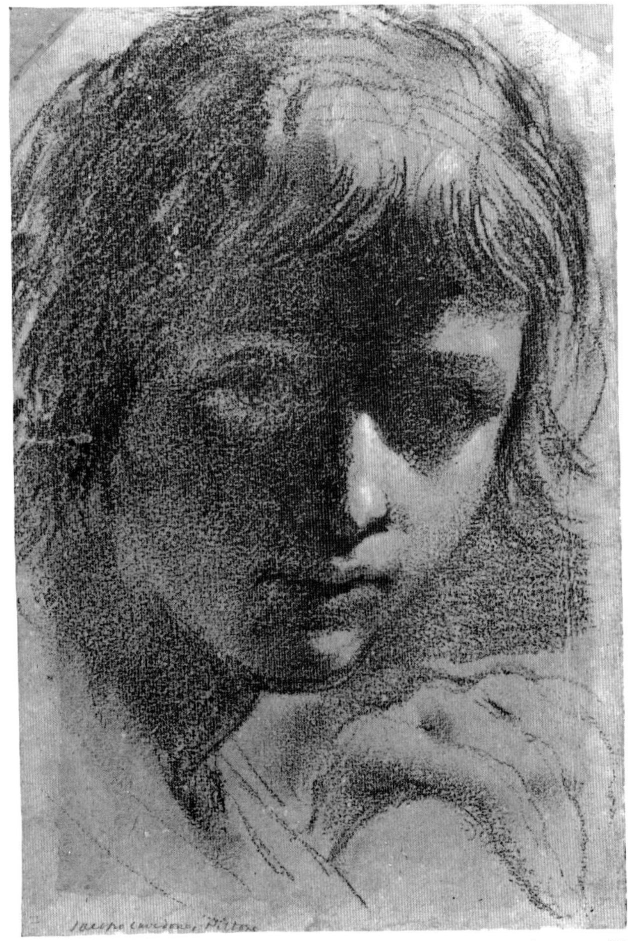

App. no. 81

82 Head of a Girl

She is in three-quarter profile to the right and looks out at the spectator.

Oiled charcoal, touched in places with white chalk, on rough, buff-coloured paper. 403 × 278mm.

1946–7–13–732. Not illustrated.

Provenance: William Young Ottley (sale, T. Philipe, London, 8 June 1814, lot 367 (as Cavedone), bt *Clarke Edinb, £7–2–0*); Sir T. Lawrence (L 2445); S. Woodburn (sale, Christie's, London, 4 June 1860, lot 213 (as Cavedone), bt with 2 others *Sir T. Phillipps, £0–4–0*); Phillipps-Fenwick; presented anonymously.

Literature: Popham, 1935, p. 135, no. 3 (as Cavedone).

Inscribed in black ink in the bottom centre of the old Ottley mount: *Jacopo Cavedone, Pittore.*; and below this, slightly to the left, in pencil: *Sir T L. Woodburn.* Numbered in pencil in the bottom left corner of the mount: *1078*; and, also in pencil, below the bottom right corner of the drawing: *81*. Again in pencil, at the top of the mount, in the centre, is the Woodburn sale number: *213/3*. On the *verso* of the drawing, in the centre, is a further pencil inscription: *Cavedone.*

See App. no. 81, which is clearly by the same hand.

3 Drawings of the School of Guercino (App. nos. 83–94)

83 Nude Woman kneeling

She kneels to the left, with her body turned slightly towards the spectator and her head halfway to the right, looking upwards; her left arm is raised as she rests her left hand on the end of a staff, which is incompletely drawn.

Oiled charcoal and white chalk on grey paper. 426 × 279mm.

5211–62. Not illustrated.

Provenance: W. Fawkener Bequest, 1769.

Inscribed in brown ink just above the bottom left edge: *Goercino* [sic] *daccinto*.

Presumably drawn from the life. The style would seem to reflect Guercino's early period, though the drawing appears too feeble to be by him and is perhaps by a follower or associate.

84 Judith with the Head of Holofernes

Her body is turned slightly to the left though her head faces the spectator; in her raised right hand she grasps the severed head of Holofernes by the hair while her left hand rests on the hilt of her sword.

Oiled charcoal, with some white heightening, on paper faded brown. 297 × 212mm; much damaged and extensively repaired.

1895–7–25–7. Not illustrated.

Provenance: L. Stephanoff, from whom purchased.

85 Nude Woman reclining on a Couch and playing with a Bird

Her back is to the viewer and her head is propped up against a large cushion to the right; her left hand is placed at the side of the cage and the bird peers back at her from its perch.

Red chalk over some black chalk on paper from an account book. 189 × 276mm.

1859–8–6–68. Not illustrated.

Provenance: (?)Casa Gennari; Mr Bouverie; Mr Hervey; 1st Earl of Gainsborough (anonymous sale, Christie's, London, 20 July 1859, lot 58, bt with 2 others, together with lot 59, *Tiffin, £1–1–0*).

The drawing has been detached from its mount which, according to Popham (note on *verso*), bore a nineteenth-century attribution to Guercino. Also on the *verso* are faint traces of a child's face in red chalk.

It may be noted that this drawing, though included in the 1859 sale of the Bouverie collection, does not bear the Bouverie stamp (L 325).

86 The Christ Child lying on the Madonna's Lap

He is naked, with his head to the right, and with his right arm raised; the Madonna's left hand supports his body.

Red chalk on discoloured white paper. 168 × 231mm.

1907–10–30–13. Not illustrated.

Provenance: N. Hone (L 2793); William Strutt, by whom presented.

The Christ Child drawn in a nearly identical pose on a cushion occurs in another School drawing, probably not by the same studio hand, which is in a private collection (with Christie's, London, 1984; A. & C. Cooper, neg. no. 22819). There the Child reaches up towards the infant St John the Baptist, while St Joseph looks on. A red chalk drawing in the Louvre, Paris (inv. no. 6865), again probably not autograph, records the pose with slight variations. In this composition the Child looks up at St Joseph, who lifts a fold of drapery with his right hand (the figure of the infant St John the Baptist is omitted). The Louvre drawing is almost certainly the one etched by W. Baillie for Rogers's *Imitations* (published in 1771).

A more distant variant of the pose appears in a *Madonna and Child* by Matteo Loves (*fl.* 1625–62) now in a private collection (B, 1986, fig. 144). The pose is reversed so that the Child lies to the left and raises his hand to his mother, who kneels before rather than behind him.

87 Madonna and Child

She is seated facing to the front and prepares to take in her arms the Infant Christ, who steps off a pedestal on the left, in profile to the right.

Red chalk. 280 × 233mm; on paper that has been exposed to the sun; worm-holes and other damage along the top margin.

1895–9–15–708. Not illustrated.

Provenance: Miss C. Goodrich; from whom bought on 12 April 1867 for £5 by J. C. Robinson (according to the annotated copy of Robinson, 1872); J. Malcolm.

Literature: Robinson, 1869, no. 256; Robinson, 1872, no. 268.

From a certain smudging of the contours, the drawing gives the impression of having once been offset.

A retouched offset of a *Madonna and Child*, which is a close variant in reverse of the present composition, is in the Uffizi, Florence (inv. no. 12476–F; 354 × 230mm). It is drawn to the same scale as App. no. 87 and could conceivably have been based on an offset from it, with substantial reworking. There are, however, numerous small differences between the two drawings, the most significant being that the block on which the child stands in App. no. 87 has been substituted by a cloud.

88 St Jerome contemplating a Crucifix

He kneels in profile to the right before a block of stone, serving as an altar, on which his clasped hands rest; on the stone is a crucifix at which he gazes.

Pen and brown ink; drawn on two sheets of paper joined vertically to the left, one fifth of the way along the lower edge. 293 × 268mm; laid down on an old canvas support; the pen lines are badly faded from over-exposure to light.

1938–11–3–2. Not illustrated.

Provenance: R. Lumb Esq., by whom presented.

Literature: de Moura Sobral, 1974/5, p. 10.

A typical School drawing.

89 The infant St John the Baptist in the Wilderness

He stands in profile to the left, naked except for the skin draped over his right shoulder, against which rests his reed cross; he drinks from a gourd whilst a sheep grazes by his side.

Red chalk. 252 × 182mm.

1859–8–6–70. Not illustrated.

Provenance: (?)Casa Gennari (on the basis of the inscription); Mr Bouverie (L 325); Mr Hervey; 1st Earl of Gainsborough (anonymous sale, Christie's, London, 20 July 1859, lot 59, bt with one other, together with lot 58, *Tiffin, £1–1–0*).

Numbered in graphite in the bottom left corner: *21*; below, in brown ink, is the inscription: *Sf.Fo.74.* (For similar inscriptions, see Nos. 10, 38 and 46; for a discussion of such inscriptions, see M & T, 1989, under no. 200, and also no. 297.) Along the bottom edge of the old mount, to the right, is a pencil inscription: *Giovanni Francesco Barbieri/called Guercino da Cento.* In the top left corner of the mount, also in pencil, is the number *11*, encircled. On the *verso* of the drawing is a further inscription in brown ink: *del Guercino.*

The drawing may well be a reworked offset.

90 Madonna and Child

She is half length, in profile to the left, gazing down at the Infant Christ in her arms; he kneels, in profile to the right, and returns her gaze, holding the neckline of her dress with his right hand and an unidentifiable object in his left (?a piece of fruit).

Red chalk. 261 × 204mm.

Ff. 2–130. Not illustrated.

Provenance: Rev. C. M. Cracherode Bequest, 1799.

Inscribed in pen on the back of the old mount in the bottom left corner: *Guercino.*

91 Woman standing in profile to the left

She stands full length and extends her right arm to the left, palm upwards, while hitching up her skirts with her left hand to reveal her left calf; a drapery which passes over her right shoulder billows out behind her.

Pen and black ink and grey wash. 228 × 148mm; the corners cut away.

5236–138. Not illustrated.

Provenance: Sloane Bequest, 1753.

Inscribed on the reverse of the old backing, top centre, in brown ink: *Guercino.*

As Louis Fagan was the first to point out (MS. catalogue of the drawings of the Italian School in the British Museum, 1888), the pose of the figure (but not the drapery) is based on that of Proserpine in Enea Vico's engraving of *Proserpine* after (?)Parmigianino. In style, the drawing itself is perhaps more reminiscent of the work of the Cremonese Giuseppe Caletti (1600–60), a follower of the Carracci, than of Guercino.

92 Landscape with a Tree in the Foreground and a walled Town in the Distance

The tree is prominent on the right and on the left is a bridge with travellers; in the middle distance, beyond the bridge, is a gully, and to the left a road with two men who make towards the town; behind the walls of the town rise two towers and in the distance is a high mountain.

Pen and brown ink. 262 × 199mm.

1895–9–15–712. Not illustrated.

Provenance: J. Malcolm.

Literature: Robinson, 1869, no. 257; Robinson, 1872, no. 272.

Popham rightly observed that the drawing is by an imitator of Guercino (note in Departmental copy of Robinson, 1872; shelfmark Cc. 5. 1); indeed, the style of the drawing is not unlike that of Guercino's nephew Cesare Gennari, by whom many landscape drawings are recorded in the 1719 inventory of the Casa Gennari (for which see Introduction). Nonetheless the drawing owes much in composition and handling to such landscape studies by Guercino himself as the small group at Windsor (M & T, 1989, nos. 247–9), though the comparison only emphasises the inadequacies of App. no. 92.

93 Landscape with a Tree in the centre Foreground

The tree is on a knoll; behind it is a stretch of water on which there is a boat containing four persons; to the left, in the distance, is a fortified town away from which three figures stroll along a road.

Pen and brown ink. 188 × 305mm; the drawing was once torn in four: the pieces have been reassembled and neatly stuck down, perhaps by Richardson.

Ff. 2–143. Not illustrated.

Provenance: J. Richardson, Sr (L 2183); J. Barnard (L 1419); Rev. C. M. Cracherode Bequest, 1799.

According to Departmental records, the back of the old mount is inscribed with Barnard's initials and his note: *N:º 653 12 by 7½ Engraved by Pond.*

Despite the inscription, it was in fact not Arthur Pond but Charles Knapton who etched the drawing in reverse, as one of their series of facsimile prints after Old Master drawings (Weigel, 1865, no. 3444; Hake, 1922, p. 342, no. 37), with the inscription: *E Museo Dni Jonathanis Richardson*. For other drawings etched in this same series, see App. nos. 58–9.

The drawing is strangely inept, the draughtsman not even grasping such essentials of perspective as the diminishing scale of figures in accordance with a vanishing point. The drawing is surely not by Guercino himself but by a close follower working in his studio. Two other landscape drawings by this same studio hand, which appear to have been torn into quarters in exactly the same way, are known: one in the collection of Jacques Fryszman, Boulogne-Billancourt, Paris (inv. no. 2.605, pen and brown ink, 185 × 286mm, inscribed on the *verso* in an old hand: *Genaro*); and another, formerly on the art market in Rome (pen and brown ink, 198 × 305mm; *Mostra di disegni italiani*, exh. cat., Centro Culturale 'Galleria Cembalo Borghese', Palazzo Borghese, Rome, 1984, no. 47, as follower of Guercino). It appears that the three drawings were laid on top of one another and torn up at the same moment.

Several other landscape drawings of a similar type to these three *disegni strappati*, with awkwardly drawn, elongated figures, out of scale with each other and often with the architectural elements in the background, may be by this same follower, even though they are sometimes given to Guercino himself.

94 Landscape with a Tree on the Crest of a Hill

The hill, surmounted by a tree swept over to the left by the wind, is slightly to the right of centre; the ground falls away to the left and beyond, a glimpse of a distant landscape is revealed; on the right, on the brow of the hill, are two figures, one on horseback.

Pen and brown ink. 111 × 189mm.

1893–7–31–5. Not illustrated.

Provenance: J. Richardson, Sr (L 2183); J. Barnard (L 1419); Earl of Aylesford (L 58; sale, Christie's, London, 18 July 1893, lot 238, with 8 others, *Colnaghi* commissioned).

Visible in the bottom right corner are traces of an inscription, mostly cut away by the bottom edge of the sheet. According to Departmental records, the back of the old mount is inscribed with Barnard's initials and his note: *N° 333 7½ by 4½*.

In our opinion the drawing is too feeble to be by Guercino himself. It may be by the same hand as App. no. 93, also once in the Richardson and Barnard collections.

4 Anonymous Copies after Guercino (App. nos. 95–107)

95 Erminia

She is seated with her body turned slightly to the right and her head facing in the opposite direction; her right hand rests on her left knee while her left hand is raised as if in surprise; she wears a plumed helmet.

Red chalk with some stumping. 337 × 250mm; the white paper, discoloured light brown, is much damaged and patched.

1943–11–13–8. Not illustrated.

Provenance: Eric Rose, by whom presented.

Literature: M & T, 1989, under no. 12 (as copy after Guercino).

A feeble copy, drawn to the same scale, of the study in the Royal Library, Windsor Castle (No. 22), for the figure of Erminia in the painting *Erminia and the Shepherd* of c. 1619–20 in the City Museum and Art Gallery, Birmingham (S, 1988, no. 61).

96 Four Putti, one holding a Bow, another a Piece of Drapery

The putto with the bow is halfway down the left side of the sheet, holding the bow in his right hand and drawing it to the left, while flying to the right; below him, another putto flies to the left, a drapery billowing behind him; to the right of the first putto are the head and shoulders of a third, turned to the left; above him is the fourth putto, also turned to the left, his face obscured by one of his outstretched arms.

Brush with light brown and light red wash over red chalk. 249 × 172mm.

Pp. 4–43. Not illustrated.

Provenance: J. Barnard (L 1419; sale, J. Greenwood, London, 19 February 1787, lot 72, as Albano, *£0–10–6*); Sir J. Reynolds (L 2364; sale, H. Phillips, London, 17 March 1798, ?lot 1166, bt with one other, as Guercino); R. Payne Knight Bequest, 1824.

Numbered in red ink on the back of the old mount, in the bottom right corner: *1166*.

The putti are copied in reverse from different parts of the fresco of *Aurora* painted by Guercino in 1621 in the Casino Ludovisi, Rome (S, 1988, no. 83; for related drawings see Nos. 32–5). G. B. Pasqualini's engraving in reverse after the *Aurora*, which is the only early print to reproduce the fresco, omits two of the putti (B, 1988, fig. 35) and is far too schematic to have been the model for the drawing. The copies may thus have been made, with the assistance of a mirror, from the original fresco rather than from a print.

The drawing was sold as by Francesco Albani (1578–1660) in the Barnard sale of 1787. The connection with Guercino's work must have been noted shortly thereafter, since the drawing was apparently sold with an attribution to Guercino at the sale of Sir Joshua Reynolds in 1798. Lot 1166, to which the number on the back of the old mount refers, contained two drawings given to Guercino. Nevertheless, the drawing entered the collection in 1824 as Albani and until 1987 was preserved with the unmounted drawings placed under his name.

The technique of brush drawing with light washes suggests a seventeenth-century Bolognese hand, close to that of Elisabetta Sirani (1638–65) or Lorenzo Pasinelli (1629–1700).

97 Rest on the Flight into Egypt

The Madonna is seated just left of centre, her head facing towards the right and her body turned slightly to the left; the Infant Christ is seated on her lap, pointing at Joseph to the right who kneels to secure a bundle with a rope; behind him the ass grazes in profile to the right, while beyond, an angel looks at Joseph and rests his right hand on the saddle of the ass.

Pen and brown ink and light brown wash over black chalk; squared for transfer in red and black ink. 258 × 410mm.

5212–57. Not illustrated.

Provenance: W. Fawkener Bequest, 1769.

Inscribed in pencil in the bottom centre of the mount: *Guercino da Cento. Vero Originale.*

As Mahon has pointed out (communication to the Department), App. no. 97 is after a drawing formerly in the collections of Dan Fellows Platt and John Davis Hatch, Jr, and now in the National Gallery of Art, Washington, D.C. (inv. no. B.30–696). The Washington drawing, which is reproduced by Bagni (1983, p. 131), is preparatory for the fresco of the *Rest on the Flight into Egypt* of 1627 in the drum of the cupola of the Cathedral at Piacenza; it is squared for transfer, even though it differs from the finished solution. The squaring on the British Museum copy does not, however, correspond with the smaller grid of the Washington drawing.

98 Madonna and Child with a Book

She is shown half length, standing at a table, with her body turned slightly to the left; she supports the Infant Christ who is seated on a cushion on the table, facing to the right; in her left hand she holds the book, the pages of which the Infant turns.

Black chalk with some stumping. 173 × 139mm.

Ff. 4–52. Not illustrated.

Provenance: Rev. C. M. Cracherode Bequest, 1799.

The *verso* of the drawing bears the following inscription, visible through the back of the old mount: *quadro in tela ben Conservato/senza niun dubio del Guercino/sula maniera sua piu vaga/senza* [. . .] *e molto Godibile/150 Zechine/*[. . .] *F. Studio.* An arrow, extending the length of the drawing, near the left edge, is marked, parallel to it: *Piedi 3 oncie 7 de inghilterra* and another spanning the width, near the bottom edge, is similarly marked: *Piedi 3 oncie 2.* The inscriptions have been transcribed, not entirely accurately, in an eighteenth-century hand (?Cracherode's) on to the back of the mount.

Popham, in a note on the backing, just beneath the first (transcribed) inscription, commented that the drawing records the particulars of a picture by Guercino which was then for sale, perhaps to an English buyer. No corresponding picture by Guercino is known to us, nor indeed do we recognise the handwriting of the inscription on the *verso*. However, the drawing's style points to a Bolognese artist such as Donato Creti (1671–1749) or a member of his circle.

99 Youth resting his Head on his Hand

His head is inclined slightly to the right and is supported by his left arm, the elbow of which rests on a horizontal surface.

Pen and brown ink, much faded. 231 × 172mm.

5211–17. Not illustrated.

Provenance: W. Fawkener Bequest, 1769.

Inscribed in brown ink in the bottom centre of the old mount: *Guercino da cento.*

As Popham observed (note on the back of the old mount), this is a copy after an engraving by Francesco Curti (1610–90), of which there is an impression in the Department (inv. no. U. 4–181; Bartsch, 1803–21, XIX, p. 31, no. 136; Bertelà, 1973, no. 509). For a comment on Curti's activity, see B, 1988, pp. 90ff. The drawing is a free copy and enlarges the figure in the print, which is one of a series of twenty, dedicated to Marchese Francesco Montecuccoli (for which see also App. no. 56). Its date of publication is not known.

100 Landscape with Boats in a Harbour

Four boats shelter in the harbour on the right, one being manoeuvred by a man with a long pole; to the left, four men converse beside two barrels and a bale of merchandise; in the distance, two more figures can be discerned to the left of a building.

Pen and brown ink. 271 × 417mm; several losses in the darks where the ink has corroded the paper.

1893–7–31–6. Not illustrated.

Provenance: Earl of Aylesford (L 58; sale, Christie's, London, 18 July 1893, lot 238, with 8 others, *Colnaghi* commissioned).

Literature: Popham & Lloyd, 1986, under no. 148.

Inscribed in black ink in the bottom left corner of the old mount: *Guercino*; in the bottom centre of the same, the number *61* is inscribed in grey-black ink.

Popham, in a note on the mount, pointed out that this is a copy of a drawing by Guercino at Holkham Hall (No. 173).

101 Landscape with a Gateway

On the left is a gateway, through which some figures pass while others converse outside the perimeter wall; a road, along which travel wayfarers, winds through the middle ground; in the background is a fortified town.

Pen and brown ink. 261 × 404mm.

Ff. 4–25. Not illustrated.

Provenance: Rev. C. M. Cracherode Bequest, 1799.

Popham pointed out (note on the back of mount) that this

is a copy after an etching by Jean Pesne (1623–1700), the third in a series of fourteen after landscape subjects by Guercino (see B, 1985, pp. 65ff.; the print is reproduced on p. 79). The original drawings, which these prints reproduce in reverse, are, with two exceptions, at Chatsworth (see Nos. 166–8).

102 Sts Roch and Sebastian with, above, the Madonna interceding before the fulminating Christ

St Roch, on the left, kneels on his left knee with his arms open and with a staff leaning against his right arm and leg; St Sebastian, on the right, faces left and looks upwards, tied with his arms behind his back to a tree stump; in the sky, the Madonna kneels on a cloud above St Roch, in profile to the right; she points down towards St Sebastian and looks up at Christ, who holds two arrows in each hand.

Pen and brown ink and red wash, over traces of black chalk. 287 × 203mm.

5226–32

Provenance: Sloane Bequest, 1753.

A copy by an eighteenth-century Bolognese hand, presumably after a lost composition drawing by Guercino for an altarpiece formerly at Nonantola but now untraced: a feeble copy of the original picture, with the head of St Francis added at the right, is now in the church of S. Michele at Nonantola (S, 1988, no. 148; see also M & T, 1989, under nos. 75–6, for an exhaustive discussion of this commission and of the related drawings). App. no. 102 only came to light among the anonymous unmounted Italian drawings of 'Groups of Saints', after the appearance of Salerno's monograph (1988) and the Windsor catalogue (1989). It records yet another phase in the evolution of the composition, other stages of which are known from two autograph drawings discussed by Mahon and Turner. The first, in pen, was formerly in the collection of Sir Robert Witt and is now at the Snite Museum of Art, University of Notre Dame, Indiana, though its whereabouts remained for long unknown (photo, Witt Library, as Witt Collection, inv. no. 1340); the other, in pen and wash, is in a private collection (M & T, 1989, under nos. 75–6, repr. fig. 15). Both these studies, like App. no. 102, show St Roch on the left and St Sebastian on the right, in contrast to the painted copy recording the finished work in which their positions are reversed. The lost study recorded in the British Museum drawing differs from the other two composition drawings in that the Madonna, and not an angel sheathing a flaming sword, is shown in the sky. This implies that it was probably executed later in the genesis of the composition.

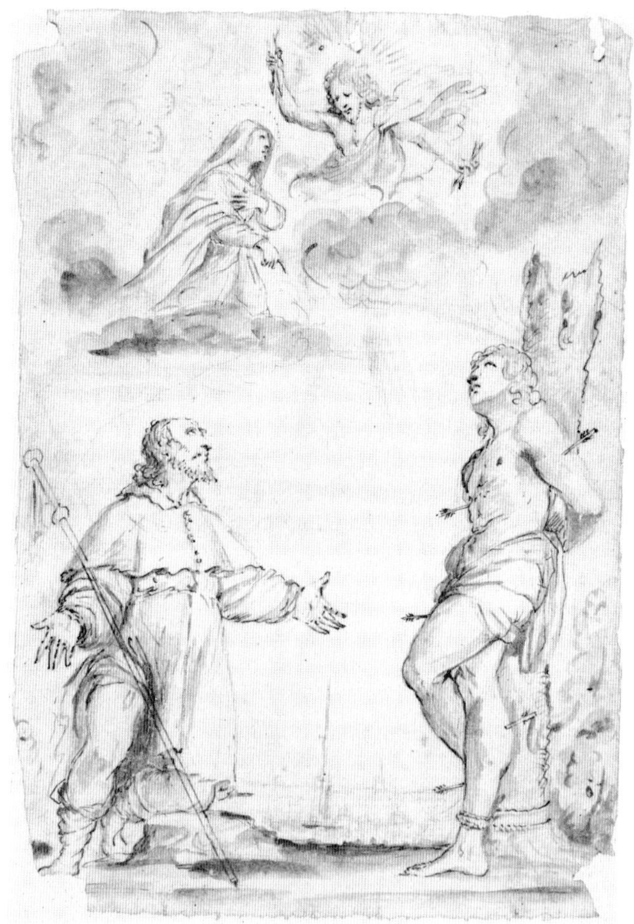

App. no. 102

103 Bishop Saint holding a Model of a Town

He stands with his body facing the spectator and with his head turned to the left, as if to converse with the cherub on the left who holds his crozier; he holds the model in front of him with both hands; his mitre rests on a ledge behind him to the right.

Black chalk with some stumping on white paper discoloured light brown, the whole much rubbed. 403 × 275mm.

Ff. 2–132. Not illustrated.

Provenance: Rev. C. M. Cracherode Bequest, 1799.

Inscribed in brown ink in the bottom right corner: *G. Reni 14*; and on the back of the old mount, in the bottom right corner: *Barbieri*. Popham noted on the back: *Possibly once Guercino but completely rubbed out and then gone over by a later hand*.

In our opinion, the drawing is entirely homogeneous, although feeble throughout. We thus find ourselves unable to support Popham's view that it is perhaps based on an erased and subsquently reworked original.

The saint could be either St Petronius or St Geminiano. The model, with one tall tower and a smaller leaning tower, suggests the city of Bologna of which St Petronius was the patron saint. However, there seems to be a certain formal relationship between the figure in the drawing and that of St Geminiano, the patron saint of Modena, in Guercino's altarpiece of the *Madonna and Child with four Saints*, formerly at Modena and now in the Louvre (S, 1988, no. 288); the model of the town that St Geminiano carries features the celebrated spire of Modena Cathedral known as La Ghirlandina. Similarities between the altarpiece and this drawing are particularly strong in the juxtaposition of the putto with the crozier and the figure of the bishop. It may be that for a representation of St Petronius a follower adapted Guercino's figure of St Geminiano from his altarpiece, which, in fact, remained in his studio from 1651 until after his death.

104 Head and Shoulders of an Ecclesiastic

He is bearded, looks upwards in profile to the left and wears a cope.

Pen and brown ink. 198 × 248mm; there is a loss in the darks on the saint's chest.

Ff. 2–138. Not illustrated.

Provenance: Rev. C. M. Cracherode Bequest, 1799.

Visible through the backing, on the *verso* of the drawing, are various insignificant inscriptions.

In pose and in type the drawing, though clearly a copy, resembles one by Guercino, also a bust of an ecclesiastic in profile, formerly on the London art market (Colnaghi's, exh. cat., 25 June to 13 July 1985, no. 28), which is a study for a print by Francesco Curti (Bertelà, 1973, no. 512).

105 Penitent Magdalen contemplating a Crucifix

She is seated with her body turned to the right, but with her head turned towards the crucifix at the left; she beats her breast with a rock held in her right hand, while her left hand rests on a skull which lies on some books.

Pen and brown ink and brown wash. 154 × 218mm.

5226–193. Not illustrated.

Provenance: Sloane Bequest, 1753.

Inscribed in brown ink, in the bottom left corner, the initials *V.P.F.* The old backing has been partially torn away to reveal, on the *verso*, a landscape with a man walking to the left, carrying a bundle on a stick over his shoulder (the sheet having been turned top to bottom).

The *recto* study is a feeble copy, presumably after a drawing or painting by Guercino.

106 Two Heads, a Man and a Woman

The man, on the left, is bearded and in profile to the left; on the right the woman looks up slightly, in three-quarters profile to the left.

Pen and brown ink and brown wash. 96 × 143mm; the top left corner cut away.

1852–11–16–83. Not illustrated.

Provenance: Rev. Thomas Knox.

Inscribed in grey-black ink in the bottom left corner: *Guercino*.

107 Landscape with Figures at a Draw-well

In the centre foreground are two trees on a small eminence, while in the background, to the left, two men draw water at a well from which a horse drinks; in the background, to the right, behind a fence and some trees, is a hill.

Pen and brown ink and brown wash. 173 × 291mm.

Ff. 2–141. Not illustrated.

Provenance: Rev. C. M. Cracherode Bequest, 1799.

Mahon has pointed out that this is a free derivative of a drawing by Guercino himself in the Royal Library, Windsor Castle (M & T, 1989, no. 258).

5 Copies after Guercino by named Artists (App. nos. 108–117)

Livio Mehus (1630–91)

108 Four caricature Heads

In the top left corner is the bust of a man in profile to the right wearing a fur-trimmed hat and with stubble on his chin and neck; in the top right corner is the bust of a man in profile to the left with a prominent forehead and a sparse beard and moustache; at the bottom of the sheet is a pair of heads in profile to the left, the one on the left with an extremely flat nose and the one on the right, wearing a cap, with a prominent beak-like nose.

Pen and brown ink and brown wash. 265 × 193mm.

1948–4–10–330. Not illustrated.

Provenance: Sir J. Reynolds (L 2364); P. & D. Colnaghi, London, from whom purchased.

Literature: M & T, 1989, under no. 296, fig. 30.

Inscribed in brown ink with the artist's monogram *L M* in the bottom left corner; and in the bottom right corner also in brown ink and also in an old hand: *Livie Meus.*

The two heads represented in the upper half of this sheet are copied from known caricature drawings by Guercino, that on the left being after a drawing in the Royal Library, Windsor Castle (M & T, 1989, no. 296) and that on the right being after one in the Art Museum, Princeton University, Princeton (inv. no. 48–1300; Gibbons, 1977, no. 286). The source, if any, of the pair of heads in pen and wash in the bottom of the sheet is untraced, but it is likely that this pair was also after an original drawing by Guercino.

Mehus was born in Oudenard in Flanders. As early as 1645, when he was only 15 years old, he seems to have arrived in Italy, where he was trained in Florence by Pietro da Cortona, who was then active in the decoration of the Palazzo Pitti. Mehus then travelled extensively in Italy, visiting, among other centres, Genoa, Milan, Rome and Venice, and returning to Florence, where he was employed by the Medici and members of their court. It is even possible that the Medici, who were avid collectors, may have sent Mehus to the Casa Gennari to purchase drawings by Guercino. This seems to be one of the earliest documented cases of an independent artist copying drawings by the master.

Another drawing attributed to Guercino, but undoubtedly by Mehus, probably after a lost study by the master, was recently on the New York art market (sale, Sotheby's, 8 January 1991, lot 200). The subject is Neptune, perhaps with Amphitrite; the drawing is executed in pen and wash and measures 284 × 200mm. As in App. no. 108, Mehus's monogram appears in the bottom left corner. An inscription in ink in the bottom right corner reads *Livio Meus*, but this is not in the same hand as the similarly located inscription on App. no. 108.

Hugh Howard (1675–1738)

109 Madonna of the Rosary with Sts Dominic and Catherine

The Madonna is seated on a cloud on the right with the Christ Child on her lap and turns three-quarters to the left; with her right hand she passes two rosaries to St Dominic who kneels on one knee, on the left, with his body facing right; opposite him is St Catherine facing left, also kneeling and gazing upwards at the rosary which the Christ Child lowers to her; in the background a crowd of the faithful look on; in the sky on the left are putti, some scattering flowers.

Red chalk; a ruled red chalk border surrounds the image 359 × 238mm.

1874–8–8–109

Provenance: Charles Howard, 5th Earl of Wicklow.

Literature: Binyon, 1898–1907, II, p. 364, no. 20, as 'after an Italian Master'.

The drawing is an excellent facsimile copy by the Irish painter and collector Hugh Howard of a composition drawing by Guercino in the Devonshire collection at Chatsworth, which was made by Guercino in preparation for his altarpiece the *Madonna of the Rosary with Sts Dominic and Catherine of Siena* of 1640–43 for the church of S. Marco at Osimo (see No. 129). The Chatsworth drawing bears the collector's mark of the 2nd Duke of Devonshire and presumably Howard copied it after it had passed into his possession.

As a collector, Hugh Howard specialised in Old Master drawings. In 1697 he set off on an extensive tour of the continent in the retinue of Thomas Herbert, 8th Earl of Pembroke, starting in Holland and continuing through France into Italy, where he is said to have remained for about three years. He returned to England in 1700 and, after a short period in Dublin, he settled in London, where he practised as a portrait painter and was employed by such patrons as the Earl of Pembroke and William, 2nd Duke of Devonshire. The Duke, with whom he shared a passion for collecting Old Master drawings, was among the artist's most consistent patrons and it was presumably while carrying out commissions for him that Howard was able to study and reproduce drawings in the Devonshire collection.

Lugt (L 2957) rightly described Howard as one of the best connoisseurs of his day, and there can be no doubt that he had excellent taste, judging from the selection of drawings from his collection that entered the Museum in 1874. His remarkable understanding of the styles of different masters is admirably shown in his facsimile copies after drawings by various artists, of which there is also a large group in the Museum, including examples after Van Dyck, Carlo Maratti, and others (Binyon, 1898–1907, II, pp. 362ff.; the artists from whom the majority of copies were taken were mostly identified after Binyon's catalogue appeared).

App. no. 110 is an offset of Howard's copy.

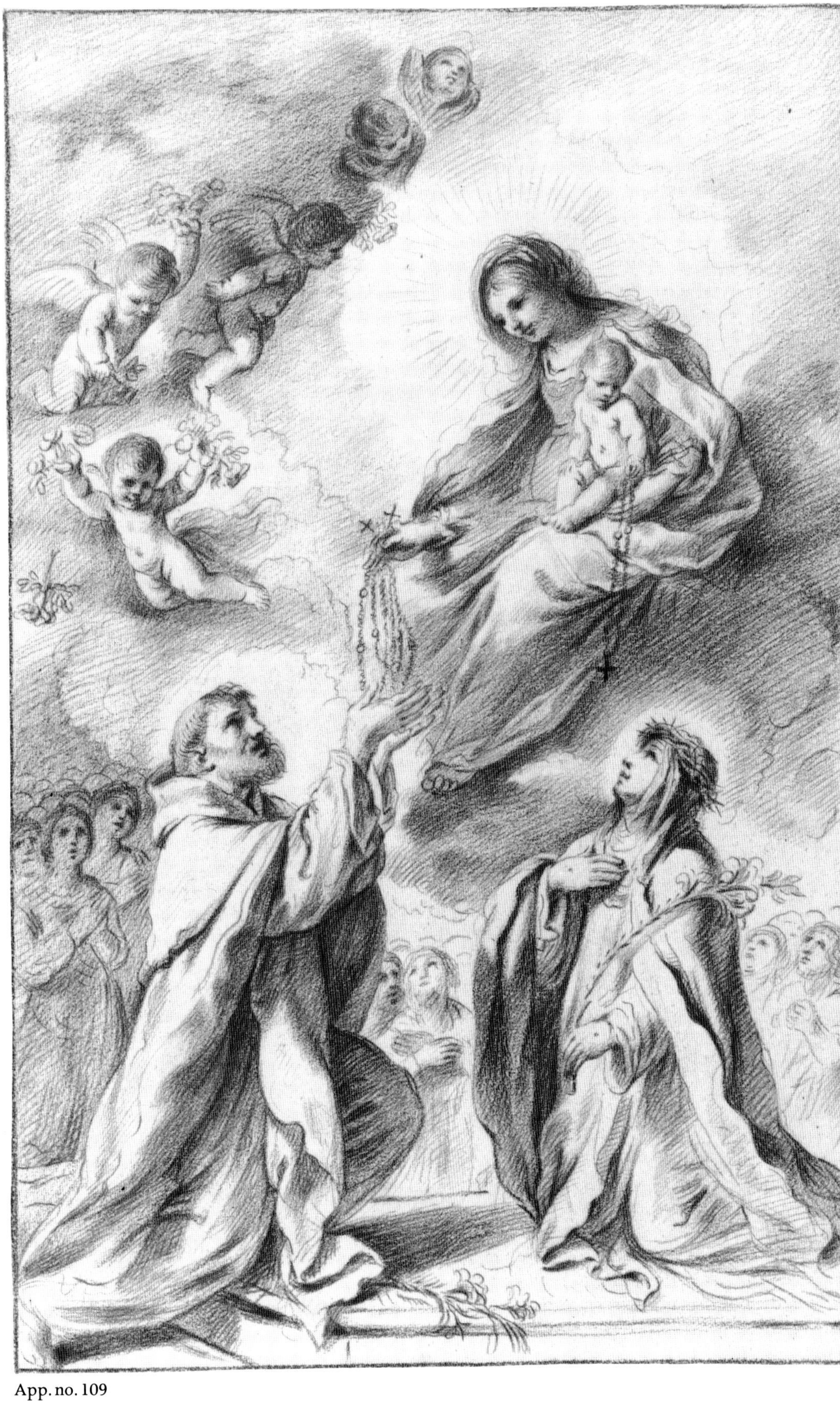

App. no. 109

110 Madonna of the Rosary with Sts Dominic and Catherine

For a description of the drawing, see App. no. 109, but in reverse.

Red chalk offset. 360 × 240mm.

1874–8–8–110. Not illustrated.

Provenance: Charles Howard, 5th Earl of Wicklow.

Literature: Binyon, 1898–1907, II, p. 364, no. 21.

The drawing is an offset of App. no. 109.

Francesco Bartolozzi (1727–1815)

111 Christ disputing with the Doctors

The youthful Christ is seated on a raised platform on the left, with his body facing right but with his head and shoulders turned in the direction of two doctors seated below him to the left; in front of him are three more seated doctors who appear to be discussing the contents of a book which they pass among themselves; two doctors stand behind this group, apart from each other, attentively observing the proceedings; in the background can be seen the heads of several spectators.

Pen and brown wash. 283 × 435mm.

Gg. 3–387

Provenance: Rev. C. M. Cracherode Bequest, 1799.

Literature: Binyon, 1898–1907, I, p. 79, no. 1.

Inscribed in brown ink on the *verso* in the centre: *Bartolozzi.*

This is a facsimile copy after a drawing by Guercino formerly in the Denon collection and now in the J. Paul Getty Museum, Malibu, California (inv. no. 84.GG.23; Goldner, 1988, no. 16). Guercino's drawing is one of a number of studies made by him to assist his follower Antonio Bonfanti, called il Torricella, with the execution of a painting of this subject, datable before 1627, for the church of S. Francesco, Ferrara (repr. Riccòmini, 1969, pl. 20).

Francesco Bartolozzi first learnt the art of engraving from his father, a Florentine goldsmith. He later entered the Florentine Academy and studied under Ignace Hugford and Gian Domenico Ferretti (1692–between 1766 and 1769). Subsequently he went to Rome to copy the antiquities there and then to Venice (1745) where he entered the shop of the engraver Joseph Wagner (1706–80). He arrived in England in 1764 at the request of Richard Dalton, Librarian to King George III, to begin work on a series of engravings after drawings by Guercino in the Royal collection (for Bartolozzi's involvement in this project, see M & T, 1989, pp. xxix–xxxi). He worked for several publishers including John Boydell, in particular, and spent most of the rest of his life in this country. In 1802 he accepted the post of Director of the National Academy, Lisbon, where he died after some years.

Bartolozzi made several facsimile copies after Guercino, probably in connection with his numerous engravings after the master's drawings, and a large group of such copies survives in the Albertina in Vienna (Stix & Fröhlich-Bum, 1926, nos. 435, 439–43, 445–8, 450, 452–6). App. no. 111 may also be an instance of a drawing made in connection

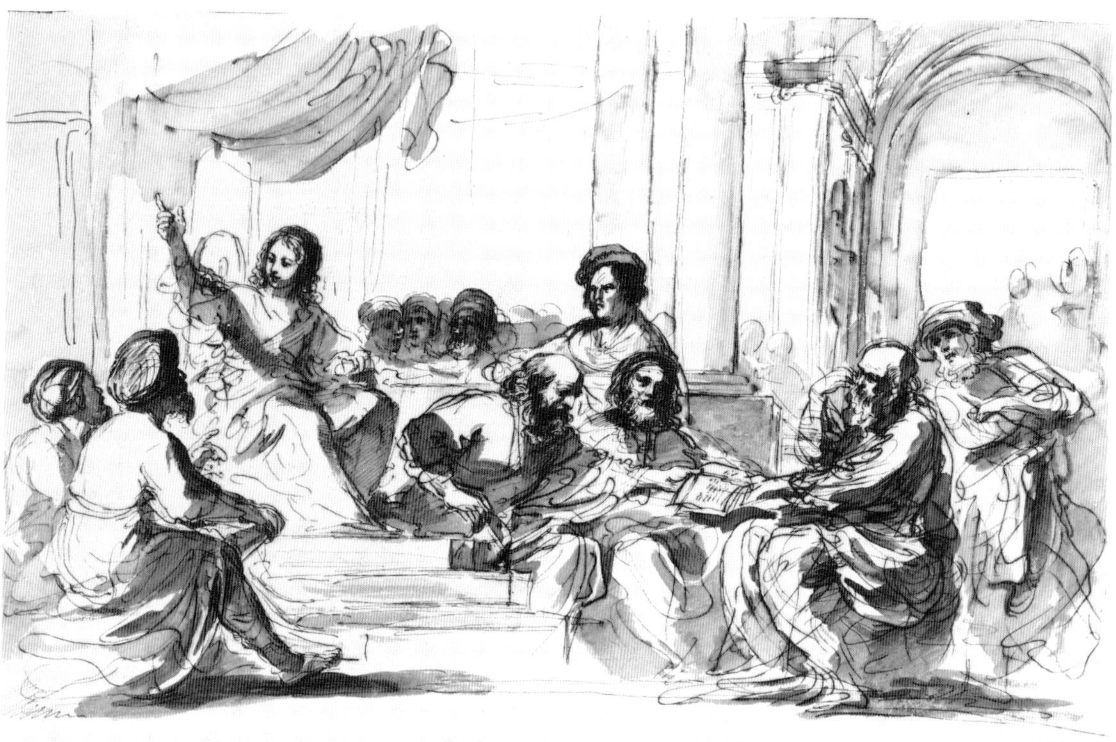

App. no. 111

with a print, but Riccòmini (1969, p. 38, under nos. 49–50), who mentions an engraving by Bartolozzi after Guercino's drawing, gives no reference, and we have hitherto been unable to trace it. The Malibu drawing was also engraved in reverse by the Frenchman Baron D. Vivant-Denon, while it was in his own collection (it bears the inscription *Tiré du Cabinet de M.r Denon.*), and is one of the plates in Albert de la Fizelière, *L'Oeuvre originale de Vivant-Denon*, Paris, 1873 (vol. I, p. xi, no. 33 in a list of plates entitled *Table Générale*, inv. no. 1876–7–8–869; there are two other impressions in the Department: U. 4–89 and 1856–2–9–836).

All of Bartolozzi's drawings of this type are remarkable for their accuracy and for the understanding they show of Guercino's style. Also characteristic of Bartolozzi is a tendency to prettify the faces of the figures, though in the case of App. no. 111 this cannot be said to be so. Since this tendency is absent or less evident in his earliest etchings after Guercino, it may indicate a relatively early date for the present drawing. Moreover, there is no evidence to show that the Malibu drawing was ever in England: indeed, as mentioned above, it was from an early date in the collection of Vivant-Denon, who acquired many of his drawings from the Zanetti Collection in Venice. This might imply that Bartolozzi could have made this copy when Guercino's original drawing was still in the Casa Gennari (for Bartolozzi's activity as a copyist of Guercino's drawings in the Casa Gennari, see M & T, 1989, p. xxx, and the Introduction to this Catalogue).

Francesco Bartolozzi or Follower

112 Two Horsemen fighting

The soldier in the foreground is seen from the rear, his horse prancing to the left; he wears armour and a helmet and wields a sword and shield; the soldier in the background, bearded and wearing a plumed helmet, strikes at his opponent with a spiked cudgel, his horse prancing to the right; behind the riders, to the right, is a tree trunk and other vegetation, while to the left is a building.

Pen and black ink and brown wash over traces of black chalk. 275 × 328mm.

Ff. 4–26. Not illustrated.

Provenance: Rev. C. M. Cracherode Bequest, 1799.

Literature: Popham, 1948, p. 11, under no. 17; Whitfield, 1977, under no. 49; Popham & Lloyd, 1986, p. 69, under no. 142.

On the back of the old mount in the centre, in brown ink and in an old hand, the inscription: *Guercino da Cento*.

In a note on the back of this mount, Popham pointed out that App. no. 112 is an eighteenth-century copy of a drawing by Guercino in the collection of the Earls of Leicester at Holkham Hall (No. 74). The style of the drawing suggests Bartolozzi, or a close follower, to whom it is here tentatively attributed. Although drawn to roughly the same scale as the original, the copy has not been traced from it. The copyist has captured the spirit of Guercino's drawing style, but has chosen to leave out the most significant pentiments (i.e., in the legs of the horses on the left).

Robert Shipster (fl. 1794–9)

113 Woman seated on a Cloud accompanied by a Putto

Her body is turned slightly to the left and she looks back over her left shoulder at the nude infant who returns her gaze; with her right arm she points upwards.

Pen and black ink and brown and reddish wash. 270 × 230mm.

1986–6–21–12. Not illustrated.

Provenance: Sir Denis Mahon, by whom presented.

Literature: Blunt, 1956, p. 76; Hammer, *et al.*, 1977, no. 35.

Inscribed in black ink on the *verso* in the centre: *R Shipster Delin 1794*, and below, again: *1794*.

Shipster, about whom very little is known, was principally an engraver and pupil of Bartolozzi. Although he is usually described as having flourished in London between 1796 and 1799, App. nos. 113–17 are all dated 1794, establishing a slightly earlier date for his activities as an artist.

As Mahon was the first to point out, App. no. 113 is after a drawing by Guercino in the Witt Collection, Courtauld Institute Galleries, London (inv. no. 1355; Hammer, *et al.*, 1977, no. 35).

114 Assumption of the Virgin

The Virgin is seated on a cloud, looking upwards, with her hands crossed over her breast; an angel, to the right, crouches on a cloud at her feet and peers downwards; in the top left-hand corner are three putti.

Pen and black ink and brown wash, with the occasional touch of red wash. 252 × 210mm.

1872–6–8–530. Not illustrated.

Provenance: J. H. Anderdon, by whom presented.

Literature: Binyon, 1898–1907, IV, p. 93, no. 1.

Inscribed in black ink in the bottom left corner: *R Shipster Delin. 1794*.

Shipster's drawing is after one by Guercino formerly in the Claude Lucas collection (sale, Christie's, London, 9 December 1949, lot 78, with one other, bt *Calmann, gns 60*), the present whereabouts of which are unknown. Guercino's drawing is a study for the upper part of the altarpiece of the *Assumption of the Virgin with Sts Peter and Jerome*, painted for the Giroldi Chapel in the Cathedral at Reggio Emilia in 1626 and still *in situ* (see No. 56 where other drawings by Guercino for this picture are considered).

115 Esther and Ahasuerus

Ahasuerus, bearded and wearing a turban, is seated on the left, in profile to the right; with his left hand he reaches out to take the limp wrist of Esther, who swoons on the right, supported from behind by another woman.

Pen and brown ink and brown wash; the drawing is surrounded by a border ruled in brown ink. 256 × 298mm.

1986–6–21–11. Not illustrated.

Provenance: Sir Denis Mahon, by whom presented.

Inscribed in brown ink in the bottom left-hand corner: *R Shipster. Delin. 1794.* On the *verso* are several insignificant sketches of soldiers and heads in black chalk. There is also a series of calligraphic squiggles in brown ink together with another inscription: *R Shipster 1794.*

As Mahon pointed out (note on the *verso*), Shipster's drawing is after one by Guercino, formerly in the Fowell Buxton collection, sold at Sotheby's, London, 23 March 1978, lot 157 (repr.), and now in the University of Michigan Museum, Ann Arbor, Michigan (inv. no. 1978/2.41). That drawing is one of a series that Guercino made in preparation for the painting of the subject, which dates from 1637–9 and is now also in the University of Michigan Museum (S, 1988, no. 180).

116 Mars holding a Sword

He is in profile to the right, striding with his right leg forward; his left arm is raised in front of him, the palm facing outwards; his right arm is drawn back and in his right hand he holds a sword; he wears armour and a plumed helmet.

Pen and brown ink and brown wash over black chalk. 309 × 224mm.

1986–6–21–13

Provenance: Sir Denis Mahon, by whom presented.

Literature: Stechow, 1976, under no. 160.

Inscribed in brown ink along the blade of the sword: *R Shipster Delin 1794.*

Shipster's copy would appear to record an untraced drawing by Guercino for a lost picture of *Cupid restraining the enraged Mars*; the appearance of this painting is recorded in a print by Giacomo Giovannini (see No. 133). Of the five surviving preparatory drawings by Guercino for this composition, none shows Mars striding in profile to the right, though the one in the Allen Memorial Art Museum, Oberlin, Ohio (inv. no. 58.154; Stechow, 1976, no. 160), shows Mars with his left arm raised, the palm facing outwards. However, a drawing by or after Guercino in the Louvre, Paris (inv. no. 6893; see under No. 134 and Fig. 21), which was brought to our attention by Stéphane Loire, shows Mars in an almost identical pose. That it is indeed Mars who is represented is confirmed by the presence in the Louvre drawing of Cupid, standing on a block at the left, restraining the figure's sword-bearing right arm (though only the arms and one foot of Cupid are visible owing to the drawing's having been cut at the left edge). For a drawing of a warrior in a very similar position, see again No. 134.

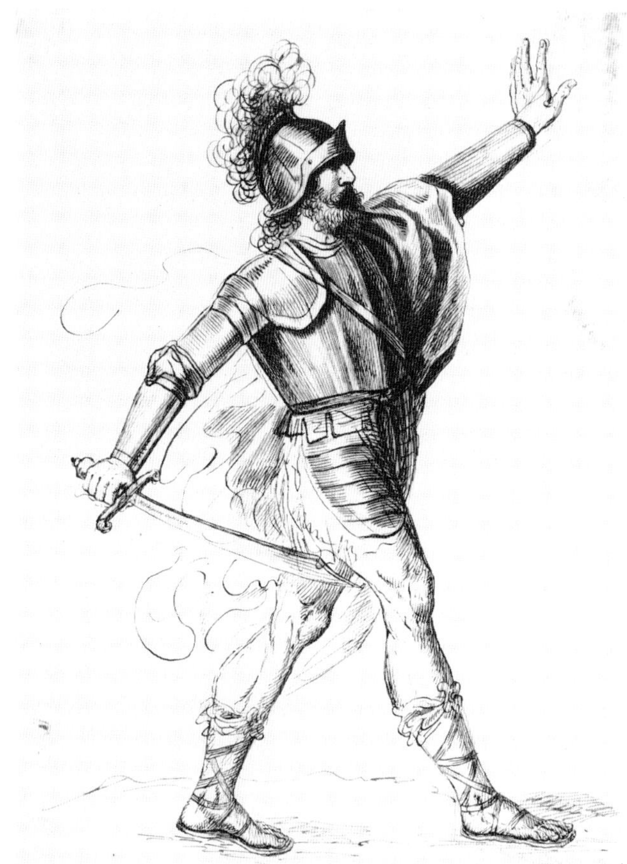

App. no. 116

117 Woman holding a Bowl

She is half length, turned to the right, and holds the bowl in both hands.

Pen and black ink; the drawing is surrounded by a border ruled in black ink. 232 × 188mm.

1986–6–21–9. Not illustrated.

Provenance: Sir Denis Mahon, by whom presented.

Inscribed in black ink in the bottom left corner: *R Shipster. Delin 1794.*

The drawing by Guercino on which this copy is based was formerly in the collection of the Earls of Gainsborough and was sold at Christie's, London (sale, 23 November 1971, lot 104, repr.). Another copy, by Bartolozzi, is in the Albertina, Vienna (inv. no. 1389; Stix & Fröhlich-Bum, 1926, no. 450), as Denis Mahon pointed out in a note on the *verso* of App. no. 117.

6 Drawings by and attributed to Cesare Gennari (1637–88) (App. nos. 118–121)

118 An old Man with a Youth whispering in his Ear

The bearded old man is on the left, wearing a cap; his head is turned to the right towards the youth who is behind his left shoulder.

Pen and brown ink. 86 × 143mm (including 6mm strip of paper added at the left edge).

1946–7–13–762. Not illustrated.

Provenance: (?)S. Woodburn; Phillipps-Fenwick; presented anonymously.

Inscribed on the *verso*, in green pencil, in the bottom left corner: *847*. The drawing appears to have been made on a scrap of paper which once formed part of a letter, or a draft of a letter, on which appears the name of Cesare Gennari. A fragment of the letter, in brown ink, reads as follows: along the top, *Francesca resto col baciarli le/mani. Bolg*[a] *li 13 Luglio/71/D*[.] *V. S. Mol*[*to*] *Ill*[*re*]; and in the bottom right corner: [?]*Ser.* [?]*suo/Cesare Genna*[*ri*: cut off by the right hand edge of the sheet].

This is surely a typical, but slight autograph study.

119 The infant St John reclining in a Landscape

He leans on a bank to the left, supporting himself on his right elbow, in the crook of which rests his reed cross; his left arm passes across his body and in his left hand he holds a (?)bowl; he looks downwards.

Pen and brown ink and light brown wash. 117 × 157mm; the paper, much holed and damaged at the bottom edge, was laid onto another sheet, extending the drawing downwards to a total depth of 138mm.

1986–6–21–7. Not illustrated.

Provenance: N. Hone (L 2793); Sir J. Reynolds (L 2364); A. M. Champernowne (L 153); M. de Beer; Sir Denis Mahon, by whom presented.

Inscribed in brown ink along the bottom centre of the sheet on which the drawing has been laid down: *Cesare Genari 14*; and, also in brown ink, but in a different hand, along the bottom centre of the old mount: *Cesare Gennari*. On the back of the mount, in the top left corner, is a pencil note in Mahon's hand: *Bought for £1/(May, 1939)/from Mr. Max de Beer*; also inscribed in pencil, about one third of the way down the back of the mount, to the right, are two numbers: *16* (encircled) and *610*.

A slight but characteristic example of the artist's work; compare the drawing of *St Nicholas of Bari* in the Mahon Collection, on loan to the Ashmolean Museum, Oxford (M & E, 1986, no. 47).

Attributed to Cesare Gennari

120 Charity

She is standing and is represented to below the waist; her head is in profile to the left and she looks down at a child lying on his back in front of her; behind him are two other children, one clinging to the woman's right shoulder.

Black chalk. 224 × 193mm; two disfiguring smears appear, one in the turban and the other in the top right.

1884–3–8–9

Provenance: (?)P. Crozat (?his number, *62*, inscribed in black ink in the bottom right corner); Mr Gowen, from whom purchased.

Although the style of the drawing reflects Guercino's late period, the execution seems not to be his. The composition is reminiscent of a picture of *Charity*, datable 1661, by Cesare Gennari in the Galleria Nazionale d'Arte Antica, Rome (B, 1986, p. 295 and p. 304, fig. 166). There are, however, many differences between the two works, the most important being that the figure of Charity is seated in the painting, and is shown bare-breasted, suckling one of the infants. In spite of these important differences, there are sufficient minor points in common to justify the conclusion that this drawing may be an early preparatory study by Cesare for this picture.

A weaker version of the drawing, also in black chalk but in reverse, is in the Uffizi, Florence (inv. no. 3676-S; 217 × 193mm, as Guercino). This is almost certainly a faint offset, retouched.

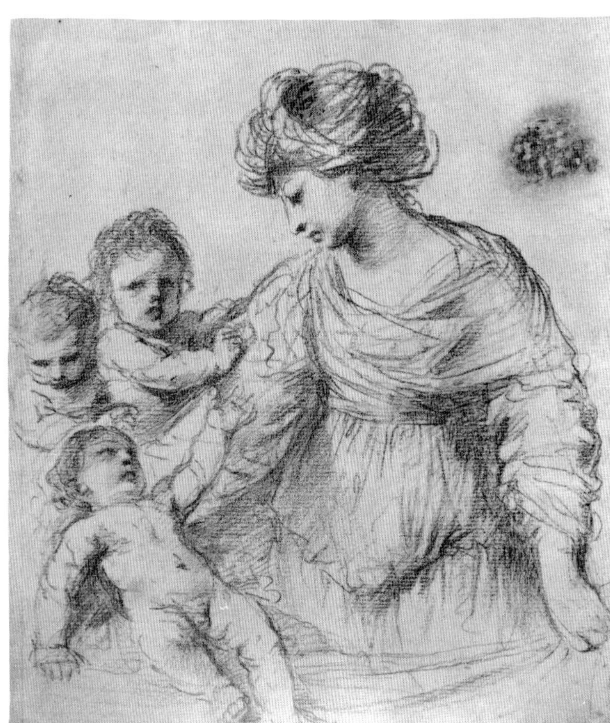

App. no. 120

?Copy after Cesare Gennari

121 The Holy Family with the infant St John

The Madonna is seated in profile to the left with the Christ Child on her lap; he looks down, over his left shoulder, at the Baptist standing in profile to the left beside her and raising his arms in Christ's direction; behind the group, Joseph leans his right elbow on a block and proffers an object towards the outstretched arms of the Christ Child.

Red chalk, heightened with white chalk. 161 × 139mm.

5212–15. Not illustrated.

Provenance: W. Fawkener Bequest, 1769.

Inscribed in pencil along the bottom of the old mount, to the right: *Cesare Gennari*.

This sketch cannot be an autograph drawing by Cesare Gennari on account of its very poor quality. We are not, however, in a position to identify a composition by him from which it might be copied.

7 Drawing attributed to Carlo Gennari (1716–90)

122 Landscape with a Woman and a Child standing by a River

The river, which is in the centre, is flanked on the left by rocks down which a waterfall courses; the child stands with the woman on the right bank, on which are trees and undergrowth; there are buildings in the distance.

Pen and brown ink and brown wash on light brown paper. 250 × 382mm.

1872–10–12–3285. Not illustrated.

Provenance: R. Udny (L 2248); W. Esdaile (L 2617).

Inscribed in brown ink in the bottom centre of the old mount (?in Esdaile's hand): *Benedetto Gennari.*; and in graphite, in the bottom right corner of the same: *Benedetto Gennari*. On the back of the mount, in the bottom left corner, is a further inscription in brown ink (?also in Esdaile's hand): *Robt Udny's coll^{n} 1803* [a cancellation]. *P 46 N 7*.

It is not possible to say with certainty whether this was one of the drawings included in lots 325–7, simply listed as Gennari, in William Esdaile's sale of 19 June 1840 held at Christie's, London. The drawing does not appear in the catalogue of the sale of 14 April 1803 and seven following days at T. Philipe, London, which Lugt (L 2248), with good reason, believed was of the third and last part of Udny's collection of drawings.

In spite of the old attribution to Benedetto Gennari (1633–1715), the drawing seems to us to be of the mid-eighteenth century and could well be by Carlo Gennari, a great-great-nephew of Guercino. It compares extremely well with the group of drawings reproduced by Bagni (1985, pp. 223–41).

8 Drawings by the 'Faker' of Guercino (App. nos. 123–126)

123 Landscape with a Building and a Bridge on the left

The bridge spans an expanse of water which opens, in the foreground, into a small cove along the banks of which couples stroll or sit; in the foreground on the right is a small tree and undergrowth and in the background are mountains.

Pen and brown ink. 272 × 415mm.

1986–6–21–8. Not illustrated.

Provenance: Anthony Wilson; Sir Robert Witt (L *Suppl*, 2228b); Sir Denis Mahon, by whom presented (for documentary interest, as an example of the 'Faker's' hand).

Literature: B, 1985, no. 66 (repr.); Jones, 1990, no. 135a.

The identity of the artist who produced App. nos. 123–6, probably in Bologna in the late eighteenth century, is unknown. He seems to have specialised exclusively in the drawings of Guercino, notably the landscapes which were very popular with collectors of the period. He concocted them from motifs taken from prints of the genuine drawings, varying these with passages of his own invention. The characteristic *brio* with which they are drawn approximates the lively touch of Guercino's own pen drawings, but has on closer acquaintance quite a different character. The forger's activity must have been lucrative, judging from the numerous examples that survive in collections in Europe and America. Although first identified in 1930 by the Hungarian scholar Edith Hoffman, his work continued, on occasion, to sell as Guercino's until the 1970s.

Bagni, in a study devoted to the 'Faker's' landscape drawings (B, 1985, p. 93), pointed out that a motif in App. no. 124 is derived from the fourth in the series of prints after Guercino's landscape drawings by Jean Pesne (for which see Nos. 166–70); the print is reproduced by Bagni as no. 58 on p. 85.

124 Landscape with Couples on the Bank of a River

The couples are seated or strolling about the banks of an inlet of water which penetrates the landscape from the left; in the distance are houses and some mountains.

Pen and brown ink. 281 × 423mm.

1875–7–10–2624. Not illustrated.

Provenance: Purchased from Mr Daniell.

Literature: Jones, 1990, no. 135b (repr.).

See App. no. 123.

125 Landscape with two Men in the Foreground

The two men are strolling to the right along an open expanse of land bounded by a tree to the right and a stretch of water to the left; beyond are a group of buildings and a mountain range.

Pen and brown ink. 280 × 413mm.

1875–7–10–2625. Not illustrated.

Provenance: Purchased from Mr Daniell.

Literature: Jones, 1990, no. 135c.

See App. no. 123.

126 Landscape with Figures and a Fortress

In the centre is a road winding back to the fortress, towards which walks a couple; in the foreground another couple are seated at the side of the road with their backs to the spectator; in the background are mountains.

Pen and brown ink. 278 × 414mm.

1875–7–10–2626. Not illustrated.

Provenance: Purchased from Mr Daniell.

Literature: Jones, 1990, no. 135d.

See App. no. 123.

Bibliography

Andrews, 1968 K. Andrews, *National Gallery of Scotland: Catalogue of Italian Drawings*, Cambridge, 1968

Artioli & Monducci, 1982 Nerio Artioli and Elio Monducci, *Dipinti 'Reggiani' del Bonone e del Guercino (pittura e documenti)*, exh. cat., Reggio Emilia, Basilica della B.V. della Ghiara, 30 January – 28 February 1982; second, corrected edn, February 1982

B, 1983 Prisco Bagni, *Guercino a Piacenza: Gli affreschi nella cupola della Cattedrale*, Bologna, 1983

B, 1984 Prisco Bagni, *Guercino a Cento: Le decorazioni di Casa Pannini*, Bologna, 1984

B, 1985 Prisco Bagni, *Il Guercino e il suo falsario: I disegni di paesaggio*, Bologna, 1985

B, 1986 Prisco Bagni, *Benedetto Gennari e la bottega del Guercino*, Padua, 1986

B, 1988 Prisco Bagni, *Il Guercino e i suoi incisori*, Rome, 1988

B, 1990 Prisco Bagni, *Il Guercino e il suo falsario: I disegni di figura*, Bologna, 1990

Bacou, 1967 Roseline Bacou in *Le Cabinet d'un grand amateur P.-J. Mariette*, exh. cat., Paris, Musée du Louvre, 1967

Bartrum, 1984 Giulia Bartrum, *Landscape in Italy: Drawings of the 16th and 17th Centuries*, exh. cat., London, British Museum, 9 February–29 April 1984

Bartsch, 1803–21 Adam Bartsch, *Le Peintre-graveur*, 21 vols., Vienna, 1803–21

Bartsch, *Recueil* Adam Bartsch, *Recueil d'estampes d'après les desseins de Fr. Barbieri dit Guercino qui n'ont pas encore été gravées, tirées de la collection de S. A. R. Monseigneur le Prince Albert de Pologne, Duc de Saxe-Teschen, de celle de Monsieur le Comte Maurice de Vries, et autres*, published by F. Piranesi, Paris, 1808

Bartsch, 1983a *The Illustrated Bartsch*, 36, formerly vol. 17 (Part 3): *Antonio Tempesta: Italian Masters of the Sixteenth Century*, ed. Sebastian Buffa, New York, 1983

Bartsch, 1983b *The Illustrated Bartsch*, 48, formerly vol. 12: *Italian Chiaroscuro Woodcuts*, ed. Caroline Karpinski, New York, 1983

Bean, 1969 Jacob Bean, 'Guercino as a Draughtsman' (Review of M, *Disegni*, 1969), *Master Drawings*, VII, 1969, pp. 428–31

Bean, 1979 Jacob Bean, *17th Century Italian Drawings in the Metropolitan Museum of Art*, New York, 1979

Bertelà, 1973 Giovanna Gaeta Bertelà, with the collaboration of Stefano Ferrara, *Catalogo generale della raccolta di stampe antiche della Pinacoteca Nazionale di Bologna, Gabinetto delle Stampe, Sezione III: Incisori bolognesi ed emiliani del sec. XVII*, Bologna, 1973

Bettagno, 1978 Alessandro Bettagno (ed.), *Piranesi: Incisioni – rami – legature – architetture*, Vicenza, 1978

Binyon, 1898–1907 Laurence Binyon, *Catalogue of Drawings by British Artists and Artists of foreign Origin working in Great Britain, preserved in the Department of Prints and Drawings in the British Museum*, 4 vols., London, 1898–1907

Blunt, 1956 Anthony Blunt, *Hand-list of the Drawings in the Witt Collection*, London University, London, 1956

BM *Repr.* *Reproductions of Drawings by Old Masters in the British Museum* (4 parts; notes to Part I signed by Sidney Colvin), London, 1888–94

Bodart, 1975 D. Bodart, *Dessins de la collection Thomas Ashby à la Bibliothèque Vaticane*, Vatican City, 1975

Bohn, 1984 Babette Bohn, 'The Drawings of Ludovico Carracci', *Master Drawings*, XXII, 1984, pp. 405–25

Bora, 1988 Giulio Bora, *I disegni della Collezione Morelli*, Bergamo, 1988

Boschini, 1676 Marco Boschini, *Gioielli pittoreschi*, Vicenza, 1676

Bottari, 1754–8 Giovanni Bottari, *Raccolta di lettere sulla pittura*, 6 vols., Milan, 1754–8

Bottari, 1966 Stefano Bottari (ed.), with notes by Renato Roli and Anna Ottani Cavina, *Guercino: Disegni*, Florence, 1966

Brejon & Volle, 1988–9 Arnauld Brejon de Lavergnée and Nathalie Volle, *Seicento, le siècle de Caravage dans les collections françaises*, exh. cat., Paris, Galeries Nationales du Grand Palais, 11 October 1988 – 2 January 1989, and Milan, Palazzo Reale, March–April 1989

Byam Shaw, 1976 James Byam Shaw, *Drawings by Old Masters at Christ Church, Oxford*, 2 vols., Oxford, 1976

Byam Shaw, 1983 James Byam Shaw, *The Italian Drawings of the Frits Lugt Collection*, 3 vols., Institut Néerlandais, Paris, 1983

Calabi, 1928 A. Calabi, *Francesco Bartolozzi: Catalogue des estampes et notice biographique d'après les manuscrits de A. de Vesme, entièrement réformés et complétés d'une étude critique*, Milan, 1928

Châtelet, 1967–8 A. Châtelet, *Dessins italiens du Musée de Lille*, exh. cat., Amsterdam, Brussels, Lille, 1967–8

Châtelet, 1970 A. Châtelet, *Disegni di Raffaello e di altri italiani del Museo di Lille*, exh. cat., Florence, Gabinetto Disegni e Stampe degli Uffizi, 1970

Clarke & Penny, 1982 Michael Clarke and Nicholas Penny, *The Arrogant Connoisseur: Richard Payne Knight, 1751–1824*, exh. cat., Manchester, Whitworth Art Gallery, 1982

Colnaghi, 1971 P. & D. Colnaghi & Co. Ltd., *Loan Exhibition of Drawings by Old Masters from the Collection of Mr Geoffrey*

Gathorne-Hardy, exh. cat., 12 October–5 November 1971, and afterwards at the Ashmolean Museum, Oxford, 20 November 1971–2 January 1972

Cresti, *et al.*, 1977 Maria Vera Cresti, Francesco Federico Mancini, Giovanna Sapori (eds.), *Cento disegni dell'Accademia di Belle Arti di Perugia: XVII–XIX secolo*, exh. cat., Rome, Villa della Farnesina alla Lungara, 27 May – 31 July 1977; Perugia, Palazzo dei Priori, September–October 1977; Spoleto, Palazzo Ancaiani, October–November 1977

Cummings, 1965 Frederick Cummings, with an introduction by Rudolf Wittkower, *Art in Italy 1600–1700*, exh. cat., Detroit, The Detroit Institute of Arts, 1965

Czére, 1989 Andrea Czére, *Disegni di artisti bolognesi nel Museo delle Belle Arti di Budapest*, exh. cat., Bologna, San Giorgio in Poggiale, Collezioni d'Arte e di Storia, 11 September–12 November 1989

Di Giampaolo, 1987 Mario Di Giampaolo, *Dal disegno all'opera compiuta: Trentacinque disegni per trentacinque dipinti*, exh. cat., Torgiano, Museo del Vino, 29 October–12 November 1987

Dirani, 1982–3 Maria Teresa Dirani, 'Mecenati, pittori e mercato dell'arte nel Seicento: Il *Ratto di Elena* di Guido Reni e la *Morte di Didone* del Guercino nella corrispondenza del cardinale Bernadino Spada', *Ricerche di Storia dell'Arte*, XVI, 1982–3, pp. 83–94

Dirani, 1988 Maria Teresa Dirani Mistorigo, *La Chiesa* [. . .] *di San Biagio Nuovo*, Vicenza, 1988

Donnithorne, 1988 Alan Donnithorne, 'Early Approaches to the Conservation of Works of Art on Paper: Cleaning, Repair and Restoration', in V. Daniels (ed.), 'Early Advances in Conservation', in *BM Occasional Paper* no. 65, British Museum, London, 1988, pp. 15–25

Emiliani, 1959 Andrea Emiliani, *Mostra di disegni del Seicento emiliano nella Pinacoteca di Brera*, exh. cat., Milan, Palazzo di Brera, 19 June–31 July 1959

Fischer, 1984 Chris Fischer, *Italian Drawings in the J. F. Willumsen Collection*, exh. cat., Frederikssund, J. F. Willumsen Museum, 14 April–3 June 1984

Galleni, 1975 Rodolfo Galleni, 'Bonaventura Bisi e il Guercino', *Paragone*, XXVI, 1975, pp. 80–82

Gathorne-Hardy A. E. Gathorne-Hardy, *Descriptive Catalogue of Drawings by the Old Masters in the Possession of the Hon. A. E. Gathorne-Hardy*, London, 1902

Gernsheim Walter Gernsheim, *Corpus Photographicum*. Photographs of drawings in public and private collections. In progress.

Gibbons, 1977 Felton Gibbons, *Catalogue of Italian Drawings in the Art Museum, Princeton University*, 2 vols., Princeton, New Jersey, 1977

Goldner, 1988 George Goldner, *European Drawings, I: Catalogue of the Collections*, The J. Paul Getty Museum, Malibu, California, 1988

Guiffrey, 1876 J. J. Guiffrey, 'Lettre du Cardinal Spada à Marie de Médicis au sujet de la Galerie du Luxembourg (1629)', *Nouvelles Archives de l'art français*, 1876, pp. 252–4

Hake, 1922 Henry M. Hake, 'Pond's and Knapton's Imitations of Drawings', *The Print Collector's Quarterly*, IX, 1922, pp. 325–49

Hammer, *et al.*, 1977 Martin Hammer, Terence O'Hair and Gerard Neill, *Drawings by Guercino and other Baroque Masters*, exh. cat., London, Courtauld Institute Galleries, February–March 1977

Heawood, 1950 Edward Heawood, *Monumenta Chartae Papyraceae Historiam Illustrantia, I: Watermarks mainly of the 17th and 18th Centuries*, Hilversum, 1950

Heinz, 1960 Günther Heinz, *Katalog der Graf Harrach'schen Gemäldegalerie*, Vienna, 1960

Hess, 1934 J. Hess, *Die Künstlerbiographien von Giovanni Battista Passeri*, Leipzig and Vienna, 1934

Horton, 1960 Anne K. Horton, 'A Drawing by Guercino', *Allen Memorial Art Museum Bulletin* (Ohio, Oberlin College), XVIII, 1960, pp. 5–19

Huchard & Laing, 1977–8 Viviane Huchard and Alastair Laing, *The finest Drawings from the Museums of Angers*, exh. cat., London, Heim Gallery, 23 November–22 December 1977; Liverpool, Walker Art Gallery, 5 January–5 February 1978; Dublin, National Gallery of Ireland, 15 February–15 March 1978; Birmingham, City Museum and Art Gallery, 21 March–23 April 1978

Illustrated Bartsch See Bartsch, 1983a and b

Jaffé, 1987 Michael Jaffé, *Old Master Drawings from Chatsworth: A Loan Exhibition from the Devonshire Collection*, exh. cat., organised and circulated by the International Exhibitions Foundation, Alexandria, Virginia, 1987–8

Joachim & McCullagh, 1979 Harold Joachim and Suzanne Folds McCullagh, *Italian Drawings in the Art Institute of Chicago*, Chicago and London, 1979

Jones, 1990 Mark Jones (ed.), *Fake? The Art of Deception*, exh. cat., London, British Museum, 1990

Kauffmann, 1982 C. M. Kauffman, *Catalogue of the Paintings in the Wellington Museum*, London, 1982

Klingsor, 1931 Tristan Klingsor, 'Un grand dessinateur méconnu: Le Guerchin', *L'Amour de l'art*, XII, 1931, pp. 349–57

Koevoets, 1976 Ben Koevoets, *Oude Tekeningen in het bezit van de Gemeentmusea van Amsterdam waaronder de Collectie Fodor, I: Italië, 15e–18e eeuw*, Amsterdam, 1976

Kurz, 1955 Otto Kurz, *Bolognese Drawings of the XVII and XVIII Centuries in the Collection of Her Majesty the Queen at Windsor Castle*, London, 1955

L; L *Suppl* Frits Lugt, *Les Marques de collections de dessins et d'estampes*, Amsterdam, 1921; *Supplément*, The Hague, 1956

Leporini, 1925 H. Leporini, *Die Stilentwicklung der Handzeichnung: XIV bis XVIII Jahrhundert*, Vienna, 1925

Lewis, *Walpole*, 1937–83 W. S. Lewis (ed.), *The Yale Edition of Horace Walpole's Correspondence*, London, 1937–83

***Libro dei Conti*, 1808; 1841** The Manuscript of Guercino's Account Book (the *Libro dei Conti*) is in the Biblioteca Comunale dell'Archiginnasio, Bologna, MS. B.331; it is published in full on pp. 59–160 in J. A. Calvi, *Notizie della vita, e delle opere del Cavaliere Giovan Francesco Barbieri detto il Guercino da Cento*, Bologna, 1808; and on pp. 307–44 in Malvasia, 1841, II

Lippincott, 1983 Louise Lippincott, *Selling Art in Georgian London: The Rise of Arthur Pond*, New Haven and London, 1983

Loire, 1990 Stéphane Loire, *Le Guerchin en France*, exh. cat., Paris, Louvre, 31 May–12 November 1990

M, 1937 Denis Mahon, 'Notes on the young Guercino', *Burlington Magazine*, LXX, 1937, pp. 112–22

M, *Studies*, 1947 Denis Mahon, *Studies in Seicento Art and Theory*, London, 1947

M, 1949 Denis Mahon, 'Guercino's Paintings of Semiramis', *Art Bulletin*, XXXI, 1949, pp. 217–23

M, 1951 Denis Mahon, 'The Seicento at Burlington House: Some Addenda and Corrigenda. I – Drawings by Guercino', *Burlington Magazine*, XCIII, 1951, pp. 56–8 (notes on some of the Guercino drawings included in the exhibition 'Works by Holbein and other Masters' at the Royal Academy in 1950–51)

M, 1967 Denis Mahon, *I disegni del Guercino della Collezione Mahon*, Bologna, 1967, corrected reprint of part of the exhibition catalogue *Omaggio al Guercino*, Cento, June–October 1967

M, *Dipinti*, 1968 Denis Mahon, *Il Guercino (Giovanni Francesco Barbieri, 1591–1666): Catalogo critico dei dipinti*, exh. cat., Bologna, Palazzo dell'Archiginnasio, 1 September–18 November 1968

M, 1968 Denis Mahon, 'Drawings by Guercino in the Casa Gennari', *Apollo*, LXXXVII, 1968, pp. 346–57

M, *Disegni*, 1969 Denis Mahon, *Il Guercino (Giovanni Francesco Barbieri, 1591–1666): Catalogo critico dei disegni*, exh. cat., Bologno, Palazzo dell'Archiginnasio, 1 September–18 November 1968; second, corrected edn, October 1969

M, 1981 Denis Mahon, 'Guercino and Cardinal Serra: A newly discovered Masterpiece', *Apollo*, CXIII, 1981, pp. 170–75

M & E, 1986 Denis Mahon and David Ekserdjian, with the assistance of Helen Davies, ed. Nicholas Penny, *Guercino Drawings from the Collections of Denis Mahon and the Ashmolean Museum*, exh. cat., Oxford, Ashmolean Museum, 29 April–22 June 1986, and London, Hazlitt, Gooden & Fox, 15 October–12 November 1986. This catalogue also figures as a supplement to the March 1986 issue of the *Burlington Magazine*

M & T, 1989 Denis Mahon and Nicholas Turner, *The Drawings of Guercino in the Collection of Her Majesty the Queen at Windsor Castle*, Cambridge, 1989

Macandrew, 1980 Hugh Macandrew, *Ashmolean Museum, Oxford: Catalogue of the Collection of Drawings, Vol. III, Italian Schools, Supplement*, Oxford, 1980

Macandrew, 1983 Hugh Macandrew, *Italian Drawings in the Museum of Fine Arts Boston*, Boston, 1983

Malvasia, 1678 Carlo Cesare Malvasia, *Felsina pittrice: Vite de' pittori bolognesi. . .*, 2 vols., Bologna, 1678; the life of Guercino is found on pp. 358–86

Malvasia, 1841 Carlo Cesare Malvasia, *Filsina pittrice: Vite de' pittori bolognesi. . .*, 2 vols., Bologna, 1841; the life of Guercino is found on pp. 255–74

Marangoni, 1920 Matteo Marangoni, *Il Guercino* (Piccola collezione d'arte, no. 9), Florence, 1920

Marangoni, 1959 Matteo Marangoni, *Guercino* (I grandi maestri del disegno), Milan, 1959

Mariette, 1741 P.-J. Mariette, *Description sommaire des Dessins* [. . .] *de feu M. Crozat*, Paris, 1741

Mariette, 1851–60 P.-J. Mariette, *Abecedario de P.-J. Mariette et autres notes inédites de cet amateur sur les arts et les artistes*, 6 vols., Paris, 1851–60

Marqués, 1983 Manuela Mena Marqués, *Museo del Prado: Catálogo de dibujos, VI: Dibujos italianos del siglo XVII*, Madrid, 1983

Mayor, 1871 W. Mayor, *A brief chronological Description of a Collection of original Drawings and Sketches, by the most celebrated Masters of the different Schools of Europe . . . formed by and belonging to Mr. Mayor*, London, 1871

Meijer & Van Tuyll, 1983 Bert W. Meijer and Carel van Tuyll, *Disegni italiani del Teylers Museum Haarlem provenienti dalle collezione di Cristina di Svezia e dei principi Odescalchi*, exh. cat., Florence, Istituto Universitario Olandese di Storia dell'Arte, 29 October–18 December 1983, and Rome, Istituto Nazionale per la Grafia, Gabinetto Nazionale delle Stampe, 10 January–20 February 1984

Meder, 1919 J. Meder, *Die Handzeichnung, ihre Technik und Entwicklung*, Vienna, 1919

Miles, 1979 Ellen Miles, *Thomas Hudson 1701–1779*, exh. cat., London, Kenwood House, 6 July–30 September 1979

Morris & Hopkinson, 1977 E. Morris and M. Hopkinson, *Walker Art Gallery, Liverpool: Foreign Catalogue*, 2 vols., Liverpool, 1977

de Moura Sobral, 1974–5 Luis de Moura Sobral, 'Etude d'un dessin du Guerchin', *Revue trimestrielle du Musée des Beaux-Arts de Montréal*, VI, no. 2, 1974–5, pp. 5–17

Nicodemi, 1921 Giorgio Nicodemi, *I disegni della Pinacoteca Bresciana Tosio e Martinengo*, Brescia, 1921

Northcote, 1813–15 James Northcote, *Memoirs of Sir Joshua Reynolds . . .*, 2 vols., London, 1813–15

Oberhuber, 1977 Konrad Oberhuber, *Renaissance and Baroque Drawings from the Collections of John and Alice Steiner*, exh. cat., Cambridge, Mass., Fogg Art Museum, 1977

Parker, 1956 K. T. Parker, *Catalogue of the Collection of Drawings in the Ashmolean Museum, Vol. II, Italian Schools*, Oxford, 1956 (reprinted with corrections, 1972)

Parker & Byam Shaw, 1953 K. T. Parker and J. Byam Shaw, *Drawings by Old Masters*, exh. cat., London, Royal Academy of Arts, 1953

Penny, 1987 Nicholas Penny, Review of B, 1985, *Burlington Magazine*, CXXIX, August 1987, pp. 542–4

Pepper, 1984 D. Stephen Pepper, *Guido Reni: A complete Catalogue of his Works with an introductory Text*, Oxford, 1984

Piccard, 1979 Gerhard Piccard, *Wasserzeichen Horn*, vol. VII in the series *Die Wasserzeichenkartei Piccard im Haupstaatsarchiv Stuttgart*, Stuttgart, 1979

Pineux-Duval, 1829 Pierre-Amaury Pineux-Duval, *Monuments des arts du dessin* [. . .] *recueillis par le Baron Vivant Denon*, 2 vols., Paris, 1829

Piranesi, *Raccolta*, 1764 G. B. Piranesi, *Raccolta di alcuni disegni del Barberi* [*sic*] *da Cento detto il Guercino, incisi in rame, e presentati al singolar merito del Sig. Tommaso Jenkins Pittore, ed Accademico di S. Luca, in atto di rispetto, e d'amicizia dall'Architetto, e suo Coaccademico Gio. Battista Piranesi*, Rome, 1764

Popham, 1935 A. E. Popham, *Catalogue of the Phillipps Fenwick Collection of Drawings*, London, 1935

Popham, 1938a A. E. Popham, 'A Drawing by Guercino', *British Museum Quarterly*, XII, no. 1, 1938, pp. 25–6

Popham, 1938b A. E. Popham, *Seventeenth Century Art in Europe*, exh. cat., London, Royal Academy of Arts, 3 January–12 March 1938

Popham, 1938c A. E. Popham, 'Seventeenth-century Art in Europe at Burlington House: II. The Drawings', *Burlington Magazine*, LXXII, 1938, pp. 13–20.

Popham, 1948 A. E. Popham, *An Exhibition of Old Master Drawings from the Collection of the Earl of Leicester, Holkham Hall*, exh. cat., Arts Council of Great Britain, 1948

Popham, 1962–3 A. E. Popham, *Old Master Drawings from Chatsworth*, exh. cat., Touring Exhibition circulatd by the Smithsonian Institution, 1962–3

Popham, 1967 A. E. Popham, *Italian Drawings in the Department of Prints and Drawings in the British Museum: Artists working in Parma in the Sixteenth Century*, London, 1967

Popham & Lloyd, 1986 A. E. Popham, *Old Master Drawings at Holkham Hall*, prepared for publication, with an introduction, by Christopher Lloyd, Chicago, 1986

Ragghianti, 1938 Carlo Ludovico Ragghianti, 'Notizie e Letture', *La Critica d'Arte*, III, 1938, pp. xvii–xxx

Reid, 1874 *Dyce Collection: A Catalogue of the Paintings, Miniatures, Drawings, Engravings, Rings, and miscellaneous Objects bequeathed by the Reverend Alexander Dyce*, with entries on the drawings, prints and etchings by George William Reid, London, 1874

Reveley, 1820 Henry Reveley, *Notices illustrative of the Drawings and Sketches of some of the most distinguished Masters in all the principal Schools of Design*, London, 1820

Riccòmini, 1968 Eugenio Riccòmini, *Il Seicento ferrarese*, Milan, 1969

Roberts, 1986 Jane Roberts, *Master Drawings in the Royal Collection*, exh. cat., London, Queen's Gallery, Buckingham Palace, 1986

Robinson, 1869 J. C. Robinson, *Descriptive Catalogue of Drawings by the Old Masters, forming the Collection of John Malcolm of Poltalloch, Esq.*, London, 1869

Robinson, 1876 J. C. Robinson, *Descriptive Catalogue of Drawings by the Old Masters, forming the Collection of John Malcolm of Poltalloch, Esq.*, 2nd edition, London, 1876

Rogers, 1778 Charles Rogers, *A Collection of Prints, in Imitation of Drawings, to which are annexed Lives of their Authors with explanatory and critical Notes*, London, 1778

Roli, 1972 Renato Roli, *G. F. Barbieri, Guercino* (Collana disegnatori italiani), Milan, 1972

Rovere, 1858 Clemente Rovere, *Descrizione del Reale Palazzo di Torino*, Turin, 1858

Rowlands, 1984 John Rowlands (ed.), *Master Drawings and Watercolours in the British Museum*, exh. cat., London, British Museum, 1984

Ruffo, 1916 Vincenzo Ruffo, 'Galleria Ruffo nel secolo XVII in Messina', *Bollettino d'Arte*, X, 1916, particularly pp. 95–126

Russell, 1923 A. G. B. Russell, *Drawings by Guercino*, London, 1923

Russell, 1925 *Catalogue of an Exhibition of Italian Art of the Seventeenth Century*, with an Introduction to the Drawings by Archibald Russell, exh. cat., London, Burlington Fine Arts Club, 1925

Russell, 1973 Francis Russell, 'A Guercino Footnote', *Master Drawings*, XI, 1973, p. 271

Ryskamp, *et al.*, 1979 *William & Mary and their House*, exh. cat., with an introduction by Charles Ryskamp, New York, Pierpont Morgan Library, 1979

S, 1988 Luigi Salerno, *I Dipinti del Guercino*, Rome, 1988

Scannelli, 1657 Francesco Scannelli, *Il microcosmo della pittura*, Cesena, 1657

Schaar, 1977 Eckhard Schaar (ed.), *Siftung Ratjen: Italienische Ziechnungen des 16.–18. Jahrhunderts*, exh. cat. (touring exhibition, 1977–8), Munich, 1977

Scharf, 1953 Alfred Scharf, 'The Exhibition of Old Master Drawings at the Royal Academy', *Burlington Magazine*, XCV, 1953, pp. 351–6

Sciolla, 1989 Gianni Carlo Sciolla (ed.), *Da Leonardo a Rembrandt: Disegni della Biblioteca Reale di Torino*, exh. cat., Turin, 1989

Scott-Elliot, 1958 A. H. Scott-Elliot, *The Paul Oppé Collection*, exh. cat., London, Royal Academy of Arts, 1958

Southorn, 1988 Janet Southorn, *Power and Display in the Seventeenth Century: The Arts and their Patrons in Modena and Ferrara*, Cambridge, 1988

Stainton, 1983 Lindsay Stainton, 'Hayward's List: British Visitors to Rome, 1753–75', *Walpole Society*, XLIX, 1983, pp. 3–36

Stampfle & Bean, 1967 Felice Stampfle and Jacob Bean, *Drawings from New York Collections, II: The Seventeenth Century in Italy*, exh. cat., Pierpont Morgan Library, New York, 1967

Stechow, 1976 Wolfgang Stechow, *Catalogue of Drawings and Watercolours in the Allen Memorial Art Museum, Oberlin College*, Oberlin, Ohio, 1976

Steinberg, 1980 Leo Steinberg, 'Guercino's *Saint Petronilla*', *Studies in Italian Art History*, I, American Academy in Rome, 1980, pp. 207–42

Stix & Fröhlich-Bum, 1926 Alfred Stix and L. Fröhlich-Bum, *Beschreibender Katalog der Handzeichnungen in der Graphischen Sammlung Albertina: Band I, Zeichnungen der Venezianische Schule*, Vienna, 1926

Stix & Leporini, 1927 A. Stix and H. Leporini, *Die Handzeichnungen der Sammlung Török*, Vienna, 1927

Stix & Spitzmüller, 1941 Alfred Stix and Anna Spitzmüller, *Beschreibender Katalog der Handzeichnungen in der Graphischen Sammlung Albertina: Band VI, Die Schulen von Ferrara, Bologna, Parma und Modena. . .*, Vienna, 1941

Sutton, 1967 Denys Sutton, 'Art and the Theatre' (editorial), *Apollo*, LXXXVI, 1967, pp. 88–93

Sutton & Garlick, 1969–70 D. Sutton and K. J. Garlick, *Italian Drawings from the Ashmolean Museum, Oxford*, exh. cat., Wildenstein's, New York and Oxford, 1969–70

Tan Bunzl, 1972 *Italian 17th Century Drawings from British Private Collections*, compiled by Yvonne Tan Bunzl and others, with an introduction by Anthony Blunt, exh. cat., Edinburgh, The Merchants' Hall, 19 August–9 September 1972

Thiem, 1979 Cristel Thiem, 'Unpublished chalk Drawings by Guercino in the Collection of Schloss Fachsenfeld', *Master Drawings*, XVII, 1979, pp. 401–17

Thiem, 1982 Cristel Thiem, *Bolognesische Zeichnungen 1600–1830 aus der Sammlung Schloss Fachsenfeld mit Leihgaben aus Windsor Castle und der Fondazione Cini, Venedig*, exh. cat., Stuttgart, Staatsgalerie, 2 March–2 May 1982

Turner, 1980 Nicholas Turner, *Italian Baroque Drawings* (British Museum Prints and Drawings Series), London, 1980

Turner, 1981 Nicholas Turner, 'Some preparatory Drawings for Guercino's early Altarpiece of *Sts Francis and Louis of France* at Brisighella', *Master Drawings*, XIX, 1981, pp. 164–6

Turner, 1982 Nicholas Turner, Review of Macandrew, 1980, *Burlington Magazine*, CXXIV, 1982, pp. 161–3

Turner, 1984 Nicholas Turner, Review of Byam Shaw, 1983, *Master Drawings*, XXII, 1984, pp. 206–12

Turner, 1985 Nicholas Turner, 'Two Paintings attributed to Ludovico Carracci', *Burlington Magazine*, CXXVII, 1985, pp. 795–6

Turner, 1987 Nicholas Turner, 'The Mind of the Master', *British Museum Society Bulletin*, March 1987, pp. 5–9

Turner, 1988 Nicholas Turner, 'Old Masters given to Museum', *British Museum Society Bulletin*, Spring 1988, pp. 34–5

Turner, 1990 Nicholas Turner, Review of Loire, 1990, *Burlington Magazine*, CXXXII, 1990, pp. 652–4

Van Hasselt, 1959 Carlos van Hasselt, *Fitzwilliam Museum Cambridge: Exhibition of 17th Century Italian Drawings*, 18 June–16 August 1959

Van Tuyll, 1990 Carel Van Tuyll, Review of M & T, 1989, *Burlington Magazine*, CXXXII, 1990, pp. 216–17

Vesme, 1897 Alessandro Baudi di Vesme, 'La regia Pinacoteca di Torino', *Le Gallerie Nazionali Italiane*, III, 1897, pp. 3–68

Vesme, 1963–8 Alessandro Baudi di Vesme, *Schede Vesme: L'Arte in Piemonte dal XVI al XVIII secolo*, 3 vols., Turin, 1963–8

Waagen, 1854 Gustav Friedrich Waagen, *Treasures of Art in Great Britain. . .*, 3 vols., London, 1854

Ward-Jackson, 1980 Peter Ward-Jackson, *Victoria and Albert Museum Catalogues: Italian Drawings, Volume Two: 17th–18th Century*, London, 1980

Waterhouse, 1941 Ellis K. Waterhouse, *Reynolds*, London, 1941

Waterhouse, 1960 *Italian Art in Britain*, with an introductory note by E. K. Waterhouse, exh. cat., London, Royal Academy of Arts, Winter Exhibition, 1960

Weigel, 1865 Rudolph Weigel, *Die Werke der Maler in ihren Handzeichnungen*, Leipzig, 1865

Whitfield, 1977 Clovis Whitfield, *Old Master Drawings from Holkham*, exh. cat., London, Thomas Agnew & Sons Ltd, 2–27 May 1977

Zampetti, 1967 Pietro Zampetti, *Note sparse sul '600*, Venice, 1967

Zanotti, 1739 Giampietro Zanotti, *Storia dell'Accademia Clementina di Bologna aggregata all'Instituto delle Scienze e dell'Arti*, 2 vols., Bologna, 1739

Concordances

Chatsworth (inv. nos.)

Inv. no.	*Exh. cat.*
513	200
514	65
515	129
522	18
526	168
533	167
544	166
550	67
551	68

Holkham Hall (Popham & Lloyd nos.)

P & L	*Exh. cat.*
142	74
148	173
149	193
150	143

London, British Museum (inv. nos.)

Inv. no.	*Exh. cat.*	*App. cat.*
5210–68		75
5210–73		76
5210–74		77
5211–17		99
5211–20		66
5211–62		83
5212–15		121
5212–57		97
5212–66		27
5226–32		102
5226–193		105
5236–138		91
Ff. 2–129		42
Ff. 2–130		90
Ff. 2–131		44
Ff. 2–132		103
Ff. 2–133		4
Ff. 2–134	99	20
Ff. 2–135	133	38
Ff. 2–136		23
Ff. 2–137		45
Ff. 2–138		104
Ff. 2–139		64
Ff. 2–140	216	63
Ff. 2–141		107
Ff. 2–142	165	59
Ff. 2–143		93
Ff. 2–144		58
Ff. 2–145		60
Ff. 4–25		101
Ff. 4–26		112
Ff. 4–52		98
Gg. 3–387		111
Pp. 4–43		96
Pp. 4–57		52
Pp. 4–58	208	65
Pp. 4–59		24
Pp. 4–60		7
Pp. 4–61		41
Pp. 4–62	36	5
Pp. 4–63	164	57
Pp. 4–130		72
1847–3–6–10		13
1852–11–16–83		106
1859–8–6–67		56
68		85
70		89
71		39
1872–6–8–530		114
1872–10–12–3285		122
1873–5–10–3534		6
3535		1
1874–8–8–109		109
110		110
1875–7–10–2624		124
2625		125
2626		126
1884–3–8–9		120
1893–7–31–3		29
4		30
5		94
6		100
1895–7–25–7		84
1895–9–15–703		34
704		25
705		26
706	54	9
707		51
708		87
709	120	36
711		10
712		92
713		11
1907–10–30–13		86
1910–2–12–3	112	28
4		21
5		8
6		40
7		43
8	113	35
9		22
1937–10–8–1	186	62
1938–11–3–2		88
1943–11–13–8		95
9		32
10		73
11		71
12		48
13		47
14		74
15		31
16		70
17		37
18		46
19		53
20		18
21		54
22		19
23		61
1946–7–13–83		81
721	9	2
732		82
762		118
1318		78
1948–4–10–330		108
1952–1–21–41		14
42		67
43		68
44		69
45		15

Inv. no.	Exh. cat.	App. cat.
1953–4–11–48		55
1954–6–10–7		12
1969–9–20–17	83	16
1979–10–6–84		3
1986–6–21–1		50
5		79
6		80
7		119
8		123
9		117
11		115
12		113
13		116
14	93	17
1987–7–25–47	124	49
1989–6–17–278	110	33

London, Courtauld Institute Galleries (inv. nos.)

Inv. no.	Exh. cat.
1327	44
1328	33
1337	111
1339	121
1341	88
1342	190
1344	71
1345	38
1346	203
1347	189
1349	132
1358	46
1359	191
1365	56
1366	107
1368	141
1369	96
1376	6
1861	154
4593	47

London, Victoria and Albert Museum (Ward-Jackson nos.)

PWJ	Exh. cat.
716	150
717	162
722	84

Oxford, Ashmolean Museum (KTP nos.)

KTP	Exh. cat.
856	29
857	49
858	73
859	20
861	185
862	55
863	135
864	183
868	184
869	153
870	206
872	66
873B	170
875	102

Oxford, Sir Denis Mahon's collection of Drawings by Guercino, on loan to the Ashmolean Museum (M & E nos.)

M & E	Exh. cat.
1	1
3	10
4	17
6	14
7	23
8	24
9	25
10	27
15	59
16	60
17	61
18	62
19	70
21	81
22	77
23	87
27	114
28	125
29	138
30	130
31	152
33	155
34	156
35	158
36	159
38	48
42	194
43	179
45	196

Windsor, Royal Library (M & T nos.)

M & T	Exh. cat.
1	2
3	3
4	5
5	7
6	8
8	13
9	15
11	21
12	22
13	26
14	28
15	31
16	32
18	34
19	35
21	39
22	40
23	41
24	42
25	43
26	45
31	51
32	52
35	53
36	57
38	58
43	63
44	64
52	72
53	69
55	76
57	78
58	79
60	80
61	82
62	85
63	86
64	90
65	91
67	89
68	92
73	94
74	95
78	98
79	97
81	100
82	101
83	105
84	108
86	115

M & T	*Exh. cat.*
88	119
89	117
90	118
91	116
94	122
95	123
98	128
101	131
110	136
111	137
113	139
115	142
117	144
118	145
119	146
120	147
121	148
122	149
128	50
130	157
133	160
134	161
139	19
147	37
149	4
150	16
168	75
183	106
236	163
238	178
240	174
247	180
249	181
253	176
254	175
255	177
256	171
263	182
277	188
278	187
280	198
282	215
287	197
289	195
307	207
318	202
319	201
329	213
334	210
339	204

Mahon, Disegni, 1969

Mahon	*Exh. cat.*
7	1
14	2
20	10
26	5
30	20
32	6
33	7
36	17
37	18
38	13
43	15
48	14
49	23
50	24
51	25
53	29
60	26
69	27
76	28
77	30
78	33
80	32
82	34
84	35
87	38
88	43
89	42
91	41
97	52
102	53
103	59
104	60
106	61
107	62
116	70
117	69
118	71
119	72
123	81
125	77
126	78
129	87
130	88
134	92
137	98
141	113
143	125
149	138
150	136
151	135
152	139

Mahon	*Exh. cat.*
159	130
160	150
161	152
166	155
167	156
172	158
174	160
175	162
178	19
180	37
183	49
184	48
185	54
187	44
192	169
196	166
197	165
201	178
203	177
204	180
205	179
208	167
213	186
214	185
215	190
216	189
217	191
220	46
223	183
224	194
227	196
230	206
231	188
232	216
233	208
234	209
237	214
241	200
245	203
247	16
250	4

Indexes to related works

Numbers in **bold type** preceded by 'No.' refer to the entries in the Exhibition Catalogue. Numbers in **bold type** preceded by 'App. no.' refer to entries in the Appendix. Works referred to in the Introduction and in the Notes to the Introduction are not included in the Index.

1. Drawings by or after Guercino or by Members of his School, not included in the Exhibition

Drawings are arranged by location and are identified by inventory or catalogue number. Where there are no such numbers, or where these numbers are unknown to us, the drawings are identified by title. Drawings in private collections are listed by name of collector. Drawings that have been sold at auction are placed under location and name of auctioneer, in order of sale date.

2. Paintings by or after Guercino, or by Members of his School